A History *of*
GEROPSYCHOLOGY
in Autobiography

A History *of*
GEROPSYCHOLOGY
in Autobiography

Edited by
James E. Birren *and* Johannes J. F. Schroots

American Psychological Association
Washington, DC

Published by
American Psychological Association
750 First Street, NE
Washington, DC 20002

Copies may be ordered from
APA Order Department
P.O. Box 92984
Washington, DC 20090-2984

In the UK and Europe, copies may be ordered from
American Psychological Association
3 Henrietta Street
Covent Garden, London
WC2E 8LU England

Typeset in Times Roman by GGS Information Services, York, PA

Printer: Data Reproductions Corporation, Auburn Hills, MI
Cover Designer: Design Concepts, San Diego, CA
Project Manager: Debbie K. Hardin, Reston, VA

Library of Congress Cataloging-in-Publication Data

A history of geropsychology in autobiography / edited by James E. Birren and Johannes
J.F. Schroots.
    p.; cm.
  Includes bibliographic references and indexes.
  ISBN: 1-55798-631-2 (alk. paper)
    1. Aging—Psychological aspects—Study and teaching—History. 2.
Aged—Psychology—Study and teaching—History. 3. Developmental
psychology—History. 4. Psychologists—Biography.   I. Title: Geropsychology in
autobiography.   II. Birren, James E. III. Schroots, J.J.F.
    [DNLM: 1. Geriatrics—history—Personal Narratives. 2. Aged—psychology. 3.
Psychology—history—Personal Narratives. WZ 112H6733 1999]
  BF724.8.H57   1999
  155.67—dc21
                                                                    99-051564

British Library Cataloguing-in-Publication Data
A CIP record is available from the British Library

Printed in the United States
First Edition

CONTENTS

CONTRIBUTORS

Paul B. Baltes, Max Planck Institute for Human Development, Berlin

Eva Beverfelt, NOVA, Norwegian Social Research, Oslo

James E. Birren, UCLA Center on Aging

Jack Botwinick, University City, MO

Dennis Basil Bromley, The University of Liverpool

Fergus I. M. Craik, University of Toronto

Linda Fagan Dubin, University of California, Los Angeles

James L. Fozard, Morton Plant Mease Health Care, Clearwater, FL

Margaret Gatz, University of Southern California

Elsie Harwood, St. Lucia, Queensland, Australia

Irene Mackintosh Hulicka, Buffalo, NY

Robert Kastenbaum, Arizona State University

Nathan Kogan, New School for Social Research, New York

Gisela Labouvie-Vief, Wayne State University

M. Powell Lawton, Polisher Research Center, Philadelphia

Gerald E. McClearn, The Pennsylvania State University

John R. Nesselroade, University of Virginia

Timothy A. Salthouse, Georgia Institute of Technology

K. Warner Schaie, The Pennsylvania State University

Johannes J. F. Schroots, Free University Amsterdam

Joel Shanan*

Hans Thomae, Bonn, Germany

Lillian E. Troll, Alameda, CA

---

*The editors are deeply sorry to inform the readers that Professor Joel Shanan passed away on September 16, 1999, in Kfar Saba, Israel. He was still teaching a course on personality development at the Hebrew University when he was struck by illness earlier in the year. His autobiography will confirm the words of his son, Amir. ''His life was a story of pain and courage, resilience and resourcefulness, morality and integrity, and above all, a loving and undefeatable belief in humanity.''

Chapter 1
AN INTRODUCTION TO A HISTORY OF GEROPSYCHOLOGY IN AUTOBIOGRAPHY

James E. Birren and Johannes J. F. Schroots

The purpose of this book is to present the history of geropsychology in the words of many of the pioneers who developed research, scholarship, and educational programs in the subject during its formative phase. Because the emergence of studies in the psychology of aging was primarily a post-World War II phenomenon, many of the pioneers are still living and are able to describe the origins of the field of study.

It is almost impossible to get a detailed view of the emergence of a field of study without consulting the people who contributed to its development. In this book we have urged the scientific pioneers accessible to us to describe the development of their careers so that we might gain an understanding of the conditions and the influences that attracted their interest and that provided support or resistance to their ideas and efforts. In addition to the purely intellectual account of their careers, the authors have been encouraged to tell details of their lives that characterize their career pathways between pitfalls and good fortune, depressions and wars, antipathies and attractions, and the influential stereotypes and social lag effects. Without an understanding of personal career pressures and attractions it would be difficult to grasp how the psychology of aging grew from its social, institutional, and personal soil.

The Value of Autobiographical Histories

Autobiographies can reveal how chance and accidents help determine the flow of events and choices, as do the shifting balances of resources and the interests of institutional administrators, family members, and peers. Autobiographies reveal different career paths to contributions and achievements and perhaps to lingering disappointments. The details of individual careers are often left out of histories of fields and overlooked are the decisions individuals make in the process of shaping their careers and that contribute to the creation of a new field.

Why geropsychology attracted its pioneers is part of its history. Was attention focused because of chance events, an encouraging mentor, reading a book, an aged relative, or a personal encounter? Elements such as these in careers are often overlooked as though they are not important forces in shaping careers and the substance of a field of study. Questions about how geropsychology became a major component of contemporary psychological study and knowledge can be answered through the personal accounts of the psychologists who opened the subject for research and systematic scholarship.

The audience for this book will be the increasing number of scholars, researchers, and students who want to answer questions about the content of geropsychology and its origins. Also, administrators need to have information about the processes of institutional and career changes to make adaptations in their institutions. Another audience for this book will be students who seek to understand how the flow of academic lives is viewed from the inside.

Students contemplating careers in geropsychology, whether in research or applied work, will have access to information that will help guide their choices.

This book presents material that helps to give insights into how creative and productive lives develop and flower. For students of career development this book will provide valuable source material about the background of choices made among institutional and personal priorities. It offers the basis for understanding career development in an emerging field. Graduate students can learn from the autobiographies of pioneers how career opportunities develop by chance or are created by individual initiatives. Colleagues can gain insight into sources of success and of pitfalls in the pursuit of knowledge. Readers in the history of psychology can learn why some topics emerged rapidly into research and why others have been neglected. Also, historical answers may be sought to questions about why geropsychology itself was slow to emerge in the landscape of psychology generally. Why did it appear at some universities and institutions and not at others? What features of the intellectual climate of a particular time and place favored the pursuit of questions about aging? In a more general way this book will contribute to understanding the nature of scholars and their personal quests for knowledge, its motivation and rewards. It may also make the products of our studies more useful in improving the course of human life.

Selection of Contributions

The autobiographies are sometimes intellectual in tone and sometimes include more personal circumstances. It is doubtful if anyone fully grasps the sources of his or her career motivations and how he or she contributed to the growth of science. The careers of these writers have been influenced by a myriad of social and economic circumstances, as well as personal misfortunes and opportunities. From the rationalizations, omissions, emphases, and personal and impersonal accounts, the reader may piece together a historical map of geropsychology. In developing this book the editors invited mature pioneers of the field to write their autobiographies and tell the stories of their careers. This is a very different task than describing the results of research in a scientific article in which logic is perhaps the strongest element.

There were some early psychologists, psychiatrists, and physiologists who gave thought to some of the issues of aging ancillary to their careers that were primarily established in other areas—for example, Carl Jung and Ivan Pavlov. These and others are represented in the biosketches at the end of this book. They provide some interesting clues about the priorities of the era in which they worked and add to the intellectual history of psychology. In addition to individual autobiographies an attempt was made to gather information about some early contributors to the field who are no longer living—for example, G. Stanley Hall, Alan Welford, and Charlotte Bühler.

Information about the history of the emergence of geropsychology in different countries was also sought by sending questionnaires to relevant persons. This information along with brief biosketches of early pioneers is presented to provide as much information as possible about the circumstances that surrounded the fledgling subject matter of geropsychology.

The origins of general psychology, experimental psychology, and other early research emphases have already been described in the autobiographies of early 20th-century psychologists in a series of volumes on the history of psychology in autobiography (Boring, Langfeld, Werner, & Yerkes, 1966; Boring & Lindzey, 1967; Lindzey, 1974, 1980, 1989; Murchison, 1930, 1932, 1936). These earlier works provided models for other areas of psychology but it remained for the present volume to bring to light the conditions of the emergence of geropsychology in autobiography.

The authors selected to write their career histories were asked to present accounts of the circumstances in which the field emerged. The selection of contributors to the volume presented several issues. As the interest in the subject has grown at a rapid rate there are relatively few first-generation geropsychologists but many second-generation geropsychologists and many persons representing subspecialties. To be a pioneer it was decided that the person should be over the age of 50 years. The editors were faced with the task of inviting authors from a wide range of subfields. A balance was sought in leaders representing subfields—for example, cognition, emotions, and social processes. Also, the development of careers of women was to be represented along with those of men. It was also decided to represent pioneering efforts in geropsychology in other countries. The need to secure some level of representativeness of the autobiographies reduce the capacity to respond to some of the more popular subfields. To aid in the process the editors sought informal advice from colleagues about what to do with representing some of the larger areas of activity. For example, cognition has attracted the most interest. If all the pioneers were included—in other words, those over age 50 who had an established reputation in the psychology of aging—at least two volumes of the present size would have been required. The editors regret that more scholars could not have been included and wish to express the view that inclusion in the volume does not represent an implicit evaluation of career contributions. Choices had to be made among countries and subfields of interest.

The reader will note a preponderance of autobiographies from the United States. This results from two factors: the rapid expansion in America of psychology as a university subject since the beginning of the 20th century and the early interaction of psychology and public health about the issues of aging in the late 1930s. These two factors resulted in a relatively early encouraging environment and growth of the number of pioneers in geropsychology.

The Relatively Recent Emergence of Geropsychology

The readers of these autobiographies may form the impression that geropsychology is solely a product of the second half of the 20th century. On the contrary, it has deep preresearch roots in the histories of cultures, religions, philosophy, and medicine. Many cultures have assumed that humankind was once immortal but lost it through its own actions. Confronted by the fact that people change in appearance and die as they grow older, it was characteristic to attribute control over the course of life to cosmic forces and to form beliefs in some form of life beyond death. Prescientific ideas about aging and death persist and may have contributed to the slow emergence of geropsychology as a scientific and scholarly subject matter.

The slow development of geropsychology was probably a result of cultural resistance to seek natural explanations for sensitive questions for which there were no obvious answers. It also trailed experimental psychology and child development for both scientific and pragmatic reasons (Merens & Branigan, 1966). Distracting attention from the study of aging were the early emphases given to child psychology and behaviorism. The need for study and knowledge about child development preempted earlier scholarly resources in a society in which children were the populous segment (Thompson & Hogan, 1996). Also, behaviorism created an unfavorable climate for exploring changes in individuals not attributable to environmental reinforcements. An exponential growth in published research literature began about 1950 and appears to be continuing today (Riegel, 1977). Specialized research units began to be created in several countries, and university faculty members began to establish careers with an emphasis on geropsychology. Multidisciplinary centers and institutes were created in universities that invited psychologists to participate. Psychology is now a major contributor to broader scientific efforts devoted to the study of aging (Birren, 1961).

Conclusion

There are several uses for this book. Among them is making available the historical background of the emergence of geropsychology, a 20th-century phenomenon. It provides the new and expanding body of undergraduate and graduate students of the psychology of aging with the details of the emergence of their field of study. Scholars interested in the history of science are given the basic material from which to draw inferences about the factors that facilitated or delayed the emergence of the new field. It provides researchers interested in the analysis of narrative material with important sources of information about the background of an emerging subject matter and the pioneer personalities.

Psychology departments that are adding the psychology of aging to their divisions will find this book to be a useful addition to their departmental libraries. The information in this book should also be attractive to general users of university and college libraries. Geropsychology is going to be of increasingly broad significance in the 21st century as societies attempt to meet the practical needs of increasing populations that are living longer. The increases in life expectancy and decreases in birth rates are leading to dramatic changes in the age composition of developed countries. With the increases in the numbers of older persons there will be greater need for research on the processes of change in adult life. This would be similar to the large share of resources that went into child development early in the 20th century.

It may be expected that geropsychology will continue to expand. The subject matter is complex, as these autobiographies indicate. It may be one of the most complex subject matters facing science in the 21st century. It will likely result in new patterns of careers not yet seen in this volume and careers that will respond to the rising interest in raising the quality of long adult lives.

References

Birren, J. E. (1961). A brief history of the psychology of aging. *The Gerontologist, 1,* 69–77, 127–134.

Boring, E. G., Langfeld, H. S., Werner, H., & Yerkes, R. M. (Eds.). (1966). *A history of psychology in autobiography* (Vol. 4). Worcester, MA: Clark University Press.

Boring, E. G., & Lindzey, G. (Eds.). (1967). *A history of psychology in autobiography* (Vol. 5). New York: Appleton Century Crofts.

Lindzey, G. (Ed.). (1974). *A history of psychology in autobiography* (Vol. 6). Englewood Cliffs, NJ: Prentice-Hall.

Lindzey, G. (Ed.). (1980). *A history of psychology in autobiography* (Vol. 7). San Francisco: W. H. Freeman.

Lindzey, G. (Ed.). (1989). *A history of psychology in autobiography* (Vol. 8). San Francisco: W. H. Freeman.

Merens, M. R., & Brannigan, G. G. (Eds.). (1966). *The developmental psychologists.* New York: McGraw Hill.

Murchison, C. (Ed.). (1930). *A history of psychology in autobiography* (Vol. 1). Worcester, MA: Clark University Press.

Murchison, C. (Ed.). (1932). *A history of psychology in autobiography* (Vol. 2). Worcester, MA: Clark University Press.

Murchison, C. (Ed.). (1936). *A history of psychology in autobiography* (Vol. 3). Worcester, MA: Clark University Press.

Riegel, K. (1977). History of psychological gerontology. In J. E. Birren & K. W. Schaie (Eds.), *Handbook of the psychology of aging* (pp. 70–102). New York: Van Nostrand Reinhold.

Thompson, D., & Hogan, J. D. (Eds.). (1996). *A history of developmental psychology in autobiography.* Boulder, CO: Westview Press.

Chapter 2
AUTOBIOGRAPHICAL REFLECTIONS:
From Developmental Methodology and
Lifespan Psychology to Gerontology

Paul B. Baltes

The editors of this volume know that I struggled with accepting this assignment. Only after Jim Birren reminded me of collegiality and my commitment to the field did I persuade myself to engage in this task. Nonetheless, I would like to summarize some of the reasons for my many reservations. They are relevant when one reads and evaluates the product that resulted.

Several factors converged to produce resistance. On the one hand, I felt I was still composing my life. The idea of a life review struck me as off time and perhaps as counterproductive. Moreover, I sensed that good autobiographies reflect a mixture of intuitive and rational knowledge. But as I thought about my professional career, what I found foremost in my mind were rationality-based knowledge structures and associated ''abstract'' mental scripts, with little room for the intuitive.

For instance, after years of working on theoretical models of lifespan development, the nature of these models seemed to dictate how to think about my own life as well. Two examples will illustrate. One of the lifespan models I have advanced and elaborated (with colleagues, as is true for much of my work) specifies three interacting influences on the sequencing, direction, and differentiation of ontogeny across the lifespan: *age-graded influences, history-graded influences,* and *nonnormative influences* (P. B. Baltes, 1987; P. B. Baltes, Lindenberger, & Staudinger, 1998). In addition, with Margret Baltes, I have outlined a model of successful lifespan development labeled *selective optimization with compensation* (P. B. Baltes & Baltes, 1990).

It is difficult for me to distance myself from these theoretical frameworks, to let my life express itself without the mental scripts flowing from lifespan theory. As soon as I begin to reflect on my biography, I ask questions about age-graded events, history-graded factors, and nonnormative events, and about their interactions. Similarly, I ask how in my life the processes of selection, optimization, and compensation operated, actively and passively, consciously and subconsciously, individually and collectively. As I anticipated writing this

---

This autobiography is dedicated with gratitude and love to my colleague and wife, Margret M. Baltes, who died unexpectedly on January 28, 1999, and after this chapter was written. Her contributions to my life and professional career were immense, unconditional, and without fail.

Note that the present author now prefers the spelling of *lifespan psychology* instead of *life-span or life-span developmental psychology* (Baltes & Goulet, 1970).

autobiography, the losses rather than the gains of such mental constraints were at the fore. Perhaps this is so because I was assailed by uncomfortable thoughts about the usefulness of these abstract models for the representation of individual lives.

There was more to feed my resistance. I feared creating a flexible and self-serving reconstruction of the past. It is a special feature of Homo sapiens that we act on and transform reality, especially if reality is projected into the past. Autobiographies, it seems to me, seduce their writers to engage in egotism and vanity. Throughout my life, I have consciously fought these vices in myself. Similarly, did I want to confront weaknesses and failures?

Yet, as I read in a commentary on autobiographies, "if autobiographies couldn't be self-serving, would anybody ever write one?" How was I to solve this motivational and intellectual conundrum, how would I contain egotism and ignore the theoretical frame of lifespan theory as I reflected on my own life? I found no solution except for making, as I do with these observations, this vexing problem transparent, and I use these self-insights as a general disqualifier. Whatever I offer in the following narrative should be taken with a grain of salt.

I will begin with some observations about my childhood and the conditions that, in my view, orchestrated the factors necessary for investing myself in my own development. In a second section, I will reflect on how my wish for advancement was channeled to psychology as a field of study. Subsequently, I will try to locate my own work in the emerging field of gerontology. Mentors, colleagues, students, and supportive institutional contexts are crucial to my assessment. I view myself as someone who has always worked in a context of interactive minds (e.g., P. B. Baltes & Staudinger, 1996) and in reciprocal relationships with people who have enriched and transformed my thinking and orientation in profound ways.

Acquiring a Sense of Proactive Agency and Upward Mobility

I was born in 1939 in Saarlouis, Germany, located near Saarbrücken, the capital of the Saarland, and the Alsace-Lorraine-Luxembourg border. Historically, the city of Saarlouis is of French origin. A liking for France was part of the soul of the Baltes-Haser-Detemple family, although my upbringing was undoubtedly German. This imaginary French connection was further enhanced when, in 1963, I married Margret Labouvie, whose family lineage included French as well.

When Germans of my age reflect back on their childhood, many wonder how and why they survived at all. Childhood in Nazi-era and postwar Germany was lived in miserable conditions. Death, hunger, war, air raids, war-forced migrations, fear of the invading foreign soldiers, an absent soldier–father (who remained a French prisoner of war until 1947)—all these factors suggest deprivation and vulnerability, risk factors en masse, with few economic and social resources. That the risks were real can perhaps be inferred from the fact that up to late childhood, I had a severe stutter. My family was concerned about whether I could enter primary school.

In retrospect, I view these early challenges primarily as opportunities. Why? The historical context taught me that bad circumstances can be transformed into stories of progress. On the one hand, I vividly remember war, hunger, and fear. But I also remember the sense of being a survivor, and I especially remember the warmth and many strengths of my mother and the larger family context that generated an experience of mastery. Given our generally low level of material resources, minor positive events were transformed into major ones and were associated with personal or family agency.

For instance, I think often about the excitement and opportunity that ensued in response to a gift I received for being the best pupil at the end of first grade in 1946. The gift came from an officer of the French occupying force and perhaps paradoxically involved a military toy tank. After having played with the tank for a day or so, I traded it to a neighbor child, whose parents owned a meat factory, for a string of delicious sausages. My mother's response was tears and pride in her son. How often she later told this story to others in my presence, thereby strengthening my belief that I was a raised in a tough situation but, through my own behavior, made a difference. Similarly, I remember pieces of chocolate that my mother had acquired for her children in trade for family jewelry. Again, this and similar events were expanded by the magic of subsequent storytelling, and I began to feel that despite my hard circumstances I was special and could bring about changes.

My sense of efficacy was enhanced by the collective success of a small family business. After World War II, we were poor. Without any financial resources, my parents started a small business. Initially, we ran a small publike restaurant along a major roadway. Over the course of a decade it was expanded to include a larger restaurant, a small hotel, and a busy service station. All three children (aside from a beloved older sister who died in 1950 at age 21, I had two older brothers) participated in making a go of the family enterprise: behind the counter as a cashier, as a bartender, as the bellboy taking luggage to the rooms, as a waiter in the restaurant, or as the gas station attendant. For me this experience started when I was 11 years old. My father suffered from a war-related illness and died early (when I was 17); my mother, with primary assistance from my eldest brother, was the household chief. These were years of hard work and serious financial insecurity, as I knew very well. I was often the one who took the daily receipts in my back pocket to school. During the school recess, with official permission, I jogged to the local bank to deposit the funds. I knew how important it was that I be on time so that none of our own checks would bounce; more than once, the cashier waited for my deposit before he presented the checks for payment. In time, however, under the firm leadership of my mother, we as a family developed a sense of accomplishment. We looked forward to, and participated in, significant upward economic mobility.

In prevention and resilience terms, I was well immunized and taught early to adapt to whatever life conditions surrounded me. Perhaps most important, I learned what it meant to have a sense of control and a purpose in life. A primary goal of life was striving toward betterment through ingenuity and hard work. Sociologists would call it a sense of upward mobility, wanting to move beyond one's family background.

The feeling of being motivated for upward mobility, in economic, social, and psychological dimensions, never left me. It is a fountain from which I still drink. I developed a worldview that contained the modifiability of reality as a basic principle, and I would not be surprised if my later interest in the modifiability in the course of aging had its foundation in this belief. This interpretation is consistent with lifespan theory, of course. As Klaus Riegel, one of my intellectual heroes, argued so eloquently in his conception of dialectical psychology (Riegel, 1976), the mastery of crises is among the critical ingredients for developmental advance.

Education as a Vehicle of Individual Development and Academia as an Outcome

Three primary circumstances channeled my sense of personal efficacy and desire for upward mobility into an academic rather than a business career. The first was that I learned quite early that, in good German tradition, my eldest brother was the heir apparent of the family business, and I accepted this without any negative feelings. I needed to look for another career. A second reason was my parents', especially my mother's, commitment to intellectual matters and her belief in education and education-related domains as better spheres of life than the family business we owned. She encouraged me to become educated and showed unwavering pride in my academic success—in addition, she largely ignored my weaknesses. To some degree I never understood why my mother had such a strong belief in education. To the best of my knowledge, nobody in her family ever attended college. Nonetheless, like her own mother, my mother was interested in cultural affairs: reading, theater, and opera. As an adolescent I became her regular companion at plays and musical performances in the nearby cities.

The third source of my evolving interest in education and becoming an *Akademiker* (university graduate) was located in the family network of my father. Although his parents came from a farming background, one line of the family was academically disposed. An older second cousin (Werner Reinert, one of the noted literary authors of the Saar), in particular, dropped by from time to time during my adolescence and encouraged me to pursue a university education. For me, this cousin and his younger brother, Günther Reinert, were models to emulate, and as inner voices they guided me to the Abitur and a university education. This story of adolescent grooming through my second cousins continued. When I entered the university, Günther Reinert (1929–1979) became my first and probably principal academic mentor. This mentorship began when he persuaded me to study psychology at the University of Saar in Saarbrücken (1959–1967), where he was a faculty member of the Psychological Institute.

Enhancing my choice of psychology as a career was a sibling rivalry with my brother Peter, four years older. He was interested in psychology and had brought home, for instance, tests of intelligence. Like chess, which was the primary field of intellectual rivalry for my father and his three sons, these intelligence tests for a few weeks provided our competitive play. My brother Peter, however, could not study psychology himself for lack of the proper educational degree (he had dropped out of the gymnasium track to become a primary school teacher). This gave me a chance to win out. A decade later, and by way of a detour in the form of a PhD from the University of Lima in Peru, my brother too was able to join the rank of academics as an educational scientist. In fact, some of his educational work on life management (e.g., P. B. Baltes, 1993) is similar in substantive orientation to my own research on wisdom and successful development.

Becoming a Developmental Psychologist at the University of Saar

In 1959, having completed the Abitur in a humanist gymnasium in Saarlouis, I entered the University of Saar (Saarbrücken). At that time, this newly founded university was in its infancy, and the atmosphere for beginning students was friendly but also highly competitive (see P. B. Baltes, 1997a). In the Psychological Institute, we were a small group of students, many of whom ended up in academe. And it was the place, where during the second semester of study, I met my wife.

The chair of the institute was Ernst E. Boesch. At that time, chairs through their status alone dominated German psychology departments. In addition, Boesch possessed a power-ful intellect, and his influence on students was intense. He also offered us a prestigious academic lineage: Boesch had been a student of the Genevan psychologists Jean Piaget and Andre Rey. For this reason, I have always considered myself a Piagetian. Boesch added to the Piagetian framework a deep interest in cultural variation and cultural psychology. It is likely that my commitment to the theoretical orientation of contextualism and the concept of "plasticity" originated here.

Piagetian developmental cognitive structuralism and Boeschean cultural-psychological theory thus were two of the cornerstones in my study of psychology. The third, provided by the guidance of Günther Reinert, was psychometrics and the developmental study of intelligence. Reinert was, next to the chair, the most senior teacher at the institute, and he functioned as an associate director.

My 1963 master's thesis under Reinert's supervision was a factor-analytic study on the differentiation hypothesis of intelligence in childhood (Reinert, Baltes, & Schmidt, 1965). This theme continues to be part of my intellectual agenda, though now with a primary focus on adulthood and old age. What is the structure of intelligence? How does it change with age? How is it related to ability and performance levels? What are its antecedents, correlates, and consequences? What do structural changes in intelligence imply for the measurement of intelligence? (See P. B. Baltes, Cornelius, Spiro, Nesselroade, & Willis, 1980; Lindenberger & Baltes, 1997.)

After my receiving a diploma in psychology (equivalent to a master's degree) and at the age of 24, I left my intellectual home territory for the first time. Primarily to learn English (my humanist education had taught me quite a bit of French, Latin, and Greek, but no English), I obtained a travel stipend from the German Academic Exchange Office (DAAD) to study in the United States. This was a big step for me, and it did not come easily. The enthusiasm of my wife was a critical factor. Margret looked forward to the adventure of spending a year in the United States. Occasionally, she tells me that this opportunity was an important reason for marrying me.

On the day after our wedding in 1963, Margret and I left for a year at the University of Nebraska. We chose that institution because Warner Schaie, who had been a visiting professor at the University of Saar a few years earlier, had invited me to be his research assistant. This was a momentous turning point in my life and career. Intellectually it opened new windows and freed me from the local constraints of one relatively isolated university, and interpersonally it reduced my perhaps all-too-tight family and homeland bonds. I often wonder what would have happened if Margret had not been the adventurous kind who was excited about going to the States and willing to nurture me through a case of homesickness. Her experience, while working as a research secretary with Schaie, marked the beginning of her interest in a career in academe, an aspiration that at that time was not encouraged in women in Germany.

At the University of Nebraska, I participated fully in what was then called a proseminar for incoming graduate students. As a result, my Genevan cognitive and developmental approach was complemented by a solid dose of American behaviorism and learning psychology. As part of the main overview seminar, I also had a brief introduction to the study of aging in the form of a couple of lectures presented by Schaie.

I learned more about gerontology in connection with my research assistantship with Schaie, where I worked on the data analysis and write-up of a study on auditory sensitivity in old age. In the process, I began to venture into the gerontological literature and copublished my first article in English (Schaie, Baltes, & Strother, 1964). Most certainly, this one-year contact with Schaie was the primary reason why gerontology became one of my areas of interest and why I joined Schaie at West Virginia University at a later time, where he, as the head of the department of psychology, recruited me as an assistant professor.

Emerging Interest in Lifespan Theory and Methodology:
My Dissertation on Sequential Strategies

Any science needs good methodology. A central part of my work on gerontology has been in developmental methodology (e.g., P. B. Baltes, Reese, & Nesselroade, 1977). How did this happen? The principal impetus stems from my dissertation work.

After my year at the University of Nebraska, I returned in the fall of 1964 to the University of Saar to obtain a doctorate. In a position comparable to a junior assistant professor or lecturer (*Wissenschaftlicher Assistent*), I taught courses in developmental (introductory and Piagetian) and clinical psychology, including a seminar on behavior therapy. In addition, I supervised several baccalaureate and master's theses on various topics, such as parent–child relationships, the role of social desirability response sets in personality assessment (jointly with Klaus Eyferth), and on age differences in optimal level of stimulation and the use of testing-the-limits as a method in clinical-developmental psychology (jointly with Lothar Schmidt). Of the students in my undergraduate classes I remember Jochen Brandtstädter and Gisela Labouvie-Vief (discussed later) most. Of fellow colleagues in my own cohort, Leo Montada stands out. Our interactions continue into the present.

Soon after my return to Germany in 1964, I began to seek a topic for my own dissertation research. My first choice, empirical studies on Boesch's developmental model of action psychology, was not received with much enthusiasm. I remember the essence of Boesch's response when I presented my idea to him in an informal conversation: "Dear Mr. Baltes, let me do this kind of research myself. Why don't you find something else?" I was disappointed. From today's perspective, this rejection generated many gains and I feel no regret. It was a turning point and set my course toward becoming a lifespan rather than Piagetian developmental psychologist. On the splendid celebration of his 80th birthday, Boesch and I exchanged our memories of this event. He could not remember it and expressed surprise, perhaps even sadness.

Relatively quickly, I decided to reorient myself and pursue the general topic of developmental methodology. In teaching developmental psychology at the University of Saar, I had covered issues of research design and measurement, including Schaie's general developmental model (Schaie, 1965) and his formulation of three sequential strategies. While at the University of Nebraska, I had already mentioned to Schaie that I was uncomfortable with his theoretical and statistical proposal for defining and unconfounding the effects of age, period, and cohort. At the same time, I was much impressed with his effort and sensed that the questions of how to index age changes, how to study development in a changing society, and how to separate interindividual differences from intraindividual age change were central to developmental psychology.

With Reinert's proximal and Schaie's distal encouragement, I proposed to Boesch to write a dissertation on developmental methodology with a special focus on a critical evaluation of Schaie's general developmental model. Boesch agreed, and in 1967 I submitted to him and the faculty my dissertation titled "Cross-Sectional and Longitudinal Sequences in the Study of Age and Generation Effects." The English article (P. B. Baltes, 1968) resulting from my dissertation became a citation classic. The friendly and supportive editor accepting the article was Hans Thomae, the 20th-century doyen of German lifespan psychology. At the time I did not know Thomae personally, but I had read his work on longitudinal methodology for my dissertation.

Apparently, an initially less than desirable "nonnormative" life event, Boesch's discouragement of my first dissertation topic, had a positive outcome. Although the substantive course of my work had been directed away from Piagetian-Boeschean psychology, when deciding on the topic of my dissertation I had selected well. Schaie, in his seminal work on cohort effects in human development, had identified a major theoretical and empirical issue; an issue, incidentally, that was of much interest in other quarters of social science research as well (e.g., Elder, Riegel, Ryder, and Riley) and attracted much attention. Any critique would be widely read, especially because Schaie's initial exposition was rather complicated.

For many, I became the intellectual opponent of Schaie. Specifically, in my dissertation I argued on the one hand that Schaie's concern with historical and cohort change in the study of development and aging was right on target. On the other hand, I criticized his specific approach and suggested that his theoretical and methodological efforts—namely, to identify age effects primarily as maturational, period effects as environmental, and cohort effects as genetic—were conceptually misguided. I argued that his categorization ignored the fundamental genetic–environmental interaction associated with each of the three components age, period, and cohort. In addition, I criticized Schaie's statistical solution aimed at unconfounding the effects of age, period, and cohort as inappropriate. To prevent misinterpretations about the causes for the sequential collected age-cohort outcomes, I suggested using Schaie's sequential strategies as "descriptive" and not "explanatory" methods of data collection. For this purpose, I introduced the labels of *cross-sectional* and *longitudinal sequences* (see also P. B. Baltes, Reese, & Nesselroade, 1977).

Regarding the issue of age- and cohort-sequential methodology, Schaie and I continued to present opposing views in the literature for several years. To the best of my knowledge, however, these exchanges did not alter our close and positive relationship. Where I am concerned at least, the associated dialogues and publications strengthened my intellectual bonds and commitment to the topic of developmental methodology. In the final analysis, in a joint paper published in 1975 in *Human Development,* Schaie and I agreed to disagree about the interpretation of age, period, and cohort effects, but to sort out, as I had argued, the descriptive from the explanatory.

Parallel to my conceptual dissertation, and in cooperation with Günther Reinert, I tested sequential methods empirically (e.g., P. B. Baltes & Reinert, 1969). While Schaie was using his model to study age and cohort-related functioning in adulthood intelligence in the United States, I conducted comparable sequential research on cognitive development in children in Germany. We clarified the so-called season-of-birth effects in IQ and showed that they were simply due to differences in the length of education that same-aged children had received as a result of fixed age cutoffs for school entry. It pleases me that this early research continues to be cited as "one of the best documented studies of the effects of schooling" (Ceci & Williams, 1997). Together with my earlier master's thesis topic, this cohort research on cognitive development in children also strengthened my lifelong interest in the study of intelligence.

Thus, beginning with my study leave at the University of Nebraska and continuing with my dissertation and dissertation-related research, Schaie's influence on me (although he was not my teacher and mentor in a technical sense) was strong. Despite our intellectual disagreements about specifics (including, later, the nature of intellectual aging; P. B. Baltes, 1993), I view him as the primary figure directing and supporting my initiation into gerontology.

Developing a Career in Lifespan Psychology

Schaie must have felt similarly positive, for he invited me, a few months before I completed my doctorate, to be a discussant at a conference on aging he arranged in 1967 at West Virginia University, where he had just moved. There I met quite a few of the elite in psychological gerontology for the first time.

West Virginia University (1968–1972)

Largely unknown to me, Warner Schaie used this invitation to persuade his faculty to offer me an assistant professorship. As the new chair of the Department of Psychology, he was committed to developing a graduate program in developmental psychology that covered the entire life span. When I returned to Germany, however, the first offer I received was not from West Virginia University but from the University of Michigan. Klaus Riegel had attended the conference and had arranged for the University of Michigan to offer me an assistant professorship.

For a German developmental psychologist, viewing human development as a lifelong enterprise comes naturally. As I have described in several publications (e.g., P. B. Baltes, 1979), the history of German developmental psychology, since the monumental work of the philosopher-psychologist Tetens published in 1777, was oriented toward covering the entire life span. When teaching at Saarbrücken from 1965 to 1967, I already had made an effort to cover lifespan topics when teaching the introductory course in developmental psychology. Joining an emerging program in the psychology of development across the life span was therefore attractive, and my wife and I knew and liked Schaie from our time at the University of Nebraska. Thus, to the surprise of many who know the hierarchy of American higher education, I chose West Virginia University over the University of Michigan. My position as assistant professor started in January 1968.

The four years I spent at West Virginia University were splendid and exhilarating, especially owing to my discovering there a new colleague, John R. Nesselroade. Nesselroade had joined the West Virginia psychology faculty a semester before me with a recent doctorate from the University of Illinois, where he had worked with Raymond B. Cattell, whom I came to admire while studying in Saarbrücken. In addition, West Virginia University was right for the development of a dual career. Following her master's degree from the University of Saar (where she had worked with Boesch), my wife joined the graduate program at West Virginia University to obtain a doctorate in 1973 in another strong program of that department, experimental-operant psychology.

Meeting, and soon collaborating with, John Nesselroade was arguably the most significant event in my professional career. Not only did we embark on a program of exciting collaborative research, we also enjoyed each other's company. Both on and off campus, we worked on issues of developmental methodology (e.g., P. B. Baltes, Reese, & Nesselroade, 1977) but also on intelligence and personality, where we applied, for instance, age-cohort sequential strategies to the study of adolescent development (Nesselroade & Baltes, 1974). This meeting of the minds continues into the present, a successful professional marriage of two careers. If there is something akin to collective agency, or collective selective optimization with compensation (M. M. Baltes & Carstensen, 1999) this is what John Nesselroade and I produced and enjoy.

An added strength of the context at West Virginia University was that Nesselroade and I had excellent doctoral students to enrich the dyad. In fewer than four years I was the primary dissertation supervisor of six doctoral students, several of whom came from my former home institution in Germany. In gerontology, Gisela Labouvie-Vief (she and I share the Reinert brothers as second cousins) and Harvey Sterns are the best known. In addition, I worked closely with William Hoyer when he changed his program affiliation from experimental to developmental psychology.

It is difficult to identify the institutional origins of a given field. When it comes to lifespan thinking in developmental psychology, however, it seems fair to argue that the lifespan developmental psychology program that evolved at West Virginia University from 1968 onward was the main catalyst during the 1970s, at least in the United States. This faculty, with its critical and collaborative mass of expertise and concentration on the entire life span, was unique and had immediate impact. Of the other colleagues on the developmental faculty at West Virginia University, Larry Goulet, Stephen Porges, Frank Hooper, and Hayne Reese were especially significant.

The program presented itself in a more public manner for the first time when Larry Goulet and I organized in 1969, with strong administrative support from Warner Schaie, the first West Virginia Conference on Lifespan Developmental Psychology. It was for that conference that we made the first effort (P. B. Baltes & Goulet, 1970) to define and explicate the term *lifespan developmental psychology*. During my tenure at West Virginia University we held two more conferences, one on lifespan methodology organized and published in 1973 by Nesselroade and Reese, the other on personality and socialization organized and published in 1973 by Baltes and Schaie.

This period also laid the foundation for my theoretical work. During my years at West Virginia University, I began to outline a basic framework of lifespan psychology with a view toward a joint understanding of the traditional processes of development and aging (P. B. Baltes, 1973a). During this time I also started to think about the modification and optimization of human development (P. B. Baltes, 1973b; P. B. Baltes & Labouvie, 1973).

A focus on the modification and optimization of human development and aging was much enhanced by the work of my wife, Margret Baltes, and her training and interest in operant psychology and behavior modification. Together with William Hoyer, Gisela Labouvie, and later Sherry Willis as well as Margie Lachman, Margret has continuously reminded me of the potential of intervention, of treating a given developmental trajectory, such as the aging of intelligence, as one of many possible ones, and of keeping in mind that any developmental outcome is strongly conditioned by environmental factors and their constraints (M. M. Baltes & Baltes, 1977). I believe it was also in this collegial and marital context that I developed and nurtured my interest in the plasticity of human aging. Later, my interest in plasticity and intervention research was intensified by other contextual conditions, such as the action focus of Penn State's College of Human Development, where my career path took me next.

The Pennsylvania State University (1972–1979)

The intellectual attractiveness of the lifespan movement, combined with the expansion of American higher education, was a significant reason why many of the faculty associated with the West Virginia program in lifespan developmental psychology were quickly recruited away. As for me, in 1972 I was offered at the age of 33 the position of director of a division with some 25 faculty members in the College of Human Development at The Pennsylvania State University. This program already contained a sizable number of successful developmental and geropsychologists (e.g., Ray Bortner, Joe Britton, Aletha Huston-Stein, and David Hultsch). The college dean, Donald H. Ford, invested with vision in an interdisciplinary conception of human development and offered me the challenge of building a strong lifespan program in psychology and sociology, combining basic research with application.

Intellectually, the hallmark of my stay at Penn State was the further evolution of lifespan theory and the implementation, jointly with Sherry Willis, of a major research program on the plasticity of intellectual aging. Here, however, I focus on institutional development. Among my first appointments at Penn State were John Nesselroade, Lynn Liben, and William Looft. Soon we were able to strengthen this group further by adding scholars in child and adolescent development who were friendly to a lifespan approach, such as Richard Lerner, but also similar minds in the sociological study of lifespan family development (e.g., Ted Huston, Graham Spanier). Richard Lerner in particular has become a significant figure in the effort to generate a theoretical field of developmental psychology that reflects the theoretical perspectives of a lifespan approach. As at West Virginia University, we also had gifted graduate students whose dissertations I had the pleasure to supervise, such as Steve Cornelius, Margie Lachman, and Carol Ryff. There were other doctoral students, such as Rosemary Blieszner, Roger Dixon, Brian Hofland, and Ron Spiro, with whom I worked closely, although I was not their primary advisor.

Max Planck Institute for Human Development (1980–Present)

In 1980 I received an offer to become a director with the Max Planck Society in Germany. Specifically, I was offered the opportunity to direct a center for psychology and human development in Berlin. At the same time, Margret Baltes was offered a professorship in psychological gerontology at the Free University Berlin.

These were attractive offers, but the pull to stay in the United States was not weak. We very much liked our new homeland. But there were also more personal reasons to remigrate. In the two years before, two people in Germany had died who were central to our lives and whom I had promised to return to Germany when an opportunity arose: my mother and my first mentor, Günther Reinert.

The Max Planck Society is a dream institution for anyone whose primary commitment is to promoting a long-term program of research and to nurturing younger generations at the international frontiers of science. Berlin enjoys a continuous stream of visiting scientists, the Max Planck Society offers financial and infrastructural support for long-term research, and one has the opportunity to recruit outstanding young scholars as doctoral students, postdoctoral fellows, research scientists, and visiting scientists. Among the visiting scientists, for instance, and restricting names to adult development and aging, Vern Bengtson, Laura Carstensen, David Featherman, John Nesselroade, and Tim Salthouse participated actively in many facets of our research program.

In Berlin my interest in and commitment to gerontology grew stronger. To a large degree this resulted from my work as codirector of the Berlin Aging Study (P. B. Baltes & Mayer, 1999; P. B. Baltes & Smith, 1997) and excellent collaboration with the coleader of the Berlin Aging Study, the sociologist Karl Ulrich Mayer. Mayer is one of my codirectors at the Max Planck Institute. Just as I am interested in advancing a lifespan approach in psychology, he is committed to strengthening the sociological counterpart, life-course sociology.

In my judgment, the affiliation with the Max Planck Society offered a new level of action and support for me and for gerontology as a field. In Germany, having the Max Planck Society devote a significant amount of its resources to a field is a symbol of high peer recognition. Not surprisingly, therefore, and due to the collaboration with a new cohort of first-rate younger research scientists, my research program showed new mental energy. During these years I also began to enjoy a number of peer-based friendly gestures such as awards, elections to important academies such as the Royal Swedish Academy of Sciences or the American Academy of Arts and Sciences, and honorary doctorates. I mention these not only because they were important to me but also because they symbolize that by the 1990s, for my generation at least, geropsychology had arrived.

Institutional Networks and Progress in Research

This last observation leads me to comment on the role of institutions and the significance of participating in institutional networks beyond one's home institution. I hold in high esteem each of the institutions I was affiliated with. But other so-called institutional or networking institutions significantly fostered my career and my interest in lifespan psychology and aging.

Especially for someone whose first academic homes were not part of the elite system of institutions, these extrauniversity institutions were of paramount importance. For my own career, six such institutions stand out: the U.S. Social Science Research Council (SSRC), the Stanford Center for Advanced Study in the Behavioral Sciences, the Berlin-Brandenburg Academy of Sciences, the John D. and Catherine T. MacArthur Foundation, the Johann Jacobs Foundation, and the European Science Foundation. Each of these institutions has contributed in notable ways to my career. Through these institutions I have also acquired several mentors and friends who have deeply influenced my career and ways of thinking about science and scholarship: Orville Gilbert Brim, David Hamburg, Gardner Lindzey, David Magnusson, Matilda Riley, and Franz Weinert.

For instance, in 1973 Brim invited me to become a member of the SSRC Committee on Work and Personality in the Middle Years. This committee, under Brim's leadership, opened up an entirely new set of perspectives and collegial relations, for instance with Gardner Lindzey and David Hamburg. Brim himself is one of my handful of significant mentors from a distance, as is Lindzey. In 1978, this committee was transformed into an SSRC Life-Course Perspectives on Human Development Committee, initially chaired by Matilda Riley and later jointly by Glen Elder and me. In my work with the SSRC, I sharpened my thinking about the nature of human development and its interdisciplinary as well as policy agenda. These interactions formed a convoy of scholars who in the long run, I am sure, helped me to gain admittance to the "real" academy, including three fellowships (1978–1979, 1990–1991, 1997–1998) at the Center for Advanced Study in the Behavioral Sciences in Stanford, California.

Let me use the Stanford center as one more example of the powerful role of extrauniversity institutions. Regarding my theoretical contributions in the field of geropsychology, my first one-year center fellowship was perhaps the most crucial one. Initiated by Matilda Riley, a seminar convened to examine basic issues of aging and its future research agenda. In this seminar, many of my ideas, especially regarding lifespan theory and the role of plasticity, achieved a new level of precision, integration, and interdisciplinary fertility (e.g., P. B. Baltes, Reese, & Lipsitt, 1980). Conversations and discussions with CASBS fellows from several disciplines, such as James Birren (psychology), David Featherman (sociology), James Fries (medicine), Matilda and Jack Riley (sociology), Martin Seligman (psychology), and George Vaillant (psychiatry), were particularly helpful. Regarding plasticity, for instance, James Fries, David Featherman, Margret Baltes, and I, each in our own way, sharpened this notion for use in intervention research and models of successful aging.

The Emerging Contours of Psychological Gerontology in the 1960s and 1970s

So far I have presented a chronological account of the antecedents and contexts of my career. In the following sections I reflect on my contributions to the field of geropsychology. Here we are most likely to encounter self-serving views of the past. More complete accounts are contained in P. B. Baltes (1987, 1993, 1997b) and P. B. Baltes, Lindenberger, and Staudinger (1998).

During the decades when I joined the field of gerontology, the 1960s and early 1970s, the field was in a *status nascendi*. For my generation, Birren's 1959 *Handbook* had set the stage. Nevertheless, there was a dearth of theory and methodology. As scholars engaged themselves, they had to ask how to open a new field of scientific inquiry. What are the interesting questions about old age and aging? What are the proper methods? What can one expect of old age as a stage in life? How is aging related to earlier phases of life?

Researchers were struggling to identify geropsychology as a field with its own theoretical and empirical Gestalt. Because of the strong developmental and psychometric training I received at my home institution in Germany, my approach to these questions was guided more by mainstream developmental psychology and methodological frameworks than by gerontology. I wanted geropsychology to be a part of psychology, not its own discipline. In fact, it is fair to conclude that I journeyed into gerontology by being pushed, not by being pulled. What interested me were fairly abstract issues of theory and method. Only a decade or so later did I become interested in aging as a substantive phenomenon.

Advancing Developmental Methodology

The triangulation of research design, measurement, and theory was one cornerstone of my psychological training. Not surprisingly, therefore, when ''pushed'' toward gerontology I became something like a developmental methodologist. This opportunity was enhanced because at that time there was much debate about issues of measurement and the degree to which our data were afflicted by inadequate methods. How to study change, how to identify interindividual differences and separate them from intraindividual change, how to move from description to explanation or from quasi-experimental designs to experimental designs, how to generate a body of knowledge that is both theoretically and empirically sound—these were the questions that I (together with others) attempted to clarify and move into the foreground (P. B. Baltes, Reese, & Nesselroade, 1977).

Historically first was, as I mentioned earlier, my critical evaluation and reformulation of Schaie's age-cohort-sequential designs in my dissertation work (P. B. Baltes, 1968). Subsequently, however—primarily in collaboration with John Nesselroade—my interest expanded to include a search for better convergence between theory and method in developmental research in general. My zealous interest in developmental theory and Nesselroade's deep competence in psychometrics and multivariate research made a wonderful coalition. Moreover, fed by discussions with experimental child psychologists Larry Goulet and Hayne Reese, I argued for an integration of descriptive, quasi-experimental, and experimental approaches in the study of development using the notion of *simulation of development* as a metaphor (P. B. Baltes & Goulet, 1971; Lindenberger & Baltes, 1995).

Lifespan Theory and Aging

The second niche that presented itself during the 1960s and 1970s was the sharpening and articulation of theory. One of the central questions concerned developmental versus gerontological frameworks of theory. What are the origins of aging, do they lie primarily in the ontogenetic past or in the conditions of old age itself, how much continuity is there in lifespan development? Is aging a transformation of development, or does it constitute the outcome of a new set of determining factors and processes that are superimposed on and interact with development?

In general, the field of gerontology had two primary options. One was to study aging as the status of being old; the second was to view aging as an outcome and part of the life course. Primarily for reasons of my psychological training in Germany, I selected the second, the lifespan option. By letting aging enter my conception of childhood-based development, I became a lifespan psychologist (P. B. Baltes, 1973a, 1987, 1997a; Baltes & Goulet, 1970). By refusing to be a gerontologist in the narrow sense, I maintained strong connections to more historically advanced fields such as child-developmental and cognitive psychometric psychology. Thus I joined those who embedded aging in a larger substantive and theoretical context and who thereby were somewhat immunized against the intellectual vulnerability of a newly emerging field. This view lingers into the present. Often I refuse to label myself as a gerontologist.

Participating in the development and elaboration of a lifespan developmental orientation was significant because it permitted me to be innovative in a dual sense. On the one hand, I contributed to the study of the precursors of aging. At the same time, however, I kept in touch with child developmentalists, thereby helping to create a new field, lifespan development (P. B. Baltes, 1987; P. B. Baltes, Reese, & Lipsitt, 1980). From this vantage point, aging is foremost an integral part of lifespan ontogenesis.

Eventually a new metatheory of development resulted (P. B. Baltes, 1997b), with a perspective that from birth onward made the simultaneous existence of gains and losses, multidimensionality, multidirectionality, and multifunctionality the centerpieces of ontogeny. In addition, I argued that selection, optimization, and compensation are the three foundational processes from which development flows. This view of the nature of ontogenetic change, which has parallels in developmental biology, is a radical departure from traditional theories of development, where either growth (early life) or decline (late life) is considered as the defining characteristic of ontogenetic change in adaptive capacity. Others, of course, joined in this effort and proposed alternative but similarly motivated theoretical conceptions; one example is the important work of my former student Gisela Labouvie-Vief (1980, 1982).

Contrary to my initiation into gerontology, the origins for my interest in the metatheory of lifespan psychology are more difficult to identify where individuals are concerned. None of my immediate mentors or colleagues was a lifespan psychologist, nor can I remember an educational experience that stimulated me to think in that direction. Most likely, aside from adding the topic of old age to my interest in childhood, this enthusiasm about a lifespan approach evolved primarily in interactions with people whom I met in diverse institutional settings and in interactions with my own colleagues and students in writing and teaching.

As I mentioned, the German tradition of developmental psychology going back to the work of Tetens and Thomae was another contributing context. As I invested myself in the historical study of lifespan psychology (P. B. Baltes, 1979), I realized that Germany had a long and distinguished tradition in this field dating back to the 18th century (Tetens). In time, of course, I became familiar with the works of 20th-century lifespan scholars such as Charlotte Bühler, Erik Erikson, Robert Havighurst, Bernice Neugarten, and Hans Thomae. But my interactions with them and my reading of them were minimal. Today I consider their conceptions (developmental task, age grading, cognitive mental representations of the life course, etc.) as very relevant as I work on articulating theoretical frameworks with substance.

Also operative were reinforcement schedules and the building of institutions, including publication outlets. In the late 1970s, for instance, I cocreated an annual research series to promote the visibility of lifespan work. From a sociological perspective, Brim had copublished two essays on socialization after childhood with Wheeler in 1966, essays that opened for me more than any other the institutional structuring of lifespan continuity and change. After I had edited the first volume in 1978, Brim joined me to edit the next five volumes of the annual series on lifespan development and behavior. During this period, and with much guidance from Brim, I developed a better understanding of the substantive processes of lifespan development and its contextual contingencies associated with individual and institutional processes of social differentiation (e.g., ethnicity, gender, social class) and social-historical change.

Geropsychology and Interdisciplinarity

In their early evolutionary states, emerging specialties reflect a holistic approach. Disciplinary differentiation comes later. This certainly was true for gerontology in the 1960s and 1970s. The study of aging is more than psychology, and psychological research on aging will profit if it recognizes the biological, social, institutional, and historical forces that shape human development. In this spirit, another marker of my intellectual history is my firm embeddedness in transdisciplinary dialogue.

I am a psychologist, of course, and would like to contribute primarily to the science and profession of psychology using psychological principles and methods. On the other hand, I recognize that psychological analysis is but part of the scientific enterprise. Therefore, I have engaged myself routinely and with enthusiasm in interdisciplinary dialogues with colleagues from neighboring disciplines such as anthropology, sociology, and biology.

Because of this spirit, for instance, I became involved in the Berlin Aging Study, in which about 40 scientists from internal medicine, psychiatry, psychology, and sociology collaborate. And this interdisciplinarity esprit led me more recently to propose an overall theory of lifespan development. This metatheory reflects two decades of interdisciplinary discourse and in its foundation is inherently biocultural; it emphasizes the conjoint action of biological-genetic, institutional, social, and individual factors (P. B. Baltes, 1997a).

Making Developmental Theory Contextualistic

Theoretical orientations in geropsychology reflect variations in emphasis associated with individualistic (organismic) and contextualist (environmental) factors and processes. Some would claim that in the history of psychological gerontology, this dynamic during the past few decades expressed itself in a movement from more individualistic theory toward more contextualistic theory. Within developmental psychology, lifespan psychology was a key player. In this instance, my primary intellectual benchmarks were Urie Bronfenbrenner and Richard Lerner.

While recognizing the defining significance of genetic factors, I have argued that the expression of human development is equally strongly conditioned by cultural and individually based agency factors. Each developmental or aging outcome is but one of many possibilities. I trace this theoretical stance to early writings (M. M. Baltes & Baltes, 1977), although more refined frameworks evolved later and in collaboration with new colleagues at the Berlin Max Planck Institute (e.g., Reinhold Kliegl, Ulman Lindenberger, Jacqui Smith, and Ursula Staudinger). In social-science disciplines, such a contextualist orientation, of course, is the norm. This, however, was not true for psychology.

From Description to Explanation and Modification:
Plasticity and Intervention Research

One theme associated with contextualism is plasticity (see also Lerner, 1984). For me, information about the range and conditions of plasticity as well as its age-related changes is the cornerstone of developmental and aging theory (P. B. Baltes, 1993, 1997a). As gerontology evolved, such an approach was less prevalent than it is today; now most of us think that knowing "what is possible and not possible" is the quintessential question of developmental and gerontological theory.

How variable, how modifiable is aging? What is optimal aging? Such questions form another stone in the mosaic of issues that shaped my intellectual motivation and contributions to geropsychology. My enduring commitment has been to use science to change the contextual and behavioral world of old age for the better (P. B. Baltes, 1973b; M. M. Baltes & Baltes, 1977; P. B. Baltes & Labouvie, 1973). In the 1960s and 1970s, such a focus was present but not at the fore. The science of aging, so my colleagues and I argued, is more than the counting of wrinkles and charting decline.

In this spirit of using science for the betterment of human functioning, I have made *intervention research* and the *optimization of human development* a significant part of my intellectual agenda since the early 1970s. Intervention, of course, is relevant to causal explanation and therefore is part of experimentation. But, for me, the significance of intervention research also has a human optimization and human policy dimension. As I have said recently (P. B. Baltes 1997a; see also M. M. Baltes & Baltes, 1977), I consider the architecture of cultural and biological evolution as essentially incomplete. Of all periods of the life span, the period of old age is the most incomplete and therefore subject to most risks and negative outcomes.

As an intervention-oriented psychologist, I have attempted to provide agency to society and individuals in the task of optimization of old age. Here, aside from collaboration with Margret Baltes, historically I owe much to a close cooperation with Sherry Willis, an educational child developmentalist at Penn State. In the mid-1970s I invited her to develop with me research on the modifiability of intelligence in old age. To this end we initiated a large program of cognitive training research aimed at exploring human potential in old age, selecting explicitly a domain (fluid intelligence) where decline was the rule (Baltes & Willis, 1982). When I left for Germany in 1980, Willis joined Schaie in matrimony and research collaboration on the same topic involving the Seattle Longitudinal Study.

The initial findings of this research program, in which Rosemary Blieszner, Steve Cornelius, Brian Hofland, Margie Lachman, and Ron Spiro played critical roles as advanced graduate students, led to much optimism. Later, as I transformed the program of research at the Berlin Max Planck Institute (P. B. Baltes, 1993) and, with the input from others such as Reinhold Kliegl and Jacqui Smith, considered methods of testing the limits, we obtained new findings on age-associated losses that spawned less optimistic considerations, as described in the next section.

Dual-Process Theory of Lifespan Intelligence and the Search
For Positive Aging (Wisdom)

Theory, method, intervention research, and models of optimal aging coalesced in one additional effort to make a contribution to geropsychology. One of the hotly debated areas of gerontological research in the 1960s and 1970s was whether intellectual decline is inevitable and ubiquitous. With verve, researchers took opposing views. Articles by Horn, Donaldson, Botwinick, Schaie, Willis, and me clashed on an intellectual battleground (e.g., P. B. Baltes & Schaie, 1976, versus Horn & Donaldson, 1977). This was an exciting time, in part because as the field advanced, it soon became clear that the questions were not phrased well, and that new research needed to be conducted to make progress.

In my case, the new work (conducted at the Berlin Max Planck Institute) made me change my thinking, which originally tended to argue for an optimistic, no-decline view. One line of my work, on the psychology of wisdom, continued this tradition of optimism. Other work, however, suggested a move toward a less optimistic and more balanced, more differentiated and multidimensional view of intellectual aging (P. B. Baltes, 1993). This change in theoretical and empirical perspectives put me, for some years at least, in opposition to some of my closest colleagues, notably Warner Schaie and Sherry Willis.

I mention this research perspective because it permits me to highlight a profound transformation in my thinking that had precursors (e.g., P. B. Baltes, 1979; P. B. Baltes et al., 1980), but largely coincided with my appointment at the Berlin Max Planck Institute and working with a new group of scholars with additional areas of expertise. In this newly configured context of minds, I worked toward developing a conception of lifespan intelligence, one that explicitly involves gains and losses, links psychometric intelligence with cognitive psychology and the study of expert systems, and furthermore is reflective of Tetens's original outlook on human development.

My principal collaborators in this newly evolving research program were (in alphabetical order) Freya Dittmann-Kohli, Roger Dixon, Reinhold Kliegl, Ulman Lindenberger, Jacqui Smith, and Ursula Staudinger. Expanding the work of Cattell and Horn on the theory of fluid and crystallized intelligence, we added new theoretical perspectives. Specifically, we considered models of expertise and the differentiation between the largely brain-biology-based "fluid mechanics" and the knowledge-based "crystallized pragmatics" of the mind. A so-called dual-process theory of intelligence resulted (P. B. Baltes, Dittmann-Kohli, & Dixon, 1984; P. B. Baltes, 1993). In addition, we developed model research paradigms of the mechanics (serial memory as operationalized by the method of loci) and the pragmatics (wisdom), and used expertise and testing-the-limits paradigms to explore zones and limits (asymptotes) of functioning in these two analogues of the mechanics and the pragmatics (P. B. Baltes, Smith, & Staudinger, 1992; Kliegl, Smith, & Baltes, 1989, 1990).

This approach permitted us, we think, to offer a new integrative conception of lifespan intelligence that is neither pessimistic nor optimistic (P. B. Baltes, 1997, P. B. Baltes et al., 1998), but that contains a modulated view of gains and losses in intelligence over the lifespan. Regarding the mechanics of the mind, the evidence is definite: decline starts early in adulthood (Lindenberger & Baltes, 1997). Regarding the cognitive pragmatics, where wisdom served as sample case, there is a potential for advance as long as the mechanics do not fall below a certain threshold. It is in the pragmatics of the mind where the interpenetration of intelligence and personality, of biology and culture, is strongest, and where culture can outwit biology (Staudinger & Baltes, 1996).

Toward Theories of Successful Aging:
Selection, Optimization, and Compensation

Throughout human history, science has looked beyond, using scientific knowledge to extend our visions and improve the human condition. This is true also for old age. For millennia, philosophers and humanists have wrestled with identifying the positive in human aging; their efforts were largely based on focusing the mind on the meaning and enjoyable experiences of life (P. B. Baltes, 1991).

In gerontology, since the 1960s, empirically minded scientists have taken up the challenge to search for a good life and optimal aging. The concept of successful aging became the mental guidepost for these efforts (M. M. Baltes & Carstensen, 1996; P. B. Baltes & Baltes, 1990; see also Rowe & Kahn, 1987). Beginning in the late 1970s, Margret Baltes and I have participated in this effort. Interrelating the work of others (e.g., Brandtstädter, Brim, Fries, Kahn, Labouvie-Vief, Lachman, Lawton, Riley, Rowe, Ryff) and our own, we have developed a theory of successful aging that reflects our best knowledge about the nature of lifespan development, the biological and social constraints of aging, and the mechanisms and factors that operate for selection, optimization, and compensation (SOC) to orchestrate an effective and good life.

The theory that Margret Baltes and I developed, *selective optimization with compensation,* is a general theory of development that can be applied to many levels of aggregation and analysis, including psychological aging. For each of the main objectives of lifespan development (growth, maintenance, and management of loss), we submit that it is important to select goals, to optimize the means for reaching these goals, and to compensate when extant means to reach goals disappear. In my view, this theory is the most direct expression of my scholarly commitment to optimization, of articulating life-management strategies that are conducive to maximizing gains and minimizing losses as we develop and age. Together with new colleagues, such as Alexandra Freund, Jutta Heckhausen, Frieder Lang, Ulman Lindenberger, and Michael Marsiske, we are currently at work, collaboratively and individually, to test the theory in a variety of settings and with differing formulations.

Observations

Throughout my life, I have been involved in collaborative relationships. More than the ones I have mentioned here were relevant at one point or another in my career. This is especially true for the fields of child and adolescent development, where an entirely different cohort of colleagues would be involved. Of close collaborators at the Berlin Max Planck Institute regarding questions of child development, for instance, the late Michael Chapman, Todd Little, Gabriele Oettingen, and Ellen Skinner come to mind.

Lifespan continuity and change also applies to professional colleagues and friends, in particular, however, were "significant others" throughout most of my career, as colleagues, cothinkers, or inner voices. In order of their entry into my life and using up to 1970 as a criterion, these were Günther Reinert, Margret Baltes, Ernst Boesch, Warner Schaie, John Nesselroade, and Orville Gilbert Brim, whose contributions to my career cannot be overestimated.

My acknowledgments of significant others would be incomplete, however, if I were not to highlight the powerful influence that some of my former students or postdocs, and by now accomplished gerontological or lifespan scholars, have had on my intellectual biography. Over the years, and beginning in the early 1970s with Gisela Labouvie-Vief, many of them have changed the nature of my thinking about development and aging in critical ways. Alphabetically and with a focus on lifespan psychology and the study of aging, I want to acknowledge especially the contributions of Jochen Brandtstädter, Steven Cornelius, Freya Dittmann-Kohli, Roger Dixon, Jutta Heckhausen, Reinhold Kliegl, Margie Lachman, Ulman Lindenberger, Michael Marsiske, Carol Ryff, Jacqui Smith, and Ursula Staudinger. Each of them has succeeded in making me think differently about one or the other of my intellectual concerns. I expect them to be among those who shape the future contours of lifespan psychology and keep geropsychology in the news of science.

In another institutional context and befitting a lifespan psychologist, as a trustee of the youth-oriented Johann Jacobs Foundation (e.g., *Johann Jacobs Foundation: Annual Report 1997*), I have the opportunity to express a commitment to another period of life: childhood and adolescence. In this context, we discuss lifespan connections between youth and old age, and occasionally I am confronted with the argument that too much societal and scientific concern for and investment into old age detracts from the future welfare of children and youth.

Finally, mentioning and thanking only in the closing paragraph my children Boris (born 1965) and Anushka (born 1971) for their many contributions to family life, reciprocal socialization, and patience with an all too often preoccupied and career-oriented father carries symbolic meaning. It is bound to give the impression of an afterthought. As it turns out and in the best spirit of reciprocal generational transfer, my children are very important to me. Moreover, they seem to understand their father very well, often better than he does himself. I hope that the fatherly neglect they may have experienced in their childhood, and the fact that we uprooted them when returning to Germany and presented our Black adopted daughter with an all-too-White environment, is compensated by a more present and resourceful late-midlife father. Indeed, my wife has remarked more than once that my fatherhood has grown in leaps and bounds as our children have become adults.

References

Baltes, M. M., & Baltes, P. B. (1977). The ecopsychological relativity and plasticity of psychological aging: Convergent perspectives of cohort effects and operant psychology. *Zeitschrift für experimentelle und angewandte Psychologie, 24*, 179–197.

Baltes, M. M. & Carstensen, L. L. (1996). The process of sucessful ageing. *Ageing and Society, 16*, 397–422.

Baltes, M. M. & Carstensen, L. L. (1999). Social-psychological theories and their applications to aging: From individual to collective. In V. L. Bengston & K. W. Schaie (Eds.), *Handbook of theories of aging*, (pp. 209–226). New York: Springer.

Baltes, P. B. (1968). Longitudinal and cross–sectional sequences in the study of age and generation effects. *Human Development, 11*, 145–171.

Baltes, P. B. (1973a). Prototypical paradigms and questions in lifespan research on development and aging. *Gerontologist, 13*, 458–467.

Baltes, P. B. (1973b). Strategies for psychological intervention in old age. *Gerontologist, 13*, 4–6.

Baltes, P. B. (1979). Lifespan developmental psychology: Some converging observations on history and theory. In P. B. Baltes & O. G. Brim Jr. (Eds.), *Lifespan development and behavior* (Vol. 2, pp. 255–279). New York: Academic Press.

Baltes, P. B. (1987). Theoretical propositions of lifespan developmental psychology: On the dynamics between growth and decline. *Developmental Psychology, 23*, 611–626.

Baltes, P. B. (1991). The many faces of human aging: Toward a psychological culture of old age. *Psychological Medicine, 21*, 837–854.

Baltes, P. B. (1993). The aging mind: Potential and limits. *Gerontologist, 33*, 580–594.

Baltes, P. B. (1997a). Ernst E. Boesch at 80: Reflections from a student on the culture of psychology. *Culture and Psychology (Special issue: The legacy of Ernst E. Boesch in Cultural Psychology), 3*, 247–256.

Baltes, P. B. (1997b). On the incomplete architecture of human ontogeny: Selection, optimization, and compensation as foundation of developmental theory. *American Psychologist, 52,* 366–380.

Baltes, P. B., & Baltes, M. M. (1990). Psychological perspectives on successful aging: The model of selective optimization with compensation. In P. B. Baltes & M. M. Baltes (Eds.), *Successful aging: Perspectives from the behavioral sciences* (pp. 1–34). New York: Cambridge University Press.

Baltes, P. B., Cornelius, S. W., Spiro, A., Nesselroade, J. R., & Willis, S. L. (1980). Integration vs. differentiation of fluid-crystallized intelligence in old age. *Developmental Psychology, 16,* 625–635.

Baltes, P. B., Dittmann-Kohli, F., & Dixon, R. A. (1984). New perspectives on the development of intelligence in adulthood: Toward a dual-process conception and a model of selective optimization with compensation. In P. B. Baltes & O. G. Brim Jr. (Eds.), *Lifespan development and behavior* (Vol. 6, pp. 33–76). New York: Academic Press.

Baltes, P. B., & Goulet, L. R. (1970). Status and issues of a lifespan developmental psychology. In L. R. Goulet & P. B. Baltes (Eds.), *Lifespan developmental psychology: Research and theory* (pp. 4–21). New York: Academic Press.

Baltes, P. B., & Goulet, L. R. (1971). Exploration of developmental variables by manipulation and simulation of age differences in behavior. *Human Development, 14,* 149–170.

Baltes, P. B., & Labouvie, G. V. (1973). Adult development of intellectual performance: Description, explanation, modification. In C. Eisdorfer & M. P. Lawton (Eds.), *The psychology of adult development and aging* (pp. 157–219). Washington, DC: American Psychological Association.

Baltes, P. B., Lindenberger, U., & Staudinger, U. M. (1998). Lifespan theory in developmental psychology. In R. M. Lerner (Ed.), *Handbook of child psychology* (5th ed., Vol. 1: Theoretical models of human development, pp. 1029–1143). New York: Wiley.

Baltes, P. B., & Mayer, K. U. (Eds.). (1999). *The Berlin Aging Study: Aging from 70 to 100.* New York: Cambridge University Press.

Baltes, P. B., Reese, H. W., & Lipsitt, L. P. (1980). Lifespan developmental psychology. *Annual Review of Psychology, 31,* 65–110.

Baltes, P. B., Reese, H. W., & Nesselroade, J. R. (Eds.). (1977). *Lifespan developmental psychology: An introduction to research methods.* Monterey, CA: Brooks Cole (reprinted 1988, Hillsdale, NJ: Erlbaum).

Baltes, P. B. & Reinert, G. (1969). Cohort effects in cognitive development of children as revealed by cross-sectional sequences. *Developmental Psychology, 1,* 169–177.

Baltes, P. B., & Schaie, K. W. (1976). On the plasticity of intelligence in adulthood and old age: Where Horn and Donaldson fail. *American Psychologist, 31,* 720–725.

Baltes, P. B., & Smith, J. (1997). A systemic–wholistic view of psychological functioning in very old age: Introduction to a collection of articles from the Berlin Aging Study. *Psychology and Aging, 12,* 395–409.

Baltes, P. B., Smith, J., & Staudinger, U. M. (1992). Wisdom and successful aging. In T. Sonderegger (Ed.), *Nebraska symposium on motivation* (Vol. 39, pp. 123–167). Lincoln: University of Nebraska Press.

Baltes, P. B., & Staudinger, U. M. (Eds.). (1996). *Interactive minds: Lifespan perspectives on the social foundation of cognition.* New York: Cambridge University Press.

Baltes, P. B., & Willis, S. L. (1982). Plasticity and enhancement of intellectual functioning in old age: Penn State's Adult Development and Enrichment Project ADEPT. In F. I. M. Craik & S. E. Trehub (Eds.), *Aging and cognitive processes* (pp. 353–389). New York: Plenum Press.

Ceci, S. J., & Williams, W. M. (1997). Schooling, intelligence, and income. *American Psychologist, 52,* 1051–1058.

Horn, J. L., & Donaldson, G. (1977). Faith is not enough: A response to the Baltes-Schaie claim that intelligence does not wane. *American Psychologist, 32,* 369–373.

Kliegl, R., Smith, J., & Baltes, P. B. (1989). Testing-the-limits and the study of age differences in cognitive plasticity of a mnemonic skill. *Developmental Psychology, 25,* 247–256.

Kliegl, R., Smith, J., & Baltes, P. B. (1990). On the locus and process of magnification of age differences during mnemonic training. *Development Psychology, 26,* 894–904.

Labouvie-Vief, G. (1980). Beyond formal operations: Uses and limits of pure logic in life-span development. *Human Development, 23,* 141–161.

Labouvie-Vief, G. (1982). Dynamic development and mature autonomy: A theoretical prologue. *Human Development, 25,* 161–191.

Lerner, R. M. (1984). *On the nature of human plasticity.* New York: Cambridge University Press.

Lindenberger, U., & Baltes, P. B. (1995). Testing-the-limits and experimental simulation: Two methods to explicate the role of learning in development. *Human Development, 38,* 349–360.

Lindenberger, U., & Baltes, P. B. (1997). Intellectual functioning in old and very old age: Cross-sectional results from the Berlin Aging Study. *Psychology & Aging, 12,* 410–432.

Nesselroade, J. R., & Baltes, P. B. (1974). Adolescent personality development and historical change: 1970–1972. *Monographs of the Society for Research in Child Development, 39* (1, Serial No. 154).

Reinert, G., Baltes, P. B., & Schmidt, L. R. (1965). Faktorenanalytische Untersuchungen zur Differenzierungshypothese der Intelligenz (Factor analytic studies on the differentiation hypothesis of intelligence). *Psychologische Forschung, 28,* 246–300.

Riegel, K. F. (1976). The dialectics of human deveolpment. *American Psychologist, 31,* 689–700.

Rowe, J. W., & Kahn, R. L. (1987). Human aging: Usual and successful. *Science, 237,* 143–149.

Schaie, K. W. (1965). A general model for the study of developmental problems. *Psychological Bulletin, 64,* 92–107.

Schaie, K. W., Baltes, P. B., & Strother, C. R. (1964). A study of auditory sensitivity in advanced age. *Journal of Gerontology, 19,* 453–457.

Staudinger, U. M., & Baltes, P. B. (1996). Interactive minds: A facilitative setting for wisdom-related performance? *Journal of Personality and Social Psychology, 71,* 746–762.

Chapter 3
STUDYING AGING IN NORWAY

Eva Beverfelt

To Write an Autobiography:
More Difficult Than I Thought

To write an autobiography with an emphasis on my career in the study on aging appealed to me as a fascinating task. An uncomplicated travel of reminiscences, easy to undertake—so I thought before starting. I was wrong! The job did not turn out to be a simple one. Yet there should be good reasons for me to present my personal life account. A number of gerontologists have indicated motives and mental health benefits related to writing autobiographies in old age. In a paper about elderly participants in autobiography competitions in Norway, I myself had suggested that "bringing order to their life histories and explaining how and why they developed like they did, seemed to be a challenging puzzle where the answer was a clarifying 'this is me—here I am' picture" (Beverfelt, 1984). Thirteen years later this challenging puzzle lay before me. So what was the problem? In brief it was to find the red thread, the main line indicating a systematic development through the stages of my personal and occupational life history. It was at that point I felt at a loss. So many red threads appeared in the picture. It became difficult to sort out the developmental trends due to my own decisions and those that were directed by various coincidences on my way.

Thus my interest in an academic career cannot be traced back to a certain stage of my youth or to particular persons. Generally education was taken for granted in my family. My mother (born in 1896) got her degree from the gymnasium in 1916, an education similar to

I regret not having left more space for international cooperation and contacts, which constituted an essential condition of my career. Meeting foreign colleagues and spending some time abroad were necessary sources of knowledge, experience, and encouragement. A grant from the Ford Foundation enabled me to participate in the preconference seminar and the Fifth International Congress of Gerontology in San Francisco in 1960. Above all, the grant included two months of travel in the United States. Together with Margaret Bucke from England and Aurelia Florea from Italy, I was invited to visit universities and institutions to exchange experiences about research and old age care. Among later great stays in the United States are those related to the White House conferences in 1971 and 1981. To participate in one of the conference committees in 1971, chaired by Donald P. Kent, was really a privilege. The way in which Professor Kent stimulated discussions of the committee became my ideal for leading a group. Thanks to kind invitations, I also enjoyed staying in New Zealand and Israel for some months. Those not mentioned are not forgotten, neither are the numerous persons who have shared their knowledge and time with me. Yet I feel that in this history a few of those who have had an important influence on my career should be mentioned by name, and they are Wilma Donahue, C. Tibbitts, and J. E. Birren from the United States; R. M. Titmuss, P. Townsend, Margret Dieck, and R. J. van Zonneveld from Europe; and Thea Nathan and S. Bergman from Israel.

the one of most of her siblings. My father (died in 1932) had been a physician. I myself was glad and proud to go to the gymnasium where my mother had been educated. Glad because I could follow in the footsteps of my mother, whom I admired very much. Proud because I was among those who passed the special entrance examination of this school. Able and devoted teachers and clever classmates were encouraging for the desire to learn through further studies. Due to the German occupation, the offer of leisure time activities was limited, and the school became maybe a more significant part of life than it otherwise would have been. My decision to go to the university was received by my family as a matter of fact. Their only concern was the choice of psychology, because they were in doubt as to whether I could earn my living as psychologist. Actually I intended to study law but changed my mind after having read some psychology literature as a part of an obligatory examination before attending the university. This introduction is meant to serve as a background for the history of my life in geropsychology, or rather social gerontology, over approximately 40 years.

From Novice to Self-Educated in the Study of Aging

After World War II Norway, with its 3.3 million people, was a nation marked by relief and optimism. The solidarity between people since the war still influenced society. Especially, we who were young at that time were convinced that whatever future might bring, it could not be as difficult to cope with as life during the five years of occupation. Rebuilding in destroyed areas, repairs of damages, and development of an ideal welfare state were considered to be only a matter of time. The idea of a welfare state was generally accepted.

In the debate of social policy, the living conditions of older people becomes one of the central themes. Increased interest from politicians was also brought about by the demographic development, implying a rapid growth of old people in number and share of the total population (8% in 1950, versus 14% today). Along with this interest came an awareness of the need for scientific studies of the conditions of older people.

Thus the research on aging started in the early 1950s. Two main features characterize the beginning. First, the field of research was introduced by a voluntary health association, the National Public Health Association (NPHA). In 1950 this association established a new section of its organization and appointed a committee of advisors. During the following years, the NPHA prepared research programs, initiated studies, and created gerontological forums and a research institute. So far there was no interest from academic circles, apart from one important exception—the Institute of Social Medicine at the University of Oslo. Professor Strøm, the head of this institute, undertook the very first studies, which focused on elderly workers and living conditions of older people in institutions and in their own homes. Second, the pioneers of the first stage were all physicians. Most were in key positions in health care and social medicine, but a few were geriatricians. At this point I do underline the fact that in spite of the professional background of the pioneers, the approach to studies of aging was not dominated by a medical view.

In 1954, the NPHA initiated the foundation of the Norwegian Gerontological Society (NGS). In his opening address, the director of the NPHA, Dr. Gedde-Dahl (1954), stressed that because the study of aging is a multidisciplinary field, research should be based on interdisciplinary approaches as well as studies within each of the relevant disciplines. Through visits to other countries the speaker had learned that it was difficult to sustain a sound balance of interest between the various disciplines: ''Where the medicine has dominated, social scientists will often feel left out, where the psychologists have dominated, medical considerations may be left in the background.'' Such pitfalls should be kept in mind when planning gerontological research in Norway.

I never heard the address of Gedde-Dahl. At that time I didn't even know about the foundation of a gerontological society. My six-year study of psychology was finished, I had just left the University of Oslo with the cand.psychol. degree, and I had accepted a job offered by the psychology division of the army. Interviewing and testing recruits and dealing with dropouts and other problem cases were far from doing research on aging. Yet my history in the field of aging started about that time, although at first it was limited to experience related to spare-time activities.

For several periods during my years as a student I worked in a central government office occupied with the distribution of pensions to civil servants. Many of the retirees came to fetch their monthly pension, and occasionally it struck me as a strange phenomenon that the human beings in this age group were no concern of psychology, as they were never mentioned in my textbooks or by the teachers. This observation only vaguely stirred my mind. My interest in aging and old people might have ceased there if it hadn't been for another incident. Like other graduates in those days I felt it an obligation to share my knowledge of psychology with people who wanted to educate themselves through evening courses. So I offered my service to The Students' Free Education, a nationwide nonprofit organization. The director of this organization had just returned from a visit to America. Among the new ideas he brought home was to organize preretirement training courses. None of the other psychologists, registered as teachers, were willing to conduct such a course. The mere thought of ''something'' related to old age was turned away. Finally I agreed to run the course, provided the subject would be the psychology of middle age and later years. The title of the course became We over 50. The course—24 sessions, attended by people 50 to 80 years of age—was succeeded by 25 more over the following six years.

Before the first course began I made serious efforts to get a minimum of information about the issue I was expected to introduce. Visits to the university library and to the Ministry of Social Affairs gave me some ideas about literature and old age care. The most valuable help was the advice to contact the NPHA, through which I learned about studies already undertaken in Norway and about the international and Norwegian societies of gerontology.

Another incident bringing me closer to the environment of aging was an invitation to serve on the board of NGS. A board member had seen my name on the list of evening course leaders. My lack of knowledge, which I clearly stated, was of no concern to the board members, who needed a psychologist in order to meet the multidisciplinary approach confirmed in the bylaws. On that condition I agreed to take a seat among this learned group of professors and others in high-level positions, mostly in medicine.

A formal connection with the Gerontological Society was inspiring and to a great extent enhanced my interest in geropsychology, which I suggested should be paid more attention in discussions on relevant research themes. Moreover, in the evening course I was conducting I was met with crucial questions such as the impact of aging on personality, cognitive functions, mental health, and adaptation. In this respect there was not much to learn from the other board members of the society, and because I could find no one else with whom to share my interest, I decided to keep myself informed about knowledge gained through research by colleagues abroad, especially in the United States. After all, my interest was still primarily attached to a spare-time activity.

My main concern had now become child psychology. I had been offered a job as research assistant in a longitudinal project, conducted by Åse Gruda Skard, assistant professor at the University of Oslo and a leading child psychologist. The job in itself was indeed attractive and the environment of work even more so because I admired Professor

Skard as an outstanding psychologist and inspiring teacher (and I was grateful for her support during my psychology study). Again I had a job in a field far from aging, certainly studying development, but at an early stage of life, among children three months to two years of age. Although I enjoyed the job, the psychology of aging was constantly on my mind. Nevertheless I was surprised when during a party Professor Schjelderup, a former teacher of mine, stated that the psychology of aging would be a challenge to psychologists in the near future. I did not ask why he had never touched on this aspect in his lectures. I was too shy.

The only trouble with the job as research assistant was that it would last only as long as the project could be financed. Especially when the American grant (which covered a main part of the budget) came to an end, the future of the study would be insecure. This aspect of my job worried me because I was dependent on earning money. The income of my husband, who was educated in law, was insufficient to support both of us. No glorious time for solicitors existed in those days. The supply exceeded the demand of the labor market, and young professionals were glad to have jobs at all. Under the circumstances I found it stupid not to accept an offer of a permanent job as consultant of aging to the NPHA. We, Åse and I, both cried when I left. For a long time I felt guilty for not having lived up to my obligations considering all she had done for me over the years. Fortunately our friendship and contact continued as long as she lived. Here and now I am glad to honor the memory of Åse Gruda Skard, one of the few Norwegian psychologists I was asked about by colleagues in other countries during the 1960s. In spite of her contribution to child psychology in the United States, Norway never gave her the recognition she deserved. Skard's memory is also related to aging as she was among the few teachers at the University of Oslo who first made an effort to make the psychology of aging visible to the students. The other university lecturer making efforts in this direction was Sol Seim. But apparently the time was not yet mature enough for this approach. Still more regrettable is the fact that teachers of today are reluctant to incorporate aging in the different psychological subjects.

My decision to accept a new job was ascribed to a matter of economy. This explanation is perhaps too simple. There may have been other motives as well. I had come to a crossroad in my career in psychology. The involvement in aging had become so time-consuming that I would have to drop it if I wanted to make myself useful in another field. Did I really want to give up the psychology of aging? If Å.G. Skard had been able to provide a permanent job for me, would child psychology have been my first choice? The question shall remain unanswered. It is mentioned only to indicate that my career in the psychology of aging was not the result of serious and thorough planning. On the other hand, I had cultivated and expanded my interest during the three years before I began my employment in the NPHA.

As consultant to the health organization, I soon realized the benefit of working in protected environments like those of my former jobs—protected in the sense that there were always psychologists close by, somebody willing to exchange experience, ideas, and opinions. Not that I appreciated all of them to the same extent. But we belonged to one and the same professional group. All of a sudden I found myself in a completely different work situation. Management and staff welcomed me with kind curiosity but apparently without any idea concerning how I could benefit the health and welfare of older people. Neither skeptical nor especially optimistic as to a future contribution of mine, they obviously expected the consultant to find out by herself what to do and how to do it. Sometimes I even wondered if I had been employed as an alibi for an up-to-date interdisciplinary section on aging or as the psychological mascot of the NPHA. Anyway, I felt professionally alone. Also among psychologists I missed my identity as a child psychologist. Luckily in a few years it became acceptable for a psychologist to work with the problems of aging and the older population. I had adopted the new identity, being a geropsychologist. This was mainly due to the fact that my job had developed in a direction far beyond what I (and probably my employer) had imagined when I started.

To explain the development, I have to go a few years back. In 1954, during the foundation of the Gerontological Society, Gedde-Dahl stated the need for a gerontological research institution (see Gedde-Dahl, 1955):

> It is desirable that this Society arrives at a joint planning and balancing of the research tasks. Preferably we should then have a research center. . . . It is evident that then also the decades ahead of retirement must be subject of investigation.

Gedde-Dahl translated words into action. Three years later the NPHA was ready to open its gerontological institute. An outline for the plan of activities to be performed had been prepared with the cooperation of the Gerontological Society and the Municipality of Oslo, and the outline had been approved by the bodies concerned.

Premises were arranged for in a new building, which was raised by the NPHA. The building was originally planned entirely as a boarding school for nursing students. At a late stage of the building process it was decided that some of the space would be allocated to a gerontological institute. The result was that the school looked on its new neighbor, the gerontological institute, as an unpleasant intruder, although both belonged to the same organization.

The scope and methods of the institute as indicated in the plan outlined were rather vague. The institute would include two units: a scientific one and a practical one. One unit would conduct research on aging from a theoretical and applied point of view, and the other unit would organize day care service on an experimental basis and thus function as a model center. Among the staff needed right from the start was a physician, a nurse, a psychologist, and a social worker. The plan stated that ''Physician and psychologist are needed not only for the practical work but also for the scientific activities.'' Besides, the physician would also be in charge of the institute because so many of the problems to be dealt with had to be considered from a medical point of view: ''It is difficult or impossible for a person educated in social science to survey the medical questions. It is then easier for a physician with socio-medical insight to survey the social questions'' (Gedde-Dahl, 1957). More quotations from the plan of the institute could be added, clearly showing its medical ancestry.

Reading the plan now gives rise to mixed feelings. A nearby question is: Where was I in the picture at that time, 40 years ago? I had not been involved in preparing the plan. Nor was the plan for the gerontological institute referred to when I was employed by the NPHA, which was actually rather strange considering the fact that less than a year later I was, so to speak, thrown into the institute. But these conditions show the power and impact of a great private health organization in those days. In contrast to public authorities, the NPHA was not hindered by complicated bureaucratic rules and formal procedures.

Also employment procedures were indeed informal. When I had announced my interest in the job offered, I was interviewed by Gedde-Dahl, who apparently was well informed about my engagement in the psychology of aging. The only point he stressed in that connection was my experience from the evening course: Did I feel comfortable when I had to introduce psychological subjects without using ''the noncomprehensive terminology of psychology''? Otherwise he was mainly concerned with my hobbies: Did they include music, literature, history, bridge? The question left no doubt about *his* interests. The point of referring to this trifle is to give a glimpse of the man who was going to be my superior. He was above all physician, emphasizing the health and medical problems of aging, while at the same time he was advocating the study of social and psychological problems as well. With his colorful and complex personality, Gedde-Dahl could inspire laypersons and his staff members to perform at their very best, yet he could be a rather ruthless adversary.

My letter of employment from the NPHA gave information on my salary and practical matters—not a word about the content of my job. The question of my salary should be included in the history of women's emancipation. I was told that because I was married and thus provided for, my salary had to be lower than for a man in a corresponding position. Only a modest, naive, or optimistic person would accept a job on these conditions. I did! I don't know the dividing line between being naive and optimistic, so I admit to being both. Significant contribution to the development of health and welfare measures had been achieved by the informal course of action of the NPHA. But the freedom of action strengthening the striking power of the organization also made it an unpredictable and often problematic employer. During the 17 years I worked with NPHA this dichotomy became a challenge, and sometimes a problem, in my career.

The first challenge appeared just before the opening of the gerontological institute— late autumn of 1957. I had been busy employing a secretary for the institute and a social worker and service personnel for the practical unit. Moreover, Viktor Gaustad, head physician of the geriatric department at the City Hospital of Oslo, had agreed to act as a medical consultant for half a day per week.

The date of the opening ceremony was announced, the minister of Family and Consumers had agreed to give the opening address, and invited guests from Sweden (two MDs) as well as Norwegian guests were ready to give papers. The only "thing" missing was a director of the new institution, *Nasjonalforeningens Gerontologiske Institutt* (NGI). No physician, with insight into social medicine or without, had been tempted by this position. But the show had to go on. So I was ordered to take responsibility for the management of the institute. There I was, faced with professional and administrative challenges rather different from those I had met with earlier. The simplest part of the job was administration. Apart from the personnel mentioned earlier, there was no one else to administer. On the other hand, the lack of coworkers made it complicated to live up to expectations concerning research.

The NPHA had decided that the board should consist of five members: two members representing its own organization and one representative each from the University of Oslo, the Old People's Health Committee, and the Social Welfare Department of Oslo City. Although composition and members of the board changed over the years, there were only five different chairs during the 37 years I was in charge of the institute. In that way the chairs gained knowledge and experience while bringing about fruitful discussions on plans and procedures. They were open for new ideas and approaches, but at the same time they served as an element of continuity.

My obligation in this respect was to work as secretary of the board. Perhaps some will associate the term *secretary* with a person who automatically receives instructions and takes notes. My experience points to quite another direction. I soon realized the possibilities of this position to influence decision making. Because it was my responsibility to prepare the matters to be dealt with by the board, I had the advantage of indirectly suggesting terms of discussion. The term *power* has a slight negative connotation. Yet because I have now retired, I admit that I felt comfortable to have some power enabling me to influence the development of NGI.

The first board of NGI had to cope with all the problems of a newcomer. The purpose of the institute was to do research on aging and to develop a model of a service center. To construct clearer definitions of subgoals and methods, the board prepared bylaws for its own activity and guidelines for the work of the institute. Still, the challenges ahead seemed enormous—exciting and promising but also frightening for a female version of John Lackland, the English king who had the title but had only a small population to rule. The comparison is not quite perfect, but it concerns a "research" director who was practically without staff.

The NPHA was, of course, ready to support the tiny child it had given birth to. Its general approach when developing a new field of work was to become familiar with the experience from corresponding fields in other countries. Therefore the NPHA took it for granted that I should participate in meetings and seminars abroad and that social gerontologists should be invited to NGI. In spite of this support, valuable as it was, problems associated with starting off the institute were difficult to cope with.

When we slowly succeeded it was to a great extent due to the contribution of Viktor Gaustad, chair of the board for the first 10 years. His professional help, encouragement, and belief in the job never failed. Since the early 1950s, Gaustad had emerged as the first in various geriatric and gerontological arenas. He had developed a geriatric hospital department, had been chair of the Norwegian Gerontological Society, and had given a paper at the Third International Congress of IAG in London (in 1954). His interest in aging and old age included social gerontological problems as well as geriatrics. Both his international contacts and broad interests became important for the development of NGI. Many great personalities, women and men, have given me the support that assumed the positive development of my career. Pointing to any particular person may be to insult others. Nevertheless, I can't restrain myself from allocating Gaustad a special place in this connection. He was strong and efficient yet never authoritarian; he was willing to compromise, but only when he considered this to be the most fruitful way of problem solving.

Everyday Life at NGI During the First Years

The conditions of research could have been better as to location of premises. Closely connected with the service center, they were rather noisy. On the other hand this busy place, with streams of older people coming and going, was a sound reminder that old age does not only exist in books. My curiosity and motivation to learn more about becoming and being old were strengthened. Moreover, subjects to be included in innovation studies and theoretical research were easily at hand. Still, the challenges seemed near to overwhelming. The feeling of insufficiency was a close attendant. Life was complicated, yet never boring.

The NPHA had left me its gerontological "library," which I started to supplement along with the efforts to continue my literature study. My main interest had been, and still was, coping behavior and strategies. The question was how to approach the problem. Theories and hypotheses discussed in thick books at hand were too highbrowed and elevated for me. So I decided to get a general view regarding the daily life of older people in the vicinity. In a random sample, 430 older people who did not use the service center were interviewed. I did most of the interviews myself. The remaining were done by a sociology student, who later joined the research team. Some results from the study were submitted in my paper at the Fifth International Gerontology Congress (in 1960). Before that I had attended two gerontological conferences abroad. The first one was in Copenhagen, arranged by the European branch of the Social Science Research Committee. The knowledge of the chairman, H. Friis, and of the outstanding participants impressed me, especially the group from England: Sheldon, Abel-Smith, Townsend, and Titmuss. A few months before, at an international congress of psychology, also in Copenhagen, I had given a paper on the development of children 1 to 3 years old. Now at the gerontological meeting, my contribution was poor. My question, kept in silence, was why I was the only psychologist. Was no one else in Europe interested in gerontology? Of course, there were geropsychologists at that time, in England, Germany, the Netherlands, and other European countries. But for some years sociologists and economists had a rather strong impact on the Social Science Research Committee.

The following year I attended the Fourth International Conference of IAG in Italy. I was still a bit uneasy and a rather passive participant, although I was grateful for the opportunity to attend the congress. I made efforts to obtain knowledge and make myself acquainted with life in the big international world of gerontology. Here it was in front of me, represented by famous gerontologists such as John E. Anderson, James E. Birren (1959), Wilma Donahue, Robert J. Havighurst, Robert W. Kleemeier, Bernice Neugarten (1968), and Clark Tibbitts (1960). I was now able to see and listen to celebrities whom I had learned about from gerontological literature. Approaching any one of them was out of the question. What should I tell about "my research"? The distance between their world and mine worried me a bit. But much more important was the positive outcome. It strengthened my motivation to continue my efforts to develop research on aging in Norway, especially in geropsychology. Besides being comprehensible for a psychologist, this was apparently a highly esteemed branch within the hierarchy of research. At least the highest and lowest level of this system seemed clear. On the top glittered biology, at the bottom was applied research, not rarely associated with social work, even with volunteers, middle-class women wearing hats. Not yet quite sure about my place in this system, I went home full of hopes and inspiration. An especially vague plan of mine had been stimulated by what Klaus F. Riegel had told me about his German standardization of the Wechsler Bellevue test.

Foothold in Research

Along with the interview study mentioned, my research assistant and I started to translate the Wechsler Adult Intelligence Scale (WAIS). The idea to do a study on mental capacity and aging was based on considerations from various points of view. The theme was of great theoretical and also practical significance. It would stress the psychological profile of NGI and, so I hoped, make it more attractive to psychologists, at least to students. Moreover, from my former work, although limited to children and recruits, I was familiar with studies on mental capacity. Most important for realizing the idea was also a request from Dr. Gaustad to develop a Norwegian test for measuring cognitive functions of middle-aged and older persons.

The WAIS project included 110 older participants (70 to 74 years old) and 111 middle-aged participants (55 to 64 years old). In addition to the psychological study as a main part, the project was composed of different medical examinations of the subjects in the oldest age group. The medical part of the project was introduced because of experience we gained through preliminary studies. Strange reactions to some of the items in the test made us suspicious as to whether we were testing mental capacity or sight and hearing. We therefore extended the project to include also sight and hearing examinations. A noticeable individual difference in physical fitness stressed the problem of the relationship between physical health and mental capacity. So we incorporated as well a check on their general state of health. Two experts acted as consultants to the project: Viktor Gaustad gave assistance on the medical part and Sol Seim did likewise for the psychological part. Seim, the university teacher I introduced earlier, took great interest in motivating able students to participate in the project, and she succeeded very well. The two students, Hilmar Nordvik and Aase-Marit Nygård, both completed their studies during the project. Nordvik, now a professor at the University of Trondheim, left NGI shortly after we finished the WAIS project. Aase-Marit Nygård remained at the institute until after I retired (in 1994). As a specialist in clinical geropsychology, she has become one of the leading gerontologists in the Nordic countries and is at present president of the Norwegian Gerontological Society.

But let me return to the time 37 years back. After a few years of hard work, my expectations when starting the WAIS project were met. We had completed a comprehensive research project, gained significant experience (also through mistakes), and we had become better equipped to deal with new challenges of research. The project had brought the institute into contact with interested students, and we could offer psychologists a Norwegian version of WAIS. The fact that Nordvik analyzed findings from the project in his cand.psychol. dissertation probably helped change the attitude among students of psychology. More of them now applied for spending their compulsory time of practice at NGI.

Dealing with this stage of my career and the favorable development of the institute, I feel obliged to add and underline a piece of information about the WAIS project and the work of NGI in general. Implementation of the WAIS study had been possible thanks to help and support from psychologists and physicians outside the institute. The honor of the Norwegian version of WAIS must be shared with the group of four psychologists who participated as volunteers in the work of translating and adjusting the test to Norwegian conditions. Professors of psychology gave advice as to relevant literature and the pattern analysis method, which we applied in relation to data collected on interests and social contacts.

Regarding the physicians, the general practitioner was a staff member employed part time by NGI. We had argued strongly to obtain such a position. Unfortunately it could not be maintained when the doctor left after a few years. But his nurse had become interested in gerontology and remained with the institute for a number of years. Anyway, the doctor and the nurse participated in the project. The specialists on sight and hearing both worked with the state hospital and took part in the study out of pure interest; their financial compensation was near to nothing. The three reports submitted by the physicians were included in the final project report, which also dealt with the relationship between psychological and medical data.

The WAIS study became a kind of door-opener to geropsychology and Norwegian psychologists. A complete Norwegian version was especially appreciated by the psychologists who so far had only superficial translations of part of the test battery. In a preliminary report from the study it appears that

> From a number of psychologists in other institutions there have been a great interest and demand for the Norwegian version of the Wechsler test prepared by NGI. On the condition that we get access to the protocols, we have lent the manual to psychiatric departments, rehabilitation institutes, a policlinic for alcoholics and a social-medical department.

The final report of the study concludes that, in spite of weaknesses, "As the first comprehensive gerontological research project, basically theoretical, in this country, we still hope the study to be of significance first of all by stimulating further research within the multidisciplinary field of gerontology" (Nordvik, Beverfelt, & Nygård, 1965). Also other professions took interest in our research. The Medical Society, a very conservative and sophisticated body, invited us to report on the WAIS study; and although mainly concerned with the medical part, the society members had to listen to the presentation of psychological problems as well.

Acknowledgment of NGI as a research institution was further affirmed by the fact that NGI was supported by grants from the National Research Foundation. Yet neither the impact of the WAIS study nor the expansion of NGI occurred overnight. Preparing plans of the WAIS study was indeed time-consuming, involving extensive correspondence with the Psychological Corporation in the United States in order to gain permission to translate and adjust the test to Norwegian conditions. Simultaneously the survival of NGI depended on meeting other obligations. The institute should have made itself visible and be useful for NPHA by acquiring and disseminating relevant knowledge. Intelligence and aging was not

its main concern. But through teaching, preparing study material for educational establish-
ments, and conducting studies on institutions and measures for older people, we succeeded
to some extent both in satisfying NPHA and in arousing public authorites' interest in NGI
and our activities. In conclusion, for my career the WAIS study meant a significant step
forward in knowledge and self-confidence. The impact of the study on the future of NGI was
also obvious, yet only one of the efforts led to the expansion over the coming years.

Encouraged by the saying about becoming a prophet in your own country, we prepared
an article for the *Journal of Gerontology.* Had it been difficult at home, it was apparently
more complicated to become a prophet in another country. Getting the manuscript back for
the second (or was it the third?) time, we were to the point of giving in when I incidentally
mentioned the matter to Professor Johan Torgersen, president of NSA where I was secretary.
Torgersen, himself a well-known contributor to scientific journals, urged us to go on, telling
that he *always* got his manuscript back twice or more. We both knew this was not true, but
anyway it was a comfort to me. The article appeared in 1964.

In 1967 Torgersen succeeded Gaustad as chair of the board of NGI. It was a privilege for
the institute and for me to benefit from the influence of this great scientist who was in learned
circles referred to as Leonardo da Vinci of the North. Although he was a professor of
anatomy, his strong interest in aging above all concentrated on cultural, philosophical, and
psychological aspects. His knowledge about these issues as well as about theory of science
appeared in books such as *Man, Wonder, and Problem Child in History of Life, Natural
Science and Cathedral,* and *Philosophy and Crime.* Many of his articles were published in
the *Norwegian Medical Journal* because the scientists, philosophers, and other authors he
was writing about were discussed from a medical point of view. A jewel among these articles
is Torgersen's interpretation of physicians in the drama by Ibsen.

Regarding organizing and administrative problems, he was of minor help. I felt guilt-
ridden when I had to occupy his time with practical and financial matters of the institute.
Kind and friendly, he would listen to my presentation of the problems but to discuss them
was beyond his interest. During a board meeting he might ask me in a whispering voice
whether the issue was account or budget. He never bothered learning the difference, which
was no problem at that time as I felt fairly competent myself. A few years later when
Torgersen had left NGI, we were in need of a chair who was ready to become involved in the
whole organizing of the institute.

NGI Becomes a Public Institution

From the late 1960s the research activities of NGI developed at a speed I had hardly
dreamed about a few years earlier. The expansion was due to improved economic conditions,
which made it possible for NGI to employ more researchers. Most of them were psychologists, indicating a growing interest in aging, although a general skepticism among psychologists was not overcome.

In 1970 the service center was separated from the institute, and three years later NGI
became a state institution under the auspices of the Ministry of Social Affairs. The takeover
by the state, simple as it seemed from outside, actually was a result of heated debates
between NPHA and NGI, and among the executive committee of NPHA, where the
members were of strong opinions for or against maintaining the ownership of the institute.
The relationship between the director of NPHA and me had become cool. NGI, created by
the association, was once a child they were proud of and wanted to educate. Now, we in the
service of NGI felt the institute to be considered a troublesome teenager struggling for
independence. Yet I was not worried about the future of NGI, sure that the national

government would assume responsibility. We had already been welcomed by the Ministry of Social Affairs as a clearinghouse and data collecting agency.

But no one on the staff was particularly happy about the thought of NGI becoming a state institute. I strongly recommended that the NPHA maintain ownership on the condition that the basic budget was secured by public funding. Apparently this suggestion was of no interest for the negotiating parties. The Parliament decided to make NGI a state institution. I had hoped for another solution but felt relieved that a stressful period of preparing special reports and of being evaluated was over and that the operating cost would be met by the state. Contact with my new peer group, directors of other state institutions, was stimulating, although not very close. On the other hand, improved economic conditions gave NGI more freedom of action, leading to more comprehensive administrative tasks for me. Under these circumstances I felt it an obligation to continue developing NGI into a sound research institute, rather than to concentrate on my career as psychologist in the study on aging.

The annual budget from 1973 that was funded by the national government supported a staff of twelve behavioral and social scientists, two research aids, one information officer, and seven administrative and support personnel. It was a big staff compared with the start 15 years earlier. A county medical officer, Gustav Vig, had become chair of the board, and for more than a decade NGI benefited from his experience gained through participation in studies and implementation of knowledge since the early 1950s.

The first 10 years as a public institution passed very smoothly. A generous grant from the government made it possible to celebrate the 25th anniversary of NGI with professional and social arrangements. Important gerontologists from Europe and the United States were invited for a seminar. And a meeting at the university was honored by the presence of H. M. King Harald, ministers, and other celebrities. Considered as a historic event, it is interesting to observe the later fate of NGI in view of the acknowledgment given by the Minister of Social Affairs (Heløe, 1982):

> When the Institute became a national institute and formally responsible to a Ministry, there was no lack of gloomy forecasts about ministry direction: there would no longer be scope for freedom of research, it would become an institute for drawing up reports, and so on. The Ministry, however, has all the time wanted, expected, and—dare I in all modesty add—made it possible for the Institute to maintain its own identity. We have felt that the Institute has been eager to meet our needs, while at the same time it has managed to carry on its activities without compromising professional principles or its own integrity. We feel—as the Institute also says it feels—that our cooperation has been a success. I hope that this cooperation will continue in the same favorable atmosphere, and that the Institute will continue to contribute as it has done. This year our collaboration has been extended to allow the Institute to cooperate more closely in the Ministry's experiments and research concerning care of the elderly.

According to a Parliament decision 14 years later, NGI emerged as a greater research institution. Even if most of the researchers are carrying on their work, the fact remains that there is no longer an institute of gerontology in Norway. I do not pretend to look at this development as a mere historical event. It makes me feel sad. That it happened two years after my retirement is a poor consolation. There is no guarantee that I could have prevented it. The point of the story is to illustrate the vulnerability of a research institution dependent on politicians in power.

It is therefore even more encouraging to observe that issues being dealt with by researchers of social gerontology today are rooted in activities indicated by NGI. I will briefly present some of them.

Research Areas

An ongoing research project on aging, memory, and learning, which started at NGI, indicates the continuous interest in the issue of *mental capacity and aging*. A most rewarding experience during recent years was my close connection with Sol Seim's study on personality and intelligence. When she retired at 70 years old, I was glad to have the opportunity to invite her to join NGI. She became enthusiastic concerning the idea to continue a former research project in which she had examined a group of persons at the ages of 13 and 30. Since Seim became member of the NGI staff she examined the same group twice, when they were 60 and 70 years of age. Seim was a valuable ambassador of NGI and contributed to the prestige of the institute on both a national and an international level. Findings from the examination of the 70-year-olds were published in November 1997, and the then 84-year-old author was subject to great attention in the mass media and otherwise.

The area of geropsychology that witnessed the greatest expansion is the clinical field, or, more precisely, research and psychological intervention concerning dementia in old age. Because NGI arranged the first seminars and conducted surveys in the 1970s, research and guidance centers have developed, some of them staffed with psychologists who originally worked with NGI. In general the activities of NGI in this area mainly consist of applied research and the teaching and training of personnel. Except for a few active psychologists, basic research has been undertaken by psychiatrists.

My interest in the study of autobiographies originated from interest in adjustment, adaptation, and coping skills. As on other occasions, environmental conditions gave the push to promote studies: Early in the 1960s NPHA, in cooperation with the University of Oslo, arranged a nationwide competition inviting people 70 years and older to write their life histories. Some years later a similar competition was carried out. On both occasions, I had the privilege to serve on the evaluation committee. It was an instructive task, although to read hundreds of pages, mostly handwritten and often in dialect, was more demanding than I had foreseen. Anyhow the experience clearly showed the value of such data as a gateway to the understanding of psychological aging. One of the very able psychologists at NGI, Kirsten Thorsen, devoted herself to personal life review research, leading to her PhD.

To witness the conditions of poor old people living in their own homes and in institutions had been sad experiences. More shocking was the conditions of work in industry as it existed when I started research on middle-aged and older workers 35 years ago. It often struck me that the psychological insight achieved during a six-year study was a bit far from reality. Moreover, I felt uncomfortable being aware of my narrowmindedness. I had grown up in a small community on the countryside where most of us were poor and used to primitive conditions. That was something else. We had fresh air, the woods, and the sea. Even poor stables and cow barns seemed more attractive than the dusty, dirty, and noisy rooms where blue-collar workers in heavy industry spent a great part of their lives in those days. Sometimes I felt embarrassed asking what their jobs meant to them. Through the job as a student, I had dealt only with the pension system of civil servants. Now I learned about the enormous difference in the private pension system of blue- and white-collar workers. Another finding was the lack of information among blue-collar workers about their rights as retirees, including the size of their pensions as well as measures offered by the employers. A psychologist who made a significant contribution to studies on older workers also took an interest in preretirement counseling. Being familiar with efforts in Scotland and England, especially the work of Alastair Heron, the NGI took the initiative of founding the Center for Senior Planning. This semipublic agency, which was launched with one psychologist from

NGI and his secretary as the only staff, today has a staff of seven and is still active in practice and research.

Because I had been active in this area for a few years, I was appointed to chair a public committee that would promote the conditions of older workers. This official support and extra research funding provided the possibility of intensifying our efforts, and former NGI researchers are still active in this field.

Research Strategies

Two underlying problems have been attendants in my service of gerontology. The first one, concerning the organization of research, became more complicated over the years. I viewed the negative impact of market-directed studies as an ever-increasing problem. This unfortunate development is a threat to the fruitful research of institutions not formally affiliated with universities. In organizing research at NGI, my point of departure was that a combination of basic and applied research would benefit both parties. For as long as possible I tried to organize the activities of NGI as a combination of research "in ivory towers," applied studies, and the dissemination of information. Perhaps a balance considered as favorable may be maintained, but the problem arises when the budget no longer permits an organization to do basic research. Once an organization has reached the point, as NGI did, when the annual grant is insufficient to cover its operational cost, the institution becomes more or less forced to grasp for income. In NGI's case that was through applied studies, which were more easily funded than basic research. In the memorial volume at the 25th anniversary, I warned against this development. My argument was (and still is) that without paying due attention to theoretical research, the quality of the general activities suffers. In the case of NGI it resulted in a negative impact on applied research as well as on the dissemination of knowledge. It is not a question of the one being more important than the other. It is a matter of living up to certain scientific norms, to ascertaining that able theorists serve as guides and are corrective as to methods and procedures, and to ensuring that the quality of research does not crumble. It is a question of avoiding the common misunderstanding that applied research is equivalent to problem solving.

The second problem is the impact of research findings on policy and practice. We can only describe the efforts of NGI. Information was disseminated in the form of research reports, textbooks, seminars, and teaching. Mass media were used to influence public opinion. To a great extent, staff members acted on public committees, and policy makers, planners, and practitioners showed great interest in publications and recommendations from NGI. Yet the extent to which the knowledge has been implemented into practice is another question. I hope my efforts and those made by NGI have not been in vain. I prefer to hope so. I can't prove it.

A Manifest

I do understand Skinner (1982) when he said: "I have been wallowing in reminiscence lately in writing my autobiography. . . . The trouble is that it takes you backward." And I am worried about the observation referred to by Havighurst (Havighurst & Glasser, 1972): "The mind never photographs. It paints pictures."

I appreciate dealing with the history of social gerontology in Norway, and I am grateful to have been an active participant. Yet the fact remains that I have been only an instrumental link. It so happened that no other psychologist was on the spot when I started. Today about 10 psychologists are active in geropsychological research, and 25 to 30 are working in clinical geropsychology.

This development would have forced itself ahead anyway. However, I like to think that the development would have arrived a bit later and been a bit slower without me. I admit to being a person who can't exist without illusions.

After a Long Life in Gerontology

Elderly people, a term that has represented a theoretical construction to me, all of a sudden—so it seems—has become a description of my contemporaries. This is definitely no original observation. Cicero discussed a similar experience 2000 years ago. In his book *Old Age,* Cicero mocks those who complain about the burden of old age that creeps on them unaware. If old age comes sooner than they have reckoned with, their calculations have been wrong, and how, asks the author, can old age be less of a burden if preceded by 800 instead of 80 years?

The wisdom of Cicero and his insight into old age bring me, the aging gerontologist, to reflect on what I have learned about geropsychology over the past 40 years. I can certainly refer to different pieces of knowledge. But mostly they are scattered, and the body of knowledge is rather fragmentary. Therefore the challenge and my continuous problem has been to integrate pieces of information into a clarifying picture of psychological aging and to suggest explanations of behavior and emotions. This is not to say that my efforts to gain information piece by piece have been worthless. I have experienced the pleasure of being curious, and I have learned to appreciate even the smallest piece of knowledge that could extend my insight. The hope to approach a synthesis of my fragmentary knowledge has given meaning to my efforts.

Over a period of years I have witnessed the short lives of various theories on aging. Nevertheless efforts to develop models and theories will be needed also in the future, even if the search for theories that can explain all different patterns of aging might look like a Sisyphean task. Anyway, the many knowledge gaps in gerontology represent a great challenge to psychologists as well as to researchers from other disciplines. The approaches and appropriate methods will depend on the theme to be studied, psychological trends related to the process of aging or behavioral patterns in later life. My hope as to future research on the psychology of aging is that the researcher will give priority to the study of the foggy border between normal and pathological changes in cognition that occur in later life.

A great part of my career has consisted of stimulating, organizing, and administering social gerontological research. In this relation I became familiar with the exposed position of a person in power. I have felt the wind that is blowing on the tops and experienced loneliness, for me the most difficult problem to cope with. My responsibility and staff participation were sometimes difficult to unite. Quite a lot of energy was used restraining my quick-tempered character. Spontanity became a luxury for me.

In retrospect I realize how slow I was in admitting the limits of democracy when it comes to decision making. Dependent on social contact, my starting point was too optimistic and rather naive. I thought that to be accepted and appreciated by everybody was a matter of negotiations, patience, and applying the appropriate procedure. Experience faded this notion, leaving strength to live with the fact that my leadership of NGI had to be based on knowledge to the best of my ability rather than on the wish to be personally popular.

Yet I was privileged to work with a staff devoted to their jobs, colleagues who, with a few exceptions, were faithful and loyal to me. Indeed, I am glad to express my gratitude to the technical staff, researchers, and chairs of the NGI board. But even with this valuable backing I should have been worse off tackling my obligations if it had not been for Bengt, my husband. He was the one patiently listening to my complaints and correcting me when I was too emotional and unreasonable. He discreetly let me understand that many of his clients had problems more serious than mine. Bengt taught me to catch salmon, which includes the unique experience of rivers and mountains at sunrise and sunset. Encouraging me to travel and participate in meetings, he firmly refused to join me. To be an attendant at conferences abroad is not his style. But in Norway and in our home, Bengt has taken care of my visitors and those of NGI as if they were his personal friends. And thanks to gerontology we have been fortunate to meet a number of people from different parts of the world. Some of them have become our friends and also in that way enrichened our life.

Gerontology provided me with a wilderness rather than a rose garden. Achievements, great experiences, disappointments, and defeats went hand in hand. Anyway, when closing the account, the result is that I owe gerontology a great debt of gratitude for the challenges and joy of my career and for possibilities to develop lasting friendships. The most significant contribution to my quality of life here and now is the certainty that friendship, in contrast to my career, is not limited by retirement age.

References

Beverfelt, E. (1984). Old people remember: A contribution to society. *Educational Gerontology, 10,* 233–244.

Gedde-Dahl, T. (1955). Research on aging in Norway. *Nordisk Medicin, 54,* 1051.

Gedde-Dahl, T. (1957). The work of the National Public Health Association for health and welfare among the elderly. *Stencil,* 19.

Havighurst, R. J., & Glasser, R. (1972). An exploratory study of reminiscence. *Journal of Gerontology, 27,* 245–253.

Heløe, L. A. (1982). The twenty-fifth anniversary of the Norwegian Institute of Gerontology. Address by the minister of social affaires.

Nordvik, H., Beverfelt, E., & Nygård, Aa.-M. (1965). A psychological and medical study of middle aged and elderly people. *Norske Gerontologiske Skrifter, 11.*

Chapter 4
I HAVE TO DO IT MYSELF

James E. Birren

Chance is clearly evident in my life. At my birth on April 4, 1918, I promptly fell on the floor in the delivery room, causing consternation for the doctor, nurse, my mother, and presumably for me, who turned purple. Years later, reconstruction of the event with my mother established that she was aware of what had happened, because the ether she had been given had worn off. Apparently the nurse had not put a clip for the umbilical cord in the obstetrics bag, and the physician complained that he would have done better had the charwoman assisted him. The nurse left the room in a hurry to find a clip while the doctor in his anger went out of the delivery room looking for one in the other direction. Meanwhile, I had been left lying on a small table adjacent to my mother, from which I was pulled by the expulsion of the placenta. When the the doctor and nurse returned to the room, I was an inconvenient mess on the floor. My mother said, ''I will never forget the look on the doctor's face when he saw you lying on the floor.'' My mother also told me that as she left the hospital with her baby, the nursery attendant mentioned that I was ''better now.'' All these events left uncertainty and the question in my mother's mind: better than what?

I have the impression that I was not expected to survive the fall from the delivery room table. In fact, the doctor must have been so rattled that he did not record my birth. Twenty years later, when I needed evidence of my birth, I discovered there was no recorded birth certificate. The doctor was still alive at that time and signed my handwritten birth certificate application. I became a rare individual in that my birth certificate is in my own handwriting. This event seems to characterize one of the underlying themes of my life: I have to do it myself.

My mother and father were simple folks, both children of immigrants from western Europe. My mother's family came from the Rhine area in Germany and bore the name Kolkmann. My father's family came from Luxembourg with the name Birren.

My father's family was Roman Catholic and my mother converted from Protestantism to marry my father. I was baptized in Saint Benedict's Church in Chicago, the same church in which my parents were married. My father, I believe, was in the second graduating class of the church's elementary school. He told me tales of swimming in the Chicago River when it was still a clean winding rural stream with trees on its banks.

When I was about $4\frac{1}{2}$ years old, my father moved the family to a then-rural area west of Chicago called Saint Charles. I could wander out of our small country cottage, and my mother did not need to worry about me. I made acquaintances with the farmers in the area and could get rides down Main Street on the farmers' horses and wagons. I found that the world was a wonderful place to explore. My confidence in people, places, and events may go back to that period of childhood exploration.

The School Years

My brother Raymond, who was two years older, was in third grade. He had the task of taking me to school on my first day. He left me outside the door of the first-grade room, where I remained standing until the nun, Sister Gregory, opened the door and asked me what I was doing there. I must have muttered the right words, for she took me into the class and pointed me to a seat. I was formally enrolled in Our Lady of Mercy School, to which my parents paid $1 a month tuition. By the time I was in third grade we moved farther northwest, and my brother and I went to Our Lady of Victory School. I became more intrigued with the mysteries of the church and wanted to be an altar boy and perhaps a priest.

I still feel my brother Raymond was brighter than I, but he was also much more belligerent. The nuns had ignored his left-handed predispositions and made him write with his right hand. I believe this forced change in his handedness contributed to his later belligerency in the classroom. When Raymond was in fifth grade he could roller-skate to the public library, about three quarters of a mile away, and get a collection of books. For some reason there was little restriction on him, and the books he checked out opened my eyes to reading, although I did not have much grasp of the facts of life. My brother would occasionally do nice things for me, but he would not have much to do with me; I was the ''little twerp.''

I graduated from the Prussing Elementary School in June of 1932 and that fall entered Carl Schurz High School. I entered a technical course at the high school because I thought I would be an engineer. In addition to the technical courses, I took the college prep courses. I had made a friend during that first year, Al Edahl, and we would occasionally walk home to save the 7¢ streetcar fare. If we accumulated our savings, we could get a hamburger for 10¢.

One of the impressive things about the high school was its size and facilities, with three gymnasiums and two auditoriums. In the main auditorium the school had installed a pipe organ. I doubt if there are many public high schools today with a pipe organ. The tech-boys went through a sequence of well-equipped classes: wood, pattern, forge, foundry, and machine shop. Looking back, I am startled to realize that we cast molten brass and steel in the foundry. Today, the mere idea of casting molten steel (at 3000° Fahrenheit) in a high school shop sends shivers down my spine. Somewhere in my crowded garage, I still have a hammer, wrench, calipers, and other things I made in these shops.

My religious upbringing presented me with a major problem in my early teens. My father was indifferent about his Catholicism, though my mother, as a convert, pursued her obligation to have my brother and me educated as Catholics. I entered into a long and fretful relationship with the Catholic Church in my teens. My brother Raymond and I were sent to Catholic schools until we moved far out to the northwest corner of Chicago, when we went to a public school.

At about age 14 I began to find myself at odds with what the nuns had taught me and I became involved in a deep struggle with the church. The scary fairy tales that the nuns had told us to keep us disciplined as children had repercussions. We had been told that God could read every mind and he always knew what we were thinking and doing. We had to be clean in thought and deed or we would burn eternally in hell; the ground itself would open up and swallow us.

The tension arose in me; I apparently felt that I had to break with the church or be broken myself. When I was 21 I retreated to a psychoanalyst's couch to resolve the internal warfare between my tendencies and my upbringing. My mentor at the Chicago Psychoanalytic Institute was Martin Grotjahn. He began to encourage me to become a nonmedical analyst. However, World War II broke out and changed his plans as well as mine.

Deciding to Go to College

No one in my family had graduated from college and there was no parental pressure for it or against it. I decided to go to the Wright Junior College and continue my interest in technical subjects. At that time I had a fantasy about going on to the University of Illinois for a degree in engineering after I finished junior college. The country was still in an economic depression, however, and getting an engineering degree did not seem to be a useful step. So with two years of math, science, and other subjects, I entered the Chicago Teachers College, reasoning that I might at least get a steady job teaching school. Instructors began to show interest in me, and I responded.

One of the influential teachers was an art instructor, Arturo Fallico, who stirred my interest in philosophy, although I had not taken a single course in it. Together we created the philosophy club.

When I turned 20, two friends and I decided to lease a gas station. I went to school during the day, one of us went to night school, and the third was working a day job but needed extra money. We paid ourselves the handsome sum of $27\frac{1}{2}$¢ an hour!

Another instructor, David Kopel, responded to my growing interest in psychology and suggested I volunteer for a summer as a research assistant at the Elgin State Hospital to learn new skills and ideas. Following Kopel's suggestion, I went to Elgin State Hospital, where my eyes were opened. The hospital was a high-level professional organization, with Phyllis Wittman in charge of the psychology department. I learned to administer intelligence tests, participate in staff meetings, and watched a neuropsychiatrist, a German refugee, perform postmortem examinations.

Another eye-opening experience for me was becoming acquainted with a group of divinity students who were in training at the hospital. They were very bright students, some from Ivy League schools, who came out of very different backgrounds, and I was caught up in a new culture. The man who was coordinating the group was Richard Eastman, a young graduate student in English from Yale University. Eastman subsequently finished his PhD at the University of Chicago and became chair of a Midwest university English department. I was so motivated by the summer experience that I decided to go on to graduate school in psychology at Northwestern University. Phyllis Wittman recommended me and I was admitted to Northwestern in the summer of 1941. But by then the war clouds were already gathering.

My brother Raymond and I had to register in 1940 for the military draft. Both of our draft numbers came up in the summer of 1941, but Raymond was deferred because he had a perforated eardrum. When I was called in to the local draft board for my physical examination, I discovered the exams were held in an empty store. Thin partitions were put up so the various local doctors could examine the draftees. As I sat waiting, I heard them discussing my status. My brother had been deferred and they did not want to defer me as a graduate student. They noted that I had a very fast pulse, which was moderately disqualifying. In any event, I was given a short-term deferment to continue my studies at Northwestern University.

Northwestern University and World War II

My wife Betty and I met in our first graduate class in psychology at Northwestern University in the summer of 1941. Thus began a relationship that is now more than 58 years old.

As a graduate student I gravitated toward Robert Seashore, who seemed to have an affinity for mechanical devices and liked measurements of motor skills. Employed as his assistant, I found myself making some instruments for measuring hand tremor and reaction time. Seashore was a good mentor for me. Because he was interested in mechanical things, he helped me make a transition from "things" to "ideas." He had a strong family orientation and once told me that a man was only one third alive until he got married and was not wholly alive until he had children.

Japan attacked Pearl Harbor on December 7, 1941, and the United States entered World War II. That Sunday morning, Betty and I had gone into downtown Chicago to have lunch with her father, because he was passing through to Cleveland where the family lived. He brought rumors about war, which sensitized us to the fact that the probability of war was not a product of a news announcer's imagination. On that Sunday afternoon the graduate students clustered around the radio and heard the news that war had broken out. About an hour later one of the professors came through and told us there was nothing to it, "don't worry." By the end of the term the graduate students were scattering into the military services and shipping out.

After Pearl Harbor there was a move in the psychology department to do war-related research. Andrew Ivy, chair of the physiology department, contacted Seashore to develop a project that would measure the use of amphetamines to relieve fatigue. The motivation for the research was apparently derived from the war in North Africa. The war there was being fought between the British under General Montgomery and the Germans under General Rommel. The Germans would pursue the British for hours beyond the usual length of day and we were told that amphetamines had been discovered in some of the captured German gear, which may have contributed to that army's ability to stay awake long hours and perform efficiently.

Ivy and Seashore organized a project on amphetamines and fatigue at Fort Sheridan, Illinois, with three graduate students: a physiologist, Stanley Harris; a psychologist, A. C. VanDusen, and I. Together with Seashore we went into the field at Fort Sheridan to measure the effects of fatigue and the counteracting effects of amphetamines. Soldiers went on long forced marches followed by continuous guard duty, requiring 24 hours of wakefulness. The troops were given alternately one of four types of capsules: a sugar placebo, caffeine, and two types of amphetamines.

This research was quickly expanded to measuring the same behavioral characteristics in tank drivers under forced wakefulness at Fort Knox, Kentucky. We then went to the army desert camp in Indio, California, where troops were preparing to go to Africa. All of this was a vast new experience for me: the travel, military camp life, and the necessity to adapt to the conditions of tent life in the desert.

After the data collection was over and the project came to an end, Dr. Ivy told me that I would have to either enter the military or go to medical school. Ivy had both a medical degree and a PhD. The medical degree, he said, was so that he could tell administrators to go to hell when he needed to. He felt he could always go into practice as a physician. That did not seem like a good enough reason for having two advanced degrees to me, so I elected to follow the military route. I was commissioned an ensign in the Hospital Corps of the U.S. Navy and told to report to the Naval Medical Research Institute in Bethesda, Maryland, on June 7, 1943. It was a privilege to get such an assignment, and it happened before I had completed my PhD. I was the least educated and least experienced person among the group of first-class scientists I was assigned to join. It was particularly odd to go from civilian life to military life overnight.

The Naval Medical Research Institute

The transformation of James Birren during the three years at the Naval Medical Research Institute was startling. There were scientists from major American universities carrying out research projects related to the navy war effort. The chief of my unit was a biophysicist, Harold Blum, a professor from the University of California at Berkeley. Also in the unit was a PhD in psychology from Yale, M. B. Fisher; a young physiologist with a PhD from Berkeley, M. Morales; and a physicist from Johns Hopkins University, Richard Lee. I was assigned to many different projects, ranging from the study of motion sickness, to the effects of oxygen deprivation, to visual dark adaptation.

The U.S. Navy had ships that were primarily intended to sail in the cool waters of the North Atlantic. In the Pacific, ships were sailing closed up under high external temperatures, which led to excessive internal heat and humidity. The navy was concerned that sailors were developing heat rash and infections and losing efficiency in response to the high heat and humidity, with consequent infection. Because of fire hazard, the men's bunks always had to be covered, which led to the accumulation of moisture in the mattresses and sheets. This was an ideal circumstance for developing skin irritation and infection. Because of this, the navy was beginning to experiment with ways of cooling the ships, and our research task was to determine if cooling improved the efficiency of the men.

Within three years I probably participated in about two dozen research reports. One project involved my collaboration with a dentist, Commander Carl Schlack. He had gotten duplicate records of dental examinations conducted in boot camps in the United States, and these data were analyzed by region and other variables (Schlack & Birren, 1946). One of the surprising findings was that Boston had the highest number of dentists per capita and its young sailors also had the poorest teeth. *Time* magazine reported on the findings from the navy dental study based on our science article and referred to me as a ''dentist'' although I served as a data analyst.

I was once assigned to work with a physiologist from Columbia University, Barry King, on the evaluation of an artificial resuscitation device. Dogs were used to test the efficacy of the machine. I knew nothing about animal experimentation, but one learns quickly under wartime conditions.

Time sped by and brought along new experiences, such as traveling from Boston to Halifax in a convoy of ships going to Europe. We were studying seasickness aboard landing craft, and we tried to evaluate the effects of antiseasickness remedies on the troops headed to Europe.

Later, I was assigned with three other colleagues to a battleship, the USS *Washington,* which was undergoing repair in Bremerton, Washington. We were to go into the Pacific theater of operations, but the war ended before we could leave port. Instead, we sailed from Bremerton through the Panama Canal to the navy yard in Philadelphia. En route, my colleagues and I made many observations about the types of factors involved in sick call. My colleague Manuel Morales, the physiologist, could find a research project almost anywhere. We collaborated and analyzed the sick-bay records of the battleship and discovered that the most frequent complaints were skin and foot problems. Occasionally a seaman would drink hair tonic or some other lotion with a high alcohol content, which would have serious side effects requiring medical care.

Our observations included the experience of being in the 16-inch gun turrets during firing practice or in the fire-control center of the ship. It was sobering to see a huge shell placed in the rifle—and the large bags of powder rammed—and it was awesome to be in the turret of 16-inch guns as they fired. The loud noise was outside; inside, it was more of a thud with a tremendous recoil of the rifle barrel into the turret area.

I learned that the guns were not fired like a shotgun, with a single pull of a trigger, but rather the command to fire was released to a mechanical computer that calculated the optimum firing time in relation to the roll, pitch, and scend of the ship, along with target characteristics involving its range and speed. A shell was fired when the computer achieved a solution to the equation. I was impressed by the similarities of the gun-firing process to the central nervous system regulation of motor behavior, involving not only our intentions to act but modifying our behavior in relation to the complex input of the vestibular apparatus, vision, and cerebellum in modifying the output of our motor system.

One custom aboard ship that stuck out in my mind was that quite a few of the men had an earring in one ear. I was told this was the privilege of men who had gone down with a ship. One could clearly see the number of experienced men on board this ship who had previously gone down with another navy ship under battle conditons.

At the end of the war, the staff at the Naval Medical Research Institute soon began to vanish as people went back to universities. Universities were expanding rapidly with the growth of returning veterans who received G.I. educational benefits. I had about a year left on my PhD at Northwestern University and obtained a predoctoral fellowship from the National Institutes of Health (NIH). I was pleasantly surprised by receiving the award of the fellowship and also an invitation to meet with the director of the NIH. Today the NIH could not afford the time of such personal contact between the director and fellowship trainees, who now number into the thousands per year. The director and I fell into a conversation about our Midwest backgrounds, and he told me he had gone to a college in Minnesota. He was a little surprised that I used the term *experimental psychology* in my curriculum vitae. He said they did not use the term *experimental* in other fields: ''We assumed that all sciences can be experimental.''

In 1946 Betty and I returned to Northwestern for the fall semester, and I took my qualifying exams from a new faculty. It was strange coming back to the university campus after spending three years working in a highly technical facility with great support staff. The new chair of the psychology department was my professor, Robert Seashore. Seashore served as my supervisor along with the physiological psychologist Donald Lindsley, who had just arrived from Brown University. The faculty allowed me to use my investigations of motion sickness as a data source for my dissertation. Because the dissertation involved a bit more physiological reasoning and Seashore was busy with the department, Donald Lindsley was my active mentor.

The Baltimore Gerontology Center

Before receiving my degree, I had already agreed to take a position in Baltimore with Nathan Shock, whom I had met during the war. He liked my broad experience with different kinds of measures because he himself had been a joint doctoral student of Baird Hastings and Louis Thurstone, a biochemist and a psychologist at the University of Chicago. Perhaps he saw in me a kind of young hybrid that reflected his background.

At the Baltimore center at that time there were physicians who owed two years of government service because their medical education had been paid for under the wartime emergency. As before, I found that I began to do research with my neighbors. In particular, in

1948, David Solomon came from Harvard University to do research as an endocrinologist. He began to do work on aging and the stress response of the endocrine system. At that time I served as a control research participant for him while I did my own research. From colleagues I learned new concepts that someone in psychology would not usually be exposed to. Clearly, from some of these I borrowed ideas.

One of my clearly borrowed concepts was from the physiologists who were working on age changes in renal-clearance capacity. I found it intriguing that they could characterize the clearance capacity of the kidney by appropriate measurements. By analogy, I thought about processing the capacity of the human brain and began to think about suitable measurements. At the same time, I was concerned with interpretation of data that indicated that older people had slower reaction times. To me, this was a diminished capacity not unlike reduced kidney-clearance capacity. How much can one's kidneys clear per unit time, or in the case of the nervous system, how much information can it process per unit time? It turned out that the concept was clearer than the related research findings because the central nervous system does not keep the same unit fixed over time.

The nervous system keeps regrouping, and what was a bit of information at one point can become grouped or clumped into a larger unit. The behavioral ''bit'' does not remain fixed. I did, however, manage to contribute to the issue of the interpretation of slowness of behavior with age, which is my major career story.

I suppose my background had a formative effect on my view of the organism as having more or less efficiency to perform different tasks. If there was a reduction in efficiency, I had to seek out the mechanisms or causes. The word *mechanism* itself is a shaping kind of metaphor or an orienting term. In recent years a visiting professor gave me a present at the end of a yearlong seminar. He presented me with an electrically driven simulator of perpetual motion. He labeled it the *mechanism* in playful recognition of my frequent use of the term in a seminar. I had assimilated the word from a tradition in which the term *mechanism* was used to express the link between cause and effect or the pathways through which cause and effect are related.

When I joined the staff of Nathan Shock, I picked as one of my research topics the slowing of behavior with age and the ''mechanisms'' that lie behind the slowing. In reading the early literature of Edward Thorndike and subsequently Irving Lorge and others, I felt they were minimizing the significance of slowing as an important factor in psychological abilities. In particular, I was impressed that the literature on the use of timed and untimed tests never settled the issue of which type of test was valid for what purpose. At that stage of the development of the subject matter it was assumed that intellectual power could not be fully expressed by older persons because the response processes slowed down. It became customary to attribute the slowness of behavior to either the slowness of the motor response or to loss of acuity of sensory and perceptual input. Little attention was given to the importance of the speed of the brain's mediation between stimulus and response.

One of the early studies consisted of age differences in the speed of doing simple addition problems (Birren, Allen, & Landau, 1954; Birren & Botwinick, 1951). I reasoned that if I lengthened the series of digits to be added from 2 to 25, the longer digit lists would have a smaller proportion of time involved in writing the answer. It follows that the correlation between a speed-of-writing test and the speed of doing addition problems should decline to zero for long problems if the slowness of writing the answers was the only relevant factor. The results showed that for young adults the correlation between speed of writing and speed of addition did decline, but it leveled off after about four digits and explained only 10% of the common variance thereafter. In contrast, the correlation in older adults declined but remained high, explaining almost 50% of the variance for long problems (Birren &

Botwinick, 1951). This instance clearly showed that the limiting factor lay not solely in writing or in the response process but largely in the central processing that shared a common variance with writing speed. If one were to partial out the speed factor as expressed in writing time related to age in such tests, one would be throwing out changes that were particularly characteristic of the central nervous system. This gave rise to the idea that the biggest portion of variance in slowing of behavior with age can be attributed to the central nervous system itself and less to peripheral sensory factors and motor response processes. This seemed to be a fairly revolutionary thought at the time because it was reversing the customary pattern of causal attribution to peripheral processes of the origin of slowness in older subjects.

Related research involved comparing reaction times using difference response modes of the jaw, finger, and foot. Surprisingly, the age differences were approximately constant across the three modes. This suggested that there was little increase with age in nerve-conduction velocity, because if there were, there would be an increase in response slowness as a function of path length; for instance, foot responses would be disproportionately slow compared with jaw responses (Birren & Botwinick, 1955a).

The University of Chicago Experience

From 1951 to 1953 I was assigned to the University of Chicago by the National Institutes of Health while new facilities were built in Bethesda, Maryland. In 1951 I had the opportunity to work with neurophysiologist Patrick Wall when he was at the University of Chicago's Department of Anatomy. He induced me to measure directly the nerve conduction velocity of rat sciatic nerves in relation to age. I found an increase in speed of conduction velocity as the rat developed, but the sciatic nerves from old rats did not show an increasing slowness trend with age. In a closely related project, I later measured speed of startle reaction in rats in response to mild shock applied to the paws or to a sudden white noise (Birren, 1955). Results showed that the older rats were indeed slower in their behavior; however, given the previous findings, we could not attribute that to the change in peripheral nerve conduction velocity (Birren & Wall, 1956).

I also attempted to define more clearly the role of perception in slowing of behavior with age. In these studies I varied the difficulty of the perceptual task. Research participants had to say as quickly as possible which was the smaller circle, the right or the left. By varying the area of the circles, one manipulates difficulty. All people are slow when you get down to a 1 or 2% difference in circle size, but what I was doing was attempting to describe the role of age differences in the speed of perceptual judgments while varying the task difficulty. Presumably, if perceptual discrimination is the only variable, then as one made the task progressively easier, older people's performance should approximate that of the young. In these studies, as in others, there is a residual difference in the speed of behavior between old and young adults after the issue of perceptual difficulty is eliminated by experimental manipulation (Birren & Botwinick, 1955b; see also Birren, Riegel, & Morrison, 1962). Slowness in speed of perceptual judgment with age is not solely explained by limitations of sensory or perceptual acuity.

These and other experiments of the period convinced me that the major fact that we were facing was that with age there was a slowness of mediation of the central nervous system of all processes. This has come to be known as the strong hypothesis about aging and slowing; for instance, that everything the nervous system does is slower with advancing age. The other hypothesis is that there are independent subfactors that account for the slowing. By analogy to the concept of general intelligence, I suggest that there is a general speed factor of central nervous system mediation that slows with age, in addition to which there are specialized processes of slowing in subsystems of the brain.

While at the University of Chicago I had academic contacts that resulted in being exposed to two scientific principles that I adopted. The first of these was from the psychologist Louis Thurstone, with whom I spent a quarter in residence. His influence on my thinking about age and intelligence is seen in a 1961 article (Birren & Morrison). In his conversations he told me that if you have only one method of measurement with which to answer a question, you are probably in a weak position. Perhaps this now might be stated in terms of convergent validity, that two or more measures of the same concept should be used to establish its validity.

Another contact was with Ralph Gerard, a neurophysiologist. He told me that after years of putting electrodes into nerves, he still had no idea about how the nervous system was organized or integrated. This leads to the statement of principle that you have to use a methodology appropriate to the level of question that you are asking. Perhaps this might be rephrased to, ''If you are trying to catch an elephant, tweezers will not do, and if you are trying to catch a bullfrog in a pond, don't use a bulldozer.'' My predilection is to go for the power of the question and then find one or more techniques that will attempt to answer it.

The National Institutes of Health

The next level of research that I undertook with colleagues was a joint evaluation of behavioral measures in concert with assessment of cerebral circulation and metabolism, psychiatric symptomatology, social functioning, and assessment of subclinical disease. The joint project was undertaken by a multidisciplinary team at the National Institute of Mental Health (NIMH). Measurements were made on a group of 47 community resident men over the age of 65, each of whom volunteered to be a resident in the institution for a two-week observation period (Birren, Butler, Greenhouse, Sokoloff, & Yarrow, 1963).

Out of that massive collection of data, we ascertained that the brain circulation and brain metabolic values in healthy older men were equivalent to those earlier reported for young adults. There was no necessary reduction with age in general metabolic activity of the brain or circulation. At the same time there were observed reductions in speed of reaction time and higher than expected scores on global verbal information. This leads to the expression of the principle that a healthy older adult continues to acquire information and store it but processes it more slowly (Birren & Fisher, 1992).

The foregoing is opposite to the paradigm found in children who are learning to read. They are slow and process each element separately. Later, they combine words into phrases and read rapidly orally or silently. Thus familiarity improves the speed of reading. Later in life it is suggested that the slowness is not related solely to practice but to an intrinsic change in speed of processing that slows the overall reading or cognitive performance. This line of reasoning has been very difficult for developmental psychologists to accept, because learning is usually studied as a function of the number of trials or amount of experience, and differences in performance are explained solely by differential practice and exposure.

One of the more general principles I have evolved is that aging is a multilayered process. Although there are patterns characteristic of us as a species, for instance slowing, there are other subpatterns that are more related to age-associated disuse and diseases. Future research will no doubt establish subpatterns by comparing psychological performance with longevity or remaining years of life, or with differences in mortality and morbidity in relation to behavior. For example, it is widely noted that women live longer than men. If there is an intrinsic pattern of aging and an intrinsic relationship between the length of life and behavior, then the performance of women in the later years should be better or change more slowly than that of men. These issues devolve into matters of whether there are behavioral markers of aging, like genetic markers, that will forecast the length of life. Somehow, behavioral markers of aging have not been as widely sought after, for example, as have genetic markers. Yet behavior is a sample of the integrity of the central nervous system, and it should have a role in developing markers of aging.

The Later Years

I left the National Institutes of Health in 1965. At that time I was responsible for the research program on aging, both intramural and extramural, within the National Institute of Child Health and Human Development. Robert Aldrich, then the director, was a pediatrician deeply interested in the carry-forward effects of childhood health and experience into adult life. After organizing the National Institute of Child Health and Human Development, unfortunately for me, he left to return to his professorship in pediatrics at the University of Washington.

The University of Southern California invited me to become the director of a new institute on aging in 1965. The president of USC had been an assistant surgeon general in the public health service and a biomedical scientist, and he had a strong interest in the subject matter of adult change and aging. Within the university I moved very quickly to establish a program of graduate education, because one of the big deficiencies in the country at that time was the lack of traineeships and scholarships to encourage graduate students in various disciplines to pursue the study of adult development and aging.

The family transition to California was not an easy one. My family had to establish roots in a new community. We had lived in Maryland for a long time and had not expected to leave. Our three children had been students in the school system there. But we did move, and I think eventually we all grew as a result. Our son Jeff had a particularly difficult time the first year in transition but became thoroughly rooted in California. The difficulty of families adjusting to moving at that period was not very well considered, because the tradition of America was one of supporting career movement, and the rest had to fall in line. I am much more sympathetic today to young careerists who have to move a family lock, stock, and barrel to a new community.

At USC I was initially startled by the lack of facilities. I was thoroughly used to the large structure and support mechanisms of the National Institutes of Health, and I was ill-prepared for the lack of microstructure and facilities. An important strength was very apparent—I was only one telephone number away from a decision maker.

I often think that some longitudinal studies of the future will begin with the conditions of uterine life and experience and follow through the expression of the human genome in the context of environmental effects. For example, what are the consequences of a stressful pregnancy and a low birth-weight child for adult development and aging and predisposition to disabilities in late life?

Perhaps I was thoroughly sensitized to the power of longitudinal studies by my colleague K. W. Schaie, whom we attracted to USC to be the director of research for the Andrus Gerontology Center. His insistence on the analysis of the compartments of variance of (a) time of measurement, (b) cohort effects, and (c) ontogenetic change remain with me now as almost a ritual or mantra of interpretation. There are obvious and large cohort drifts in the population of older persons since we began studying psychology in the latter part of the 19th century.

Another intellectual influence on me at USC was my colleague James Henry, a physiologist. He showed that the necessary and sufficient condition for producing cardiovascular disease in mice was the social environment in which the animals lived. Clearly, genetic potential varies the magnitude of the effect, but nevertheless, inbred strains of mice will or will not show a rise in blood pressure with age and length of life as a consequence of the social environment. In the analysis of patterns of aging, I believe an ecological orientation is essential.

An example of institutional inertia was one that I experienced at the National Institute of Mental Health. In 1960, Robert M. Butler and I proposed that we establish a laboratory within the NIMH to study the issues of adult development and aging. At that particular time there was a dominant view that the organization of behavior was laid down early in the life of the child and that the basic pattern was lived out or expressed in the daily events of life. The thought that interactions and new factors could arise during adult life seemed far-fetched, and the senior administrators turned down the proposal. Subsequently, social and scientific pressures built, which led to the creation of the National Institute on Aging. Ironically, I was offered the opportunity to head the new institute, but I was well anchored at USC. Fortunately, Robert Butler was able to become the first director of the National Institute on Aging (NIA) in 1975.

When I came to USC in 1965 I was 47 years old and had not been heavily involved in teaching. I was not bored with student interactions, as perhaps some of my colleagues were at that point in their lives, and I volunteered to teach courses in psychology. I discovered that there was a pattern of burnout and disenchantment in midcareer faculty who had been teaching throughout their careers, in contrast to my midcareer enthusiasm and energy. Also, I was not competing for and with the graduate students, as were the younger faculty members who were asserting their intellectual dominance, nor was I trying to minimize my interactions with students. Because my career was already established, I could be more openhanded in supporting the students in their steps toward creating careers. I welcomed the interactions with the graduate students, and I used to say openly that the students had the obligation of teaching me new things. For me, it was a wonderful period of growth at USC from 1965 to 1989, and we tackled many complex and new topics in research and teaching in the psychology of adult life and aging as well as, more broadly, in gerontology.

One of the sources of ideas and stimulation was the creation of the Institute for Advanced Study in Gerontology and Geriatrics at the Andrus Gerontology Center at USC. Funded for five years by the Andrew Norman Foundation, it brought together each year a study group on some topic of aging. The fellows came mainly from psychology, sociology, and biology, though a few came from other disciplines. There are too many names and publications to quote from these productive seminars, though I continue to appreciate the contributions of Hans Schroots and the late Pauline Robinson. I believe this program of seminars was one of my distinct contributions to the field. It is perhaps fitting that the volume on emergent theories of aging was its last publication as a kind of summary of intellectual progress made (Birren & Bengtson, 1988).

In 1989, when I was 71 years of age, I became emeritus at USC and faced an uncomfortable atmosphere surrounding the question of what to do next as the professor who had been the founding dean of the Andrus Gerontology Center. At the same time, David Solomon at the University of California at Los Angeles was looking for a director to organize the Borun Center for Gerontological Research. He recruited me, and I enjoyed the rapid transition and taking on another opportunity for guiding the growth of a research program. In 1995 I became the associate director of the UCLA Center on Aging.

What did my most recent experiences at UCLA teach me about the principles of academic life and geropsychology? I came to recognize again the great inertia that is built around existing subject matters and the complex rationales that surround academic decisions. Apparently it will take a generation for organizational changes to occur that will encourage the support of scholarship, research, and teaching about the course of adult life. Being convinced of the scientific importance as well as the practical implications of studying adult development and aging, I am somewhat impatient with institutions and individuals that appear blind to the significance of the subject matter. Aging appears to be one of the most complex subjects facing science in the 21st century. In addition to studies of particular facts, the pursuit of the subject needs theory, integration, and good questions to guide research.

References

Birren, J. E. (1955). Age differences in startle reaction time of the rat to noise and electric shock. *Journal of Gerontology, 10,* 437–440.

Birren, J. E., Allen, W. R., & Landau, H. G. (1954). The relation of problem length in simple addition to time required, probability of success and age. *Psychometrika, 16,* 219–232.

Birren, J. E., & Bengtson, V. L. (Eds.). (1988). *Emergent theories of aging.* New York: Springer.

Birren, J. E., & Botwinick, J. (1951). Rate of addition as a function of difficulty and age. *Psychometrika, 16,* 219–232.

Birren, J. E., & Botwinick, J. (1955a). Age differences in finger, jaw and foot reaction time to auditory stimuli. *Journal of Gerontology, 10,* 429–432.

Birren, J. E., & Botwinick, J. (1955b). Speed of response as a function of perceptual difficulty and age. *Journal of Gerontology, 10,* 433–436.

Birren, J. E., Butler, R. N., Greenhouse, S. W., Sokoloff, L., & Yarrow, M. (Eds.). (1963). *Human aging.* Washington, DC: U.S. Government Printing Office.

Birren, J. E., & Fisher, L. M. (1992). Aging and the slowing of behavior: Consequences for cognition and survival. In J. J. Berman & T. B. Sonderegger (Eds.), *Psychology and aging. Nebraska Symposium on Motivation, 39* (pp. 1–37). Lincoln: University of Nebraska Press.

Birren, J. E., & Morrison, D. F. (1961). Analysis of the WAIS Subtests in relation to age and education. *Journal of Gerontology, 16,* 95–96.

Birren, J. E., Riegel, K. F., & Morrison, D. F. (1962). Age differences in response speed as a function of controlled variations of stimulus conditions. Evidence of a general speed factor. *Gerontologia, 6,* 1–8.

Birren, J. E., & Wall, P. D. (1956). Age changes in conductive velocity, refractory period, number of fibers, connective tissue space and blood vessels in sciatic nerves of rats. *Journal of Comparative Neurology, 104,* 1–16.

Schlack, C., & Birren, J. E. (1946). Influences on dental defects in naval personnel. *Science, 104,* 259–263.

Chapter 5
A FORTY-YEAR CAREER IN GEROPSYCHOLOGY

Jack Botwinick

At this writing I am completing my tenth year of retirement. With the start of 1988 I became professor emeritus of psychology in arts and sciences of Washington University and of neurology in the School of Medicine of the same university. My active career began about 40 years before then in what is now the gerontology branch of the National Institutes of Aging. I spent almost all of the 40 years in the study of aging.

How Did It Begin?

It all began by chance. I was discharged from the U.S. Army at the end of the Second World War and like so many veterans I was without direction, not totally comfortable with my old surrounds and certainly not thinking of a professional or scientific career. I concluded my BA at Brooklyn College and got a temporary job at the United Nations, which was then located in Long Island, New York. My evenings were far from full and to do something about this I enrolled in evening and Saturday morning courses at Brooklyn College, which could (and which for me eventually did) lead to the MA degree in psychology.

I took a job with the New York City Department of Welfare as a "social investigator" and continued with my course work. Toward the end of the semester, I walked out of a morning class with a classmate I barely knew, and this event was a turning point in my life. He said to me, "Did you file for the civil service test?" Not only hadn't I filed but I hadn't heard of it. He told me that it was the last day to file for a government position in psychology. It should be noted that tests are not given today for civil service jobs but they were required years ago.

Together we went to the filing station and did what was required. The test covered general psychology, and although by this time I had taken many courses, I did not have confidence that I could pass such a test. However, I did and received an offer of a job. I reported to the then gerontology section of the National Heart Institute in Baltimore, where Nathan W. Shock was the director. My new boss introduced himself and told me his name—James E. Birren. Jim was only a few years older than I, but he was already an experienced researcher.

I Found My Niche

Jim was a very good teacher and I needed teaching. He got me working on his research and instructed me as necessary. Jim shared authorship on publications with me even when he didn't have to do so.

I was a good student mainly because I enjoyed the research process so much. I even enjoyed the menial details of research that graduate students today often are spared, or, when not, are sometimes able to ''farm out.'' In those days, all data collection was completely manual and all statistical analyses were carried out with the Monroe or Frieden calculator, not with computer packages so routinely used today.

I learned quickly and developed confidence. After some time on the job, Jim took a leave of absence but I was able to continue on my own. I began a study, carried it out on my own, and published it. I now felt I was a psychologist and decided to get a PhD. The Baltimore stint was short, but what an important time it was.

Back to School

With the help of the G.I. bill, I became a candidate for the PhD at New York University. There were no aging training programs at NYU, nor were there such programs I knew about elsewhere, although some existed. This didn't bother me, however, because at that time I was simply interested in research with the substantive research area not of special importance to me. It seems to me that this is backward, not the way it works out in most cases (or how it is rationalized retrospectively in most cases).

My PhD attitude was not an admirable one in that my goal, simply stated, was to do what I needed to do to get the degree and spend as little time as necessary at school acquiring it. I already had research experience, so getting to a research topic and starting a doctoral dissertation came quickly to me. My dissertation topic was a popular one in psychology at that time (stimulus generalization) and it was completed without special note.

Early Job Experiences

I received the PhD in 1953 and accepted employment while looking for an opportunity to get me going in a career way. A psychologist I met at NYU offered me a job in a New York City engineering company. He and I were the only psychologists in the company; his responsibility was to bring in military grants and I was supposed to know something about human engineering research. It was a most peculiar job.

This engineering company was headed by a retired admiral. Everyone, myself included, stood up from our chairs whenever he passed by. Thankfully, he did not pass by very often. My formidable task was to develop, through research, a cockpit display for aircraft night landing on aircraft carriers. Normally, I would have been overwhelmed by such an assignment but I knew there wasn't the slightest possibility that my research plans would be carried out. This was because there were no facilities to do research and, more important, no expectation for it to be done. I had more variables in interaction than was possible to analyze without computers, which were not available at that time. It was fun for a while but soon I became bothered by the boondoggle character of what I was doing. It became worse when a naval officer in charge of the whole project visited and showed us a picture of how he wanted the end product, the cockpit display, to look (this regardless of my research assignment). Worse still, he made it clear by saying something like this: ''I don't want any P 0.05's or 0.01's or any of that kind of statistical stuff you psychologists give me.'' I quit in about three months.

My next job was with an education research office at Brooklyn College. Surprisingly, this office was headed by a physicist named Louis Heil, a very nice man of far-seeing ideas. One of them was to develop training films for students to learn by, rather than by the typical lecture method. This, of course, is a common teaching method now. It seemed like a good idea to me then except that he had me write the scripts. I don't remember completing any one script because I was greatly unprepared and was without skills to do this. We discussed the matter and my script writing was discontinued. There were no negative feelings.

I have spent time describing these two very short term jobs because they left impressions on me. First, the notion of job integrity became an issue of primary importance. I believe it would have been important to me without my engineering company experience, but the experience brought the issue of integrity up front. Second, I realized there are all kinds of research and not all of it is for me. Third, I realized that while I was focused on research process and not on substantive research topics, there were limits to this in that I did find some things more interesting than others.

In Geropsychology to Stay

I went to an American Psychological Association (APA) conference mainly for the purpose of finding more meaningful and satisfying work and I was lucky in running into Jim Birren. Jim was in the early stages of establishing an aging laboratory within the Laboratory of Psychology of the National Institute of Mental Health (NIMH) in Bethesda, Maryland. I was very glad to join him and start work and begin a career path. This Bethesda experience, which started in 1955, was a satisfying, productive eight-year venture.

I worked with Jim and I worked independently. I had two research assistants, one of whom was Joseph Brinley, a PhD from Catholic University. We worked closely, published together, and, I hope, he feels he benefited from our association as I feel I benefited from it. Eventually, he accepted a faculty position in the Psychology Department of St. Louis University, in time becoming a full professor.

It was a busy time and not only did I do what I liked doing—research—but Jim got me doing what I didn't like doing. He urged and encouraged me to present my data at national conventions and to be involved in national society affairs. I had had an extremely negative experience in an undergraduate speech class. This was a required course where the teacher wanted us to speak like upper-class Englishmen instead of in our native Brooklyn accents. Even more than the others in the class, the teacher would not let me go beyond the first two or three sentences of my required speech making because my word pronunciations didn't pass muster.

Now you might think this humiliation was a minor event in growing up, but the fact is that when Jim suggested I present my data "in front of people," I said no; I didn't want to expose myself to such humiliation again. But Jim urged (he was my boss after all) and mainly encouraged, and I complied.

Fortunately, my first talk went well and after that I had no difficulty. After some time, I immodestly say, I became a very good public speaker. With my research publications, my talks, and my society activities, I developed a national prominence so that during these Bethesda years I was able to serve as president of Division 20 of the APA and also president of the Behavioral and Social Science Section of the Gerontological Society (now of America), as well as serving in other capacities in these societies. Later, I was in the Council of Representatives for Division 20 of the APA.

I observed and experienced many events and situations during these years. Here are some thoughts and issues regarding them.

How to Train for Research on Aging

In the later 1950s, gerontology as a broad movement was still in its early stages and there was discussion of how to train students. Some of gerontological leaders of that time believed it essential that training should be multidisciplinary. Others believed as strongly that training should be within a discipline with emphasis on aging. In the main, the latter opinion won out, and as things developed, it could hardly have been otherwise.

The thought of training research gerontologists in the biochemical, biological, behavioral, and social sciences seems ludicrous today but it wasn't so back then. The field was small with relatively few research people and relatively few research publications. It is now hard to believe that at that time, in the 1950s, I tried reading all the literature on aging.

Research Experience Is Necessary

The aging laboratory was but one of several in the NIMH. This means there were many behavioral and other scientists close by. We were fortunate in that we had no need to develop research grant money; research assistants were available; equipment needs were met; statistical consultants were at hand; interesting informative lectures were frequent. Many of the research investigators were bright, young, new PhDs out of the best universities. I felt I was part of an elite world. There were no administrative duties for most of us, no teaching, no pressures, only the expectation of research accomplishment. What wasn't said, but I think felt, was that given all this, the research had to be exemplary. This could be a great pressure but whatever the reason, my surprise was how difficult it was for so many of these bright people to get going on productive research careers. Some seemed to take years to get their research going, and when they did, the research was not all that exemplary. I don't mean to suggest that this was the majority experience but it seemed to me this was the situation in too many cases.

Why was this so? I can think of two reasons. One, it has been my experience that not many people find contentment in full-time research. Not many people have the luxury of the NIMH opportunity—academic faculty must teach, work with students, develop research funds, make reports, serve on committees, and do research. All this is far from easy. At the same time, however, it makes for a more varied work experience, and for many people a more desirable one.

Two, many of the new PhDs at the NIMH came to the job with only their dissertations as research experience. More experience than this was needed. Nowadays postdoctoral training is almost expected for academic careers. It is true that many new PhDs accept postdoctoral training because of the difficulty of securing satisfying employment. Whatever the reasons, postdoctoral or other further research training serves a good, even necessary, experience for many new PhDs.

Creativity

There were frequent research lectures at the NIMH presented by outstanding people around the country. Often, after such lectures in behavioral research, a group of us would gather to discuss our impressions. Rarely were there disagreements regarding the soundness of the research as it was carried out. When it came to evaluations of whether such research was creative or even "just" important, agreements were far from unanimous. I saw this so often that I began to doubt whether evaluating anyone on the basis of creativity was a fair thing to do. Is creativity in behavioral research basically in the mind of the beholder?

Geropsychological Research

Much, if not most, of research in aging takes the form of applying ideas within the general discipline to aged sample populations. This is fine and much has been learned from such research. This suggests that it is not necessary to be a geropsychologically trained researcher to do aging research. This is so but I believe that, all things being equal, the research is more likely to be better if carried out by investigators steeped in gerontological concerns.

Here is an example of a simple application of a general concept in a series of aging studies that might have made for better studies had they been carried out by geropsychologists. In several studies old and young groups were compared in the acquisition and extinction of the conditioned response. These studies, briefly reviewed by Botwinick (1967, pp. 80–82), were carried out well but the geropsychologist might more likely have asked an important question that was not asked by these researchers: Was there an age difference in the response to the unconditioned stimulus (UCS)? If the older group experiences the UCS (typically a noxious sensory stimulus) with less feeling than the younger group—that is, if the UCS was functionally less intense for the older group—then the findings of the study could have been explained on this basis rather than on age difference in conditionability.

It seems to me that research topics that stem from the needs and characteristics of older people have more intrinsic applied value than research ideas that arise from the general literature. Studies of "plasticity" in cognition is an example of such a study. Plasticity is inferred when older adults are trained or practiced on a task and demonstrate improvement in performance. However, often lacking in such studies are young control subjects. When young control groups were tested—as, for example, Erber (1976)—the results showed the young in starting at higher performance levels than the old also improved with practice and remained higher. These studies indicated that older people do learn, no surprise here, but they also suggest to me that "able to, and do learn" is a concept more immediate to the data and probably more correct than "plasticity." Training and practice studies are important, but they would be even more so if the tasks were those of everyday life rather than the typically used laboratory procedures.

Aging Decline?

Early during my first year in the aging laboratory, I attended a conference that Jim Birren organized. It was exciting for me to meet leaders in the field whose names I knew and to meet others whose names I did not. It was an interesting conference but one thing above all impressed itself on me. One by one, the biologists presented their data emphasizing aging decline; with little exception, the behavioral and social scientists did not. If anything, they talked about maintenance of function. Why was this so? Is behavioral function, I asked, so independent of biological function? In the years that followed it became clear that this disparity in viewing human aging was a pervasive issue in gerontological research.

The controversy regarding decline with age took its most active form in behavioral research in intelligence testing. The data have been clear in showing decline in many functions, with maintenance or relative maintenance in others. It is possible to look only at the head of the elephant and see one thing and look at the back and see another. Look at the whole elephant and you have a complete picture. There is no question in my mind that the complete picture includes cognitive decline in aging.

Most of the research focused on group trends, with individual differences given less attention than they deserved. People decline at different rates. If we accept the reasonable assumption that decline and maintenance functions are distributed more or less normally (bell-shaped curves) then finding an intact old person should not be seen as evidence of no age decline. It should be seen that this intact person represents the tail end of the normal curve.

The popular literature in newspapers and magazines, taking the lead from some of the leading researchers in the field, tend to report no decline with age. We sometimes even see this in the quasi-scientific literature. Is this just wishful thinking?

Mandatory Versus Voluntary Retirement

This was a hot topic in the gerontological literature during the 1950s and 1960s, spilling into the popular press and even in the halls of the U.S. Congress later in the 1970s. The policy question was simple: Should older workers (usually meaning 65 years or older) be obliged to retire on an age basis, or should retirement be voluntary irrespective of age? The question has since largely been resolved in favor of voluntary retirement, not, I believe, on the basis of convincing research but rather on humanitarian values. I had been ''fence-sitting'' on this issue and I still am.

During the period of vehement debate an argument in support of the voluntary position was that older workers should be evaluated individually on the basis of their competence on the job. This is a lot easier to say than to do, but is this really a good idea? In the case of an esteemed, elderly tenured professor, for example, whose productive days are long passed, and who, in fact, shows signs of faltering, an evaluation of competence might result in an expression of something like this: ''Sorry, but you have to go—not because of age discrimination but because you are no longer competent.'' This is less humane than a recognized retirement because of age. There is also the matter of fairness to the well-trained new PhD waiting in the wings for an opportunity.

Clearly, there are many competent older professors—many on the tail end of the normal decline curve—and retiring them on the basis of age is wrong. That's why I ''fence-sit.''

Personal Reflections

A Kindness

Within the first year of my NIMH employment I developed an odd malady that, although without any pain whatsoever, it was potentially dangerous for me to live alone. It was even more dangerous for me to drive a car, even if only to and from work. Very fortunately, this malady was short term and never to recur, but I didn't know this at the time. Jim Birren and his wife, Betty, took me into their home to stay for a while. They had three young children in a busy household and a busy work life. They made me feel welcome. I tried to be unobtrusive, but obviously, I was a stranger in their midst. They housed me, fed me, and I rode to and from work with Jim. I never forgot this kindness.

Will I Be Sorry Later?

Another personal experience was related to research but tangentially. I was a research member of a large-scale multidisciplinary study of extraordinarily healthy men aged from about 65 to 100. These individuals were highly selected on the basis of health so that they were not considered representative of men their ages. Two of the investigators on the research team were young psychiatrists, one named Robert N. Butler and the other Seymour Perlin. Both later became eminent in their fields.

Butler and Perlin had just concluded a series of clinical interviews of these healthy men and were walking down one of the long National Institutes of Health (NIH) Clinical Center corridors animatedly discussing their findings. I tagged along listening to what they found. This incident, small as it may be, had a lasting impact on my life in that it bore on two major decisions I later made.

In the interviews, Butler and Perlin were saying, one man after another told of the regrets they had in life. These regrets were of things they could have or should have done, but didn't. Regrets were not expressed about mistakes they made or of things they did. In other words, regrets were of omission behavior or decisions, not of commission efforts.

Somehow, this affected me. Right then and there I decided to raise the question whenever an important decision came up: Would I be sorry later if I didn't act positively?

Marriage and the Family

A little more than a year after coming to Bethesda, Joan Betty Garfein and I married. It was and remains the best thing I ever did.

Ours was a traditional household with father working and mother at home taking care of just about everything, including our three lovely daughters. The culture was different then and there was no thought of doing otherwise. A difficulty arose later in that I got busier and busier and my at-home time with family suffered in terms of my availability and attention.

The problems that may exist in a one-career, two-parent household are nothing compared with those of the two-career households. I am totally in favor of the current access women have to academic and other careers, but I don't envy what young men and women now have to experience. I never had the sense that the going was easy for me or that there weren't hurdles to overcome, but when I now think that my career started in the general economic upturn after the war that made for job opportunities and relatively easy access to research grant funding, I think that, relative to now, it was easy. I didn't have to find work where my spouse would find work; I did not have to share in child care, home care, or do any of the things that are now correctly demanded in two-career families. More difficult still is the single parent with career responsibilities. I admire all those who manage these difficulties and I wonder whether I could have been successful under these arduous, demanding, competitive pressures.

Time to Move On

My NIMH experience was a satisfying and productive one. Still, a time came when I felt the need for a new experience and, perhaps, a broader one. I decided to investigate the NIH extramural program, that part—the main part—of the NIH that evaluates and funds research and training programs.

I received a welcome, encouraging response with information that the extramural program provides opportunity for involvement and influence in research and training throughout the country. I accepted a position that placed me ''in charge of NIMH predoctoral training.'' In this move I received a promotion to GS-14.

This high-sounding job was a big mistake. Within only a few days I began to realize this. I was bored with what I was doing and saw no way to influence anything, even if I cared to. In three weeks I couldn't see myself continuing and so informed my immediate supervisor, Bertram Booth. He was surprised and displeased; he told me that much time and paperwork went into the transfer from my laboratory, intramural position to the present one. I was apologetic as I should have been.

A few days later, I was called into the office of the man in charge of the whole extramural program, Phillip Sapir. He asked why I was dissatisfied and I told him, truthfully, that I accepted the position in good faith and had looked forward to a long association but either the language used in describing the work or the perception of what my task responsibilities entailed were different from mine. Again, I apologized.

To my surprise, he described several positions that were available and asked me to choose any one of them that appealed to me. I was tempted but refused them with thanks because I was afraid that I might react the same way and tarnish what was a good reputation. At this point he said for me to continue working as best I could and be free to look for different work opportunities. I was lucky to have had such nice bosses.

Despite this negative experience, very important learning took place. I did grant-related administrative work, attended some study-section (grant evaluation) sessions, met some of the extramural personnel, and, accordingly, became knowledgeable about the NIH grant system.

My Next Station

In seeking work possibilities I became interested in the Gerontology Center in the Department of Psychiatry of the Duke University Medical School. Ewald W. Busse was chairman of the department and director of the center, and with his support, I applied for a Research Career Development Award (RCDA). It was approved and this took care of my salary. The move to Durham, North Carolina, in 1963 started what turned out to be six contented, productive years.

Hitting the Ground Running

Adjustment to this new Duke experience was as easy as could be. I came with ideas that I didn't get a chance to work on when at the NIMH. Literally on day one, I got working on them. Simultaneously, I wrote a successful research grant proposal so that I could get equipment and research assistance.

Not surprisingly, I found Bud Busse a most able and fair director and chairman of the department, and he was personally likable. One of the unexpected positives was Larry Thompson, whose office was next door to mine. Larry had and has many high-level skills for behavioral research, and, in fact, I have yet to meet anyone with as many. My skills complemented his and together we published ten studies. I enjoyed his company and was very glad for his presence.

I wrote my first book during this time, *Cognitive Processes in Maturity and Old Age* (Botwinick, 1967). This title emulated the then name of Division 20 of the APA—that is, *Maturity and Old Age*. When I was more than half finished writing the book, I wrote to six major book publishers asking whether they would like me to send them what I had written for possible publication. Each returned my letter in about six weeks and each had the same response—they referred to their market research department and found that there was an insufficient market for such a book. None of the six publishing companies cared to see what I had written.

Discouraged, the writing continued; on completion, a member of the psychology department advised me to contact the Springer Publishing Company. The response was positive, possibly because Springer was interested in developing a gerontological specialty, which this far-seeing company has since done.

The sales of this book reflected that the six major publishing companies knew what they were doing, but the response to this book among gerontological researchers and teachers was encouraging. I was complimented personally at national meetings and I might have taken these compliments as nothing more than social platitudes, except two of these made me think that perhaps it was otherwise. Years later, a research physician whose name I now don't remember referred to a subsequent, more popular book and said, ''Your older book was better.'' Not much of a compliment, I agree, but it did point to his perceived value of the earlier book and suggested its appeal to include nonpsychologists. The other compliment was more sustaining. Leonard Gottesman, a psychologist then at the University of Michigan who was teaching a course in the psychology of aging said, ''Thank God for your book!'' He said it made his teaching very much easier.

I accepted this compliment because I knew where my writing called for the most labor and ''creativity.'' Even within the restricted domain of cognition, the literature was diverse with respect to areas and types of investigations, quality of work, and the years in which they were published. The literature was amorphous—a mess really—and I took the job of imparting an organization to it. The effort seemed successful because the organization of the literature appeared so natural to those who read the book. Certainly, it seemed so to Gottesman.

Many years later I had a different response to the book. A graduate student in a here unnamed university was given a task by his mentor to write brief biographical sketches of selected persons in the field. I was sent my sketch for comment. *Cognitive Processes in Maturity and Old Age* was seen as yet another publication focusing on aging decline. I returned the sketch with comments of displeasure.

Time to Move On Again

There were three reasons I thought I should consider relocation even though I did not feel any need to move, in fact, didn't want to leave. The Vietnam War was heating up and I saw the possibility that, progressively, NIH grant funds would be more difficult to get. My RCDA provided my salary and other grants provided the means to carry out my research. All this was ''soft money'' and despite my tenured professorship, I thought it best to start thinking about ''hard money.''

There were two other reasons for thinking about leaving, although less important ones: First, I began to think of a psychology department as a more natural home for a psychologist. Second, I had already spent so much time doing hands-on research, I thought I would have something special to offer undergraduate and graduate students. Accordingly, I let the word out that I had interest in employment in a psychology department.

A few offers came my way but I was not interested in them. Shortly, Marion Bunch, then chair of the Psychology Department of Washington University in St. Louis (WU), offered me a one-year visiting professorship. I told him I was interested but I would not move my family to St. Louis for one year. He arranged for me to fly to St. Louis every other week for two or three days to teach a graduate seminar for PhD candidates in the department's aging program. I did this while continuing my work at Duke.

I expected an offer for a regular appointment as the year was ending and when it came I was pleased, but also conflicted. I knew the situation at WU very well by this time and it was all positive, but I really didn't want to leave Duke. A factor that pushed the decision to go was the question I learned to ask when at the NIMH, ''Will I be sorry later when I am old?'' In 1969 we packed once again and moved to St. Louis to a tenured professorship and a sizable increase in salary.

My Last Career Station

My WU employment lasted 20 years, including my year as a visiting professor, just about half the duration of my career. As much as I didn't want to leave Duke, I was pleased with WU. Had the decision to leave Duke and come to St. Louis been a failure, would I still have valued the "will I be sorry" question? Fortunately, I never found out.

First Order of Business

The department had a long-standing but expiring predoctoral training grant for Geriatrics-Gerontology. Robert Kleemeier had been the original director and from all accounts it had been a viable training program, conceived at least partly as multidisciplinary. When I arrived in St. Louis the program was in shambles with Kleemeier deceased seven years.

Graduate students were languishing without direction in the study of aging, many were in the program in name only having no interest in aging. Some graduate students were there a long time without having started their dissertations.

I assumed the role of the director of training in successfully applying for a training grant refocusing the direction of study. The grant was titled "Aging and Development," with the specified goal of training PhD candidates in traditional psychology with special expertise in research on aging. The grant also included the training of postdoctoral students, with both predoctoral and postdoctoral candidates receiving generous stipends, whatever university tuition costs were necessary plus supply and travel stipends. One of our postdoctoral students, Joan Erber, became a major collaborator with me in research and teaching. She is now a tenured professor at Florida International University in Miami.

Existing and new students of aging were made to recognize that this was a program of research in aging and that other academic interests were to be no more than auxiliary. I held graduate seminars to this end discussing ideas in the research on aging and focusing on dissertation planning.

Simultaneously, I made an effort to enlist interest among the general departmental faculty to work with the students of aging. Here I had success but, as might be expected, only among a limited number of the faculty. The predoctoral training program was improved to the point that I like to think of it as one of the better ones in the country. Funding for the program was continuously renewed during the time I was an active member of the faculty and the program exists today under the very able direction of Martha Storandt.

Research

When I arrived at WU, the chair of the department, Marion Bunch, asked Martha Storandt to help me, and help me she did. She was a relatively new PhD who enthusiastically helped in developing the training program and she helped me in my research. Before long she became a very important research collaborator and together we published many studies made possible by a series of research grants. I often said Martha "made me look good." Martha is now a professor of psychology and a leader in geropsychology and is often called on by the APA for counsel and service.

Among the studies we did was a series on memory. We used many procedures, all collected on the same subjects; because of this and because some of the studies were based on simple procedures that probably were not publishable on their own, we decided to publish all of them as a book with a chapter integrating all the data. The book was named, *Memory, Related Functions and Age* (Botwinick & Storandt, 1974). We thought it a thorough examination of what the title reflected, but the book did not achieve a wide readership and this was disappointing. We tried to bring some of the findings to gerontologists' attention through reviews of the literature.

My most successful book was *Aging and Behavior* (Botwinick, 1973), which was revised and enlarged in 1978 and revised again in 1984. The original 1973 edition was reproduced in Braille by the N.Y.C. Lighthouse for the Blind and this pleased me very much. The 1984 edition was largely a new book with the same format calling for almost as much effort as the original one. I thought about a new title and publishing it as a new book but decided otherwise in order to take advantage of the popularity of the original. I served on NIH study sections and in a few grant applications I saw sections of this book taken at what appeared to be verbatim. I took this as a compliment.

I also published a short book, *We Are Aging* (Botwinick, 1981), that I thought might be of interest to research-oriented high school students or community college students. Based on sales, this book was not successful. In looking at it now I can see that I really did not do the intended job. I was amused to learn, however, that in 1987, *We Are Aging* was translated and published in Japanese.

My journal publications covered a variety of areas but almost always in the context of age. The most prominent areas of study were of cognitive functioning and psychomotor behavior, particularly the role of expectancy in speeded responses. There were studies on perception, relocation to nursing homes, Alzheimer's disease, and others.

My labors were recognized in honors that I received. There were the Brookdale and Kleemeier Awards of the Gerontological Society of America, The Distinguished Contribution Award of Division 20 of the APA, the Keston Memorial Lectureship Award of the University of Southern California. I presented in the APA Master Lecture Series.

Undergraduate Teaching

It may be recalled that one of my reasons for coming to WU was that with my hands-on research experience I thought I would be an asset for teaching undergraduate and graduate students. I believe I was good for graduate students, but my hands-on experience was little use to undergraduates. With exception, I found them not only uninterested in my research, but uninterested in research period.

My early years at WU took place during the height of the Vietnam War. The students were not the same before or after this period, and my disappointment regarding their lack of interest in research was nothing compared to how the war affected classroom behavior. It seemed to me that hostility permeated the classroom—it felt as if it had a weight. Several of the students showed signs of being on drugs. There was little response to what I was trying so hard to do. I would leave the classroom with a wet shirt and damp jacket.

Students in groups roamed the halls doing I knew not what. There was a report of a physics teacher whose data files had been destroyed. A building was burned. I took to duplicating all my papers—research and teaching—and keeping one set at home. Some of the faculty members who were against the Vietnam War discussed the war in class and counseled students accordingly. I believed this to be wrong and never discussed the war with students even though my personal sympathies were with them, if not with what many were doing. I never mentioned that I had stood silent vigils against the war with a Quaker group in the hot summer sun of Durham, North Carolina, during several lunch hours.

A year or two after one of these difficult classes, a student came to visit me. He was one of the students I remembered because his behavior was contrary to what I just described. I told him how hard it was for me and he told me that he felt it was harder for him. He said that I would ask a question and when he tried to respond he was chastised by those around him.

In time the students reverted to usual ways and university life became normal. I had come to WU from Duke prepared to subordinate my research to teaching, but during the hectic Vietnam days I began to devote less time to students and more to research. I never fully moved back to my intention of subordinating research for the sake of students, and I attributed this to having been ''burned.'' In retrospect, however, this may have been rationalization in that I probably belonged more in the laboratory than in the classroom.

Centers

I received a phone call from Robert Felix, who suggested we meet for lunch. This surprised me because he had been director of the NIMH when I was there but his lofty station and mine were far apart. I think I met him only once. At the time he phoned me he had just retired as dean of the medical school of St. Louis University.

At lunch he told me that he was in contact with the Veterans Administration (VA) and wanted to establish in St. Louis a Geriatric Research Educational and Clinical Center (GRECC) that the VA was planning for several cities around the country. We started work on this but for some reason he lost interest and the project languished. Not long afterward a VA employee contacted me to help rejuvenate this effort and I was glad to try again.

I did all that I could to help and the St. Louis VA got its GRECC. I really don't know how instrumental my help was, but the VA chief of staff allowed me to name two psychologists for appointments to GRECC. One appointment turned out to be a disappointment to me, even if not to the VA. The other appointment was a winner. Carol Dye was a clinical psychologist trained in the old Kleemeier program at WU and retained a major interest in aging. Her work in GRECC was valued and after a while she transferred to become chief of the VA psychology service. I was familiar enough with this service to know that she did an excellent job, all the while giving prominent clinical attention to the aging veteran. Carol died a few years ago and with this my contact with the VA stopped.

I had another more satisfying and continuing involvement in establishing a center. Leonard Berg is a neurologist in the WU medical school who long had interest in Alzheimer's disease and organized a small group to study clinical issues and literature in the field. In 1979 a member of this group visited me to see what interest and help I might provide. Before long, Martha Storandt and I became active in efforts to develop research grants to study Alzheimer's disease. This small beginning developed in 1984 into the Alzheimer Disease Research Center (ADRC), now a world-class center, and also the Memory and Aging Project, continuously funded by a program project grant. Martha and I became codirectors of clinical research of the center with several of the PhDs we trained working in it.

Although we were influential participants in achieving and contributing to the center, it is Leonard Berg who was the real force behind its success. He is now recognized as one of the foremost leaders in diagnosing, treating, and researching Alzheimer's disease. It is hard to find a nicer person than Len Berg.

Retirement

Why Did I Retire?

The decision to retire was not easy to make because I knew that once retired it was irreversible. I had several reasons for retirement, but the foremost one was that I felt spent. After all these years I no longer was taken by what I was doing. Things that interested me, perhaps even excited me, no longer did. I read the literature and some of it seemed like old ideas in new formulations. Even my own new ideas for research seemed familiar. I no longer felt vital on the job. I thought it time to close shop, referred to the question, ''Will I be sorry later?'' and retired at age 65.

In all candor, had I not had the economic means to retire, or had the home context not been a desirable option, I would have continued work. I might have revitalized, I might not have, but for me, retirement has been satisfying.

Looking Back

I don't know what importance my research will have in the run of time. I do look back with satisfaction, however, that although my bibliography includes some ''quickie'' studies, all my work, ''quickie'' and otherwise, was carried out with as much quality as I could apply. I have enough ego to appreciate the honors and awards I received. My collaborators and assistants were treated with fairness and respect, and when warranted, with gratitude. I have satisfaction in knowing that many benefited from association with me.

I am pleased with the aging and development training program of the WU psychology department, where we had fine predoctoral and postdoctoral students. I take pride in their accomplishments.

I feel particularly good about the start and achievement of the ADRC of the School of Medicine. This is a major resource. Finally, my retirement would not be a successful one if it were not for my wife, Joan. I feel blessed.

References

Botwinick, J. (1967). *Cognitive processes in maturity and old age.* New York: Springer.

Botwinick, J. (1973, 1978, 1984). *Aging and behavior.* New York: Springer.

Botwinick, J. (1981). *We are aging.* New York: Springer.

Botwinick, J., & Storandt, M. (1974). *Memory, related functions and age.* Springfield, IL: Charles C. Thomas.

Erber, J. (1976). Age differences in learning and memory on a digit-symbol substitution task. *Experimental Aging Research, 2,* 45–53.

Chapter 6
A PERSONAL PERSPECTIVE FROM
THE UNITED KINGDOM

Dennis Basil Bromley

In one sense, my career in geropsychology began in 1945, toward the end of World War II, when I was serving with the Royal Air Force (RAF). At that time, I was considering what I wanted to do with my life, which was to do anything other than going back to my old office job. I happened to read a short book on the history of science, which concluded with a chapter on psychology, hailed as the science of the future. I was sold on the idea, and I was on my way, but with little notion of where I was going.

Academic Career

I was fortunate enough to benefit from the relatively easy access to a university education in the United Kingdom in the postwar years. I found myself in the company of other ex-servicemen keen to take advantage of the opportunity. I studied at the University of Manchester, and graduated in 1950 with a BA (Hons) in psychology, Class I. Shortly afterward, I became a junior lecturer in the Department of Psychology at the University of Liverpool. I was responsible for teaching social psychology. I soon discovered, the hard way, that the most effective way to learn is to teach. It is useless to speculate about the contribution to geropsychology I might have made had I taken up an alternative offer of training in clinical psychology at the Maudsley hospital.

Early Years

When invited to contribute to this publication, I retrieved all the small academic diaries I had kept from the year 1954. These were not diaries in the literary sense, but rather collections of memoranda related almost exclusively to my academic activities. For example, in the academic year 1954–1955, I was busy recruiting and testing volunteer subjects for my PhD research. I was also teaching, examining, reading, administering, making contact with researchers in aging, and beginning to write up my ideas.

Professor Hearnshaw, head of the small department at Liverpool, was keen for staff to cooperate on one main research issue—namely, conceptual or abstract thought. In the 1950s, abstraction and generalization were believed to be essential to high-grade intelligence. They were susceptible to conditions of brain damage and mental illness. They remain contemporary research issues. Hearnshaw developed a new type of high-grade intelligence test designed to measure what he called "temporal integration," the extent to which respondents could establish abstract relationships between successive stimulus arrays. The serial presentation of stimuli effectively added short- and medium-term memory components to a task involving visuo-spatial perception and logical inference, thus operationally defining "temporal integration." Nowadays, dealing with this sort of task is described as "information processing." Hearnshaw's test took about an hour to administer to individuals or to small groups by means of a slide projector. I acted as an occasional research assistant to Hearnshaw and helped to calculate some of the statistical results.

Although Hearnshaw did not succeed in generating widespread interest in the theoretical and practical aspects of temporal integration, my involvement did bring home to me the importance of psychometrics and neuropsychology. Unfortunately, I was hampered by mediocre talent in mathematics, lack of training in physiology, and heavy teaching commitments in personality and social psychology. Somehow, I found myself asking, "What happens to conceptual thought (abstraction and generalization) in normal people in later life?" This question was prompted when I read about higher mental processes and about Wechsler's work on adult intelligence. It provided a focus for my PhD research.

I did not use Hearnshaw's test of temporal integration. Instead, I devised a test battery made up of some standardized measures of general intelligence and some novel tests. These included individually administered pencil-and-paper tests and performance tests. Among others, they included the Wechsler-Bellevue Form 1, the Porteus mazes, the Hanfmann-Kasanin block-sorting test, the Shaw Test, and a self-constructed proverb interpretation test. The test battery took the average volunteer about two hours to complete. I tested a cross-sectional sample of 256 men and women volunteers evenly distributed across the adult age range. I spent two years collecting the data at my expense of time and money and then spent about eight years analyzing the data. I did this first by hand, then with the help of an electromechanical calculator, then with help of the Hollerith facilities at a local company, and finally with the university's newly installed DEUCE computer. This machine occupied a large floor and took about four seconds to calculate one correlation.

By 1956–1957, I was using research data to explore normal age differences in incidental learning and creative thinking. Lehman's work on age and achievement (cited in Bromley, 1988) provided a strong stimulus. By 1958–1959, I was hard at work on my PhD thesis. In those days, university staff could pursue a research degree without supervision, so I was free to do whatever I pleased whenever I pleased. I enjoyed several conferences abroad—in New York, San Francisco, and Copenhagen—which enabled me to meet other research workers and exchange ideas.

I was awarded my PhD in 1962 for my thesis titled "Ageing and Intellect." I had been sensible in deciding to publish individual parts of my research findings as they emerged rather than concentrating on completing my PhD. Even by 1962, I had data that I had not analyzed, but by that time some of the tests seemed old-fashioned or unlikely to reveal anything of interest.

My domestic circumstances in the period between 1952 and 1961 were difficult, an unsuitable marriage and low pay making it necessary to take on additional employment in the evenings. I could not work properly at home, so the department of psychology became a sort of refuge—I could feel myself relaxing as I settled into my office each day. I read voraciously and without much discrimination, in virtually all areas related to psychology, and read everything on aging that was available. I was in charge of the library accessions for psychology, a role that I enjoyed.

From about 1953, I began to take an interest in philosophical issues in the behavioral sciences. That interest has continued up to the present, and it provided the background for my research activities. Then, as now, there were pressures on academic staff to publish their research findings, although the emphasis on large-scale team research was not so great, at least in psychology.

While engaged in the statistical analysis of my PhD research data, I became impressed with Siegel's (1956) book on nonparametric statistics. I decided to apply these methods almost exclusively, and I even developed a nonparametric method of cluster analysis, soon overtaken by alternative methods. I suspect that one of my PhD examiners did not like my emphasis on conceptual and methodological issues and my concern with the statistical analysis of psychometric survey data. Nevertheless, while my research on intelligence and aging was under way, I had the benefit of help, encouragement, and advice from Welford and Birren and, of course, Hearnshaw. They seemed then, and proved to be, impossible acts to follow. The books by Welford (1958) and Birren (1959) came out at an opportune time for me.

The academic climate in which my career developed was friendly and helpful, although there was little financial support. Research on aging was a small-scale enterprise. At conferences or through visits or correspondence, I was able to talk to almost everyone with related interests.

Psychological Research in Aging in the United Kingdom, 1950–1970

In the 1950s, the Nuffield Foundation supported notable psychological research in human aging in the United Kingdom, carried out under the direction of Welford at the University of Cambridge. Welford (1958) described this work on cognitive and psychomotor skills.

In 1955 the members of the Medical Research Council in the United Kingdom thought it desirable to link research in psychology to the occupational aspects of aging. This followed a report by the National Advisory Committee on the Employment of Older Men and Women, a government committee set up in 1952. This report drew attention to the need for increased knowledge of the fitness and capacity for work of older people, and recognized the adverse effects of age prejudice and occupational discrimination. Hearnshaw had experience in industrial psychology, and Liverpool had the necessary industrial contacts.

Consequently, the major development in psychology at Liverpool was the setting up, in 1955, of the Medical Research Council unit on the Occupational Aspects of Ageing. The scope of the MRC unit's research work was wide and covered vision, hearing, functional age, vigilance, sleep, decision processes, intellectual functions, memory, imagery, learning, and personality. The work was carried out partly with the help of a panel of volunteer subjects (respondents) in laboratory settings and partly in industrial settings. Although notionally concentrated on the second half of the working life, the research included studies on young adults and retired people. Hearnshaw (1971) summarized the research on human aging carried out in the Department of Psychology and the MRC unit from 1953 to 1970. See also Heron and Chown (1967), cited in Hearnshaw (1971).

The main reason for setting up the MRC unit was the official belief that the United Kingdom faced a national worker shortage and that ways should be found for retraining older workers. In any event, the worker shortage was short-lived, quickly overtaken by technological change, increased female employment, and economic recession.

I need not describe the administrative, interpersonal, financial, and technical circumstances accompanying the work of the MRC unit. Heron directed the unit from 1955 to 1963. Hearnshaw directed it from 1963 to 1970, except for the academic year 1964–1965, when I was acting-director in Hearnshaw's absence. I was the honorary scientific advisor from 1962 onward. During this time, of course, I was a full-time lecturer in the Department of

Psychology, with a wide range of teaching, research, and administrative duties. In the early stages, my contribution to the work of the MRC unit was minimal, although later on I acted as supervisor to some of the staff registered for postgraduate degrees.

Over the years, I had personal contact with virtually all 20 members of the research staff in the MRC unit. It would be invidious of me to pick out individuals for special mention. Sufficient to say that some are still active, even eminent, in research in aging; see the list of references in Hearnshaw (1971).

According to my diaries, the years between 1963 and 1970 were busy and productive, helped by a settled domestic situation. I became more involved with the work of the MRC unit and participated in international activities in gerontology. In 1966 I published my first book. Also by that time I had contributed 11 journal articles to the literature on aging. Against all expectations, and presumably catching a tide of interest in aging, the book went into a second and a third edition with several reprints (see Bromley, 1988). I suppose these inexpensive textbooks were my most significant contribution to the psychology of aging, at least in the United Kingdom, meeting an educational demand and drawing attention to the multidisciplinary nature of gerontology. I regret not being able to refer to all the main publications that had influenced me by this time. The various editions of these Penguin Books contained more than 600 names of researchers.

My research interests extended well beyond the psychology of aging. I tried, with varying degrees of success, to keep up with advances in psychometrics, personality study, social psychology, clinical psychology, and the philosophy of the behavioral sciences.

Between 1956 and 1960 my domestic problems had stimulated an interest in legal evidence and argument. My reading in these areas forced me to revise my ideas about the philosophy of science and its practice. In time, these ideas came to fruition in my book on the case study method (Bromley, 1986). This followed up my earlier books on personality description (Livesley & Bromley, 1973, cited in Bromley, 1977, 1986). I showed how the case study method is basic to scientific inquiry in the social and behavioral sciences. I also rejected the dogma that "science is not concerned with the individual." Contrary to traditional opinion, general rules in the behavioral sciences can be formulated, and modified or refuted, through the examination of individual cases, as in legal science. This is linked to what is nowadays called "case-based reasoning." I was pleased to contribute to a symposium on the case study method at the APA convention in Boston in August 1999.

Middle Years

In 1970, I inherited the remains of the MRC unit as a personal research grant. This helped to maintain the panel of volunteer subjects. I used my MRC grant to follow up a research interest in the language of personality description. Earlier, I had supervised a research student investigating the development of person perception in childhood and adolescence. He collected data on children's written descriptions of themselves and other people. We developed a method of content analysis with a range of descriptive categories to find the main effects and interactions for the different age groups and the two genders. We eventually published an account of this research in Livesley and Bromley (1973, cited in Bromley, 1977, 1986), as mentioned earlier. I intended to use the same method to look at age and gender differences in the language adults use when writing personality descriptions.

The reasoning behind my choice of this research topic argued that the traditional psychometric approach to personality assessment was misguided; a more functional ap-proach was needed. This approach would not try to identify basic, universal personality factors but try to discover what sorts of information observers use in making sense of their own and other people's behavior. It would also aim to identify the conceptual frameworks we use in understanding and dealing with individual cases. This echoes the historical distinction between the study of persons, and the study of individual differences. When one examines observers' descriptions of themselves and other people, one finds that personality traits form only a part of their account. Our self-concepts, and our concepts of other persons, are functional (practical and field-dependent) systems of beliefs. They are based on various assumptions and on all sorts of information (derived from a multiplicity of sources and organized in complex ways).

My immediate research problem was to identify the relevant categories of information observers use and to test for possible age and gender differences among normal adults. I had assumed that the method of content analysis used with school-age children would apply to adult descriptions of persons. The assumption proved untenable. I underestimated three things: the complexities of adult language, the length of adult descriptions, and the range of individual differences in the way adults choose to conceptualize people.

An avalanche of data soon buried me. Even with the help of two hard-working clerical assistants, the problems of semantics and coder reliability blocked the proposed quantitative analysis. This was before the arrival of convenient computer-assisted methods of transforming and analyzing typewritten transcripts. With the end of research funding in sight, I decided to draw a sample of 240 descriptions from the 2250 I had collected. I produced an impressionistic qualitative analysis instead of the intended quantitative analysis. I was unable to draw conclusions about age or gender differences, but I published an account of how ordinary adults conceptualize and describe each other (see Bromley, 1977, 1986, pp. 27–34).

In the 1970s I attended conferences in Amsterdam, Nijmegen, Kiev, Vichy, Tokyo, and Washington. These conferences marked the growing international interest in gerontology. I helped to set up the British Society for Social and Behavioural Gerontology (BSSBG), now known by a more economical title and acronym, the British Society of Gerontology (BSG). Many of us were keen to establish a national institute of gerontology in the United Kingdom, like the Gerontological Society of America. This required the joint action of several organizations. The BSSBG represented mainly psychologists and sociologists. The British Society for Research in Ageing (BSRA) represented mainly biologists and physiologists. The British Geriatric Society (BGS) was exclusively medical, represented mainly by geriatricians and psychiatrists. The British Association for Service to the Elderly (BASE) represented mainly social workers, nurses, and voluntary bodies. Representatives from these organizations formed a British Council of Ageing (BCA), supported by the Nuffield Foundation, and held discussions about the proposed gerontological society. The discussions went on for some years without agreement. The United Kingdom still has no national institute combining the interests of all concerned with gerontology. The reasons for this include financial constraints, differences in the size and status of the various organizations, continuing lack of interest on the part of the relevant professions, and a lack of charismatic leadership.

I became a fellow of the British Psychological Society (BPS) in 1962 and a fellow of the Gerontological Society of America in 1972. My diaries reveal an academic life packed with teaching, research, and administration. I also spent a lot of time helping to plan a new building for the department of psychology at Liverpool, completed in 1973. Somehow I found time to keep fit, to read fiction, and to take part in the activities of the university air squadron. My interest in aviation sustains a long-term memory of Jeanne Gilbert telling me that she held a private pilot's license. I greatly enjoyed her book, published in 1952 (cited in Bromley, 1990).

In 1975 I became professor and head of the department of psychology at the University of Liverpool. The number of people involved in research in aging in the United Kingdom was still quite small, so that interdisciplinary contacts were easy and frequent. I well remember being impressed with the dedication of the geriatricians with whom I came into contact. Demographic changes were making it increasingly clear that gerontology would have to grow in spite of the low level of scientific interest and the prevailing social prejudice. Unfortunately, working with the elderly was not a popular option among psychologists or doctors. I was unable to persuade staff in my department to make research in aging a collective enterprise. Perhaps my attempts to draw attention to the psychological aspects of death and dying contributed to the general apathy! For a time, my interest in this area drew me into voluntary work associated with bereavement.

My duties as head of the department slowed down my research into adult age differences in person perception. Nevertheless, I managed to pursue my interest in the study of individual cases, with special reference to the modes of reasoning we use to account for a person's behavior (Bromley, 1986).

Earlier in my career, my interest in person perception and social psychology led me to carry out a small investigation into serial changes in reputation. Apart from a brief report to a conference, the data lay fallow until my retirement from the university in 1990. I then had time to reexamine them in more detail, and to investigate the phenomenon of reputation in a more systematic way. This enabled me to write what I believe is the first book on this topic (Bromley, 1993). I mention this fact because it illustrates how events sometimes have unplanned, long-term consequences for research.

Sabbatical Leave

In 1969 I took up the offer of a sabbatical year at the Philadelphia Geriatric Center (PGC). My proposed role was to help monitor the effectiveness of a new hospital designed for geriatric patients. Delays in the hospital project meant that I had to look around for alternative research topics. Researchers at the PGC worked on existing projects outside my main areas of interest and expertise.

One of the reasons I was attracted to the PGC was the possibility of studying human behavior in real-life settings. I arranged an exercise to continuously observe a day in the life of one patient. The results revealed typical behaviour cycles but did not seem to justify the time and effort required for this sort of investigation. Some years later, however, a colleague in the United Kingdom used behavior sampling to study the disturbed sleep patterns of elderly patients.

I spent some time devising a form board test that would measure individual differences between, and serial changes in, patients with very low levels of intelligence. These were patients with zero or near zero scores on a minimental scale. I achieved some success in obtaining differential test scores from such patients, but I was unable to make much progress because of limited time and resources. Nowadays the way forward for this sort of research is through computerized displays and on-line data analysis.

My main academic contribution during this sabbatical year was a book chapter on theory construction in the psychology of aging (see references in Bromley, 1988). This made use of important but neglected ideas about ''substantive logic'' derived from Toulmin (see references in Bromley, 1986). Formal logic does not provide a complete solution for the analysis of substantive arguments—that is, practical or real-world arguments. I was able to clarify the substantive logical structure of the widely discussed theory of disengagement and subsequently showed how substantive logic could be used in case-studies, as discussed earlier.

The quality of the proceedings at various conferences and seminars I attended in the United States impressed me. One conference was on death and dying—a topic that I helped to popularize (if that is the word) on my return to the United Kingdom. My family and I enjoyed several holidays exploring parts of the United States, and we retain happy memories of the PGC and its dedicated staff.

From 1979 to 1980 I enjoyed a sabbatical year in Calgary, Canada. Against my better judgment, I was persuaded to help evaluate a day center for geriatric patients; the temptation was too great. I had spent over a year in Canada in the 1940s training as a pilot in the RAF. I thought Canada was a marvelous country and constantly berated myself for not migrating there. However, following my arrival it took me a long time to register the complicated administrative and local political conditions that affect evaluation research. Lacking formal authority, I was like an anthropologist who not only fails to understand the culture he is visiting but also fails to recognize his failure. I found myself having to collect or estimate figures on quite basic issues such as epidemiology and local amenities. I produced a report. However, the diversity, the rapid turnover of staff, and the limited time available made it impossible for me to find out what effect, if any, my report had on facilities for geriatric patients. Besides playing my main role, I carried out some clinical assessments and counseling sessions and gave talks on the psychology of aging to various groups across Canada. The frustrations of an ambiguous social role were greatly eased by good friends, Alberta blue skies, walks in the mountains, and cross-country skiing.

I had intended using any free time in Canada to begin writing a textbook on the psychology of aging—long promised to my publisher. I had even shipped out much of the necessary research literature. It was only in the last few weeks of my visit, however, that I made a start on the book, and even that was a false start—Alberta outdoors beats everything!

Later Years

The prospect of resettling in Canada at what seemed to be the late age of 56 seemed daunting; so in 1980 I returned to Liverpool to resume my normal workload. The University of Liverpool established a local interdisciplinary Institute of Human Ageing (IHA). This was one of a number of local initiatives throughout the United Kingdom. The BSSBG transformed itself into the BSG with a pronounced shift toward the sociology of aging. Its *Journal of Ageing and Society* began publication in 1981.

By 1982 I was reacting against the emerging enthusiasm for life-span developmental psychology. I felt that the study of adult aging had little in common with juvenile development; it had different concepts, methods, and applications (see Bromley, 1988, pp. 27–30; 1990, pp. 29–31). I felt that the study of human aging had first to develop as a science in its own right, then the long-range connections between juvenile development of adult aging could be investigated. To bring the two areas together prematurely would dilute, and possibly misdirect, research efforts. Later on, I found myself reacting against the emphasis on large-scale research methodology in geropsychology (see Bromley, 1990, pp. 352–355). I also reacted against the use of sophisticated statistical analysis on relatively crude and insufficient data. At the same time, I felt that geropsychologists, including myself, have not been sufficiently inventive and rigorous in the construction and standardization of psychometric measures.

At the back of my mind was the possibility of writing a book on aging, which would build on my long-standing interest in social psychology. Instead, for some reason, my nose for relatively unoccupied niches in psychological research identified the topic of motivation and emotion in later life. I included a chapter on this topic in Bromley (1990, chap. 7, pp. 263–315).

Also by 1982, I was beginning to see that my interest in the effects of aging on the language of personality description could contribute to research into the effects of aging on language generally. My original intention was to examine the forms of language used in personality descriptions as one possible semantic framework that might stand comparison with other sorts of semantic framework. I had already described the main content areas in personality description, but I had not so far formulated a ''semantics'' of personality description. I started by finding suitable examples from personality descriptions to illustrate the sorts of concepts and arguments typically found in introductory books on semantics. Unfortunately, the hoped-for new ideas on the semantics of personality description remain stubbornly dormant. Other half-finished work on case-based reasoning languishes for want of critical and constructive feedback (or, more likely, because of competing interests).

Nevertheless, I published an article on aging and written language (Bromley, 1991), focusing on the sorts of issues identified by other researchers. This was an interesting research exercise, and I learned a lot from my background reading and reviewers' comments. Unfortunately, it did not contribute much to my understanding of semantics or the ''functional'' nature of personality description—that is, the way meanings about the self and others are conveyed and used. Perhaps the ''pragmatics'' of the language of personality description will prove to be a more rewarding line of inquiry.

By 1985 I had completed my 10-year period as head of the Department of Psychology. This decreased my administrative workload but kept me busy with the usual rounds of teaching, examining, and research. Three years later, Penguin Books published the third revision of my book with a new title (Bromley, 1988) to mark a substantial shift in the contents. In the 1980s I was active in the BPS, the BSG, and the Liverpool IHA.

Retirement

I retired in 1990 at the age of 66 when circumstances seemed propitious. I must confess that by this time I felt I wanted a holiday from aging, and I had other interests that I had neglected over the years. One of the reasons for my feeling burned out was that the textbook on aging that I had long promised my publisher appeared (Bromley, 1990). Producing this book had taken considerable time and effort, and I had to omit a great deal of material that was relevant to the psychology of aging. I drew the conclusion that there was now too much information in this area for one person to master or for one book to deal with in any sort of depth. On the other hand, I may have spread my energies too thinly over too many areas of interest.

Following my official retirement from the university, I taught a third-year option on the social psychology of reputation on a part-time basis and published a book on this topic in 1993. I did not completely abandon my interest in aging, and I fully intended to continue to work on the research data available to me. This tends to confirm the typical pattern of retirement for university professors.

One of the topics I had lectured on to outside bodies was preparation for retirement. I found this easier to preach than to practice. For a few years beforehand, I occasionally reflected on what I would do in my retirement. I was relieved to find that my general lack of concern with long-term financial planning had resulted in what appeared to be a reasonable financial state of affairs for me on retirement. The realization of what might have happened led me to take a self-taught, crash course in economics and financial planning, which proved to be at least as interesting as psychology. The subsequent recession brought, and continues to bring, family and financial commitments not anticipated in preretirement planning.

By 1993 software developments in computing encouraged me to restart the massive task of analyzing my data on adult age and gender differences in the language of personality description. Unfortunately, I overestimated the benefits of this software, and progress has been painfully slow. So far, I have produced provisional findings on adult age and gender differences in the use of emotionally toned words and the use of content categories in self-descriptions. For example, my data suggest that the terms of reference used in adult self-descriptions are similar for both men and women. The only obvious effect of aging is a steady and substantial increase in references to life-history events—hardly worth a Nobel Prize.

A few years ago, a colleague invited me to write a short contribution to a proposed book on the ways in which gerontologists have coped with the process of aging. Surprisingly, he found himself short of contributors and abandoned the proposal. In my contribution, I half-jokingly said that I hoped to write an article on learning to fly again 50 years after I first learned. I started flying again in 1994 at the age of 70. I obtained my private pilot's license in 1996 and continue to fly (and pass the twice-yearly statutory medical examinations) at the time of writing. I published my article on the effects of relearning this complex psychomotor skill in late life (Bromley, 1996).

Clearly, I have not unduly extended my holiday from aging. I still enjoy facilities at the university. I recently contributed to gerontology conferences in Amsterdam, Liverpool, and Manchester. I presented a paper titled ''The Aging Self and the Changing Self-Concept'' at the Fourteenth Nordic Congress on Gerontology in 1998. I offer occasional advice connected with postgraduate research into Parkinson's disease caregivers, and health education for elderly persons. At the same time, I am trying my hand at screenwriting. I have completed, but not yet managed to market, a film script and a children's book portraying the legend of Gilgamesh—geropsychology's first hero, whose search for eternal life was unsuccessful. I first came across this legend in Zeman's (1944–1950) marvelous contributions to the history of aging, and I have consulted a number of authoritative sources.

I walk daily and weight-train regularly; mild arthritis in a hip joint has forced me to give up jogging. I fly, but only in visual meteorological conditions (rare enough in the United Kingdom). I work in the garden and promise myself to work out a feasible research project while there is still time. Fortunately, family demands are minimal. I have not yet followed in G. S. Hall's footsteps (Hall, 1923, cited in Bromley, 1990), but I have made a start. He reported making a bonfire of a lifetime's accumulation of academic books and papers.

My interest in gerontology has kept me fully aware of my time horizon. I have experienced some of the annoyances of later life firsthand: poorer vision and hearing, decreased strength and stamina, a prostate operation, and a slight arthritic condition and, ironically for a geropsychologist, a rodent ulcer. Nature is witty! In case I should have forgotten the proximity of my vanishing point, the BPS persuaded me to provide a videotaped interview for their archives. The request to write an autobiographical contribution to the history of geropsychology was another reminder of my greatly foreshortened expectation of life. That is all in a day's work for a gerontologist.

Conclusion

As indicated earlier, my main contributions to psychogerontology have been academic—books, articles, lectures, and so on—in spite of an underlying preference for applied psychology. This is partly a consequence of the academic culture covering the major part of my career. I suppose it is also partly a consequence of my personal preferences and abilities for working with ideas rather than with people.

Naturally, my ideas have changed over the years. I entered psychology when it was still trying to emulate the physical sciences, with a strong emphasis on experimentation, quantification, and general laws. I welcomed the gradual shift toward the systematic observation of behavior in natural (real-world, familiar, recurrent) situations. I welcomed the analysis of qualitative data with its emphasis on descriptive accuracy rather than on convenient, and sometimes spurious, measurement and statistical analysis. My preferences are for the study of individual cases (of persons and situations), small-scale surveys, quality assurance research methods and data analysis, and close attention to the logic of substantive real-world arguments.

References

Birren, J. E. (Ed.). (1959). *Handbook of aging and the individual: Psychological and biological aspects.* Chicago: University of Chicago Press.

Bromley, D. B. (1977). *Personality description in ordinary language.* Chichester, England: John Wiley & Sons.

Bromley, D. B. (1986). *The case-study method in psychology and related disciplines.* Chichester, England: John Wiley & Sons.

Bromley, D. B. (1988). *Human ageing: An introduction to gerontology* (Rev. ed.). Harmondsworth: Penguin Books.

Bromley, D. B. (1990). *Behavioural gerontology: Central issues in the psychology of ageing.* Chichester, England: John Wiley & Sons.

Bromley, D. B. (1991). Aspects of written language production over adult life. *Psychology and Aging, 6*(2), 296–308.

Bromley, D. B. (1993). *Reputation, image and impression management.* Chichester, England: John Wiley & Sons.

Bromley, D. B. (1996). On learning to fly again after 50 years. *Generations Review, 6*(4), 2–4.

Hearnshaw, L. S. (1971). *The psychological and occupational aspects of ageing: Liverpool researches, 1953–1970.* Liverpool, England: Medical Research Council.

Livesley, W. J., & Bromley, D. B. (1973). *Person perception in childhood and adolescence.* Chichester, England: John Wiley & Sons.

Siegel, S. (1956). *Nonparametric statistics for the behavioral sciences.* London: McGraw-Hill.

Welford, A. T. (1958). *Ageing and human skill.* London: Oxford University Press.

Zeman, F. D. (1944–1950). Life's later years. Studies in the medical history of old age. *New York Journal of the Mount Sinai Hospital,* parts 1–12.

Chapter 7
AGING MEMORIES:
A Career in Cognitive Psychology

Fergus I. M. Craik

When I was at the University of Liverpool in the early 1960s, our research group was visited by an eminent scholar from London—a Professor Fry as I remember. Our group was made up of young postgraduate students, and when we were introduced as researchers of the aging process, the professor remarked "Hmm, studying it from some distance it seems!" Less true today, alas! However, living through the aging process does at least afford the researcher the opportunity of thinking out his or her earlier pronouncements in a way that is not usually possible for students of other developmental, comparative, and abnormal phenomena. Looking back at my earlier work I am torn between pleasure at being "right" from the start—at least in the limited sense of still holding the same view today—and dismay at my rigidity and lack of progress. In this essay I will attempt some accounting of the switch/stay ratio in the ideas that have guided my experimental research over the past 40 years.

I was born in Edinburgh, Scotland, in 1935, and later went to high school and university in that chilly but beautiful city. I also met my wife Anne there, so we look on it as our home

Careers in geropsychology are very varied, as this volume demonstrates, and I suppose mine is no more unusual than many others. In my cognitive aging corner of the field, and in my generation (plus or minus 20 years), it is not uncommon for researchers to be active contributors to the parent discipline of cognitive psychology as well as to cognitive aging—Tim Salthouse, Leah Light, Pat Rabbitt, Denise Park, Lynn Hasher, and Rose Zacks are some of many names that come to mind.

I would like to express my gratitude to the many people who have helped my career at various points; mentors and colleagues in Edinburgh, Liverpool, London, Toronto, and elsewhere. Apart from my difficulties as a medical student I have had it easy, thanks largely to these helping hands. Much of my empirical work and many of my ideas are attributable directly to interactions with my graduate students and postdoctoral fellows over the years, and it is to them that I owe the most. Of the 16 PhDs who worked with me as their primary supervisor and who had qualified by the end of 1997, only five worked primarily in aging research (Mark Byrd, Joan McDowd, Ray Shaw, Karen Li, and Nicole Anderson). In contrast, I have had some 21 postdoctoral fellows, and 17 of these worked on aging topics. I will ponder these data for a while before drawing any major theoretical conclusions.

Finally, I owe an enormous debt of gratitude to my family for putting up with me over the years. My wife Anne and children Lindsay and Neil were often shortchanged while I toiled to meet yet another deadline. I was somewhat taken aback on one occasion by being asked by one of my children's friends (teenagers at the time) whether I was "actually a workaholic," but my alarm was reduced when the same youth later commented to my wife (who, like me, has mildly leftist views) that "he had never met a real communist before!" So everything is relative I suppose. And now the children have children of their own, who regard their grandpa with a mixture of affection and tolerant amusement. From the Beatles to babysitting—it didn't take long! Oh well, still time to write one or two more decent papers with any luck.

town although we have lived and worked happily in Canada for many years. My father is now aged 90, and is a living testament to the beneficial effects of a daily dose of Scotch whisky on successful aging. At the time of my birth he was an ambitious young executive in the Bank of Scotland and was appointed manager of the branch in Lockerbie—a small town in the southwest of Scotland that achieved unhappy fame many years later as the site of the TWA plane disaster. Growing up in a Scottish town was a satisfying experience; my first career aspirations were modeled, naturally enough, on some of the local figures who seemed to spend their lives in interesting ways. Around the age of 4 or 5 I debated whether to become a minister or a joiner (the Scottish term for carpenter). I wonder now whether these two vocations appealed, respectively, to my future interests in teaching and empirical work; whatever their origins, I soon decided that being a joiner would be more fun.

My first school was Lockerbie Academy, and there I learned the basics of arithmetic and grammar. My parents were ambitious for me, and so sent me to an excellent high school in Edinburgh at the age of 12. My best subjects there were English and physics—a slightly unlikely combination. I liked science in general (except for the mathematics) and biology in particular, so a career in medicine seemed a sensible choice. I think I was the first person in my family to go to university, although it seemed entirely appropriate that I should do so— almost all of my friends from school were also going on (most to Edinburgh University), my parents expected and encouraged it, and Scottish attitudes were very much in favor of the best possible education. Although Scotland is a small country, and not a particularly wealthy one, it has had four universities for 500 years or so. The tradition there (certainly in my day) was for students to attend their local university, so I applied to the medical school at the University of Edinburgh (my *only* application) and was duly accepted in 1953.

Medical school was not a success, unfortunately. The first year was basic science—no problems there—but I had immediate difficulties when I started studying anatomy in the second and third years. I found it tiresome and onerous to learn catalogs such as the 47 anterior relations of the kidney, and I just could not find general principles to make the learning meaningful. I soldiered on grimly for several years despite being a mediocre student and despite a growing realization that I rather disliked the company of sick people; not a good attitude for a potential physician. I did enjoy neurology, however, and was intrigued by the psychiatric cases that I saw. I read some books on psychosomatic medicine and was impressed by the obvious power of the mind to influence apparently mechanistic bodily systems. The interaction between brain and behavior was thus a topic of early interest, and I strongly suspect that if I had graduated in medicine I would have ended up as a researcher in this general area, doing much the same work as I do today.

However, my medical aspirations ended in 1958, partly as a function of my own growing dislike of the program and partly as a function of my failure to satisfy the steely eyed examiners of the Edinburgh Faculty of Medicine (my fault, not theirs, in both cases). I was able to salvage the courses I had passed in medicine (physiology, biochemistry—even anatomy) and transfer them to the science faculty; I graduated from the psychology program in 1960. At that time British university departments were usually quite small, and had a single professor—"the Prof"; other faculty members were lecturers, senior lecturers, and readers. The professor at Edinburgh was James Drever, a pleasant scholarly man whose interests reflected the department's origins as the Department of Mental Philosophy. He was not an experimentalist, but he encouraged me in my empirical interests and clearly felt that the discipline would make progress by virtue of scientific findings as well as by theoretical analysis. The final-year honors class had a weekly seminar with Drever in which we read a series of books, then critiqued and discussed them. Drever's selection in 1959 was interesting and forward looking when considered from the vantage point of 40 years later; we read Gibson's *The Perception of the Visual World* (Drever was a friend and admirer of J. J. Gibson), *The Organization of Behavior* by Hebb, *Learning and Instinct in Animals* by W. H. Thorpe, and *Motivation* by Dalbir Bindra. We also read some Hull, but behaviorism was never a major force in British psychology. I was therefore exposed early on to Canadian biological psychology, in the shape of Hebb's and Bindra's ideas, and also to the evolving views of the ethologists like Lorenz and Tinbergen. Perceptual theory also appealed to me, especially the ideas of transactional functionalism (so much more satisfying to roll round the tongue than phrases like "pulmonary embolism" or "ventricular fibrillation") and the writings of Helson and Brunswik.

Ian Hunter taught a course on memory and learning that I enjoyed but that did not capture me entirely. The article that really knocked me sideways was George Miller's classic paper on the Magical Number Seven, so for my thesis project I decided to merge information theory with the perception of time and devised an experiment in which the participants ("subjects" at that time) made absolute judgments of varying complexity and were later asked to estimate how long they had been working. The study yielded a nice function linking subjective judgments of duration to the rate of information processing—possibly before its time in 1960, although I did not think of publishing it. But the experiment did have a practical spin-off; it seemed acceptable to approach young women to ask them if they could help out by participating in a psychology experiment—I ended up testing 120 participants, possibly the largest scale study that I have ever run. But I did the decent thing and married one of them—my wife, Anne.

Designing, running, and analyzing my experiment on time perception was a formative experience. It confirmed my interest in experimentation and demonstrated the satisfaction to be gained from a pattern of data falling neatly into place. I still love to see a tidy pattern of numbers, even in the simplest experiments. In my lab class on human memory we gather data on free recall of word lists and I plot the results with rising excitement (the primacy effect! the recency effect!) while the students yawn and gossip in the background. Professor Drever approved of my experimental interests and suggested that I apply for two possible postgraduate research positions; one was at an institute of ophthalmology, but the work there seemed a little too narrow for my tastes; the second was at the Medical Research Council (MRC) Unit on Occupational Aspects of Ageing at Liverpool University, and this was definitely more attractive. However, I also felt that I had spent too many years as an undergraduate and was keen to get into "a real job," so I applied for a position in the research department of a large London advertising agency. I was actually offered the job and had provisionally accepted it when I was told that, unfortunately, the budget for the position had not been approved. So, in a way, the MRC unit was my second choice, and it is interesting to reflect on the role of chance in a career. My suspicion is that temperament, interests, and abilities will generally govern the broad outlines of the type of work a person does, but chance may play a major role in determining the exact form the work takes.

University of Liverpool, 1960–1965

In postwar Britain, research into old age and the aging process had been sponsored by the Nuffield Foundation, and in 1946 a research unit into problems of aging was established at Cambridge University under the direction of A. T. Welford. This group flourished for 10 years, conducting research into aspects of human skilled performance, including perception, learning, memory, attention, and reaction time. The results of their investigations, framed by a broad theory of human performance, were later published in *Ageing and Human Skill* (Welford, 1958). This book, along with Donald Broadbent's *Perception and Communica-*

tion (1958), was a major inspiration to my early work in the experimental psychology of aging. In 1955 the Medical Research Council decided to support further work on the psychology of aging, but to tilt the research toward applied and occupational aspects. The Liverpool unit was therefore set up in 1955 with Professor Leslie Hearnshaw as the director and Dr. Alastair Heron, first as the deputy director and later as the director.

When I arrived in Liverpool in the autumn of 1960, Dr. Heron had planned four research topics spanning the fields of experimental and occupational studies of aging; these topics were taken on by four young researchers. Roger Wilson was to study flicker fusion frequency and other aspects of visual functioning, Norman Wetherick explored age differences in problem solving and concept attainment, Ken Elliott looked at labor mobility as a function of age, and I studied age-related changes in confidence and decision making. The thinking behind this last topic was that an age-related decline in self-confidence might impose an artificial ceiling on an older person's abilities—especially when learning new skills. My first experiments on this topic were carried out in the framework of Julian Rotter's level of aspiration theory. I inherited an aiming task in which participants estimated their future performance at various levels of practice. Some evidence was found to support the idea of a general trait of confidence, and I also confirmed a tendency for older adults to seek more information before committing themselves to a decision. I found the ideas rather too vague for my tastes, however, and the experimental results were not very clear-cut, so I switched my allegiance to the relatively new ideas stemming from signal detection theory, propounded by Tanner, Swets, Birdsall, and others. This framework suggested more rigorous experiments in which younger and older adults listened for faint auditory signals in a noisy background. Signal detection theory permits the separation of sensory and motivational factors, and my studies in this area provided evidence for greater caution on the part of older adults and a tendency for older people to restrict the range of their decision criteria when using a rating scale—they were less risky at the risky end of the scale and less cautious at the cautious end. I submitted all of these studies as a PhD thesis in the Department of Psychology at the University of Liverpool and was awarded the degree in 1965.

As an MRC employee at Liverpool, it was easy to visit other MRC research units, and Alastair Heron greatly helped my career by sending me on several trips to the applied psychology unit at Cambridge. This group was certainly the strongest team of experimental psychologists in Europe. It was led by Donald Broadbent and also had some promising young researchers: Alan Baddeley, John Morton, and Pat Rabbitt, for example. These visits opened my eyes to the exciting new world of cognitive psychology—to studies of attention and short-term memory, to experiments on stress and vigilance, and to sophisticated theories of reaction times. I proudly returned to Liverpool with a copy of tape-recorded dichotic digits. I still have the tape somewhere—the digits were spoken by Margaret Gregory (later Margaret Broadbent) and the recording was obviously made on a summer evening, as the sounds of birdsong from Cambridge gardens can be heard quite clearly.

In my last two years at Liverpool (1963–1965) I therefore started to conduct experiments on age changes in memory and attention; this is the line that stuck with me and led to later work in London and in Toronto. Apart from the support and encouragement I received from Alastair Heron and Professor Hearnshaw, other colleagues and friends provided ideas, criticism, and suggestions. I should single out Dennis Bromley especially, since he supervised my thesis work after Dr. Heron left to take up a position in Africa. Dennis had broad interests in cognitive and social gerontology and provided wise and careful guidance in a good-humored way. He and I went once a week to the Kardomah Tea Room to eat supper before teaching in an evening class. We were sometimes joined by Roma Grundy, later his wife but then a girlfriend; Dennis and Roma would conduct a genteel flirtation over the teacups as I munched away embarrassedly at my fish and chips. "Well, you know what my name spells backwards? . . ." said Roma coyly on one occasion; "What—Yd-nurg??" responded Dennis in mock innocence. Terry Rick was another pal from the psychology department; he and I shared the teaching in one of the evening classes. Ann Davies from the MRC unit met one of our students socially, a retired academic with a pronounced Eastern European accent. Hoping to get some gossip, Ann asked him how he was enjoying the course. "I hev two teachers" said the man after a reflective pause, "Krick und Krock. Krick is vonderful, but Krock is ebsolutely awful." Terry and I both loved the story—each convinced that *he* was the vonderful Krick of course.

As is usually the case, there is no clear line dividing a category of people who were influential scientifically from those that were simply friendly and helpful, but I certainly profited greatly (and in some cases continue to profit) from conversations with Ann Davies, Sid Tune, and Norman Wetherick at the Liverpool unit. We had a visit from Patrick Rabbitt, and I remember being vastly impressed by Pat's prolific list of suggestions for possible future research topics. Alastair Heron was a major help and influence; apart from advice on experimental issues, he facilitated contacts with the Cambridge group, and funded trips to the International Congress of Gerontology in Vienna and to the APA annual meeting in Washington, DC. Liverpool in the 1960s was an interesting and satisfying place to live and work; I remember those days with affection.

Birkbeck College, 1965–1971

After receiving the PhD from Liverpool I decided to look around for another position. I would have dearly liked to move to the Applied Psychology Unit at Cambridge, but they had no openings at that time. A faculty position in a university department seemed the next best thing, so I applied for a post as a lecturer at Birkbeck College in London and was appointed there in 1965. Birkbeck is part of the federated University of London, and the Department of Psychology was chaired by Arthur Summerfield, with Peter Venables as the second professor. Peter was a big influence, especially; his work was in schizophrenia and in electrophysiology. Although clearly the cognitive difficulties experienced by older adults must have a different cause from those underlying schizophrenia, there are some interesting parallels nonetheless, and my thinking benefited from considering the methods and theories used by Venables and his students.

At Birkbeck I was under no obligation to pursue research in aging, and in fact I became progressively more interested and involved in research on short-term memory in the late 1960s. The age variable played a part in some studies, however; for example, in experiments concerned with the identification and measurement of a "pure" primary memory component in free recall. We found that age had no effect on primary memory but that the secondary memory component declined with advancing age. These experiments were published in a book edited by George Talland and also as one of my first international journal articles in the *Journal of Verbal Learning and Verbal Behavior* (edited at that time by Leo Postman) in 1968.

George Talland played a crucial, if inadvertent, role in my career by offering me a position with his Boston group around that time. I had met George at various conferences, and he had been supportive and encouraging; for my part I greatly admired the manner in which he blended theory and experiments. I was keen to spend a year in an American lab, but had no thoughts of leaving Britain permanently, so Talland's offer posed a real dilemma. My boss at Birkbeck, Arthur Summerfield, offered a solution by promising me a year's leave of absence in the near future if I could find a congenial (and sufficiently wealthy) temporary haven in the new world. (I should mention that it *was* unusual for junior faculty members to be granted a leave so early in their careers.) As it happened, Donald Broadbent had invited me to a NATO-sponsored conference on memory at Cambridge in the summer of 1967, so I took the train to Cambridge armed with Summerfield's offer.

The meeting lasted two weeks and involved many of the major figures in memory research such as the diplomatic Arthur Melton, the enigmatic Donald Norman, and the charismatic Endel Tulving. I hesitantly approached Tulving to see if there was any chance of spending a year in Toronto, and to my mild amazement he responded that it might well be possible if I was prepared to teach a couple of courses. Was I prepared to? Absolutely! And so it came about that I spent the 1968–1969 year at the University of Toronto—instantly transformed from a mere lecturer in the United Kingdom to a visiting associate professor in Canada. I ended up teaching a course in memory and a lab class in human and animal learning, despite my feeble protestations that I had never taken a course in animal learning and had never so much as handled a laboratory rat in my life. No problem—here's your white lab coat, a pair of gloves, and a manual of possible experiments; let me know if you have any questions, OK? (This was Glenn Macdonald, the dryly humorous chair of the Toronto department.)

I enjoyed the year in Toronto. The Department of Psychology was very active in research, with several meetings a week devoted to problems of memory. Also, I found the general attitude to research in Canada and the United States to be very positive and supportive; new ideas were welcomed and encouraged, unlike in Britain where they were questioned and disputed (reflecting perhaps the difference between an empirically based intellectual culture in North America and a rationally based culture in Britain). Or was it attributable to the fact that psychology in Britain was still loosely connected to philosophy and thus to advances by argument and rhetoric rather than by experimental demonstrations? I'm not sure, but I know that I relished the empirical-theoretical atmosphere in Toronto and other North American centers. My family also liked living in Toronto; we went back to London in 1969 after my year as a visitor but returned to Toronto as permanent residents in 1971.

Aging research was thus not my primary interest while in London between 1965 and 1971, but I remained active in the field. One topic, mentioned already, concerned age differences in short-term and long-term memory; another was the interface between attention and short-term (primary) memory. Dichotic listening was a dominant methodology in Britain, following Broadbent's pioneering work in the 1950s, and I carried out some experiments using this paradigm. I also continued working with signal detection theory measures; one suggestion that caught *my* attention was that the sum of the squared signal strengths (d'^2) from two or more simultaneous discriminations (e.g., shared attention between the two ears) gives a measure of total processing capacity for the discriminations in question. Some of the available capacity is lost in the divided attention situation—possibly because it is needed to control the sharing procedure—and I found that more capacity is needed for this purpose in the older listener. This work is based on an interesting paper by Martin Taylor and colleagues and was never really followed up, although the topic of divided attention retains its interest for me today. One last important event around that time was an invitation to another NATO conference—this time in Thessaloniki, Greece, in 1966. The conference was organized by James Birren and Alan Welford and dealt with age-related changes in decision making in various theoretical and practical situations. It was stimulating and agreeable to share a relaxed week or so with some big names in the field. As I remember, I lectured on the use of signal-detection theory in studies of aging to a large group of polite but somewhat bemused students from Turkey and Greece. It was a very pleasant few days; I do hope that NATO's objectives were advanced in some small way.

University of Toronto, 1971–2000

I took up my position as an associate professor of psychology at the Erindale Campus of the University of Toronto in the fall of 1971, and I have been at the university since then. The Erindale Campus is situated about 15 miles west of downtown Toronto in the booming suburb of Mississauga. The buildings are pleasantly situated among trees and parkland (well, car-parkland these days), and in 1971 the faculty members were young, bright, and research oriented (now they are middle-aged, bright, and research oriented). I had decent research space, reasonable funding, and excellent colleagues, both at Erindale and on the downtown campus where I retained my close research ties with Endel Tulving, Bennet Murdock, and Bob Lockhart, among others. The highlight of each week was the departmental memory seminar—the Ebbinghaus Empire—set up by Endel Tulving and George Mandler in the early 1960s and still going today.

My first few years in Toronto were dominated by the development of the levels of processing framework for memory research. While still in London I had been impressed by the attentional theories of Anne Treisman, then at Oxford. She had suggested that perceptual information is subjected to a series of analyses, with each successive level acting as a kind of pass-fail test. The tests work on signal detection theory principles, such that an incoming signal can "pass the test" and proceed to higher level analyses *either* on the basis of its signal strength (d') *or* because the criterion for a passing grade (β) is set at a lenient level. This system modified and elaborated Broadbent's original filter theory of attention, allowing for both bottom-up, perceptual (d') and top-down, conceptual (β) factors to play a role in what gets through to conscious awareness. Hierarchical models of this sort have always appealed to me, as have models involving gradual and continuous changes as opposed to sharp categorical divisions, and it seemed to me that memory (or at least the encoding aspects of memory) might be thought of as the products of these various levels of analysis. Thus both the amount and the qualitative nature of incoming information encoded into memory would depend on the attention paid to an event and how the event was processed. These ideas were quite vaguely thought through when I returned to Toronto in 1971, but I was delighted to discover that my colleague Bob Lockhart had been thinking along the same lines. We had mentioned these notions to Endel Tulving, who had been encouraging and who suggested that we write them up as an article for the *Journal of Verbal Learning and Verbal Behavior* (Craik & Lockhart, 1972). Tulving was the editor of the journal at that time and was enormously helpful in shaping the Craik and Lockhart piece. He also became interested in the empirical aspects of levels of processing, so he and I collaborated on an experimental article that came out in the *Journal of Experimental Psychology: General* in 1975.

Meanwhile my interests had turned back to problems of aging. The key event here was an invitation by Jim Birren and Warner Schaie to contribute a chapter on age-related differences in memory to the first edition of their *Handbook of the Psychology of Aging* (Craik, 1977). When Birren called me about this in the summer of 1973 I was initially quite surprised as I had not been heavily involved in aging research in recent years. However, he persuaded me that this distance from the field would give my views some perspective and objectivity, so I started reading the latest articles and thinking about the issues again. At that time I think it is fair to say that the field of cognitive aging lagged a few years behind its parent fields of "straight" research in perception, attention, memory, learning, and thinking. I had that impression, at least, and thus was emboldened to offer various gratuitous suggestions on how research on memory and aging should proceed. Having made these insightful suggestions, of course, I was then tempted to follow them up myself—so I was drawn back into the field.

I completed the first draft of the *Handbook* chapter at the end of 1974 and sent off the final revision in May 1975, commenting in a letter to Jim Birren that I had *enjoyed* writing the review and that it had rekindled my interest in the research on aging. I had received helpful suggestions on the first draft from several people, but I might single out the Canadian psychologist David Schonfield in particular—he wrote me a four-page letter with detailed and insightful points. In his letter Schonfield mentioned his concept of ''remembering to remember''—a notion that grew into the current research topic of prospective memory, that of remembering to carry out an action at some future time. It is interesting to reflect that Schonfield was thinking about such issues in the early 1970s. One other letter I received in connection with the *Handbook* chapter was from Alan Welford. In reply to my inquiry he said he had nothing new to report on the topic of memory but added that he was surprised to see my address and sorry that I had been ''lost to Britain.'' The pangs of guilt I might otherwise have felt at this mild admonishment from a much-respected senior figure were mitigated, however, by the fact that Welford's letter came from Adelaide, Australia, where he had moved as head of department some years before.

The conjunction of the *Handbook* chapter and my experimental work on levels of processing set me thinking about possible age differences in depth of processing. Was it possible that part of the typical age-related drop in memory performance is due to a failure of older people to process words and other events in a sufficiently deep and elaborate fashion? An exploratory study was carried out by Sharon White, a senior undergraduate at Erindale, and this yielded the interesting result that older people recalled and recognized fewer words than their younger counterparts when instructed simply to learn a list, but that the age difference was eliminated by the combination of a semantic orienting task at encoding and a recognition test at retrieval. That is, the simple device of asking a semantic question at the time of acquisition (e.g., Is the word a jungle animal? TIGER) coupled with a recognition test appeared to ''repair'' the deficiencies in older participants' encoding and retrieval processes. Although it was only an undergraduate thesis we thought that this interesting result was worth including in the *Handbook* chapter.

This basic result and the ideas that it engendered were developed over the next five or six years in conjunction with various postdocs and graduate students—Eileen Simon, Jan Rabinowitz, Brian Ackerman, and Mark Byrd were some of my main collaborators. We postulated that the aging process was associated with a reduction in ''processing resources''—essentially the amount of attention that could be devoted to information processing—and that this reduction curtailed the rich and meaningful analysis of perceived events that occurs spontaneously in younger people. We pointed out that when attentional resources are experimentally curtailed in young adults by having them perform two tasks at once (a memory task and some further attention-demanding task), the resulting pattern of memory performance is essentially the same as that seen in older people working under full attention conditions. These findings bolstered our faith in the notion of depleted resources, although (for reasons I have never fully understood) the idea of a general reduction in processing resources has never met with much favor. The further idea was that whereas depleted resources would typically be associated with inefficient encoding and retrieval processes, these impairments can be alleviated by guiding appropriate processing at encoding by means of orienting tasks, and guiding appropriate processing at retrieval by providing cues, context, or reproviding the event itself in a recognition test (Craik & Byrd, 1982; Craik & Simon, 1980; Rabinowitz, Craik, & Ackerman, 1982).

The salient events around this time included a sabbatical year spent in the Department of Psychology at Stanford University in 1977–1978. The Stanford department had a stimulating group of visitors that year—nobody in aging as such, but a number of researchers in perception, cognition, and developmental psychology. I shared an office with Jim Cutting and talked a lot to Ann Brown and Rochel Gelman, as well as to various locals including Gordon Bower, Ellen Markman, and John Flavell. In the summer of 1978 I attended the first Talland conference in Boston, organized by Lennie Poon and others. I found this meeting enormously rewarding and enjoyed making some new research contacts, including Tim Salthouse. A couple of years later Sandra Trehub and I organized a conference on aging at the Erindale Campus of the University of Toronto. We tried to cover a range of topics related broadly to age differences in cognitive processing—from the biological basis to social implications. Thanks to the support of various groups such as our local Program in Gerontology headed by Blossom Wigdor we were able to attract a galaxy of aging stars (as it were) including Pat Rabbitt, Marion Perlmutter, John Horn, Nancy Waugh, David Arenberg, Marcel Kinsbourne, and Paul Baltes. The papers were uniformly excellent, and Trehub and I later brought out an edited version of them in book form (Craik & Trehub, 1982).

Like any involved researcher I have served on the editorial boards of a number of journals over the years—British, Canadian, American, and European journals dealing both with mainstream cognition and with cognitive aging. My one stint as main editor was with the *Journal of Verbal Learning and Verbal Behavior* from 1980 to 1984. This journal, known popularly as *JVLVB,* was probably *the* major journal of human memory and learning in the 1960s and 1970s. By 1980, however, the emphasis was switching to experimental studies of language, and when Marcel Just and Patricia Carpenter took over the editorship in 1985 they changed the name to its present title, *Journal of Memory and Language,* to reflect this change. I checked back through the contents of the four volumes that I edited to see whether my presence as editor had encouraged a wave of articles on aging. The numbers for the four years were, zero, zero, one, and two for 1981, 1982, 1983, and 1984, respectively. An optimist might perceive a trend here, but it is hardly a flood.

I spent the 1982–1983 year back at Stanford, this time at the Center for Advanced Studies in the Behavioral Sciences. Several other memory researchers were there at the same time, including Matthew Erdelyi, Bobby Klatzky, and Bob Crowder, so we formed a stimulating and useful discussion group. Someone, it may have been Tom Trabasso, urged me to read Herbert Simon's book *The Sciences of the Artificial,* and I was very taken with Simon's stress on the role of the external environment in both engineering and biology. That is, to be adaptive, a device or an organism must function well in its particular set of external circumstances, and in that sense the external environment shapes, constrains, and supports the inner environment of the system in question. It can be argued that babies and very young animals are quite dependent on a benign external environment and react rather passively to environmental changes. As the baby matures into infancy and childhood, he or she becomes progressively less tied to the here and now, and begins to act *on* the external world rather than react to it (this is one of Piaget's fundamental ideas on cognitive development). It seemed to me that older adulthood might be associated with some reversal of this trend, so that the older person's mental processes are again acted on by the external environment rather than acting to control the outside world.

These ideas can help us understand the varying patterns of age-related losses in memory. A retrieval test that is well supported by environmental context or by the representation of stimuli (as in recognition memory) will show only slight age-related losses, whereas a test with little environmental support (like free recall of a list of items) will require a lot of self-initiated activity and will show substantial losses with age. This dissociation between recognition and recall had been demonstrated by David Schonfield and was shown again in a more complex experiment published in 1987 by Joan McDowd and myself (Craik & McDowd, 1987). At the time of acquisition, a task requiring self-initiated processing is one in which participants are simply instructed to "learn this material," whereas environmental support can be provided by, for example, organizing the material into a form compatible with the learner's current store of schematic knowledge. I presented these ideas first at a symposium on memory organized by Donald Broadbent at the Royal Society in London and subsequently at a meeting in Berlin commemorating the centenary of the publication of Ebbinghaus's groundbreaking book *On Memory.* The written versions of these talks were published later in the proceedings of the two meetings (Craik, 1983, 1986).

I have always been interested in the biological mechanisms underlying behavior, and my research in the past 10 years has been progressively concerned with the neural correlates of memory. Following the pioneering work of Brenda Milner and her colleagues in Montreal, the hippocampus and its surrounding structures in the medial temporal lobes have been viewed as the crucial structures for the formation of new memories. More recent work has suggested that the frontal lobes also play an important role; for example, my colleagues Morris Moscovitch and Gordon Winocur have proposed that the medial temporal structures function in a rather automatic way during acquisition and retrieval, whereas the frontal lobes function in a more strategic fashion to select and control what is encoded and what is retrieved. These ideas are of great interest to cognitive aging researchers, because there is evidence for a similarity between normal aging and frontal lobe pathology—older people behave in some ways like patients with frontal lobe damage. One function of the frontal lobes appears to be the integration of information about an event with its temporal and spatial context. Thus, frontal lobe patients may exhibit "source amnesia"—that is, they can remember facts but are unable to recollect where and when they learned these facts. John McIntyre is a colleague from Winnipeg who spent some months in Toronto, and he and I carried out some experiments to show that normal aging is also associated with a mild form of source amnesia; older people show a disproportionate loss of contextual information relative to focal or factual information (McIntyre & Craik, 1987). My colleagues and I later followed up this finding by showing that, within a group of older people, those who showed the greatest loss of contextual information also tended to score poorly on neuropsychological tests of frontal lobe functions.

The recent emergence of neuroimaging techniques has allowed neuroscientists to look rather directly at these problems. The University of Toronto acquired a Positron Emission Tomography (PET) scanner in 1992, and I have been involved in some exciting studies using this new methodology. A group led by Shitij Kapur found that "deep" processing of words was associated with specific activation of an area in the left dorsolateral prefrontal cortex, for example; thus our 1972 ideas on levels of processing were given some neurological justification in 1994. Endel Tulving then pointed out that several PET studies had shown that encoding processes were consistently associated with *left* frontal activation, whereas retrieval of the same material was associated with *right* frontal activation. At first it seems strange that information should "go in one lobe and out the other," but it seems likely that these frontal structures are mediating *control* processes for encoding and retrieval and are not the actual storage sites, which are probably located in posterior regions of the cortex.

I have been fortunate throughout my career to have had excellent students, postdoctoral fellows, and faculty colleagues; my own thinking has been influenced greatly by the suggestions and theoretical ideas of these various collaborators. In the mid-1980s, for example, Robin Morris came over from Britain to work with me, and he, I, and Mary Gick collaborated on a series of studies on working memory and age. Robin had been one of Alan Baddeley's students and so came primed with the latest ideas from Cambridge. This joint collaboration resulted in a series of studies illustrating age-related changes in the ability to hold and manipulate information held in the mind; older people are poorer at this, especially if they have to carry out a second operation while attempting to perform the primary task. As Welford had suggested in 1958, this type of age-related difficulty may lie at the heart of many cognitive difficulties experienced by older people.

Another important idea, whose implications we are investigating at present, was proposed by my friend and colleague Larry Jacoby. His suggestion is that most cognitive operations reflect a mixture of specific, consciously controlled processes and more general, unconscious, automatic processes. Normally it is impossible to specify the proportions of each type of processing involved in a complex task, but Jacoby has devised an ingenious opposition procedure to dissociate the processes and measure them separately. This procedure has been used by Jacoby and his students to study age differences, with the finding that age-related losses in memory are confined to consciously controlled process; it seems probable in fact, that older people make *greater* use of stereotyped automatic processes, in compensation for their loss of specific control. These ideas and preliminary findings have exciting implications for tying together notions of frontal lobe function and dysfunction, the underlying neurology, and the consequences of reduced cognitive control in perception, attention, memory, and thinking.

In the past 10 to 12 years, two events that were significant for my involvement in research on aging were, first, the formation of the Canadian Aging Research Network (CARNET) and, second, the foundation of the Rotman Research Institute. In the late 1980s the Canadian government decided to allocate a large sum of money to research; not to the existing research councils but in the form of a new competitive program for research coalitions or networks. Its idea was to involve collaborative groups of researchers from across Canada in various research endeavors and also to steer this research in ways that would benefit the country by requiring that each research network should involve partners from the private sector. These conditions were not immediately appealing to a theoretically oriented university researcher like myself, but Blossom Wigdor persuaded a group of us that a network addressing the social and psychological aspects of aging might well be attractive to the politicians who ran the program. And so CARNET was born. After some initial reversals, the network was funded with Victor Marshall as director. Victor is a sociologist of aging who was at the University of Toronto at that time, and so two of the three groups that coalesced (loosely) to form CARNET were made up of sociologists and the third, headed by myself, was composed of cognitive aging researchers from across Canada. One initial hope was that the sociologists and cognitive psychologists would join forces to tackle problems of mutual interest (the effects of different living arrangements on cognitive performance, for example), but this happened to a very limited extent, I must confess. The cultural divisions between community-oriented sociologists and biologically oriented cognitive psychologists are surprisingly impermeable. In other respects, the CARNET venture (which ran from 1990 to 1995) was quite successful; the funds enabled Canadian researchers of cognitive aging to meet and discuss issues on a regular basis, and the funding philosophy also pushed a number of us to apply our ideas to real-world problems. The bureaucracy of the federal program was a major downside, on the other hand, and (as the PI of the psychology group) I was not sad to see the funding end in 1995.

The Rotman Research Institute was set up in 1988 owing to the efforts and vision of Joseph L. Rotman, a Toronto-based businessman and entrepreneur. The institute is part of the Baycrest Centre for Geriatric Care; its director is Donald Stuss, a neuropsychologist specializing in frontal lobe function, and its mission is to study normal and abnormal cognitive processes as they occur in normal aging, pathological aging, and as consequences of brain damage. I was initially involved in planning the institute when I chaired the psychology department at the University of Toronto (1985–1990) and have since been an associate scientist with the group. In 1997 I was honored to be appointed to the Glassman Chair in Neuropsychology—a University of Toronto position but designed to strengthen the links between the university and Baycrest. So at present I spend one or two days each week at the Rotman Institute, carrying on my research into cognitive changes in normal aging but also becoming involved in studies with brain damaged patients and in the development of rehabilitative techniques. So I am now using neuropsychological tests routinely, as well as traditional laboratory methods, and (as mentioned previously) I am getting involved in the exciting new world of neuroimaging. Perhaps my early medical school training will come in useful after all.

References

Broadbent, D. E. (1958). *Perception and communication.* London: Pergamon Press.

Craik, F. I. M. (1977). Age differences in human memory. In J. E. Birren & K. W. Schaie (Eds.), *Handbook of the psychology of aging* (pp. 384–420). New York: Van Nostrand Reinhold.

Craik. F. I. M. (1983). On the transfer of information from temporary to permanent memory. *Philosophical Transactions of the Royal Society of London,* Series B, *302,* 341–359.

Craik, F. I. M. (1986). A functional account of age differences in memory. In F. Klix & H. Hagendorf (Eds.), *Human memory and cognitive capabilities, mechanisms and performance* (pp. 409–422). Amsterdam: Elsevier.

Craik, F. I. M., & Byrd, M. (1982). Aging and cognitive deficits: The role of attentional resources. In F. I. M. Craik & S. E. Trehub (Eds.), *Aging and cognitive processes* (pp. 191–211). New York: Plenum Press.

Craik, F. I. M., & Lockhart, R. S. (1972). Levels of processing: A framework for memory research. *Journal of Verbal Learning and Verbal Behavior, 11,* 671–684.

Craik, F. I. M., & McDowd, J. M. (1987). Age differences in recall and recognition. *Journal of Experimental Psychology: Learning, Memory, and Cognition, 13,* 474–479.

Craik, F. I. M., & Simon, E. (1980). Age differences in memory: The roles of attention and depth of processing. In L. W. Poon, J. L. Fozard, L. S. Cermak, D. Arenberg, & L. W. Thompson (Eds.), *New directions in memory and aging* (pp. 95–112). Hillsdale, NJ: Erlbaum.

Craik, F. I. M., & Trehub, S. E. (Eds.). (1982). *Aging and cognitive processes.* New York: Plenum Press.

McIntyre, J. S., & Craik, F. I. M. (1987). Age differences in memory for item and source information. *Canadian Journal of Psychology, 41,* 175–192.

Rabinowitz, J. C., Craik, F. I. M., & Ackerman, B. P. (1982). A processing resource account of age differences in recall. *Canadian Journal of Psychology, 36,* 325–344.

Welford, A. T. (1958). *Ageing and human skill.* London: Oxford University Press.

Chapter 8
TEN YEARS WITH AGELESS ALBINO RATS AND COLLEGE SOPHOMORES LED TO A THIRTY-SOMETHING-YEAR CAREER IN GEROPSYCHOLOGY

James L. Fozard

The title of this chapter makes the point that my formal training and early experience were in experimental psychology and ergonomics as known in the 1950s, a time when psychological knowledge was based mostly on studies of successive cohorts of college students and albino rats.

This chapter covers several main topics: (a) how I made geropsychology a career (a lucky accident for me—I was offered a job doing research in aging by persons willing to take a chance on someone who had no previous background in aging); (b) what I brought to geropsychology (training, experience, and a conviction that meaningful work is critical to one's self-esteem); (c) how I adapted to a career in geropsychology (I had many opportunities to learn geropsychology rapidly—assuming ongoing projects, reviewing, and journal editing); (d) my major accomplishments (research in many areas of gerontology and significant work roles in two major longitudinal studies of aging; development of applied gerontology including gerontechnology and geriatric medicine and long-term care); and (e) what I have learned from a career in gerontology (humility as a scientist, a respect for individual differences and a knowledge that they can be scientifically described, and the importance of the physical and social environment as determinants of personal aging).

I would place myself in the second generation of geropsychologists following World War II. Members of the first include Drs. Anderson, Birren, Botwinick, Kleemeier, Welford, and Shock. At Shock's 80th birthday party given by colleagues and former students, Leonard Hayflick presented him a commemorative issue of *Experimental Gerontology*.

The most important people influencing my initial research in cognitive aging were George Talland and Nancy Waugh. My later research on aging has benefited from interactions with many professional colleagues and collaborators in gerontology and geriatrics, especially my research colleagues at the NIA. The leaders in gerontology I have known since beginning my geropsychology career have consistently strengthened and enhanced my commitment and devotion to the field—Jim and Betty Birren, Robert Kastenbaum, Nathan Shock, Alan Welford, Paul Haber, Merrill Elias, Reubin Andres, Carl Eisdorfer, and others.

I am grateful and proud that I can be a part of geropsychology and gerontology in both research and applied settings in a time of great development of these fields. I appreciate the many friendships I have with colleagues in gerontology. I especially appreciate the love and enthusiasm of my wife, Marian, who always encourages us both to take on new adventures and challenges as we age. As long as I live, I will delight in the development of my children and their families. As long as I am able, I will continue to garnish my working career with musical activities.

Shock classified several guests as spiritual descendants. I was a spiritual grandson. I responded, "Dr. Shock, you just named Dr. Reubin Andres (a highly respected colleague) to be your spiritual son even though he is only seven years older than I."

"Yes," Shock said, "but age isn't the point; you just weren't around early enough."

Major Influences in My Background and Training

Work Ethic

My father died when I was 12. He was 63, two years before the mandatory retirement age as the general manager of a large mine in a remote area of Arizona. Having anticipated retirement, he had been in the process of purchasing a cattle ranch, "large enough so I won't be bored," as he had put it. My father had had few hobbies and he had enjoyed his work. It was obvious to me as a boy that he did not like the thought of retirement. One effect his preretirement plans had was to make me search for an occupation that could continue beyond an arbitrary retirement age. The other effect resulting from his death came later; I learned to value independence and self-reliance at a young age.

In my family, people wanted and were expected to continue meaningful, paid work well into old age. Also, both my parents and relatives, particularly on my mother's side, placed a high value on doing "useful and practical" work. Except for my father, who earned a degree in electrical engineering at the University of California at Berkeley, I was the only one in my family to attend college. My mother and her siblings were for most of their careers self-employed and worked until very late in their lives (all but one lived into their 90s). Separating work and retirement was not part of their thinking. But prizing independence was. After receiving her training as a nurse and serving in World War I, my mother moved from New York City to LaTouche, Alaska, in 1919, where she was the nurse in several clinics, including the one used by the mine run by my father, the mining engineer who became her husband. This background has strongly influenced both my sister and myself—neither of us has plans for full-time retirement even though we are both over 65 when this was written. My sister, now in her 70s, continues to run and expand a two-acre nursery and greenhouse operated earlier by her now deceased husband and her.

Religion and Love of Music

Family members on my mother's side who influenced me as a youth had strong religious convictions and most were very active in fundamental Protestant sects. My aunt founded an inner-city Christian mission in which she taught and played piano for 45 years. An uncle led a prayer meeting group at work for more than 30 years. Many family members supported large evangelistic enterprises such as Billy Graham's crusades with money and donated work time. As an adult, I joined and reared my own children in the Unitarian Church, but my early experiences have made me appreciate the motivational importance of stable, well-articulated systems of beliefs, although mine are quite different from those of my parents.

Music has been an important part of my life since early childhood. I played and sang at home with family. I studied piano and trombone in high school, majored in music for two years in college, and studied music performance at the Music Academy of the West in Santa Barbara for three summers. I have performed in and led amateur and semi-professional music activities almost all of my life, mostly in jazz and wind band groups. At the time of writing I have completed nine years as the leader of the Starvation Army Band, a New Orleans jazz and swing music group that performs at Maryland-area concerts, weddings, retirement homes, and even funerals. In the press of work, time is somehow always found for this significant personal and social activity.

Early Education

My grammar school education included attending one-room schools in Idaho and Arizona reached by students on horseback and two rural Arizona schools with combined grades. Later I attended Roger Ludlowe High School, a large suburban high school in Fairfield, Connecticut—a complete shock after a grade school education in rural Arizona. Because my elementary school education was deficient in mathematics, I took remedial arithmetic along with regular high school math. In college, required courses in mathematics and statistics continued to be a challenge. However, my difficulties helped me become a good undergraduate statistics teacher because I understood my students' problems.

Undergraduate School

At the University of California at Santa Barbara I changed majors from music to psychology in my junior year. Robert Gottsdanker had the most influence on my decision to study psychology in graduate school. After taking his courses in statistics and experimental psychology I became his student assistant. Years later, Dr. Gottsdanker conducted important research on age differences in reaction time. Thirty years after graduation I was very honored when he invited me to give a research seminar on that topic at my alma mater where he was still actively teaching.

Master's Degree Training

Except for full support in my first year in college and limited help thereafter, I supported myself as an undergraduate working part time in a supermarket and as a bass trombonist in local musical groups. Paying for graduate school training necessitated obtaining an assistantship. Partly because of Dr. Gottsdanker's recommendation, I was admitted to the master's degree program at San Diego State College with a research assistantship that was important to my later career.

I helped prepare an exhaustive annotated bibliography for human factors engineering by selecting and abstracting hundreds of scientific articles in many disciplines contributing to the new discipline. The efforts were led by Drs. Alphonse Chapanis and Arnold Small, pioneers in ergonomics and human factors who strongly influenced my thinking. The transactional view of person-environment interactions is not unique to ergonomics, but that is where I first learned about it. Later, Chapanis and Small played leadership roles in relating human factors to aging, Chapanis by writing one of the first papers on human factors and aging and Small by founding the Technical Group on Aging in the Human Factors and Ergonomics Society.

More School?

Although Dr. Small and my professors at San Diego State encouraged me to continue graduate study, I was tired of school, and in 1956 I accepted a job for a large defense research company. During my orientation, the person who had offered me the position surprised me by saying, ''Don't take this job, continue graduate school.'' I followed that advice, and in retrospect I am very grateful to that man, whose name I cannot recall with certainty.

My training at San Diego led to limited but intense work experiences in human factors engineering in two navy laboratories and at the Space Guidance Center of International Business Machines, Inc. The most interesting was my work with Robert Lockard at the U.S. Naval Ordinance Test Station on a scheme to use a signal from the eye to track a moving target. We found that with appropriate magnification of the target image, the eye's tracking accuracy provided the information needed to drive a tracking device without manual guidance. Years later a commercial eye tracking system was developed based in part on our study.

Doctoral Training

In 1956 I was accepted into the new experimental psychology doctoral program at Lehigh University, and I was the first to graduate from it. My training emphasized conditioning, perception, social psychology, vision, and audition. I was the teaching assistant for the undergraduate introductory and experimental psychology courses, and for two years I was the psychologist on a team that developed and implemented a peer-counseling program for freshmen in the university dormitories. Part of the effort involved creating a professional and social organization for the upper-class counselors, which was named the Gryphon Society. I was pleased to be a charter member of that group, which celebrated its 40th anniversary in 1997.

My advisor was Solomon Weinstock, known for his research on the partial reinforcement extinction effect. My research evaluated an extension of Estes's theory explaining the advantage of distributed over massed practice in operant conditioning (Fozard, 1966). Weinstock, a fine teacher, often taught his students how to critique research by example. This experience left an indelible impression on me. In seminars he would select an article at random from a recent edition of the *Journal of Experimental Psychology* and examine it from hypotheses to conclusions with fiery and devastating criticism worthy of F. Lee Bailey.

Work, Then More School

After Lehigh, I spent three great years teaching at Colby College in Waterville, Maine. Colby provided a high-quality liberal education. To increase student enthusiasm for the required courses in experimental psychology, I replaced the sequence of formal laboratory experiments then used with a simpler but more labor-intensive process for the teacher in which students conducted one or two studies from conception to reporting.

Wanting more research than was possible at Colby, I planned a postdoctoral fellowship in human learning and perception, a plan that solidified during a summer spent in a National Science Foundation (NSF)–supported program for young faculty held at the University of Michigan with Professor Arthur Melton, then a giant in research on learning and memory.

After a year of teaching in the University of Maryland European Division, I began a two-year postdoctoral fellowship (1964–1966) with Douwe Yntema, head of the psychology group at the Massachusetts Institute of Technology Lincoln Laboratory. My research concerned subjective judgments of the relative recency of remembered events—work purporting to show that remembering is largely a reconstructive process and that cues based on temporal information provided a partial basis for memory search (see Fozard, 1970, for a summary).

Later, Yntema contributed to aging research by adapting a procedure he devised called Keeping Track of Many Things at Once. The subject received a sequence of items consisting of messages—for example, the face cards of the four suits of playing cards are interspersed with questions about the most recent exemplar of a category such as the queen of spades. As his part of the Design Conference on Memory and Aging (Poon & Fozard, 1976), Yntema and colleagues developed a version of his paradigm that vividly documented the vulnerability of older persons to proactive interference effects, as reported by Fozard (1981a).

The Transition to Research on Aging

After completing my fellowship, I took a teaching position at Southern Methodist University as one of five new faculty recruited to implement a doctoral program in psychology. The project was aborted unexpectedly in its first year by the university, resulting in the voluntary exodus of six faculty, including myself.

Yntema then introduced me to Dr. George Talland, a psychologist in the Psychiatry Department at Harvard Medical School, who collaborated with the Normative Aging Study (NAS) initiated in 1963 by the Veterans Administration (VA) Outpatient Clinic in Boston. Talland conducted studies in short-term memory with the NAS and was a consultant to the NAS director for finding a replacement for the first psychologist with the Normative Aging Study, Dr. Peter Comalli. The requirements for the job were strong credentials and potential in experimental psychology (cognitive or perceptual); knowledge of or prior interest in aging was not required. I was quickly offered the job that completely changed my career.

It was not an easy decision, one that is hard to imagine now. One of my references, Arthur Melton, warned me that I was risking my reputation by working in a nontraditional setting; indeed, when I gave a seminar at the University of Michigan that year, it was on judgments of recency, not aging. For me at the time, it was very challenging to consider the significance of studying research participants of various ages. I had associated such research with clinical applications. Creating and understanding the distinctions between normal and pathological aging were to become a lifetime concern for me as they must for any person who does research in gerontology.

Full-time research was also a new experience. I was given a clinical faculty appointment at Harvard Medical School in the Department of Psychiatry Research, which hosted the completion of my NSF-supported research project on judgments of subjective recency. Short, intensive courses, often team taught, formed the core of the curriculum for medical students and fellows. Indeed, in 12 years at Harvard, I only taught seminars on aging in my last two years; prior to that I taught psychological testing and, with Nancy Waugh, courses in clinically oriented statistics and the effects of head injury on memory and cognition.

Learning by Doing in Geropsychology

My adaptation to geropsychology involved three intertwining paths: development of a research program around significant perceptual, memory, and learning issues in adult aging; participating in interdisciplinary research in the NAS; and learning some pragmatics of the gerontological enterprise, such as the politics of aging research, how to work in multidisciplinary teams, and dealing with the reputation and quality of research on aging in various fields.

Identifying Significant Perceptual, Memory, and Learning Issues
in Adult Aging

Lessons From George Talland

Talland gave me my initial reading list: Welford's *Ageing and Human Skill;* the Birren/ Welford *Aging of the Nervous System;* Botwinick's *Cognitive Processes in Maturity and Old Age;* and Talland's own edited book, read in galley form.

I participated in a conference on the psychopathology of aging that he organized; the major goals were to promote interest by the experimental psychologists in problems related to aging as defined by clinicians and for clinicians to learn how the concepts and research tools of the experimental psychologists might be applied to their work on aging. I was not acquainted with the clinically oriented people, but I knew the experimental psychologists who represented a veritable who's who of that time (e.g., Arthur Melton, Leo Postman, George Miller, Donald Broadbent, and Michael Posner). Although interesting, the conference did little to increase the shared interests between the two groups, a frustrating outcome for Talland. I strongly shared Talland's goal to increase the involvement of experimental psychologists in aging research. Leonard Poon and I vigorously encouraged this kind of activity first in the Design Conference on Memory and Aging (Poon & Fozard, 1976), and later in the Talland Memorial Conferences (Poon, Fozard, Cermack, Arenberg, & Thompson, 1980). The money for these activities was supplied by the National Institute on Aging (NIA) and much wisdom in their formulation was provided by the NIA's Dr. Walter Spieth.

Finally, I completed some of Dr. Talland's research following his death from cancer in March 1968. Talland's chief at Harvard and my supervisors at the outpatient clinic requested that I complete Talland's work with the NAS. His program, supported by the National Institute of Child Health and Human Development, had a dozen experiments that addressed interference effects in retrieval from short-term memory, response time in paced inspection, and choice reaction. The results of some of the studies were partly analyzed. I could only publish results from part of the research because it was not possible to eliminate competing explanations of the results of all the ongoing work. Reporting on Talland's experiments provided me with some very rapid training on the special problems of research on cognitive aging.

Mental Performance and Aging

Geropsychologists agreed that reaction time slowed with age, but they did not agree about how much or how important the slowing was. The existing literature on aging and short-term memory indicated that both speed and quality of mental performance worsened with age, an important observation in planning my research. I engaged Dr. Nancy Waugh, then at Harvard Medical School, as a consultant to the NAS. We developed Mental Performance and Aging, a program to study age differences in speed of retrieving information from sensory, primary, secondary, and very long term or tertiary memory. One goal of the research was to show that the age effects differed for the different memory stores using procedures designed to minimize the confounding effects of age differences in the quality of memory.

The project was productive and exciting. Nancy Waugh's sharp thinking and creativity were important ingredients. Waugh moved to Oxford University, but we continued to collaborate. The project supported a young scientist manager—first Dr. John C. Thomas, then Dr. Leonard Poon. Both wrote several papers with Waugh and me (summarized in Fozard, 1981b). Thomas and I prepared a talk on human factors and aging that was the starting point for later essays I developed. Poon combined a background of engineering and experimental psychology; he has become a well-known leader in gerontology.

Several young scientists developed careers while working there as fellows or employees: Terrance Hines, Nancy Bowles, Nancy Treat, Gordon Carr, and Terry Anders, a postdoctoral fellow with Nancy Waugh. The two papers Anders wrote with me are some of the most widely cited in the gerontological literature (e.g., Anders & Fozard, 1973). John Cerella, then a graduate student with Dr. Herrnstein at Harvard, got his start in geropsychology by programming the computer-controlled experiments used in the Mental Performance and Aging program.

Psychology of Aging and Interdisciplinary Research in Gerontology

When I joined the NAS in Boston, the recruitment of the NAS cohort of more than 2000 men was just being completed. Charles Rose, assistant director of the NAS and a social worker at the outpatient clinic, was the driving force behind the recruitment. Following this effort, Rose, then in his 50s, returned to graduate school where he proceeded to earn a doctorate in sociology. Although we disagreed on many things, I always helped and supported the administrative and planning efforts of Dr. Rose, who did so much to develop the NAS.

Research on Abilities, Personality, and Interests

Psychology was well represented in the NAS. In addition to the programs of Comalli and Talland, four standardized psychological tests recommended by consultant Dr. Ronald Nuttall had been administered to more than 1200 men. The General Aptitude Test Battery (GATB) was widely used in employee selection. The others were the Cattell Sixteen Factor Personality Inventory, The Strong Vocational Interest Blank, and the Allport Vernon Lindsey Scale of Values. In most cases, the NAS had more data on these instruments for men than were available from their norms, a fact used in my data analyses.

I had the data machine scored and began work, first on the GATB. Fortunately, Nuttall was an expert on factor analysis and he taught me most of what I know about those techniques. After creating a socioeconomic status (SES) score for each participant, we factor analyzed the GATB test scores in relation to SES and age. Subsequently we replicated our results on the standardization data of the GATB, on the basis of which we recommended changes in the test profiles used in selecting workers that took into account age and SES.

Because of the complex history of development of the Cattell 16PF, my initial plan was to factor analyze the items to determine the factor structure. It was not technically feasible to do this at the time, so the initial descriptive study presented scale scores by age and SES.

Personality and vocational interests were areas where my experience and knowledge were limited. During a consulting job, I met Dr. Paul Costa. His training and knowledge impressed me very favorably, and I arranged for him to start work with the NAS on the personality and interest data. Costa and Dr. Robert McCrae, then a graduate student, initiated work that led to their seminal research on the stability of personality in adulthood, work that continues at the NIA. Costa and McCrae have built outstanding careers; we have collaborated on several projects over the years.

Dr. Robert Kastenbaum arranged for NAS scientists to prepare reports for two special issues of *Aging and Human Development*. Most interesting was an effort in which each investigator used his or her data to predict the participant's chronological age; I used data from the GATB and the 16 PF. Dr. Nuttall helped us combine the data from the different NAS domains. When chronological age was controlled for in the analyses, very few correlations of interest tied the various measures together. From this we learned early on that chronological age is not a good outcome variable when constructing composite indices of aging.

The NAS Computerized Data Bank

I played an unplanned leadership role in the early development of the computerized database for the NAS, mostly because I had the most machine-readable data of any investigator. A comprehensive NAS database was created, from which customized data files could be created easily. For over a year, I dealt with problems of reliability, documentation, standardization, formats, and other practical issues. We soon learned that data management in the NAS could and should be a full-time job, and I was pleased when Dr. Arthur J. Garvey was hired to take charge of that activity. However, the NAS experience was useful in my later career with the Baltimore Longitudinal Study of Aging (BLSA) and the Florida Geriatric Research Program (FGRP), both of which have a large and complex longitudinal database.

Learning About Psychology of Aging From Reviewing Grants and Journal Editing

Peer Reviewing

I learned much about gerontology serving as a site reviewer for the National Institutes of Health (NIH) and the VA Medical Research Service. My first three NIH reviewing assignments involved projects proposed by Drs. James Birren, Jack Botwinick, and Carl Eisdorfer. I was especially impressed with the efforts and plans of these pioneers to build training programs for young gerontologists. Before that experience, I had known these leaders only through their writings.

Journal Editing

I was the associate editor for psychological and social sciences of the *Journal of Gerontology* from 1972 to 1976. A major issue then—and now—was the status of the *Journal of Gerontology* as a place to publish articles relative to journals in the parent fields of persons working in gerontology. Taking my cue from Drs. Shock and Birren, the first two editors of the *Journal,* I adopted three strategies to improve the quality of my part of the *Journal.* First, most manuscripts were reviewed by a subject-matter expert outside aging, as well as by peers in aging. Second, I challenged or required authors to show the relevance of the background data provided about the participants to the research outcomes. The question of whose aging is being researched is of central importance. Writing this reminds me of a funny, three-beer conversation I had with Dr. Richard Adelman, then the *Journal*'s associate editor for biological sciences. We attempted to enumerate all the requirements for the perfect subject for pure gerontological research—rodent or human. What a long list it was! Third, my letters regarding revisions to or rejections of a manuscript contained detailed explanations of what was needed to make the report acceptable or suggestions for doing the research in such a way as to make its report acceptable for resubmission. Usually, the letters were long. Colleagues sometimes remind me of the lengthy letters they received from me. I miss editing. I was greatly honored by offers to be the initial editor of *Psychology and Aging* and later the *Journal of Gerontology: Psychological Sciences*. The demands of my work prevented me from taking advantage of these opportunities.

Guest Editing Human Factors *and Some Unplanned Long-Range Outcomes*

I guest edited the first special issue on aging of *Human Factors,* dedicated to Ross McFarland. This activity later helped me to make unique contributions to gerontology and to develop a meaningful worldview of aging.

Dr. Small arranged for me to give an invited address at the 1975 meeting of the American Psychological Association (APA), from which I developed an important thought piece (Fozard & Popkin, 1978) proposing many interventions on the environment and with people related to the challenges of aging. The paper acknowledged my intellectual debt to Powell Lawton (Lawton & Nahemow, 1973); its title was inspired by Birren's ''Translations in Gerontology—From Lab to Life,'' published in the *American Psychologist* (1974).

I helped Arnold Small promote the growth of the Technical Group on Aging in the Human Factors and Ergonomics Society. From difficult beginnings, the technical interest group has grown to some 300 members and has well-attended sessions. During its growth, I chaired the group for several years until we had sufficient members to hold a legitimate election.

As aging became an issue in human factors, the NIA, under the direction of Dr. T. Franklin Williams, considered supporting research in the area. I recommended a panel of experts to advise Dr. Williams, including Drs. Richard Pew, Edwin Fleishman, and Alphonse Chapanis. Subsequently, extramural funds were allocated to stimulate human factors research, and Dr. Robin Barr was appointed to coordinate the initial effort. Barr did an outstanding job; he was succeeded by Dr. Jared Jobe.

Most important, my activities led to my participation, starting in 1990, in the development of a new multidisciplinary discipline—gerontechnology—research and development of technical products, services, and environments on behalf of aging and aged people. This development will be discussed later in the chapter.

Career Transitions: Research Administration and Development of Geriatric and Long-Term Care Programs in the Department of Veterans Affairs

Leading a Geriatric Research, Educational, and Clinical Center (GRECC)

In the 1970s the Veterans Administration initiated its GRECC program; the first installments were implemented on a competitive basis, including the one at the outpatient clinic. I helped develop the clinic's proposal. My personal interest was to develop an experimental memory and learning clinic that would complement my research program and address common problems of older persons related to memory and cognition.

The GRECC program provided a platform for career transition because I became codirector of the Boston division of the Boston/Bedford GRECC with Dr. Jeremiah Silbert, a physician recently appointed as the second director of the NAS. Although I continued my research in memory and cognition with the NAS, I sharply curtailed my other involvement in the study in order to develop other clinical research programs.

Developing a GRECC program at an independent outpatient clinic proved to be an administrative challenge. Successful use of GRECC resources depended partly on recruiting biomedical researchers who had enough clinical responsibilities to justify paying their salaries from patient care as opposed to research funds. Clinic appointments that included academic and research responsibilities required approval of a committee representing the deans of the medical schools of Harvard, Tufts, and Boston University because the faculty appointments of the clinic staff were at one or sometimes two of the three schools. This system proved to be very difficult for linking clinic and faculty appointments. We did not solve the problem; years later Dr. John Rowe, successor to Silbert and me, arranged to transfer the Boston division of the GRECC to West Roxbury VA Medical Center, affiliated only with Harvard Medical School.

A Personal Change in My Life Resulted in a Major Career Change

In 1976 my marriage of 12 years ended in separation and a divorce that was official in 1977. Several months after our separation, my wife required medical treatment lasting more than a year. During the time, I moved back to our home to rear our three children, a responsibility that became permanent. This change in parenting roles was the basis for a major career change and a move. I could not support a large-scale research operation run on soft grant money that I generated, carry out my new duties with the GRECC, and do a good job of raising a family at the same time. Because my duties as the first VA program specialist on research on aging required me to track all gerontological research in the entire VA system, I was in a good position to consider alternative employment possibilities.

A Different World—The Long-Term Care and Geriatric Programs of the Veterans Administration

In 1978 I became the director of Patient Treatment Service in the Office of Geriatrics and Extended Care at the VA central office, the second person appointed to the position. The position brought new career opportunities, a promotion, and the establishment of a home in which I could function as a working, single parent in a location that allowed my children to visit their mother. Being a single parent brought me very close to all aspects of the growth and development of my children, a very precious personal experience. The downside to the new job was a radical decrease in my research. A book describing 10 years of work in mental performance and aging never got completed. Significant parts of the planned book were presented in abbreviated form in a chapter (Fozard, 1981b). Some applications of the research were described in my Division 20 presidential address (Fozard, 1980) and by Fozard and Popkin (1978).

Extended Care

The new position required fast-paced administrative activity, and management and long range planning for nonhospital extended care programs (e.g., VA-operated nursing homes, contract nursing homes, VA domiciliaries, hospital-based home care, and the board and care homes). During my tenure between 1978 and 1985 these programs grew substantially. In addition we initiated new programs: a medically oriented adult day health care program, a hospice program, a respite care program, and the geriatric evaluation units (GEUs). Activities included preparation of guidelines and manuals specifying levels of care, space, staffing, and regulations for extended care programs; review of building plans for new VA-operated nursing homes and domiciliaries; preparation of budget proposals; drafts of enabling legislation for new programs; surveys of program utilization and quality; and system-wide administration and training programs. Routine activities included preparation of reports to Congress and correspondence to beneficiaries and members of Congress, most of which was prepared for the signature of government officials up to the level of the president according to a complex set of rules.

Paul Haber and Program Development in Geriatrics

The extended care programs represented about a third of the VA medical system workload. They, along with several other geriatric programs, were the overall responsibility of the assistant chief medical director for geriatrics and extended care, the person to whom I reported. Paul A. L. Haber, MD, was the initial incumbent, and he returned to the position for a time while I was there. Haber, the VA's greatest champion of geriatric clinical programs and the founder of the GRECC program, was a dynamic visionary. Working for him was a great experience. His expectations of me included high-quality programs, increased linkages among the extended care programs, and the systematic development of an interdisciplinary team approach to patient care. My lack of clinical experience was considered a plus by Dr. Haber, who said he had all the clinicians he needed. He wanted a gerontologist who could critically evaluate and review his rapidly developing programs and believed that I filled that role.

I quickly learned the difference between program development and program evaluation from Dr. Haber. For example, one of my specific jobs was to expand and strengthen the GEU program in the VA. I learned about GEUs, including where the good ones were, and proudly brought Haber a five-year development plan. The plan, he said, was excellent in concept but weak on strategy, too complicated, and too drawn out. Chastened and wiser, I adopted Haber's strategies, the most important of which called for carefully selected staff to promote the GEU concept throughout the VA medical center system and at the medical schools affiliated with the hospitals. As Haber predicted, interest in establishing GEUs snowballed. Although no new funds were provided to operate new GEUs, special funds were allocated with which I was able to initiate a competitive program for hospitals to receive training for interdisciplinary teams that would staff GEUs. The training was conducted at two VA medical centers that had outstanding GEUs. Within a few years, GEUs were implemented in well over half of the VA medical centers. An external program review conducted years later confirmed the usefulness of the programs. My experience in the process was described in my APA invited address given when I received the Distinguished Contribution Award from the APA division on adult development and aging. At a retirement ceremony honoring Haber, I playfully characterized his contribution to the GEU story as the ''Wizard of Oz'' approach to program development, because it depended on helping people to recognize and to build on their strengths and knowledge rather than new program money.

Transcending Bureaucratic Hurdles

The growth of extended care programs often required cooperation among many VA offices and I quickly learned that sharing credit and responsibility was a critical ingredient for progress. One of my jobs was to increase the interest and quality of physicians in extended care programs. Although the VA provides the clinical training for a high percentage of young physicians in the United States, the training seldom included extended care programs where most medical problems of the patients were classified as chronic. For many, assignment as the physician for a nursing home or a hospital-based home care team was seen as a professional downgrading. We improved the medical side of our extended care programs by attracting excellent clinicians from the VA geriatric fellowship and GRECC programs.

Similar programs were developed by leaders of nursing and social work. Clinical psychologists were underutilized in VA extended care programs even though the VA is the largest employer of clinical psychologists and the largest provider of clinical training for young psychologists. I frequently used the opportunities provided by my program visits to hospitals and lectures at medical schools to urge psychologists to take a more active interest in the extended care programs in addition to their usual work with psychiatry and mental health services. One of my principal activities as the chair of the APA task force for the 1981 White House Conference on Aging was to further develop this theme, particularly at an interdisciplinary conference on mental health that was cosponsored by the professional societies for psychiatrists, psychologists, nurses, and social workers.

My experience in the VA central office provided a number of interesting and challenging experiences. I was the VA representative on the secretary of HHS task force on dementia and the federal interagency committee on research on aging. I served as a consultant to the American Medical Association panel on dementia for three years. I managed the preparation of and helped write the first and second editions of the VA book on diagnosis and dementia, now in its third edition (Patient Treatment Service, Veterans Administration, 1980).

Leaving the VA

Although there were no formal guidelines, jobs at my level in the VA central office were usually time limited, and properly so. They were typically filled by persons from the system of VA medical centers who ultimately returned to such settings. By 1984 my goals for geriatrics and extended care had been largely attained. Synergistic relationships among the extended care programs had developed, and the capable program specialists on my staff were working very well individually and as a team, thanks in part to the skills of my deputy, James R. Kelly, my successor. The development and expansion of programs had far exceeded my expectations. The VA commitment and approach to care of the aging veteran had been well articulated in a major planning document published in 1984. I resigned from the VA after 18 years during which I had the equivalent of three careers: performing research in the psychology of aging in a major longitudinal study of aging, developing and directing a multidisciplinary GRECC program, and directing the VA programs in extended care.

The NIA and the Baltimore Longitudinal Study of Aging (BLSA)

I became chief of the newly created longitudinal studies branch (LSB) in the NIA intramural research program, a job that involved full-time administration and research with the BLSA. The BLSA, which celebrated its 40th anniversary in 1998, had already become famous after 27 years. I had been a consultant to the outside peer review evaluators of the BLSA on three occasions, so I had some knowledge about the strengths and weaknesses of the study.

The new position coincided with my marriage, in 1985, to Marian Singer, a teacher of English as a second language and a professional editor and writer whom I courted for several years. In addition to our love for one another, we share an enjoyment of music. Marian gracefully assumed the challenging role of stepmother especially as it affected her and my two teenage children who lived at home during the first six years of our marriage.

When I reported for work, most of the current BLSA scientists had been working with the study for more than 20 years. The BLSA founder, Dr. Nathan Shock, was a NIH scientist emeritus, and I was pleased that he was chosen to be part of my newly created branch. The BLSA is a resource shared by scientists assigned to laboratories appropriate to their expertise. My leadership responsibilities were shared with an internally comprised BLSA steering committee that advised the scientific director on research directions and the composition of the group of BLSA participants. This collective approach to leadership was appropriate for a multidisciplinary research effort. It was necessary because most of the financial and personnel support for the BLSA came through the laboratories represented on the committee. I strongly supported this approach because it helped maintain a commitment to the BLSA by scientists whose work in the study is part time, and it provided administrative continuity during times of change of leadership in the NIA. However, decision making in the context of the committee was often difficult and turbulent. As one colleague put it, "Working this way is like trying to herd cats."

My job was to manage BLSA operations, to assume responsibility for several ongoing but underused studies, to develop new research, and to share leadership responsibility as described earlier. I later learned that BLSA research and its participants received substantial media attention, which required my involvement in more than a dozen interviews yearly.

Managing BLSA Operations—Participants, Clinical Evaluation, and Data

BLSA Participants

The BLSA staff schedules and manages participant visits and handles reports and communications between visits. The schedule includes continuing and first-time participants, the latter drawn from a waiting list according to research needs. I successfully addressed four issues related to BLSA participants: (a) a rationale for the size and composition of the participant group, including minority participation; (b) a system to track inactive participants; (c) a quality information system for deceased participants and an autopsy program; and (d) administration of the participant waiting list. Overall, BLSA operations are very smooth, largely because of the work of a competent and dedicated support staff.

Clinical Evaluation

The clinical characterization of participants is important in BLSA research and required improvements. Because of inconsistencies in the clinical evaluations, I established a corps of nurse practitioners and physicians' assistants who perform the evaluations under the supervision of a single physician. The medical history, diagnosis lists, medication use logs, and many questionnaires were redesigned to be appropriate for a longitudinal study (Fozard, Metter, & Brant, 1990).

BLSA Data

The BLSA started before computers were widely used, so BLSA data management evolved with changes in the database and technology. Staff members prepare files suitable for analyses by scientists. At the time of this writing they are installing a user-friendly system to allow investigators to create their own working files. Great care is taken to protect the confidentiality of the data.

Research Activities—Taking Charge of Underutilized Data and Starting New Projects

Changing ongoing BLSA research requires committee decision, mostly because of the links among studies. Each of the many outside collaborators has an inside-BLSA partner who facilitates the conduct of the research and assures that it meets NIH requirements. I spent significant amounts of time promoting research with outside collaborators.

Underused Data

I assumed responsibility for many ongoing projects including those on vision, hearing, the speed of reaction and movement time, self-reported activities, the clinical database, and pulmonary function. The diversity of subject matter was challenging, and for most areas I assembled working groups to evaluate and, where appropriate, to report the results. The pulmonary data and laboratory provides an example. To achieve quality control, consultant Dr. Melvyn Tockman and I made the BLSA an additional satellite in the ongoing Atherosclerosis Risk in Community Study, which had a central facility for evaluating ongoing data collection. Historical and contemporary data were blended by tracing the old paper records with an electronic pen so that all records could be machine graded using contemporary research standards. Although laborious, this process yielded unique data allowing us to show that rapid changes in pulmonary function is an independent risk factor for cardiac death (Tockman et al., 1995) and to show that age-associated changes in pulmonary function in healthy adults follows a constant percentile (Pearson et al., 1998).

Describing Individual Differences

The underused data had missing data and records of unequal lengths, which started and stopped at different times. The heterogeneity of the individual longitudinal paths was striking, confirming Nathan Shock's frequent comment that aging is a very individual matter. These issues were addressed by me and Dr. Larry Brant, a mathematical statistician, who successfully adapted multilevel regression techniques to characterize individual longitudinal changes and to address practical problems of analyzing repeated measures in many areas, including hearing thresholds, prostate aging and disease, and pulmonary function. In our studies of aging and hearing, we used these techniques to demonstrate that elevated systolic blood pressure was an independent risk factor for hearing loss at all ages across the adult life span (Brant et al., 1996). Dr. Jay D. Pearson, a postdoctoral fellow with Brant and later a staff scientist, and Professor C. H. Morrell of Loyola College were major contributors to these seminal BLSA efforts.

Developing New Longitudinal Research

Developing longitudinal studies appropriate to the BLSA is a continuing activity for all BLSA scientists. I am particularly proud of two of them. In 1988 I convened a study group to reintroduce strength assessment in the BLSA; the group included Drs. Jerome Fleg, a cardiologist, E. Jeffrey Metter, a BLSA medical officer and a neurologist, and Ben Hurley, a kinesiologist at the University of Maryland. In 1992 we implemented a longitudinal study of strength in the BLSA. Using a different subject population, we developed an intervention study to investigate age-related differences in response to strength training. The studies were embellished by Dr. Metter and his colleagues to study the firing patterns of motor units that stimulate muscle action. Still more recently a study of genetic factors contributing to differences in muscle mass has been added. This productive study now involves many BLSA scientists; its first publication was by Lindle et al. (1997).

I facilitated and developed the team that studies prostate aging and disease. In it, prostate growth and anatomy are being assessed noninvasively by magnetic resonance imaging, and urinary symptoms and function are measured; using current and historical material, serum assays of prostate-specific antigens and male hormones are determined. The goal is to describe the interrelated changes in these factors that sometimes lead to benign prostatic hyperplasia and prostate cancer (e.g., Carter et al., 1992). This longitudinal study is redefining the boundaries between prostate aging and disease; by 1998 it had yielded 25 publications and significantly influenced practice.

Looking Back at About Thirty Percent of the Life of a Continuing Study

My 13 years with the BLSA covers only about a third of its history. Many of the scientists and staff who were there when I joined the NIA continue their work there. Recently, I presented a group award to members of the BLSA 40th anniversary committee who planned the anniversary package (video, articles, etc.) sent to present and past BLSA participants, BLSA scientists, and friends of the BLSA. I was reminded that two of the awardees had helped mount the BLSA's 25th anniversary celebration! Its history is recorded in more than 900 scientific publications and described in dozens of media productions; its unfolding future is contained in several research protocols and planning documents, which reflect the interests of a new generation of scientists as well as continuity of existing research.

I am proud of my work with the BLSA. My managerial and organizational activities improved participant management, the clinical evaluation of participants, data management, and the interactions among scientists who work with the BLSA. My scientific work improved methods for describing variability in patterns of aging and resulted in the analysis and reporting of many studies and the development of new research. I accumulated experience and knowledge about many areas of aging, mostly documented in reports coauthored with members of the teams I built. I have benefited from working with excellent scientists, mostly named in the references, and from the competent and dedicated staff who operate the BLSA.

Describing Aging in Relation to Environmental Factors

Altering the physical and social environment to improve human performance and adaptability is the central idea in ergonomics, and I have discussed the application of this idea to aging. BLSA and NAS reports typically describe individual aging without explicit reference to the context in which it occurs except for selected medical and social information. How can the physical and social environment be manipulated to alter the course of aging as well as the adaptation of a person to the opportunities as well as the challenges of aging? Along with colleagues including biologist Dr. George Baker, I have tried to develop useful concepts for linking descriptions of human aging to contemporary descriptions of the physical and social environments in which aging occurs (Fozard, 1997).

During my years with the BLSA the opportunity to develop these ideas resulted from my involvement with the development of a new multidisciplinary field called ge-rontechnology—the development of products and environments that could influence the course of aging as well as adaptation to it. The activity was initiated by engineers Jan

Graafmans and Tonni Brouwers and Professor Herman Bouma at the Eindhoven (Netherlands) University of Technology. I was an advisor and a keynote speaker for the first
conference held in 1991 at Eindhoven.

In my view, gerontechnology provides a rational approach for developing preventive
and adaptive interventions related to aging. I took a yearlong sabbatical (1993–1994) from
the NIA to serve as a visiting professor at the Eindhoven University of Technology where I
participated with Dutch and other colleagues in Europe to develop educational and research
initiatives that defined the new field. I was particularly interested in long-range planning of
physical and social environments and technology for noninvasive monitoring of physiology
and behavior that could help prevent or delay age-associated declines in function. I also
explored the potential of technology that would help older persons better use the opportunities for making new social interactions, new learning possibilities, and other opportunities
associated with retirement. The year in the Netherlands also led to new, productive
collaborations for the BLSA with Dutch engineers.

Gerontechnology has grown. In 1996 the second international congress on gerontechnology was held in Helsinki, Finland (Graafmans, Taipale, & Charness, 1998), and
the third was held on October 10–13, 1999, in Munich, Germany. In September 1997 the
International Society for Gerontechnology was founded in Germany; its headquarters is the
Eindhoven University of Technology.

Summation and a Look to the Future

Influences on Me

My attitudes toward personal aging, family, and the proper mix of work and play were
shaped by my early experiences and my love for music. As indicated by the chapter title, my
formal training in experimental psychology and human factors engineering provided the
academic basis for my career in geropsychology. However, my career in geropsychology
was not a direct result of my training; it started with an unexpected contact while I was job
hunting. Indeed, I would not be writing this chapter if my supervisors at the NAS had
required formal training in aging or development.

My Influence on Others

Most of my geropsychology career has been in government research laboratories,
medical school settings, and government offices. The number of graduate students and
young scientists I have mentored one-on-one is relatively small—most were named earlier
in the chapter. My major influence on other psychologists has been through my writings and
professional activities, especially my efforts to involve experimental psychologists in
research on aging (e.g., the Talland Memorial Conference and the conference book, *New
Directions in Memory and Aging*). My work in gerontechnology in Europe has given me an
opportunity to help develop a new discipline that I believe will become a very important
partner to gerontology.

Accomplishments

My accomplishments cover the four parts of my geropsychology career: psychology of
aging; longitudinal studies of aging; ergonomics and gerontechnology, and program
development in geriatrics and extended care. With respect to psychology of aging, many of

my research articles in memory and aging continue to be widely cited despite several changes in theories of cognitive aging. My chapters in the *Handbook of the Psychology of Aging* and the Bocklehurst *Textbook on Geriatric Medicine and Gerontology* are part of the reference literature in gerontology. My involvement with longitudinal studies of aging spans almost 25 years and covers work with three such studies, including two of the largest longitudinal studies in the United States and work as an advisor to several others in Europe and Asia. Research in the BLSA and Florida Geriatric Research Program to which I have contributed is multidisciplinary in nature; only a fraction of it directly involves geropsychology. I am especially pleased with my contributions to ergonomics and the expansion of this field to gerontechnology with European colleagues. Advances in applied gerontology as well as a full scientific description of aging requires a description of the physical, social, and internal environments in which aging occurs. The expansion of long-term care and geriatric medicine to which I contributed has, I hope, increased the quality of geriatric medicine and the delivery of long-term care.

The Future

At the time of publication, I will have retired from 32 years of government service to assume a position as the director of geriatric research at the Morton Plant Mease Health Care System in Clearwater, Florida. The activities include directing the organization's 25-year-old longitudinal study of aging, the Florida Geriatric Research Program, and developing applied studies oriented toward developing and evaluating new medical and nonmedical clinical programs. While continuing to work with longitudinal studies of aging in the United States and other countries, I expect to devote more of my remaining working life to the development of gerontechnology and ways to study changing person/environment relationships with aging. Research as well as my personal experience of aging makes me realize the increasing importance of the physical and social environment for a good quality of life as we age.

References

Anders, T. R., & Fozard, J. L. (1973). Effects of age upon retrieval from primary and secondary memory. *Developmental Psychology, 9,* 411–415.

Birren, J. E. (1974). Translations in gerontology: From lab to life. *American Psychologist, 29,* 808–815.

Brant, L. J., Gordon-Salant, S., Pearson, J. D., Klein, L. L., Morrell, C. H., Metter, E. J., & Fozard, J. L. (1996). Risk factors related to age associated hearing loss in the speech frequencies. *Journal of the American Academy of Audiology, 7,* 152–160.

Carter, H. B., Andres, R., Metter, E. J., Fozard, J. L., Chan, D. W., & Walsh, P. C. (1992). Early detection of prostate cancer using serial PSA measurements. *Journal of the American Medical Association, 267,* 2215–2220.

Fozard, J. L. (1970). Apparent recency of unrelated pictures and nouns presented in the same sequence. *Journal of Experimental Psychology, 86,* 173–184.

Fozard, J. L. (1980). The time for remembering. In L. W. Poon (Ed.), *Aging in the 1980s: Selected contemporary issues in the psychology of aging.* Washington, DC: American Psychological Association.

Fozard, J. L. (1981a). Changing person-environment relations in adulthood. *Human Factors, 23,* 7–27.

Fozard, J. L. (1981b). Speed of mental performance: The costs of aging and the benefits of wisdom. In

G. A. Maletta & F. J. Pirozzolo (Eds.), *Advances in neurogerontology* (pp. 59–96). New York: Praeger.

Fozard, J. L. (1997). Aging and technology: A developmental view. In W. A. Rogers (Ed.), *Designing for an aging population: Ten years of human factors and ergonomics research.* Santa Monica, CA: Human Factors and Ergonomics Society.

Fozard, J. L., Metter, E. J., & Brant, L. J. (1990). Next steps in describing disease and aging in longitudinal studies. *Journal of Gerontology, 45,* 813–820.

Fozard, J. L., & Popkin, S. J. (1978). Optimizing adult development: Ends and means of an applied psychology of aging. *American Psychologist, 33,* 975–989.

Graafmans J. A. M., Taipale, V., & Charness, N. E. (Eds.). (1998). *Gerontechology: A sustainable investment in the future.* Amsterdam: I.O.S. Press.

Lawton, M. P., & Nahemow, L. (1973). Ecology and the aging process. In C. Eisdorfer & M. P. Lawton (Eds.), *The psychology of adult development and aging.* Washington, DC: American Psychological Association.

Lindle, R. S., Metter, E. J., Lynch, N. A., Fleg, J. L., Fozard, J. L., Tobin, J., Roy, T.A., & Hurley, B. F. (1997). Age and gender comparisons of muscle strength in 654 women and men aged 20–93 years. *Journal of Applied Physiology, 83,* 1581–1587.

Patient Treatment Service, Veterans Administration, Department of Medicine and Surgery. (1989). *Dementia: Guidelines for diagnosis and treatment.* Anonymous Program Guide prepared by J. L. Fozard & A. M. Kennedy (2nd ed.). Washington, DC: Veterans Administration.

Pearson, J. D., Kao, S. Y., Brant, L. J., Metter, E. J., Tockman, M. S., & Fozard, J. L. (1998). Longitudinal change in forced expiratory volume in healthy, non-smoking men and women: The Baltimore Longitudinal Studying of Aging. *American Journal of Human Biology, 10,* 171–181.

Poon, L. W., & Fozard, J. L. (Eds.). (1976). *Design Conference on Decision Making and Aging.* Normative Aging Study and the Bedford/Boston Geriatric Research, Educational and Clinical Center, Technical Report 76-01.

Poon, L. W., Fozard, J. L., Cermak, L. S., Arenberg, D., & Thompson, L. W. (Eds.). (1980). *New directions in memory and aging: Proceedings of the George A. Talland Memorial Conference.* New York: Erlbaum.

Tockman, M. S., Pearson, J. D., Metter, E. J., Fleg, J. L., Koa, S. Y., Rampal, K. G., Cruise, L. J., & Fozard, J. L. (1995). Rapid decline in FEV: A new risk factor for coronary heart disease mortality. *American Journal of Respiratory and Critical Care Medicine, 151,* 390–398.

Chapter 9
A CASE OF CHANCE AND CHOICE

Margaret Gatz

In this chapter, I offer an accounting of how I came to be a clinical geropsychologist and how my primary research concerns have developed. The format and coverage reflect the guiding questions provided by the volume's editors.

Personal and Contextual Events That Have Influenced My Career in Psychology and Aging

I have a strong belief in the role of chance encounters as influential turning points in the shaping of a career. I found aging by chance. I did not have particularly warm and important relationships with grandparents, and formative volunteer experiences helping older adults characterized neither my Girl Scout nor college days. When I received my PhD in clinical psychology at Duke University, I was not affiliated with gerontology in any way whatsoever. Although I had completed my clinical internship in Morgantown, West Virginia, the internship was centered on the medical school campus. The life-span development group, which included people I now recognize as giants (Warner Schaie, Paul Baltes, John Nesselroade), was located in the psychology department downtown. I met them, but I completely failed to appreciate the significance of what they were doing. Obviously, life-span developmental theory was not an intellectual influence during my time in Morgantown. At Duke, interpenetration was minimal between the psychology department and the medical school, where the aging center was housed. Carl Eisdorfer, who was to become a major figure in mental health and aging and the director of Duke's Center for the Study of Aging and Human Development, was then on the faculty in psychiatry. He provided some instruction in the graduate program in clinical psychology; however, he taught assessment and community psychology, not aging.

The connection to aging was perhaps inadvertently accomplished by Marcel Kinsbourne. Marcel, then on the medical school faculty at Duke, served as an informal advisor on my dissertation research, in which the participants were children. After the dissertation was completed, he persuaded me to apply for a postdoctoral fellowship at the Center for the Study of Aging and Human Development, assuring me that I could continue to study development in children and adolescents while I was a fellow.

Then started the string of coincidental encounters and occurrences that established my interest in aging. Among several subsequently distinguished scholars in my postdoctoral ''class'' was Ilene Siegler. It was Ilene who truly introduced me to gerontology. Her unofficial tutorial was composed of lunches, coffee breaks, and dinners during which she described notable people and their contributions to the study of aging. When I took a field trip to Dorothea Dix State Hospital with a law school faculty member who was teaching a course in law and mental health, I invited Ilene and we visited the units at Dix that housed the aged. We learned that a group of aides was initiating a geriatric therapeutic community and the staff wanted someone to study their innovation. This study became my first gerontology research project. It shared a number of features with many projects started later: it was collaborative and interdisciplinary (the research group included Ilene, a developmental psychologist, and Susan Dibner, a field sociologist), the project both addressed research questions of interest and had applied implications, we sought (and received) a grant to fund the research, and students were included on the research team. Providentially, the student who asked to join our team was Mick Smyer, then a first-year graduate student in the clinical program at Duke.

The postdoctoral year was further remarkable for the seminar series, where the guests included Warner Schaie, Paul Baltes, Gisela Labouvie, Sandra Howell, Klaus Riegel, and others. Listening to these speakers, I formed the opinion that those who studied aging had a far more interesting approach to development than those who studied children.

I think that I was the first clinical psychologist on a Duke postdoctoral fellowship. I certainly was the first clinical-community psychologist. Community psychology came to my attention shortly after its invention. President Kennedy signed the Community Mental Health Centers Act in 1963. The Swampscott Conference, which marked the beginning of community psychology, took place in 1966. In 1967 the need for summer employment fortuitously led me to a research assistantship reading state hospital records for a study of pathways of mentally ill patients. In earlier decades, patients were admitted as young adults to state hospitals, where they lived out their lives. Under community mental health, earlier intervention in the community was intended to prevent admissions to state hospitals, while deinstitutionalization was supposed to reintegrate patients into the community. In the summer of 1968, at Duke, the entire first-year clinical psychology class was given a seminar in community psychology and taken to a small eastern Carolina town to administer cognitive screening batteries to students about to enter first grade in order to identify problems early for preventive intervention. In subsequent years at Duke, students were taken or sent on trips to a community in the southern part of the state, where we learned about mental health consultation. No one breathed any connection between community psychology and aging; however, as a postdoc, I began to put the two together.

The significance of community psychology for my thinking was a matter of timing and luck. Mine was the cohort of the Civil Rights movement and antiwar demonstrations. Beyond the historical circumstances that touched my entire generation, a key formative influence in my own life was moving as a preadolescent from the Midwest to the South. The South meant ''Dixie,'' the confederate flag, the Bible belt, and ''Whites only.'' Although at first I had but a dim understanding of the situation, I was aware that something seemed wrong. Rudimental form was given to my feelings when I encountered some members of our White Southern Protestant church who espoused the righting of social wrongs in the name of ''Christian action.'' As a college student, I linked up with desegregation efforts, primarily at churches, movie theaters, and my own college. During graduate school, I connected with community organizers who were trying to transform economic and educational opportunities for disenfranchised Black residents. Community psychology gave an academic voice to these sociopolitical concerns.

If graduate school brought together my modest civil rights background with the community mental health movement, the postdoc allowed me a first opportunity to combine community psychology and aging through studying a geriatric therapeutic community.

However, although I continued to see the reciprocal relevance of gerontology and community psychology, the job market during this postdoctoral year did not include advertisements for such a combination.

Harking back to my dissertation and perhaps to my experience with adolescents on my internship, I ended up at the University of Maryland in a child-clinical slot. Coincidentally, Forrest Tyler, the director of clinical training, was a visionary in community psychology. Then, during a Model Neighborhoods meeting attended by a University of Maryland faculty-student delegation, two older women active in their senior citizen's association made a plea for help in reaching isolated older adults in the community. Thus another chance event reconnected me to aging. With Forrest Tyler, Oscar Barbarin, and a graduate student team, we launched a peer outreach program funded by the Administration on Aging in which we trained older adult volunteers to contact older persons in their communities and to educate them about community resources. Ilene Siegler, Linda George, Forrest Tyler, and I also carried out a project using the Duke Longitudinal II sample and the Maryland sample to try to apply concepts borrowed from positive mental health to characterizing successful aging. Also, Mick Smyer, by now at Penn State, and I continued to find reasons to write together.

Ilene Siegler introduced me to the Gerontological Society. From attending these meetings, I learned that the University of Southern California (USC) housed perhaps the most important gerontology center in the world. In another fortuitous connection, Larry Thompson, who had been a preceptor to Ilene and me as postdocs, was now on the USC faculty. He hoped to promote training in clinical psychology and aging. What seemed clear was that, to institutionalize training in clinical psychology and aging, the clinical psychology faculty needed someone with expertise in aging but also with mainstream clinical credentials. In January 1979 I packed up and moved west.

At USC my primary commitment lay in establishing a mental health and aging PhD track. My students and I even began to study the factors that attracted clinical students to study aging. It was an exciting time for mental health and aging, including opportunities to participate in an American Psychological Association book called *Aging in the 1980s* edited by Lennie Poon, another member of my postdoc class; the Mini-Conference on the Mental Health of Older Americans, held in conjunction with the White House Conference on Aging; and the Conference to Train Psychologists for Work in Aging (otherwise known as ''Older Boulder''). At USC, Steve Zarit had established the Andrus Older Adult Center (AOAC) for counseling older adults and their families. The clinical cases at the AOAC increased my interest in understanding the various sources of memory complaints and memory problems in older adults. The hospital where AOAC was then housed indicated an interest in expanding their services to older adults, and I set up a community needs assessment as a class project. One of the clinical-aging students learned about a new city-sponsored program that provided emergency alert response services to low-income older adults, and we formed a team to conduct a program evaluation. Another chance opportunity arose from the USC context when Vern Bengtson invited me to collaborate in the longitudinal extension of the Study of Three Generations.

The next turning point with respect to my research again arose totally serendipitously. Mac Klein, soon to become my husband, suggested that I consider coming to Sweden on my sabbatical, because he had been invited to be a visiting professor in sociology at Stockholm University during the fall of 1985. I pointed out that I had not been invited to do anything, and I set about finding something to fill that need. Mick Smyer recommended that I contact Nancy Pedersen at the Karolinska Institute in Stockholm, where he had recently visited. He also told me about the Gerontology Institute in Jönköping, directed by Stig Berg. I wrote letters to Nancy Pedersen and to Gerald McClearn, principal investigator of the Swedish Adoption/Twin Study of Aging (SATSA), introducing myself, and was informed that I could have a place to sit in Stockholm. Sandy Finkel, a geriatric psychiatrist with whom I had worked on the Mini-Conference on the Mental Health of Older Americans, encouraged me to join the International Psychogeriatrics Association (IPA) and attend the IPA congress in Umeå, Sweden, in late August of 1985. I wrote up a beginners' description of classical twin research and was awarded airfare from USC's Faculty Research Innovation Fund. The trip to Sweden was on.

Umeå in August was enchanting, a town of birches with daylight lasting long into the evening. At the IPA congress, I met Stig Berg and many other Nordic gerontologists. Sitting with the SATSA group afforded an unusual collaboration between adjacent fields. Behavior genetics analyzes the relative contributions of genes and environments for purposes of explaining individual differences in a population. The idea with SATSA was to use behavior genetics to explain influences on aging and to do so in a longitudinal design. I was captivated by the possibilities, and I eagerly began learning from Nancy Pedersen and her colleagues. In turn, I could contribute expertise in mental health and in gerontology to the SATSA research group. For example, at one meeting when the group was discussing the SATSA cognitive battery, I casually remarked that some percent of the sample eventually would become demented and that maybe they would want to include some sort of simple mental status measure. Safe to say, I had no appreciation of where that thought would later take me.

The next summer I returned to Sweden, attended the Nordic Gerontological Congress, and presented some results with the mental health variables in Swedish Adoption/Twin Study of Aging (SATSA). During that visit, during the next visit, and the next, and by fax and Bitnet, Nancy and I set up mechanisms to screen for dementia not only among SATSA longitudinal participants but also among SATSA dropouts and nonresponders. We got some seed funding from USC, received generous guidance from Jim Mortimer and Terry Radebaugh, the latter then at the National Institute on Aging (NIA), and were rewarded by a two-year NIA grant, followed by a five-year NIA grant. In August 1997 we were awarded yet five more years, this time to expand the study of dementia beyond the SATSA sample to the entire Swedish Twin Registry. A twin design has exciting features. Comparing identical and fraternal twin pairs lets one estimate relative influences of genes and environmental factors in explaining disorder. In identical pairs, differences in the occurrence of disorder point to potentially modifiable risk factors in the earlier affected twin or to protective factors in the unaffected (or later affected) twin. Finally, unaffected partners of twins with dementia represent a population for studying early changes and early detection of dementia. My need to find something to do in Stockholm had serendipitously evolved into a mammoth research enterprise that will continue to dominate my research life for many, many more years.

Back in Los Angeles, we had drought, we had fires, we had mudslides, we had the civil disturbance following the Rodney King verdict, and we had the Northridge earthquake. The civil disturbance became the occasion for renewed commitment to community psychology. Northridge afforded an opportunity for learning about natural disaster research and for obtaining National Science Foundation support to interview the Three Generations families who were affected by the earthquake.

Organizationally, the 1990s brought another White House Conference on Aging and the associated miniconvention on the mental health of older adults; this time I was asked to edit the miniconvention book (published by the American Psychological Association) and was able to attend the White House Conference as an issues expert. Division 12 (Clinical) of the American Psychological Association now has a section on aging. As a class project for a graduate seminar, we applied the Division 12 criteria for empirically supported treatments to the aging literature, in part to assure the inclusion of older adults in the directions being taken within mainstream clinical psychology, in part to transfer more rapidly into gerontology the developments being made in mental health more generally. I spent a term as associate editor of *Psychology and Aging*. The American Psychological Association (APA) established a permanent committee on aging, of which I became a member. That committee has the mandate of forcing older adults into the awareness of the APA. Geropsychology is now recognized as a proficiency by the APA.

Influential Teachers, Mentors, and Books

I attended college at Southwestern-at-Memphis, which has since changed its name to Rhodes College. I never seriously envisioned any field of study other than science, perhaps reflecting my having grown up with a father who had a PhD in zoology and who taught anatomy in medical school. Consequently, I indicated an intention to major in chemistry, a subject that my high school French teacher had urged me to select (my lack of talent in foreign languages already having manifested itself). Pursuit of a liberal education led me to an introductory psychology course taught by Llewellyn Queener. Queener, who had both a divinity degree and a doctorate in psychology from Yale University, exposed us to learning theory, social psychology, and the excitement of the field. He became a confessor figure. Psychology—the Queener version thereof—provided an academic container sufficiently large for diverse issues that roused or fascinated me: from racism and civil rights to the effect of chemicals on the mind.

Margaret Donaldson arrived at Southwestern-at-Memphis as an exchange scholar and introduced me to developmental psychology. In search of a transforming experience, I applied as a nondegree student at Edinburgh University, took a leave of absence from Southwestern, and sailed (literally, on the *Queen Mary*) for Scotland. There I enrolled in English literature, moral philosophy, and a graduate course in developmental psychology in the School of Education. It was taught by Margaret Donaldson, who had herself studied with Piaget, and she arranged laboratories for her class to observe how children's minds deal with cognitive tasks. Durng that year, I also played on the Edinburgh University women's varsity basketball team, which practiced in an unheated gym. I returned to Southwestern as a psychology major.

Graduate school brought new mentors. At Duke I was assigned Robert Carson as my clinical supervisor. At the time I believe that the Duke faculty regarded me as one of their admissions errors. Bob Carson taught me a lot about psychotherapy; he also made it clear that he believed in me. I treasure my copy of his book that he inscribed to me.

My clinical internship was at the Department of Behavioral Medicine and Psychiatry at West Virginia University Medical Center and at the Robert F. Kennedy Youth Center, both in Morgantown. The psychiatry department was special in its use of behavioral science and in its creative model of group intervention, borrowing from principles of therapeutic community, gestalt strategies, and learning theory. My primary supervisor, Marion Jacobs, was my first woman mentor since beginning graduate school. Moreover, she was a remarkable clinician and talented clinical supervisor, and she exemplified the scientist-professional model, involving me in research to study group process.

Later, my colleagues—Mick Smyer and Nancy Pedersen—also served as my mentors, and my students have been teachers as well as learners. The privilege of being a faculty member is the constant opportunity for learning. Among many students, at the University of Maryland, Dan Hurley represented social action and nonhierarchical organizational structures, forcing the recognition of these values even when it was not comfortable within the context of social science and academe. At USC, Cynthia Pearson was a perfectionistic and challenging coauthor and coinvestigator, prohibiting intellectual shortcuts in any review chapter, article, or project. Charles Emery cajoled me into joining an aerobics group while he was starting his research on physical exercise in older adults. Many students received advisement while serving as my jogging partner. Bob Corb took me to the swimming pool and remains an annual companion on the Los Angeles Marathon bicycle tour. Conversations in lab meetings (the USC term for weekly gatherings of all graduate advisees with their faculty mentor) have had unforeseen impacts. Michele Karel's concern with explaining depression in older adults led me to bring more order to my own theory of mental disorder in older adults. Susan Turk Charles's passion for health psychology persuaded me to place increasing importance on health and illness, a perspective reinforced by recent experiences when members of my family have suffered from both major illnesses and ordinary aches and fatigue. Julie Wetherell made me think about anxiety; Amy Fiske, about suicide.

Many articles and books have also made a difference in the direction I took. I submit that the reason a piece of literature is influential reflects an interaction between the particular piece of literature and what issues the reader is wrestling with at the time. Among gerontological writings, some examples of selections that affected my idea system include Paul Baltes's "Prototypical Paradigms and Questions in Life-Span Research on Development and Aging" (1973), Lawton and Nahemow's "Ecology and the Aging Process" (1973), Riegel's "The Dialectics of Human Development" (1976), Costa and McCrae's "Still Stable After All These Years: Personality as a Key to Some Issues in Aging" (1980), and Kahn's "The Mental Health System and the Future Aged" (1975). Baltes gave an early overview of key propositions that he continues to elaborate from his base in the Berlin Aging Study. His propositions, particularly as they have subsequently matured, offer conceptual justification for extending the idea of prevention to encompass cognitive aging. Lawton and Nahemow translocated person–environment fit into gerontology, reminding the field that people's competence varies according to the demands of their context and bringing theoretical legitimacy to interventions that target the environment. Riegel focused on processes of change, from intrapsychic to mega-historical. Costa and McCrae focused on varieties in ways to characterize a person's change, for example, change in level versus change in the psychometric structure of a psychological attribute. Kahn analyzed older adults in relation to the history of the mental health system, took controversial positions against intervening too intrusively into older people's lives, and brought to the fore the distinction between lifelong mental illness and disorders arising anew in old age.

The combination of reading someone's writings, hearing the person talk, and having the opportunity to interact with the person has meant the most to my own growth. Each of the selections mentioned here comes with the recollection of a presentation at a seminar or conference and one-on-one interaction. I have found the generosity of senior figures in gerontology to be remarkable. For example, Powell Lawton has been especially supportive, ever since I first met him at a hotel breakfast counter during a convention. During his Penn State years, Paul Baltes was available as a career consultant whenever I made the trip to State College. Martha Storandt is always willing to provide input and is one of the most broadly knowledgable folks I know with respect to mental health and aging.

My Approach

A central theme throughout my career in aging has been to bring clinical aging into mainstream clinical psychology. This effort has encompassed theory, professional practice, and research. Theoretically, I suggest ways that concepts from adult development and aging can inform clinical psychology more generally and, conversely, how trends in clinical psychology thinking can supply insight to those interested in older adults. Professionally, I have sought to expand opportunities for training in clinical aging and to expand the role of psychologists in working with older adults. Empirically, I have been concerned with characterizing age-related change and influences on change, including influences due to history and cohort. Bringing these threads together is a concern for the implications of principles of development for programmatic intervention and a concern for evaluating our efforts to enhance people's lives.

Reevaluating Established Perspectives

My way of doing what I do has four defining features. The first is to question prevailing wisdom, raise definitional issues, and react to poor reasoning. Numerous examples exist. In 1978 Mick Smyer and I noted that there seemed to be a small surge of interest in mental health and aging. It seemed to be taking place outside of organized clinical psychology, and there was an emphasis on the unique issues in clinical work with older adults. We found the emphasis on uniqueness to be troubling, both conceptually if one takes a life-span developmental perspective, and strategically, because it sends the message to clinical psychology that older adults should not be included in their purview. We wrote an essay published in the *American Psychologist* (Smyer & Gatz, 1979) arguing for the applicability of theoretical principles from community psychology to working with older adults and urging that an entire new field did not need to be invented.

A concept that has long been particularly attractive to me is sense of control. With older adults, there are many obvious ways in which policies, environmental design, and other systemic factors conspire to remove control. At the same time, there are real dependencies, particularly those brought about by chronic health conditions. It is not a simple matter to figure out how to optimize control. Sometimes it is necessary to provide assistance. Some efforts to empower are superficial and not meaningful. The challenge is to optimize independence and hence control and to make the granting of control genuine. This concern has repeatedly filtered in and out of my writings. For the most recent, see Gatz (1995), ''Questions That Aging Puts to Preventionists.''

I also was disturbed by literature proposing that older adults inevitably became more external with age due to their losses and other insults to their independence. In reaction, I participated in examining locus of control first using the Duke Longitudinal II sample (Gatz, Siegler, George, & Tyler, 1986) and later both SATSA (Pedersen, Gatz, Plomin, Nesselroade, & McClearn, 1989) and the Three Generations data (Gatz & Karel, 1993). The Three Generations data were especially exciting, because the study has now continued for long enough that the original middle generation has become the age of the grandparents at the first time of measurement, whereas the original third generation has become the age of their parents. Thus, it is possible to look at both longitudinal change and generational differences. Our findings from Duke Longitudinal II and from the Three Generations data highlighted the difference between cross-sectional and longitudinal designs. In both studies, the cross-sectional data implied increasing externality, but the longitudinal data contradicted such an inference. Different dimensions of control behaved differently: In the Duke Longitudinal II analyses, we distinguished control over the occurrence of events from control over one's handling of events. The SATSA data showed the influence of one's childhood rearing on one aspect of control—belief in luck.

Similarly, I reacted to literature suggesting that depression went up as people became older. In presumably well-intended efforts to show that older adults were in need of mental health services, several widely disseminated reports suggested inexorable increases in depression decade by decade. Consequently, I have participated in looking at self-reported symptoms of depression in community samples, both with Three Generations (Gatz & Hurwicz, 1990) and subsequently with SATSA (Gatz, Pedersen, Plomin, Nesselroade, & McClearn, 1992). Our results suggested a more nuanced understanding of age and depression, with greater emphasis on the integral role of health and more appreciation of the difference between lowered happiness and active depression. In addition, depression has been the featured example in my thinking about the nature of mental disorders in older adults, including distinctions between symptoms and clinical disorder and between lifelong patterns and late-life onset disorder.

Challenging existing wisdom does not necessarily mean that it is entirely wrong. Rather, it is that a perspective is missing. Cynthia Pearson, Max Fuentes (now Fuhrmann), and I (Gatz, Pearson, & Fuentes, 1983) took on the task of considering the myths of aging that are challenged by the Facts on Aging quiz or otherwise debunked as part of workshops to introduce gerontology. Myths are negative stereotypes, such as older people being ill, not having very much money, being demented, and not engaging in sexual behavior. The Facts on Aging quiz views these answers as incorrect and promotes positive images of aging supported by empirical data. We used the term *countermyths* to describe these positive images, and we concluded that the myths tended to include a kernel of truth, also upheld empirically, and should not be entirely discarded in favor of countermyth. With respect to mental disorders, the reverse has been true. Empirical data are cited not to counteract negative images but to establish that there is overlooked mental disorder. Still, it would seem likely that the same principle would apply, affording some truth to the alleged myth and bringing some skepticism to the countermyth.

Tackling New Problems

A second feature of my work is that I perpetually take on new problems. For example, with each new edition of the *Handbook of the Psychology of Aging,* I find myself signing up for a new topic, typically one about which I had no special expertise but did have an agenda. For the second edition, I selected psychological interventions because I was exasperated by claims—both in mainstream clinical psychology and by experts in mental health and aging—that there was no literature on psychotherapy with older adults. For the third edition, I picked caregiving, with several issues in mind: the epidemiology of caregiving was largely unknown, there was a critical definitional issue with respect to who regarded themselves as caregivers versus who performed caregiving roles, and the point of view of the person being cared for was almost entirely overlooked. For the fourth edition, I elected to examine mental disorders, with the purpose of bringing together aging and current thinking in clinical psychology about the nature of psychopathology.

Dementia was another new problem for me. It seems clear that the causes of Alzheimer's disease will prove to encompass multiple genetic factors as well as other factors; in other words, despite the prevailing scientific climate, it is preposterous to be searching for "The Gene." In the Study of Dementia in Swedish Twins, we have come to the view that cognitive reserve is a useful construct. Conditions that reduce reserve are risk factors. Anything eventuating in greater reserve is a protective factor. Indeed, these need not necessarily be specific to Alzheimer's disease. A question that emerges from this conceptualization is the extent to which factors that explain normal cognitive aging overlap factors pertinent to Alzheimer's disease. We have a lot of work ahead, and I will not run out of new things to learn.

Establishing Stimulating Collaborations

The third characteristic of my way of doing work is strategic collaborations: I work with people I enjoy. I think that research should be fun. I enjoy working with people from adjacent disciplines: sociology, psychiatry, behavior genetics, neurology, and anthropology. I have no doubt about the scientist-professional model, because it is so clear that my applied experiences (both with individuals and with institutions) influence my research and that my research affects my approach as a clinician.

A special category of collaborations involve international colleagues. My career begets travel opportunities; I have attended Nordic gerontology congresses in Finland and Sweden, IPA congresses in Rome and Berlin, and a Behavior Genetics Association meeting in The Netherlands; I have met Beth Meyerowitz and her colleague in Czechoslovakia; I have been invited to Max Planck Institute; and I have participated in Jackie Lomranz's forum "Towards Theories on Aging and Mental Health" at Kibbutz Shefayim in Israel. Thanks to my husband's travels and connections, I was also included as an invited professor at the University of Castile-La Mancha in Spain, and consequently have the opportunity to analyze Spanish data that parallel other studies in which I have been engaged. Finally, international collaborations have enriched my appreciation of the role of culture.

Staying Interested

The fourth characteristic is a capacity easily to become interested in things and to remain interested. For example, I continue to think that development is a life-span affair. Child development has been a subtext for me since I took the class with Margaret Donaldson. My internship included work in a federal correctional facility for adolescents. My dissertation concerned children's learning to represent perspective. At the University of Maryland, I worked with two different school-based intervention projects. More recently I found myself back in the schools. I was looking for a community intervention project for graduate students taking a community psychology seminar. Concurrently, Steve Danish telephoned looking for someone to be his Southern California coordinator for a program that he created, called Going for the Goal. Going for the Goal teaches life skills to adolescents: helping students to set positive goals and teaching them the skills necessary to reach those goals. Of course, Going for the Goal became the class project and continues even now. Implementing the Going for the Goal program had the additional element of redintegrating all the issues of community consultation. At the same time, having a husband who studies street gangs has led to other tangential collaborations, including an article in the newsletter published by APA's office for international affairs about the development of European variants of the American street gang.

Finally, sport has always been a part of my life. My mother had been a physical education teacher at a liberal arts college. As a child, she was my track coach. I attended college before Title IX, although—as noted—I played on Edinburgh University's women's basketball team. Years later, in another of those fateful coincidences, I was asked by USC's president to serve as the institution's faculty athletics representative to the National Collegiate Athletics Association (NCAA). This role, and all of the related committee assignments on campus and in the Pacific-10 Conference, provided me with a truly special and different view of the university community. Being on NCAA's research committee has further enabled me to consider the place of intercollegiate athletics in academe. As a spin-off, in response to a request from a USC alumnus about sports and violence, several on our campus have established an informal institute (called a steering committee), and the steering committee organized a national conference on sport, youth, violence, and the media. Currently, two colleagues and I are editing a book based on the proceedings. I continue to insist that there are ways to link these activities intelligibly.

An Assessment

The editors of this volume asked what I liked best among my own work. Looking now, I like the description we wrote about the implementation of the geriatric therapeutic community (Gatz, Siegler, & Dibner, 1980). Rather than a traditional evaluation, we explicated the ideology that inspired the innovation and then depicted clashes between that ideology and the practicalities of transforming an institution. I like Mick's and my efforts once each decade to make sense of trends in mental health care and their meaning for older adults (Gatz & Smyer, 1992; Smyer & Gatz, 1979). I believe that the Study of Dementia in Swedish Twins can provide genuinely important information about Alzheimer's disease. And I enjoy being able to look back at some less promising efforts. Did I really begin a discussion section (see Gatz, Pedersen, Plomin, Nesselroade, & McClearn, 1992) with this sentence? "The results provide new evidence relevant to the interrelated set of interests that launched the inquiry."

References

Baltes, P. B. (1973). Prototypical paradigms and questions in life-span research on development and aging. *Gerontologist, 13,* 458–467.

Costa, P. T., Jr., & McCrae, R. R. (1980). Still stable after all these years: Personality as a key to some issues in aging. In P. B. Baltes & O. G. Brim (Eds.), *Life-span development and behavior* (Vol. 3). New York: Academic Press.

Gatz, M. (1995). Questions that aging puts to preventionists. In L. Bond, S. Cutler, & A. Grams (Eds.), *Promoting successful and productive aging* (pp. 36–50). Newbury Park, CA: Sage.

Gatz, M., & Hurwicz, M-L. (1990). Are old people more depressed? Cross- sectional data on CES-D factors. *Psychology and Aging, 5,* 284–290.

Gatz, M., & Karel, M. J. (1993). Individual change in perceived control over twenty years. *International Journal of Behavioral Development, 16,* 305–322.

Gatz, M., Pearson, C., & Fuentes, M. (1983). Older women and mental health. In A. U. Rickel, M. Gerrard, & I. Iscoe (Eds.), *Social and psychological problems of women: Prevention and crisis intervention* (pp. 273–299). New York: Hemisphere/McGraw-Hill.

Gatz, M., Pedersen, N. L., Plomin, R., Nesselroade, J. R., & McClearn, G. E. (1992). The importance of shared genes and shared environments for symptoms of depression in older adults. *Journal of Abnormal Psychology, 101,* 701–708.

Gatz, M., Siegler, I. C., & Dibner, S. S. (1980). Individual and community: Normative conflicts in the development of a new therapeutic community for older persons. *Aging and Human Development, 10,* 249–263.

Gatz, M., Siegler, I. C., George, L. K., & Tyler, F. B. (1986). Attributional components of locus of control: Longitudinal, retrospective, and contemporaneous analyses. In M. M. Baltes & P. B. Baltes (Eds.), *Aging and the psychology of control* (pp. 237–263). Hillsdale, NJ: Erlbaum.

Gatz, M., & Smyer, M. (1992). The mental health system and older adults in the 1990s. *American Psychologist, 47,* 741–751.

Kahn, R. L . (1975). The mental health system and the future aged. *Gerontologist, 15,* 24–31.

Lawton, M. P., & Nahemow, L. (1973). Ecology and the aging process. In C. Eisdorfer & M. P. Lawton

(Eds.), *The psychology of adult development and aging.* Washington DC: American Psychological Association.

Pedersen, N. L., Gatz, M., Plomin, R., Nesselroade, J. R., & McClearn, G. E. (1989). Individual differences in locus of control during the second half of the life span for identical and fraternal twins reared apart and reared together. *Journal of Gerontology: Psychological Sciences, 44,* P100–P105.

Riegel, K. F. (1976). The dialectics of human development. *American Psychologist, 31,* 688–700.

Smyer, M. A. & Gatz, M. (1979). Aging and mental health: Business as usual? *American Psychologist, 34,* 240–246.

Chapter 10
FOOTPRINTS ON THE SANDS OF TIME:
An Autobiography

Elsie Harwood

To write an autobiography, however brief, is for me an experience of retrospection in which each change or demand as it occurred seemed merely to represent the next thing to do. To have been born into a family characterized by encouragement and support was good fortune indeed, although we were minimally endowed in the economic sense. When contemplating questions about my career that would inevitably be asked by psychologists whose careers and training can be fitted into a pattern of present-day normality, I realized that such questions would be virtually inappropriate. I called on Shakespeare's fund of wisdom (Hamlet V, 2, 10):

> There's a divinity that shapes our ends,
> Rough-hew them how we will.

Without being presumptuous, and not knowing Shakespeare's concept of divinity, I felt that these lines seemed in some sense to epitomize the formation of my career, with my entry into the broad field of psychology and, among other specialties, the field of geropsychology.

Early Years

I was born in London on May 22, 1911, in what I was later to discover had been the inaugural year of lectures at the University of Queensland, on the other side of the world. In 1914, I migrated with my family to Australia and, in due course, took my primary education at the Manly (Brisbane) State School. This culminated in a scholarship, which gave me entry in 1926 to the Brisbane Girls' Grammar School. In 1930 I matriculated with an open scholarship (one of 20 in the state of Queensland), which allowed me to attend the University of Queensland in Brisbane. The university had opened its doors with 80 students distributed in the foundation faculties of arts, science, and engineering. Other essential faculties were added in 1935. When I entered in 1931, 800 students were enrolled. Having been awarded

It is a matter of regret to me that many of the men who believed in me and shaped my end are deceased long before my end could be realized. I can but name them: Professor Michael Scott-Fletcher (philosophy), Professor J. L. Michie (classics), Professor W. M. Kyle (philosophy-psychology), Associate Professor Stanley Castlehow (classics), and Associate Professor George Naylor (psychology).

Two professors of psychology (Donald W. McElwain, retired, and Peter Sheehan) are aware of my gratitude for their assistance and support in many ways; and Professor Bob Milns earns sincere thanks for including me in a classical exercise that would have the enthusiastic approval of any geropsychologist who believes in mental regeneration in the later years.

the language prizes in all years at the grammar school, I chose to take the classics honors course—Latin, Greek, and ancient history. I was awarded a BA degree with first-class honors, which led in 1935 to an appointment as tutor (junior lecturer) in classics and psychology. In the Great Depression, after World War I, the combined title of my appointment was due to lack of funds for more than one new appointment in the faculty of arts, where there was already one such appointment, in English and Foreign Languages, held by James Charles Mahoney on return (1933) from Oxford, where he attended as Rhodes scholar. Later he became a French professor but died in retirement in 1997. Faced with a decision, the heads of classics and philosophy (in which psychology was a small part) had agreed to share a divisible person. Philosophy I, which contained psychology, had been an undergraduate requirement of the classics honors course—a small psychology course, indeed, as a precursor to a life and career in the profession of psychology! In 1937 I was awarded the classics MA degree for a thesis embodying a history of the Island of Rhodes from 411 B.C. to 167 B.C.

My work in psychology was essentially concerned with supervision of a small laboratory and the organization of experimental designs. We had obtained some equipment, including a Hipps chronoscope, an ergograph, a psychogalvanometer, a kymograph drum, and the current color-blindness tests. Sensation testing was to be set up in relation to visual, auditory, gustatory, and olfactory sensation. There were models of eye and ear for dismantling, so that attention could be given to function and dysfunction, especially in the visual and auditory modalities. This led me to consider sensory problems in the disabled and the aged. One other item, to which I gave little attention, was a phrenology head, although it may have been subtly responsible for my subsequent engagement in neuropsychology. This was a time of vocational guidance and selection, and we were affiliated with the Institute of Industrial Psychology, founded and managed by Dr. A. H. Martin, a senior member of the Sydney University Department of Psychology, which had been a separate department since 1929. I was able to spend time, to my advantage, talking with Dr. Martin, on various occasions.

After three years on the classics staff, two of which were spent concurrently in the psychology section of philosophy, I was advised by Professor J. L. Michie (classics) to obtain experience in secondary school teaching, and I received an appointment as senior mistress in classics at St. Margaret's, a highly reputed Anglican School with grades from kindergarten to the senior (matriculation) level.

World War II

At the end of three years of secondary teaching (1938–1940), I was invited to accept a university assistant lectureship in psychology, and in 1941 my future career seemed to have been preordained. With World War II in its early phase, and philosophy still a composite subject including logic, psychology, ethics, metaphysics, education, Greek philosophy, and divinity, the staff consisted of Professor W. M. Kyle, E. C. D. Ringrose, a senior lecturer in education, and myself. Our experience in vocational guidance and selection (then unique in Queensland) led to a request in 1941 from the Australian Army Camp Hospital to visit the camp two days a week on a voluntarily basis to assess soldiers being returned as unfit from the Middle East campaign and to advise the colonel-in-charge on treatment, retraining, transfer, or discharge. The superintendent of the large mental hospital, Dr. Basil Stafford, had become the colonel-in-charge.

The returned army men had been enlisted without benefit of psychological assessment, and many of them were quite unsuitable for service—some even illiterate. It was not until

1942 that an army psychology unit was established, headed by Fowler and McElwain. (Donald McElwain was to become the first professor of psychology when the chair was founded in 1955 at the University of Queensland.) Being relieved of our camp hospital duties, we then received a request from the colonel-in-charge of recruits for assistance in selecting men suitable for officer training. We administered group tests and scored them by hand. On the basis of these results we made our recommendations, and men were selected after army interviews had confirmed their suitability.

An interesting aspect of these early days of the American "invasion" of Australia en route to the Pacific war zone was that, like the Australians in 1939, men had been transported overseas without benefit of psychological or psychiatric personnel and without assurance of their fitness to serve or to adapt in foreign parts. An amusing outcome was that the American army was able to lend the camp hospital two medical specialists who were at that stage surplus to requirements—an ear, nose, and throat specialist and a gynecologist-obstetrician. They had accompanied the army, but claimed to having no psychological-psychiatric skills or experience. They gave welcome assistance in the medical examinations until returning to their U.S. Army service.

As a result of our joint contribution at that time, we at the university were able to accept referrals from the U.S. Army to examine and advise on the outcome in relation to servicemen whose "breakdown" condition in this foreign country had rendered them unfit for duties. We continued to serve in this advisory situation until further U.S. units included appropriate services, but not before some of the first arrivals had been returned (on our advice) to their peacetime—often farming—duties in their familiar environments.

We learned a lot from these wartime experiences, reminiscent of the clinical services given by Elton Mayo at the end of World War I. But our war was far from over. Mayo had been a foundation appointment to the philosophy department in 1911. He became a professor in 1923 and then transferred to Pennsylvania and later to Harvard, becoming famous for his industrial psychology in the United States. There was a Mayo tradition at the University of Queensland in my student days. He had graduated in the University of Adelaide.

Shortly after my 1941 appointment, I went to Sydney to observe the daily work of the Institute of Industrial Psychology. In the army contact my interest in clinical psychology was alerted, with experience of sufferers from neurosis, psychosis, and other problems such as illiteracy and malingering, which had resulted in the men's hospitalization. In Sydney, in the unavoidable absence of the psychologist, Dr. Martin passed all the listed cases to me, and I completed the week's normal clinical program for the institute. With the outbreak of World War II, George Francis King Naylor, who had been the institute psychologist for 10 years, was seconded to the Royal Australian Air Force, where he took charge, as squadron leader, of the testing and selection of air force recruits for the duration of the war. Originally a geologist, with the Sydney University Medal and the geology prizes, Naylor had undertaken the Sydney University course in psychology, and had been appointed to the institute as deputy director and psychologist. Already a master of arts and master of science, in 1947 he came to the University of Queensland as the senior lecturer in psychology. In 1952 he was awarded the PhD degree. My candidature for the PhD degree had begun in the early 1950s, and the degree was awarded in 1957 for a thesis titled, "Mental and Social Development of Australian Adolescents." In those days staff candidates had somehow to fit their research into a busy lecturing, clinical, and administrative schedule. To collect data for my project it was necessary to drive (in vacations or weekends) throughout the large area of South-East Queensland to meet with adolescents in their local habitat. I had one research assistant. From 1950 to 1957 I was the first subdean of the faculty of arts.

From Philosophy to Psychology

Doctor Naylor's arrival had reinvigorated the pressure on the university administration for a department of psychology and separation from philosophy. In the 1940s, because of my classical expertise, I had been assigned to provide a course in Greek philosophy. During those years I had been preparing a textbook titled *Introduction to Greek Philosophy,* which would enable another philosophy lecturer to undertake the course and so relieve me of the last philosophy assignment as we progressed inevitably toward a department of psychology. My book was published in 1948 and was used as a text for some years thereafter.

But it was not until 1955 that a Department of Psychology was established. In 1947 Naylor and I had already established an honors course in psychology, and offered or shared the various specialist sections according to our respective interests and strengths.

The story of my career and my entry into psychological specialties, including clinical neuropsychology and geropsychology, is largely a matter of supply and demand. As an instance, the postwar increase in motor vehicle accidents and other causes of head injury had led to an increase in civil suits for damages, and lawyers were becoming aware of the need for expert evidence of psychological effects in these cases. Dr. Naylor and I responded, and in my case the ''medico-legal'' work continued from 1955 to 1997. This was pioneering work, predating the appearance in court of several government psychologists who had been our students. Because of this record, I was invited in 1970 to join the neurosurgical case conference of the Mater Hospitals, and this involved examinations of babies, children, adolescents, and adults of all ages. It was also an opportunity to involve selected honors and postgraduate students in the hospital experience. My appointment as honorary medical psychologist emeritus continued until I terminated it in 1997. All cases were under the care of neurosurgeons, and I was able to attend at their operations on the brains of some of the patients whom I had examined. During this period I extended my knowledge in neuropsychology by visiting and talking with overseas practitioners, and much of my 1971 sabbatical year was devoted to pursuing experience in the fields of neuropsychology and geropsychology in the United Kingdom, as the Queensland research project was then in its fifth year. From 1957 to 1997 I attended overseas centers in Europe, the United Kingdom, and the United States, holding discussions with neurologists, neurosurgeons, neuropsychologists, and those concerned with hostel or nursing home care of the aged.

In the department I was promoting clinical psychology and offering a course, which prepared students for competent professional work. Some of these students assisted in the early stages of our research project into aging. This course was organized at a time when test training involved the introduction of a number of tests and their application in clinical practice, whether with babies, children, adolescents, or adults. At the end of the academic year, a one-day open book examination enabled the students to opt for the test paper, which would deal with a child, an adolescent, or an adult. They were then given raw scores, responses, and minimal life data based on cases fully examined by me but new to the students. In each case, five tests had been used, and students were expected to perform statistical treatment where necessary, to score various responses in personality tests, and to write a diagnostic report. Most students wrote reports that compared more than favorably with my known conclusions. It was a demanding exercise, and some of those students, now in middle-age and in elevated academic positions, have told me that they have used my methods in their own clinical training courses.

In the first year of the longitudinal study of elderly subjects, when financial aid was not yet available, a number of these trained clinical students gave up their time to complete much of the first round of Wechsler Adult Intelligence Scale testing, and when it was decided to make a parallel, alternative form of WAIS, which was to be used for the second, fourth, and sixth rounds, it was these students who made themselves available for many hours. The logistics of this undertaking can be appreciated as by no means a simple matter.

This brings me to the earliest of my three sabbatical years. While in Brussels in 1957 I first met Professor David Wechsler. Until the publication of his Wechsler Bellevue Scale (1944), we had been reliant on group tests for adult assessment, the Binet test being for children and quite inappropriate for adults. Wechsler's decision to convert the group tests then available into an individual adult scale had been a brilliant and welcome landmark in the history of testing. I also visited Wechsler at the Bellevue Hospital, and found that, when WAIS was made in 1955, there had been no parallel form because of the lack of enough alternative items. This produced a technical problem for users of WAIS when research or clinical and hospital practice necessitated serial repetition of cognitive assessment, which should be uncontaminated by the patient's recognition of previously seen performance items. Among other techniques used by Wechsler was the cross-sectional comparison of elderly persons with young adults. It was probably due to this that, in thinking of research into change with age in the elderly, we decided to use the longitudinal method—admittedly more costly and slower to produce the conclusion.

First Longitudinal Study

The first longitudinal study of the elderly in Australia was thus instituted in 1966, when the expectation that Dr. Naylor and I would be retiring in 1976 caused us to think in terms of a 10-year project. The journalist who assisted in raising the sample of willing participants for the research was also responsible for its fortuitous identification as Operation Retirement. This unexpectedly appealed to the elderly, who identified themselves as belonging to a large group. Within one week, 350 applicants had responded, as being over the age of 60 and willing to be available to us for 10 years. Some were in their 90s. Within a few months we had added another 56, most of whom had turned 60 in the interval. At the end of the 10 years, the University of Queensland had appointed us both as honorary research consultants, and the question of termination of the project did not arise.

The first round of testing, using Wechsler's WAIS was undertaken before funding could be sought from commonwealth grants, and much of that year's testing was done by my successful clinical students who had proven to be competent and who willingly visited and tested the subjects, to everyone's satisfaction.

We then contemplated the next step and, being unwilling to use the same test a second time, we had to make an alternative scale. Here, again, we had the services of my clinical students, who spent many hours testing another sample of adults with WAIS and obtaining their responses to a large number of potential items from which Dr. Naylor with his acclaimed flair for test making was able to select the appropriate items. Thus the Naylor-Harwood Adult Intelligence Scale, known as NHAIS, was made, published in 1972 by the Australian Council for Educational Research (ACER). The NHAIS was also published under license from the Psychological Corporation of New York, which had published Wechsler's tests. There was one limitation. The test was not to be sold outside of Australasia. When the revision of the WAIS *(WAIS-R)* came out, we were disappointed to see that some easily remembered performance items were repeated, but Wechsler's tests are still deservedly in vogue.

Financial Support

Once the first round of testing was completed, generous grants were provided for nine years from three commonwealth research funds and, after retirement of the principals, the next 10 years were financed by the Utah Foundation. Throughout the 20 years, the department generously supported the project, and at all times attendance at international conferences was encouraged by the vice chancellor's special funds. Vigorous experimentation was performed during the first 10 years, and four rounds of testing were completed: WAIS, NHAIS, WAIS, and NHAIS.

Death of George Naylor

It was a matter of deep regret and loss that, four years after the completion of the projected 10 years, Dr. Naylor died suddenly in 1980. His personal contribution was irreplaceable, and much of my theoretical and practical skills must be attributed to his sharing and inventive attitudes, and to the privilege of working in partnership with him, which I did from 1947 to 1980. His death came after the four rounds of cognitive results had been analyzed, but the Utah Foundation made it possible for me to extend the plan, with the continued support of three men (all my former students and colleagues) who were retired, or close to that event. They were Lex Irvine, Laurie Enticknap (deceased in 1998), and Richard Mortimer Tanner. Throughout the 20 years of the collection of data, the most frequent research assistant was Margaret Scally, whose visiting and testing of the panel members ensured that, by 1987, data collection was complete and ready for ultimate analysis, based on six cognitive assessments (WAIS-NHAIS-WAIS-NHAIS-WAIS-NHAIS). These were spaced so that each scale was experienced at an interval of approximately five years and tended to be accepted by the aging subjects as a new operation, especially as all the items in NHAIS were different from those in WAIS. At the end of the longitudinal study, and with numbers reduced to 87 survivors, 67 who had completed all six cognitive assessments were found collectively to have produced an annual average decrement of less than 1%. The average, as usual, masks the fact that some individuals had a greater or lesser decrement. In fact, a few people showed no decrement at all throughout the study.

Group Tests

During the first 10 years, other functions had been tested experimentally. Control groups of young adults were used in relation to speed of perception and in testing memory (spontaneous recall and recognition). The most memorable experiments were concerned with learning (to translate German into English, and to play the recorder). In fact, once these experiments were reported nationally and internationally at gerontology conferences or in publications, we found that people believed that we did nothing else but teach German and recorder playing!

Experiments

Before Dr. Naylor's death we made group tests of intelligence and interests, producing age-norms for the elderly. These were self-administering or usable in groups, designed to be used to guide elderly people into various forms of retirement activities, especially pointing to possible new learning or even relearning. These tests were free of copyright and could be used by members of any profession or by the people themselves. They were circulated nationally and internationally, to promote mental or physical activity in retirement. One gerontologist in Germany proposed to translate these tests for use in his country.

Longevity

Later in the research program a study of longevity was organized, in view of the great age of the surviving panel members and their knowledge of the history of their forebears. A table of life expectancy was assembled to include the birth and death dates of as many generations as possible, and a longevity quotient (LQ) was proposed, which would have 100 as the average when death coincided with the life expectancy age. The formula could be used with calculation of a provisional longevity quotient for those not yet deceased.

Perception

Two of the experiments using control groups of young adults can be briefly mentioned:

1. Speed of perception certainly favored the younger group in that, whereas they could process and report, on average, 24 bits of information per second in a timed exposure of digits, the elderly could achieve on average only 15 bits in their 60s, 14 in their 70s, and 12 in their 80s. There were, of course, some of the elderly group whose score exceeded the average for the control group.

Memory

2. In a test of spontaneous recall of 20 pictured articles exposed 2 seconds per card, a criterion of 80% with, if necessary, repetitions of exposure, was set. Without warning, 1 month later, all subjects were again tested for recall. At this stage, the elderly recall was 40% of their original recall; that of the control group was 54%. To test for recognition, 40 more items were interleaved, making 60 in all. In the spontaneous recall, the elderly had achieved 74% of the control score, but with recognition this had risen to 87%. Clearly, the elderly had accepted and stored information, which could not be retrieved without the benefit of recognition. It is important to consider this finding when estimating the memory of frail or possibly dementing people.

3. In 1969 the German learning group was subjected to a translation test of equal difficulty to the translation passages normally set for the school-leaving (senior-level). The test was set, and the scripts marked, by the head of the Institute of Modern Languages. Of the 55 participants who took the test, 8 were given A passes, 12 were assessed at B, and 18 at C, all at the senior level. Nine others reached the intermediate or junior level and 8 performed below the junior level. These panel members refused to resign and, for 10 years in all, they continued to learn and enjoy the German language. At one stage, a member of the group who had learned and been tested with the group became the group's teacher.

4. The same enthusiasm was shown in 1972 by the 80 members of the recorder-playing group, and they also learned and practiced together for 10 years. Dr. Naylor had taught the German, and our research clerk, Robin Kempster, taught the music and the recorder playing. In both groups there were members who, having been beginners with the others, became the teacher or a conductor, and in both cases the condition had been upheld that group members must be beginners. The oldest successful German student was 90 years old, and the oldest recorder player was 97 at the end. Both groups gave up the meetings at an average age of 80 years.

In 1970 the department instituted the first national psychology course in gerontology. To be admitted to this second-year course, students needed to have passed in Psychology I. Enrollments at first reached a little more than 200. Students came from different faculties and professional courses, and we made it possible to devote half of the course time to a small group contribution from their particular areas of study, training, and experience. Each week we introduced a different perspective. When Dr. Naylor and I retired, this course was maintained by Mr. Lex Irvine, who had always been associated with the research and the course.

Beginning in 1966, I was regularly requested or invited to present papers to national and international conferences. We often needed to resort to cross-sectional results, which we also did when applying for grants from the commonwealth funds. I presented papers at national conferences in all capital cities—Canberra, Sydney, Melbourne, Hobart, Adelaide, Perth, and Brisbane—and at most international meetings that I attended in London, Singapore, New York, Melbourne, Auckland, Acapulco, Ljubljana, and Liège.

Awards and Affiliations

As the research progressed toward an inevitable end in the formal sense, acceptance of its value was expressed to me in the form of awards, which would have been shared with Dr. Naylor if he had survived. In 1988 I was awarded the first David Wallace address and the medal and life membership of the Australian Association of Gerontology. Dr. Wallace had been a president of the association and a much admired gerophysician. In 1985 my contribution to the university and to the welfare of the aged through research was rewarded by the conferral of a doctorate of science degree, honoris causa. To receive such an award from my own university was an honor of the highest order, especially as the conferring chancellor was Sir Walter Campbell, chief justice of the Supreme Court in Queensland and shortly then to become the governor of the state of Queensland. He had been one of my most valued students in the immediate postwar years.

In 1985 I was also honored by the Commonwealth of Australia with the award of membership (AM) in the General Division of the Order of Australia. This was for my contribution to the welfare of the aged. This award too was invested by the governor, Sir Walter Campbell, at Government House.

In 1992 The Australian Psychological Society, through the group known as Psychology and the Elderly Interest Group, instituted the Elsie Harwood Award, to be given for high academic standard in a fourth year honors thesis about aging for a student from any Australian university offering an accredited psychology honors course. I was able to present the award to the first winner at the annual conference of the society and to give the keynote address to a very large audience, among whom were numbers of my former clinical students, many of them in high academic positions. As the title given to the conference was ''Fresh Looks,'' I took the opportunity of presenting a succession of metamorphoses through which my career had taken me, and a nostalgic reception made the occasion one of the most enjoyable of my entire academic life.

In the current years of ''retirement,'' I have terminated membership in some organizations, but I maintain a few of these activities, including a governorship of the Freemasons' Geriatric Medical Foundation, which has established in perpetuity the first chair of geriatric medicine at the University of Queensland. The foundation has raised capital of approximately $2.5 million, which is ongoing toward a projected $3 million. The department in now thriving clinically, educationally, and in research.

I continue membership in the College of Clinical Neuropsychologists but am no longer accepting medico-legal referrals. I also continue membership in the University of Queensland Foundation because it provides seeding funds for staff with selected new research projects. For some years I have been a fellow of the Australian Psychological Society and an associate fellow of the British Psychological Society. These keep me in touch with developments within the profession.

I have ceased to function on behalf of state and commonwealth governments, but formerly I was chair of a forum for the aged in Queensland and member of the National Forum in Canberra. During my tenure as chair we saved the acoustic laboratory from abandonment and saw it converted into the Australian Hearing Services for pensioners and ex-servicepeople with hearing impairment; we persuaded the government to produce a remote controller for the hearing aid and were partially responsible for a switch in Queensland to an enduring power of attorney.

Illness and Insight

On the assumption that autobiographies in the area of geropsychology will be read by our colleagues, I feel that not to include here a strictly biographic detail would fall into the category of unethical suppression of information. I trust that this brief account will be read in that spirit. In 1975 I was assailed by an illness that threatened my life—bacterial pneumococcal meningitis and encephalitis. Two weeks of unconsciousness and two months in the hospital, followed by six months of slow and partial recovery, gave me very good insight into the textbook problems of our patients—young and old—for which a diagnostic term can only hint at understanding. To have experienced protracted residual effects of such a disease, short of death, can provide a better understanding of conditions seen in geriatric wards and neurological hospitals than can be obtained from the best of textbooks, but this is not a recommendation to opt for the disease!

I was later informed that at my lowest state, apart from severe paralysis, the effects included aphasia and profound deafness. As consciousness slowly returned, I experienced vertical diplopia, prosopagnosia, memory failure, and imbalance when I was stood up. Aphasia evolved into nominal dysphasia. Monoaural hearing slowly returned, but I was unable to judge the direction of the source of sounds, which is a well-known effect. Many of these problems are still detectable after 24 years, but disablement is not acceptable when adaptation is the focal process. Because we are discussing the field of geropsychology, I find it necessary to accept that those residual effects that are resistant to further recovery will inevitably be compounded with the normal effects of the aging process. In my case, I have only recently realized that this is so. However, in terms of the longevity study spoken of earlier, my LQ in 1975 was 106. Today my longevity quotient (LQ) is 145, which is stern proof that I have considerably outlived the expectations of my life span. My return to university work after some nine months of ''rehabilitation'' was a useful exercise, and it illustrated the effect of my recommendation to patients to work with rehabilitation ''on the job,'' which is why it is so important with geriatric patients to find out what they had done in their premorbid state. I returned slowly to hospital and legal work, and my university students said that I was much better at the end of the semester.

Conclusion

I am often asked what I do in retirement. My reply is more of the same, but I add that I spend enjoyable time weekly with the classics and ancient history department. In 1992 a chance meeting with Professor Bob Milns of the classics department resulted in an invitation to join a Friday afternoon Greek and Latin reading group. This came 60 years after my last reading of Homeric Greek, and 46 years since I had lectured for one year (in addition to my own schedule) in Latin, Greek, and Greek art and literature. This was due to the serious illness of Professor J. L. Michie, who died in June 1946.

Two groups were meeting weekly. The first group was reading Homer's *Iliad* and *Odyssey,* whereas the second group—with some overlap between the groups—was at first concentrating on Latin (e.g., *Confessions of St. Augustine, Letters of Abelard and Héloise,* and the 150 psalms) and latterly Vergil's *Aeneid* of classical times. I accepted the 1992 invitation and then realized that this was an opportunity to study relearning. No statistical experimentation was necessary. I was able to observe my own recovery of the two languages and that of the mostly retired professional men whose Latin predated their university days, and one or two of whom were learning Greek for the first time. The group, at the time of writing, consists of four medical men (one a practicing gynecologist-obstetrician, one a retired member of the same college, and two who are still practicing medicine), one a retired Supreme Court judge, two retired members of the English department, one a Russian lecturer, two mature age classics students, and several postgraduate classics students. Professor Milns chairs the groups and enjoys—as we do—the interprofessional discussions of the content of the Latin and Greek texts.

Finally, it is reasonable for me to revert to my initial words of Shakespeare, in that there must be people who think my ''end'' that was never preplanned was, indeed, rough hewed! But my gratitude will always be directed to those who ''shaped my end'' by causing me to progress in keeping with their unvoiced expectations so that it was never necessary for me to apply for a position or to regret the events or demands that formed part of my movement from one stage to another.

Chapter 11
ELDERLY MENTORS AND THE NEPOTISM RULE

Irene Mackintosh Hulicka

I may be the only person in the world who can attribute interest in aging to the nepotism rule. Until the age of 32, I had almost no interest in or experience with elderly people and definitely no career aspirations with respect to gerontology.

I grew up in a very rural area of Saskatchewan at a time when farmers were desperately poor because of repeated crop failures. All adults in our local community had emigrated from Europe or Eastern Canada. The "older people" were men and women who had "homesteaded" on previously unfarmed land. When I was a child this "older" generation ranged in age from about 35 to 50. Grandparents were nonexistent or thousands of miles away. I attended a one-room country school with 35 to 40 other children in grades 1 through 8. There was no high school in our community. I studied grades 9 and 10 by correspondence, and for grades 11 and 12 I attended a town school 30 miles from home where I paid high tuition and worked for my room and board, not an easy assignment.

When I graduated from high school, my knowledge of career opportunities was exceedingly limited. I knew few high school graduates and only three or four people who had gone to university. No teacher or adult other than my parents had discussed career opportunities with me or suggested a university education. It was assumed that women who wanted a premarriage career should choose from among nursing, teaching, and secretarial work. I didn't want to be a nurse. My mother predicted that I would be a disaster as a secretary because of my inability to "suffer fools gladly." Canada was heavily engaged in World War II; I believed I could simultaneously serve my country and acquire training by joining the army. Although recruiting officers promised me officer training, a parental permission statement (signed by my little brother) didn't offset my underage status. I was told I would be "called up" in a couple of years.

When I completed high school, my parents offered to pay the initial tuition fee for a one-year teacher training program. I had no aspirations to be a teacher, but some training was better than no training. I had never been in a city, but the first day there I found living quarters (a 9-by-12-foot "light housekeeping" room shared with another student) and part-time employment as a waitress. I was required to sign a statement promising not to accept a teaching position before I was 18. Standardized tests were administered, and the authorities announced that because of the teacher shortage the top 10 scorers would be immediately granted temporary teaching certificates. I was terrified to learn I was one of the top 10. At 16, and with only six weeks of useless teacher training, I was placed in charge of a one-room country school with 25 pupils in grades 1 to 8.

Despite my trepidation and inexperience, I was reasonably creative and competent as a teacher. The temporary teaching certificate was my gateway to further education. After a year of teaching (at $4 a day and no pay for holidays, sick leave, or bereavement) I had saved enough to go to university. Further, the teaching certificate enabled me to obtain full-time teaching positions during the three-to-four-month summer break from university classes. Typically my spring–summer teaching positions were in remote areas that had been unable to recruit a teacher or in schools that had lost or removed a teacher because of severe disciplinary problems. For example, when I was 18 I was principal of a three-room school in a northern lumbering village. The 40 students in my class, aged 12 to 17 and in grades 6 to 11, had helped the former principal to have a "nervous breakdown." On my first day of school, I found desks overturned and hostile sullen students, a few of whom were inebriated on lemon extract. I was terrified. However, there was no escape. The village was served by a train only once a week, and I needed to earn money. A combination of firmness, humor, presenting interesting materials, and perhaps a basic sense of fairness on both sides of the desk had a calming influence. Before long those sullen young "thugs" became a highly motivated group of students. At their request, special catch-up sessions were held before and after school and on Saturdays. Contending with the problems and challenges presented by so-called difficult schools enriched my appreciation of human diversity and strength. Some of the lessons I learned as a young teacher helped me to see and appreciate the strength and courage of people in later adulthood.

The summer teaching positions, supplemented by scholarships and part-time work during the academic year, enabled me to become a full-time student at the University of Saskatchewan. No academic advisement had been provided by the high school or the university. Perhaps because of the narrowness of my horizons, I did not take the initiative to explore various career options. During my freshman year I enjoyed and did well in economics. My economics professor advised me that economics is a man's field in which women could not excel. I decided to major in economics. I do not remember any mention of aging or the aged in any economics class or in any undergraduate or high school class, with the sole exception of Shakespeare "All the World's a Stage" passages from *As You Like It*. His seventh stage of life was interpreted as justified mockery of the doddering incompetence of old age.

As I neared completion of a BA in economics, I noted with consternation that although economics classes and assignments interested me, I did not enjoy discussing economics with my classmates (all men) at social events. During my senior year, I took my first course in psychology, probably the most dreary, boring class in my undergraduate curriculum. It was taught by a nice philosophy professor, who may have had insufficient interest in or knowledge of psychology to make the class interesting. I sensed that despite the drabness of the lectures and text, there might be excitement in the study of human behavior. The war was over and the university was expanding. A psychology department distinct from the philosophy department was established. I completed a honors degree in economics (a year of graduate study, plus a comprehensive exam) and simultaneously sampled psychology courses. I found psychology more exciting than economics and stayed at the University of Saskatchwan to complete an MA in psychology. My master's thesis measured depth of hypnotic state and the relationship between hypnotizability and two tests of suggestibility.

As I approached completion of my MA, I tried unsuccessfully to find employment that would use my knowledge of psychology. A high school in the Province of Alberta advertised for a teacher in midsemester. My handwriting has always been terrible, so it is not surprising that the school officials responded to Mr. Ian Mackintosh. With tongue in cheek, I signed I. Mackintosh to all subsequent correspondence, and they continued to communicate with Mr.

Ian. The position was offered, with a salary substantially higher than that of many professors. After all, Mr. Ian was assumed to be a middle-aged man who had experience in several schools and had completed three university degrees. When I arrived, the school officials were aghast that they had promised such a high salary to "a mere 22-year-old girl." For the next two years I had no reason to complain about my salary.

After two years of high school teaching, I was ready for a change. I applied casually to several Canadian, American, and British universities for graduate training in psychology. I was amazed that most universities accepted me, and several offered graduate student stipends. For idiosyncratic reasons, including a distaste for large cities, I chose the University of Nebraska at Lincoln. I have never regretted the choice, though my husband, who has a PhD from Berkeley, can't understand how I could choose Nebraska over Berkeley, especially because Berkeley offered a much higher stipend. The Nebraska psychology department had a small, well-qualified, diligent faculty who were interested in the education and welfare of the graduate students. The initial courses with heavy emphasis on psychophysical methods, physiological psychology, and methodology were rather tedious, but gradually, as my competence increased, so did my interest. I particularly valued the training in statistics and methodology.

My dissertation research reflected a tendency that is evident in most of my gerontological research—namely, an attempt to relate laboratory research to real-life observations. In a Friday statistics class, I had enjoyed learning to use complex analysis of variance. That weekend I had to prepare a research design for another class and cast about for a problem that could use complex analysis of variance. I thought about the rather simplistic studies on learning and extinction that were currently in vogue. One of the ideas that hit me was that laboratory rats learn quickly to quit making a response if reinforcement is no longer forthcoming. In real life, some learned responses tend to be stubbornly retained. I dashed off an experimental design to test the hypothesis that resistance to extinction should vary as a function of the degree of irregularly in the acquisition of responses. The next week, I was amazed to be congratulated by professors for an interesting dissertation proposal. Parenthetically, the ease of designing the dissertation was offset by problems in designing, building, and paying for components of the apparatus, and data collection time. Nevertheless, I was amazed to complete all requirements for the PhD in less than two years. I have no memory of any mention of aging in the doctoral program.

My first postdoctoral appointment was as an assistant professor at a liberal arts college in Kansas. At this college, the apparently unwritten recruitment rule was to hire only single women and married men. The line between town and gown was firmly drawn by the president. There was a faculty club for men only and a women's association, which I did not join, for wives and female faculty members. Perhaps I was becoming aware of my own aging; I did not like the prospect of social life over the years being limited to a gala Saturday night with the girls. The college president appeared unsympathetic to my reason for resigning, but subsequently his recruitment policy changed slightly.

My next move was to the University of Oklahoma. The university had well-qualified faculty members, a strong graduate program in psychology, and many competent graduate students. I was able to use the animal laboratory facilities of the pharmacy department and set up a research program involving both graduate and undergraduate students. My research was thriving, I was getting research grants, and students were highly motivated to do well in my graduate and undergraduate courses. I was even selected by students as one of the three outstanding professors on the campus. Apart from working 60 to 80 hours a week at a lower rank and for less pay than male colleagues with credentials no better than mine, this was a wonderful academic position. However, I began to question whether I wanted to continue as an academician. Tangible rewards were not commensurate with effort expended, nor with accomplishments. I was sickened by petty politics, which on occasion victimized students or even faculty members. I debated whether to leave psychology and academia, perhaps for medicine, law, or business or to take postdoctoral training in physiology and neurology in order to investigate learning and memory mechanisms more fully. Then I met my future husband. We had a whirlwind romance and after more than 40 years of marriage still express gratitude to the University of Oklahoma for making possible the improbable meeting of a woman from rural Saskatchewan and a man from cosmopolitan Prague, Czechoslovakia.

Our marriage put a new slant on my career. The nepotism rule, which prohibited members of the same family from working for the same institution, was strongly practiced by most academic institutions, including the University of Oklahoma. I had been at the university longer than my husband and I had tenure, but he did not. He could not be considered for tenure unless I relinquished mine. The university was located in a small town with few employment opportunities for psychologists. My department was willing to rehire me on a year-to-year basis, but we recognized that my unbridled tendency to protest inefficiency and unfairness could endanger yearly reappointments.

Employment opportunities were generally much better for psychologists than for political scientists and historians, my husband's specialities. We decided he should accept employment in a large city where I should be able to find work or, if I chose, to go to medical school. The medical school alternative was less available to women in the late 1950s than it has been in recent years. Some medical school admission committees considered gender, pregnancy, and old age (31) salient reasons for rejecting an otherwise qualified applicant. Not all medical schools were so bigoted. The University of Buffalo accepted my application for medical training and offered my husband a faculty position. We decided to move to Buffalo, a move we have never regretted. Before we left Oklahoma, we were grief stricken by personal tragedy. Our infant son died, almost certainly because of medical mismanagement. For perhaps illogical reasons, I rejected the medical school option.

The psychology department staff at the University of Buffalo fought valiantly over several years against the nepotism rule, hoping to offer me a faculty position. They did not succeed. In the early 1970s the nepotism rule was rescinded in the State University of New York system. Of the career options available to me in Buffalo, the most appealing was a postdoctoral clinical psychology internship at the Veterans Administration (VA) Medical Center. (My salary at the VA for a 32-hour-per-week internship was $5,400 in contrast to my faculty salary of $5,600 at the University of Oklahoma for a 60 to 80 hour workweek).

The VA internship met well my needs for learning, creativity, service, and independence. On my first day, the director of the medical center asked me to try to help the hospital's many long-term elderly patients. Here was a challenge to explore a field I knew nothing about. I had no training in geropsychology, virtually no exposure to elderly people, and no experience with people in either short-term or long-term facilities. Because of the nepotism rule, I found a new challenge, a new interest, and a new path in my career.

I could not have asked for a better situation or set of opportunities. My psychology supervisor, chief psychologist of the outpatient mental hygiene clinic, was a competent clinical psychologist for nonhospitalized patients. He had no experience with old people and an apparent aversion for people with physical illnesses and losses. I was never able to persuade him to visit wards with me. He was very helpful with respect to the selection, administration, and interpretation of psychological tests. Sometimes he didn't understand when I said testing was unnecessary or impossible.

The internship was an exhilarating growth experience. I had almost complete freedom to define my sphere of action, my tasks, and approaches. Initially, I spent much time on the wards, observing and interacting with patients, staff, and family members. I began to get many referrals. Usually the referrals requested psychological testing, but the unstated request was to help the patient deal with loss, pain, depression, and fear or to help the staff deal with behavioral problems. I read what I could find on psychological assessment and treatment of elderly people; I found little and had serious questions about the quality of what I did find.

During my first week in the hospital, I received impetus for a research project. An 84-year-old patient was interviewed at a meeting convened to consider his disposition. A physician administered items from a mental status scale. The patient responded correctly to questions such as ''Who is the president?'' and ''Who is the governor?'' but not to ''What day is it?'' He was judged to have memory problems and some dementia. A few days later the patient, who had seen me only at the meeting, greeted me on the ward, despite his impaired memory. After chatting for a few moments, he asked ''What day is it?'' I hesitated before I said, ''Thursday.'' He laughed and retorted, ''You had to think too before you could answer.'' Then he explained that he often did not know the day because one day is just like another in the hospital; he does not see well enough to read newspapers; radio and TV announcers do not consistently identify the day; and no big-print calendars were available on the ward. (Such calendars were available shortly thereafter.)

It occurred to me that much of what is blamed on poor memory in old people might be due to poor learning, for whatever reason, as in the case of the old man's lack of information about the day of the week. I reviewed the research literature on age differences in memory. Many studies reported age differences, but no study measured the original level of learning. This simple observation made clear the need for controlled research on age differences and changes in memory. Before my internship ended, I had completed one such study, with others in progress. Also during the internship year, several types of group therapy sessions for older patients were established, a practice that ward personnel and most of the participants valued. On the whole, the internship was a positive experience. The limitations imposed by the nepotism rule were used constructively.

When the internship was completed, I was offered a full-time clinical position with the VA Medical Center. My position was on the medical service, and hence I was not affiliated with the psychologists on the neuropsychiatric service or the mental health outpatient service. As the only psychologist on the medical service, I was free to take referrals from any service in the hospital except neuropsychiatry, though geriatrics and physical medicine and rehabilitation had priority. I spent much time working with elderly patients and severely disabled patients of all ages. It was a wonderful position.

My elation was short lived for personal reasons. I was pregnant again with constant threats of miscarriage. Further, I was diagnosed with a life-threatening disease. My husband and I were frightened. Perhaps for therapeutic reasons, I continued to work diligently. When our son was born healthy, we concentrated on our happiness rather than fears about my health. Gradually, over the years, the health problem disappeared, providing informal evidence that positive emotions can affect health positively just as negative emotions can have adverse effects.

The next five years at the VA were happy and productive. I expanded my clinical expertise with elderly and severely disabled patients. Graduate clinical psychology trainees and research assistants including Harvey Sterns and Joel Grossman developed interest in geropsychology, either from a clinical or research point of view. We did research to explore age differences and age changes in learning and memory, made constructive suggestions to improve methodology, and developed research materials that were less biased against the elderly than many that had typically been used. I was frequently asked to give research papers at scientific conferences and educational or clinical papers at conferences for nurses, therapists, physicians, and volunteers. Some of my clinical publications and lectures on geropsychology topics were used in educational programs for persons who work with the elderly.

In the spring of 1963, I sent a note to the program chair of the Eastern Psychological Association suggesting that the EPA organize a symposium on some aspect of aging. A few weeks later, the program chair called to ask me to organize and chair such a symposium. The only problem was that he needed the details of the program within 24 hours. Although pessimistic, I decided that if it were to be done, I should aim big. I called Dr. James Birren, who said he would be pleased to participate, as did Dr. Edward Jerome from the National Institutes of Health. As a third participant, I wanted Dr. David Wechsler, but when I called he had just left New York for Los Angeles. Later that day Dr. Wechsler called me. He had been paged and was calling from the LA airport. He said he would be delighted to participate. Thus within seven hours, the first EPA symposium on a psychogerontological topic was organized, with three distinguished speakers.

I was thoroughly enjoying my work at the VA and blessing the nepotism rule for its contribution to a new direction in my career. The patients, physicians, nurses, and the hospital manager seemed to appreciate my work. The VA central office was also supportive. Unfortunately, our VA manager reached mandatory retirement age. I genuinely regretted his retirement. The new manager seemed to have a bias against whatever the former manager initiated or liked. A few months after the new manager took over, the chief of staff was sent to my office with ''something interesting to tell me.'' The hospital had to reduce its staff and my position had been chosen ''because after all you are not a bread winner.'' I was stunned. I could not believe that an institution would victimize me, regardless of the quality of my work, simply because I had an employed husband. This was in 1963. Had it happened in 1983 the explanation would necessarily have been different.

I left work a half hour early that day. I was amazed, and if the truth be told, furious. I did two things. I contacted Dr. Richard Bugelski, a distinguished professor at the university. I am not sure what he did, but I think he initiated protests from two universities that elimination of my position would negatively affect their graduate training programs. A few days before I was given the ''interesting information,'' a central office official who had visited our hospital left a message requesting a report on one of my projects when it was completed. I wrote to him thanking him for his interest but regretting the project would not be completed as my job had been eliminated because I was not a breadwinner.

I do not know what went on behind the scenes, but about two weeks later I was asked to continue with the VA as a research psychologist. Perhaps the offer was intended to undo an injustice and at the same time save face for the local administrator. The manager told me pompously that much time and many long-distance calls had been used to find a way to retain my services. Injudiciously I retorted that the taxpayers' money had been wasted resolving a problem that should never have occurred. The manager had the last laugh; a couple of years later when the VA central office offered me a substantial promotion, he refused to sign the necessary papers. The central office offered to have me move with the promotion to any of several VA centers where my work on aging could be continued. This would have been disruptive to my family life. With regret, I decided to leave the VA and return to academia.

In looking back, I think of the years at the VA as among the most productive and rewarding years in my career. The VA established a study group on the psychological aspects of aging to address basic issues and issues pertaining to treatment programs for the elderly. The study group met twice a year for two days, often choosing the time and location to enable members to attend the meetings of the Gerontological Society. The study group meetings brought together psychologists such as Neil Coppinger, Jack Lasky, Richard Filer, David Cohen, Allen E. Edward, Rayman W. Bortner, Roy M. Hamlin, Robert E. Canestrari, Leonard F. Jakubezak, Elston Hooper, Peter E. Comalli, and Robert Kleemeier. The meetings, involving a small number of people, provided for exchange of information and ideas and mutual help on research projects. One outcome of the study group was a volume of the *Gerontologist* edited by Neil Coppinger titled ''The Psychological Aspects of Aging'' (1967). I had two articles in this volume: ''Research Problems with Reference to Treatment Programs for the Elderly'' (subsequently entered into the Hearings of the Senate Committee on Aging) and ''Age Changes and Age Differences in Memory Functioning: Proposals for Research.''

The camaraderie among members of the VA study group on aging was also found at the meetings of the Gerontological Society and Division 20 of the American Psychological Association (APA). As a newcomer to geropsychology, I appreciated the warmth and encouragement of Charles Taylor, Jack Botwinick, Joseph and Jean Britton, and many others. The meetings of Gerontological Society of America (GSA) and Division 20 consistently served as sources of encouragement and stimulation.

After I left the VA, my opportunities to focus on research were diminished. I was affiliated first for two years with an excellent Catholic undergraduate college and for over a quarter of a century with State University College at Buffalo, a primarily undergraduate college distinct from but in the same city as the State University of New York at Buffalo. Because ours was an undergraduate college with no research assistants and virtually no support or reward for research, it was difficult to find time for research. My major task at Buffalo State College was to establish and develop a psychology department. During the demanding department-building period, and subsequently when I served as dean of natural and social sciences, I continued to do research and writing in geropsychology and particularly to accept invitations to address service provider groups with the goal of presenting information that might modify attitudes toward and treatment of elderly persons. Further, I was able to interest many departmental colleagues in geropsychology with the result that several included sections on adult development and aging in classes on personality and abnormal, experimental, and developmental psychology. We introduced two undergraduate courses on the psychology of aging, and many students over the years chose an aging emphasis in their careers. Several have graduated from doctoral programs that emphasized geropsychology, some have studied law or medicine or physical or occupational therapy with an emphasis on aging. A few entered politics, where their influence has been used to improve programs for the elderly.

Although basic research has been a primary interest since I was a graduate student, and geropsychological research has been a primary interest since my internship at the VA, I have had consistent interest in geropsychological education. This interest has manifested itself in a number of ways, such as incorporation of geropsychology into our college's psychology curriculum, encouraging other departments (e.g., biology, sociology, English, economics) to attend to aging in their educational programs, addressing groups of service providers and educators, and writing articles about education in aging. One of my closest collaborators in educational projects is Dr. Susan K. Whitbourne. Among our joint educational projects are two APA workshops on teaching the psychology of aging, other more local workshops, and several articles, including one in *The Teaching of the Psychology of Aging,* edited by Parham, Siegler, and Poon (1990). We also published a small book titled *Teaching Undergraduate Courses in Adult Development and Aging* (1979).

One of my most valuable educational projects has been collaboration with the medical school of the State University of New York at Buffalo, where my title is research professor of medicine. I have worked extensively with people like Dr. Evan Calkins, former head of the Department of Medicine, to design, develop, and offer educational experiences for medical students and residents. For a number of years a geriatrician and I coinstructed a course on geriatric medicine (the first formal instruction in geriatric medicine offered by our medical school).

I participated as a section chair at the Boulder Conference on Gerontological Education (1981). One of the outcomes of the conference was a book edited by Santos and VandenBos (1982). I was responsible for the chapter on recruitment. Throughout the years, I have answered innumerable letters and phone calls from people who have been assigned to teach a course on the psychology of aging or adult development and aging. I have shared course outlines, reading lists, and suggestions for assignments, and I have figuratively held the hands of novices in the field.

My research on aging has consistently had a humanistic or from-life-to-laboratory flavor in contrast to the more theoretical or from-laboratory-to-life emphasis of many esteemed colleagues. Because my introduction to aging and the aged occurred in an institutional setting, and I first became interested in gerontology from a clinical as well as research point of view, I have had and used opportunities to interact with and learn from older people in institutions, laboratories, social groups, and as clients in my clinical practice. I have learned from them much about the subjective experience of late adulthood.

Our observations during research projects indicated that some of the inefficiency of older people in performing laboratory tasks derived from their reaction to the type of tasks used and the temporal conditions imposed by investigators rather than from age-related cognitive deficits. For example, when we attempted to use the then popular one-bun, two-shoe, three-tree imagery technique to facilitate memorizing lists, older people didn't do well and some said they were angered or humiliated by being asked to engage in such ''child's play.'' Likewise, when we replicated someone else's research using their nonsense equation stimulus material older people expressed anger at the request that they should learn such nonsense. Older people may be more discerning and selective than college sophomores in their choice of materials to be learned. We found that observed age differences in cognitive efficiency as measured by laboratory task performance could be reduced by choice of materials to be learned or remembered, by instructions to use specified learning strategies, and by use of self-selected presentation and response intervals. Our work on the use of mediational strategies was among the first to demonstrate that older people can learn to improve their strategies for learning and for retrieval.

One of the observations that appalled me in my review of pre-1960 research was the inappropriate selection of research participants. For example, one investigator compared a young sample of nurses and medical residents in a mental hospital to an elderly sample composed of long-term mental patients. Because of the prevalence of confounding age, health, education, native language, and many other age-related variables, we did some straightforward research to demonstrate the need to be sensitive to confounding. For example, in a study that attempted to equate young and elderly participants for health status (number of diagnoses and length of hospitalizations), age differences in cognitive performance were markedly reduced. Further, young hospitalized patients performed less well than elderly (65 years or older) nonhospitalized volunteers. We refrained from using the comparison of hospitalized young people and community-dwelling old people as evidence of an age-related increment in cognitive efficiency.

Research pertaining to fears of the elderly was initiated a few years ago. The impetus for the fear research began when I was asked to see a patient immediately who refused to eat or to talk to anyone. With no time to get background information about the patient, and accompanied by six interns, I was introduced to a 68-year-old patient. He was exceedingly thin (I learned later that he weighed 68 lbs), and his pale face was dominated by large tearful eyes. When we were introduced, I said "I've been looking forward to meeting a brave man."

"Who might that be?" he said.

"You," I replied. "I understand you have been facing some big problems bravely." I don't know why I said *brave* but perhaps the word *brave* was a key to initiating conversation. He began to pour out his fears: fear that he would be sent to a nursing home, that treatment in the nursing home would be poor because of limited finances, that he would never be able to return to his apartment, fear of abandonment, fear of falling in the bathroom, and so on. The man was apparently starving himself to death to escape his fears. His bony fingers held my hand tightly for 45 minutes except when I persuaded him to eat ice cream from the snack tray. I provided whatever legitimate reassurances I could, and when he asked me to come back I promised I would but not for two weeks as I would be out of town. Before I left the hospital, I told a physician the man's near-starvation situation and his fears. The physician said that if he were to gain some strength he could return to his own apartment, with daily help from health care aides. I was optimistic. However, reassurance came too late. The patient died three days after my visit.

Both the physician and I were deeply affected. We argued that if we addressed and identified fears of individuals we might, through providing information, making procedural or environmental changes, and providing reassurances be able to reduce or eliminate some debilitating fears, perhaps releasing energy for the fearful individual to deal more effectively with other reality-based fears. Working with local colleagues, we developed a Fears and Worries checklist, which can be used for research purposes. In one project we assessed the fears and worries of people about to move from their homes to nursing homes. Approximately two weeks after the relocation, fears and worries were reassessed. As expected, fears were lower after a settling-in period. Identification of and attention to preadmission fears would probably reduce preadmission trauma.

The literature on fears of older people tends to focus almost exclusively on fear of death. Our research suggests that stronger and more prevalent than fear of death are fear of the circumstances of death, fear of becoming more sick and helpless, being more dependent on others for physical care, loss of eyesight or hearing, loss of spouse, unwanted relocation, not being able to help others, and having nothing to anticipate with pleasure. In my clinical work I have found attention to personal fears valuable with people of all ages.

My colleagues Drs. Jack Morganti and Jerry Cataldo and I have been considering the effects of latitude of choice on self-concept and life satisfaction. One of the events that directed us to this area of research occurred when I was conducting group therapy sessions for elderly veterans. Often there were requests from nurses, physicians, or therapists to observe a group session. I opposed use of a one-way mirror, and established a policy that a guest could attend a session, provided an invitation had been obtained from a group member (patient). The participants liked this rule, which apparently supported a sense of control. A nurse had been invited to attend over a two-week period. One morning as the group was assembling, the nursing supervisor announced that she was sending Miss Y instead of Miss X. I pointed out that Miss Y needed an invitation from a group member. The supervisor argued firmly but unsuccessfully that permission from the two of us was enough. When the group assembled, a quiet gentleman said, "You done right, Doc, you done right. It ain't that we don't want her here, but we got the right to decide." It was decided Miss Y was welcome, and there was practically a wheelchair race to invite her.

It does not take acute observational skills to detect tendencies to deprive older people, particularly people with physical disabilities, of choices they are fully competent to make.

We prepared a questionnaire that rates the importance to the individual of making his or her own choice in a specific situation and whether he or she has ordinarily no, some, or much choice. Our reasoning was that limitations on choice about an important item or event is more negative than choice limitations on events personally judged as unimportant. Our cross-sectional findings indicated that latitude of choice tended to peak in the 60s and 70s, and to be higher in the 80s than in adolescence (ages 14 to 16) and roughly equivalent to young adulthood and middle age (ages 45 to 54). Older people in institutional settings had much lower latitude of choice scores than like-aged people in noninstitutional settings. Perceived latitude of choice (based on both choice and importance scores) correlated significantly with self-esteem and life satisfaction. We have used research findings such as these to sensitize service providers and family members to unnecessary restrictions on choice.

My interest in efficiency of memory functioning in late adulthood has continued. Questions that I have asked, many of which I have not answered, pertain to issues such as the nature and extent of memory decrements associated with aging, how memory problems affect meeting the demands of life in a nonlaboratory environment, uses that elderly people make of memory, constraints on activities created by memory deficits, and strategies used to adapt to memory impairment. Questions might be raised about the prevalence and intensity of fear of memory loss, and when such fear exists, how it affects behavior, psychological well-being, and perhaps even memory itself. Our research shows that elderly people are more likely to complain about poor memory than younger people are, but correlations between complaints and objective measures tend to be low. Questions of considerable interest are the use that older people make of memory, and whether there are age differences in the use of episodic memory. Our observations suggest that cognitively intact older people can draw equally well from all temporal periods in their personal history. Memories selected for conversational purposes tend to reflect perceptions of audience interest. Events of 70 to 80 years ago might be judged potentially more interesting to fairly new acquaintances than recent events in an unstimulating environment.

During the past few years, I have concentrated more on direct clinical contact with people of all ages and less on research and education. Frequently, I see patients in a hospital who are depressed, fearful, or withdrawn after major losses such as double amputation, cerebral vascular accident (stroke), heart attack, or surgery. Although many of these people are ''down'' because of recent losses and fears for the future under changed circumstances, some downplay present problems to dwell on past hurts or long-standing problems, such as resentment over a parent's favoritism to a sibling or pain over an early adult broken romance. One 79-year-old woman in intensive care announced her decision that 59 years with an abusive husband was quite enough; she needed my opinion about the propriety of leaving him. She did, and she enjoyed three years of glorious freedom somewhat tinged with guilt before she arranged for his funeral. She died shortly after he did.

Elderly people who make appointments with me on their own initiative bring a vast array of problems, most of which are not unique to old age. Problems include fears for the future, guilt over long continuing lust, inadequate parenting, having been an uncaring child, concern over problems of offspring, unresolved grief, unrequited romantic love, self-dissatisfaction, and the whole gamut of human difficulties.

As I review my career, I am amazed that I was asked to prepare my autobiography for a book on the history of geropsychology. My accomplishments seem limited in comparison to those of many people whom I consider leaders in the field. I had no formal education in geropsychology, no exposure to the study of aging, and no mentor to influence me. Apart from my one year as a postdoctoral intern and five years as a clinical or research psychologist in the VA, my work on aging has been peripheral to other responsibilities of my position. If I had to judge the value of my contributions, I would consider the three following categories:

1. *Research.* My research and publications on age differences and age changes in memory and learning addressed some important methodological issues and identi-fied problems that needed attention. Perhaps also my humanistic from-life-to-laboratory approach encouraged other scientists to attend more closely to the personal qualities and situations of the persons whose cognitive and emotional processes were being studied.

2. *Gerontological education.* I have attempted rather consistently to introduce or improve the quality of gerontological education through the development of educational programs, broader curriculum development, workshops on teaching the psychology of aging, and articles addressing the need for education in geropsychology. Locally, I contributed to the inclusion of geriatric medical educa-tion in our school of medicine. I have given hundreds of lectures to service providers and administrators of programs, always attempting to encourage more sensitive and appropriate services to the elderly.

3. *Clinical work.* I was probably one of the first psychologists to have and to publish articles on group therapy for elderly persons. Well do I remember practical problems of conducting group discussions with 10 or more elderly men in wheelchairs, of whom one was completely deaf and another was completely without speech. These sessions were learning experiences for me and for trainees who assisted me. For example, I learned that many of these old veterans experienced a sense of noth-ingness when a fellow patient with whom they had shared a ward for months died. The usual practice was that patients were moved to the other end of the ward when the body was removed; their knowledge that a fellow patient had died came from an empty or newly occupied bed. Patients had no opportunity to attend a memorial service or convey condolences to family members. Almost certainly they recognized that their own death would also be treated by hospital personnel as if they had never existed. In the group sessions, I would give them an opportunity to talk about death and the person who had died by saying something like, ''I was sorry to hear Mr. L. died.'' Usually the entire session would be devoted to reminiscing about the deceased or a discussion of death and dying. After a few such ''memorial'' sessions, the announcement of a death usually came from a group member. Once when I was on vacation, two graduate students conducted the groups. A popular member of one group, Mr. T., attempted suicide because of terrible pain from cancer. It took him 5 days to die. The graduate students were uncertain about their ability to handle the group discussion about his death, particularly because of the suicide attempt. They sought help from every psychologist around. However, in subsequent meetings, not one patient mentioned Mr. T's death. When I returned, the graduate students told me that they feared the patients were so traumatized by the suicide attempt and death that they couldn't talk about Mr. T. The first meeting with me had barely begun when someone told me Mr. T. had died after a suicide attempt. The entire meeting, with tears and laughter, was devoted to reminiscing about Mr. T. and discussing death and suicide. As the meeting ended, I asked the men why they hadn't talked about Mr. T.'s death at earlier meetings. Several of them looked at each other, then one said quietly, ''We talked it over among ourselves and decided if we talked about his death in the meeting, it would be much too hard on the boys.'' I was impressed by their sensitivity.

In my clinical work with older people, I have attempted to attend to their wisdom, problems, points of view, and limitations. What I have learned in clinical endeavors has been used in the training of future clinicians, educational programs, and the design of research.

I was asked to identify my mentors in the study of aging. My mentors were not my professors, none of whom, as far as I know, had the slightest interest in aging or the aged. Although I cherish professional contacts with many of the most outstanding people in the field of geropsychology, I cannot identify one whom I could consider a mentor. In all truth, my mentors in the study of aging were the elderly people with whom I have interacted for the past 39 years. By letting me interact with them, by telling me about their lives, successes, problems, and fears, and by serving as my research participants and clients, they taught me much, which, in combination with information from the research and writings of expert geropsychologists, I have attempted to convey to students and practitioners and to use in my clinical work. I am grateful to these elderly people who have been my mentors and to the nepotism rule that indirectly put me in the position to interact with older people and to study the aging process.

References

Coppinger, N. W. (Ed.). (1967). The psychological aspects of aging: A prospectus for research in the Veterans Administration. *The Gerontologist, 7,* 1–80.

Hulicka, I. M., & Whitbourne, S. K. (1979). *Teaching undergraduate courses in adult development and aging.* Mount Desert, ME: Beech Hill Enterprises.

Parham, I., Siegler, I., & Poon, L. (Eds.). (1990). *Aging curriculum content for education in the social and behavioral sciences.* New York: Springer.

Santos, J. F., & VandenBos, G. R. (Eds.). (1982). *Psychology and the older adult: Challenges in training for the 1980s.* Washington, DC: American Psychological Association.

Chapter 12
DR. PALEG'S SKULL:
On the Geropsychologizing of Robert Kastenbaum

Robert Kastenbaum

My task in this chapter is to chronicle the experiences of a person who was as surprised as anybody when he discovered he had become a geropsychologist—a career option that few if any of his generation knowingly pursued.

A Dead End as a Beginning

Bonner Place was a typical enclave of the working poor in the South Bronx of the 1930s, one pile of tenement apartments next to another, all well along in the aging process. At the very cul of the sac a mystery dwelt. Here the childhood curiosity was granted access to the seething depths of the underworld. It would be many years before I learned that Greek legends had been nourished by steaming fissures on Mount Olympus. In the meantime, we had our sewer opening. Only an iron grating separated us from the nether regions. Paul DeAngelis and I personally saw a baby dinosaur emerge from the sewer one evening, although our report did not meet with universal respect. We suspected that there was more to the world than our parents and teachers let on.

"What Do You Want to Be When You Get Old?"

In this intense little world there were mostly boy games, totally girl games, and whoever-is-good-at-it games. Making and launching small flying objects was a mostly boy pursuit, as was shooting off rubber bands from wooden guns or impersonating the action movie characters we saw in the Fleetwood Theater whenever we had a nickel for admission or the nerve to sneak in. Tag and chase games were for all who wanted in, and talent alone determined who could participate in the most prestigious marble-shooting contests. If memory serves, though, girls and only girls played at being real grown-ups. The sidewalks would resound to the familiar chant: "*A* my name is Alice. I live in an ant hill and my husband's name is Andy." "*B* my name is Bertha. I live in a box and my husband's name is Bernie." This invocation of the future was enacted over a chalked grid on the sidewalk and required a degree of dexterity as well as a solid grasp of the alphabet. *Nobody played games about being old.*

"What do you want to be when you grow up?" was a question that adults would occasionally pull on us. The girls of Bonner Place and P.S. 35 responded dutifully in terms of wife and mother, teacher and nurse. Boys mostly didn't have a clue. Fireman or doctor is what we might have told inquisitors just to get them off our case. If we had secret fantasies they were not to be exposed for adult scrutiny. But it didn't matter much what we might say. Growing up was a remote prospect. Who knew?

Adults had always been adults. Old people had always been old. We did have some idea of past and future, though. For many of our parents and grandparents, there was an "old country," resembling a storybook once-upon-a-time land. The past had a gravitational attraction for the adults. How things were had a lot to do with how things were supposed to have been. This past referencing helped to shape our identities within family lines. Readings from the Old Testament also provided a sense of a past that was somehow still with us. A child might easily believe most of the really important stuff had happened a long time ago.

Futurity also spoke to us. The reality of passing time and directionality was institutionalized in the progression from one grade to the next. Physicality also made its point. Last year's clothes were not fitting us, so we would receive hand-me-downs from older children who were getting even older. Social expectations also changed. One day I would become old and responsible enough to go by myself to the Fleetwood Theater. Still later I could take my little brother with me. "Getting older" meant becoming more useful and independent, and living in a larger world.

More subtle was the tension system generated by parents and other adults. Our parents were hard working and hard pressed. Everybody worried about money. The challenge of coming up with next month's rent payment was part of a specific recurring time-tension system. The adults kept themselves going through their belief or hope in better times to come. Eventually we kids would have to make something of ourselves. We did not fully understand the stakes or effort involved but realized that a lot was riding on our success in a future that still had little tangible reality for us. It could not have been reassuring when my parents kept receiving report cards with such comments as "Could do better" and "Needs improvement."

Meanwhile, we showed a proper, unquestioning respect for the elders in our lives and cheerfully ran errands for them. Old people usually were nice. They didn't yell at us much, and they sometimes gave us cookies or told us interesting stories. Nevertheless, nobody ever asked us, "What do you want to be when you get old?" The connection between our child-selves and the adults we would become was elusive enough. How much more difficult it was to imagine ourselves *old!* How could we comprehend the strange workings of time that would lead us to walk in their shoes? Playing at action hero, firefighter, or baseball star, not a one of us could imagine devoting our lives to the study of aging. The world of the old was even more distant than the incomprehensible city that surrounded our little dead-end street or the mysterious depths that lurked below the sewer grating.

Some Markers Along the Path

Although I did not realize it at the time, several influences and dispositions were already preparing me for some kind of activity that involved the inquiry process. Included in the mix were such ingredients as the following:

- *The work ethic.* I grew up with the belief that it was useful, necessary, and satisfying to do good work. One did not always like the kind of work that needed to be done, but there was inherent satisfaction in completing a task and knowing that one had contributed somehow to the proper order of life. There was nothing "workaholic" about this orientation: doing what needed to be done seemed to be a big part of what life was all about.

- *All kinds of people.* The sidewalks (and classrooms) of New York were not the melting pot of diverse peoples that this phrase implies. Families often organized themselves around traditions they would defend against people from other traditions. Old-world animosities continued to flourish in the new world. Nevertheless, most of us dead-enders seemed to realize that we were all struggling with pretty much the same life situations. We needed each other. Compassion as well as conflict were frequently in evidence. I played, fought, and schooled with children from diverse backgrounds, years later puzzled to discover that all schools were not integrated. Old and young, White and Black, ''normal,'' disabled, and ''touched'' were all in the flow of our life. It would not have occurred to me that being old made a person less interesting or valuable.

- *Growing up Jewish.* From ground level this meant that my Catholic friends would go some places and do some things I didn't, and vice versa. It also meant that we didn't eat pork or ham. (Years later I asked my father, then in his mid-80s, why we *did* eat bacon. His unassailable reply: ''Because I *like* bacon.'') The main thing about being Jewish was other people making a thing of it. I came to realize that being Jewish meant being set aside in a special category, about which some people had strong negative feelings. I was responding to being a marginal person without understanding all that was entailed. It was uncomfortable and sometimes infuriating to be treated that way, but it also gave one a different perspective and encouraged paying attention to what people said and did.

- *Look after the horse first.* My father was a musician who opted for the less satisfying but more secure work of a milkman when he took on family responsibilities during the Depression. The milk wagons were still being drawn by horses in those days. I remember his respect and affection for his horse. One looked after the horse's thirst, hunger, and comfort before attending to one's own. I was fascinated by the otherness of horses, dogs, cats, birds, snakes, yes, even rats and the dubious baby dinosaur. Later as a graduate student and newly minted psychologist caught up in a world of human constructions and concerns, I would find a kind of saving grace in the otherness of animals. There was a living reality beyond partial reinforcement, factor analysis, the MMPI Minnesota Multiphasic Personality Inventory, or the ratio of human to animal responses on the Rorschach. Psychology was to be taken seriously, but so was the dog's new strategy for winning her favorite chair or the profoundly sad eyes of a caged bear.

- *Books, books, books.* I would read practically anything. Fiction was great, but so was history and biography. Early on, I developed a bad habit. Once a book had caught my interest I would construct my own variations and launch my own questions and imaginings. There would be two books in process: the one I was reading and the one I was making up as I went along. This habit has stayed with me, requiring special discipline to suppress when my task is to learn the author's message and just that. There were lots of books in our apartment, and I also became a frequent visitor to the local library. Soon I was learning about microbe hunters and other daring scientists and explorers. At age 6 I was ready to place my skills at the disposal of any intrepid scientist or explorer who needed a bit of help, as long as it didn't interfere with playing stickball or make me late for supper.

- *Dr. Paleg's skull.* Samuel Paleg was our family physician. He would make the occasional home visit, but more often we went to his office on Grand Avenue—in those days indeed a grand and spacious boulevard much superior to our cramped little tenement row. In my eyes, Dr. Paleg was a very old man who knew everything there was to know about everything. He promised that I when I became a doctor he would give me that terrific skull he kept in his office. Wow! I did in fact learn some things about doctoring that were unusual for my age, and became the unofficial class medic when a nose was bloodied or some other minor mishap occurred. In its silence the skull seemed to speak about mysteries I might some day understand. That skull may have been an advance marker for my subsequent interest in death-related phenomena, and Old Doc Paleg became an enduring model of a wise, effective, and warm-hearted adult. (Meeting him 30 years later, I was astonished to find that this ''very old man'' had just then retired!)

The Academic Beginnings of a Geropsychologist

Geropsychology was as much an unknown in the corridors of a graduate program in psychology circa 1955 as it had been on the sidewalks of New York in the 1930s. *Gero-*anything was known to but a few scattered pioneers. The Gerontology Society of America (GSA) had started in 1947, but I never heard mention either of the GSA or the word *gerontology* throughout my academic studies. There was a close parallel with another dimension of the human experience: the study of our symbolic and actual encounters with death. *Thanatology* was also unknown at the middle of the 20th century except by those who rummaged through history's more obscure and forbidding closets. Students preparing for careers in the social and behavioral sciences rarely were exposed to lectures, readings, or field assignments in which either aging or dying/death/grief were salient. The same neglect of aging and death issues prevailed in the education of nurses, physicians, and clergy, as well as other sociobehavioral scientists.

Most students of my generation emerged from the academic labyrinth with a blinkered model of human life in which aging and death scarcely mattered. If anything, academia had taught us to ignore issues that could not be manipulated and controlled. Our teachers bristled or retreated when life occasionally flung up a situation involving aging or death—few of our mentors had addressed themselves to their own mortality. Death was indeed a pervasive sociocultural taboo, as Feifel (1959) would later reveal. Society acknowledged death only in fleeting and peripheral flashes. A lurid murder would be good for a few days of media coverage, for example, but the intrinsic human relationship to aging and death was tacitly avoided. Woe to those who dared violate this taboo! Eager to advance itself as an independent field of inquiry and practice, the academic psychology of the 1950s eschewed messy, unpopular, or unscientific topics (i.e., those we could not quantify, control, and neutralize). Curious though it may seem today, psychology for the most part contented itself with studying hypothetical people who did not age or die.

Here is one graduate student's experience of aging or death related issues in the late 1950s. I was in the clinical track at the University of Southern California and became a Veterans Administration (VA) trainee after completing the bulk of the course work.

Only once was the subject of aged people brought up in the classroom. The professor was a creative person who had pioneered an emerging specialty area. She was admired for the passion and courage she brought to the issues that concerned her. But Prof. X charged into this seminar session in high sputter. She was furious about an incident that had just occurred during her morning's consultation visit to a Veterans Administration facility. A psychologist had been speaking to an old man. Imagine that! But it was worse, much worse. She had seen the psychologist shouting into the old man's ear, ''WHAT DO YOU THINK ABOUT DEATH?'' The professor branded this as the most disgraceful action she had ever seen performed by a *psychologist. She hoped that none of us would ever do anything like it. In five years of graduate work, this was the only classroom moment that focused on aging and/or death.*

Woodworth and Schlossberg's mammoth *Experimental Psychology* was the revered bible for the basic experimental course. I still have my well-worn copy. We were made to understand that almost everything worth knowing about psychology could be found between its covers. How about human aging? Well, there was a footnote. *A footnote.* Apparently a psychologist by the name of Birren had studied the reaction times of Navy men. He found that the older mariners were slower. (My girlfriend's mother, who was back in the dating game, claimed that aging tars were still much too fast.) Other than that lonely footnote in one textbook, I learned nothing about geropsychology from the required readings throughout my doctoral studies. Not quite true. I learned that aging was not a matter of interest to psychology. It certainly would not be on the exam.

In the clinical sphere we did meet plenty of elders. I was one of many clinical students who sought apprenticeships with the VA, which was highly regarded for its quality of mentors. The more naive of us—me, for one—discovered that we would be plying our nascent craft or sullen art primarily with elderly men, each of whom had a suitcase of chronic problems. Where, oh where, were the brilliantly neurotic young women who had resposed so alluringly on Freud's couch? Of what use were recondite theories and state-of-the-art techniques when we were dealing with a man three or four times our age who had been worn down by life, left adrift by society, and now clung desperately to the VA lifeline? Nothing in my grad school experience had prepared me to work effectively with elders. There had also been little preparation for helping people whose problems were biosocial as well as psychological. During my fairly intensive apprenticeship with the VA I worked exclusively with men, many of them aged. I can see their faces now. I can see them trying to put a face on a life that had not panned out or that had come disastrously unraveled. I did not learn how to become a geropsychologist from these men, but I did develop an appreciation for all that I did not know about coming to terms with a long life.

Death was also excluded from psychological literature and pedagogy. Woodworth and Schlossberg had devoted 1,128,000 words to core psychological topics. Of this total, 166 were given to death-related topics: .0001 of the total word count. E. G. Boring's classic *A History of Experimental Psychology* (1949) was even more firm in its rejection of death as a topic of psychology's attention—total word count: 0. Throughout my grad school years I never heard a lecture nor received a reading or other assignment that dealt directly with dying, death, or grief. Around the world, millions were still grieving for World War II deaths, and health statisticians were already tracking the increasing longevity of many populations, noting that the course of life and death was undergoing a significant change. Neither these phenomena nor cold war anxieties nor the unrelieved suffering of terminally ill people were able to permeate the halls of academic psychology. Or maybe that was just Southern California in the 1950s!

The rare psychologist who did consider death to be a relevant issue was regarded as a disagreeable eccentric. This was certainly the case with Herman Feifel, the clinical psychologist who had drawn the wrath of my professor, but who has since received deserved honors from the American Psychological Association and many other organizations for his pioneering studies of death attitudes. Near the end of my clinical internship I would meet both Feifel *and* the elderly man into whose left ear he had been shouting, ''What do you think about death?'' (As it turned out, this gentleman could hear tolerably well if you spoke close to his *right* ear in a setting free from the usual hub-bub of the VA center.) Clinical learning aside, I had found virtually nothing in my undergraduate or graduate studies of psychology that prepared me for living in a world of fellow mortals who grow up, grow old, and die.

Time: In or Out?

Gradually it dawned on me that it was not just aging and mortality that were missing from our education in psychology. We were also giving limited attention to that flowing matrix that is inseparable from aging and death: *time*. Despite a wealth of sociocultural associations, it is difficult to grasp this insubstantial substance that waits for nobody and that, in passing, takes lives, relationships, empires, and even the monuments that were intended to preserve great names and events. Under Chagall's brush, time is a kind of river that flows from an inconceivably distant past to an unknown future. We may call ''time out'' and try to ignore the flow, but on it goes, replacing youth with maturity, maturity with age, life with death, and, in the alchemy of regeneration, death with life.

We graduate students experienced an odd sort of relationship with time. Many of us felt ourselves to be in a time chamber that was isolated from the natural developmental flow. We had been schooling for many a year, and now it seemed that we might spend our portion of eternity within the university environs. This perception may have been heightened by the fact that our ranks included midlife students who were still moving toward their degrees with glacial stealth. Had there really been a life before graduate school? Was there really an afterlife? Was the graduate school experience a preparation or a replacement for our real lives? Our inadequate conception of the total life course contributed to the confusion. The developmental theories we encountered usually were limited to the early years of life and treated as though peripheral to general psychology. Similarly, our own socialization had focused on getting through childhood and becoming responsible and self-sustaining adults. What was supposed to happen after that? If anybody knew, they weren't telling. There was just very little sense of what a whole life trajectory was all about and therefore what to make of our prolonged immersion in the student role. Academic psychology had not created this dilemma all by itself, but the lack of attention to the riper years of the life course had certainly contributed to our ambiguous and unsettling relationship with time.

I was perhaps especially attuned to the paradoxes of time because I had fallen into philosophical studies on my way from Bonner Place to graduate school. In fact, the unexpected scholarship that made it possible for me to enroll at University of Southern California was in philosophy. I brought along a little philosophical knowledge and the irksome habit of questioning when I transferred to psychology. Although I would find many psychological issues stimulating and challenging, I could never quite subdue my interest in philosophical problems.

Psychology's disposition of time (circa 1955) proved to have something in common with the grand line of philosophical thought. Plato had set the tone with his downgrading of time to imperfection and illusion. Through centuries of philosophic dialogue and diatribe, those who considered time to be of the essence were generally booted to the sidelines. A philosophy apron-stringed to church dogma much preferred that which is not subjected to the vagaries of time. Not just the true, but the good and the beautiful and the moral were all characteristics of the everlasting. In laboring to support this proposition, philosophers had to take leave of much of daily experience, if not of their senses. Your average respectable philosopher within the Western tradition said very little about the sort of time we might call psychological, phenomenological, or organismic. A wall of abstractions and distractions separated the established philosophies from the time that real people experienced in the real world.

I soon discovered that psychology also regarded time as a subject of secondary interest. Academic psychology had taken up the customary philosopher's trick of converting time to space whenever possible. This was not merely an attitude; it showed up in measures, analyses, and theoretical models. Time most often would be represented as a single dimension with spatialized markers. Time was a place in space or a line through space. It is much easier to deal with space than it is with time. We detect space primarily through the visual system, whose physical structures and pathways are fairly well understood. By contrast, there is no palpable time receptor system, no simple parallel to the perception of space.

If seeing is believing, then time is less credible than space. Time is also too personal, complex, and subtle to suit the experimentalist's temperament. It is much too protean, alive, and wriggly for the reigning spatialized research design models. There also seemed to be pleasure in the exercise of control for its own sake. We will show time who's boss! For example, the dominant behavioral-experimental paradigm during my grad days presented time as chained conditioned responses—time itself in chains.

Time had been pretty much relegated to a point reiterated through space. There was nothing remotely timelike about this representation. The time line did not move, did not take itself with itself as it crossed from the left to the right margin, did not even tick. Academic psychology had persuaded itself that time could be reduced to a single quantifiable dimension, no different from any other variable that could be so represented. In fact, this reduced representation of time was perhaps the most boring because it was the most predictable of dimensions commonly used in psychological research and measurement. Test scores, for example, had some inherent interest because they might differ at different ''points in time.'' But those points in time had no choice but to advance in lockstep—that is all the societal and scientific timekeepers would permit them to do. Academic psychology had succeeded in replacing that most subtle, complex, and mysterious insubstantial substance— time—with a simple-minded and boring representation. Even a poorly made artificial flower had more affinity to the lillies of the field than did the psychologist's brain-dead flat line to the flow, intimacy, and power of time. The spirit of scholastic thinking flourished within the halls of self-consciously modern behavioral psychology.

A partial exception was the study of time perception. Since the early days of experimental psychology, many researchers had investigated the perception of time under various conditions (e.g., ''filled'' or ''unfilled''). Unfortunately, these painstaking and sometimes ingenious studies had not established useful generalizations or influenced theory, although they had at least kept alive the concept of time as a characteristic of human cognition and experience.

Outside the friendly confines of experimental psychology one could find some thinkers with fresh approaches. Perhaps the most appealing in the late 1950s was Jean Piaget, whose contributions were becoming influential in the United States. I was excited by his approach to human development. After a while, though, I could not help but notice that reality for Piaget was that which is constant and permanent. The child's awareness of time melting like an ice cream cone was almost equivalent to the concept of error variance. Awareness of transience and loss was significant only as a marker of progress toward the concept of object permanence. This prodigious thinker and researcher had turned his back on inconstancy, impermanance. Was change not real? Was transience not real? Was it not adaptive to comprehend the fleeting and the perishable?

Well—enough! About midway through my grad studies I felt that time was much neglected by psychological theory and research and that this neglect seriously undermined our mission. How strange it was. We were learning how to be researchers and service providers yet given every encouragement to ignore time, aging, and death.

I Make My Escape

My escape was abetted by several developments:

- Lawrence K. Frank's seminal (1939) article on time perspective came to my attention through the kindness of a good samaritan. Later I was fortunate to meet Frank, a probing and original thinker who offered words of encouragement and had laid the foundations for inquiry into our relationships with time within a sociobehavioral framework.
- I became aware of philosophers who had started to turn the tide toward time-relevant theory, starting mostly in the second half of the nineteenth century. Henri Bergson (1912) and Samuel Alexander (1920) were my favorites. Furthermore, the quantum leap in physics was accompanied by intriguing new investigations of time, such as Hans Reichenbach's *The Direction of Time* (1956). The invigorating ideas that had unsettled traditional views of time must have implications for psychology—but what implications? I also came upon the emerging existential literature, which encompassed both philosophy and psychology. I began to realize that, away from the mainstream of psychology, there were quality thinkers who had much to say about the meaning of time.
- I lucked on some of the early literature on the psychology of creativity. Years later this would become an active and enfranchised area of research. At that time, however, creativity was a peripheral topic that was encountered almost as rarely as aging and death. Perhaps the major exception was taking place just down the hall where J. P. Guilford, a luminary of the University of Southern California (USC) psychology department, was studying intellectual abilities. From Guilford I learned about the personality and cognitive traits that seemed to favor creativity. Outside of Guilford's research, creativity was almost always defined in terms of its products. I became especially interested in the *process* of creativity and came up with a little theory about the ability to integrate and transform past, present, and future elements into new configurations.
- My proposal for a dissertation on the creative process was shot down, perhaps deservedly so. ''Creative process'' came across as a fuzzy notion and I could not show that it had been established as an official concept in psychological research. I turned to Plan B: a study of future time perspective in adolescents. Fortunately, Larry LeShan had recently (1952) published an article close to that topic in the green journal *(Journal of Abnormal and Social Psychology)*. Waving this article under several faculty noses succeeded in the acceptance of this project as legitimate. When the original committee chair cleverly skipped town (a year's sabbatical), I was fortunate in securing the services of J. P. Guilford, the factor-analysis maven, who comprehended the study in a flash and encouraged me to do a—surprise!—factor analysis. The findings contributed to my growing interest in the later adult years: the adolescents in this sample had an intense sense of hurtling forward rapidly into the future but little idea about what would happen when they got there. The further off the future, the more global and undifferentiated the view. Furthermore, their anxieties about who they had been in the past seem to have been projected ahead into who they might become in the later adult years. The basic dissertation results became the basis of one of my first journal publications and I had also (Kastenbaum, 1959) published on the age-and-death findings in Feifel's (1959) groundbreaking book, *The Meaning of Death.*

Real Life, Real Death

I was fortunate to receive a National Institute of Mental Health (NIMH) postdoctoral fellowship to work with Heinz Werner at Clark University. I had become aware of his distinctive contributions while looking for something else at the USC library. Werner was a fount of innovative research methods but also a scholar in the grand tradition whose philosophical roots were intriguingly different from mainstream psychology. I became more aware of the relationship between developmental history and immediate situational context, as well as more tuned into what would later be called a holistic approach to human experience and action. Werner was friendly enough, but his attitude toward my interests was mostly of ironic amusement: "Bob, you take care of studying aging and death around here. I am too busy doing it." That was true.

I was now able to devise and conduct academic research on time perspective while expanding my knowledge of Werner's developmental-organismic approach. However, I soon tumbled into an obsolete health care facility in which obsolete people had been gathered. Cushing Hospital, originally an army, then a Veterans Administration facility, was now being operated by the Commonwealth of Massachusetts for some 600 geriatric patients. There is quite a long story here, and I have told some of it elsewhere (e.g., Kastenbaum, 1996). Basically, I started a department of psychology and with the help of the new superintendent, J. Sanbourne Bockoven, MD, was able to launch a research program with federal funding. First we studied the effects of tranquilizers and stimulants on geriatric patients (these were given routinely throughout the nation, but there were no dependable data on their effectiveness). This project led through curious turns of fate to a continuing series of studies on the social and physiological effects of moderate use of alcohol (mostly wine). Morale, self-esteem, and interaction improved markedly when geriatric patients were given the opportunity to sip a glass of wine or two and treated like human beings in the process. Use of psychotropic drugs declined markedly as the patients' quality of life improved. This was actually a theory-driven project (I called it a "Mutual Gratification Model"), and it was indeed gratifying to see how staff members altered their perceptions and interactions with patients who now showed themselves to be more individual, resourceful, and pleasurable to be with than had previously been the case. Eventually this clinical research program would lead to building and operating The Captain's Chair, a neighborhood pub within the confines of a structurally unneighborly institution. This series of studies (and some that we continued in other venues) became a national model for improving the quality of life within congregate care facilities. Not everybody approved. I remember a letter from a woman in Elkhart, Indiana, who reviled me for this unholy innovation. I replied with statistics documenting increased church attendance as a consequence of wine/beer interventions. Actually, most clergypeople were very supportive of this effort.

Before long we had another project going—a demonstration effort intended to help institutional staff to be more responsive to the needs of terminally ill elders. At that time there were no journals, textbooks, or courses on this subject. My colleagues and I would soon help to fill these gaps, but at that moment we were heading into *terra incognita*—make that, *terror incognito.* Quickly we learned that most of the assumptions and techniques we started out with were pretty near worthless. Fortunately, Avery D. Weisman, the distinguished existential psychoanalyst, came aboard as an invaluable consultant, and we started to share our own learning experiences with others (e.g., Weisman & Kastenbaum, 1968).

There was a good deal of personal learning involved, beyond the specific findings from these two major projects and several smaller studies. In my dual education for clinical and research activities there had been a strong emphasis on the individual. Now I could not help but become more aware of contextual dynamics, how each one of us—hospital staff, family, and researcher as well as patient—were participants in a complex mutual-influence situation. I still cared mostly about the individual and so shaped my theoretical models, but it was obvious that one had to take into account the larger time-space-person-attitudinal manifold if we were going to understand the individual. I would continue to draw on my education as a psychologist, but was on my way toward a more interdisciplinary orientation.

Most evident was the heavy strangeness of the institutional atmosphere—something akin to an airport terminal in which most everybody was a stranger disconnected from the other strangers, few feeling quite at home, and therefore not really their usual selves. And everybody waiting—waiting. Sam Beckett, that master of depression and the absurd, could have taken some instructive notes here. What did life mean in this no-place place? What was the point of providing care for those who would only get older and more infirm, and then perish? And what, if anything, could we do to protect cherished meanings and enhance quality of life? These same considerations circled around every study or clinical intervention.

Speaking of interventions—there was essentially no database for selecting or devising psychological service programs for the institutionalized aged. Impaired elders were seldom referred to psychologists or psychiatrists, except for fairly perfunctory assessments that would have little bearing on the generic custodial care that was available. In trying to find my own way, particularly as a therapist, I organized one of the first symposia on therapy with elderly people, held right smack in the middle of the hospital itself to call attention to the possibility of improved care. The paper that I wrote for this occasion, ''The Reluctant Therapist'' (1963), attempted to analyze our own hesitancies, fears, and value priorities as obstacles to entering into therapeutic relationships with elderly people. That little paper seemed to come along at the right time, offering challenge and encouragement to a new wave of psychologists (or should we call ourselves ''geropsychologists'' now?).

Working within the constraints of a hospital environment I had to learn to respect boundaries, turfs, and hierarchies. A study or clinical program would not have the opportunity to test its merits unless there was understanding and goodwill on the part of many people, such as the directors of the medical, nursing, and social work services. How was a freshly minted young psychologist supposed to earn this kind of cooperation within a conservative environment that did not welcome new kinds of people or programs? I had not learned any of that stuff in grad school, so I set about to make as many mistakes as possible as quickly as possible and then try to learn as fast as possible to keep my head on my shoulders. It is more amusing in recollection than it was at the time. Graduate programs in geropsychology today would certainly be doing a *mitzvah* for their students by preparing them for understanding and working with people of various disciplines in complex real-life situations.

My fondness for clean-cut experimental research had to give way to devising ways of learning what we could about the matters most close to the bone within complex, conflicted, and shifting real-life situations. As if I needed the reminder, my office was one door down from the hospital morgue. The white-haired Swedish immigrant who had stunned me with the story of his life yesterday morning was now under Dr. Tedesco's scalpel. ''I can tell you what he died with,'' Tedesco often said, ''but not what he died of. Perhaps life. People sometimes die of life, you know.'' I *didn't* know, but I was starting to learn. My previous interest in the experiences and meanings of time deepened through interactions with many of the residents, and I perhaps helped to encourage others to heighten their appreciation of the phenomenological life of elderly men and women.

What I have said here does not begin to capture the excitement and stress of confronting the existential issues of meaning and death along with the limits of one's own knowledge within an institutional structure with a high priority for the status quo and damage control. Somehow, our common humanity in face of the intractable facts of aging, illness, and death seemed to pull us through (at least some of the time).

Gerontology was starting to take hold elsewhere as well. The pioneering Institute of Gerontology at the University of Michigan, under the resourceful direction of Wilma Donahue, was a harbinger of other centers to come. Detroit's Wayne State University decided to expand its own nascent gerontology program, in collaboration with the University of Michigan. To my own surprise, I had become a professor of psychology at Wayne State University and was supposed to teach stuff that I was still trying to learn.

Detroit Is Burning: Geropsychology in a Tinder Box

Police cruisers lined the street. Ranks of tense officers equipped with riot gear stood shoulder to shoulder, glaring at the long columns of Wayne State students and faculty who were obeying the order to evacuate. We realized that somehow *we* were supposed to be the threat. From our standpoint, the officers posed the menace, just itching for an excuse to pummel us. This was how my very first day as a professor came to a rather early close.

I cannot say precisely how the civil unrest of the late 1960s influenced my work as a psychologist interested in life-span development, aging, death, and creativity. Nevertheless, one always was aware of the tension, the instability, the possibility of violence and disorder. Wayne State University was very much an urban university, and therefore spared no political demonstration or criminal action. Paradoxically, perhaps, it was also a situation rich in the opportunity to establish new kinds of interpersonal relationships and innovate new academic programs. It was a vibrant, if also a disturbing time.

I was able to create the Center for the Psychological Studies of Dying, Death, and Lethal Behavior with the help of kindred souls on and off campus. We attracted some talented and fearless people who were soon engaged in research, educational, and service programs. It was about this time that I also offered what seems to have been the first regularly scheduled seminar on the psychology of death anywhere. In later years the instructor would know a lot more about the subject matter, but we probably had more mutual astonishment and fun those first couple of times. Soon the course transformed itself into the multidisciplinary Death, Society, and Human Experience, very likely the longest running university class of its kind. Eventually I would write the first textbook for such a course (Kastenbaum, 1977, 1998), though before then I had tried to figure out what our subject matter might or should be with *The Psychology of Death* (1972, 1992, 2000).

It was also about this time that I lucked into the opportunity to start a journal. Offered the invitation to start a journal on aging and death, I was able to persuade a publisher to make that two: one journal for aging, the other death. There was a lot more to aging than death, I suggested, and it was not only the aged who were touched by death. From a moment of casual happenstance we were able to launch both journals simultaneously in 1970: *The International Journal of Aging & Human Development,* and *Omega, Journal of Death and Dying.* The existing gerontological journals at that time were invaluable, but not especially adventuresome. *IJAHD* was intended to be more open, more on the edge. There was no peer-reviewed journal devoted to the broad range of death-related issues at that time, so the need here was obvious. Richard A. Kalish, social psychologist and close friend, had worked with me in producing a mimeographed give-away publication called *Omega* years before. He agreed to serve as editor of *Omega,* but "had it up to here" with the frustrations and pressures of a new publication and decided to go back to having a real life. I took over as editor of *Omega* on a temporary basis, along with similar responsibilities for *IJAHD.* These temporary arrangements continued until 1999 when I slipped out of academe and persuaded two stalwart people to take the editorial reins. Having read more manuscripts than I would care to count, I must have learned something from them in all these years.

It was the launching of these new journals that led to my most direct involvement in the civil rights ferment. I thought it would be useful to devote an issue of *IJAHD* to Black aging, a topic that had received very little attention. Hobart Jackson, director of the leading care facility for Black aged, agreed to edit this issue. We soon felt, though, that more action was needed in that direction. A White House Conference on Aging was on the horizon. We gathered some kindred souls and came up with a proposal for a Black House Conference. We did a little of this and a little of that, and "suddenly" the White House Conference added a set of minority issues to the official agenda, and the Senate Select Committee on Aging invited several of us to become consultants for ethnic and racial issues. The Black Caucus on Aging created itself at this time, and now, many years later, is still going strong. This was an invigorating experience in participatory democracy and the opportunity to work with some brilliant, committed, and warm-hearted people I might not have otherwise known.

Another invigorating experience should have turned into complete disaster. I got myself into the dilemma of writing and producing a theatrical event for the city of Detroit (an idle suggestion that somebody actually took seriously). The only way out of it seemed to be getting through it. I wrote, then cast, rehearsed, and acted in an evening's entertainment called, *All Fall Down: A Multi-Media Celebration of Love and Death.* This enterprise had every right—indeed, an obligation—to fail miserably, but somehow it all came together at crunch time for a memorable evening. Having survived this risky shift from academia to theater, I would try my luck again and again. *Why Does the Fireman?,* an existential farce, took the place of my presidential address for the Division of Adult Development & Aging of the American Psychological Association. This proved to be the forerunner of a number of other theatrical pieces, including the opera *Dorian* (music by Herbert Deutsch), an updated revisioning of Oscar Wilde's novel. The libretto for this opera was then incorporated in *Dorian, Graying: Is Youth the Only Thing Worth Having?* (Kastenbaum, 1995a). This unlikely seeming mix of opera, historical analysis, and psychological reflection is one of my continuing attempts to synergize the potentials of sociobehavioral research with the arts and humanities. *Closing Time,* a music drama involving an encounter between an acutely suicidal young man and a chronically suicidal old man, has since been performed, and *American Gothic,* a tale of a Kansas farm family trying to survive the Dust Bowl and the Depression, will soon be on the boards. Other works are in various stages of progress, regress, or stalemate. After some years of theory development it now seems to me the inherent *drama* of life-span development, aging, and death might best repay our attention (Kastenbaum, 1994). With the drama excluded, what we have left is too often a collection of disembodied facts and high-polished and refined numbers that have little bearing on the intense stakes involved in real lives and real deaths.

Forty Years Down the Road

After several years of professoring at the then-new University of Massachusetts at Boston, I returned to the geriatric hospital in which I had stumbled through my ad hoc apprenticeship as a geropsychologist, but this time as the superintendent. Another terrific learning experience awaited me, along with another fine collection of bumps and bruises. My hope of building on the strengths of this facility to develop a new kind of center for care, research, and education had to be set aside in favor of sheer survival. Political and economic forces were running against the continued operation of an aging geriatric facility, yet no viable alternatives were on the horizon. I would succeed to the extent of keeping the hospital open and functioning responsibly, but I could introduce only a few new and limited clinical, educational, and research programs. Singing ''When Irish Eyes Are Smiling'' with Bob Hope and Governor Ed King seemed to have been the single most effective action to keep the hospital going, although, befitting the off-pitchness of my vocalization, I sang very quietly.

I also had the opportunity to help plan and analyze the National Hospice Demonstration Project which, within a few years, would provide the database for making hospice care in the United States a keeper from the federal support standpoint. I would continue my long-term interest in terminal care right up to the present (e.g., Saunders & Kastenbaum, 1997). It has been a privilege to be associated with one of the most redeeming movements in recent social history.

It was off then to Arizona State University where we established an interdisciplinary program on aging and human development. I then moved into the Department of Communication, discovering it to be a virtual miniuniversity of its own with colleagues representing a broad spectrum of disciplines and interests. Naturally, I became even more interested in communication, and some colleagues and students have also taken aging and death to their hearts.

In some ways I have made no progress at all: I still don't understand time, the course of life-span development, the secret of life, the meaning of death, or what exactly constititutes a balk. However, my assumptions about what constitutes ''understanding'' and what kinds of understanding are possible are still changing. I do not need convincing that our *relationship* with our subject matter must be considered in both qualitative and quantitative approaches. As students of the human condition we have the opportunity to be (though imperfectly) both inside and outside our subject matter. We also have the opportunity to cherish the individual, the situation, and their fleeting but decisive relationship, but also the general flow of people through situations. Integrating what we know and guess into one meaningful framework is the challenge. If there is a trick to meeting this challenge, it will have something to do with the kind of person we have been making of ourself.

In thinking these kinds of thoughts, I try many little experiments, some empirical, some more in that realm we may decry as fantasy or welcome as imagination. These efforts have been including such topics as the future of death (Kastenbaum, 1997), the philosophical assumptions behind death education and counseling (Kastenbaum, 1995b), our constructions of the deathbed scene (Kastenbaum, 1993b; Kastenbaum & Normand, 1990, Kastenbaum & Thuell, 1995), the psychological and political mind-set of ''encrusted elders'' (Kastenbaum, 1993a), and the attempt to create a future elder self to save one's present youthful self (Kastenbaum, 1989–1992).

My career line has not conformed to a tidy profile and still shows no signs of doing so. For what it's worth, I do feel a connection not only among the various projects of my adult life, but also with my early fascination with inquiry, discovery, and the limits of things (including the limits of our ability to understand the limits).

I have not seen a baby dinosaur emerge from a sewer grating for some time now, but I would not be surprised to be surprised by life in any place at any hour. Dr. Paleg's skull is entitled to speak for itself, I think, or to remain silent.

References

Alexander, S. (1920). *Space, time, and deity* (2 vols.) London: Macmillan.

Bergson, H. (1912). *Time and free will.* London: George Allen.

Boring, E. G. (1929, 1949). *A history of experimental psychology.* New York: Appleton-Century-Croft.

Feifel, H. (1959). (Ed.). *The meaning of death.* New York: McGraw-Hill.

Frank, L. K. (1939). Time perspectives. *Journal of Social Philosophy, 4,* 293–312.

Kastenbaum, R. (1959). Time and death in adolescence. In H. Feifel (Ed.), *The meaning of death* (pp. 99–113). New York: McGraw-Hill.

Kastenbaum, R. (1963). The reluctant therapist. *Geriatrics, 18,* 296–301.

Kastenbaum, R. (1972, 1992, 2000). *The psychology of death.* New York: Springer.

Kastenbaum, R. (1977, 1998). *Death, society, and human experience* (6th ed.). Boston: Allyn & Bacon.

Kastenbaum, R. (1989). Old men created by young artists: Time transcendence in Tennyson & Picasso. *International Journal on Aging and Human Development, 28,* 81–109.

Kastenbaum, R. (1992). Creativity: A lifespan approach. In T. Cole, D. Van Tassel, & R. Kastenbaum (Eds.), *Handbook of humanities and aging* (pp. 285–306). New York: Springer.

Kastenbaum, R. (1993a). Encrusted elders: Arizona and the political spirit of postmodern aging. In T. R. Cole, W. A. Achenbaum, P. L. Jakobi, & R. Kastenbaum (Eds.), *Voices and visions in gerontology* (pp. 160–183). New York: Springer.

Kastenbaum, R. (1993b). Is there an ideal deathbed scene? In I. B. Corless, B. B. Germino, & M. Pittman (Eds.), *Dying, death, and bereavement* (pp. 109–122). Boston: Jones & Bartlett.

Kastenbaum, R. (1994). *Defining acts: Aging as drama.* New York: Baywood.

Kastenbaum, R. (1995a). *Dorian, graying: Is youth the only thing worth having?* New York: Baywood.

Kastenbaum, R. (1995b). What should we expect from philosophy? In J. Kaufmann (Ed.), *Awareness of mortality* (pp. 3–16). New York: Baywood.

Kastenbaum, R. (1996). The cave at the end of the world: How the unknowing studied the unknowable. In M. R. Marrens (Ed.), *The Developmental Psychologists* (pp. 289–310). New York: McGraw-Hill.

Kastenbaum, R. (1997). The future of death. In S. Strack (Ed.), *Death and the quest for meaning* (pp. 361–380). New York: Jason Aronson.

Kastenbaum, R., & Normand, C. (1990). Deathbed scenes as imagined by the young and experienced by the old. *Death Studies, 14,* 201–218.

Kastenbaum, R., & Thuell, S. (1995). Cookies baking, coffee brewing: Toward a contextual theory of dying. *Omega, Journal of Death and Dying, 31,* 169–180.

LeShan, L. L. (1952). Time orientation and social class. *Journal of Abnormal & Social Psychology, 47,* 589–592.

Reichenbach, H. (1956). *The Direction of time.* Berkeley: University of California Press.

Saunders, C., & Kastenbaum, R. (1997). (Eds.). *Hospice care on the international scene.* New York: Springer.

Weisman, A. D., & Kastenbaum, R. (1968). *The psychological autopsy: A study of the terminal phase of life.* New York: Behavioral Publications.

Chapter 13
ON BECOMING MORE GENERAL WITH AGE

Nathan Kogan

Childhood and Precollege Years

I am preparing this final revision of my autobiography in Paris, where I am spending the current semester on a sabbatical leave. Approximately 30 years ago, I lived and worked here for a year and a half, and had acquired sufficient fluency to offer lectures on my research in French. Through disuse, however, the acquired capacity to speak and comprehend a foreign language slips away. Relearning the language at age 71 does not proceed as efficiently as it did 30 years earlier. I stand in envy of the fluency of my wife, who is working at UNESCO, and of my younger daughter, who is enrolled in a French lycée.

Viewed in the context of a successful academic career, the sense of inadequacy one feels when floundering in a foreign language is a truly sobering and humbling experience. I am forced back to my childhood to find any sort of parallel. As is probably the case for preadolescent boys almost everywhere, participation in sports is exceedingly important, and I certainly shared that value. As hard as I tried, however, to excel in baseball, touch football, and gymnastics, I lacked the upper body and arm strength to hit a baseball with power, to launch a long pass in football, and to hang on to an overhead bar in a gymnastic exercise. These deficiencies were immediately apparent to my peers and were cause for personal embarrassment. In much the same way, I am embarrassed when my efforts at communicating in the French language fall short.

Just as my current difficulties with French should be viewed against the background of my career accomplishments, so should my childhood athletic inadequacies be placed in the context of my broader childhood experience. My parents, Jewish immigrants from eastern Europe, established a retail jewelry business in Bethlehem, a steel town in eastern

I must offer special notes of thanks to the people who contributed so much to making my career a productive one. I need hardly say more about my principal mentors at Harvard, Gordon Allport and Jerome Bruner. My erstwhile collaborator, Michael Wallach, in both temperament and scientific outlook served as a near-perfect complement to me, enabling us to reach heights of productivity over a 10-year period. Effective collaboration is a delicate matter that cannot be forced. Thus, it was evident after our years of satisfying collaboration ended that both of us had to go our separate ways. I owe a special debt to Sam Messick who helped to create the kind of ambience in the ETS Research Division in which I could prosper. Finally, I am indebted to the numerous graduate students in the Psychology Department of the New School who, over the years, became my research assistants. They are the coauthors of many of my articles and often served as a source of inspiration. Before my arrival at the New School, I worked with other professionals and postdocs whom I have also credited with coauthor status. The pursuit of research is very much a team effort, and I have been especially fortunate in the choice of individuals who have been part of my team.

Pennsylvania. I grew up in the shadow of the Bethlehem Steel works along with most of my age peers, many of whom were also the offspring of immigrant parents. Many of these parents brought with them the anti-Semitic attitudes they had acquired in Europe, and these attitudes in turn were transmitted to their children. As one of a handful of Jewish children in my elementary school, I had to endure much verbal abuse. Ironically, it was during this period—the mid-1930s—when the Nazi campaign against the Jews was gathering steam. Obviously what I endured, though emotionally upsetting, was quite mild in comparison with what was to come throughout Europe.

Consistent with that aspect of my childhood, my elementary school experience on the whole was basically an unhappy one. The authoritarian practices of the school along with the prevalence of corporal punishment for largely minor infractions yielded an environment largely governed by threat and fear. The school authorities were able to implement these policies with impunity, given relatively uneducated immigrant parents who could not conceive of challenging the system. It should also be kept in mind that the Pennsylvania requirement for a teaching license at that time consisted of two years of postsecondary education in a teacher-training institution, hardly the type of instruction likely to generate inspired teachers.

Did my childhood offer any compensatory pleasures? Academic learning posed no problem for me. Despite my athletic shortcomings, I recall enjoyable hours spent on playing fields, where performance mattered more than did ethnic identity. But a special source of gratification was provided by my participation in my parents' business from an early age. As a preadolescent, I accompanied my parents on trips to New York City to buy merchandise from jewelry wholesalers who were astonished at how much I had learned about the nature of the business at so young an age. By the age of 8 or 9, I was doing minor watch and jewelry repair and writing business letters to wholesalers. I actually began to wait on customers at a time when my head barely cleared the display cases. During the Christmas shopping season, my assistance was virtually indispensable. By contrast, my younger sister remained completely detached from the business throughout her life.

As I entered adolescence, my involvement in my parents' small business continued, though with a growing ambivalence. There were so many ways in which I felt the business could be improved, but my parents were unresponsive to almost all of my suggestions— from the aesthetic (making the outdoor window display more attractive) to the interpersonal (treating customers in a more considerate manner). With the arrival of World War II, and the resultant scarcity of civilian merchandise, my father would recondition old clocks, for example, and sell them at inflated prices—an activity that offended my ethical sense. I nourished the fantasy of gaining control of the business and forcing my parents into retirement. As I approached high school graduation, another jewelry store in a choice location in the town was going out of business and its owner approached my parents with the opportunity to buy it. I pleaded with them to do it in the expectation that I could eventually take it over and make a success of it. My parents were not risk takers, however, and the deal was never sealed.

Another factor in the equation concerned my parents' strong conviction that I was destined to be more than a jewelry store proprietor. They were well aware of my academic success in high school and were very gratified to learn that I had earned a partial scholarship at Lehigh University. As much as I wanted to rescue my parents' business, I knew they would not really relinquish control, and to pass up a university scholarship would have been a foolish act. As events turned out, after World War II ended, my parents moved their store to the periphery of the business section with the result that days went by without a customer in sight. It was painful to watch my father pacing the store and glancing outside for hours at a time. It had become apparent that there was little choice but to sell the business. By that time, I was already in graduate school, and any desire I once had to become a small-town business proprietor had long since vanished.

College and Army Years

When I entered Lehigh University at the age of 17, it was evident that I could squeeze in no more than three semesters of study before induction into military service via the draft. I was advised to pursue an engineering program (Lehigh's major strength at the time) on the grounds that it would prove useful to me in the army. Contributing to this advice was the fact that I had performed well in basic science courses in high school. Although I obtained B-level grades in Lehigh's engineering courses, it had become clear to me that I would not pursue engineering as a future career. I simply did not find mechanics, engineering drawing, and chemical qualitative analysis, among other similar topics, especially interesting. Nevertheless, on completion of my army basic training, I was assigned to the Army Specialized Training Program at North Carolina State University for further training in electrical engineering. I actually expressed a preference for the Japanese language program at the University of Minnesota, but with a prior year of engineering study in my background, my fate was sealed.

The nine months of additional engineering study at North Carolina State left me totally disenchanted and in search of other potential career options. V-E day arrived and V-J day was imminent, but I had close to a year of army service remaining. It was important that I used the time constructively to select a major area for completion of my bachelor's degree. Harking back to my earlier fondness for geography (taught by the one elementary-school teacher toward whom I felt some positive attachment), I contemplated the study of international relations as a prelude to entering the Foreign Service. Somewhere along the line, however, I was given the false impression that the Foreign Service demanded an independent income, and that seemed to be an insuperable obstacle. Ironically, my wife, Katherine, is the daughter of a former American career ambassador to Poland, the Soviet Union, and West Germany (Walter J. Stoessel). That is about as close as I was able to get to the Foreign Service.

Let me return now to the second year of my two years of army service. The army was making correspondence courses available to its personnel, and I decided to take advantage of the opportunity. But which of the numerous course offerings should I choose? For some time I had known about an older first cousin, Leonard Kogan, who had earned a psychology PhD at the University of Rochester and acquired a reputation as an outstanding statistician and research methodologist. In my family's eyes, he was the very model of a successful professional. This was enough of an incentive for me to find out what the field was all about. I subscribed to an introductory psychology correspondence course and soon became hooked. The field held a special appeal for me because it would allow the opportunity to use my scientific and quantitative skills with the focus on people rather than on electrical power and electronics.

With psychology as my intended field of concentration, I made a concerted effort to transfer to another institution from Lehigh University. Essentially, I did not wish to return to the declining fortunes of my parents' business. But I had no choice; as the massive numbers of veterans descended on colleges and universities at the war's end, there was little room for transfer students. Accordingly, I returned to Lehigh to major in psychology and was informed by the chair of the department (on his becoming aware of my engineering background) that I would have little difficulty with the prescribed courses. He was right; my grade performance moved from its previous B-level in engineering to A-level in psychology. Whether this reflects the greater difficulty of engineering or the stronger motivation that I brought to psychology study has to remain a moot point.

Although I was doing very well academically (graduating summa cum laude and with a Phi Beta Kappa key), the two postarmy years to the BA were emotionally wrenching. I had essentially given up on the possibility of reviving my parents' jewelry business, but I could not avoid involvement by virtue of living at home. Whatever personal independence I had gained living away from home in the army was threatened by an overcontrolling mother. With hindsight, I realize that I should have moved into a dormitory on my postarmy return to Lehigh. Given the support offered by the G.I. bill, living away from home would have been financially feasible. Apart from distancing myself from the emotional maelstrom of my family, such a move would also have permitted stronger bonds to form with undergraduate classmates. One of the major regrets of my life is the lack of a complete full-blooded undergraduate experience.

The Lehigh Psychology Department in the mid-1940s consisted of four faculty members. Given the university's engineering emphasis, industrial psychology was well represented, but courses covered the full gamut of psychology specialties at the time. With the small number of faculty, comprehensive coverage of the discipline of psychology placed a heavy teaching burden on each faculty member. I cannot recall much research activity taking place, nor was a research-based honors thesis required for graduation. Classes were small, however, permitting the faculty to become well acquainted with the few psychology majors. They obviously wrote highly favorable letters of recommendation for me, for I was accepted by several top graduate schools. With my interests gravitating toward social-personality psychology, the choice of Harvard seemed sensible on the basis of the specialty areas of its faculty. Furthermore, over and beyond two additional years of G.I. bill eligibility, Harvard offered me modest scholarship assistance.

Graduate School Years

When I entered Harvard's Department of Social Relations in the fall of 1948, one of the department's major missions was to produce an integrated social science encompassing sociology, social anthropology, and large sections of psychology. The primary figures in this movement were the sociologist Talcott Parsons, the anthropologist Clyde Kluckhohn, and the psychologist Henry Murray. As an undergraduate psychology major at Lehigh University, I had taken one sociology course and had not been exposed to anthropology at all. Much of the effort during my first graduate year was devoted to mastery of the new vocabulary needed to build an integrated social science theory. Quite frankly, this noble aim did not engage me, and I began to have serious doubts about my capacity to survive a program that seemed incompatible with my career goals in psychology.

By the second year, the situation had changed quite dramatically. I worked as a research assistant in Richard Solomon's laboratory, where he was conducting avoidance learning studies with dogs. This was the period when learning theory dominated experimental psychology, and it became a major focus of my thinking as I systematically constructed a file containing every avoidance learning study published up to that point in time. I actually opted for learning theory as my special topic on the PhD qualifying examination.

My enchantment with learning theory, however, did not continue beyond my second year. I was not taken with the idea of pursuing a career as an animal psychologist—what seemed a likely fate if I were to undertake a doctoral dissertation on avoidance learning. By the third year, I had completely shifted gears. At this time, Jerome Bruner had launched the research that came to be known as "The New Look" in perception. In due course, my dissertation was cast in "The New Look" paradigm. In addition, there was another major source of influence on my work at this time. Although Gordon Allport is best known for his contributions to personality psychology, he also had an abiding interest in the study of attitudes. In the early 1950s, he turned his attention to issues of racial and religious prejudice and discrimination, and in 1954 he published what came to be known as a classic in the field, *The Nature of Prejudice.* As a student in Professor Allport's seminar in the early 1950s, I became familiar with *The Authoritarian Personality* and eventually blended it with "The New Look" in perception in formulating my dissertation topic on the link between authoritarianism and repression.

It can be readily seen that my graduate training was completely lacking in any exposure to gerontological or even to broader developmental issues. Piaget's writings had not yet begun to penetrate American academic psychology, and the geropsychological research of the time (what little there was of it) had not made any impact on the Harvard Social Relations Department in the late 1940s through the early 1950s. To the best of my knowledge, geropsychology has never gained a foothold at Harvard, but child-focused developmental psychology became a dominant force with such luminaries as Roger Brown, Jerome Bruner, Jerome Kagan, Lawrence Kohlberg, and Sheldon White.

Before moving on to my postdoctoral years, I should say a few words about the changes in my personal life. With the move to Harvard, I had finally put my parents' business concerns behind me. On the few occasions when I visited them in Bethlehem, it was their declining health that became my primary concern. Following the all-male environment of the army and Lehigh (which only later became coed), I finally found myself in a situation where it was possible to meet and socialize with women. As a high-school student, I was too socially awkward to interact comfortably with girls. The Harvard environment offered the first opportunity to develop the interpersonal side of my life with female peers. Of course, I developed strong friendships with male peers as well. But the confidence building came with the discovery that I could date women who actually looked forward to seeing me again. These were the 1950s, however, a period that did not encourage the acquisition of sexual experience. Perhaps this contributed to an unfortunate choice in my first wife. Despite the birth of my older daughter, I endured a dozen years of incompatibility that finally culminated in a legal separation and divorce in the mid-1970s. I refused, however, to permit this personal anguish to cripple my productivity. Indeed, my work offered the personal satisfaction that at least partially compensated for the stresses associated with my life at home.

Harvard also offered me the opportunity to reengage with sports. I became a devotee of squash racquets, an activity that I pursued well into middle age. I also became a modestly competent tennis player. Somewhat later, with the encouragement of my wife, Katherine, I began to enjoy long-distance trail hiking in mountain regions and the countryside in New York State and New England. She has played a major role in guiding me toward a more balanced life of work and play that includes a healthy dose of physical activity.

Early Postdoctoral Years

After earning the PhD in 1954, I stayed on at Harvard in a postdoctoral capacity for three additional years, dividing my time between institutional research for the Harvard administration and social-psychological research on person perception in the Harvard Laboratory of Social Relations sponsored by the Group Psychology Branch of the Office of Naval Research. In the latter case, eight journal articles jointly published with Renato Tagiuri or Jerome Bruner appeared between 1955 and 1960 in a diversity of journals. All of this is prelude, of course, to my move into geropsychological work in 1957. At that time, a gerontological research and service unit—the Age Center of New England—had been established in Boston by Hugh and Natalie Cabot, and I accepted a position as research coordinator for a two-year period. It became my job to recruit investigators throughout the greater Boston area who might have interests in seeking federal grant funds for research making use of the center's pool of approximately 500 elderly adult volunteers. My level of success in this task was modest at best, but fortunately my affiliation with the center offered the opportunity to embark on some research of my own.

One might well ask why I did not seek a tenure-track academic position at this stage of my career. First of all, I remained attached to the Boston-Cambridge area and in fact retained my postdoctoral research appointment at Harvard. Second, the opportunity to gain a foothold in a relatively unexplored field proved exceptionally attractive. I envisioned a publication track record that would inevitably be of use to me later when the time came to seek a tenure-track position. Third, I anticipated a fruitful collaboration with my erstwhile colleague Michael Wallach, an anticipation that was realized many times over. Fourth, I was not particularly motivated to embark on teaching at that point in my career. In sum, the decision to move to the Age Center is one that I have never regretted.

With my fund of social-psychological knowledge about attitudes toward racial and religious minorities, I felt that it should be possible to apply this information to what one investigator at that time called the "quasi-minority of the aged." A thorough search of the available literature on the topic yielded two names that loomed large—Jacob Tuckman and Irving Lorge. These two psychologists dominated the field of geropsychological belief-attitude studies in the 1950s, and unless one could demonstrate inadequacies in their work, there would have been little point in pushing such research further. Those familiar with my work know that I found the Tuckman-Lorge studies faulty in several respects.

In an effort to improve on the state of affairs at the time, I set out to build a new instrument that would remedy most of the shortcomings in the Tuckman-Lorge approach. At the time of its publication, the Kogan (1961) "Attitudes Toward Old People" (OP) Scale offered a fairly reliable, strictly attitudinal scale that controlled for acquiescent response tendencies through the use of items in matched pairs (i.e., of comparable content but worded in opposite positive versus negative terms). Ever since its publication more than 35 years ago, there has been a steady stream of requests for permission to use the OP Scale in research and evaluation contexts. Many of these requests come from nursing researchers and students who wish to study the impact of training programs designed to enhance the favorability of nurses' attitudes toward elderly patients. Although the OP Scale continues to attract new users, I make no claim that it represents a final word in attitudinal assessment in its domain. Indeed, I will later explain why I now have serious doubts about the wisdom and efficacy of attitude-scale methodology.

The construction of the OP Scale could be described as the centerpiece of my early geropsychological research, but a number of other approaches were also explored. Attitude scales provide for each respondent a number on a continuum extending from positive to negative. This represents useful information, but such scores hardly begin to do justice to the qualitative aspects of beliefs and attitudes. Accordingly, my colleagues (P. Golde and F. C. Shelton) and I built sentence-completion instruments in which sentence stems referring to the needs, fears, wishes, and sources of gratification of elderly persons had to be completed by respondents. Responses were categorized and compared with those generated for "people-in-general."

Still another approach to assessing attitudes was based on my previous experience in person-perception research at Harvard. Rather than ask the individual to respond to the generalized class of older people, why not have him or her respond to a sketch of a particular person, young or old, and possibly varying in other characteristics as well? One can readily ask respondents to make personality trait inferences, including among these some of the well-worn aging stereotypes (e.g., absent-minded, dogmatic, cautious, and, of course, on the positive side, wise and serene). An initial experiment along these lines appeared in published form with Shelton as coauthor in 1960. The next study to use the person-perception approach with young versus old targets appeared 12 years later. It is evident that our work on this topic was years ahead of its time, but I was pleased that the study was included in the Kite and Johnson (1988) meta-analysis of the research on attitudes toward younger and older adults. From the early 1970s to the present day, the person-perception application to aging has flourished, though it may now be called social cognition, and different theoretical schemes are employed.

Still another approach to the study of attitudes and beliefs became available with the development of Charles Osgood's semantic differential. Together with my collaborator, Michael Wallach (about whom I shall say more later), we published in 1961 the first geropsychological study to take advantage of this new measurement tool. A diversity of age-relevant concepts (e.g., retirement, future, middle age, older people, death) were presented to samples of male and female younger and older adults for rating on a set of bipolar adjective scales. The semantic differential did not begin to receive wider application in the field of aging until the construction eight years later of the Rosencranz-McNevin Aging Semantic Differential.

During the period of my association with the Age Center of New England, I was able to acquire a set of passport photographs from a local photography studio. The photos represented male and female individuals ranging in age from late adolescence through advanced old age. At the time, I was aware of studies that used photos to study young children's awareness of and attitudes toward different racial groups. There were no empirical studies examining children's awareness of and affective feelings toward age differences in adults. Accordingly, in 1961 my colleagues (J. W. Stephens and F. C. Shelton) and I conducted a study using 4- to 6-year-old children who were asked to rank-order separate sets of male and female photos by age and to express their degree of liking for each of the photos. Approximately eight years passed before the publication of another article on children's age perceptions as the research took on a distinctly Piagetian flavor with investigators inquiring into the role of bodily size and physiognomic cues in young children's inferences about age.

Earlier, I made reference to Michael Wallach, my collaborator on the semantic-differential study. Mike and I overlapped in our affiliation with the Age Center of New England. Both of us had been Harvard graduate students in psychology, and we had both been strongly influenced by Jerome Bruner. In due course, Mike Wallach and I addressed the issue of the possible relation between the implicit risk-regulatory processes in categorical judgment tasks (an issue that concerned Professor Bruner and his associates) and the explicit forms of risk taking represented by decision-making tasks. We carried out a study comparing younger and older men and women on both kinds of tasks and reported a pattern of significant age differences in confidence and extremity of judgment and in explicit levels of risk taking on the Choice-Dilemmas questionnaire (CDQ) (Wallach & Kogan, 1961). The CDQ proved to be a popular instrument in the study of risk taking and cautiousness in the elderly.

In sum, the time spent at the Age Center of New England proved to be one of the most prolific periods in my research career. New assessment methods were devised or applied to geropsychological problems—attitude scaling, the sentence completion technique, the semantic differential, person-perception methodology, and photo ratings by young children. Most surprising in all of this is the length of time it took geropsychology to catch up with many of these new developments (anywhere from 8 to 12 years). All of this testifies to the importance of the zeitgeist in influencing the kind of research that is carried out.

These time lags were less evident in the case of my collaborative research with Mike Wallach on age differences in risk taking. As indicated earlier, the CDQ proved to be highly popular and in short order became the focus of further empirical work in the late 1960s by Jack Botwinick (as summarized in his *Aging and Behavior* textbooks). Although both Mike and I left the Age Center in 1959—he moving to MIT and me moving to the Research Division of Educational Testing Service (ETS) in Princeton—our collaboration continued for an additional 10 years. The forthcoming decade of the 1960s proved to be exceedingly productive for both of us.

Ten Years Doing Other Things

By the spring of 1959, it had become quite clear to me that the time had come to seek an academic or research position with the prospect of eventual tenure. I was particularly intrigued by the position available in the Research Division of ETS because it offered the opportunity to continue my engagement with research without the distraction of teaching. Further, it appeared that ETS was willing to support basic research in psychology that had little connection with its primary testing operations. I was aware of the strong psychometric orientation of the ETS research staff at the time, an orientation in which I had not been systematically trained, but I viewed this as an opportunity to acquire new methodological skills.

My first year in the ETS Research Division was not a particularly happy one. My group leader, John Hemphill, was working on the development of "in-basket" techniques (i.e., the simulation of the kinds of items that a business manager or executive might find accumulated in his or her in-basket on a particular day). The respondent's handling of these materials was then scored on a wide range of categories and dimensions. There was nothing in my background that prepared me for this kind of applied research. With the growing feeling that the work was not compatible with my strong preference for conceptually driven research, I began to give serious thought to seeking another position. Fortunately, Samuel Messick, the head of the Personality Research Group, became aware of my plight and a personnel transfer was arranged whereby a member of that group shifted to a more appropriate placement in John Hemphill's unit, and I shifted over to Sam Messick's group. From that point forward, I felt secure in the knowledge that I could make a significant contribution to the mission of the ETS Research Division.

The first year at ETS was not a total loss, for it did offer me the opportunity to draft several of the geropsychological papers published in the early 1960s that were based on Age Center data. Although supportive of a broad band of psychological research, the atmosphere in the ETS Research Division was not particularly conducive to the study of gero-psychological issues. With the support of grants from the National Science Foundation (NSF), Mike Wallach (now at Duke University) and I continued our collaborative work on risk-taking behavior at both the individual and group level. I was able to obtain a visiting lectureship at Princeton University and, as a consequence, gained access to the laboratory facilities essential for carrying out individual and small-group studies of risk-taking behavior. Also around this time, Mike Wallach and I embarked on our joint research on the creativity–intelligence distinction, culminating in the book *Modes of Thinking in Young Children* (1965).

During this period, Sam Messick had been awarded a large National Institute of Mental Health (NIMH) grant to study individual differences in cognitive controls and cognitive styles. I collaborated with Sam on that aspect of the project with which I was most familiar—styles of categorization and conceptualization—and several joint publications emerged from that effort.

At some point during the 1965–1966 academic year, I met the eminent French social psychologist Serge Moscovici, who was spending that year at the Institute for Advanced Study in Princeton. We talked about some of our mutual interests in group decision making, and he invited me to come to Paris in the fall of 1966 to join him at the École Pratique des Hautes Études for a year. During this period, I was supervising the doctoral dissertation research of Helmut Lamm, a German student in the Princeton University Psychology Department, who had accepted a position in the Institut für Sozialwissenschaft at the University of Mannheim in West Germany (under Professor Martin Irle's direction). It became evident that I would have the opportunity to pursue transnational research on group decision making in France and Germany. I drafted a proposal to conduct such research there, and it was funded by the Advanced Research Projects Agency in the Defense Department. Several published studies with French and German collaborators emerged from this work.

In February 1968, I returned to ETS. As much as I enjoyed the research ambience there, it soon became clear that I could not remain at ETS much longer. Although I had an academic connection at Princeton University, fundamental personnel changes were taking place in the Psychology Department that made future access to students and research facilities quite unlikely. In addition, my first marriage had disintegrated to the point where I no longer felt comfortable living in Princeton. The time was ripe for a change, and when I was offered a tenured professorship in the Graduate Faculty of the New School for Social Research, I decided to accept it.

The Return to Academia

Against my better judgment, I agreed to assume the chairmanship of the Psychology Department on my arrival in the fall of 1969. It could best be described as baptism under fire. The 1969–1970 academic year was distinguished by the ongoing crisis of the Vietnam War and the critical events of the secret Cambodian bombing and the Kent State shootings. In May 1970, our building was taken over by a radical group of students, and the end of the academic year was completely disrupted. The university eventually recovered from this event, and I went on to complete my three-year term as chair. In due course, I served two additional terms as chair (11 years in all). In retrospect, I consider those to be self-sacrificial years. My research and writing suffered as I devoted hours to administrative work that carried heavy responsibilities without commensurate power or influence.

It was not until 1972 that I began to think seriously about gerontological issues again. I really cannot say what lured me back into the geropsychological fold. Perhaps, after a decade of research with children and young adults, I yearned to extend my work across the life span. No doubt, the invitation to participate in the West Virginia Life-Span Conference in 1972 served as an impetus, for it forced me to think about the life-span implications of my work on cognitive styles and creativity (Kogan, 1973).

There were other inducements to pull me back to the geropsychological enterprise. The Gerontological Society chose to hold its annual convention in Puerto Rico in December 1972, and I found it hard to resist renewing acquaintanceships in that locale at that time of year. Attendance at that meeting signaled my renewed interest in geropsychological issues and eventually led to invitations to submit chapters to edited volumes. When 1977 came into view, the time seemed particularly appropriate for a close look at the attitude-belief area to see how much progress had been made and to possibly encourage promising new directions. Accordingly, I organized a symposium on the issue for the Gerontological Society meeting that year in San Francisco. The year 1977 was of special significance because it marked the 25th anniversary of the first Tuckman-Lorge publication. If one were going to take stock, the quarter-century mark seemed to be an especially appropriate time.

My stance in the symposium paper was quite critical of research in the field, and I directed some of this criticism against my own earlier work. The symposium paper raised the possibility that attitude scales might have prompted us to ask the wrong question. Instead of asking about the degree of positivity or negativity in views held about older people, one might more profitably ask how differentiated is a respondent's view of older persons. It will be granted that investigators have made efforts to differentiate subcategories of older persons (e.g., Neugarten's distinction between the young-old and the old-old and the contribution of Marjorie Brewer and her associates in distinguishing among elder statesmen, grandmotherly types, and senior citizens using photo-sorting techniques). Whether this latter threefold classification is the best we can hope for remains a moot issue, but there is little doubt that the work described helps to account for some of the contradictory qualities (e.g., serene and irritable) that are assigned to the elderly. As yet, however, we know little about individual variation in the extent of differentiation of elderly targets.

Midcareer Integrative Reviews of Selected Topics

The advance of scientific knowledge within any domain requires both well-designed empirical studies and the eventual integration of the publications that derive from such studies. Over the course of the decade extending from the late 1970s to the 1980s, I undertook a series of reviews, some at the request of editors compiling chapters for books. Some of these reviews concerned selected topics within geropsychology and were intended to offer readers an indication of the nature of the work accomplished up to that time. Three major reviews were prepared in the areas of age stereotyping, cognitive styles in aging, and personality and aging. Briefer reviews on the topics of person perception, cautiousness, and creativity were prepared for the first edition of the *Encyclopedia of Aging* edited by Maddox.

Age Stereotyping

In the course of preparing my review article (Kogan, 1979) on this topic, I closely examined aging-relevant research that fit within the person-perception paradigm to see whether any firm conclusions could be drawn. I confronted a pattern of contradictions. Some studies reported prevalent stereotyping of older people; other studies found no evidence whatsoever for age stereotyping. How could one account for these discrepancies? For all of the relevant research published through 1978, I was able to discern a pattern that could conceivably account for the presence or absence of stereotyping in the experimental contexts used. Relevant research published after 1978 did not completely conform to the pattern, and hence I had to modify my ideas somewhat. The new ideas were presented at a conference organized by Simon Fraser University and subsequently published in the conference proceedings (Kogan, 1982b).

Before 1979, in all of the studies where respondents made comparative judgments of target persons of varying age, age stereotyping was prevalent. By contrast, where respondents judged a single target person—whether older or younger—age stereotyping was conspicuously absent. Younger and older targets were judged similarly. Hence, the critical determinant proved to be the use of multiple-judgment (within subjects) versus single-judgment (between subjects) experimental designs. This difference did not come as a complete surprise, for a comparable effect emerged in the research that my colleague F. C. Shelton and I conducted almost two decades earlier. Further, the foregoing design contrast proved to be a significant contributor to the level of age stereotyping in the Kite and Johnson (1988) meta-analysis.

As indicated earlier, the pattern changed somewhat by 1979 in the face of further published studies, and the sharp distinction between the impact of multiple versus single-judgment designs could no longer be sustained in its simple one-dimensional form. In the pre-1979 studies, investigators employed sketches of stimulus persons that offered a modest amount of affectively neutral information (e.g., marital status, number of children, common hobbies and interests). Of course, sketches do not have to be written at this middle level. One can strip the stimulus down to the bare essential of age—a 25-year-old versus a 65-year-old. Such impoverishment of stimulus information not surprisingly evokes negative stereotyping even in the single-judgment case for the obvious reason that the judge is only given age information to work with.

At the other extreme, one can enrich the sketch provided of the stimulus person. This important contrast between relatively impoverished versus enriched stimulus targets as delineated in Kogan (1982b) became acknowledged as the specific versus general variable in the Kite and Johnson (1988) meta-analysis. General (impoverished) stimulus-person descriptions generated more negative age stereotyping than did specific (enriched) descriptions.

Where does all of this leave us? It is apparent that the experimenter can manipulate the stimulus information provided about younger and older persons so as to obtain virtually any pattern desired—no stereotyping, negative stereotyping, or positive stereotyping. Note further that the specific negative and positive stereotypes favored are not random. There clearly are culturally acquired stereotypes about age that people assimilate and invoke dependent on the situational context. The fact remains, however, that stereotypes do not have to be invoked; age information may well be of lesser salience relative to more prominent demographic attributes such as occupation, education, and gender. In general, age stereotypes are latent in people's minds by virtue of the common cognitive currency of our culture but only become manifest under particular circumstances. The nature of those circumstances could well become the focus of a research project in its own right.

Cognitive Styles in Aging

As I have already indicated, theory and research on cognitive styles have been a major focus of my work throughout my career. My orientation to the topic has been developmental with a primary focus on the childhood and adolescent years. However, I had prepared an earlier review on cognitive styles from a life-span perspective (Kogan, 1973), and when Gordon Finley as a coeditor of the *Review of Human Development* asked whether I would prepare an updated review (Kogan, 1982a), I agreed to do it. At the time the review was prepared, cognitive styles could hardly be described as a hot topic in geropsychology. One found a limited number of adult age-comparative studies on the cognitive styles of reflection-impulsivity and field independence-dependence. On the other hand, interest in conceptualizing styles from an age-comparative perspective, an area in which I had conducted empirical work, was a flourishing geropsychological enterprise, much of it inspired by the work of Nancy Denney.

The principal issue at the time concerned the meaning of the observed shift from early to late adulthood in preference for thematic, complementary groupings. Given young children's preference for such groupings, a cognitive-regression interpretation received serious consideration. It soon became apparent, however, that the alternative mode of grouping by similarity (abstraction) is influenced by Western schooling, and that complementary grouping reflects the contiguity and functional relatedness of objects in the real world. From such a perspective, older adults long removed from the required abstraction of formal schooling, were in fact performing in a natural, adaptive manner in the studies at issue.

Although the reflection-impulsivity research initially instigated by Jerome Kagan and his associates and the field independence-dependence research initially formulated by Herman Witkin and his associates were generating much empirical research and theoretical controversy in the late 1970s and early 1980s, they have virtually disappeared from the current psychological literature. Indeed, in Sternberg (1997), the foregoing work is assigned to a historical chapter describing older approaches in the field. This shift whereby psychological constructs once popular become consigned to a ''historical dustbin'' is deserving of the attention of the historically inclined members of our discipline. Within the past dozen years, I participated in two conferences on the topic of cognitive styles, both leading to published volumes to which I contributed chapters. My final contribution to the topic in 1994 took the form of an entry in the *Encyclopedia of Human Intelligence* edited by Robert Sternberg. These relatively recent contributions demonstrate how I have experienced both extremes. As indicated previously, my earliest contributions predated further development in certain areas by a decade (plus or minus two years). In stark contrast, my final publications on cognitive styles appeared after the topic had more or less run its course. Ironically, the impact of being too far ahead of or behind the times is more or less the same—general neglect by the relevant potential audience. Nevertheless, the investigator ahead of his or her time can at least take personal satisfaction in observing the field as it catches up. No such pleasure is available to the investigator writing about topics that have peaked and moved out of view. There can only be regrets at having stuck with a topic area just a bit too long.

Personality and Aging

With Gordon Allport as a major mentor during my graduate-school years, it is hardly surprising that I have maintained a firm interest in personality over the course of my career. I have taught the basic graduate-level personality course at the New School for almost 20 years and have done my best to follow the personality journals diligently over that time. I have also served as an associate editor of the *Personality and Social Psychology Bulletin* and on the editorial boards of the *Journal of Personality* and the *Review of Personality and Social Psychology.*

Accordingly, when I was invited to write the ''Personality and Aging'' chapter (Kogan, 1990) for the third edition of the *Handbook of the Psychology of Aging,* it represented an opportunity to apply my knowledge of the personality area to life-span and geropsychological issues. With few exceptions, contemporary research on personality and aging is distinguished by the use of longitudinal designs. At the time that I prepared the *Handbook* review, the major longitudinal projects collecting personality information had been functioning for periods of up to 50 years. Although I had never been personally involved with these long-term projects (extending over most of the life span), I found it very challenging to attempt an integration of longitudinal studies that had employed a diversity of personality measuring instruments.

Late Career Focus

My interest in sex and gender issues can be traced back to the early and middle stages of my career as I explored sex differences in cognitive styles, risk-taking dispositions, and creativity. In the late 1970s, I embarked on further research on age categorization based on photos, and much to my surprise I found pervasive gender differences lurking in the data. In broad terms, the research pointed to a stronger youth bias in judgments by males relative to judgments by females and greater salience of the age dimension on the part of male in comparison to female respondents.

My interpretation of these gender effects leaned heavily on Susan Sontag's sociocultural ideas regarding a "double standard of aging." Within that perspective, the Western media have promoted the more rapid aging of women relative to men through such means as age-based gender biases in the choice of models in advertisements and in the choice of male and female actors for film roles. This type of sociocultural interpretation seemed quite congenial to me at the time and for several years thereafter, even though no effort was made to locate a culture where the double standard was absent.

As the late 1980s came into view, I began to notice the emergence of a new field assigned the label of "evolutionary psychology." This new field suddenly began to talk about such issues as sex differences in age-of-mate preferences and how these differences were influenced by chronological age differences. Data obtained from a diversity of countries and across different historical periods pointed to striking cross-cultural and cross-time uniformities. It had become evident to me that a new way of thinking about geropsychological issues of age and gender might prove fruitful. Accordingly, my colleague and I drafted a paper using both old and new data on gender differences in age cognitions and preferences that explicitly compared an evolutionary and sociocultural approach to explaining the outcomes (Kogan & Mills, 1992). As might be expected, it is not possible to declare one or the other approach "a winner." What evolutionary psychology offers is a source of new hypotheses and a new way of looking at issues and problems in the geropsychological area. If recent issues of geropsychological journals are any sort of guide, investigators in the field have shown virtually no interest in what is already one of the more active and controversial areas within the discipline of psychology.

In regard to my own current research, my students and I have returned to the issue of age norms, a topic first studied by Bernice Neugarten and her colleagues more than 30 years ago, with the goal of exploring gender effects from an evolutionary perspective. Three Gerontological Society of America (GSA) poster presentations have taken place, and it is my intent to gather all of this material together for a multistudy article.

Epilogue

When asked to identify what kind of psychologist I am, I generally reply that I am a general psychologist. I have acquired Fellow status in APA Divisions 1, 7, 8, 9, 10, 15, and the AAAS, in addition to Division 20 and the GSA, and hence it should be apparent why it is difficult to label myself as anything other than a general psychologist.

Review of research proposals and journal manuscripts has occupied large chunks of my time. For four years I was a member of the Personality and Cognition Research Review Committee of NIMH, and I have participated on an ad hoc basis for numerous granting agencies. I have served on the editorial boards of the major aging and gerontological journals: *Psychology and Aging,* the *Journal of Gerontology,* and *The Gerontologist.* Earlier, I referred to my editorial role on personality and social psychology journals.

Reflecting my ongoing interest in the study of metaphor, I continue to serve on the editorial board of *Metaphor and Symbol*. In addition, I have had a long-term abiding interest in the arts and have served on the editorial board of *Empirical Studies in the Arts* since that journal's inception in 1983. My involvement in that area is further reflected by my election as president of APA Division 10 (Psychology and the Arts) on two occasions (1980–1981, 1989–1990), and as APA Council Representative from that division. I should also note my service on the executive committee of Division 20 as a member at large (1978–1980).

With my growing interest in evolutionary psychology and my older interests in the arts, it was merely a matter of time before I attempted to bridge these domains. I have published two papers seeking the origin of the performing and visual arts in our evolutionary history (Kogan, 1994, 1997). Geropsychology obviously focuses on ontogenesis—the stability and change of living organisms over time. Linking aesthetics and evolutionary theory has forced me to think about phylogenesis—that is, what changes took place over millennia in the human species that could account for the emergence of the arts. In the course of this work, I have had to familiarize myself with the writings of historians, archeologists, and evolutionary biologists. To accomplish my goals rather late in my career, I have found it essential to become more interdisciplinary. Recall how aversive such an interdisciplinary orientation struck me during my first year of graduate study. At a time when one is trying to establish a disciplinary identification, interdisciplinary discussion can be a distraction. Once such an identification has been achieved, one can respond to and even deliberately choose to work on problems and issues that extend beyond the boundaries of scientific psychology.

Summary

Given my humble beginning as the son of poorly educated immigrant parents, I have clearly led an upwardly mobile life. It would have been easy to stumble along the way, but fortunately I never completely lost control of my life and I was incessantly driven by an urge toward competence and achievement. I recognized that continued involvement in the jewelry business meant parental control, that a career as a less-than-talented engineer represented a path to oblivion, and that the guilt that permeated my first marriage eventually had to be lifted if I expected to gain control over the emotional side of my life.

Of course, favorable external events and circumstances have helped to smooth the path for me. The G.I. bill vastly reduced the financial strain of my later undergraduate and early graduate years. Meeting the woman who became my second wife made it possible for me to experience an emotionally balanced life—to love as well as to work. The choices of Harvard, the Age Center, ETS, and the New School's Graduate Faculty were positive in the extent to which they offered supportive research or scholarly environments. If given the opportunity to choose again, I might well depart the Graduate Faculty rather than hang on as I have for close to 30 years. Over that period, I turned down several job offers that appear more attractive in retrospect than seemed to be the case at the time. Regrettably, for one reason or another, they fell short of my fantasy of an ideal institutional environment. The inertial tendency to stay put was simply too strong.

References

Kite, M. E., & Johnson, B. T. (1988). Attitudes toward older and younger adults: A meta-analysis. *Psychology and Aging, 3,* 233–234.

Kogan, N. (1961). Attitudes toward old people: The development of a scale and an examination of correlates. *Journal of Abnormal and Social Psychology, 62,* 44–54.

Kogan, N. (1973). Creativity and cognitive style: A life-span perspective. In P. B. Baltes & K. W. Schaie (Eds.), *Life-span developmental psychology: Personality and socialization.* New York: Academic Press.

Kogan, N. (1979). Beliefs, attitudes, and stereotypes about old people: A new look at some old issues. *Research on Aging, 1,* 11–36.

Kogan, N. (1982a). Cognitive styles in older adults. In T. Field, A. Houston, H. Quay, L. Troll, & G. Finley (Eds.), *Review of human development* (pp. 586–601). New York: Wiley.

Kogan, N. (1982b). Research on beliefs and attitudes about old people. In G. M. Gutman (Ed.), *Canada's changing age structure* (pp. 299–332). Burnaby, BC: Simon Fraser University Publications.

Kogan, N. (1990). Personality and aging. In J. E. Birren & K. W. Schaie (Eds.), *Handbook of the psychology of aging* (3rd ed., pp. 330–346). San Diego, CA: Academic Press.

Kogan, N. (1994). On aesthetics and its origins: Some psychobiological and evolutionary considerations. *Social Research, 61,* 139–165.

Kogan, N. (1997). Reflections on aesthetics and evolution. *Critical Review, 11,* 193–210.

Kogan, N., & Mills, M. (1992). Gender influences on age cognitions and preferences: sociocultural or sociobiological? *Psychology and Aging, 7,* 98–106.

Sternberg, R. J. (1997). *Thinking styles.* New York: Cambridge University Press.

Wallach, M. A., & Kogan, N. (1961). Aspects of judgment and decision-making: Interrelationships and changes with age. *Behavioral Science, 6,* 23–36.

Wallach, M. A., & Kogan, N. (1965). *Modes of Thinking in Young Children.* New York: Academic Press.

Chapter 14
REASON AND EMOTION ACROSS THE LIFE SPAN:
A Personal View

Gisela Labouvie-Vief

I am standing near the ocean, on sandy terrain overgrown with wild grasses and sloping toward the beach on the right. Before me is a house of yellow brick, lit up by a brilliant sun. It is a two-story structure, with a roof sloping over the front porch, a cozy, inviting kind of a house, though I am a little startled at the yellow color of the brick. As I watch the house, my mother arrives for a visit. She looks radiant and alive, a big smile on her face. She tells me how beautiful my house is, how excited she is to visit me. She adds, "I'm so sorry I did not come visit earlier—I had no idea!"

Throughout my adult life, I have kept a journal of my dreams. Though I always had a love of things logical and formal, dreams and art seemed to form a counterweight, a force insisting on balance and integration. Not surprisingly, as I pondered how to approach writing an autobiographical statement, I had the dream of the yellow house.

Dreams, like the story I was invited to tell in this chapter, have many layers. There is a personal layer—restoring to me, a woman at midlife, a radiant, gold-lit "mother," a new sense of my feminine self, symbolized by the house in the dream. There is, second, a more collective and cultural layer. That layer speaks of the role of the "mother," the generalized feminine, and how this role has emerged and is being transformed in the subcultures and cultures that have sustained me. At the juncture of these two layers lives the story I am asked to address: the story of a woman's dream, and one that has been lived largely in academia.

In their study *The Seasons of a Man's Life* (Levinson, Darrow, Klein, Levinson, & McKee, 1978), Levinson and colleagues detail transformations in men's dreams as they progress from young to middle adulthood. "Dream" in this instance does not refer to the kind of night dream I just related, but rather to the vision or general plan that structures our life's course, even if that plan is rather intuitive and only partly conscious. And, because it is often more a sense of direction toward which we feel drawn than a clear plan, I believe that our nights' dreams help define that direction by commenting on deviations from that course and applauding as we return to the main pathway.

Levinson claimed that he was speaking of universal matters when he described the evolution of the life dream. To an extent I think he is correct. Women do have their dreams

I gratefully acknowledge the input of Jason Allaire, Jan Calle, Lois Robbins, and Karen Sutton. Comments by James E. Birren and Johannes Schroots have helped improve this version of the chapter.

that over time become transformed just as those of men do. But the realization of the dream of a woman is, I think, subject to somewhat different forces, as women traditionally have not been encouraged to dream of the heroic and extraverted journeys men claimed for themselves. Rather, their journeys often form a counter landscape to the extraverted heroism of the traditionally masculine part. Thus, the particular way in which my own dream took shape is influenced by no theme more profoundly than that of gender, of my being a woman.

In my own life, the way that life dream took shape through my role in academia and the study of adulthood and later life interweaves several story lines. While these lines have some chronological significance, they present themes—forces and tensions—that were present at all life stages, though they might take on particular significance at one time but recede into the background at another. The first of those story lines deals with the core of my life dream and involves a tension between two ways of viewing the world—the "masculine" and "feminine" or, as I refer to them more generally in my book *Psyche and Eros* (Labouvie-Vief, 1994), between logos and mythos. The second line deals with the unique way in which that dream has been shaped through the rewards and disappointments of academic work and its environment. Of those, the single most important is the result of being a woman in academia at a particular point of historical time and in a particular culture (a culture where, as Kant had it, women gifted with the powers of logic and analysis "might as well even grow a beard"; see Labouvie-Vief, 1994, p. 220). Both lines involve joys and upheavals that ultimately caused the dream to be reborn in a richer, more fully integrated form—a form that offers the unique reward of a blending of personal and academic quests.

Between Two Houses

I am in San Francisco, standing in front of two houses. Both are old Victorian buildings that have been remodeled. The one on the right has been completely overhauled, all of the nooks and crannies and gingerbread decor removed to give it clean, modern lines. It is painted a light orange. I think what a pity it is that the house has been so modernized, most of the charm taken away and done over to yield a somewhat bleak appearance. Inside the house, a party is going on: People I know are conversing and walking around—some of them very important and powerful. I notice a hallway with a staircase. As I watch, the stairs to the upper floor rise and close access to the second floor. I have an ominous, fearful feeling of being shut out of something significant and vital. Just then I turn to the house on the left. It also has been remodeled, but none of the charm has been removed. Next to the door there is a small round towerlike structure. The house is covered with shingled siding and painted in beautiful rose, magenta, and purple tones. It looks enchanting and inviting, and I turn to the male companion on my left and say, "Let's go in!"

Growing Up German

A core theme that permeates my own life story is a certain tension between two loves of mine: that for formal elegance and precision and that for the expressive, if sometimes diffuse, depth of music, art, and myth. One of them is symbolized as the house of logos in the dream, the house where powerful men walk, carrying on important conversation that excludes me. The other house is the house of mythos with its enchanting colors and textures.

Formal matters appealed to me as a result of a natural inclination, because from childhood on my mind was drawn to the symmetry and certainty one could achieve by engaging in formal and rational analysis. But from an early age, I was also friendly with the muses. My love for art and music was nurtured by a rich cultural tradition that made these important parts of my daily life. The castles and churches that spotted the countryside were filled with murals, wall hangings, frescoes, paintings, and other priceless art. Opera, symphony, and chamber music were ever present in school and religious observances. Many hours of my childhood and adolescence were spent drawing or painting or playing the violin or recorder. I also acquired an early love of myth; indeed, one of the first books I ever bought with my own money was a dictionary of myth.

Yet I recognized early that these two modes of looking at the world do not always relate comfortably. On one hand, my parents put their own faith in matters academic and thought of the products of the mythos mode as more of a luxury than a necessity. Also, my cultural heritage had asserted an oppositional relationship between the rational and the nonrational, and it was the rational that usually won out. Yet it seemed to me from an early age that the less formal voice of mythos often provided a comment on the more formal one of logos by displaying through metaphor and image the very intentions denied by the other voice. In fact, it seemed to me that logos often amounted to a defensive attitude to which we resort when we need to create clarity and beauty in the midst of chaos. And both my culture and my family had placed me in the middle of chaos.

I was born in Germany in the fall of 1945, after World War II ended, and the postwar scene forms part of my earliest memories. Not that I had personally experienced war, or that war was an adult concept to me. Rather I picked up a sense of its devastation from the constant fear of the adults surrounding me. For example, whenever a fire or police siren sounded, I sensed the terror they evoked in individuals who had been used to gathering their loved ones and running to bunkers to escape bombing. Food was scarce, and I remember my mother and grandmother setting out early in the day with a shopping tote or two and returning later with perhaps a bag of potatoes or a small amount of meat or fish. Then there also was the physical landscape, scattered with the remnants of houses that were destroyed during the war. Wall remnants were standing here and there, with signs of habitation such as doors, stairs, or windows still attached.

When I grew older, a darker and even much more ominous tone was added to the difficulty of daily existence: the gradual realization that the weight I had sensed from my earliest days was not just a matter of daily survival struggles but of a barely nameable event. My grandmother would tell me that the bedroom set of beautiful mahogany wood had belonged to Jewish friends, a family my grandfather had helped cross the border to France to help them escape the Nazis. When I asked her why this family fled and if she still visited these friends, she told that they had died after the Nazis invaded France. Similar fragments of stories slowly exposed that something indescribably awful had happened during the war, although it was extremely difficult to know just what had happened. To a child's mind, the Nazi's became something mythical, a bit like the all-pervasive Devil of my Catholic upbringing.

As we grew a little older my siblings and I began to learn concrete details about the war and the Nazis. We wondered about the pervasive silence around us, the difficulty we had getting clear details. Germany was in a state of shock, and there was little public talk about recent history for a decade or two after the war ended. My family remained mostly silent, too, and did not talk much about this, perhaps in an effort to spare us. It was only years later we found out my grandfather and my father had resisted the Nazi regime. Indeed my own godfather, a friend of my father's from their medical school days, had been part of a famous Nazi-resistance group, the White Rose.

To know about such facts would have been a source of comfort and pride to us and boosted a sense of moral well-being. Instead, we grew up under a sense of pervasive shame that lay on many German people—the sense of having a basic moral fault, of being German, of being part of a culture that had systematically arranged for the destruction of so many human lives. This notion of collective guilt shaped the identity of Germans of my generation. In some, it raised moral sensibility; in others, it supported a defensive moral complacency.

In my own case, these experiences sharpened the moral differentiation between the power of social systems and more general laws that might transcend the voice of social power. It always seemed a matter of urgency to me that I behave according to a vision dictated not by my immediate needs for self-protection, but that was oriented by a vision of the dignity, rights, and values of every living being. Years later, this understanding supported friendships with individuals—such as Klaus Riegel and Larry Kohlberg—who were able to help me affirm that vision and who understood that it arose out of a deep need for self-integrity rather than an "unfeminine" stubbornness!

To return to my youth: To live in such a climate was a challenge for a child and adolescent, and that challenge was all the more formidable because my parents—themselves having been raised in a culture that was adult centered and quite authoritarian and that thought of children as unruly creatures who should be taught to value reason and obedience as early as possible—were the first in their respective families to get advanced degrees and to become physicians. Thus the real difficulty of surviving in a postwar era, the horrors of the war, and a deeply rooted sense that breaking with a tradition of farming and small business had left them unmoored from tradition—all of these factors added to a pervasive sense of threat and the notion that we must demonstrate superior academic achievement to "make it," to give proof of our worth.

All of these circumstances led me to give up mythos interests when I entered adolescence. I had, as already mentioned, bought a dictionary of mythology and set out to trace the stories of the different divinities—mostly Greek—whose tales had been a part of my upbringing. It was briefly thereafter, at about the age of 12, that I began to find the study of myth very confusing. Stories that previously had clung to my memory suddenly were difficult to understand or remember, and I was so disturbed that I laid this passion of mine to rest, at least for the time being. I also turned away from another passion: drawing and painting. These activities had somehow become vaguely fearful. It was only years later that I seemed to understand the reason for this (see Labouvie-Vief, 1994). Whether in myth or in art (or, for that matter, in real life), it seemed to me that the roles of men and women were displayed in profoundly asymmetric ways. The men were the ones that ventured out, became heroes, ruled the heavens. But the women were the ones confined to passivity and suffering.

As Gilligan (Brown & Gilligan, 1992) suggested, such experiences give girls growing up the sense that something is wrong with them. Reading Freud, to whom I turned because of my love of myth, sharpened the vague sense of feeling that something was wrong with my being a woman. But reading Freud felt akin to an assault on my femininity. I felt rather alarmed and was less and less able to follow his arguments, whose objective tone cataloged an endless array of women's deficiencies. So when I began to study psychology, I found the writings of Piaget much more palatable, giving as they did a clear and cool picture of the mind.

Coming to the United States

Eventually I left Germany and entered the life-span developmental program at West Virginia University in 1968. I did so with the encouragement and sponsorship of Paul Baltes, whom I had met at the University of Saarbruecken, where I received a prediploma in 1966. The life-span program at West Virginia University, headed by Warner Schaie, then was the focal point for exploring developmental themes beyond youth and across the entire life course. With its sense of mission, this program was an exciting one for graduate students who could feel at the center of something new and vital. With a series of conferences exploring the meanings of development through life, I and my fellow graduate students were part of the exploration of new frontiers in theoretical development. There, I met many of the people who had shaped the study of development in later life and from whose work I drew tremendous inspiration. Jim Birren, Klaus Riegel, Bernice Neugarten, Larry Kohlberg, Lillian Troll, Larry Goulet, John Nesselroade—all of these were individuals I first met while at West Virginia University, and all of them have been important in shaping my work. In addition to these "teachers," I also met my fellow students, themselves noted gerotologists, Harvey Sterns, Bill Hoyer, and Joseph Fitzgerald.

Coming to West Virginia and the United States created in me a sense of being relieved from a heavy burden of formal authority structures I had begun to experience as stifling in my German training. The attitude of American universities seemed to me open, friendly, and extraverted. Of course, I was to learn over the years that this extraversion itself was a cultural attitude that concealed its own rigidities. Nevertheless, for the time being I felt like breathing the fresh air that comes from a system that is less heavily weighted with tradition and hierarchical lines of authority.

At the same time, with its strong emphasis on cognition and methodology, the West Virginia program suited my logos needs and laid the basis for my early work in academia. I worked on issues of ontogenetic and generational change with Warner Schaie. With Baltes, I began to work on theoretical issues. I especially became interested in issues of plasticity in later life and collaborated on research on training cognitive skills in the elderly.

The work at West Virginia defined my entry into an academic career when I joined the Department of Educational Psychology at the University of Wisconsin in 1972. There, with the help of Judy Gonda, I performed my original study on training in fluid abilities in the elderly. This work, opposing as it did the old dogma of inevitable and irreversible decline in the elderly, helped support the sense of mission that drives many a young assistant professor. I received a good deal of attention, because the notion that intellectual skills in the elderly could be trained was nothing short of astonishing two or three decades ago. This brought excitement to the early stages of my career.

Yet even in these early stages of my career, a more introverted streak of mine began to assert itself. I began to wonder about the motivation for my research. I have always experienced a tension between doing work that is politically convenient and work that impresses me as psychologically important and true (even if it goes counter to established "wisdom"). So it struck me that, while my research created a lot of excitement on the conference circle, the participants who helped me produce the results that were so controversial in the professional arena confronted me with their own doubts about the presuppositions of my work. They were not at all convinced that they wanted to be trained to improve on intelligence tests, and they surely did not feel that such improvements would add to their lives. This argumentative engagement in the purposes of my research struck me as a singularly intelligent attitude to take, and the dream ripened in me to make the study of that form of intelligence the focus of my future career. More and more it seemed to me that our ways of looking at the elderly often had arisen out of an assessment methodology that had been uniquely established in the context of young people. What was missing in this was a developmental account of adulthood—an attempt to trace how youthful competencies evolved through different life stages to give each period of life its own unique character that was not reducible to earlier life stages, even though it evolved from them.

Perhaps with some felicity, a grant I had submitted on intellectual training in older adults was not funded—although it did result in a recommendation that I apply for a Career Development Award. So I decided to devote my career to the question to the relationship between cognition and emotion in adulthood—the questions that had occupied me and that had ripened in me over some time. This investigation became my major endeavor after I took on the position of an associate professor and came to Wayne State University in 1976, following a four-year stint as an assistant professor at the University of Wisconsin. In some ways, this move signaled my entry into another house.

Creating in the Dark

I am in the house of a woman, a dark, poorly lit structure that has a somewhat shabby appearance. I watch her work around in her kitchen, and I notice a dark room behind the kitchen. It looks like a basement room or garage, with no windows or doors. Nor does it have lights, and overall it looks like the kind of ill-lit room one might encounter in a Dickens novel. In this dark room, the woman has arranged a number of flowerpots along the back wall. Each of these pots contains a luscious strawberry plant with beautiful, luminous strawberries, brilliantly red. When I return a day or so later all of the strawberries have disappeared, and only some wilted gray leaves and stems are left. I learn that a man has entered the basement and stolen the strawberries, leaving nothing but the devastating sight of wilted stuff.

Growing Strawberries

Coming to Detroit in some ways was akin to entering the house of mythos—the second of the houses in the dream I related in the previous section. As I was to learn, that house offered many opportunities for growth and development. But it also confronted me with a darker side—symbolized by the predator in the current dream—that created an enormous tension.

At Wayne State University, I immediately began the line of work that would constitute the mainstay of my career for the past 20 years or so: To work on an account of adulthood that was informed by developmental theory. Most studies of adulthood and later life at the time simply consisted of comparisons of younger and older individuals, often invidiously selected from college populations in the case of the younger individuals and nursing home residents in the case of the older. It seemed to me that results from this research often were uninterpretable, because they deleted a series of links that define continuities from one life stage to another.

My training in the University of West Virginia only had a minor component of traditional developmental theory, and so I set myself the goal of reading some of the classic developmental theorists, such as Freud, Piaget, and Werner. I was fortunate, in this effort, to have as a colleague Sandor Brent, who himself had Heinz Werner as a mentor. I remember a moment when we were discussing theoretical interpretations of aging and rigidity, and Sandy stated that it was necessary to differentiate *rigidity* from *stability*. Comments such as those catalyzed—for me—a new and exciting way of thinking.

Of the theories I studied, that of Piaget was the most appealing to me. In those readings I saw a vast layout of theoretical problems that I had not been aware Piaget had tackled. In fact, it seemed to me that behind the popularization of Piaget's work was another, even much richer thinker who outlined a dynamic, systems-oriented view of development, from biological to psychological levels. Reading Piaget I was introduced to the writings of such individuals as Bertalanffy, himself an early systems theorist of biological systems. Yet comparing Piagetian writings with those of Freud and Werner, it also was obvious that Piaget had left out a whole arena of psychological problems. In his adolescence, Piaget himself had written a novel detailing the inner struggle of a young man with diverse ways of knowing: one of reason and scientific thinking and the other based on faith and the processes I was to refer to as mythos. Just as in the novel, Piaget resolved that struggle by turning toward reason rather than offering a full integration of the two modes. Thus the socially situated dimensions of our thought and behavior, the emotions that are related to our social nature, and the symbolic, mythic, and ritualistic dimensions of development all were given rather short shrift. I sensed that this deletion of a major pole of the mind was the reason his theory had not been able to offer a rich, or even useful, account of adulthood and later life. To fill in that deletion, I began to immerse myself in a study of writings in mythology and Jungian psychology.

I applied to the National Institute on Aging for a Career Development Award, and after I received that award I was freed to write a series of papers that systematically dealt with these issues. Beginning in 1980, I published a series of papers (e.g., Labouvie-Vief, 1980, 1981, 1982, 1984) in which I proposed that mid- and later life development involved integrating these devalued dimensions of thought into rational structures. The core assumption here was that reason and emotion never acted independently. Yet the relationship could be modulated and deformed as censorship was imposed on either side of the reason-emotion equation. Specifically in childhood, this synchrony became displaced because the process of growing up in a complex culture required that the individuals temporarily repress many needs and emotions and accommodate to prevailing social rules, norms, and institutions. In contrast, I suggested, adulthood brought the chance for a reintegration of those modes. Thus adults would be able to develop a way of reasoning that blended what was experienced as deeply significant personally with the needs for formal coherence and structure—a marriage of mythos and logos often celebrated as the ''divine marriage'' in myth and story (Labouvie-Vief, 1994).

A core theoretical theme in this endeavor hinged on the notion that issues of growth and adaptation or decline and regression could only be meaningfully resolved within a theoretical structure that was clearly explicated. Within such a structure, the decline of some processes (such as the child's interest in detail, or the loss of brain cells in the earliest stages of development) actually would be interpreted as *growth,* while some increases (e.g., of contextually based responses in later life) would be interpreted as overall functional *decline.* Thus I proposed, more generally, that development involves a series of trade-off functions, in which growth and decline, or gain and loss, were interwoven or trade-off processes.

In a similar way, I proposed that a decline in mythos-based thinking that appears to characterize early development is in the service of the growth at the collective level and in fact is part and parcel of development in a culture. We trade in individual creativity and self-expression for cultural efficiency, but in the process we also become alienated to an extent from our own self-core. I suggested adulthood brings a corrective movement where we realign with that mythos-based self-core.

In these writings, I also spelled out a number of implications of such a view for the study of mature adulthood and aging. In that view, integrating logos and mythos were essential not just for the well-being of the individual but for his or her relation to the culture at large. As adults became less concerned with individual survival needs, they could take on the roles of elder, teachers, mentors, wise counselors, and guardians of the deeper, more permanent aspects of the human condition.

From these general proposals, I also began to build a comprehensive research program (see Labouvie-Vief, 1997). The general program was oriented by the notion that, as individuals grow older, they reorganize their sense of what is true and real. From the extraverted structures of youth—structures such as those as Piaget had outlined—they begin to explore the inner and psychological dimensions of reality. In a first step, I examined how individuals of different developmental stages looked at issues of certainty and truth. Working with Cynthia Adams and Julie Hakim-Larson, we showed that young adolescents often think that truth is inherent in a problem. For example, when probed about their inferencing from single logical problems, these youngsters would say, ''but it says so right there!''). More mature adults, on the other hand, became succinctly aware of two decision problems, one related to ''logic'' and the other to ''intuition'' or ''everyday experience.'' In many adults, these decision systems were experienced as an opposition, but some adults maintained that correct or true answers could only be ascertained if one attempted to integrate the two decision systems.

With its epistemological cast, this exploratory research was not easy to market to funding agencies or journal editors. So as a next step we began to explore how this shift from a literal to an interpretive style was expressed in processing specific information. For example, we had individuals read, or listen to, stories that had a strong symbolic-interpretive dimension, such as fairy tales and fables. Cynthia Adams joined me in that effort, and in a series of studies we showed that with such materials older individuals were more likely to focus on psychological interpretations than on specific details of the story.

Responses such as these suggested to me that older individuals admitted to their realm of evidence the very arena of mythos thinking that is deleted in early life. This movement from taking information as something outer and objective to something that has inner and subjective components is part of a much more general trend in development. The outward movement is particularly important in youth, because it allows the individual to master the rules that permit him or her to regulate behavior in accordance with cultural dictates. However, it also carries with it certain disadvantages. In the process of adaptation to outer reality, the youth needs to be able to dissociate impersonal, abstract, and collective meanings from ones that are more concrete and personal and that carry a great deal of organismic significance. In contrast to the outward movement, adulthood may bring a compensatory movement inward. A focus on inner dynamics, on private experience, and on rich organismic experience and emotive content now comes to the fore—a process Gutmann refers to as the ''greening'' of the mature individual.

One domain in which this process is significant is the area of emotions. After I received a grant from the National Institute on Aging, I set out, with the help of Fredda Blanchard-Fields, Julie Hakim-Larson, and Marlene DeVoe, to examine that topic more specifically. Our research showed that from youth to later adulthood, individuals reorganize their understanding of emotions from one that is outer oriented and ''objective'' to one that is personal and expressive. Thus, whereas younger adults are more likely to experience emotions as something troubling and difficult to control, the older individuals were able to accept that emotions have a lawful regularity of their own that may oppose our concepts about them, these individuals evolved means of control that allowed a fuller acknowledgment of their emotional experience.

In more recent research, Lucinda Orwoll, Manfred Diehl, and a set of gifted graduate and undergraduate students helped me extend the emotion work to individuals' conceptualizations of themselves and their parents. Younger or less mature individuals framed self and others in terms of a conventional perspective. Self and others were described in terms of an abstract set of role expectations. That perspective becomes transformed in older or more mature adults. At that more developed level, the institutional values become susceptible to doubt and criticism; for example, such values can be ''carried too far.'' Instead, a dynamic perspective evolves in which descriptions of self and others convey in vivid language the unique and evolving experience of individuals within the context of their particular life histories. Lives now are understood in the context of multiple frames—cultural, social, and psychological, for example. There is keen insight into the psychological dynamics that are at the root of human diversity, yet an understanding that such diversity appears to be regulated by a common human heritage.

Encounters With the "Predator"

Of all the influences on my work in adult and late life development, probably no single set of factors was as important as my being a woman in a field that had been virtually dominated by men. Psychology had been a collective voice of men who had created one particular language of development—one rather devaluing of the processes of emotion, intuition, and expressiveness that often were belittled as feminine. Beginning to explore the role of this language of mythos therefore was a difficult and often heart-wrenching endeavor. I felt involved in a combat between these two languages and their voices in me. One, the "feminine" voice, seemed to direct my work and give it vitality. The other, "masculine" voice was a severe and sometimes tyrannical critic that easily crowded out the sense that I had embarked on an important and vital direction. That feeling slowly crystallized into words when I read Virginia Woolf's *A Room of One's Own*.

Much as Woolf, when she set out to study the role of women in literary writings, had wondered about the why of so many masculine voices that spoke of women's inability for deep and original thinking and for intellectual leadership, so I began to understand that definite emotions lurked behind the ubiquitous, seemingly rational pronouncements of women as weak in ego processes, poor in rational and moral abilities, and driven by emotions. My own work on emotions had not showed any important gender differences in men's and women's ability to integrate cognitions and emotions—much to my surprise, I confess. Neither had my own experiences in academia suggested that male teachers or colleagues acted more rationally than the women I knew. If anything, it seemed to me that women, being newcomers to the field, saw aspects of it with the new freshness of outsiders. They perceived not only its intellectual excitement; they also tended to see the complicated system of territorial and dominance structures that governed the ways in which individuals were admitted or ruled out of participation.

If there was a single factor in my career that encouraged me to trust my own voice, it was the intellectual companionship of other women. Being able to see these social dimensions of academia not from the youthful and idealizing perspective, as an awesome display of intellectual battle, but rather as a Wittgensteinian language game with its own particular motivations opened a new intellectual world for me. It is no exaggeration when I say that from that point on, my main mentors, real and abstract, became women who themselves had analyzed the role of gender in intellectual history. It was from these encounters—friendships with women colleagues and graduate students, women friends struggling to empower their own voices, and even the writings of women who had lived before me—that I drew the deepest inspiration for my work and encountered a deep affirmation of it. I am especially grateful to the support over the years I had from women such as Joan Robertson, Nancy Datan, Norma Haan, Bernice Neugarten, Ravenna Helson, Marlyne Kilbey, and Carol Magai.

These women helped me see that my inner struggles had many parallels in the outer and political dimensions of the field. I, like many women of my generation, had entered academia with a wide-eyed sense of naivete, hoping that I could prove our intellectual worth by important work. Yet I entered this new world untutored, except for a history of writings that proclaimed our inferior status as thinkers and creators. That history made it very difficult to receive effective mentoring. To begin with, as a woman who had been trained to be pliant and accommodating, the combat and competition of daily institutional life left me stunned: I did not know how to enter it. I had entered academia without advice about how to plan a career, how to encounter competition, how to make a mark. It was an especially painful experience that, when I began to make a mark of my own, my mentors seemed to me to be ambivalent at best. With the wisdom of hindsight, I realize that my tugging at the very foundational language that had marked the beginning of psychological gerontology well might have been construed as a betrayal on my part. Yet as a young woman, I felt eager not to have such terms as *competitive, grandiose,* and *self-centered* or even *egomaniacal* applied to me. Such language had been directed by tradition toward women engaged in creative activity, and I found it applied to me too. Yet it did not sound to me like a compliment in reverse; I did not take it as meaning that I might have the stuff it takes to endure in a career or even thrive in it; rather it seemed the most loathsome and shameful language anybody could apply to me.

This is why I am all the more grateful for Klaus Riegel who, when I visited him a few days before his death, looked at me and said, "Gisela, I know you can do it!" I barely understood what he meant, but the ring of his voice in my mind carried me over many dark moments, thus nourishing the development of my own voice over time. I also was deeply moved by the friendship Larry Kohlberg extended to me. Whenever I made it East, I could count on him to be on call to meet me for dinner and to have a spirited discussion on the philosophical foundations of the tension between reason and emotion.

These women and men encouraged me to search deeper for the creative voice so easily intimidated. Yet paradoxially, it was no less bold than it was easily disturbed, and it asserted itself in dreams, artwork, and even my academic writings. As a result, I withdrew from much of the overt activity of the field and created a more introverted and protected space in which to pursue my work. As part of that endeavor, I set out to explore this inner struggle between the two voices. Most significantly, I had discovered the writings of Carl Gustav Jung, and these writings encouraged me to look for the "logic" of that voice and to embark on a Jungian training analysis. In time, this inner work produced a series of paintings and drawings in which I explored the symbolism that undergirds our ways of thinking about reason and emotions. These paintings began to flow out of me, gradually amplifying and fleshing out my academic writings, which often had been rather abstract and dry. Indeed, it is no exaggeration to say that the integrations I came to write about first were fleshed out not in the medium of academic language but in that of artistic work.

As far as my academic work is concerned, these experiences—supplemented by a wide reading in myth, philosophy, religion, and anthropology—firmed my conviction that the language of mythos, rather than being an inferior language, actually provides a foundational language that enfolded our ways of thinking about reason and emotion, masculinity and femininity. Our usual discourse about the nature of reason and emotion throughout the ages had presented a very distorted picture of the actual workings of these modes (Labouvie-Vief, 1994, 1996). These musings began to reach farther back into time as I began to understand that the myths I had so loved in childhood dealt with those very workings, too powerful and disturbing for a young girl to put into words. The heroic depiction of men in those stories, paired with the self-sacrificing surrender of female protagonists, seemed to me to parallel the very structure of the theories that discussed adulthood primarily in terms of the victory of reason (construed as masculine) over the dark (and feminine) forces of the unconscious. Thus, our discourse about the nature was hopelessly confused with our thinking about gender relationships. And, I felt, a fuller theory of adulthood could be constructed if we looked at the relationship not through the metaphors of competition and combat but through those of cooperative relationships.

The results of this examination led to my book, *Psyche and Eros* (Labouvie-Vief, 1994). In that book, I discussed development not from the perspective of the hero Reason but from the landscape of mythos that thus was ravaged. That structural line was not only evident in stories and myths around the world but also became part and parcel of the structure of our major philosophical and religious systems and finally of our psychological theories of development. Yet, I suggested, a fuller theoretical account of adulthood could be offered by treating the two modes *and* the two genders not as oppositional categories but rather as the evolution of a relationship between two partners. Such a view suggests not only an altered account of gender development and its inherently relational and coconstructed nature. It also asserts that mental activity always consists of the interaction of two modes, both of them potentially rich and complementary aspects of the mind that can develop in tandem. Thus, the metaphor for maturity becomes the dance between two sets of forces, which themselves are theoretically uncoupled from gender.

Making Music

I am taking a cello lesson with my cello teacher. She encourages me to find an accompanist, a pianist with whom I can play cello sonatas. I wonder how to find such a person when I get a phone call from a woman pianist. She asks me to play the Elegy *by Fauré, and she begins playing the piano accompaniment. I join in, a little nervous and insecure at first. But somehow the music supports me, and my tone grows stronger and richer. I move with the melody, which seems to fill my whole being. I am surprised at the flow of rich sound and proud that I am able to play so well. As I play along, the woman gradually phases out her accompaniment, and as she does so, I continue to play the beautiful and haunting melody. When I tell my cello teacher about this experience, she says to me, "And you did not think you could play well!"*

I began to play the cello at the age of 46. I had continued to play the alto recorder throughout my adulthood. But in my mid-40s, I developed a longing for sound that had a deeper resonance and color. I was struck, too, when reading myths around the world, that the flute was often associated with the head and reason. Perhaps by more than accident Apollo and Athena, for example, both were associated with flutes with their heady and bright tones. But according to eastern wisdom, midlife is a time when our energies rebalance and integrate. So the cello seemed to invite me to a new era, and I was eager to accept that invitation.

At this time of my life, my earlier interests are coming full circle. A theme that had formed in my youth and early adulthood had taken on new depth. In my early career, I had understood certain theoretical linkages in a very abstract yet rather intuitive way. I often was told that these early writings are very dense—and indeed they were supported not only by personal experience but by a set of powerful intuitions for which I gradually needed to develop a language. Yet at the current stage of my life, that density is unfolding into a structure that is enriched with personal knowledge and that, in turn, encompasses a plethora of concrete detail about development across the life course.

I am sometimes told that my work often can be somewhat abstract and idealistic. If so, those features were necessary in evolving a map within which to talk about cognition-emotion relationships over the life course. However, even though I do believe that the ideal of cognition-emotion integration is important as a *theoretical standard,* in reality, the next important step is to formulate those mechanisms that cause individuals to deviate from such ideals. Just as in the domain of health, we work with idealized views of health to understand which *deviations* produced realized and nonperfect health states, so I think life-span developmental theory needs to move on to describe how individuals, because they do not live in perfect situations, come to deviate from an ideal pathway.

In my current work, I am applying this notion by examining cultural and familial mechanisms that are related to individuals' coming to adopt mechanisms that are not integrated but rather distorted. For example, one common mechanism of distortion relates to emotion repression, which is known to have negative consequences for psychological and emotional health. Yet such mechanisms may be encouraged by social regulation mechanisms related to asymmetric power distributions, such as those of gender or ethnic minority. Thus, a long exploration of the relation of cognition and emotion to gender and power and, ultimately, health issues important for collective well-being is coming to fruition, and questions I began to ask even in my childhood are beginning to yield important answers.

Following up on the work of Jung and David Gutmann, in *Psyche and Eros* (Labouvie-Vief, 1994) I suggested that women often experience their later life as a "release from interiority." In my current work, I do experience a movement outward, away from the inner explorations that have been the major theme of the building of my career. On a personal perspective, my dreams have begun to applaud. In the cello dream, making music involves the interweaving of two voices, cello and piano—the cello with its feminine curves and its sound that marries melancholy and jubilation, the piano with its powerful and commanding tone. But these "feminine" and "masculine" elements no longer are separate but integrated. As the piano's tone swells and recedes to support the cello, and as the cello takes its own turn, which in time yields to the voice of the piano, the melody weaves these two voices into a single whole. And the dream locates these two voices in a single player, for whom "masculine" and "feminine" no longer are outside forces. Instead, they have moved inward to symbolize the center of the true self.

References

Brown, L. M., & Gilligan, C. (1992). *Meeting at the crossroads: Women's psychology and girls' development.* Cambridge, MA: Harvard University Press.

Labouvie-Vief, G. (1980). Beyond formal operations: Uses and limits of pure logic in life span development. *Human Development, 23,* 141–161.

Labouvie-Vief, G. (1981). Re-active and pro-active aspects of constructivism: A life-span model. In R. M. Lerner & N. A. Busch-Rossnagel (Eds.), *Individuals as producers of their development: A life-span perspective.* New York: Academic Press.

Labouvie-Vief, G. (1982). Dynamic development and mature autonomy: A theoretical prologue. *Human Development, 25,* 161–191.

Labouvie-Vief, G. (1984). Culture, cognition, and mature rationality. In H. W. Reese & K. McCluskey (Eds.), *Life-span developmental psychology: Cohort and historical effects in life span development.* New York: Academic Press.

Labouvie-Vief, G. (1994). *Psyche and eros: Mind and gender in the life course.* New York: Cambridge University Press.

Labouvie-Vief, G. (1996). Emotions, thought, and gender. In C. Matalesta-Magai & S. H. McFadden (Eds.), *Handbook of research on emotions.* New York: Academic Press.

Labouvie-Vief, G. (1997). Cognitive-emotional integration in adulthood. In K. W. Schaie & M. P. Lawton (Eds.), *Annual review of gerontology and geriatrics* (Vol. 17, pp. 206–237). New York: Springer.

Levinson, D. J., Darrow, C. N., Klein, E. B., Levinson, M. H., & McKee, B. (1978). *The seasons of a man's life.* New York: Ballantine.

Chapter 15
CHANCE AND CHOICE MAKE A GOOD LIFE

M. Powell Lawton

The sociologist Harold Wilensky analyzed working lives in terms of "orderly careers" and "disorderly careers" (1961), finding that the orderly type is associated with more favorable personal outcomes and that a cadre of people with orderly careers is essential to the maintenance of the order of society. It is unlikely that there are many geropsychologists of my generation who could qualify for the orderly variety (this book's senior editor being a notable exception). Therefore any reading of this portrayal of my intellectual biography that discerns a grand and organized plan should be immediately revised. It is full of caprice and coincidence. The semblance of orderliness is often exaggerated by an account that is organized chronologically. Perhaps a little more order is possible when continuity of concepts and values is the focus. I shall treat the chronological facts in brief dismissive style and then concentrate on the concepts.

The Chronology

I am a southerner by birth, parentage, and desperate efforts by my family of origin to feed my southern roots. Responding to the economic stresses of the Depression and under their personal protest, my family moved to a Pennsylvania steel town during my public school years. Given this taste of the North, followed by some later unhappy years in the prewar insular and racist city of Atlanta, I could not wait to return to the North and I entered Haverford College in 1941. World War II interrupted, which I spent in civilian public service, the alternative to military service for conscientious objectors. During this time I worked clearing a swamp, working as a psychiatric aide in a mental hospital, and serving as a human guinea pig in a hepatitis B experiment. After the war I finished college and received my doctorate in clinical psychology at Teachers College, Columbia University. I spent a total of about 15 years as a clinician in the Veterans Administration, the Pottstown, Pennsylvania, Mental Health Clinic, and the Norristown, Pennsylvania, State Hospital. My career in gerontology began in 1963 and continues today.

Personal Themes

Threads that have laced together the disordered sections of my life are music and visual aesthetics, personal attachments, and spirituality. That first category is better thought of as *sensorimotor stimulation,* because there is more to it than music and art. My father was a good amateur musician and avid listener. Nothing could have pleased him more than my relatively sudden awakening to the world of music during my middle teens. I played the saxophone and clarinet, with a switch to the oboe when I was 15. The pinnacle of this career came at age 17 when I was a finalist for Leopold Stokowski's Youth Symphony. I wasn't really good enough to become a professional, however. I haven't played since I was about 21, but listening to recorded and live music continues to be my passion. It is important also that, to me, music is different from most of the other arts because it provides stimulation at the megalevel. Music seizes one's entire auditory apparatus and allows no competition. Whether its scale is that of a solo voice, chamber group, symphony, or opera it is totally possessive of the frequency and intensity range of human auditory perception and across the time its performance lasts. A contrast might be made with the visual arts, where varying proportions of the entire visual field may be the focus of attention. A visual aesthetic experience, for example, the tiny detail of a jewel's setting, may command only a small part of the view or, like the view inside a cathedral or across a landscape, may consume the entire field. My preference has been for the largest scale, which gives me all of music, architecture, and geography (but a deficiency in the perception of the nuances required for maximum appreciation of painting and sculpture). A vehicle for appreciation of the visual environment came early in my life in the many travel experiences provided by my parents. My early photo albums show selective emphasis on interesting buildings and topographies. My developmental growth spurt in this type of enjoyment came when I was allowed to walk alone in Pittsburgh (age 12 or so). I walked all possible blocks in the Golden Triangle with a sense of newness in each configuration of buildings, pedestrians, stores, and greenery. To this day, a favorite hobby is to collect new cities or areas; the experience is understandably enjoyable when the cities are great, such as St. Petersburg or Sydney, but it is also enjoyable to scan a new (to me) section of Northeast Philadelphia or a small town like Moodus, Connecticut. Another facet of large-scale environmental experiencing comes when caring for the several acres of land on which we live. It is heavily wooded, hilly, and threatens to return to a scrub-growth and honeysuckle jungle if not persistently tamed. Cutting wood and brush and walking through the changing forest is my type of outdoor work, not small-plot gardening or lawn manicure.

Novelty in this realm of sensorimotor stimulation also contributes strongly to enjoyment. Although I like many types of music, my taste is fixed especially on what appear to me to be relatively neglected masterpieces—music by Schütz, Monteverdi, Berlioz, Janacek, or Weill, for example, or classic musicals of the 1930s. The urge to explore visually and motorically has special rewards in new places or those markedly different from what we're accustomed to.

Personal attachment in my own life has much in common with that of people in general. I knew a great-grandmother and a grandfather well through my early adult life. My parents had a strong sense of family history, which bored me. But they left a legacy of family pictures and documents, which our children value more appropriately than I did, despite their knowing few of the southern cousins who populate Georgia and South Carolina. It was a family of early privilege that was impoverished by the Civil War and that spent the 20th century trying to regain its lost prestige. I think my interest in family was dimmed by the underlying themes of past glory and self-ascribed aristocracy with which the family tree was presented. I try now to reappraise and appreciate the scenario as history. My mother at age 99, now in a nursing home, still comes alive most when she tells stories about people and places from her own childhood.

My wife Fay and I celebrate our 51st anniversary this year. We love to do things together. Having moved through a good part of our own lives already, we enjoy seeing our three children and two grandchildren at work traversing that time line. Our children help us in dealing with some of our unfulfilled dreams by their professions. They are, respectively, a jazz pianist, a photographer and poet, and a painter, talents in one or the other of us that have tended to be overshadowed by competing obligations. Fay's poetry has recently begun to flourish again, however, rewarded by a poetry prize and her first published book. Fay and I both specialize in maintaining a small number of close friendships (mostly from our earlier years) and enjoying a wider circle of good but not close friends. Yet we both experience social overload relatively easily. I see as I write this that in the social realm my preference for the megalevel and for novelty of stimulation doesn't fit at all.

Spirituality is a not-quite-accurate term for a realm where I try to operate but feel least adept. I was from a southern Protestant background. Although my parents were true southerners, each had a streak of rebellion. My mother was impatient with the idiocies of segregation and several times caused consternation on a streetcar by taking a seat beyond the color line. My father was politically conservative but sought out ethnic friends as musical companions and led me to what might be considered unconventional tastes in music and food. Little stood out in my spiritual development until I was 17, when I initiated discussions with ministers and Sunday school teachers about the moral issues in war and violence. That was 1940, and my questions were viewed as curious or outrageous. My mother was totally supportive (my father died around that time) and in fact was very pleased when this concern led me to Haverford because it was a Quaker college. I had never known a Quaker, but I had learned enough about the Quaker social philosophy to find it appealing. I attended silent meeting while in college and became a Quaker shortly thereafter. The silence has always been as meaningful as the action component of Quakerism, but my practice in both arenas falls short enough of my goal to make me wish for a term less idealized than *spirituality.* The values are firm but the flesh is weak. I combat distracting thoughts about gerontology while sitting in the silence of Quaker meetings, and I struggle to counteract creeping racism in my behavior. It seemed easier to find time for action in my youth, as we made family pilgrimages to peace marches and tested real estate markets for fair housing compliance, than in my cluttered later years.

Organizing three personal themes in this manner represents an attempt to impose greater order into my scientific life than is warranted. In the succeeding sections I shall seek intellectual analogues of these themes.

Becoming a Geropsychologist

Becoming a psychologist was the direct result of working at the state mental hospital. The field of mental health was just getting its new post–World War II start, assisted in a very substantial way by social outrage at life in the mental hospitals. The many such units staffed during the war by conscientious objectors were part of this pressure, as were other pioneers such as the newspaper columnist Albert Deutsch and the mental hygiene leader Sidonie Gruenberg. This first occupational thought was certainly an active and reasoned choice of mine, but the two major influences on my future research were the fortuitous result of my returning to Haverford and finding that the main resource for studying psychology was at Bryn Mawr College. The chair, Harry Helson, was already a well-known psychologist. His adaptation-level theory (1964) was just being developed. Although I dutifully read his papers and performed tasks as participant and experimenter for his research, I really didn't see at the time how this perceptual theory could ever have much to do with human mental health. That would come later. The other professor was Donald Mackinnon, who was one of Henry Murray's select circle at Harvard. Mackinnon never published much himself but he had a major influence on the growth of dynamic personality theory at the Institute for Personality Research in Berkeley. Our personality course's textbooks were Murray's *Explorations in Personality* (1938) and Lewin's *Field Theory in Social Science* (1951).

These theoretical orientations faded quickly as I went through graduate school and my period of journeywork in clinical psychology. One of the threads of lifelong continuity of interest came in the form of my dissertation research; it took more than a decade, however, for me to recognize that one of the major themes of my later research had its origin in my dissertation research. At the time, the clinician's route to expertise in personality assessment came through the use of projective techniques such as the Rorschach test. These methods involved analysis of the way personal themes, goals, anxieties, and unconscious fantasies were "projected" onto ambiguous stimuli such as inkblots or indistinct pictures. Psychopathology was indicated, among other signs, by responses of poor resemblance to the object depicted or by amorphousness of form. My own clinical experience and skepticism about the extremes of intrapsychic causal explanations of behavior led me to be cautious in the interpretation of such responses as invariably indicative of inner psychological disorganization. The projective stimuli themselves represented a range of structure, from relatively formless to highly structured. For my doctoral research I constructed a set of projective stimuli that fell on a continuum from high to low structure and tested it on several groups of people representing a range from normality to high pathology. I predicted that the form quality of responses would be affected negatively by *both* poor stimulus structure and psychopathology, which was solidly confirmed (Lawton, 1956). But at no time did I think of Lewin's ecological equation or of Murray's need-press model.

After graduate school, while working as a clinician I did small clinical research studies as time allowed. But it was totally by chance that I received a preview of what the life of a researcher might be. A clinical colleague of mine, Al Goldman, had met the administrator of the Philadelphia Home for Jewish Aged, Arthur Waldman. Waldman's board had given him leave to investigate the possibility of establishing a research component at the Home (now the Philadelphia Geriatric Center [PGC]). Waldman therefore asked Goldman to accompany him to the Third International Congress of Gerontology, hoping to interest Goldman in moving into gerontology. At the last minute, Goldman accepted another job but persuaded Waldman to use the air ticket on me, despite my protest that I knew nothing about aging. I did attend that 1960 congress and met Birren, Busse, Eisdorfer, and Havighurst, among others. I learned a little about aging also, but took several more years to think about research as a career. When I became restive in clinical practice, I contacted Waldman again, among a number of other leads to research positions. The position at PGC had been established, and the search for a scientist had just begun. Still with anxieties about whether gerontology would be able to catch my interest, I accepted the job.

In one important way I had good reason to think it might work. I was clearly expected to perform research that would benefit the lives of older people, a goal that was consistent with the action aspect of the Quaker philosophy. Waldman's expectation that I should generate knowledge useful in application to service issues was thus highly appealing. But once again chance intervened in the form of an opportunity to do research on two service programs of PGC that were at that time in the planning stage: a new congregate housing apartment building for elders and a program for the care of the "mentally impaired aged" (Alzheimer's disease had at that time not become redefined to include the majority of the mentally impaired group). These endeavors determined the direction of my first applied research in aging.

Both innovative programs were created by Art Waldman. His congregate housing and program for dementia were "firsts" in American multicare residential settings for older people, as were other later programs that also received research attention. I am firmly convinced that it is usually clinicians, service deliverers, and policy makers who create inventive new programs. Lucky is the researcher who can maintain a working affiliation with a program-oriented visionary who at the same time respects evidence and empirically derived knowledge, as Waldman did.

Both of these projects led me to the environment and to the cluster of psychologists who at that very time were defining the field of environmental psychology: Robert Sommer, Joachim Wohlwill, Irwin Altman, and the originator, Roger Barker, and his notable students Robert Bechtel, Edwin Willems, and Allen Wicker. The work of Robert Kleemeier (1959) and Frances Carp (1966) preceded me in gerontology. In the process I rediscovered the earlier intellectual thread of environmental psychology that had led me to study the transactions between environmental and personal factors in my dissertation research. Carp's work has and continues to pace me as we search for better integration of environmental and psychological principles.

The housing research yielded gross findings that the move into planned housing offered several benefits to older people. These findings were also the source of what I called the ''environmental docility hypothesis,'' which stated that as the competence of the individual decreased, behavioral and affective outcomes would be increasingly determined by environmental factors. The affirming data relevant to this hypothesis showed that those tenants who were in the best health chose tenant friends from a broad range of locations within the housing, presumably affording them choices made on the basis of positive criteria such as common interests, compatibility, and shared values. Less-healthy tenants were more geographically restricted, choosing as friends next-door and same-floor tenants, in effect greatly constricting their likelihood of achieving their preferences in friendship formation. My research in this area led in turn to several other projects in which I could study large samples of planned housing environments and some of their design features. Design informed by behavioral knowledge was also the focus of our evaluation of the care center for dementia (the Weiss Institute). Although design principles for dementia have advanced considerably since then, the design itself and its postoccupancy evaluation provided models for many later care facilities and their evaluation.

Geropsychology as a Medium for Playing Personal Themes

These early research endeavors may be linked to some of the personal themes. Environmental psychology was a perfect venue for indulging my love of sensory stimulation, novelty, and, in particular, the large-scale environment. Visits to interesting buildings, developing measures to assess buildings and neighborhoods, and interactions with creative innovators in the design professions provided a recurring source of uplifts in daily life. Some of the most enjoyable measurement development I have done was in working out the methodology for ''behavior maps'' of institutional and housing environments and observational surveys of the ecological character of neighborhoods. The smaller details of behavioral design did not engage me so much. I spoke with architects about general behavioral principles rather than producing drawing-board-level ideas. I framed the environmental docility hypothesis and, with Lucille Nahemow (Lawton & Nahemow, 1973), embedded it into the more general ecological model of aging, which has served as a useful conceptual background for many designers. Our attempt to draw a broader ecological model of aging was done in about three minutes. The illustration caught on and has been reprinted in many gerontological and environmental publications.

We chose to characterize the person in terms of a bundle of competences (e.g., physical health, functional health, cognition, positive uses of time, social behavior). We characterized environment in terms of Henry Murray's concept of "press," the extent to which an environment demands a response from the person. We schematized this relationship between personal competence and environmental press, as shown in Figure 15.1, where the evaluated quality of outcome of the behavior or internal state occasioned by a person of a particular level of competence faced with environmental press of a particular level is represented by a point on the surface of the figure.

This characterization illustrates that favorable behavioral and affective outcomes are likely to result from a match between personal competence and environmental demand. An excess of press over competence at a particular time occasions maladaptive behavior and negative affect, as does a deficiency of press with respect to competence. We compared overdemand to stress and underdemand to deprivation. Among other principles, we determined that there is no level of competence so high as to be invulnerable to extraordinary press levels and no level of competence so low as to have no range of positive outcome. Another principle appeared to be that a given amount of objective change in press level would affect the outcome disproportionately more for low-competence people than for high-competence people—the environmental docility hypothesis.

The environmental docility hypothesis has been used widely as the theoretical rationale underlying the attempt to encourage favorable outcomes by special environmental design targeted to people with lowered competence. Ideally an incremental improvement in the environment should disproportionately enhance outcomes for the more disabled as compared to the effect of the same improvement for the most competent—take, for example, the effect of adding a ground-floor-level toilet to a two-story home occupied by a fully competent person versus the effect of this addition on a disabled person.

Such a strategy puts the professional in the active role and the older person in the passive role—that is, the older person is a recipient and user of a built environment designed by others. This one-way effect of environment on the person is, of course, only part of the story (Lawton, 1989). Our colleagues Frances and Abraham Carp (1984) pointed out that we had not dealt as well with people's needs and preferences as with their impairments. She also noted that the environment was characterized not only by demands but by resources and opportunities. It seemed clear that this thinking represented a good focus for improving the model.

It is possible to substitute personal resources for competence and environmental resources (its continuum ranging from few to many) for press. At low levels of personal resources, there is a relatively narrow range of environmental resources available and usable to the person within the "favorable outcome" zones. Environmental opportunities beyond that range are presumed to be unusable by the low-competent person, either because they are too demanding, not personally salient, or simply out of reach and therefore irrelevant. For the person of higher competence, the environment is richer because the greater proportion of all that is "out there" in the objective environment is presumably within range of use, should the person's needs and preferences point in that direction.

The environmental proactivity hypothesis thus states that the greater the competence of the person, the greater the number of environmental resources that may be used in the pursuit of personal needs and wishes. A response may be prevented or shaped by environmental demand; but conversely the person may shape her or his own environment in such a way as to afford a desired response.

The "adaptation level" represents all points at which competence and environmental press are exactly matched. A mild excess of press over competence is called the "zone of

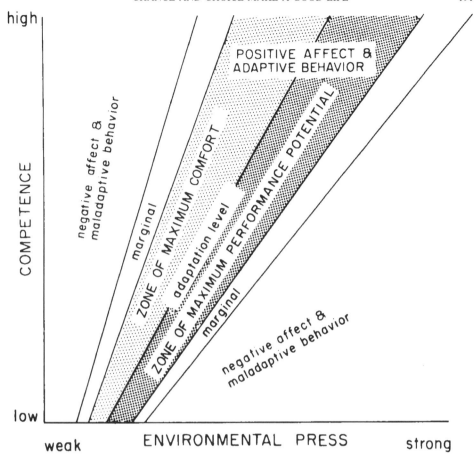

Figure 15-1. Ecological model (Lawton & Nahemow, 1973 (p. 661). Copyright American Psychological Association, reprinted with permission.

maximum performance potential," where stimulation, motivation, and learning occur. A mild deficit of environmental press is called the "zone of maximum comfort," where relaxation of effort occurs. There are clearly benefits to the person who flirts with these borderline zones.

This model is not specific to elders. Departures from normal adult competence may come in children, the disabled, the mentally ill, and the victims of poverty. Departures from normal press levels occur in catastrophes, social deprivation, racism, and peaks of personal stress. Thus this manner of thinking may help us define which personal characteristics of a user group are relevant to a design problem and which environmental features are most central to the user's ability to have a good life.

The theme of spirituality in action was, of course, well served by this research. A high level of reinforcement for performing environmental research stemmed from the social policy milieu of the day. In addition to the growing interest of the design professions, social policy makers were also concerned with the directions in which national housing programs should move. Congressional committees, officials of the Department of Housing and Urban Development and the then Department of Health, Education, and Welfare, and the nonprofit housing constituencies were hungry for knowledge regarding issues such as age segregation, ethnic mixing, services delivered within the housing context, fear of crime, and many other issues. Our housing research made substantial contributions to practice by studying such social phenomena. Looking back now, however, it is the environmental design knowledge drawn from my research that has become embedded into everyday practice and educational curricula for the design professions. Unfortunately, other social issues that my earlier housing research addressed have become neglected over the nearly two decades since housing the poor lost political appeal and new construction ceased in the federal public housing program. Social and service programs for the 700,000 older people living in these now-old projects are difficult to support, and this major need group has become a lost generation.

Environmental exploration led me naturally to mental cataloging, while at the same time leaving me bothered that the cataloged details don't always seem to fit together. Streets sometimes don't run in parallel. North and west get juxtaposed, and the mental map resists completion. Collecting, cataloging, and integrating, I suggest, represent a basic personality trait whose outcomes lead to interests in both measurement, at the bottom (descriptive) level, and concepts, at the top level. There is quite a sizable middle that has appealed to me less but where I still entertain some hope of making a firmer contribution to understanding the psychological mechanisms that connect person and environment.

Although I try to do my psychometric duty, the fine points of intensive instrument development and refinement of measures are not what seem to engage me. Especially interesting to me is the attempt to measure attributes not previously measured, or those considered very resistant to formal assessment—once more, novelty and the search for the large picture. The classic activities of daily living (ADL) had been operationalized by epidemiologist Sidney Katz (Katz, Ford, Moskowitz, Jackson, & Jaffee, 1963) just before I moved into gerontology. My colleague Elaine Brody and I (Lawton & Brody, 1969) then defined the concept and developed the still-used measures of what we called ''instrumental activities of daily living'' (IADL), daily behaviors that are more complex, somewhat more elective, and more dependent on environmental context than the physical ADLs. IADL measurement has become a generic form of health assessment. The physical and instrumental ADL measures appear in all the major surveys of aging and furnish important data on which social planning for long-term care is based. The IADL scale may well be my most enduring contribution to gerontology. By contrast, the ecological measures derived from behavior mapping and neighborhood observation were situation specific and did not lend themselves to the development of generic instruments. More recently, with several other environmental-research colleagues, I have been attempting to capture the megacharacteristics of care environments for elders with dementia, in the construction of the Professional Environmental Assessment Protocol (PEAP; see Lawton, Weisman, Sloane, Norris-Baker, Calkins, & Zimmerman, in press). Also in the past decade, several measures of emotion in older people have resulted from my research in this area: factor-derived measures of multiple affects, brief positive and negative affect scales suited for repeated measurement, measures of styles of experiencing emotion, and an observational method for assessing affect in people with dementia. Again, these measures generally represent first attempts to tailor measures of familiar phenomena to the special situations of older people.

Emotion in aging, and particularly the interestingly different action patterns of positive and negative feelings, have been the focus of much of my recent research. Although positive and negative emotion have sometimes been found to be inversely related and at other times uncorrelated, they show enough independence from one another across all studies to raise many questions about the conditions under which they are independent and those when they are simply opposite poles of a single continuum. In a series of my own research findings, there has been a strong tendency for positive emotional states to occur in older people who are more engaged with other people, leisure activities, and their environments. One of my current ideological missions is to promote the idea that a neglected route to positive mental health for older people is to find ways of enhancing such engagement. A much more difficult idea for research is whether there are other less extroverted means by which people can enhance their engagement with their own goals, thoughts, or memories—engagement for introverts. My colleague Miriam Moss and I are now measuring a construct we call ''valuation of life'' and determining whether this characteristic predicts a person's attitude regarding the end of life, life-sustaining behaviors, and what actually occurs as the person's life ends.

An important focus of this research has been to define the eliciting circumstances for positive and negative emotions—daily events, hassles, uplifts, attachments, and environmental features. Applying such questions to the life of the patient with Alzheimer's disease has been a further challenge. So far our research on this topic has demonstrated affective responsiveness appropriate to the context that extends into even late stages of dementia. Someday we hope that ''reading'' the nonverbal signs of emotion in such patients may enable family and staff caregivers to understand their preferences and aversions and help caregivers reinforce behaviors that lead to more positive outcomes.

Once again, personal themes fit well into the emotion research. Contrary to any previously stated megalevel preference, I have always thought of myself as possessing greater than usual capacity to appreciate small things in everyday life. I reconcile this contradiction with the hypothesis that it is necessary to scan the largest scale environment in order to locate particular facets that, if one is lucky, meet one's needs and preferences. Such experiences have been abundant, whether from the great people I love, my friends and coworkers, music, or the natural and humanmade environment. Black moods are not unknown to me either. For years I felt almost guilty over the repeated realization that despite all those wonderful things that I experience, I must be insufficiently grateful because when things look bad, none of the uplifts can counteract depressed or anxious moods. Emotion researchers have often demonstrated such differential effects; that negative events are more effective in producing negative affect than in diminishing positive affect and that positive events enhance positive affect more than they counteract negative affect. My research has repeatedly confirmed such findings in older people. John Reich and Alex Zautra (1981) demonstrated that when instructed to do so, research subjects could produce positive events in their daily lives. I really think that these scientific facts may be used in one's personal life as well as provide a basis for advising older people how they can increase the quality of their lives.

In my own life, as in most lives, there is always tension between the ease of the familiar and the risk of trying something new. But it is mainly the latter that brings about an uplift— that is, a combination of positive feeling together with a slight increment of activation. There is also tension between the comfort of relaxing and the challenge of learning a new task. Only the latter maintains practice. In the tradition of Reich and Zautra, it is possible to give oneself an informal quota of tasks to undertake that either intimidate one a bit or seem silly or simply unfamiliar. It is also possible to choose pursuits from categories known to provide small uplifts—in my case, live music (this requires the effort of traveling away from my chair), taking down a tree (have I become clumsy with the chain saw?), or driving a new route (will I get lost?) are examples of rationally directed choices that I force on myself as a way of staying engaged. Those who work directly with elders apply the same basic principle in their ever-present advice that older people should ''keep busy.'' I feel that if operationalized more explicitly, as Reich and Zautra have done, and made concrete in terms of establishing a weekly quota of novel or known pleasant events, this neglected aspect of mental health can be fortified. And for the introvert, ways of making one's interiority more novel, challenging, and appealing, as perhaps in self-guided reminiscence, is a task for future clinicians.

Gerontology and Personal Themes Today

I am 77 and am still working full time at PGC. Looking backward, it is hard to see how any life circumstances could have been better arranged to throw me, the pawn, to a position where advancement to the opposing king's row would become possible. Both history, the important people in my life (Fay and I met on a blind date), and the opportunities to find gratifications for personal preferences seem to have been predominantly fortuitous. I have to remind myself, however, that I also gritted my teeth to take Helson's forbidding experimental psychology, chose Columbia (near my love) over Penn (more comfortable geographically) for graduate study, left clinical practice for the unknowns of gerontology, wrote half a dozen unsuccessful grant proposals before the first hit, and dared chair my first meeting of members who were senior scientists. Both chance and choice with a bit of risk taking were thus determinants of how my career proceeded.

At present, my ideas seem as good as ever, and colleagues continue to call on me for various scholarly and organizational duties. Nonetheless, I am having little success with new funding and some difficulty getting new research reports published. Social-scientific ageism explains almost none of this unwelcome trend. Nonetheless it seems worthwhile to speculate about explanations for such a drop-off. The major reason may be due to the flourishing of gerontology. The successful establishment of this multidisciplinary field has brought many new investigators and a substantial number of eminent scholars from other branches of psychology into the research arena. The competition for grant funds and journal space far outstrips the resources available. I like to remember the good old days when one could request grant funding and assume one would get it. No more!

On the personal side, I can see that despite my denial of any cognitive slippage, I contribute equally to the problem. As I asserted earlier, I have a built-in preference for the large picture and the unexplored terrain and some disinclination to probe in depth and in detail. When geropsychology was new, this stance was rewarded because so much of the terrain was new. My megaconcepts are imprecise and my assessment devices more developmental than finalized. The need now is clearly for greater precision. In addition to my lesser comfort at this level, I also detect some measure of the old-pioneer arrogance: Reviewers should be willing to take for granted the intrinsic worth of my proposals and writings. Perhaps there is another factor based in cognitive-personality processes. The growth of science occurs partly through the introduction of new methods, new concepts, and new terms, and a natural part of this evolution is that fashions, as well as major improvements, in these arenas also change. A natural task for the motivated new scholar is to be hypervigilant to such changes and quick to incorporate them into one's own work. Serving on a study section is the perfect milieu for such continued learning. As an old-timer I feel less able to capture all the sources of input for such new learning, and furthermore I am impatient with spending the time and effort on the portions of such learning that seem to me to represent fashion and form rather than substance. Scientific progress demands that such changes occur. Nonetheless, my experience with personal aging has made me less tolerant of this aspect of our science and certainly has contributed to the reduction in my recent visible success.

Moving away for the moment from the personal, I sometimes worry about whether we are allowing form to consume a larger segment of the geropsychological environment than it should. Although I am an enthusiastic consumer of new statistical methods, I see a growing tendency for statistical issues to dominate in collegial critiques. I see the elegance of sampling schemes triumphing over the purpose and content of the data sought in research proposals. I see threats to random assignment or intrusions of ecologically complex factors increasingly invoked as reasons for disapproval. One piece of good news is the recent attempt by the National Institutes of Health to revise the general criteria for evaluating grant proposals so as to weight the creative idea more heavily, along with other more methodological criteria. I wish I could attribute to the right person the wonderful generalization that biomedical study sections search for the redeeming virtue in a proposal whereas behavioral science study sections search for the fatal flaw. Of all my long wish list for the future of geropsychology, the elevation of the creative idea to the top of the criteria for high quality would be my strongest. For the people of my scientific generation, we have the contributions of people like James Birren and Robert Kastenbaum to thank for the value geropsychology places on creativity.

Another such strong wish is that our journals strive to remain part of gerontology's nurturance system for new talent. Gerontology is by definition multidisciplinary, probably one reason why it is so satisfying to certain people. I have found the necessity for learning something about nonpsychological sciences to be one of those rewarding sources of repeated uplift. I have learned immeasurably from Elaine Brody in social work, Ruth Bennett in sociology, Walter Beattie in social policy, Robert Rubinstein in anthropology, and Victor Regnier in architecture. The ability to speak and write comprehensibly for other disciplines is an art, which sometimes requires compromises with expressive styles that may gain maximum in-group reward. Even within geropsychology the range of interests and subspecialties represented requires an enlarged view of how we should communicate. The goal of maintaining a broadened consumership puts a burden on the editing process to instruct authors in how to present their findings and, if necessary, to suggest how they may improve their concepts and methods in their next try. This generative editorial role is different from what we see in traditional disciplines where the pressure of an excess number of high-quality manuscripts may force an editor to take short-cutting measures simply to get the job done. I hope that geropsychology can remain at a scale that allows an editor the luxury of personally acting as another referee and an editorial counselor to all authors. Some journal review guidelines specifically enjoin referees from taking space to suggest how the author can improve a manuscript if it does not have a prospect of being accepted. Other editors feel it is not their job to censor vituperative, ad hominum critiques. My conviction is that gerontology is inspiring because it thrives on diversity and one of the prices of high-quality diversity is the extra work required for a nurturing editorial system. I have to say that the capstone of my career was my designation as the first editor of American Psychological Association's *Psychology and Aging* (with equal effort from Donald Kausler, who fulfilled ideally the role of discerning critic and supportive mentor for the areas of experimental and cognitive geropsychology). Our success in being nurturing critics was clearly far from complete, and the effort cost us a great deal of time lost from other pursuits. To us it was worth the effort. I hope editors of the future will take seriously this special mission.

In conclusion, the major change I have observed in gerontology was its move from a small group of on-the-fringe scientists to its present large, differentiated, and leading-science position. The movement of eminent scientists from other fields into gerontology has been especially notable. In psychology the major conceptual change I have observed is the move from the view of the elder as a pawn of biology and society toward one with overwhelming self-determining capacity. For the future, no area of present knowledge in the psychology of aging is unworthy of continued exploration. The young gerontologist should be especially attuned to her or his own personality style and seek matches for these in choices made at various stages of their careers. I have attempted to caution future gerontologists that there are dangers in becoming too preoccupied with method and style and the pursuit of flawless science and published reports. The best insurance against such misdirection will come from the educational systems in gerontology, where both excellence and collegial supportiveness can be trained. I would love to have been through such a system, but I also feel secretly proud to have been able to use coincidence and opportunity where specific teaching of gerontology was not yet in place.

References

Carp, F. (1966). *A future for the aged.* Austin: University of Texas Press.

Carp, F., & Carp, A. (1984). A complementary congruence model of well-being or mental health for the community elderly. In I. Altman, M. P. Lawton, & J. F. Wohlwill (Eds.), *Elderly people and their environment* (pp. 279–336). New York: Plenum Press.

Helson, H. (1964). *Adaption-level theory.* New York: Harper & Row.

Katz, S., Ford, A. B., Moskowitz, R. W., Jackson, B. A., & Jaffee, M. W. (1963). Studies of illness in the aged: The index of ADL: A standardized measure of biological and psychosocial function. *Journal of the American Medical Association, 185,* 914–919.

Kleemeier, R. W. (1959). Behavior and the organization of the bodily and the external environment. In J. E. Birren (Ed.), *Handbook of aging and the individual* (pp. 400–451). Chicago: University of Chicago Press.

Lawton, M. P. (1956). Stimulus structure as a determinant of the perceptual response. *Journal of Consulting Psychology, 20,* 351–355.

Lawton, M. P. (1989). Environmental proactivity and affect in older people. In S. Spacapan & S. Oskamp (Eds.) *Social psychology and aging* (pp. 135–164). Beverly Hills, CA: Sage.

Lawton, M. P., & Brody, E. M. (1969). Assessment of older people: Self-maintaining and instrumental activities of daily living. *The Gerontologist, 9,* 179–185.

Lawton, M. P., & Nahemow, L. (1973). Ecology and the aging process. In C. Eisdorfer & M. P. Lawton (Eds.), *Psychology of adult development and aging* (pp. 619–674). Washington, DC: American Psychological Association.

Lawton, M. P., Weisman, G., Sloane, P., Norris-Baker, C., Calkins, M., & Zimmerman, S. I. (in press). A Professional Environmental Assessment Procedure for special care units for elders with dementing illness and its relationship to the Therapeutic Environment Screening Schedule. *Alzheimer Disease and Associated Disorders.*

Lewin, K. (1951). *Field theory in social science.* New York: Harper & Row.

Murray, H. A. (1938). *Explorations in personality.* New York: Oxford.

Reich, J. W., & Zautra, A. (1981). Life events and causation: Some relationships with satisfaction and distress. *Journal of Personality and Social Psychology, 41,* 1002–1012.

Wilensky, H. (1961). Orderly careers and social participation: The impact of work history on social integration in the middle mass. *American Sociological Review, 26,* 521–539.

Chapter 16
AN AGING GENETICIST

Gerald E. McClearn

I don't think that it has been a purely random walk, but I certainly am impressed by the role that accidents have played in my career.

Probably the most significant accident was the timing of my birth with respect to the Second World War. Fortuitously, I was young enough to get into the military only toward the end of that conflict, but it was enough to earn entitlements under the G.I. bill, and those benefits settled the question of whether I could afford a college education. There was no tradition of higher education in my family—with origins in farms and coal mines of western Pennsylvania—and, indeed, if memory serves, the general attitude in our small town was that graduation from high school was a good thing, but anything further was viewed with some suspicion. I'm quite sure that many in the community perceived college education to be unnecessary for the careers to which the class of 1944 of Sandy Lake High School should aspire.

It happened that I was 16 years old at graduation and had a few months before becoming eligible for the draft. I cannot recall a time in my life when I did not want to become a flyer, and my most fervent hope was to become an army or navy aviator. The word was out that the aviation training programs preferred applicants with some college background, particularly in engineering, so I went to Stetson University in DeLand, Florida, for about half a year in a preengineering program. As I neared draft age, none of the flight training programs was accepting new students, but by now I had persuaded myself that it would be better to be an officer, flying or otherwise, than an enlisted man. So I signed up with the U.S. Merchant Marine Cadet Corps (USMMCC), the only program I could find with prospects of a commission. Through an intense instructional program at San Mateo, California, and a subsequent stint at sea in Victory ships (where my geographic horizons were extended by trips to Holland and to Japan), I learned a lot about the maintenance and operation of steam boilers, turbines, evaporators, generators, and so on. In all my previous life, I had shown no interest whatsoever in mechanical things (apart from airplanes), so it was a considerable surprise to discover that I actually liked the life of a marine engineer. I presumed that I had found my career. We cadets were in the U.S. Naval Reserve and had prospects of a vocation either in the merchant service or in the navy. I thought the life of an engineer on a navy ocean-going tug would be just the thing.

About six months before my class was scheduled to graduate, the war ended. The USMMCC extended greatly the time we would have to spend back at the academy at King's Point, and many of us resigned in protest. Our cadet status had not satisfied our service obligation, so I joined the U.S. Coast Guard, attracted by the fact that this service had a useful role in peacetime. I was offered an opportunity to go to the U.S. Coast Guard Academy, but, having already had my fill of the life of a cadet-midshipman, I refused. As a fireman first class, I became a member of the base personnel manning coal-fired boilers at the base at Constitution Wharf in Boston. In this job, I developed the strongest physique I have ever had, but I also developed a back problem that eventuated in a medical discharge.

By this time, there was no equivocation in my wish to get a college education. But there I was, released from the service in October 1947, after all college semesters had begun. I went through the procedure that was in place for veterans' counseling before college entrance and had chosen, from among the many splendid small liberal arts colleges in the area, one about which I had heard especially good things—Allegheny College in Meadville, Pennsylvania. Unfortunately, I would have to wait nearly a full year before starting.

I got a job with the Pennsylvania Highway Department as a draftsman to fill the time until the next semester. Like many other returning veterans, due perhaps to a sense of lost time, I was impatient to settle down and start a family. A young woman named Nancy Dye who lived a few blocks from me had matured astonishingly in the three years I had been gone, and she, now a high school senior, strongly attracted my attention.

One of my best high school buddies had a medical problem that had kept him out of the service, and he was by now an advanced engineering student at Grove City College. One day I was riding around with him as he performed some errands. One of these errands was taking much longer than planned, and I became increasingly bored as I waited in his car. Casting about for something to read, I scanned his textbooks, which had been tossed into the back seat. Most of them concerned advanced engineering of one type or another, and I wasn't up to reading them for recreation. One book was different. It was Vaughn's (1939) introductory text in psychology, a course my friend was taking as an elective. I had been aware that courses in psychology were available at Stetson, but I had wondered why anyone would want to waste time studying anything so soft-headed as I presumed that topic to be. This prejudice was, of course, based on total unfamiliarity. I had never before opened the pages of a psychology text; for that matter, I do not recall ever having talked to anyone who had. But I was desperately bored, so I gave it a try, and to my amazement (and, perhaps, some private embarrassment) found it to be interesting. In fact, it was *very* interesting. I remember specifically being intrigued by the illustrations of negative afterimages, and the discovery that psychology was concerned with the neural substrate of behavior. Any textbook that could speak of ''nonmedullated postganglionic neurons,'' as this one did, must have something going for it!

So I borrowed the book, to my friend's amusement (he had taken the course as a last resort and was unimpressed by the subject matter), and I stayed up most of the night reading it. I asked him to get me a copy for myself, and I read it from cover to cover in a few days. It was a ''where has this been all my life?'' experience. Why had I not heard about it in high school? How had I managed not to discover it at Stetson? I became very impatient for the new academic year to begin so I could come to grips systematically with this psychology stuff. This impatience was tempered somewhat by some nagging doubts about whether I could handle college-level instruction at all. To be sure, I had done well in high school, but this was going to be a new game.

Allegheny College: The Undergraduate Years

Gradually, after the early examinations during the first semester, I began to believe that I could, at least, hold my own at the college level. In no small part, I think this was attributable to the academic atmosphere of Allegheny, on which I now look back—after a career in academe—with a sense of awe. I also had the advantage, shared with other returning veterans, of a certain level of maturity that accompanied years and experiences in the service. We were intensely motivated, and, by virtue of our example, we were the dismay of the students who had just arrived fresh from high school.

During the freshman year, I decided that I didn't want to wait any longer to get a family started, and persuaded Nancy to marry me. She was in a secretarial college program at the time, and we had a commuting marriage for a year. Without doubt, the married state, which eliminated the necessity for time-consuming courtship, contributed to the possibility of concentrating hard on the business of learning all of the fascinating stuff offered to me. The breadth requirements opened all sorts of new intellectual windows, but my primary interest remained in psychology, the introductory course of which was taught by one Frank Palmer. Frank was finishing his doctorate at the University of Pittsburgh and needed some help with his dissertation research on postelectroconvulsive-shock amnesia in rats. He had spotted me as an enthusiastic student in the introductory course and offered me a job as his research assistant. Frank was a remarkably patient mentor, explaining with great care the need for scrupulous observance of the experimental and control procedures. Some issue that I no longer remember arose, and I asked him about how we should deal with it. He told me to go to the library and look up in the *Journal of Comparative and Physiological Psychology* how a similar matter had been handled by some other investigator. I dutifully went to the library and inquired where this journal was to be found. I was ushered into the stacks and got my first glimpse into the system of primary literature. So *this* was the repository of the facts that were condensed and summarized in the textbooks; this was how the ''they'' who found out all these things communicated with each other. What a powerful epiphany! All the rules I had been learning in my apprenticeship about control procedures and systematized uniformity in testing the animals, and the early hints I had had about upcoming statistical analysis, weren't just Frank Palmer's idiosyncrasies. They represented a shared domain of understanding among a community of scholars about how reliable knowledge could be acquired. And I had been doing some of it myself! Without realizing fully what was really meant by it, I knew at that moment that I wanted to join the ''they.'' I wanted to become a behavioral scientist.

Among my laboratory duties was the arrangement of matings, weanings, and general husbandry of the rats, all of which were albinos. A pet rat that had outgrown its cuteness (I think that it had bitten the little girl to whom it had been given) was donated to the lab. It was a black-hooded male, and I put it in the mating schedule, awaiting the resultant pups with great curiosity. My naïve expectation was that they would all be gray-hooded animals, and I was surprised and puzzled when there was a variety of coat colors and degrees of hoodedness in the litter. I inquired of the botany/genetics teacher who occupied a laboratory next to Palmer's, and his explanation involved the puzzling notion that the albino females had coat color genes. I incubated this idea for a few days, but it didn't acquire any more plausibility as time went by, so I went back for further explanation. I got the same story again, and it still didn't make sense, so I resolved to take the course in genetics that was given by this gentleman the next time it was offered.

I did, and during the semester I learned about the ubiquity of influence of heredity. (I also learned about the epistatic interactive effects that allowed the albino gene to mask the effects of other coat color genes.) We used a text that was strongly oriented toward agricultural matters, but there were examples of genetic influence on all organ systems, including the sensory apparatus, the endocrine system, and the nervous system. These systems, of course, were generally acknowledged to be part of the mechanistic substrate of behavior by those psychology texts that concerned themselves with the matter. So it seemed obvious to me that heredity, by influencing these systems, could affect behavior. But here was the rub. My beloved psychology sought its explanations almost solely in the environment. True, isolated references to heredity would sometimes be encountered in the texts, most particularly to some early twin studies and to selective breeding studies, especially that by Tryon, on rat learning ability. These references, however, seemed never to be incorporated into the fabric of the psychological matters being presented. Indeed, the idea of genes influencing behavior was generally ridiculed. John B. Watson's claim that appropriate training could direct the development of any child into any specified outcome had been widely accepted as a demonstrated fact rather than an unsubstantiated extravagant claim. Heredity was deemed to be at best irrelevant to behavior and at worst, in some obscure way, anathematic. For a while, I wrestled with what seemed to be a necessary choice between the fascinating phenomena of behavior and the fascinating science of the origins of individual differences. I dithered about changing majors, nursing a glimmer of hope that it might be possible to combine the interests. In my senior year, this hope was fanned into full flame by the publication of *Steven's Handbook of Experimental Psychology,* which included a chapter by Calvin Hall (1951) that reviewed the evidence on ''The Genetics of Behavior.'' For me, that was it; the combined field existed, and I wanted to contribute to it.

Over the semesters, it had become evident that a BS degree in psychology was not going to prepare me particularly well to support my wife and a daughter, Deedra, born during my senior year. The prospect of several years more of perhaps genteel, but certainly uncomfortable, poverty as a graduate student was not attractive, but it was clear that the extra investment had to be made. An immediate problem was that I could not find any graduate program that offered training in behavioral genetics. As a default, I applied to two or three departments with strong experimental psychology programs.

At this point, another most unlikely event occurred that strongly shaped my career. It was traditional for the Allegheny psychology faculty to take selected senior majors to an annual symposium at the University of Pittsburgh on the topic of ''New Frontiers in Psychology.'' The speakers in 1951 were a brilliant group, and I remember the presentations by Harry Harlow and David Krech as particularly scintillating. At a coffee break, Frank Palmer (who, after receiving his PhD had left Allegheny for another position but who was attending the conference) joined our little group of Alleghenians. He asked about our impressions of these giants of the field. Among the chorus of awestruck comments, mine about Harlow must have stood out, for Frank asked me if I would like to study with Harlow. My reply was something like, ''You must be joking!'' Frank took me by the elbow, led me to a knot of people standing around Harry, introduced himself and me, and told Harry that he was missing a bet if he didn't accept me as a graduate student immediately. Harry seemed amused, asked me a few questions, and said, ''Okay. You'll do.'' Flabbergasted, I replied that I hadn't even applied to Wisconsin. Harry dismissed my objection with a wave of his hand and told me whom to telephone and tell that he had approved me! I made the call, and shortly the paperwork appeared indicating that I had, indeed, been accepted as a graduate student for the fall of 1951.

Graduate School at Wisconsin

My general training in the psychology program and the specific experience in Harlow's Primate Laboratory were of the no-nonsense, hard-headed experimentalist type. My particular cohort was encouraged to regard correlational studies as weak science at best and multivariate statistics as largely smoke and mirrors. I have subsequently had much cause to appreciate the rigorous experimentalist training but also to regret profoundly the early gap in my training with respect to multivariate, associational research.

The Wisconsin program required that graduate students pursue a strong minor in some area other than that of major concentration. I opted for genetics, naturally, and became the first psychology graduate student ever to have done so. (For several weeks, my fellow students in a genetics seminar, all geneticists, thought I was a cytology student with poor enunciation.) It required quite a bit of extra paperwork, as I recall. Jim Crow became my minor professor, and with his exemplary guidance, I was introduced to the subtleties of the theories and methods of quantitative and population genetics.

Yale University and a Return to Allegheny

A son, Duane, was born in 1953. I received the PhD in 1954 and went to Yale for my first position. It was a good year in some respects, particularly in the opportunity it provided to become a junior colleague and friend of Frank Beach. But the fit between Yale and me was not a good one, so I began looking for another position almost immediately. Fortuitously, a position opened in my old department at Allegheny, and I applied with alacrity. My application was successful, and I moved back to Meadville, Pennsylvania, fully intending to pursue the rest of my career in a liberal arts college setting. While at Yale, I had applied to the National Science Foundation for a research grant to study the genetics of activity and learning in mice. I was able to transfer the grant to Allegheny, and I was assigned Palmer's old laboratory where I had been an apprentice scientist. Now I was on my own.

With the heavy teaching load expected in a liberal arts context (15 units a semester), and with the research program, it was a busy first year, but an extraordinarily rewarding one. Working with bright, dedicated undergraduates can be very satisfying, and the psychology majors at Allegheny certainly did (and apparently still do) fit that description. So I was tired most of the time, but I was happy in my work.

About half way through the year, I received a letter from Leo Postman at the University of California, Berkeley, offering me a position with the opportunity to build a program in behavioral genetics. I learned later that the motivation of the department was to resume the interest in heredity represented by Tryon's research program, which had been interrupted by World War II. My name had been put forward both by Harry Harlow and by Frank Beach when they were consulted about possible candidates. This letter of offer was not particularly welcome. The academic ambiance of Allegheny College and the proximity of both Nancy's and my family were strong reasons to stay put. I had no interest whatsoever in returning to the ''big leagues.'' Had the offer been couched in terms of experimental, or comparative, or physiological emphasis, I'm sure I would have declined. But the emphasis on behavioral genetics was ultimately irresistible, so with considerable angst, we packed the station wagon and migrated to Berkeley.

One dark night en route, after a hard day's driving, we stopped at a motel in Estes Park, Colorado. Neither Nancy nor I had been in the Rocky Mountains before, and we were almost literally staggered by the scenic grandeur when we emerged from our room the next morning. Memories of that glorious, crystalline morning, the sense of standing on top of the world, and the beauty of the subsequent drive through the Rockies remained vivid over the years and played a not inconsiderable role in a later career decision.

University of California, Berkeley

The Berkeley Department of Psychology was a good place to be, with a roster of superstars, including Dave Krech, who had so impressed me at the Pittsburgh meeting. Dave had joined forces with Mark Rosenzweig in using the descendants of Tryon's maze-bright and maze-dull strains of rats in their studies of neuropsychology, and their interest had been instrumental in establishing the position I now held. The department was thus atypically tolerant of ideas about genetics and behavior. There were, furthermore, several distinguished geneticists on campus who were enormously helpful and supportive. Berkeley thus provided a very congenial intellectual base of operations in which to begin to define myself academically.

Behavioral Genetics and the Behavioral Sciences

At this time the field of behavioral genetics itself was coalescing on the basis of the work of a small group of investigators who were gradually generating a persuasive body of research literature. The seminal text by Fuller and Thompson (1960) and the edited volumes by Hirsch (1967) and by Manosevitz, Lindzey, and Thiessen (1969) provided general overviews that not only gave a sense of identity to the field itself but also provided accessible information for all behavioral scientists wishing to avail themselves of it. One of my own contributions to this literature was a chapter on the history of the development of ideas on the genetics of behavior that Leo Postman invited me to provide for his book *Psychology in the Making.* This invitation gave me both the opportunity and the motivation to explore the historical roots of my chosen field more deeply than I ever had before, and I came away from that effort with a much heightened appreciation of the acumen of previous generations of scholars. It's not just that the current generation of scholars stands, as the adage has it, on the shoulders of their predecessors. Often the ''old'' ideas, if restated in current terminology, sound remarkably like the cutting edges of today's work. I suspect that there are many such ideas, shouldered aside by the juggernauts of new paradigms, that would handsomely repay revival and exploitation by modern methodologies. This might be an argument for a revival of interest in courses in the ''history of psychology,'' a currently undervalued topic.

The books and chapters cited here give a good representation of the evidential base in behavioral genetics that was building in the 1950s. This base included demonstrations of the effects of single, major, classical, Mendelian genes on categorical behavioral phenotypes (usually some abnormality of behavior), as well as evidence of genetic influence on the normal range of variation of continuously distributed variables. The most comprehensive body of theory pertinent to this latter case, and the one that best represented the nascent *Weltanschaung* of behavioral genetics, was that of quantitative genetics. This model posits the influence of many genes on a particular phenotype, each contributing only part of the phenotypic variance. (It can also accommodate the major Mendelian genes as a limiting case.) Of the greatest importance is the fact that the model explicitly and necessarily is concerned with the environmental sources of variation as well as the genetic ones. It is thus a paradigm for the comprehensive description of the sources of individuality. From the perspective of palatability to the behavioral science world, however, it is poorly and misleadingly named. ''Quantitative genetics and environmental influences'' would be more accurate, though rather cumbersome. I've attempted, with conspicuous lack of success, to promote ''differential model'' as a brief and accurate label. The important point is that genes and environmental forces are not antagonistic or alternative agencies, but that they coact to produce the complex phenotypes that are of central concern to behavioral and biological scientists. Some of this coaction is additive, but there is scope for different types of interaction. One type is the circumstance in which the difference in phenotype between individuals with different forms of a particular gene depends on what form of some other gene is present. My puzzlement with coat color genes in white rats was due to this type of ''epistatis,'' and many, many other examples can be cited. The other principal type of interaction is that of genes and environment. The effect of an environmental difference may depend greatly on the genotype of the individual. An animal-model example with some gerontological relevance is that of Fosmire, Focht, and McClearn (1993), who showed that only two mouse strains of five tested showed elevated brain levels of aluminum when fed an aluminum-enriched diet.

In the study of these underpinnings of individuality, a descriptive statistic, heritability, is frequently employed. It is simply the proportion of the total phenotypic variance that can be ascribed to genetic differences among individuals. Obviously, subtracting the heritability from 1.0 yields an index (environmentality) of the proportion due to environmental sources.

This perspective, which seemed so balanced to us behavioral geneticists, was not immediately and automatically persuasive in the behavioral sciences. Indeed, behavioral genetics became a major jousting arena in the nature/nurture controversy. Watson had driven heredity out of psychology with his outrageous claims. Hard-headed psychologists with stringent criteria for evidence about all other aspects of their fields of study seemed to accept his unsupported assertions as self-evident. One of the difficulties was that a pattern of discourse on the issue had emerged that led to categorical thinking—an attribute had to be due to heredity *or* environment. To some extent, perhaps, this tendency was promoted by Galton's unfortunate terms that made the facile nature *versus* nurture formulation so attractive. As a consequence, many behavioral scientists, operating in this either-or mode, could point to vast bodies of empirical data showing the influence of environmental factors on behavior and conclude therefrom that genes could not possibly be of any importance. Among the audiences of some of my early seminar presentations I remember well the unconcealed, adamant disdain for anyone who could believe that flexible, variable, adaptable behavior could be influenced by the content of chromosomes. This was a common experience of behavioral geneticists at the time. *Ad hominem* verbal attacks were not infrequent, and an opinion that genetics might influence behavior was equated by many with fascistic racism. Particularly vivid is the memory of one symposium at which all of the speakers were called together by the chief security officer of the campus and shown where we should retreat for protection in case the audience charged the stage. The passion of the environmentalists was undoubtedly based, at least in part, on a perception that genetics had been a motivating factor in the horrendous Nazi programs of eugenics and genocide. Revulsion at those consequences prompted a denial of genetics, no matter that that science had been grotesquely twisted and distorted in justification of political decisions already made on prejudicial grounds. (A detailed discussion of this matter is inappropriate here; some of my own perceptions are provided in McClearn and DeFries, 1973, chapter 11. I note also with some satisfaction my concluding remarks in a presidential address to the Behavior Genetics Association in 1975 in which I observed that I found racism to be abhorrent, not in spite of being a behavioral geneticist, but because of it.)

The Berkeley Research Program

The Department of Psychology facilities that were immediately available for my program were quite limited. After some time, my plight became known around campus, and Ken DeOme, director of the Cancer Research Genetics Laboratory (CRGL), generously offered me accommodations. This was my introduction to the operation of barrier facilities, and the lessons I learned there were to be very important in later years. I worked in the CRGL facilities until the psychology department was able to move into the newly constructed Tolman Hall. My facilities there were high quality but quite limited in size, and that limitation had later repercussions.

My principal research method at that time was the comparison of inbred strains of mice. This method was a standard one within the growing literature on behavioral genetics, and differences among inbred strains had previously been described with respect to a wide variety of behavioral phenotypes. The logic of inbred strains was, and is, clear and simple. The process of inbreeding produces groups within which animals are essentially identical, genetically. Different inbred strains will have different ''homogenized'' genotypes. Therefore, if several strains are maintained and tested under the same conditions, the differences among strain means will reflect genetic differences, and the within-strain variance will be a reflection of environmental influences. Even this simplest of methods demonstrates that the quantitative genetic model is a vehicle for examination both of genetic and of environmental influences. I believe that the *ipso facto* quality of the evidence provided by strain differences played an important role in the gradual, and still continuing, acceptance of the once-heretical notion that genes might influence behavior.

I was concentrating on demonstrating the existence of genetic influence on activity level and on learning performance in various types of maze. One of my departmental colleagues, a clinical psychologist named Dave Rodgers, jokingly suggested that I should do something with somewhat more relevance to the human condition. After a while, the joking became serious, and we decided to collaborate on a project that would model some phenomenon of clinical relevance. We finally settled on alcohol consumption, and within a few days we had evidence of dramatic strain differences in alcohol preference. One strain drank about two thirds of its daily liquid consumption from the alcohol bottle. Other strains drank little or no alcohol. This was the start of a research program on genetics and alcohol-related phenotypes that continues today.

Shortly after this project began, I was fortunate to be awarded a National Academy of Science/National Research Council Fellowship to study quantitative genetics with Douglas Falconer at the Institute of Animal Genetics in Edinburgh, Scotland. The institute was a treasure trove of theoretical knowledge and methodological sophistication in exploring the genetics of complex traits, and the scholars there were enormously helpful, though bemused by having a psychologist, whom they sometimes referred to as their ''behavior merchant,'' in their midst. On my return to Berkeley I set about trying to emulate their success in applying selective breeding and other procedures to my own phenotypes of interest. One consequence was two lines of mice that differ greatly in their central nervous system sensitivity to alcohol. These lines have been useful in studies of mechanisms of alcohol sensitivity in a number of laboratories, illustrating the still insufficiently appreciated potency of selective breeding to generate animal models to specification.

Bill Meredith joined the department. We quickly teamed up, and he began the remedial training in multivariate thinking that had been neglected in my graduate curriculum. Several graduate students were attracted to the group. Among them, Kurt Schlesinger and Jim Wilson (a student of Frank Beach, who had in the meantime moved to Berkeley) would have particularly important influence on my later career. I started a course in behavioral genetics, taught several other courses, did my committee work, and got tenure. The family was growing: a daughter, Diane, was born shortly after the return from Scotland. I seemed to be settled in to finish out a career as a Californian. Other events were conspiring against this straightforward trajectory, however.

One of the PhDs from the Berkeley program, Dan Bailey, had obtained a position at the University of Colorado, which was enhancing its Department of Psychology under the leadership of Stuart Cook. Somehow, Dan, who had worked with Tryon on cluster analysis at Berkeley and had inevitably picked up an interest in genetics, persuaded the Colorado department that behavioral genetics would be a good area to develop. Dan was authorized to approach me to determine whether there were any conditions under which I could be tempted to move to Colorado. Feeling particularly cramped for space at that moment, I responded to this first overture by what I thought was an utterly frivolous request for a building of my own. Within a few days, I was startled to receive a phone call from Stuart Cook, wanting to explore matters further. I asked if Dan had relayed my stated condition; I was prepared to apologize for my brazenness. But Stuart said yes, and the negotiations began. Things proceeded rapidly, I made several visits to Boulder, and I was soon faced with another difficult choice. I asked Nancy if she wanted to visit Boulder herself to see what it would be like raising a family there. Remembering that breathtaking Colorado morning in Estes Park, she said she was ready to move. So we went to Boulder in 1965, where I was expected to develop a program of behavioral genetics within the Department of Psychology, with a building of my own that included a specific-pathogen-free, barrier mouse colony and laboratory.

University of Colorado, Boulder

The reception of behavioral genetics within the Department of Psychology was generally very cordial and supportive, but some issues did arise concerning the necessity of recruiting trained geneticists regardless of their ability to teach in the psychology curriculum. Stuart Cook and I took the problem to the dean of the graduate school, Jim Archer, and the upshot of that meeting was the establishment of a separate Institute for Behavioral Genetics. The program flourished. In the early days, we received a training grant, along with several research grants, mostly to work on alcohol-related phenomena. Collaborations were established with Dick Deitrich of the Department of Pharmacology and Gene Erwin of the School of Pharmacy. R. C. Roberts, my office-mate at Edinburgh, came over for a year to provide the background in quantitative genetics until John DeFries could join the group permanently to provide that expertise. From Berkeley, Jim Wilson became research associate (and later the associate director) in the institute, bringing an endocrinological perspective; Kurt Schlesinger, working on neurogenetics, obtained an appointment in the Department of Psychology, and Agnes Conley came as administrative assistant. (Jim Wilson, incidentally, was a pilot; we bought a plane together, and I finally realized my early dream to become a pilot.) Other new appointees in the Department of Psychology and the institute included Ron Johnson and Steve Vandenberg, both with human developmental research interests. Wilson Crumpacker joined the Department of Environmental, Population, and Organismic Biology and the institute, bringing expertise in *Drosophila* genetics. Robert Plomin, with doctoral training in genetics and early behavioral development, was recruited for the Department of Psychology and the institute.

As the institute matured, more individuals became associated with it, numerous graduate students were supported by the training grants while pursuing their degrees in a variety of programs—chemistry, pharmacy, psychology, anthropology, biology—and postdoctoral fellows ranged from political science to biophysics. It was an exciting time. The work in the pharmacogenetics of alcohol continued as a main thrust; the Colorado Adoption Project was initiated; a human family study on cognitive functioning and other behaviors was established in collaboration with the University of Hawaii; a study on dyslexia was initiated; a twin-family study on tobacco use was initiated in collaboration with the Karolinska Institute in Stockholm. I had a semester fellowship at the Galton Laboratory in London and came back refreshed and invigorated. Now, surely, I was settled down. In fact I was, until 1981.

I had long had an avocational interest in gerontology. I now found myself becoming increasingly intrigued with the possibility of studying the genetics of aging processes. From the evolutionary point of view, from the genetic point of view, from the psychological and every other point of view, aging was fascinating. In exploring the possibilities, I arranged a symposium at Boulder featuring some gerontological luminaries from around the country. Included among them were John Nesselroade and Paul Baltes, both then in the College of Human Development at The Pennsylvania State University. For me, as predisposed as I already was, the scope and promise of gerontological research laid out by these scholars was nothing less than thrilling. However, the institute faculty was so committed to successful ongoing projects as to be wary of any further extension. I must have been vulnerable through another of what appears, in retrospect, to be recurring midlife crises. Thus, my interest was piqued when I saw an announcement of the availability of a position as associate dean for research at the College of Human Development at Penn State. The contact person was John Nesselroade. On impulse, I called John to ask about the position. Again, one thing led to another, and I soon faced another decision. It was, indeed, a very difficult one. The institute at Boulder was thriving, with high-quality faculty, many highly motivated graduate students, an excellent support staff, and well-funded research programs. On the other hand, Penn State was clearly one of the best places in the world to develop a program in gerontological genetics. One of the big attractions of the position was the new dean, Evan Pattishall, whose aspirations for the college's research stature were exciting. The combination of the challenge of being on his administrative team and the opportunity to develop my own research program within the context of the gerontological hotbed of the College of Human Development proved to be irresistible, and in January 1981 I moved back to Pennsylvania. Nancy, uncomplaining about earlier moves, was (very) reluctant to leave Colorado. The compromise solution was that we left the house in Boulder as it was, with daughter Diane in charge, and moved with two suitcases each to start housekeeping afresh in a small apartment in State College.

The Pennsylvania State University

My position at Penn State began on January 1, 1981. En route to State College from Boulder, I stopped in Washington, D.C., to participate in a five-year planning process of the National Institute on Aging. I'm not sure to whom I'm indebted for the invitation, but it was a very important event for me as an aspiring gerontologist, for I came to know and interact with some of the leading figures in the field. Everything I experienced at that meeting validated my admittedly scary decision to leave a successful and comfortable situation to plunge into this new area in a new setting.

So I undertook my duties at the College of Human Development in an upbeat frame of mind. The atmosphere in the college was particularly refreshing in its interdisciplinary orientation, and one of my responsibilities as associate dean required that I promote interdisciplinary endeavors, which was a mission dear to my heart. I don't know why such ventures at disciplinary interfaces have such a strong personal appeal to me, but one insight I have gained about myself is that I revel in this sort of situation. I actually find myself feeling sorry for those who haven't discovered the sheer intellectual delight of interdisciplinary pursuits. (There is an associated burden, however. I'm at considerable pains to warn my students that if they go into a heavily interdisciplinary area such as gerontological genetics, and if they are doing it right, they will always feel ignorant about something or other. This shifting but continuing ignorance promotes humility. It also promotes team efforts, because no one person can ever know everything that is needed in putting multidisciplinary questions to nature. This fact helps to explain the long list of persons to whom I am indebted.)

In addition to promoting the research and graduate training functions of such departments as individual and family studies; nutrition; administration of justice; health planning and administration; hotel, restaurant and institutional management, and nursing, I was able to initiate my own research program. My first major gerontological research effort was a collaborative, interdisciplinary, total life-span study on the genetics of aging in mice. This project, which required renovating a laboratory to barrier standard, involved faculty from the Colleges of Agriculture (Fred Ferguson and Channa Reddy) and Science (Bob Mitchell) as well as Human Development (Frank Ahern, John Nesselroade, Tobey Stout). In parallel, we began the development of a human research program, using a rare resource. Robert Plomin and Nancy Pedersen (a former doctoral student of mine from Colorado who was coordinating the Karolinska tobacco study) found that many Swedish twins had been reared separately for significant parts of their infancy and childhood. Such separated twins offer a particularly incisive method of apportioning phenotypic variance into genetic, shared environmental and unshared environmental components. This was the origin of the Swedish Adoption Twin Study of Aging (SATSA), a still-continuing longitudinal investigation. The project was facilitated enormously when Robert Plomin moved to Penn State, with a major objective of merging the approaches of quantitative genetics with those of molecular genetics in the study of behavioral development. To provide a platform for the developing program, a Center for Developmental and Health Genetics was established within the college, and Robert became its director. Elana Pyle joined in the essential role of administrative assistant.

Early during this period, I was invited to join the MacArthur Foundation Research Network on Successful Aging, under the leadership of Jack Rowe. This was an extraordinary opportunity for someone trying to break into gerontology. The members of the group were stellar informants about gerontological matters, the meetings were invariably stimulating, and the financial support was a generous addition to the support we had obtained from the National Institute on Aging.

In the course of designing SATSA, we made the acquaintance of Alvar Svanborg of the University of Gothenburg and learned much from his experience with the Gothenburg H-70 longitudinal study. He, in turn, had referred us to his colleague and former student Stig Berg, a psychologist, who had played a major role in the psychological aspects of the H-70 project and who was now director of the Institute for Gerontology in Jönköping, Sweden. The liaison with Stig and with his research group grew into a multifaceted collaboration in which students, staff, and faculty move easily and often, seminars are conducted via teleconferencing technology, and our twin research effort has expanded into two more projects. The first of these, OCTO-Twin (with Boo Johansson as project leader) concentrates on twins 80 years of age or older, and the second, GENDER (Bo Malmberg as project leader), compares unlike-sex dizygotic twin pairs as a method for exploring sex differences in longevity and age-related health problems.

Some Administrative Diversions

As these various research programs were developing, I became increasingly restive as an associate dean and resolved to get back to the best job in academe—that of a professor. My opportunity came when the College of Health and Human Development was formed from parts of the College of Human Development and parts of the College of Health, Physical Education and Recreation. My resignation was accepted with a two-year delay to help in the transition to the new college. When my term was up, I began to savor the (nearly) full-time research role. Then I was asked to start a new PhD program in biobehavioral health.

I agreed to a two-year effort. After about 18 months, I was asked to take the position of dean of the college. I did this for 27 months, at which point a MERIT award from the National Institute on Aging provided the opportunity for me to retire from academic administration. I am now enjoying the research role to the fullest, playing catch-up in a fast-moving game.

Genetics and Aging

In the course of all this, I have metamorphosed (I hope that I can make the claim) from a behavioral geneticist into a gerontological geneticist, being now concerned with, among others, phenotypes of pulmonary function, body mass index, blood lipids, collagen cross-linkage, and natural killer cell activity. I have joined a substantial and talented group of scholars who have for some considerable time been bringing various genetic perspectives to bear on aging processes (McClearn, 1987). Evolutionary genetics has featured strongly in comparative studies of different species in longevity; evolutionary and population genetics considerations have been central to prominent theories of aging, such as that of antagonistic pleiotropy or disposable soma; molecular genetics has explored issues of somatic mutation, protein anomalies and oxidative stress, among other current salient topics; single Mendelian genes have been sought in progerias and progeroid conditions. As already noted, the kind of genetics projects that I and my colleagues have undertaken address individual differences in the normal range of variation of age-related phenomena—the hunting grounds of the differential model. This normal range is a central issue and motivating force in much of gerontological research, both because understanding the origins of individuality within this range will necessarily illuminate basic aging processes and because of urgent policy implications of the inexorable aging of the populations of the developed world. It is, therefore, a particularly attractive research target for gerontological genetics.

What have studies of this sort—ours and others—contributed to gerontological thought? No detailed summary can be given here, but a few generalizations are in order. First, it is clear that the relative mix of genetic and environmental factors influencing age-related processes can vary greatly from process to process. There is no single number to describe the heritability of all aging processes. Furthermore, it is clear that the gene/environment mix can differ across age groups. Again, depending on the genotype, there is a wide range of outcomes. In some cases, heritability, either high or low, is quite stable over the life span. Other phenotypes conform to the general gerontological expectation that (presumably due to a lifetime of accumulated environmental effects) variance of age-related traits will be increasingly of environmental origin. Much of the present evidence is cross-sectional, and there is a good possibility that observed changes in genetic and environmental variance components might be due to selective attrition. People with particular genotypes, or having experienced particular environments, may not have survived. It is also possible, of course, that change is actually occurring in the number and identity of genes that are influencing the phenotype. Longitudinal data are now becoming available to clarify these issues.

Changes in expression of genes with age are the subject matter of developmental molecular genetics, one of the most exciting current cutting edges in biological research, and one with obvious import for the genetics of aging. Heretofore, demonstrations at the molecular level that genes may be turned on or off have affected the world of quantitatively distributed phenotypes principally by providing empirical justification for the hypothesis that such changes can occur as well in polygenic systems. Prospects for tangible application of changes in gene expression to the complex phenotypes remained limited, however, until recent developments in genome mapping. It has now become possible to identify some of the elements within the hitherto anonymous polygenic systems. With individuation of these "quantitative trait loci," the prospects of studying gene-gene and gene-environment interactions have become enormously brighter, both in associational studies in human beings and by mating manipulations in animal model systems. The means for bridging the gulf between quantitative and molecular genetics are now at hand. I believe that this is an extraordinary opportunity. It provides a powerful platform both for the further pursuit of the reductionist science that has been so spectacularly successful in the genetics of the past several decades and for the integrationist science that, it is increasingly realized, will be essential for the understanding of the functioning of complex systems of whole organisms. So the future of gerontological genetics is particularly bright. I'm looking forward to some role in it as an aging geneticist of aging, and the excellent team with which I'm now working makes the prospect even more attractive.

Envoi

It was flattering to be asked to provide this autobiographical sketch. Are there any lessons to be drawn from it? I don't know. It might be the observation with which I started. A lot of the details of a career are accidental. Perhaps it would be better to say that opportunities can present themselves unexpectedly. I have no prescription, however, for distinguishing unexpected opportunities from unexpected traps. I caution, however, that it's not always easy to avoid administrative roles.

It is highly instructive to have the occasion to identify the people who have played a significant role in one's career. I have identified quite a few here, but have been constrained by space considerations from even trying a comprehensive listing, which would, in any case, run a serious risk of omissions. They—fellow faculty, academic administrators, students, postdocs, technical and clerical staff—know who they are and, I hope, know how profoundly grateful I am. Thanks to them all, and I hope they'll forgive me if the general course of the narrative did not offer an easy opportunity to identify them by name.

References

Fosmire, G. J., Focht, S. J., & McClearn, G. E. (1993). Genetic influences on tissue deposition of aluminum in mice. *Biological Trace Element Research, 37,* 115–121.

Fuller, J. L., & Thompson, W. R. (1960). *Behavior genetics.* New York: John Wiley & Sons.

Hall, C. S. (1951). The genetics of behavior. In S. S. Stevens (Ed.), *Handbook of experimental psychology.* New York: John Wiley & Sons.

Hirsch, J. (Ed.). (1967). *Behavior-genetic analysis.* New York: McGraw-Hill.

Manosevitz, M., Lindzey, G., & Thiessen, D. D. (Eds.). (1969). *Behavioral genetics method and research.* New York: Appleton-Century-Crofts.

McClearn, G. E. (1987). The many genetics of aging. In A. D. Woodhead & K. H. Thompson (Eds.), *Evolution of longevity in animals: A comparative approach* (pp. 135–144). New York: Plenum Press.

McClearn, G. E., & DeFries, J. C. (1973). *An introduction to behavioral genetics.* San Francisco: Freeman Press.

Vaughn, W. F. (1939). *General psychology.* New York: Odyssey Press.

Chapter 17
GETTING HERE WAS HALF THE FUN

John R. Nesselroade

"You don't expect me to know what to say about a play when I don't know who the author is, do you? . . . If it's by a good author, it's a good play, naturally. That stands to reason."

—George Bernard Shaw

Friday the Thirteenth: The Curtain Rises

Who can say when the developmental pathway through which I have passed in reaching the point of writing this chapter truly began? The portion with which I have closest acquaintance started about noon on Friday, March 13, 1936, in Silverton, West Virginia, in the home of my maternal grandparents, Bessie and Theodore Suck (pronounced *Sook*). My parents, John S. and Emma E. Nesselroade, both native West Virginians, were residing at the time on the south side of Parkersburg, West Virginia, but Mother had gone "home" to give birth to her second child, me. My older brother, Edward, had been born in the same house less than two years earlier. Theodore owned and operated the mill in Silverton and made a comfortable living grinding grain. He was a determined, crusty, tobacco-chewing, badly crippled workaholic who was well respected in Silverton's environs. He loved his family but, I have inferred from stories told by my mother, was not very adept at showing it.

Growing Up in West Virginia

My dad worked for the Parkersburg Rig and Reel Company. He had only an eighth-grade education, but he had taken a correspondence course in management from the LaSalle Extension University (his diploma hung on our living room wall for many years). Dad worked his way into a foreman position and was a valued employee until the company changed hands near the time of his retirement. After nearly 40 years, Dad's pension was some $37 per month. My mother, who was a high school graduate, was devoted fully to Dad and her children. She scrimped and saved and managed our finances probably as well as the leanness of our situation allowed. I recall how she would "figure" the bills each month deciding how best to deal with the inevitable discrepancies between income and outgo that would surface before Dad's next payday. For years after the end of World War II, Mother

It is appropriate for me to acknowledge the highly influential papers on factorial invariance published by Bill Meredith (Meredith, 1964a, 1964b) at the time I was completing my master's thesis. Meredith's clear and powerful thinking has been a strong influence on my work for more than 30 years.

kept a 25-lb bag of sugar under her bed. She enjoyed baking and making fudge and after having done without sugar during the war was determined that it wouldn't happen to her again. When teased about this little cache, she would reply that she "wanted to get it before the hoarders did."

I was formally educated in the public schools of Wood County, West Virginia, between 1943 and 1954. From the first grade, I was what was described then as a good student, reading with the "bluebirds" rather than the "robins," often winning the class spelling bees, earning high grades in all subjects, and generally staying out of trouble.

Although there was no tradition of higher education in my family, my paternal grandmother, Nellie R. Nesselroade (nee Robinson), of whom I have some vague memories, would occasionally write and sell pieces to magazines and newspapers to augment whatever funds my grandfather Earl sent home from "roughnecking" in the oil fields of Kansas and Oklahoma. Among my treasured possessions is a book, *Voices from the Fields: A Book of Country Songs by Farming People* (Houghton Mifflin, 1937), which contains the poem, "All Serene," with the byline Nellie R. Nesselroade, West Virginia. Grandpa Earl, who was badly crippled by the time I knew him, was a big, quiet man whose physical strength was once legendary in the Nesselroade family. Ed and I got to spend quite a lot of time with Grandpa Earl when we were little and I can recall how he stressed such virtues as honesty and sobriety, but he also liked to tease and did so often and with remarkable subtlety.

My brother Dale was born two years after me and he was followed about five years later by Kenneth. Three years after Ken came David and a year after that our only sister, Nancy, was born. Family income was not able to keep pace with family size, and by my third- or fourth-grade year we were not doing very well financially.

For two years my family lived in the little town of Rockport, West Virginia. At first seven and then eight of us lived in a five-room house that boasted running water (supplied by electric pump from our own well) but no bathroom. We had an outdoor toilet—a "two-holer"—from the use of which I can attest to the validity of all the jokes one has ever heard about Sears Roebuck catalogs and the cold wind whistling through the cracks in the wintertime. We boys bathed in the kitchen in the winter and often in the creek in the summer. But thanks to mother, we always had clean clothes to wear.

I attended fifth and sixth grades at Rockport Elementary, which housed eight grades in only three rooms. Dale and I built the fires in the three rooms' coal stoves during the winter months. Mother and Ed swept the schoolrooms each evening while Dale and I dumped the wastebaskets, cleaned the blackboards, cut kindling wood, and prepared the fires for lighting the next morning. I believe that we received 40 dollars per month for our collective efforts. During these two years at Rockport, Mother began to manifest symptoms of the strain of bearing six children in 13 years (the last two only about a year apart) and trying to feed, clothe, and rear them with too little money, and her grip on reality would occasionally loosen. With lots of intrafamilial cooperation and the "nerve" medicine prescribed by Dr. Yeager, she continued to manage our day-to-day living as well as she could. My dad was always a strict disciplinarian, and during those two years he kept a particularly tight rein on us because of Mother's tenuous hold on her sanity. Mother was a survivor; she lived to regain her mental health and quite happily defined her own success in the accomplishments of her family. That all six of their children earned at least bachelor's degrees and built successful careers was a source of great pride for both of my parents.

When I was 13 years old, we moved back to Vienna, West Virginia. Our family fortunes had changed enough that we moved into a five-bedroom house, which seemed palatial compared to the house in Rockport. Our next-door neighbors told us several years later that they were aghast when they learned that a family with six children, the five oldest of whom were boys ranging in age from 15 to 3, was moving next door. Because of the rather narrow limits defining the envelop of my dad's view of permissible behavior for his sons and his zest for reminding us when we pushed it, we behaved, property values held, and the neighbors stayed on in relative tranquility.

In my seventh-grade year, I was one of two seventh graders to make the football traveling squad. I think we traveled three times, each time about 10 miles—round-trip! In my ninth-grade year, I played center on the football team, forward on the basketball team, ran the low hurdles on the track team (not particularly well), was captain of the school patrol, played the lead in the class play, *Grandad Steps Out,* and won an annual award given by the principal, Mr. Shutts, to one male and one female in the graduating class—a certificate in recognition of qualities of leadership and a little book titled, *I Dare You,* by William H. Danforth. The book was an exhortation to lead a life of courage, honor, sacrifice, and self-discipline, thereby ensuring success. I took pride in having won "the little book" and read it carefully several times over the next few years. A key precept was that one should dare to reach for greater success in life than one might otherwise expect to attain.

During my junior year at Parkersburg High, I worked after school and on weekends in the Market Street Garage for the magnificent sum of 50 cents an hour. Although I did not suddenly acquire a lavish lifestyle, mine was greatly improved by the spending money I received from my garage job. For example, after years of having my hair cut by my father, a situation that my adolescent soul found demeaning, I could now afford to go to Loving's barbershop and have my flattop groomed by a professional. I recall Dad asking me once how much I had to pay for a haircut at Loving's and his nonverbal but unmistakable rebuke when I told him. I believe it was $1.25.

By my senior year I was 6 feet 4 inches tall and was a creditable basketball player. Under Coach Sam Mandich, a former marine who had surrendered part of one ear to a Japanese flamethrower at Iwo Jima, the 1953–1954 Parkersburg Big Reds lost only one regular season game, won their sectional and regional tournaments, and traveled to the state playoffs. Sadly for us, we were defeated in the state tournament by a team that we had beaten handily during the regular season. The state tournament was played in the field house at West Virginia University in Morgantown and that was my initial visit to the institution where, 13 years later, I would hold my first tenure-track appointment.

One final memorable experience during those last three months in high school was performing in the senior class play. A desperate dramatics teacher, Grace-Marie Merrill, came to basketball practice one evening in February or March and pleaded for some of us to try out for the senior class play. For reasons I never fully apprehended, I complied and won the role of Dr. Emmett in *The Curious Savage.* As we said in those days, "It was a blast!" Those of us who weren't members of the thespian society were made honorary members for our efforts. Trying to be an effective lecturer in methods courses year after year forces one to reach deep into one's resources. No doubt somewhere in my own bag of tricks are included remnants of my stage experiences.

Between High School and College: Earning the G.I. Bill

I enlisted in the Marine Corps three weeks out of high school, in part to take advantage of the Korean G.I. bill. I knew I should go to college even if I wasn't sure why. Basic training at Parris Island, South Carolina, was an experience that cannot be adequately described. One really has to live it. Suffice it to say that, in the expanse of 10 weeks, I experienced some of the best and some of the worst in human behavior. I remember sitting up with my dad the first night of my leave home after boot camp and telling him some of my experiences;

experiences there was no need to embellish. He looked me squarely in the eye and said, ''Why Son, they don't do things like that in the United States.'' When I assured him that ''they'' did, he muttered that it was hard to believe and made his way off to bed.

While in the Marine Corps I scored well in the various classification tests and was sent to the Marine Corps Air Wing instead of the ''ground pounders.'' I went first to Airman Prep School in Jacksonville, Florida, for two months of training in simple shop mechanics, electricity, and so on, in preparation for placement in more advanced schooling. My two months extended into four months because I was playing basketball for the JAX Marines. January 1955 found me in Millington, Tennessee, just a few miles from Memphis, enrolled in a seven-month course in electronics operated by the U.S. Navy. The curriculum focused mainly on troubleshooting and repairing various radio transmitters and receivers and some radar equipment. This was not an easy school. We were assessed weekly and the tests nearly always involved a timed performance component. Our reward for successfully managing the first 27 weeks included a flight in the 28th week during which we got to take over as radar operator and guide the pilot via intercom to a series of objectives. For a 19-year-old whose world for the first 18 years of his life was limited to portions of West Virginia and Ohio, these were heady experiences.

The higher one finished in the electronics course, the greater the choice of the next duty station. This was a very practical lesson in being rewarded directly for hard work and effort. I got to go to Japan and with that began a long-term enjoyment of international travel.

When I returned to the United States for the Christmas holidays in December 1956 after 16 months in the Orient, I found my parents both doing very well. My dad, although continuing to work for the Rig and Reel, had successfully undertaken a rather extensive reading course and series of examinations and had become an ordained minister in the Evangelical United Brethren Church. He was serving as minister for a circuit of three churches scattered around Wood County. This was one of my first close encounters with the notion that important life changes of a positive nature can be accomplished successfully relatively late in life.

I still remember my younger brother Dale's grin when I awakened him that first morning home from Japan and he unfolded 6 feet 6 inches of frame from what used to be my bed and looked down into my eyes. That both he and my older brother, Ed, were in college was an added impetus for me to do the same when I reentered civilian life.

Higher Education

After serving three years in ''the Corps'' I was separated from active duty in June 1957 and drove home from Cherry Point, North Carolina, with strong feelings of accomplishment, optimism about the future, several hundred dollars in mustering-out pay, and no small sense of relief. A postscript to the electronics training I received is that despite the school having been a very good one, the curriculum featured vacuum-tube theory. Within a short time, vacuum tubes had largely been replaced by transistors and I remember having a distinct sense that I was ''obsolete'' at the age of 22. During that first several months of civilian life, I labored for a plastering contractor and applied to and was accepted at Marietta College in Marietta, Ohio, about 10 miles from Parkersburg.

I began at Marietta College in February 1958, enrolled in the electrical engineering curriculum. When I asked the registrar about transferring six credits (algebra and philosophy) that I had earned in Japan from University of Maryland extension courses, the rather discriminating clerk announced that it would depend on how well I performed in my courses at Marietta that first year. The six credits were accepted, and by taking extra credits most semesters I was able to complete my BS in 3½ years. Marietta had a strong liberal arts orientation so, in my second year, I enrolled in Professor Bruce Blackburn's introductory psychology course. Blackburn, who had never quite completed his PhD, was nonetheless a knowledgeable spokesperson for psychology. I was taken with him and his introductory course and soon told him about my interest in psychology. He expressed his pleasure and then surprised me by telling me to take all the mathematics I could. He added, "I don't care whether or not you take my psychology courses. We'll get you into a good graduate program in psychology." Although I was grossly unfamiliar with graduate and postgraduate study and advanced degrees, I knew they were "good" and was repeatedly advised by Professor Blackburn to keep my sights on graduate school.

Throughout grade school and high school, mathematics had come easily to me but early on at Marietta College, I came close to a serious "flubbing" of my lines. I began with a course in trigonometry. For a variety of reasons, not all of which come readily to mind, I did not apply myself to mastering the trigonometric identities with a level of enthusiasm commensurate with Dr. Hutt's expectations. Consequently, I performed miserably on his midterm examination. When I went to talk to him about my test score, he literally dismissed me with the comment, "My advice to you is to drop the course. If you stay in it you will flunk." Being on the verge of flunking was a novel experience for me and to this day I don't know if Dr. Hutt's warning was to have been taken literally or as a challenge. I accepted it as a challenge and through no small effort managed to complete the course with a final grade of B. A grade of B, I hasten to add, was a very respectable grade at Marietta in those days.

When I completed analytic geometry I had satisfied the liberal arts mathematics requirements that I needed to meet to be a psychology major. But, in keeping with Professor Blackburn's advice, I enrolled in the differential calculus course next and never looked back. I took integral calculus, advanced calculus, differential equations, mechanics, and modern abstract algebra and earned mostly As. Nevertheless, at some point in the advanced math courses I took, often with no more than eight to ten other students, I would see the occasional person who simply thought about and did higher mathematics differently (and in a superior manner) than I did. I was envious of such people but, at some level, I think my perception of a qualitative difference between us probably strengthened my resolve eventually to go into a field other than mathematics. I like to do things well.

In my first semester I had to take the zoology course that was taught by Professors Paul Seyler and David Young. A lot of memory work was involved, including large amounts of taxonomy. To my delight, I "broke the curve" on the final amid a large number of premed fellow students. My success in the zoology course provided some balm for not doing so well in the trigonometry course. When I was speaking with Dr. Seyler several years later, he told me that he and Mr. Young at first thought that I must have cheated on the final exam but, after several biology courses—including a two-semester comparative anatomy course in which we dissected Rana pipiens, Squalus acanthias, and Felix domestica (I split my minor between biology and physics)—they were satisfied that I had not.

The credit largely belongs to my advisor, Professor Blackburn, but I have always been grateful for the undergraduate background I received spanning mathematics, biology, and physics taught within a strong liberal arts environment. It was an excellent training regimen from which to move into the study of behavior.

Enter My Costar

My developmental pathway was forever enriched that February of 1958 when I was introduced to a lovely brunette named Carolyn Sue Boyles. Both Carolyn and I recognized that we had been in high school together but, in that large class of more than 600 students who graduated with us in 1954, we had been only barely acquainted. From the night we first double-dated (each of us with someone else) to the present we have been "an item." We were married in July 1959. More than 10 years after we were married we discovered that we had indeed signed each other's high school yearbooks. I had written "to a nice girl" in hers, and she had written "lots of luck" in mine. My youthful assessment of her continues to be valid and her early wishes on my behalf have been fulfilled a thousand times over.

My Ticket Out Arrives via Special Delivery

At the proper time I applied for graduate school to three psychology programs: University of Illinois, University of Iowa, and University of Pittsburgh. Professor Blackburn's advice to prepare by taking lots of mathematics had been sound. I was accepted at all three universities. My letter of acceptance from Iowa was signed by Kenneth W. Spence. Initially, I accepted the University of Pittsburgh's offer and was set to enroll in fall 1961. In the meantime, Professor Blackburn had written a letter to Raymond B. Cattell at Illinois and had told him about me, expressing his belief that I would be a good candidate for a research assistantship in Cattell's laboratory.

I had received my BS from Marietta and for the summer was working a 40-hour week at a local ESSO service station and running a bowling alley several nights of the week. One day a letter came that had a major impact on my career. The letter, which arrived via special delivery, was a handwritten invitation from Professor Cattell to come to Illinois for graduate school and work in his laboratory as a research assistant. Moreover, I could start that summer, as soon as I could get there. After consulting with Professor Blackburn, I wrote to Pittsburgh and secured a release, gave notice to my employers, and about three weeks later Carolyn, Cynthia Anne, our daughter who had been born October 12, 1960, and I were on our way to Champaign-Urbana. As were my dad and grandpa Earl, I tended to be rather tight-lipped, and for years afterward Carolyn would tease me by telling people that when we loaded the car and a U-Haul trailer with our meager belongings and set off for graduate school she was under the impression that we were headed to Pittsburgh and was surprised when we ended up in Illinois.

As I've noted elsewhere (Nesselroade, 1990), the combination of a half-time research assistantship in the beehive known as the Laboratory of Personality Assessment and Group Behavior (changed about 1962 to the Laboratory of Personality and Group Analysis), which Cattell ran with incredible involvement despite a heavy travel schedule, and the proseminar for first-year graduate students in the Department of Psychology at Illinois in the early 1960s made basic training at Parris Island seem tame in many ways. Apprenticing in Cattell's laboratory was exciting and instructive. Regardless of how insignificant some of my tasks seemed to be, the sense of important work going on in the laboratory was widely shared. I was elated to be a part of it. Several of us were on half-time research assistantships that required us to work 20 hours per week. Cattell's laboratory clock, however, hung high on the wall of aspiration and was powered by satisfaction for a job well and quickly done. There were important projects to be completed and that was what we were there for—the 20 hours per week was a meaningless number.

Among the resident research associates in Cattell's lab at the time were John D. Hundleby, Kurt Pawlik, and Arthur Sweney. There was also a constant parade of visiting scholars to Cattell's laboratory from around the world. They included Cyril Adcock (Australia), Åke Bjerstedt (Sweden), Sam Hammond (Australia), Akira Ishikawa (Japan), Jos Jaspers (The Netherlands), Klaus Schneewind (Germany), Bien Tsujioka (Japan), Karl

Uberla (Germany), Graham Vaughan (New Zealand), and Frank Warburton (England). Graduate students working in Cattell's laboratory at the time I arrived included Richard L. Gorsuch and John L. Horn. John, with whom I have had a special relationship for nearly 40 years, started teaching me the first week I arrived at Cattell's laboratory when I was assigned to help him collect data, and I am still learning from him.

The laboratory setting, which afforded me the opportunity to interact and learn from a wide variety of psychologists, contributed greatly to my graduate education. In part, because I quickly picked up some computer skills that these visiting scholars found helpful, I engaged with most of them at length during the course of their stay in the laboratory. The mainframe computer at the time was called ''the Illiac'' (Illinois automatic computer) and my recollection is that there was about 35 kilobytes available for access by those writing programs for data analysis.

The psychology faculty at Illinois was a star-studded and awe-inspiring one. In addition to Cattell, Charles Erickson, Lloyd G. Humphreys, J. McV. Hunt, O. Hobart Mowrer, Charles E. Osgood, Ledyard R. Tucker, and Jerry S. Wiggins were some of the graduate faculty who lectured in the proseminar my first year. Not only did I feel greatly intimidated by these stalwarts of our discipline but I also became aware quickly of how many very smart graduate students had been brought into the program. In those days, the selection process was continued on site in many graduate programs. Sixty-six new graduate students began that highly competitive situation in 1961 and yes, Department Chairman Lloyd Humphreys did tell us that half of us would not be there next year. And yes, half weren't. I heard some years later that perhaps 25% of us eventually earned the PhD from Illinois.

As thrilled as I was to be working in Cattell's laboratory, I was, at the same time, just as unsure of myself with regard to the proseminar. My lack of advanced training in psychology was evident to me and most likely to the professors with whom I had a chance to interact. Sadly, mathematics still provides few answers when the questions are psychological. I cannot say that I distinguished myself in the proseminar—the screening device for rooting out half of our class. One or two more un- or incorrectly answered questions in either the midsemester or final examination of that spring session and I would have been among the casualties who started but never completed graduate school at the University of Illinois and, most likely, I would not be writing this story today. That first year was a toughening one. I've no doubt that earlier experiences, including those in ''the Corps,'' helped me persevere at those times when I literally wondered, ''What am I doing here?''

In my third year of graduate school, 1963, again on Columbus Day, our second daughter, Jennifer Sue, was born. My lofty goals for supporting my family well notwithstanding, during graduate school, ours was a rather penurious existence. Carolyn made most of the girls' clothes and managed the other necessities on my stipend plus some money she made for scoring tests at home for Cattell's laboratory. Needless to say, family recreational activities were severely limited not only by the lack of money but by my schedule. We did have many enjoyable outings at Lake of the Woods and Crystal Lake Parks although Carolyn still maintains that my invitations usually took the form, ''Okay, let's go picnic. I'm free between 12:30 and 12:45.'' After I passed the qualifying exams, Cattell appointed me research associate and my salary went from less than $4,000 a year to $9,000 per year. We left graduate school with our car paid for and a few hundred dollars in the bank.

Seminars with Cattell, Lloyd Humphreys's course on human abilities, Tucker's scaling course, and Henry Kaiser's factor analysis course were particular highlights for me. When we would return to West Virginia for holidays, I would sometimes go to visit Professor Blackburn at his home in Marietta. Invariably, he would smile and say, ''Well, tell me about Cattell.'' It was clear that he, as did many of us, recognized the important role that Cattell played for so many years in the history of psychology as a quantitative science. As I reflect on those Illinois times from my perspective of today, one of the critical experiences for me was being introduced to P-technique factor analysis and the idea that strong quantitative methods could be applied to repeated multivariate observations of the single case as a way to study intraindividual variability. Early in my tenure in his laboratory, Ray Cattell began writing his chapter on P-technique and differential-R technique factor analysis for the book *Problems in Measuring Change,* edited by Chester W. Harris. I read an early draft of that chapter and was forever changed by its content. The interest in studying intraindividual variability kindled then has grown with time and continues to be a focal point of my research and scholarly activities.

During my graduate student years, Cattell dedicated tremendous effort and energy to starting the Society of Multivariate Experimental Psychology and helping to launch its journal, *Multivariate Behavioral Research.* In 1964–1965 he was also editing the first edition of the *Handbook of Multivariate Experimental Psychology* (Cattell, 1966). On several successive nights in his lab as the handbook was nearing completion, I helped Cattell prepare the final reference list. On those evenings he would smuggle in a bottle of red wine to facilitate our perambulations through the hundreds of index cards. On those evenings we swapped stories and joked at a level of complexity designed to relieve the boredom of the task while not threatening the accuracy of the 1601 eventual entries. Nearly 20 years after the first edition of the handbook was published, Cattell invited me to serve as senior editor for the second edition; he was coeditor (Nesselroade & Cattell, 1988). That was more than a decade ago. In the not too distant future, I hope to extend a similar invitation to a younger colleague concerning the third edition.

I considered myself very fortunate to be working so closely with such a broad and powerful intellect. Later, I realized my good luck also in being exposed so relentlessly to ''the multivariate orientation.'' Clearly, those experiences profoundly affected my own development and helped to shape my career.

My doctoral committee was composed of Raymond B. Cattell (chair), Lloyd G. Humphreys, Donald M. Peterson, Maurice M. Tatsuoka, and Ledyard R. Tucker. This formidable quintet administered one last lesson in humility at my ''dress rehearsal''—the dissertation defense—but then passed me while requiring only minor modifications to my dissertation. Although it occurred more than 30 years ago, I have a vivid recollection of walking with Cattell back to his laboratory afterward. Quite unexpectedly, he said to me, ''I think it would be okay if you were to call me Ray from now on.'' Of course, this meant a great deal to me but it was at least another two years before I could bring myself to try it. Subsequently, the timing of my own entrance onto the academic stage afforded me the great fun of tendering similar lines to my earliest PhD students before the distinctions between faculty and graduate students that rendered possible such polite gestures were dropped with the major rewriting of scripts that occurred in the late 1960s and early 1970s.

Opening in West Virginia

K. Warner Schaie was largely responsible for my joining the faculty at West Virginia University (WVU) when I completed my PhD. In November of 1965, I drove with Ray Cattell in a university car from Champaign-Urbana to Madison, Wisconsin, to attend one of the earliest annual meetings of the Society of Multivariate Experimental Psychology as Cattell's guest. Warner was at that meeting in Madison and Cattell introduced us. In a brief conversation in the elevator Warner encouraged me to get in touch with him when I was ready to enter the job market.

I recall the drive back from Madison to Champaign-Urbana on a Saturday night quite vividly because we were treated to a specialty of the Midwest at that time of year—a significant snowstorm. I drove while Ray, in part to keep me awake and alert, recited poetry, quite literally for several hours. His vast repertoire ranged from Shakespeare and Words-worth (one of Cattell's favorite poets) to some of the earthiest limericks that I had ever heard, despite my time in the Marine Corps.

In the fall of 1966, I let Warner Schaie know that I expected to finish by the next summer and was beginning to look for a job. At the time, Warner was director of clinical training in the WVU psychology department, but it was pretty clear that he was heir apparent to the chairmanship. I was invited to Morgantown to visit the department and did so while we were visiting our families in West Virginia during the Christmas holidays. I visited the department and met several faculty members, but I was not even asked to give a talk. It was never made clear to me why I didn't have to make a presentation, but I was pleased because I had had little experience on that side of the podium and was not at ease in such situations. In any case, I was offered and accepted a tenure-track, assistant professor position in 1967.

During my initial two years at WVU, Warner arranged a half-time appointment for me in the Human Resources Research Institute, which essentially amounted to freeing me of half of my teaching load without imposing other obligations on me. Thus, I was able to write some Fortran programs for data analysis and begin my research and scholarly work. The very first course I taught was on multivariate analysis in which, along with about 15 graduate students, some five or six faculty decided to sit. Even though I was completely untested, I honestly did not feel threatened by having faculty members in my audience. Indeed, I performed so effectively that by the time I finished two weeks of matrix algebra and linear combinations of variables my faculty colleagues had apparently learned all they wanted to know because they had stopped attending.

I learned and benefited much from my relationship to Warner Schaie. He was eager to raise the quality of the psychology department at WVU and saw the development of young faculty as one key to realizing his goal. A side of Schaie that many people have never seen, I'm sure, was exemplified by his offer in early 1968 to help me complete my 1967 income tax forms. Warner assured me that several benefits were available when one made the transition from graduate student to assistant professor. I had never heard, for instance, of income averaging. Warner devoted much of one Sunday afternoon to my financial affairs and as a result, our income tax return was very substantial. As I recall, it enabled Carolyn and me to purchase a piano for our home.

Enter Paul Baltes

Among other inducements to accept the position offered me at WVU, Warner Schaie told me that he was bringing in another new PhD, from Germany, with whom he thought I would get on well. I began in fall 1967 and, indeed, in January 1968, Paul Baltes joined the faculty. At West Virginia, I was a member of the personality-social program. Despite the fact that Paul was in the developmental group, in very short order we became collaborators and very close friends. We have remained so for 30 years. At that time at West Virginia, a small group led by Baltes and Schaie was beginning to pump new life into life-span development. Coincidentally, the senior member of the personality-social program took a position elsewhere, and Schaie, who by then was department chair, disbanded the personality-social program and encouraged the survivors to affiliate with other programs in the department. I first toyed with the idea of joining the experimental group but soon became a developmentalist in part because of a long-term interest in the problems of measuring change and in part because of my relationship with Paul.

As a junior faculty member I knew well my lines in some scenes and had to ad-lib frantically in many others. Working in Cattell's laboratory had been a priceless intellectual experience to be sure, but Ray Cattell was inclined to be neither tolerant nor diplomatic about it when it came to requests on his time not involving his own research program. Thus from Paul Baltes I learned much, both substantively and professionally. In addition to helping me identify some of the interesting methodological issues in aging research, including distinguishing rigorously between quantitative and qualitative change, Paul educated me about many of the obligations incumbent on a member of a profession. Constructing letters of recommendation and evaluation and reviewing manuscripts and proposals, for instance, were novel activities for me. I was very fortunate to have colleagues I respected who were also wise and willing to make their counsel easily accessible to me.

The first intellectual discussion that I can recall having with Paul Baltes took place in the Mountainlair (the WVU student union) where, over coffee, we argued about the nature and implications of factorial invariance. This discussion led to the first of more than a score of joint publications, many of which focused on developmental research methods (Baltes, Reese, & Nesselroade, 1977). Paul and I applied for and were awarded two significant research grants by the National Institute of Education, which led to the publication of several papers and a monograph (Nesselroade & Baltes, 1974) describing a short-term longitudinal study of adolescent personality and ability changes. In 1970, in a strong show of leadership that included overtly rewarding the kind of professional behavior of which he desired to raise the frequency, Warner Schaie engineered promotions for Paul and me to associate professor with tenure when we were just three years out of graduate school.

I quickly learned that I thoroughly enjoyed being involved in graduate education. In addition to having several fine graduate students of my own, including Thomas Bartsch, Dana Cable, Joe Fitzgerald, John Friel, Erich Labouvie, and Michael Lebo, I also worked closely with many of Paul's students.

Carolyn supported my flurried efforts to get my career in high gear by minimizing responsibilities on the home front. I tried to juggle family and professional demands in a responsible way, but my family was probably short-changed more often than my profession. Had that profile been different, however, I well might not be writing this piece. I am happy to say that both my daughters, who are highly professional, productive citizens of whom I am extremely proud, appear to have forgiven me any earlier excesses.

On to Penn State

In the summer of 1972, Paul went to The Pennsylvania State University as director of the Division of Individual and Family Studies in the College of Human Development. Soon after Paul had accepted his position, he had recruited me to go along. This process was smoothed via the good offices of Dean Donald H. Ford so expeditiously that the Balteses and the Nesselroades moved from Morgantown, West Virginia, to State College, Pennsylvania, in the same moving van. A significant portion of the contents of that van was a large number of IBM card-filing cabinets.

I spent 19 productive, enjoyable years in the Human Development and Family Studies (HDFS) program at Penn State. During the first 10 years at Penn State, I continued to work with Paul and also collaborated with Don Ford, Dave Hultsch, Ted Huston, Richard Lerner, Fred Vondracek, and Sherry Willis. Later colleagues and collaborators included Chris Hertzog, Gerry McClearn, Robert Plomin, and Alex von Eye. Chris, in particular, had been a frequent critic (but a supportive one) of my manuscript drafts for many years. While I was affiliated with the HDFS program, I mentored a large number of PhD students, many of whom have gone on to make their own marks in aging research. The list includes Sherry Corneal, Roger Dixon, Bill Hays, Karen Hooker, Constance Jones, Rudy Kafer, Linda Mitteness, Judy Plemons, Rachel Pruchno, Marsha Roberts, Ron Spiro, and Linda Thompson. Although they were not my students per se, I also collaborated with Cindy Bergeman, Rodney Cate, Steve Cornelius, Margie Lachman, Michael Rovine, and John Schulenberg.

My tenure in the HDFS program was especially a time of moving more and more into aging research issues. I was closely affiliated with the Adult Development and Enrichment project of Paul Baltes and Sherry Willis and later worked with Gerry McClearn, Robert Plomin, and Nancy Pedersen on the Swedish Adoption/Twin Study of Aging study. Both involved repeated measurements of older subjects. Shortly after Paul left to take a Max Planck Institute directorship in Berlin in 1980, I was reunited with Warner Schaie, who moved from the University of Southern California to Penn State. Other collaborations that I began while I was at Penn State and that have meant much to me professionally include work with M. Powell Lawton and Mort Kleban at the Philadelphia Geriatric Center, Ursula Walsh and Todd Petr of the National Collegiate Athletic Association, and Robert Ellsworth, who was then with the Veterans Administration.

In the mid-1980s, under the deanship of Anne C. Petersen, I started the Center for Developmental and Health Research Methodology. About that same time, we obtained a training grant from the National Institute on Aging and began training postdoctoral fellows in aging research methodology. Postdoctoral fellows who came to study and work at the center included Jeffrey Burr, Bruce Pugesek, Verneda Hamm, Scott Hershberger, Tenko Raykov, Charles Scialfa, Adrian Tomer, and Phillip K. Wood.

In 1977 I had begun serving on the National Institute on Aging's Aging Review Committee and soon thereafter met Dr. John W. (Jack) Rowe, then at Harvard University Medical School. In 1985, I became a member of the John D. and Catherine T. MacArthur Foundation Research Network on Successful Aging, which Jack Rowe chaired. It was through the support of Jack and the other members of the network that my friend and colleague David L. Featherman and I implemented a study of week-to-week variation in a wide array of cognitive, psychological, and physical variables, many of which are taken to be stable, in older adults. The resulting papers are now appearing in the literature (Eizenman, Nesselroade, Featherman, & Rowe, 1997; Ghisletta, Nesselroade, Featherman, & Rowe, 1998; Kim, Nesselroade, & Featherman, 1996; Lang, Featherman, & Nesselroade, 1997) and will, I hope, help to establish some new items on the agenda for research in aging over the next decades.

Mr. Jefferson's University

In August 1991, Carolyn and I moved to the University of Virginia where I was appointed Hugh Scott Hamilton professor of psychology. In addition to having my longtime friend and collaborator, Jack McArdle, as an immediate colleague and one from whom I continue to learn, I have formed several important personal and professional relationships with other members of the department. To hold a chaired professorship at ''Mr. Jefferson's University'' is for me a great honor. The PhD students with whom I have worked since coming to UVA have come from both the quantitative and developmental areas and have also been an excellent lot. They include Steve Boker, Al Damas, Dara Eizenman, Paolo Ghisletta, Jungmeen Kim, Jonathan Meyers, and Xinzi Wu. It has been my pleasure to work closely with Jack McArdle's students as well.

Touring Abroad: The Max Planck Institute

I am pleased to be able to acknowledge the deep gratitude and special regard I hold for the Max Planck Institute (MPI) for Human Development in Berlin. Thanks to Paul Baltes, who went there as a director in 1980, I have been privileged to work at the MPI whenever my university commitments permitted. The arrangement has been a felicitous combination of having a second important professional affiliation and my own private center for advanced study.

Early on in my first visit to the MPI, my not inconsiderable bulk was proximal cause for the premature disintegration of the assigned office chair, and I was permitted to order a rather sturdy and somewhat more elaborate chair by the office staff. I'm sure that a halo emanating from my obvious ties to Paul brought about this acquisition but, in any case, some of my slightly envious younger MPI colleagues jokingly referred to it as ''the Nesselroade chair.'' For 17 years I have sporadically occupied ''the Nesselroade chair'' and interacted with the MPI faculty and staff at many levels. I have a strong sense of belonging and take a deep measure of pride in the institute's scientific accomplishments and the successes of its personnel.

Support for intellectual activity at the MPI is unmatched in my experience and many of the papers I have written with which I am most satisfied were either drafted, improved, or finished while I was sitting in Zimmer 204 at Lentzeallee 94 in Dahlem. There I have been fortunate to have interacted with a large number of permanent appointees as well as visiting scholars. The former includes the late Michael Chapman, Roger Dixon, Alexandra Freund, Jutta Heckhausen, Reinhold Kliegl, Kurt Kreppner, Shu-Chen Li, Ulman Lindenberger, Michael Marsiske, Ellen Skinner, Jacqui Smith, Ursula Staudinger, Alexander von Eye, and Todd Little. The latter includes scholars in aging such as Tim Salthouse, Ron Abeles, and Neil Charnoff. It was also during my first year at the MPI (1981–1982) that I got acquainted with Jack McArdle when he breezed into Berlin from working with Herman Wold and Jan Bernd Lohmöller in Switzerland and southern Germany, respectively.

The Denouement

Clearly, it has been my good fortune to be in professional situations where a great deal seemed to be happening that influenced the development of our science. Cattell's laboratory was in its heyday in the 1960s. That period was a hallmark of his entire lifetime of important scientific contributions, and I have it in his words that I was a salient part of it. In a copy of one of his dozens of books, he inscribed to me in 1971 ''Thanks for one of the most productive periods in the history of the lab.'' When I arrived at West Virginia, the life-span emphasis was just beginning, and I moved to Penn State with the program in Human Development and Family Studies poised to became a force in the developmental arena. My sense of excitement about the future continues to be high as my role develops further at Virginia.

At this point in my career, I am closely occupied with two general themes. One is a personal (and sometimes painful) reassessment of the merits and limitations of the study of individual differences. Because this is the tradition in which I grew up intellectually, it is particularly difficult for me. I hope to unscramble my thoughts enough to write something on this topic in the near future. Concurrently, I have become ever more interested in modeling intraindividual variability and change. I am trying to master some of the exciting work in modeling of process and have begun a promising collaboration with Peter Molenaar at the University of Amsterdam even as I continue working on similar problems with Jack

McArdle, Steve Boker, and other colleagues and graduate students at UVA. My firm belief in the importance of modeling processes of change via intensive, repeated measurements of individuals has never wavered in the 30 years since I earned my PhD. A long line of excellent graduate students have helped to push this methodology while at the same time recognizing the scientific utility of general laws by conducting their studies of the individual with multiple concurrent replications—what my former Penn State colleague Don Ford and I called multivariate, replicated, single-subject, repeated measurement (MRSRM) designs. I am more convinced than ever that considerable damage has been done by the *premature* aggregation of data across individuals. Playing out these concerns in the context of adult development and aging research is an important driver of my current professional behavior.

My family continues to be very important to me. Carolyn and I have been married now for 38 years and my heart still skips a beat when I see her coming toward me. She has anchored our family with grace and dignity while generously always making the world a better place for those less fortunate than we. My daughters, Cindy and Jen, are ever greater sources of pride as they vault up the corporate ladder. Carolyn and I have lost our parents, but our family has gained as sons-in-law Joe Morrisroe and John McNeil, a trade that gives us much comfort. On March 1, 1995, Jonathan Patrick McNeil raised our number to seven. Naturally, he shows all the signs of brilliance and we will nurture him and guarantee his future to every possible extent. Jonathan's brother, Colin James, further augmented our numbers on June 18, 1998.

These dramas we call developmental pathways are complex overlays of events and influences concerning which even the presumed advantages of hindsight cannot guarantee an accurate identification and cataloging of details. Nevertheless, it has been fun to construe 6 decades of experiences in terms of my current situation with something of a license to embellish the memories that are generated in the process. Thus, developing this story line has been a rather uninhibited exercise in self-construction, the form of which may say as much about me as the content. I hope I have made it clear that I have relished my role and that I am deeply beholden to the other members of the cast who have supported me so grandly. Clearly, my interest and work in the field of aging and developmental methodology were influenced most profoundly by my dear friend and colleague Paul Baltes, but I also owe much to the others I have mentioned, too. My current professional associations, which include the continuation of some of my oldest ones, are exciting and promising to me. My extended family, in which I number my graduate students past and present, are sources of comfort, pride, and, indeed, further motivation to keep working on the difficult problems of studying behavior process and change. I sincerely hope that a few more scenes will feature those problems I believe to be key before the curtain falls.

References

Baltes, P. B., Reese, H. W., & Nesselroade, J. R. (1977). *Life-span developmental psychology: Introduction to research methods.* Monterey, CA: Brooks/Cole.

Cattell, R. B. (Ed.). (1966). *Handbook of multivariate experimental psychology.* Chicago: Rand McNally.

Eizenman, D. R., Nesselroade, J. R., Featherman, D. L., & Rowe, J. W. (1997). Intra-individual variability in perceived control in an elderly sample: The MacArthur Successful Aging Studies. *Psychology and Aging, 12,* 489–502.

Ghisletta, P., Nesselroade, J. R., Featherman, D. L., & Rowe, J. W. (1998). *The structure of weekly variability in health and activity measures and its relationship to mortality: The MacArthur Successful Aging Studies.* Department of Psychology, University of Virginia.

Kim, J. E., Nesselroade, J. R., & Featherman, D. L. (1996). The state component in self-reported world views and religious beliefs in older adults: The MacArthur Successful Aging Studies. *Psychology and Aging, 11,* 396–407.

Lang, F. R., Featherman, D. L., & Nesselroade, J. R. (1997). Social self-efficacy and short-term variability in social relationships: The MacArthur Successful Aging Studies. *Psychology and Aging, 12,* 657–666.

Meredith, W. (1964a). Notes on factorial invariance. *Psychometrika, 29*(2), 177–185.

Meredith, W. (1964b). Rotation to achieve factorial invariance. *Psychometrika, 29*(2), 186–206.

Nesselroade, J. R. (1990). Adult personality development: Issues in assessing constancy and change. In A. I. Rabins, R. A. Zucker, R. A. Emmons, & S. Frank (Eds.), *Studying persons and lives* (pp. 41–85). New York: Springer.

Nesselroade, J. R., & Baltes, P. B. (1974). *Adolescent personality development and historical change: 1970–72,* 39, whole No. 154.

Nesselroade, J. R., & Cattell, R. B. (Eds.). (1988). *Handbook of multivariate experimental psychology* (2nd ed.). New York: Plenum Press.

Chapter 18
DEVELOPMENT OF AN ADULT DEVELOPMENTAL PSYCHOLOGIST

Timothy A. Salthouse

Throughout my childhood my father was serving as an officer in the United States Army. That had two important consequences for my early life. One consequence was that the level of discipline in our family was fairly strict, in part because at that time actions of one's children could affect on the career progress of military officers. I have sometimes wondered whether my early observations of differences in family environments among my childhood friends contributed to my later interest in psychology and human behavior. The other important consequence of growing up as a military dependent was the necessity of having to move approximately every two to three years. Among the states where I lived as a child were California, Kentucky, Indiana, Missouri, and Virginia. All of this relocation finally seemed worth it when I spent my last two years of high school in Hawaii. Although I was not a particularly serious student in high school, which I attribute to a strong influence of the external environment at this time of my life, there was never any doubt that I would attend college. Both of my parents were college graduates, and I had always loved to read.

My Introduction to Geropsychology

My choice of psychology as a career occurred while I was an undergraduate at the University of California, Santa Barbara. One of the factors that influenced my decision was an early experience as a research assistant. I was taking a course in experimental psychology when, for reasons that I still don't understand, I came to the attention of the instructor, Robert Gottsdanker, who hired me to work in his laboratory. His research at that time involved studying reaction time as a means of investigating the preparation and maintenance of attention. My responsibilities as a research assistant included testing subjects and preparing "programs" for experiments by designing and implementing wiring diagrams for digital logic modules such as AND and OR gates, which were used before the availability of inexpensive computers. I was intrigued by the precision with which aspects of human behavior could be measured, and began reading as much as I could about the emerging field of cognitive psychology. Neisser's *Cognitive Psychology* (1967) had recently been published, and I remember thinking that it was one of the most fascinating academic books I had ever read. Gottsdanker was very supportive of my interests in psychology, and one way he encouraged them was by inviting me to participate in a graduate seminar while I was still an undergraduate.

Because of my interests in aspects of human performance, I applied and was accepted to graduate school at the University of Michigan in Ann Arbor, where I worked in the Human Performance Center. The center at that time was headed by Arthur Melton and was a collection of human experimental psychologists interested in memory, perception, decision making, and motor skills. All of the faculty and students associated with the center were interested in various issues related to limitations of human performance, and most were heavily influenced by the information-processing perspective on cognition.

My initial advisor in graduate school was Richard Pew, who worked in the area of motor skills. For my master's thesis I conducted research on mental models of the internal dynamics of an apparatus that launched projectiles to a target. I did not do the computer programming for the task; the study was conducted on one of the first microcomputers, a PDP-1, and the programming had to be done in assembly language. Pew went on leave and my dissertation on selective interference in memory for verbal and spatial information was completed under the supervision of Daniel Weintraub. Two articles describing research based on the dissertation were published in 1974 and 1975 in the journal *Memory & Cognition.*

My dissertation was completed in 1973, but I had no success in the job market and therefore I stayed another year in graduate school and officially received my PhD in 1974. The competition for jobs was still very high in 1974, and I remember hearing that there were 300 applicants for some positions. The only offers I received were from military laboratories, but I decided I was not really interested in that type of career. In the spring of 1974 I was offered and accepted a two-year postdoctoral position in aging and psychology with Jack Botwinick and Martha Storandt at Washington University in St. Louis. At the time I had never taken a course in aging and didn't know anything about the field.

My first exposure to the area was reading Botwinick's undergraduate textbook, *Aging and Behavior* (1973). I soon came to the conclusion that the field could be quite interesting because of the opportunity to combine the experimental approach and my interests in cognition to a domain, age-related differences in cognition, of considerable practical importance.

As a postdoctoral fellow I did a great deal of reading in the area of aging and cognition and was especially influenced by Alan Welford's *Ageing and Human Skill* (1958). I was allowed considerable independence while a postdoc and worked some with John Stern, a psychophysiological psychologist from whom I learned how to record and analyze eye movements and other psychophysiological measures. Although I did not collaborate with him on any published research, his influence was later manifested in several studies I conducted with students investigating eye movements. During my postdoctoral period, I also carried out several small studies on age differences in speed, iconic memory, and perceptual closure, as well as a study on the formation of abstract categories among college students.

After two years as a postdoc I was in the job market again and was still not very successful. I received only one interview and that was in the spring of 1976, which was rather late for academic positions. Fortunately for me, I was offered and accepted the position as an assistant professor in the Department of Psychology at the University of Missouri, Columbia. I rose through the academic ranks and left Missouri in 1986 as a full professor.

I was initially hired primarily to teach courses on sensation and perception, but after teaching a total of eight different courses in my first four years, my regular courses were perception, cognition, history of psychology, and research methods. Only once in my 10 years at The University of Missouri did I teach a course on the psychology of aging.

I was strongly influenced at Missouri by Donald Kausler, who was a highly respected researcher in the area of learning and memory. Earlier in his career he had done some research on aging, and he was returning to those interests when I arrived. The two of us were active participants in a brown-bag series where our research and that of students and colleagues was discussed. Eventually the two of us collaborated on a major project sponsored with special funds from the University of Missouri.

One of our motivations in this collaborative project was to explore different methods of recruiting and testing subjects because of the limited number of older adults in the community of Columbia, Missouri. Another motivation from my perspective was a desire to assemble a data set that would allow me to examine age relations simultaneously in multiple variables. Kausler and I developed a proposal to administer a battery of cognitive tests on small portable computers (i.e., Apple IIc computers), and when it was funded we employed examiners across the state of Missouri to recruit and test adults from 18 to over 80 years of age. Eventually data were collected from a total of more than 360 adults in the project. Several reports describing different aspects of the project were published in 1988 (e.g., Salthouse, Kausler & Saults, 1988a, 1988b).

I received my first research grant from the National Institute on Aging in 1978. The purpose of that research was to determine whether age differences in perceptual and motor skills could be eliminated with extensive practice. A graduate student, Ben Somberg, and I designed four tasks that were embedded in a video game, and then we paid young and old adults to perform the tasks for a total of 50 sessions over a period of several months. The major findings of this project, published in 1982 (Salthouse & Somberg, 1982), were that age differences were stable when participants had at least moderate amounts of practice.

This initial grant was followed by a series of grants from the National Institute on Aging. The grant that I received in 1986 for research on reasoning and spatial abilities was renewed twice and was classified as a MERIT (Method to Extend Research in Time) award in 1989.

In 1980 I attended the Summer Institute on Life Span Developmental Psychology at the Stanford Center for Advanced Study in the Behavioral Sciences. The institute was organized by Paul Baltes and David Featherman and was designed to expose young researchers to the life-span perspective on human development. This was a very stimulating time for me because of the formal and informal interactions with the directors, Baltes and Featherman, and with many of the other participants such as Carol Ryff and Gisela Labouvie-Vief.

At about this time I began working on a book reviewing the research literature in aging and cognition. This small monograph, titled *Adult Cognition,* was published in 1982.

In the 1982–1983 academic year I was on sabbatical at the University of Southern California Institute for Advanced Study in Gerontology and Geriatrics, which was directed by James Birren. Birren stimulated my interest in deeper and more fundamental questions than those I had studied as an experimental psychologist. He was particularly intrigued with the question of how behavior was organized and with the role of age as an organizing force in behavior. I believe that some of those same concerns are recognizable in my work in the 15 years since that time.

While on sabbatical I was appointed associate editor of the second edition of the *Handbook of Psychology of Aging* (1985), which further expanded my exposure to different areas of psychology of aging. I continued in that role for the third edition, published in 1990, and the fourth edition, which was published in 1996.

In 1983 I received a five-year National Institutes of Health (NIH) Research Career Development Award, which released me from normal teaching responsibilities to concentrate full time on research. Because I had just returned from a sabbatical, there was a span of six years in which I taught very few courses and was able to devote most of my time and energy to research. In retrospect this was probably one of the most important periods in my career because I take teaching very seriously, and the ability to devote time to research that would normally have been committed to teaching allowed me to both broaden and deepen my research activities.

In 1985 I made the first of several visits to the Max Planck Institute for Human Development and Education in Berlin, which was directed by Paul Baltes. In those visits I was further exposed to the life-span development perspective, in which cognition was viewed as just one aspect of psychology and aging was viewed as just one segment of the life span. This was another of a series of broadening experiences that led to a gradual shift from my original experimental, information-processing, perspective. In addition to learning much from Paul Baltes about psychology, science, and even aspects about managing one's own career, I had many intellectually stimulating interactions with some of the extremely bright and motivated junior scientists in the institute, in particular Reinhold Kliegl and Ulman Lindenberger.

In 1986 I accepted an offer to move to the Georgia Institute of Technology as a professor in the School of Psychology (which is Georgia Tech's label for what nearly everyone else refers to as a department). Anderson Smith had been there for many years and had done important early research on aging and memory. He was serving as chair of the department at that time and was in the process of assembling a group of faculty interested in aging and cognition because in the previous year Christopher Hertzog had joined the department.

The evolution of this group occurred in a rather unusual fashion. The department had received authorization to recruit a junior developmental psychologist, and Hertzog was hired for that position. However, he had just received a Research Career Development Award that paid his salary for five years, and thus the dean authorized a search for another position. I was hired the next year, but because I also had a Research Career Development Award, the dean kept the position open and we eventually filled it with another life-span developmental psychologist, Fredda Blanchard-Fields.

Shortly after I arrived, Smith, Hertzog, and I were returning together on an airplane from the 1986 American Psychological Association convention when we first discussed what evolved into the Cognitive Aging Conference. This conference has become very successful largely due to Smith, who was not only an effective organizer but also had access to valuable resources, first in his role as department chair and later as an associate dean. In the late 1980s I attempted to review as much of the available literature on aging and cognition as possible, and a monograph summarizing my interpretations of that research was published in 1991 (1991b).

From 1991 to 1997 I served as editor of the journal *Psychology and Aging*. This was another experience that provided me with a broad perspective on the field, in addition to the opportunity to exert some influence on the direction of research. Although I enjoyed the chance to see research reports in their early stages and to help shape them into published articles, it was not always pleasant to be caught in the middle between authors anxious to learn about the status of their manuscripts and reviewers who were usually overburdened with other demands on their time.

Changes in My Research

My initial research focused primarily on perceptual-motor skills and attention, and it was conducted as an experimental psychologist working from an information processing perspective. Beginning in the early 1980s, my interests shifted to the interrelations of cognitive variables with age and with one another. I also changed my focus from lower level measures of attention and perception to aspects of higher level cognition such as memory, reasoning, and spatial abilities.

I gradually came to believe that the psychometric and experimental approaches were dealing with essentially the same phenomena, but that this was not generally recognized because practitioners in the two areas did not communicate with one another. Psychologists working within the experimental tradition tended to focus on a single task with samples composed of relatively small numbers of young and old adults, whereas those trained in the psychometric tradition examined correlations among many variables in moderately large samples across a wide age range. Both groups of researchers were therefore interested in questions of the relation between age and cognition, but perhaps because of the different methods being used there seemed to be little interaction between researchers in the two areas.

I started combining the two approaches in my research by using correlational methods with measures derived from the experimental tradition. This merger started with projects on transcription typing (Salthouse, 1984), and the previously mentioned collaboration with Kausler (Salthouse, Kausler & Saults, 1988a, 1988b). The hybrid approach continued in later research on working memory (Salthouse, 1991a), on the influence of different types of speed on age differences in cognition (Salthouse, 1993, 1994), and on the role of experience on age-cognition relations (see Salthouse, 1992, for a summary of much of this research).

Two major questions have dominated my research efforts in aging. The first is what is responsible for the age-related declines apparent in many cognitive variables, and the second is why are there so few consequences of these differences in life outside the laboratory? One line of research in my laboratory has therefore examined possible reasons for age differences in cognition. Some of the projects within this category have investigated hypotheses about the role of processing resources like working memory and processing speed as potential mediators of age-cognition relations. A second line of research has investigated the role of experience as a possible moderator of age-related influences. This work started with my first NIA grant, and has continued with projects involving typists (Salthouse, 1984), architects, and musicians.

In the past several years I have become interested in determining the extent to which age-related influences on different cognitive variables are distinct and independent or are shared and in common. I believe that this research will eventually be informative about the types of explanatory mechanisms that will ultimately prove viable in accounting for adult age differences in cognition. Birren's influence is probably evident here because one way of characterizing my current interests is in terms of the question of how many distinct age-related influences are operating and at what level in a structural organization of cognitive abilities are they most pronounced?

Although most experimentally oriented researchers tend to focus on single cognitive tasks, it may be that many age-related effects operate at a broader level and contribute to the age-related effects on many different tasks. The challenge is determining how this possibility can be investigated. This is a different question than that confronting most researchers, and it requires different sets of analytical procedures that are still in the process of being developed. However, if it were eventually discovered that large proportions of age-related influences on cognitive variables are shared, then it may be more important to investigate broad and general determinants than those that are specific to particular cognitive tasks. Some of these ideas have been expressed in two monographs, published in 1985 and 1992, and in articles published between 1992 and 1996.

Changes in the Field

When I started doing research in aging in 1974 the field was perceived somewhat like a poor, slightly disreputable relative of mainstream (i.e., based on college students as the research participants) research. The topic of aging was viewed with some reservations, either because of a suspicion that the phenomena were not real (because the methodology was sometimes rather weak) or because of the feeling that if they were real then doing research in the area would be discouraging or depressing. There were only a small number of active researchers, and very few articles were published in the most prestigious journals. Only one journal was devoted to publishing research on aging, the interdisciplinary *Journal of Gerontology.*

The situation has changed radically in the past 25 years. One of the key factors contributing to this change was the formation of the National Institute on Aging in 1975 and the subsequent availability of research funds to study behavioral aspects of aging. Stimulated in part by these research funds, cognitive aging has evolved into a legitimate subdiscipline of cognitive psychology. The field now has many researchers, including some of the most respected scientists in the field of cognitive psychology. Furthermore, the Cognitive Aging Conference, under the leadership of Anderson Smith, attracts researchers from around the world and is considered by many to be the most valuable scientific conference for researchers in this field.

Articles with a focus on aging appear regularly in prestigious mainstream journals, including the various sections of the *Journal of Experimental Psychology, Psychological Bulletin,* and *Psychological Review.* A separate American Psychological Association journal devoted to aging, *Psychology and Aging,* was started in 1986, and several other journals reporting research on aging and cognition have been started in the past decade.

I believe that there has also been a gradual shift in the nature of the research from an exclusive focus on description to a growing concern with explanation. This transition is still evolving because there is not yet a consensus on the nature and levels of appropriate explanation. Nevertheless, the trend is reflected in the fact that many researchers would no longer consider it interesting merely to report that an age difference exists in some measure of cognitive functioning without an accompanying explanation of why the difference occurred.

Major Factors Affecting My Career

Two major factors have contributed to any success that I have had in my career. One is perseverance. This characteristic proved valuable early in my career when I had little success in the job market and had serious doubts about whether I would be able to pursue a career as an academic psychologist. However, things eventually worked out, and I have become convinced that one must work hard to be in a position to capitalize on opportunities when they ultimately become available.

The second salient factor in my career has been the importance of mentors and senior colleagues. These people may not always know that they are influencing their students and junior colleagues, but they often do so by example if not by design. I know that I have been affected by their commitment to the field, by their attitudes toward students, and by their perspectives on issues. Among those who have had major influences on my career were Bob Gottsdanker, Dick Pew, Dan Weintraub, Jack Botwinick, John Stern, Don Kausler, Jim Birren, and Paul Baltes. I hope that some of what I have learned from them is being communicated to the talented and motivated students with whom I have had the pleasure to work.

References

Botwinick, J. (1973). *Aging and behavior.* New York: Springer.

Neisser, U. (1967). *Cognitive psychology.* New York: Appleton-Century Croft.

Salthouse, T. A. (1982). *Adult cognition: An experimental psychology of human aging.* New York: Springer-Verlag.

Salthouse, T. A. (1984). Effects of age and skill in typing. *Journal of Experimental Psychology: General, 113,* 345–371.

Salthouse, T. A. (1985). *A theory of cognitive aging.* Amsterdam: North-Holland.

Salthouse, T. A. (1991a). Mediation of adult age differences in cognition by reductions in working memory and speed of processing. *Psychological Science, 2,* 179–183.

Salthouse, T. A. (1991b). *Theoretical perspectives on cognitive aging.* Hillsdale, N.J.: Erlbaum.

Salthouse, T. A. (1992). *Mechanisms of age-cognition relations in adulthood.* Hillsdale, N.J.: Erlbaum.

Salthouse, T. A. (1993). Speed mediation of adult age differences in cognition. *Developmental Psychology, 29,* 722–738.

Salthouse, T. A. (1994). The nature of the influence of speed on adult age differences in cognition. *Developmental Psychology, 30,* 240–259.

Salthouse, T. A., Kausler, D. H., & Saults, J. S. (1988a). Investigation of student status, background variables, and the feasibility of standard tasks in cognitive aging research. *Psychology and Aging, 3,* 29–37.

Salthouse, T. A., Kausler, D. H., & Saults, J. S. (1988b). Utilization of path analytic procedures to investigate the role of processing resources in cognitive aging. *Psychology and Aging, 3,* 158–166.

Salthouse, T. A., & Somberg, B. (1982). Skilled performance: Effects of adult age and experience on elementary processes. *Journal of Experimental Psychology: General, 111,* 176–207.

Welford, A. T. (1958). *Ageing and human skill.* London: Oxford University Press.

Chapter 19
LIVING WITH GERONTOLOGY

K. Warner Schaie

This chapter describes how I came to be a gerontologist, or in my case, how I became intrigued with the study of psychological development from young adulthood to advanced old age. Inevitably, it is also an account of how my career became interwoven with a program of scientific inquiry conducted by me, my associates, and my students over the past 40 years that has come to be known as the Seattle Longitudinal Study (SLS; Schaie, 1996).

When I entered the field of gerontology in 1951, few people knew how to spell the name, let alone being able to offer a meaningful definition. Those who did would be most likely to respond to a young student interested in gerontology by asking, "Why do you want to worry about old people, why not do something mainstream?" That was, for the most part, the response I received from my teachers and peers at the time. Hence, this autobiographical account also contributes to the story of how what once was considered an idiosyncratic interest eventually developed into a lifelong career that today nobody would doubt to be in the mainstream. Given the small number of early geropsychologists, I may have been privileged to have had at least some small influence on the progress of our field. For this opportunity I am very grateful to a number of teachers, colleagues, and students whose influences on my own scientific development I will attempt to trace in this chapter.

Childhood and Adolescence

I was born in 1928 in the town of Stettin, which then was the provincial capital of Pommerania, one of Germany's pre–World War II political subdivisions. My parents were Jewish middle class; my father and mother owned a small outfitters store for the then rapidly

In 1996 I published an autobiographical account of my pursuits as a developmental psychologist, focusing more specifically on the Seattle Longitudinal Study under the title of "The Natural History of a Longitudinal Study," in M. R. Merrens & G. G. Brannigan (Eds.), *The Developmental Psychologists* (pp. 232–249). New York: McGraw-Hill. The present chapter represents an expansion of the personal autobiographical material as well as a greater emphasis on my career development in gerontology. But one can live only one life, and the reader who is familiar with the earlier work will notice, of course, considerable overlap that was necessary to present a coherent story.

The program of research that has formed the scientific basis of much of my career, including preparation of this chapter, has been supported since 1963 by various grants from the National Institute of Mental Health and the National Institute on Aging. It is currently supported by research grant R37 AG08055 from the National Institute on Aging.

growing crowd of motor bikers. My native town was a sleepy provincial city of about 150,000 inhabitants (involved primarily in the garment industry, ship building, and fish processing) as well as a terminal for transferring grain and coal from the river barges to freighters that went to Scandinavia, Russia, and beyond. It was also a major garrison town, and as Germany rearmed the barracks multiplied and colorful parades were common. The big excitement for me was a visit to Berlin, which was an hour's train ride away. We usually stayed with two of my grandmother's widowed sisters, my first intensive interaction with old people.

The Great Depression began in Europe shortly after I was born, probably the major reason why I remained an only child. Not very long thereafter the unemployment lines lengthened, the Weimar Republic went on a course of self-destruction, and Hitler and his Nazis soon took over. When I was 6 years old and the time came to start elementary school, I therefore attended a private school that had hastily been formed by the local Jewish community to protect its children from the daily harassment experienced in the public schools. I attended that school through the middle of fifth grade, learning enough basic skills such that I can still converse in German and write grammatically correct prose in that language, although my German is studded with archaic colloquialisms that were common in the 1930s.

While in the middle of fifth grade, there came Crystal Night (November 9, 1938), the systematic destruction of Jewish synagogues and stores by Nazi hooligans, as well as the incarceration of most Jewish men in concentration camps. My parents' store was destroyed, but my father was able to avoid being taken to a concentration camp by going into hiding. He now began desperately to seek a way for our family to leave Germany, because the likely consequences of our remaining had become convincingly clear. By that time hardly any country was willing to accept Jewish refugees from Germany. The question thus became primarily one of how to get out, regardless of where one might end up going. My father discovered that it was possible to book passage on an Italian cruise ship that plied a route through the Suez Canal, then around India and Malaysia, ending up in the port city of Shanghai, China.

In June 1939, my parents and I took the train from Stettin to Trieste (the two anchor points in Winston Churchill's famous iron curtain speech) and embarked, not really knowing where we would wind up. After several futile attempts to obtain permission to go ashore along the way we finally were allowed to enter Shanghai. At the time Shanghai was still an international settlement governed by the consular representatives of 17 nations that were signatories to the so-called unequal treaties. Through these treaties, during the 19th century, foreign concessions had been created on Chinese soil that were not subject to Chinese law. The reason we were allowed to land was primarily because of the fact that the amorphous local government had not been able to get its act together to keep us out!

The trip to the Far East and the bustling and exotic streets of Shanghai seemed high adventure to an 11-year-old. Hence, I gave little thought to the uncertain future facing my family. There was a large foreign population in Shanghai, with a substantial Jewish community that had settled there during the expansion of Western trade in China or who had taken refuge from the Bolshevik revolution in Russia after World War I. Some of these people had even acquired great wealth, and they formed charitable organizations that attempted to provide shelter and food for all the refugees and education for the young. I attended a school for refugee children for about two years, acquiring English language competence and completing an educational program that would approximate that of an American junior high school. Then came Pearl Harbor, my English and American teachers were interned by the Japanese authorities, and at age 14 I became an involuntary high school dropout.

After the Japanese authorities made all the refugees relocate to a ghetto area, vocational options became quite restricted. I was fortunate enough to find a job as an apprentice in a small print shop, where I learned some typesetting skills. When the war ended in 1945 and the local English-language newspaper reopened, I managed to get a job in their print shop and learned how to use a Linotype machine and to typeset newspaper advertisements. The labor unions were already dominated by the communists, and they did not like a foreigner looking over their shoulder in the print shop; they soon forced me out.

During my final months in Shanghai, I had the opportunity to work as an untrained social worker with the American Joint Distribution Committee working with people about to be resettled in the United States. Here I first became intrigued with the infinite variety of individual differences in life experiences and reactions thereto, as well as in the resilience of adults in adapting to profound stresses and adapting to externally imposed changes of life conditions.

Young Adulthood

The communist armies were beginning to approach the gates of Shanghai. My father had died of a stroke in early 1947, and my mother was too distraught to actively participate in planning our future. Thus in 1947, I unilaterally decided it was time to resettle myself and my mother to the United States, and to our great relief we were able to leave Shanghai in November of that year on a former troop transporter (the SS *General Gordon*), arriving in San Francisco on December 17. I still vividly remember sailing under the Golden Gate Bridge in the morning fog, wondering what lay in store for me in a new country.

I have often been asked whether coming to San Francisco was a strange and stressful experience. My response has always been that, to the contrary, it seemed much more like a homecoming. Shanghai had presented us with the need to adapt to a totally different culture, within a strange environment, whose language and customs we did not understand, where water and many foods were unsafe, and many familiar foods were unavailable. By contrast, having acquired fluency in English, in San Francisco I could understand what everyone said, I could read all the signs, food and water were safe, and many of the conveniences of life we once knew were once again available to us.

After a week in San Francisco, I met with a caseworker from the agency that had sponsored our immigration to the United States to discuss the future. I was informed that the Eugene, Oregon, Jewish community had agreed to sponsor us and that a job had been found for me as a busboy in a restaurant. I pondered for a minute or two. As a brash 19-year-old, I then revved up my courage to tell the caseworker that this plan didn't quite match what I had expected would be possible for me in America. I thanked her politely and told her that I would first see what I could do for myself during the next few days. Indeed, the next day I had found a minimum-wage job in a small print shop, and the following day I moved my mother and myself into a small apartment; I promptly informed our sponsors that I had completed resettling us and that their help was no longer needed.

My printing experience had served me well in making it easy to find my first American job and it continued to help. By the summer of 1948, I had managed first to move to a better paying job at a suburban newspaper and, after being admitted to the printer's union, was able to find work in the composing room of the *San Francisco Chronicle* typesetting and making up display advertisements. The *Chronicle* was and remains a morning newspaper, which means that printers typically work at night. Hence, there was little to occupy my afternoons. One day, placing some of the display advertisements into a newspaper page, I noticed a story on a high school program for adults at the local community college. Never having completed high school, on the spur of the moment I decided that it might not hurt me to have a high school diploma. I enrolled at City College of San Francisco, took courses in civics, American history, and chemistry, but was able to test out of most other requirements (including high school English) and obtained a diploma from the San Francisco Unified School District at the end of the first semester.

Becoming a Geropsychologist

It became very clear to me that I did not wish to seek a lifelong career as a printer and that I wanted somehow to become an educated person. But why did I choose to eventually enter geropsychology? As will become clear from this section, I started college primarily interested to embark in some social service field, but serendipity soon intervened, and by the end of my junior year it was almost certain that I had found my niche in the study of aging. Moreover, another serendipitous choice of the research population studied for my dissertation would point me toward centering on the aging of intellectual competence as my central academic concern.

The College Years

The environment at San Francisco City College was very pleasant. It was a great opportunity to make new friends, the work was stimulating but not unduly demanding, and I was well able to get it done even while holding a full-time job. Having gotten used to and liking the college setting, I decided to go on, building my program of studies primarily around those courses that were offered in the afternoon so that I could sleep in the morning following my night shift as a printer. Because most science labs were offered in the morning, this meant that I was destined to concentrate on social science topics.

At City College I was influenced particularly by my English composition instructor, Donald Snepp, who with great patience helped me hone my writing skills and also exposed me to an understanding of the many metaphors in both classical and modern English and American literature that are the bane of the nonnative English speaker. Even more important was Ralph Granneberg, my instructor in the introductory courses in psychology and sociology, who first exposed me to principles of experimental psychology. He probably single-handedly convinced me that psychology was a science that should be taken seriously.

The California higher education system allowed automatic transfer to the state university system on graduation from junior college with a C average or better. Thus, after obtaining my AA, I transferred to Berkeley as a psychology major. Being a newcomer to the States, I really had not been fully aware of the world-class caliber of the University of California—Berkeley campus. Berkeley was an exciting place to be in the 1950s, and all of a sudden I found myself being taught by the people who had done the research and written the textbooks. Not only was the faculty outstanding and intellectually demanding, but the undergraduates were extremely competitive, and most of my smaller upper division classes had mixtures of graduate students as well. After some hairy times, more intensive work, and lower grades than I had come to expect at junior college, I managed to find my footing and made good use of my time.

The highlight of my first semester at Berkeley was an exciting tests and measurement course from Read Tuddenham, to whom I promptly shifted as my advisor. Once again I was having trouble building a full schedule confined to the afternoon. I therefore asked Tuddenham to do a directed study with him. Discussing various possibilities, I idly mentioned that I had thought his class discussion of Thurstone's (1938) primary mental abilities (PMA) work interesting, and wondered whether there had been any work done on the PMA in adults. As a good teacher, Tuddenham told me to go to the library and find out.

Thurstone in the 1930s had analyzed more than 60 measures of mental ability with large samples of children and adolescents in Chicago. Applying his new method of centroid factor analysis he discovered that individual differences on these measures could be accounted for by no more than 10 factors, which he thought of as the "building blocks of the mind." Thurstone published a formal test of the five most important of these ability factors. They were Verbal Meaning (a measure of recognition vocabulary), Space (a measure of being able to rotate abstract figures in two dimensional space), Reasoning (a measure of the ability to induce rules from common features of an activity), Number (a measure of addition skill), and Word Fluency (a measure of word recall).

A thorough search of *Psychological Abstracts* revealed that there were substantial data on children and adolescents but that nothing had been done with adults. Hence, I proposed a directed study to determine whether the low correlations among the different abilities reported in childhood would also prevail in adults. Tuddenham agreed that this was an interesting and appropriate question for a term project and told me to go ahead.

But where does an undergraduate find adult subjects beyond college age? As serendipity would have it, I was still being treated for the aftereffects of the malnutrition experienced during my Shanghai years. My family physician, Robert M. Perlman, happened to be interested in geriatrics. When I mentioned my subject problem to him, he offered to provide me with testing space in his practice and allowed me to recruit subjects in his waiting room. He also introduced me to Florence Vickery, then director of the San Francisco Senior Citizens' Center, one of the first to be established in the United States, who permitted me to recruit and test subjects at her facility. My first aging study was under way.

I was able to test several dozens of subjects ranging from the 20s to the 70s and found not only that the primary mental abilities remained distinct in adulthood but also that age differences were not identical for all abilities. As compared to the normative data for adolescents, it turned out that young adults and those in early middle age, on average, did better than the high school students. There were significant age differences thereafter, and in particular older adults did less well on Space and Reasoning than they did on their verbal and numeric skills. Administering the test to a subset of study participants under untimed conditions, further showed that the age difference patterns were even more pronounced when the speed restriction was removed.

While the data collection was proceeding, Dr. Perlman received an announcement for the Second International Congress of Gerontology to be held in St. Louis, Missouri. He suggested that I submit a proposal for a convention paper with him as a coauthor. The paper was accepted, but in order to report respectable statistics I now had to recruit a friend, Fred Rosenthal, who was a semester ahead of me, to run the t-tests that I had not yet mastered. Thus, in August of 1951, I mounted the Greyhound bus for my first long American trip to go to St. Louis for the Congress.

Gerontology was still a very small affair and the Second International Congress had about 200 registrants, two thirds of whom were Americans. Perhaps no more than 30 participants were psychologists. I do not remember much about the scientific sessions, but I vividly recall meeting many of the founders of geropsychology, including James Birren, Robert Kleemeier, Irving Lorge, and Robert Havighurst. This was very heady stuff for a college junior, and I was even more excited when the editor of the *Journal of Gerontology,* John Esben Kirk, invited me to submit my paper, titled "Differential Deterioration of Factorially 'Pure' Mental Abilities," as a journal article and promptly accepted it (Schaie,

Rosenthal, & Perlman, 1953). My entry into adult developmental psychology and gerontology was obviously determined by these events.

During my last semester at Berkeley I did some more reading on individual differences and became interested in the concepts of behavioral rigidity and perseveration studied by psychologists such as Kurt Lewin, Abraham Luchins, Jacob Kounin, and Charles Spearman. They suggested that the boundaries between different domains of behavior would rigidify with age, and that there would be increasing interference in shifting away from old and no longer appropriate strategies to the adoption of new and more appropriate problem-solving strategies. If this was the case, I thought that perhaps age differences in the primary mental abilities might well be explained by a progressive reduction in cognitive functions for those who were more rigid to begin with or who became less flexible as they aged. I attempted to test this proposition in another directed study, but although the effort was too ambitious to succeed then, it became the basis of my research in graduate school.

Graduate School

With my Berkeley experience coming to an end, I now turned to apply to graduate programs. Cocky as ever, I unrealistically considered only the top schools. Rejections from Berkeley, Stanford, Michigan, and Harvard put me in my place. But my backup, the University of Washington, came through. I suspect that the article in press in the *Journal of Gerontology* probably helped get me accepted into the University of Washington clinical psychology program. In the fall of 1952, I therefore headed north to Seattle, actually the first time I had been entirely on my own. The psychology department had not committed any financial support, quite usual for the time, and so once again I supported myself by working as a nighttime printer in the composing room of the *Seattle Post-Intelligencer.*

In contrast to most of my classmates, I early on had found an intellectual niche in geropsychology and I also had a set of specific research objectives at the very beginning of my graduate training. In addition to obtaining the necessary clinical training to become an academic clinical psychologist, I wanted to focus my research on the interesting puzzle of why it is that some people maintain their intellectual powers into old age while others begin to decline at an early adult stage. I did not realize at the time, of course, that I was posing a challenge, the response to which would occupy my entire career.

Having had excellent preparation in the conventional statistical methods at Berkeley, I was able to skip the usual first-year methods sequence and immerse myself directly into multivariate and factor analysis (Paul Horst) as well as scaling methods (Allen Edwards) and Q-methodology (William Stephenson was a visiting professor that year). I was thus ready to begin instrument development to provide me with formal operations that would measure the rigidity-flexibility concept I had become interested in at Berkeley as a possible explanatory variable for individual differences in cognitive aging. From the research literature I identified a set of 10 potentially appropriate measures of the construct of rigidity-flexibility that I adapted for use with a population ranging in age from young adulthood to old age. I was able to test about 300 subjects in several months' work and was then ready to conduct a multiple group factor analysis (on a Monroe desk calculator!), in which I showed that the different measures of rigidity-flexibility could be represented as a three-factor structure. I replicated the factor solution on another sample and eventually published this material as the Test of Behavioral Rigidity. This work was accepted by the end of 1953 as my MS thesis (directed by Charles Strother, Paul Horst, and Sidney Bijou).

Returning home to San Francisco for the summer of 1953, I married my first wife, Coloma John Harrison, whom I had met at a leap-year party in San Francisco the previous year. During the summer I also attended sessions of the annual meeting of the Gerontological Society in San Francisco, which I had earlier joined as a student member; that year I also became a student member of the American Psychological Association (APA).

It is important to note here that no one on the Washington psychology faculty was particularly interested in adult development or aging, and it was necessary therefore to create my own academic support system. At the 1953 Gerontological Society of America (GSA) meeting I sought advice from some of the people I had met earlier at the St. Louis congress, notably Harold Jones and a University of Washington academic physician, K. K. Sherwood. Returning to campus in the fall, I also discovered a latent interest in gerontology in a number of other departments, and I was able to convince the dean of the graduate school to sponsor a Committee on Gerontology, which my advisor, Charles R. Strother, the director of clinical training, generously agreed to chair, even though he was not particularly interested in aging. Other active members of this committee were Joseph Cohen (a sociologist interested in elder housing, who later on became the outside member of my dissertation committee); Norman Kunde (an exercise physiologist); Robert Lampman (a labor economist); and Victor Howery (then dean of the School of Social Work). The committee needed an executive secretary, and in the fall of 1953, I was finally able to give up working nights as a newspaper printer, as I now received fellowship support (from one of the first National Institute of Mental Health [NIMH] institutional training grants in clinical psychology) in return for agreeing to staff the new committee as well as pursuing my own research on aging.

To focus the work of the new committee, I proposed an intensive study of a group of well-functioning elders that not only would encompass psychological variables but would include an examination of health status, physical activities, and environmental contexts. A small grant from the University of Washington research council to Charles Strother permitted the recruitment of 25 men and 25 women over the age of 70 years who had completed a college degree or beyond. This work occupied much of my third year of graduate study, as well as the completion of a rigorous set of the then in vogue broad comprehensive examinations across the entire breadth of psychology.

As would not surprise us today, the advantaged group of elderly still maintained high levels of functioning and activity on virtually all of our measures. Several reports emerged from this study, the first presented at the 1955 APA meeting in San Francisco. This meeting was important also because it presented an opportunity to renew my acquaintance with James Birren and to start a friendship and many professional collaborations that have lasted to this day.

Other activities initiated by me under the auspices of the University of Washington Committee on Gerontology included a Northwest Conference on Aging in 1954 that, among others, brought Wilma Donahue and Clark Tibbits to campus. There were also talks on gerontology to local professional groups, and in 1955 I organized and led the first gerontology course ever offered at the University of Washington, supported by the continuing education division and staffed by members of the Committee on Aging. About that time, I also became a full member of the American Psychological Association and of the Gerontological Society.

Origins of the Seattle Longitudinal Study

Having passed my comprehensive examinations, it became time to propose a dissertation project. My mentor tried to interest me in taking a critical incidents approach (a la Flanagan) to the study of the process of psychoanalysis at a pioneering hospital for adolescent schizophrenics at which he was a consultant. After several months it became clear that whatever observational or descriptive scheme I proposed the analysts perceived as effectively changing the process! I was therefore allowed to return to my primary interest, which was to put together my pilot work on rigidity-flexibility and intelligence. As serendipity would have it, Charles Strother, my advisor, had just been named chair of the lay board of trustees of the Group Health Cooperative of Puget Sound, one of America's first (and now one of the largest) health maintenance organizations (HMOs). The HMO was interested in doing a consumer satisfaction survey but had neither staff nor financial resources to allocate. A deal was struck. I was allowed to collect my dissertation data on a random sample of the adult HMO membership under the condition that I conduct the consumer satisfaction survey at the same time. Other members of my doctoral committee included Paul Horst (who as a student of L. L. Thurstone was very sympathetic to my work and provided most of the methodological guidance), Sydney Bijou, George Horton, and Joseph Cohen as outside member). At the last minute my department head, Roger Brown Loucks, added himself to the committee to make sure, in his words ''that I wasn't going to get away with something.''

I randomly selected about 3000 persons evenly spaced across the age range from 20 to 70 years and administered the Thurstone Primary Mental Abilities (PMA) test and my own rigidity-flexibility test (the TBR) until I had assessed 25 men and 25 women in each five-year interval. I was able to replicate my earlier findings on differential patterns of age differences in intelligence by ability as well as to show that peak ages of performance had risen since the earlier work by Wechsler and others and were now to be found in the 30s or even later. Substantial positive correlations were also found between rigidity-flexibility and the ability measures, but I did not find the predicted causal relationship; that, as it turned out, required longitudinal data (Schaie, 1958).

Postdoctoral Training

When I obtained my doctoral degree in 1956 there were no employment opportunities for someone who wanted to specialize in gerontology. My mentor therefore advised me to strengthen my clinical skills through a year of postdoctoral study and then seek employment as an academic clinician. This was accomplished at Washington University in St. Louis, then an important place in the development of gerontology. There I had the opportunity to do some research with James Weiss (later chair of psychiatry at the University of Missouri), who then directed the Washington University Psychiatric Outpatient Clinic, to develop a Q-sort instrument assessing the attributes of complaints that brought older patients to the clinic, reinforcing my interest in older populations.

My Academic Career

It was now time to enter academia. My postdoctoral training had prepared me for then-burgeoning opportunities in academic clinical psychology. As will be described in this section, I began my career focusing on psychological assessment in adults, but soon was able to return to basic research in the development of adult psychological competence as well as the formulation of novel longitudinal research methodologies. Although my first academic position was that of a traditional teacher/researcher, my career has also heavily involved academic and research administration, from the very beginning focused on interdisciplinary efforts related to the study of aging.

The University of Nebraska, Lincoln

In the summer of 1957, Marshall R. Jones offered me an appointment as assistant professor at the University of Nebraska to teach adult cognitive and personality assessment and to supervise students in the psychology clinic associated with the clinical training program. In this context my interests turned to issues of objective psychological assessment. A visit by Raymond Cattell to speak at the Nebraska Symposium on Motivation aroused my interest in unobtrusive personality measurement, as well as the equivalence of self-ratings and observer ratings in personality measurement. The work with Weiss on defining symptoms that bring patients to the clinic was also continued off and on through 1960, during which year my son Stephan was born. That year I also passed the ABEPP examination in clinical psychology and was promoted to associate professor.

During my last days in St. Louis I met my successor as a postdoctoral fellow, Ottfried Spreen, who returned to Germany to lead a new clinical psychology section at the University of Saarbrücken. The psychology department had received the gift of a first-generation computer (the IBM 650) from a steel company that was upgrading its equipment. Spreen knew that I had some computer skills, and in the summer of 1961 he asked me to help him and his colleagues to think through how to use this computer.

At Saarbrücken I met Günther Reinert (later founding chair of the psychology department at the University of Trier) who was then the chief scientific assistant to Egon Boesch (the department head). Reinert introduced me to his mentor at the University of Freiburg, Robert Heiss, who had done a lot of work with a color preference test, the Color Pyramid Test (Farbpyramiden-test), first introduced by the Swiss psychologist Hans Pfister. This test seemed to offer an unobtrusive method for objective personality assessment via the relation of color and personality. On returning to Nebraska, I began to study schoolchildren as well as mentally retarded and mentally ill persons in state institutions. This work led to my first book, *Color and Personality* (Schaie & Heiss, 1964).

Although the work on color and personality almost let me to abandon my interest in gerontology, it incidentally also led to the inception of my long-standing friendship and collegial association with Paul and Margret Baltes. Günther Reinert wrote me that he had a promising young student who he thought could use some American experience. I was able to get a research assistantship for Paul for the purpose of collecting color pyramid data in Nebraska schools. He and Margret joined me during my final year at Nebraska (1963–1964), and Margret began working for me as an assistant and secretary when the first Seattle Longitudinal Study (SLS) follow-up was funded.

Converting a Cross-Sectional to a Longitudinal Study

It took me a long time to convince my Nebraska colleagues to use my training in developmental psychology. But in my fourth year at Nebraska, I was finally asked to teach the developmental section of the departmental proseminar and was allowed to introduce a unit on adult development. In preparing for that seminar, I was confronted with addressing the discrepancies between cross-sectional and longitudinal findings in the study of adult intellectual development. I soon became convinced that this issue needed to be addressed by following a structured cross-sectional sample over time, such as the one that I had collected for my dissertation. I therefore designed a follow-up inquiry that converted my original cross-sectional study of cognitive aging into a series of short-term longitudinal studies, each extending over the same seven-year period. My graduate school mentor, Charles Strother, then at the height of his professional career, graciously agreed to front for me as principal investigator. Funding for the study was received from the National Institute of Mental Health, and with the continuing cooperation of the HMO, I went into the field in 1963 to conduct this follow-up. Additionally, I drew a new random sample from the HMO membership that permitted comparison of panels tested at the same age but at different times (known as "Schaie's most efficient design"). Thus the Seattle Longitudinal Study (SLS) was now in place and I was once again firmly entrenched in geropsychology!

The second cross-sectional study (1963) essentially replicated the findings of the base study. The short-term longitudinal study, however, disclosed substantially different information about peak levels and rate of decline. Publication of findings was therefore delayed until a theoretical model could be built that accounted for the discrepancy between the longitudinal and cross-sectional data. These analyses suggested that comparisons of age group means needed to be conducted for the repeatedly measured samples as well as for successive independent samples drawn from the same cohort.

Results were reported that called attention to substantial cohort differences and that questioned the universality and significance of intellectual decrement with advancing age in community-dwelling persons. While the cross-sectional data implied peaks in early adulthood with decline beginning in middle age and becoming severe as the 60s are reached, the longitudinal data, by contrast, suggested little age-related decline before the 60s and only modest decline during the 70s.

The first longitudinal follow-up of the SLS provided some answers but it also raised sufficient methodological and substantive questions to initiate a continuing program of studies (by now including seven major and several collateral data collections) that is still in progress. The longitudinal research program was first supported by the NIMH, has been continuously supported by the National Institute on Aging since 1970 and is currently funded to continue through 2004. The initial follow-up was also instrumental in forming my methodological efforts in understanding the relationship between cross-sectional and longitudinal data sets, which led to an influential *Psychological Bulletin* article (Schaie, 1965) that for many years has been required reading for geropsychology graduate students.

West Virginia University

An opportunity arose for me in 1964 to use my academic clinical skills to organize a clinical training program at West Virginia University. I was rather skeptical at first about a move to Appalachia. But a visit in May, when the grime of the coal mining communities is hidden by the lush greenery of the Appalachian spring, and a university president (Paul Miller, who later became assistant secretary of education) with a vision to move his sleepy state university into modern times convinced me. After a summer spent on the University of Washington campus to tie up the longitudinal follow-up, I thus moved to Morgantown, West Virginia. With the help of an NIMH development grant, I was able to bring the clinical psychology effort forward to APA accreditation, helped the first set of PhD candidates finish, and put in place a working relationship with the region's VA hospitals. I was also able to bring in some contract research with the National Center for Health Statistics to help support graduate students.

In 1965 Stanley Ikenberry (until recently president of the University of Illinois and now president of the American Council on Education), who had just become dean of a new College of Human Resources and Education, asked me to be the founding director of a Human Resources Research Institute whose mission was to provide intellectual links between his college and the traditional social science disciplines in the College of Arts and Sciences. In the context of this institute I oversaw research on the effects of the community action programs sponsored by Lyndon Johnson's "war on poverty" as well as statewide evaluations of the effects of early Headstart programs. With respect to adult development I was able to organize an international seminar for the study of social change in mining communities with meetings in Morgantown and Saarbrücken.

More important with respect to gerontology, I was able to conceptualize and receive funding for one of the first institutional training grants awarded by the National Institute on Child and Human Development (NICHD) to develop the concept of training in life-span developmental psychology. I had talked earlier with James Birren (then the aging section program officer in NICHD) about developing a training grant in geropsychology, but he had cautioned me on the need to first gain greater faculty depth. Thinking back to my early conversations with the developmentalists at Berkeley as well as having read some of the work of Charlotte Bühler, I thought that it might be propitious to reintroduce the concept of life-span development in the United States. Moreover, if I could combine faculty interested in child, adolescent, and adult development, I would then have a critical faculty mass on which to base a credible application.

I also wrote a conference grant application (modeled after my experience with the Nebraska Symposium on Motivation) with the support of APA's Division 20 (Adult Development and Aging). This conference, held in 1967, had specialists in geropsychology review the literature in core topics of the field, with critiques provided by substantively relevant psychologists who were studying children or adolescents. The conference and the publication arising therefrom was the predecessor of the series of conferences and monographs known as the West Virginia Life-Span Series, which is still continuing under the guidance of Hayne Reese. That year I was also promoted to full professor.

In 1968 I was prevailed on to "simplify" my life by becoming chair of the Department of Psychology, in which role I served until 1973. One of my first acts as chair was to recruit Paul Baltes and John Nesselroade to join the departmental faculty and to take an active interest in geropsychology. Both Paul Baltes (now a director of the Berlin Max Planck Institute for Education and Development) and John Nesselroade (now professor of psychology at the University of Virginia) have continued this interest, both men eventually serving as presidents of APA's Division 20.

Next I once again returned to the study of adult cognitive development. Soon after the completion of the first longitudinal follow-up it had become evident that conclusions based on data covering a single seven-year interval required further replication, if only because two occasions of measurement permit the examination of cross-sectional but not of longitudinal sequences (the latter requiring a minimum of three measurement occasions). Only longitudinal sequences allow designs that permit contrasting age and cohort effects. Hence, plans were made for a third data collection, conducted in 1970. The results from the third data collection seemed rather definitive in replicating the short-term longitudinal findings, but they also showed further progression of the ability-related cohort trends discovered earlier (Schaie & Labouvie-Vief, 1974). This research marked a close association with Barbara Buech, whom I had recruited during the Saarbrücken mining conference and who became my Seattle field office coordinator, and with Gisela Labouvie-Vief, my chief research assistant (now professor of psychology at Wayne State University).

The University of Southern California

The heady expansion days financed by the Great Society programs and other endeavors to develop the Appalachian region had come to a close, and a new conservative university president began to talk about retrenchment and his perception that West Virginia could not afford a first-rate university. Having brought the psychology program to a nationally recognized level, I was not willing to preside over its return to mediocrity and decided that it was time to move on. At the same time, my first marriage had deteriorated to the point where a decision to bring it to an end had become inevitable, and a new beginning was needed as well to reinvigorate my personal life.

My old friend James Birren had founded the Andrus Gerontology Center at the University of Southern California in 1965. In 1973 he invited me to join him as associate director for research (later director of the Gerontology Research Institute) and as professor of psychology. At USC, I directed the interdisciplinary doctoral training program in aging and was instrumental in developing and overseeing a number of project-program efforts to bring to bear the skills of scientists in the biological, behavioral, and social sciences on major basic issues in the aging process.

Discrepancies between findings in the repeated-measurement and independent-sampling studies suggested the need for a replication of the 14-year longitudinal sequences, and it also seemed useful to follow the original sample over as long as 21 years. A fourth data collection was therefore conducted in 1977. Continuous funding also made possible addressing a number of other bothersome questions. These included analyses of the consequences of shifting from a sampling without replacement model to a sampling with replacement paradigm, an analysis of the effects of monetary incentives on participant characteristics, an examination of the aging of tests, as well as causal analyses of health and environmental factors on change or maintenance of adult intellectual performance. Doctoral students who participated in this round of the SLS and who have continued to be active in geropsychology included Christopher Hertzog (now professor of psychology at the Georgia Institute of Technology), Margaret Quayhagen, and Michael Gilewski.

At USC I also started a new longitudinal study of cognitive aging (including memory functioning), which I followed only over a three-year period but which is now being continued by another of my former USC students, Elizabeth Zelinski. Beyond the research area, I was able to make an impact on many budding gerontologists by routinely teaching the course on research methods in aging that was part of the annual USC gerontology summer institutes. I was also involved in helping organize the Leonard Davis School of Gerontology, the first of its kind, and was active chairing committees for the recruitment of its first director and psychology faculty. In many ways, both the environment at the Andrus Gerontology Center and the gentle but intellectually stimulating leadership of Jim Birren helped me broaden my understanding of the role of geropsychology within the larger context of the study of aging and convinced me even more that interdisciplinary efforts in our field are a necessity, rather than a luxury.

The Pennsylvania State University

While at USC I had met Sherry Willis, who taught at the Pennsylvania State University. As our personal and professional interests began to merge, we decided that we should give up transcontinental commuting and be at the same institution. I therefore left USC at the end of 1981 to accept an appointment as professor of Human Development and Psychology at Penn State and to marry Sherry. Since 1985 I have directed the Penn State Gerontology Center, and in 1986 I was honored by the university with an appointment as the Evan Pugh Professor of Human Development and Psychology.

The fifth (1984) SLS cycle also marked the assumption of a major role in the study by Sherry Willis, who brought her skills in designing and implementing cognitive training paradigms. A major part of the fifth cycle was therefore devoted to the implementation of a cognitive training study with our long-term participants aged 64 years or older. This study was designed to determine whether cognitive training in the elderly remediates cognitive decline or whether it increases levels of skill beyond those attained at earlier ages. In this study we found that almost two thirds of all subjects benefited significantly from a five-hour cognitive training program and that 40% of those who had reliably declined could be brought back to the performance level they had shown 14 years earlier. Training was also shown to remove the so reliably demonstrated gender difference on spatial orientation.

From the beginning of the SLS we had followed what was then the conventional wisdom of assessing each primary ability with that observable marker variable, which was thought to be the most reliable and valid measure of a particular ability. With the widespread introduction of modern methods of confirmatory (restricted) factor analysis, it became obvious that we needed to extend our concern with changes in level of intellectual functioning in adulthood to the assessment of structural relationships within the ability domain. This concern argued for collecting further data with a much expanded battery in which each ability would be multiply marked. Finally, this cycle saw the introduction of measures of practical intelligence, analyses of marital assortativity using data on married couples followed over as long as 21 years, and the application of event history methods to hazard analysis of cognitive change with age.

Penn State has had a long history of scientific and educational efforts in gerontology. The Penn State Gerontology Center was founded by Joseph Britton in 1967, with an interdisciplinary training grant supported successively by NIMH, NICHD, and since its inception by the National Institute on Aging (NIA), which has now been continuously in place for more than 30 years. The Gerontology Center had concentrated for a number of years on training service providers for local and state agencies. My early efforts were to refocus on research and education. These efforts included putting in place a pilot study support program for new faculty, the development of an annual research conference (known as the Social Structures and Aging series) with published proceedings, the showcasing of faculty by means of a reprint-preprint service, and by encouraging efforts to broaden the extramural funding for research related to aging. Of great help and continuing collegial support has been my assistant director Steven Zarit, whom I had originally recruited to USC and persuaded to follow me to Penn State.

In the education area we put in place graduate and undergraduate minors in gerontology and have been supportive of training teachers at small colleges by encouraging visiting appointments and being active in support of teaching workshops sponsored by Association of Gerontology in Higher Education (AGHE). I have also been active in encouraging regional cooperation through efforts such as the joint exhibit of Pennsylvania gerontology centers at professional meetings and participating in a consortium with Temple University and the University of Pittsburgh in operating the Pennsylvania Geriatric Education Center, which offer continuing professional education over a wide spectrum of health-related professions. Current efforts include entry into the world of the Internet, trying to share Penn State's aging-related resources with the broader community.

Returning to my own scientific odyssey, I began a new cycle in 1991 that markedly expanded the scope of the SLS. First, with the collaboration of Robert Plomin, a noted developmental behavior geneticist, we began a study of cognitive family resemblance in adulthood. We did this by recruiting the participation of a large number of adult offspring and siblings of our longitudinal panel members. Second, we abstracted health histories on our panel members and have conducted detailed investigations of the relationship between health and maintenance of intellectual functioning, showing both the influence of chronic disease on maintenance of intellectual functioning and the importance of intellectual competence in postponing the onset of chronic disease. Third, we conducted a seven-year follow-up on the cognitive training study, showing continuing effects of the training intervention, and replicated the initial findings with a more recent cohort of older persons. Fourth, with the first longitudinal replication of our expanded test battery, we were able to conduct longitudinal analyses of cognitive ability structures, demonstrating the greater stability of longitudinal data, and further update our normative data.

Most recently, I have been able (with support from the NIA) to broaden my interdisciplinary interest even farther through new collaborative studies with the University of Washington Alzheimer Center and Department of Pathology, to study genetic markers in our longitudinal subjects, to investigate the relationship between our measurement system for the study of normal aging with the diagnostic procedures used by neuropsychologists interested in diagnosing dementias, and the relation of predeath behavioral correlates of eventual structural changes in the brain.

Other Influences

I should be remiss in not acknowledging the important role of international experiences in my professional development. Given the international scope of gerontology I always learned much from attending international congresses, such as the International Congress of Gerontology or the International Society for the Study of Behavioral Development. My German language skills were useful in accessing important professional relationships in the German-speaking countries, once I was able to resolve my feelings about the injuries of the past. I spent interesting sabbatical years as the University of Trier and the University of Bern, as well as at the Gerontological Center of Lund, Sweden. Most stimulating also was a year at the Center for Advanced Studies in the Behavioral Sciences at Stanford, California.

What Have I Learned as a Geropsychologist?

As part of my scientific work, I have been able to chart the course of selected psychometric abilities from young adulthood through old age. An important contribution of this work has been the detection of substantial generational differences in intellectual performance. Also identified were a number of contextual, health, and personality variables that offer explanations for differential age change and that provide a basis for possible interventions. Cognitive interventions were designed that have been successful in remediating carefully documented declines and that have improved the cognitive functions of many older persons who have remained stable. I have also studied changes in cognitive ability structures across age and different cohorts, have conducted analyses of the relative effect of speed and accuracy in age decline and training gain, have investigated the relevance of cognitive training to real-life tasks, and have studied parent/offspring and sibling similarity in adult cognitive performance. The dialectic process between data collection and model building that has been characteristic of my work has both increased our knowledge base and led to a number of methodological advances in the design and analysis of studies of human development and aging.

Over the course of my research career I have focused on five major questions, which I have attempted to ask with greater clarity and increasingly more sophisticated methodology as time progressed. These questions are the following:

1. *What is the differential life course of intellectual abilities?* Our work has shown that there is no uniform pattern of age-related changes across all intellectual abilities.

Hence, studies using an overall index of intellectual ability (IQ) are of only limited usefulness for an understanding of age changes and age differences in intellectual functioning in individuals or in groups.

2. *At what age can we observe a reliable decline in intellectual abilities and how large is the decline?* Our general finding has been that reliable average decline in mental abilities does not occur before age 60 but that reliable average decline may be found for all abilities by age 74. Detailed analyses of individual differences in intellectual change demonstrated that even at age 81 fewer than half of all observed individuals experienced reliable decline over the preceding seven years. These findings provide a normative base that can help determine at what ages declines reach practically significant levels of importance for public policy related to issues such as ages for retirement eligibility, age discrimination in employment, or the determination of the population proportions that can live independently in the community.

3. *How do successive generations differ in intellectual performance?* The prevalence of substantial generational (cohort) differences in psychometric abilities has been conclusively demonstrated. When cross-sectional data are used as a first estimate of age changes within individuals, they tend to overestimate age changes before the 60s for those abilities that show negative cohort gradients and underestimate age changes for those abilities with positive cohort gradients.

4. *What are the causes of individual differences in age-related ability change in adulthood?* The most unique contribution of a longitudinal program of research on adult development stems from the fact that one can investigate individual differences in antecedent variables that lead to early decline for some persons and maintenance of high levels of functioning for others well into very advanced age. Variables that we have identified as being important in reducing the risk of cognitive decline include (a) The absence of cardiovascular and other chronic diseases; (b) a favorable environment that is often a consequence of high socioeconomic status; (c) involvement in a complex and intellectually stimulating environment; (d) flexible personality style at midlife; (e) marrying an intelligent spouse; and (f) maintaining high levels of perceptual processing speed.

5. *Can age-related intellectual decline be reversed through educational intervention?* Findings from our cognitive training studies suggest that intellectual decline observed in many community-dwelling older people is likely to be a function of disuse and is therefore reversible for many persons.

What Lies Ahead?

Life as a professional gerontologist encourages one to believe that scientific productivity can be maintained well into advanced old age. Consequently, because mandatory retirement for academics has ended, my future plans do not include formal professional retirement. Current work in my laboratory has just begun to examine the rate of intellectual aging in families and a seventh SLS cycle began in 1997, which includes a further follow-up on the effects of cognitive training and another set of longitudinal data waves. We have also begun to study the relationship between the psychometric measures of cognitive behavior and neuropsychological assessments to explore the possibility of earlier identification of risk for dementia, the relationship between cognitive change and prevalence of the high-risk allele of the Apo-E gene, and recruitment of participants who will allow us to conduct a postmortem to study directly anatomical and cellular features of the normal aging brain and their relations to cognitive behavior.

Longitudinal studies have a life of their own; they involve multiple generations of students and investigators. As all serious researchers know, there are no final answers or critical experiments. We continue to build on the work of those who came before us, and we hope our students will continue the quest. For those of us whose science also serves to help make meaning of our own lives, the study of gerontology is immensely rewarding; I could not have chosen a better or more intellectually exciting vehicle for my professional odyssey.

References

Schaie, K. W. (1958). Rigidity-flexibility and intelligence: A cross-sectional study of the adult life-span from 20 to 70. *Psychological Monographs, 72*(462), Whole No. 9.

Schaie, K. W. (1965). A general model for the study of developmental problems. *Psychological Bulletin, 64,* 92–107.

Schaie, K. W. (1977/1978). Toward a stage theory of adult development. *International Journal of Aging and Human Development, 8,* 129–138.

Schaie, K. W. (1996). *Intellectual development in adulthood: The Seattle longitudinal study.* New York: Cambridge University Press.

Schaie, K. W., & Heiss, R. (1964). *Color and personality.* Bern: Huber.

Schaie, K. W., & Labouvie-Vief, G. (1974). Generational versus ontogenetic components of change in adult cognitive behavior: A fourteen-year cross-sequential study. *Developmental Psychology, 10,* 305–320.

Schaie, K. W., Rosenthal, F., & Perlman, R. M. (1953). Differential deterioration of factorially ''pure'' mental abilities. *Journal of Gerontology, 8,* 191–196.

Thurstone, L. L. (1938). *The primary mental abilities.* Chicago: University of Chicago Press.

Chapter 20
E CINERE RESURGO:
Autobiography of a Geropsychologist

Johannes J. F. Schroots

Nomen est omen—the name is a sign. I have good reason to bear the name of Schroots, which means "scrap" or "junk" in English.

I was born in the ruins of bombed Rotterdam on June 5, 1943, two days before James E. Birren started his career in gerontology. My father was a simple clerk who survived forced labor of the Nazis, lent a helping hand to the Dutch resistance, and went into hiding during the last years of war to escape the raids of the German occupying forces. Working very hard, he ended his career as executive director of an international shipping company and as vice president of the Amsterdam shipping trade society. My mother took care of me and my older brother, who was born at the beginning of the Second World War. My younger brother, the third and last child in the family, was born just after the war. Not until 50 years later, when I had two children of my own, did I understand what a difficult time my mother must have had during the war; we had hardly anything to eat, she was pregnant, and, besides that, she also had to care for two young children. With unmistakable dramatic talent, she imitated much later how we—almost starving to death—spitted out the chalk water that passed for milk. Besides her dramatic talents—she was a fairly good amateur player—she had other talents as well, which she never could develop much to her regret; she was and continued to be a housewife, as usual in those days. The orthodox Roman Catholic belief of my parents, which strictly prohibited the use of any contraceptives, explains why we were born in spite of the terrible war conditions.

Free Spirit or Professor

Postwar Rotterdam was a heavily mutilated city where street kids had the time of their lives playing in deserted neighborhoods between the ruins of bombed houses and only half-finished apartment buildings. I had a free spirit and together with my older brother and a neighbor boy we loved to explore our environment all day. We took sandwiches with us and set off on adventures, preferably to garbage dumps in the neighborhood where the most exciting things were waiting to be discovered under the rubbish: a broken toilet bowl, parts of stairways, doors and windows, a rusty spring mattress, pieces of broken glass in all colors of the rainbow, and, most of all, lots of rubble. Everything was broken, rusty, or in an advanced state of decomposition, but we could not have cared less. We wished for nothing more than throwing stones, hammering at broken sinks with an iron bar, collecting undefinable parts, and studying the mechanics of a lavatory. Driven by a searching mind, I believe that I picked up my later interest in gerontology at the garbage dump. As a matter of fact, I also had a nice grandfather from my mother's side who loved practical jokes, played games with his grandchildren, and initiated me into the first principles of carpentry by coaching us in straightening bent, rusty nails before reusing them. Environmentally friendly or ecologically correct, it would be called now, but in those days—right after the war—it was dire necessity that arose because the shops were empty. From rusty nails and waste wood I constructed my first workbench. It never got beyond that stage.

When I was barely 5 years old, I started primary school, too young actually, and during the first two trimesters I performed very poorly. The low marks of my Easter report made my father ask whether I wanted to be a garbageman, because that would be my fate if I did not do better in school. Fortunately, I flourished in the last trimester and so did my marks. Apparently, I could already read fairly well, as I remember the comics of an absent-minded professor at the back of the Catholic youth magazine *The Guardian Angel (De Engelbewaarder).* The professor had a very traditional style of dressing with a top hat and a morning coat, contrasting sharply with his chaotic behavior, such as putting salt in his tea or sitting on his top hat. Obviously, the ambition to become a professor, even an absent-minded professor, was existing early in my career.

One bad day, I was hardly 8, the family moved to Amsterdam. All at once, I lost almost everything: my friends, the street and the pieces of wasteland, the neighbors who took care of us, Grandpa and Grandma, and all other members of our extended family. From one day to the next, I became a good boy who lived in the exquisite neighborhood of South Amsterdam, studied the piano, was pestered about his heavy Rotterdam accent, and attended a reputable Catholic boys school, which also prepared students for a preuniversity education (VWO). I never played in the streets again, I did my homework dutifully, but I was a very fast sprinter, though, alas, mediocre in soccer. Thanks to studious piano playing, I scored triumphs in accompanying class singing on a rickety harmonium driven by pedals and windbags.

When I was a sixth grader, my marks were high enough to take the entrance exam for a preuniversity education. Because of the permanent rivalry with my older brother who attended the Gymnasium, the highest level of education in The Netherlands, I also wanted to go to the Gymnasium at any price. As my brother was not doing well, my father wanted me to go to a lower level high school. Crying on my knees I begged my father to give me the opportunity to also go to the Gymnasium. If my father had known then that the Gymnasium education fosters an academic career rather than a business one, he would have never let me go to the Gymnasium.

Alpha, Beta, or Gamma

The classic, six-year Gymnasium of the 1950s was, no doubt, an orthodox education: the final exam consisted of no less than 14 subjects, varying from Latin and Greek to physics and mathematics. The elite Gymnasium of the Ignatius College, the Catholic Eton for day pupils, was—if possible—even more orthodox, because the Jesuits, the Counter-Reformation soldiers of Christ, were running the school. There was a stringent, almost militaristic regime with a strict schedule: mass at 8:00 a.m., classes from 9:00 a.m. to 4:30 p.m., homework, piano study, and bedtime at 9:00 p.m., day after day. When I reached the fourth year of the Gymnasium relatively smoothly, I had to make a choice between the alpha or beta division. Alpha emphasized the humanities, beta the sciences. I was neither a typical alpha, nor a beta. As the classics teacher once told me in jest: ''Schroots, you are not an alpha, you are not a beta, no, you are''—and all students held their breath—''a gamma!'' The beta division was absolutely the most competitive education and offered practically unlimited opportunities for admission to whatever academic study I would choose. As I did not know yet what I wanted to do in academia, I decided to keep all options open by making a choice for beta—however, I had reckoned, without the Jesuits, who were struggling in that year with too many beta pupils and with insufficient space. As I was neither fish nor flesh, the Jesuits exerted some pressure on me, and on my parents as well, to choose alpha instead of beta. Crying, I had to fall again on my knees before my father so that I could realize my academic aspirations.

The more I reached puberty, the more pessimistic I grew. I made difficulties out of almost everything and about my choice of career in particular. I was constantly at odds with my father (not forgetting myself) and read low budget paperbacks such as Eysenck's *Uses and Abuses of Psychology* and *Psychological Testing (Mensen testen)* by the Dutch psychologists Deen and Bokslag. My later interest in differential psychology must stem in part from these two books. As I struggled with my future—and my parents with me on the rebound—it seemed sensible to take a psychological test. The outcome of the testing, which was meant to solve the problem of my choice of career, generated a new problem: I could be almost anything I wanted to be, but I was most suitable for forestry, biochemistry, medicine, or psychology. After being torn by doubt for two years—I even considered for a moment to study law or economics to please my father—I finally decided to study psychology at the Protestant (!) Free University in Amsterdam. The leftist neighboring University of Amsterdam was negatively recommended by the Jesuit fathers, because they believed that psychology was related more to the soul and spirit of the individual than to one's mind and behavior, a notion that was still widely accepted at the Free University in 1962. I wondered a long time about whether I should study medicine instead of psychology. Fortunately, my older brother was already studying medicine, and he had to work very hard. When I noticed how he slaved in studying, I thought, wisely, that it was quite nice to be a medical doctor but not to become one. Besides, I had still other ambitions.

Art or Science

While I was studying at the Gymnasium I practiced the piano diligently, sometimes for two hours a day, but I also played in ensembles of all types with much enthusiasm. When I was having a hard time, the piano was my best friend, and at school I was known for my skills as a meritorious pianist of classical music. As soon as I passed the Gymnasium beta exam, I enrolled for the introductory class at the Amsterdam Conservatory. Starting two full-time studies, psychology and piano, didn't seem much of a problem, if only for the fact that the six-year study of psychology didn't amount to much in those days. Compared with the purgatory of the gymnasium, the academic study of psychology was my earthly paradise: I did hardly anything, joined the university (night)life with enthusiasm, but still took my exams with ease. The conservatory, however, was quite another story; to make any progress at all, I had to put in long hours of practice. After a year of solfège and four daily hours of piano playing without much progress, I dropped out of the Conservatory. I decided to become a music psychologist, but only after I had finished my university study. It took me at least two years before I had the courage to look the hard truth of my failure straight in the eye—in music I was and still am a mediocre talent, and I had never had before the experience of mediocrity. The disillusionment was so severe that I did not touch the piano for at least 10 years. Nevertheless, I am still proud that, as a second-year student of psychology, I played the concertante harpsichord part of Bach's *Fifth Brandenburg Concerto* on a harps' chord with a piano touch, and accompanied by a student orchestra. These days, I play the real harpsichord.

In the beginning of my study I suffered from a constant lack of funds. I did not have a scholarship because my father earned too much, and my parents' allowance was absolutely insufficient. I decided to make a virtue of necessity and accompanied ballet classes on the piano. This activity, however, didn't bring much in. Therefore, I lost no time in applying for the half-time job of research assistant when this new position for students of psychology was created at the Laboratory of Physiology (Free University) in my second year. I was the first applicant to be hired, even though I had yet to take the physiology exam. From that moment, I was financially on a bed of roses, but more important was the feeling of excitement that from now on I could also satisfy my interest in the biological substrate of human beings. My job was primarily to assist psychology students, who, for the first time (1965–1966), were required to take a physiology lab, a subject that I myself had never taken. In the summer of 1965 I received some practical training and was instructed how to decapitate frogs, to excite tetanic contractions, to measure basal metabolism, and to carry out numerous other physiological tests. During that summer my interest in human physiology was aroused once and for all.

Irrespective of my age and lack of experience, I was supposed to do both teaching and research. As third-year student of psychology, I felt like an outsider who was pestered by narrow-minded physiologists (medical training only) because of my academic interest in psychology. Therefore, I thought that it would be sensible to join the mainstream of research at the physiology lab (i.e., ballistocardiography or the graphic recording of the stroke volume of the heart). What I didn't know then was that the method of ballistocardiography (in which the heartbeat results in motion of the body, which in turn causes movements in a suspended special table) went out long ago, but the advantage was that I belonged to the medical club. One day Prof. dr. A. Knoop, head of the lab, suggested that a psychologist *in statu nascendi* like me would be interested in Welford and Birren's recently published book, *Behavior, Aging and the Nervous System* (1965). Well, that was putting it mildly. I almost devoured the book, because a solution was offered for the frustrations I experienced in my research. In particular Birren's chapter on *age changes in speed of behavior* appealed to my imagination, because he referred to an electronic instead of mechanical multiple reaction time device that I could use very well in my own research. At Knoop's advice, I wrote a letter to Birren with a request for information, signed with Dr. J. J. F. Schroots (according to Knoop, Americans would not reply unless signed with ''Dr.''). By return post I received the answer: Unfortunately, it was impossible to provide the information (the factory was no longer interested in production), but why didn't I come around the new gerontology institute at the University of Southern California (USC) to have a look at the electronic miracle? Signed: Dr. James E. Birren.

New World

America in the pre-Vietnam War era was the promised land for foreign students like me. I seized Birren's invitation with both hands, the more so because it enabled me to visit the proverbial Dutch uncle in America, who had a motel in Vermont. I scraped all my savings together, bought a $99 ticket for the Greyhound bus (which offered three months of free travel in the United States), and went aboard to the New World. I was 23 years old and felt the adventure beckoning at the horizon. Europeans don't have any idea of distances in the United States. After a relaxed month in Vermont and with $100 in my pocket (barely enough to live on for six weeks), I took the Greyhound and traveled nonstop via New York to Los Angeles in four days and three nights. I was exhausted, but if you want to see America, this is the way to do it.

On a hot Friday afternoon in August of 1966, I—a 23-year old student with a BA in psychology—walked into Dr. Birren's office at the USC campus. I introduced myself but didn't get any sign of recognition. I had to spell my name, and—wonder of wonders—the letter that I had sent before had been filed. Dr. Birren read the letter, looked at me with a searching glance from above his reading glasses, and said finally, "*Doctor* Schroots?" I could have died from embarrassment and explained hastily that the signature was not my bright idea. Fortunately, Dr. Birren took it well and after a tour of the gerontology institute late that Friday afternoon, he invited me to come back next Monday because, he said, there was always an empty desk where I might work. Alas, the magic reaction time machine, for which I came the whole way from Amsterdam, didn't work and was still waiting to be unwrapped and set up by an expert after the move from Bethesda to LA. My initial disappointment, however, disappeared quickly when Dr. Birren, in the following weeks, organized a seminar on behavior, aging, and the nervous system especially for me. Moreover, he helped me write a bibliography on the relations between Aging, Reaction Time, Cerebro- and Cardiovascular Disease, and Personality. My first introduction to geropsychology couldn't have been more successful, the more so because Dr. Birren gave me a grant of $200 when he heard of my financial problems. A whole new world of science and research was opened, and no doubt I would have stayed on and gotten my PhD, made a career, and become a professor in geropsychology if only I wasn't being eaten with homesickness in no time at all: I missed my friends, my piano, and the Amsterdam university life immensely. Filled with inspiration and feelings of lifelong friendship for Jim Birren, I returned to The Netherlands. On August 27, 1966, I signed Birren's visitor's book (no doctor's title) on the same page as did Bernice Neugarten.

Psychology or Gerontology

Back from the United States, I plunged with enthusiasm into the second, more specialized phase of my study. I was crazy about psychology and I wanted to know about everything except child psychology, because all the oldish, house-playing students of pedagogics exerted anything but an attraction. Besides, I had and still have an irrational dislike of Jean Piaget. To please my father, I chose industrial psychology as my major specialty. The subject was taught by Prof. dr. P. J. D. Drenth (future Rector Magnificus of the Free University Amsterdam and president of the Royal Netherlands Academy of Arts and Sciences), who was an admirer of Lee Cronbach, the American expert in psychodiagnostics and psychometrics. Drenth's lectures on psychodiagnostics had made a deep impression: his lucid explanation of the theory and construction of psychological tests, as well as the prospect of advanced classes in personnel assessment, were part of the reason I chose industrial psychology. However, only one major specialty was not enough for me; by choosing experimental psychology as second major, in combination with nearly all other subjects, seminars, and workshops that I could take, I devoured the best part of psychology taught at the Free University, and even more; with special permission of the dean of the psychology faculty (I happened to be its first student), I also took classes in neuroanatomy and neurophysiology in the Free University's medical school. I was an omnivore with a clear preference for "hard-headed" science. In the multidisciplinary field of geropsychology I felt at home from the very beginning.

With the knowledge amassed at USC, I was eager to get back to work as research assistant at the Laboratory of Physiology. I initiated an exploratory study of CVA patients and introduced the following variables: intelligence, tapping, Bourdon-Wiersma (attention, speed, concentration), BCG, ECG, and blood pressure. Soon, however, I found that the

Department of Physiology was not interested in supervising my research and most likely not in a position to do so. I felt so miserable that from then on I confined myself to assisting at the physiology lab. Nevertheless, to make use of my newly acquired gerontological knowledge, I joined a study group of clinical psychologists, chaired by Joep Munnichs, the future professor of psychogerontology at the Catholic University Nijmegen. The study group visited nursing homes and hospitals with geriatric facilities, stimulated scientific discussions and applied research, but the scientific interest of the participants was so directed toward clinical–phenomenological subjects that I resigned my membership of the group after a few years. Clinical geropsychology failed to hold my attention—probably a matter of temperament—because I didn't and still don't have enough patience for the interaction with patients. After a few sessions I know all about it, and such an attitude does not tend to promote therapeutic understanding.

Scientific Paradise

By pure chance (I was looking for information about a tapping test at the same time that Dr. A. F. Sanders, the future professor of psychonomy at the Free University, was looking for a research assistant), I succeeded in being able to work at the world-famous TNO Institute for Perception (Soesterberg), which is part of the National Defence Research Organization. Andries Sanders, who was in charge of the Department of Experimental Psychology, knew that I needed a traineeship and he offered me a position as research assistant on the spot. Before I knew it, I was doing experimental work on short-term memory for three days a week from early morning till late at night. Because of the distance and for the sake of convenience, I was staying at the Sanders's home, but the rest of my time I spent in swinging Amsterdam. I was living in two utterly different worlds: Amsterdam with its provos, hippies, Dam sleepers, Paradiso, and Vietnam protest on the one hand, Soesterberg with its military, bourgeois mentality, conservatism, and Cold War attitude on the other. As Sanders's research assistant, however, I was only marginally involved in those issues. I have rarely learned so much in such a short time. Andries Sanders is an excellent teacher; what's more, he is obsessed by experimental research. One night at home we needed a table of random numbers and didn't want to wait till the next morning. Andries calmly took his hat from the hall stand and threw quite a heap of paper scraps into it, each scrap with a number under 10 written on it. Next he asked me to draw the scraps one by one and to return each paper scrap to the hat. This was Sanders's pragmatic and creative approach to psychological experiments. As reward for all the hard work, I was allowed to attend a NATO-sponsored conference on memory in Cambridge (United Kingdom), where such well-known researchers as Donald Broadbent and Sir Frederic Bartlett could be admired and where Fergus Craik and Pat Rabbitt were also attending. So in a natural way I was exposed to the stars of experimental psychology at a young age, got to know their culture, and had a mentor—in brief, nothing seemed to stand in the way of a shining career. Not even 24 years old, I had reached the Valhalla of experimental psychology. I am still very proud of being Andries Sanders's coauthor of three short-term memory articles in the *Quarterly Journal of Experimental Psychology* (1968/1969).

During a period of almost two years, I worked for nine months at the TNO Institute for Perception. The remaining time I used for, among other things, a compulsory traineeship in industrial psychology at the TNO Institute of Preventive Health Care (NIPG/TNO) in Leiden. I had set my mind on the development of a test battery for measuring functional age (including tapping) and Andries Sanders had drawn my attention to functional age research by Dr. J. Dirken (the future professor of industrial design and rector magnificus of Delft University). I applied for a traineeship, was accepted at once, and—on top of that—was paid as a research assistant. The times have definitely changed since then. Dirken's research was relatively advanced in those days. Applied research on personnel decisions in industry was done in multidisciplinary teams of psychologists, physiologists, biochemists, ergonomists, and statisticians. The main question was, "How can one differentiate workers who are, functionally speaking, older or younger than their chronological age would indicate?" Hundreds of workers were studied with an eight-hour test battery. I assisted with the psychological assessment part of the study, which included a multiple reaction time task. In addition, I analyzed reliability and validity data of the so-called Personal Arousal Characteristics (HAB) questionnaire under supervision of Hans Dirken. Generally speaking, the concept of functional age was mildly criticized in the 1980s (for an overview, see Birren's and Cunningham's chapter in the 1986 edition of the *Handbook of the Psychology of Aging*). However, the richness of the data as reported in Dirken's *Functional Age of Industrial Workers* (1972) turns this study into a frequently quoted source to this day. Speaking for myself, not only did I owe my future job to this study, but I was also left with a lifelong interest in the subject, which, who knows, may someday be translated into research of my own under the title of *Functional Markers of Aging*.

Immediately after my traineeship at the NIPG/TNO, and driven by interest in the neurosciences, I worked for four months as research assistant at the well-known Netherlands Institute of Brain Research in Amsterdam. The research in which I was involved made an indelible impression on me, because I was confronted for the first time in my life with the deadly consequences of uninhibited outbursts of sexual desire. After I had implanted electrodes in rat brains on the spot where the (sexual) pleasure center was located, the rats were placed in a Skinner box where they could stimulate themselves electrically and without limit, until blood showed on their mouth and legs and they finally would meet their death (but before that time we saved the rats for the next run of our experiment, in which the effect of Librium on the intracranial self-stimulation behavior was tested). The findings of this experiment in neurophysiological psychology have never been published as far as I know, because the project leader ran off with the data prematurely.

In spring of 1969 Andries Sanders invited me to accept the position of junior researcher at the National Defence Research Organization/TNO Institute for Perception. I accepted eagerly; the scientific paradise was gained and, at the same time, I could do my military service. In July of 1969 I was to join the TNO (and the army).

Paradise Lost

And I would have started to work in July of 1969 if I hadn't had to take a few exams, hadn't lived and loved in magical Amsterdam for seven days a week, and hadn't become more and more a pacifist and more and more reluctant to do classified military research. I came into a moral dilemma, and with sweaty hands I studied for my final exam the 12 solutions of cognitive dissonance knowing that only one solution would solve the dilemma: Look the problem straight in the eye and act accordingly. After a few months of moral struggle, I wrote a letter to Andries Sanders, in which I informed him with all the arguments I could come up with that I decided, much to my regret because of our close ties, not to take the job at the TNO Institute for Perception. I could no longer reconcile the two utterly different worlds of defense research and the humanistic ideal. Relieved, I mailed the letter to Andries Sanders, but only a few days later I realized that with the letter I had closed the door to paradise.

Politics or Business

I graduated, cum laude, with a degree in experimental psychology and plunged immediately into a deep depression. Everybody was on vacation, I didn't have anything to do, and I had no plans for the summer. To earn a living, I walked into a marketing office hoping for the best and, purely by accident, the office happened to be involved in the development of a survey of the aged population in support of the VARA radio program "Growing Older" (with now-famous TV talk show host Sonja Barend). I was just the person they needed: I was thrown in the depths at once, and was volunteered to be project leader; otherwise I had to figure it all out by myself. Thank God, I had a very nice supervisor, Karel Slootman, who informed me about the customs and traditions of commercial survey research and imparted to me—with a touch of irony and an incredible amount of humor—that the world is less simple than I wanted in my idealism to believe. Much later I would meet Kareltje ("little Karel," he was not exactly a tall guy), once again in entirely different circumstances.

I worked for Veldkamp Marketing almost half a year, but the half-time job was not satisfying me because the research was just too simple. Because I didn't have a clear future perspective and also thought of *career* as a dirty word, I began to miss the warm nest of my alma mater and the exciting, revolutionary atmosphere of the student movement in those days, which reached its apex at the Free University in 1969–1970. Everything and everybody was democratized, everybody had a say in everything—one man, one vote—and the Board of Governers of the University made desparate attempts to steer the democratization in the right direction. An official University Steering Committee with wide powers and representing all university parties was installed. The committee members then looked for an executive secretary, but only half-time as the process of democratization should not cost too much. Thanks to my contacts in the student movement, I got the job and I spent all my time— besides the research activities for Veldkamp Marketing—on work that I hate to this day: administration, organization, and coordination of Steering Committee activities that had no scientific content. But the worst thing was that my job had to be done in an absolutely ruined and political corrupt atmosphere. Paradoxically, I felt a victim of the very democratization that I had previously advocated. Once again, for how many times in history I don't know, the saying came true that the revolution devours her own children. I left the Steering Committee prematurely, passed the last exam, and graduated cum laude with a degree in industrial psychology and with the knowledge that for a few months at least I could make a living as neuropsychologist/consultant of the NIPG/TNO project minimal brain dysfunction. Science was victorious once again.

Part-Time Researcher

But my heart wasn't in it. In the spring of 1970 I asked myself the question, "What will I do with the rest of my life?" After the disillusion of the TNO Institute for Perception, the unsatisfactory work at Veldkamp Marketing, and the even more serious disillusion of the Steering Committee, I had to decide whether I should carry on with science and research (but less ambitiously) or continue with the free lifestyle of students (but without politics and with a simple job for purely financial reasons). I was 27 years old and I couldn't have it both ways; thus, I reached a compromise by changing my job as consultant for the NIPG/TNO into the part-time position of junior researcher at the NIPG/TNO so that I would have enough time to widen my mind, travel, listen to music and, not forgetting, engage in love affairs. It was a turbulent and romantic time. The part-time job at the NIPG was exactly after my heart: reviewing neuropsychological tests and brainstorming about the design of a study of minimal brain dysfunction (MBD) in children. I worked on a team of six people: two pediatricians, one child psychologist, one social worker, one medical physicist, and one EEG technician. In those days hardly anything was known about MBD in The Netherlands (e.g., one still used the term ''organic test'' instead of ''neuropsychological test''). I decided therefore to combine science with pleasure and to participate in a neuropsychological workshop given by Ralph Reitan in Indianapolis, where I became acquainted at length with the Halstead-Reitan neuropsychological test battery. After this productive learning experience, I traveled with a friend to Mexico for a relaxed vacation, but only after my pride was shattered because my long hair was cut under duress at the Mexican border. The Mexican customs officials didn't like hippies, and I felt humiliated by the violation of my physical integrity. However, the warmth and hospitality of the Mexican people saved my vacation and since then I have been to Mexico several times.

Back in The Netherlands I (as well as two colleagues) came into conflict almost immediately with the very friendly but also very incompetent project leader/pediatrician about the design of the MBD study. Fortunately, the director at the NIPG/TNO, Prof. dr. J. de Kock van Leeuwen, was a sensible man, for he gave the three of us enough room to start our own research. By then I was again crazy about research: I wrote my first Dutch article on neuropsychological tests (Schroots, 1972) and organized a well-attended seminar on psychodiagnostics in brain dysfunctions (with lectures by my new guru, Henry Mark), which was published in 1972 by the NIPG/TNO. Next, I made a start with the design of my own study on the early detection of learning disorders and applied for a four-year grant, which, contrary to all expectations, was awarded in 1973. I was as happy as a king, but not for long as I would soon find out.

Thanks to the fact that I worked part time, there was enough time left for other nice things in my life. As a university student I had taken jazz-ballet classes, and when I looked over a newspaper ad for a refresher course in dance expression at the Amsterdam Theatre School, I decided to sign up immediately on the pretext of ''It is fun to dance in an artistic environment and to take a teacher's certificate in addition.'' After two years of part-time dance classes, I still didn't have a certificate, but on the other hand I had a wide circle of female friends and a serious interest in dance education. As a continuation of the dance classes, I taught an introductory course in psychology at a private Institute of Dance Expression and Therapy *(Bewegingsexpressie-en therapie),* which was much later recognized by the government, until I discovered that it was more fun to dance than to teach. I must confess that I stopped teaching and dancing as I became increasingly busy at the NIPG/TNO. Dance expression is a form of dancing that doesn't use special techniques and is, therefore, very appropriate for older people. Unfortunately, dance and gym teachers fail to recognize this. Missing, nowadays, is an evening class in dance expression for working people like me.

PhD or Project

In the wake of student revolution, the early 1970s—democratization burst out at the NIPG/TNO as well. The scientific hierarchy was turned upside down and in no time at all the buffs, not necessarily the best researchers, floated up to the surface on a groundswell of stencils. As I had had my bellyful of political mimeomania and could predict the outcome of the process, I withdrew into my own research as much as possible. I felt protected by an experienced school doctor, Flora van Laar, who enjoyed the political games very much, and, because of this, she became my informal mentor at the NIPG/TNO. However, she was no match for the new director, Dr. M. Hartgerink, a real tyrant who, after the early departure of De Kock van Leeuwen, ruled the NIPG/TNO with an iron hand, reversed the democratization in no time at all, and turned the NIPG/TNO research institute into a strictly bureaucratic organization. Experienced senior researchers left the NIPG/TNO, and junior researchers like me were left behind as potential victims of the whims and tempers of the ex-pediatrician

Hartgerink, who—just like the former project leader/pediatrician—didn't have a clue about the question of conscience in doing research. I asked myself many times whether I should stay at a research institute with such a suffocating work climate, but each time my personal investments in research made me decide to stay on and to take my PhD as soon as possible. Moreover, I had successfully conducted the pilot study and was on the verge of starting the four-year main study (in collaboration with the Free University and School Advisory Center Den Bosch, subsidized by the government), which would make me less dependent on the bureaucratic routines and obstruction of the NIPG/TNO.

One fine Sunday afternoon, when I was working at home, the phone rang: "This is Maarten Hartgerink. I am sorry to disturb you, but is it true that you want to take your PhD two years from now and also turn over the position of project leader to somebody else?" Yes, it was true, and part of my plan was to leave the NIPG/TNO with a PhD as soon as possible. But I also sensed danger and, therefore, I mumbled a noncommittal statement, which was interrupted immediately by, "If it is true, then your research will not be continued and your grant will be returned." At that stage of my research, I had no other choice but to tell him that I, of course, would be project leader for the duration of the main study, but that I also would like to take my doctorate very much. "In that case we have understood each other very well, first the project and, after that, I will allow you to take your PhD." To my utter amazement, Hartgerink kept his promise, but it was 1978 before I could make a start with my PhD thesis on the basis of pilot data from 1973.

Full-Time Researcher

Lacking any experience as project leader but being very ambitious, I plunged into the project activities, which essentially boiled down to the construction and validation of a sequential testing procedure for the early detection of children (four to eight years) with learning disabilities. The multidisciplinary research project included not only a physical examination by the school doctor and a neurological examination by a specialist/pediatrician, but it also included the development, construction, and validation of a standard test battery (the Leiden Diagnostic Test, or LDT), the development of advanced assessments methods (i.e., limit testing), the construction of flowcharts for the automatic analysis and reporting of test profiles (paper-and-pencil computer), and the application of Bayesian statistics in the assessment of learning disabilities. In addition, the LDT was standardized on a sample of 1200 4- to 8-year-old children, representative of the Dutch population. All this was enough for four years of good teamwork and very inspiring scientific research.

I soon realized that a part-time position didn't fit the amount of work I had to take as project leader and *auctor intellectualis* of the study. If I had to work full time, then I also wanted to be paid full time. Therefore, I decided to expand my position to a full-time job. By that, alas, my long-cherished ideal of living and working in a playful and harmonious manner evaporated halfway through the 1970s. From now on I had to take life seriously, but to this day I have trouble working regular office hours. Creativity in science, however, cannot be forced in the armor of utilitarian principles. My best ideas emerge in the morning when I am shaving, and I am working on my papers in the afternoon and evening, as well as on the weekend. Obviously, there is a price for everything, but fortunately the contacts with my colleagues made up for it—that is, the work climate was friendly and cooperative and all team members worked very hard to make a success of the project in spite of bureaucratic opposition. The project became such a success that it attracted wide attention. The prolongation of project activities was stopped, therefore, on the principle that the project no longer fitted in the policy of the NIPG; the research team was offered another job (or the contract was simply not renewed), and I—? Well, I was given an opportunity to work on my thesis.

Getting a PhD

In those days it was not common practice at the NIPG/TNO for researchers to aspire to get their PhD. In a way I felt privileged, because I could work on my thesis under the supervision of my favorite tutor, Prof. dr. Pieter J. D. Drenth, with no other obligations. Thus, after years of project management and hard work, I had enough reasons to complete my life's work in good spirits, for in 1978, a Dutch PhD thesis was still looked on from the perspective that it closes a career instead of the other way round. Little by little, however, I got depressed. The relation with a girlfriend was almost over, I missed the contacts with my team very much, I was *blessed* with a high level of achievement-motivation, and, to make matters worse, I had to analyze 1973 pilot study data that had academic value for the most part. Nevertheless, I managed to finish my thesis in about a year and it contained what is still a very interesting part on learning potential and limit testing (Schroots, 1979). I had clearly profited from previous learning experiences in writing papers.

Twenty years later I wonder what the first NIPG/TNO period of nine years has really meant to me. The first thing that comes to mind is the failure of the combination of play, life, and work. The emphasis had been more and more on work, so that the element of play was lost and maybe life also, if one may believe Huizinga's *Homo ludens.* The development of a career like that doesn't do any good for science, and for people either. Looking back, it appears that most ideas that formed the basis of the project were created in the first three years of my part-time work at the NIPG, during the pilot phase of playing and working. I strongly believe, confirmed by later experiences, that the time spent on playing with ideas pays back twice and more scientifically. Unfortunately, creative playing is on bad terms with the utilitarian thinking of the market, which has overrun Dutch universities and research institutes with the help of bureaucratic government's mania for economics.

A second issue of significance concerns my self-image. It is more than likely that my reputation has an individualistic and nonconformistic connotation. Much to my surprise I was able to lead a multidisciplinary team of peers, who at the beginning were rather skeptical about their project leader. However, I radiated enthusiasm and I got good teamworkers in return, a very special experience.

All ideas that formed the basis of my work—the third issue—can be summarized under the title of ''integration.'' As a student, because of my broad interest, I became acquainted with widely divergent views and schools in psychology, which, on first thoughts, did not have much to do with each other. For example, cognitive psychology with its experimental methods and techniques seemed unrelated to differential psychology, which relied heavily on psychometrics. In practice, experimental psychologists and psychodiagnosticians were (and are) living in two different worlds. The innovative feature of the Leiden Diagnostic Test (LDT) is that the eight tests of the LDT battery were constructed on the basis of two integrated models: a factor analytic model, à la Guilford's *Structure of Intellect,* and a developmental model of cognitive functioning, derived from the pioneering work of Henry Mark (see his 1962 *Science* article, *Elementary Thinking and the Classification of Behavior*). Also, I attempted to accommodate experimental and differential psychology by means of limit testing, an experimental testing procedure that assesses the individual's learning potential. Developmental psychology, as well as geropsychology, is involved in limit testing through Vygotsky's concept of ''zone of proximal development.'' Finally, my team succeeded in improving clinical judgment in psychodiagnostics by using decision-theoretical principles, derived from Bayes's *theorema* and Tversky's and Kahneman's work on *heuristics and biases in judgement under uncertainty* (*Science,* 1974). As far as possible the complete assessment procedure, from clinical judgement to psychological report, was computerized by means of flowcharts, playfully called the paper-and-pencil computer. I missed this inspiring climate immensely in the months before my PhD graduation on Thursday, September 20, 1979, from Free University, Amsterdam.

Then I received a letter from Jim Birren who invited me for a sabbatical year at the Ethel Percy Andrus Gerontology Center of the University of Southern California, Los Angeles. I jumped out of my depression, applied for a research fellowship with the International Fogerty Organization, and on Easter of 1979 celebrated that exactly a year before I met Marla Kleine, my beloved for life, who many years later presented me with the two most precious gifts of my life, Anna and Eva Schroots, but that was all hidden in the future.

Paradise Regained

In autumn 1979, three weeks after taking my doctoral degree in the faculty of social sciences, I bade melancholic farewell to my beloved and left for a year for the United States. Jim and Betty Birren are the most hospitable people I know, and I very gratefully enjoyed their hospitality for the first four months of my fellowship. Their Spanish-Mexican home is situated in Pacific Palisades, a heavenly spot in a paradisiacal environment. The garden of the house looks most like the Garden of Eden as Henri Rousseau would paint it, with hummingbirds and magic bushes. It was a nice place to stay in an ambiance of peace and quiet, but that did not last very long. Shortly thereafter I became pessimistic, because my stay at the Andrus Gerontology Center was not going quite as I had planned.

After many years' responsibility as project leader, I had been eagerly looking forward to finally working with other people and, in this way, to learn something about a subject I didn't know anything at all (i.e., the evaluation of Birren's *Guided Autobiography*). In my arrogant opinion, this was a soft-headed subject that I didn't take very seriously, but it appeared fascinating enough to stimulate my curiosity. Unfortunately, the project leader got maternity leave as soon as I arrived, and I had to figure out everything by myself. Worse, however, proved to be my problematic status at USC: I was registered as a so-called 999, a number that is only given to people nobody knew what to do with. As a Fogerty fellow I was finally dumped in the category of postdocs, the foreign labor of American universities (nowadays also Dutch universities). All at once I was confronted with a new world: After 10 years of scientific research I had to start all over again and to "enjoy" the status of a recently graduated psychologist-researcher who still had to learn his trade. And from another perspective, I had to start all over again because from one day to the next my knowledge of cognitive child psychology proved to be absolutely irrelevant for people who were interested only in the elderly. My problem was even more poignant, because to this day I am not interested in specific age groups, whether they are children, rats, or older people. As soon as I study a subject for a longer time, my intellectual curiosity is aroused and in no time at all I want to know more about it. My later efforts to unravel the underlying ontogenetic relation between developmental psychology (child psychology) and geropsychology can be traced back to this very frustrating experience. After three months of USC I was depressed and felt so sick for home that I wanted to go back. Fortunately, my beloved came over for Christmas, we had Birren's beautiful home for ourselves, and I didn't need to make a decision for the time being. However, I hadn't reached rock bottom yet.

That happened a few weeks later, when I felt lonely and alone in my apartment. I was writing a letter to my beloved when I suddenly became aware that I no longer wanted to do other people's work. If nobody was interested in my expertise, then I would at least do my own thing. For a Dutchman from a bleak climate, this means something like sitting in the sun with a book under a palm tree. Much later, I realized that not only was this moment decisive for the success of my fellowship, but it also provided the root metaphor of my *Branching theory* (Schroots, 1995a, 1995b). At the lowest point in my career—metaphorically called transformation, bifurcation, or *branching point*—I went my own scientific way and didn't go back home empty handed, which might have been quite possible. Order was created out of the disorder of my life through a process of self-organization, but this explanation of events will be elaborated on later.

In finding my way in life, Jim Birren has been very helpful, if not essential, and he did this in his own characteristic way of the Socratian dialogue interspersed with a good joke and long walks around the USC campus. In those days Jim was interested in the psychological characterization of short autobiographical essays on the major branching points in life. During one of our walks we made a thorough search for a single personality description, which would reflect both unique and more general traits of the individual (an impossible task), and the animal metaphor seemed to be a good candidate. For example, what is more appealing to the imagination than that we think of a person as a hyena or a lion? Immediately we see a different person. (On being asked, Dennis B. Bromley, who published *Personality Description in Ordinary Language* in 1977 and who happened to visit USC in 1980, also pointed out the contradictory nature of single personality descriptions.) When I was looking for some very easy reading in the campus bookstore and the animal metaphors were still running through my mind, my attention was suddenly drawn to Ortony's *Metaphor and Thought* (1979) with an interesting chapter by R. J. Sternberg. On impulse I decided to buy the book and went on to read it at one sitting under my favorite palm tree. This was the relaxed Californian way of life I had dreamed of. Fortunately, Jim opened my eyes by regularly asking about my reading experiences; otherwise I wouldn't have done anything during that year. I told him the story of my quest in the kingdom of metaphors, how essentially all theory is based on it, and how much fun it is to create something new by playing with metaphors. ''Why don't you write a couple of pages about metaphors?'' asked Jim *quasi* innocently, and so he brought me back, imperceptibly, to the path of science with gerontology as its destination. Before I knew it, I was the proud coauthor of three papers that all contain sections on constructivism in science and metaphors of growth and development versus senescence and aging. What started as curiosity out of pure frustration turned soon into a scientific gold mine. Thanks to my interest in metaphors, two conferences were organized: the unpublished 1982 Vancouver Conference on Metaphors in the Study of Aging (with, among others, Bengtson, Birren, Craik, and Neugarten as participants) and the very successful 1990 New Brunswick Conference on Metaphors of Aging in Science and the Humanities (with, among others, Achenbaum, Birren, Cole, Dannefer, Kenyon, Mader, Manning, Shephard, and Yates; Schroots, 1991).

By the end of my year at USC I had come to like gerontology. I asked everybody to depict the ups and downs of his or her life on a piece of paper (i.e., the primitive precursor of the later Life-line Interview Method), and I prepared myself for a vacation in Ecuador (Galápagos Islands) and Peru by taking free Spanish classes in the LA downtown Senior Citizen Center. The teacher thought that I was a bit slow in Spanish and once said to me, ''Hans, if you want to survive in Los Angeles, you better speak faster,'' but she completely forgot that even though I was speaking English, I was still thinking in Dutch. I left USC with a feeling of relief. I had learned a lesson that can only be learned with great difficulty in the dominant quantitative research climate of Dutch psychology—sophisticated, quantitative research (mathematical, statistical, or psychometric) does not automatically mean high-quality, creative research. Quite the contrary, the brute force of quantitative methods and techniques too often masks the paucity of ideas, theories, and findings. Once I had reached the Galápagos Islands with the tame iguanas, giant tortoises, and Darwin finches, I knew that I had regained Paradise.

Chaos

Back in The Netherlands the management of the NIPG/TNO immediately put me in a health care for the elderly position, and by that action I was cut off from my expertise, once and for all, under penalty of discharge. This authoritarian decision was taken during my sabbatical, in spite of the fact that I had asked for consultation before I left. Therefore, I was obstructive for at least two years before resigning myself to my fate. Besides, in the same period I received several invitations for a chair in child psychology or educational psychology, and what's more, I was president of the child psychology division of the Netherlands Psychological Association *(Nederlands Instituut van Psychologen)*. As it turned out, gerontology has won the game because the complexity of aging is more of a scientific challenge to me than is child psychology.

It was a chaotic, but at the same time creative period. I read almost everything and anything I could find in the field of natural philosophy, general systems theory, gerontology, and life-span psychology, inspired by my favorite book from under the palm tree, Gregory Bateson's *Mind and Nature* (1979), with essays about form and process, convergent and divergent sequences, quantity and quality, Darwin, Lamarck, and D'Arcy Thompson. Bateson's erudite essays are the basis of my later interest in Ilya Prigogine's work, as explained in his popular book *Order Out of Chaos* (1984). But before I was engaged in chaos theory, I made an attempt to develop the new field of *ontogenetic psychology,* which I defined as follows:

> Ontogenetic psychology is concerned with the description and explanation of the ''coming-into-being'' of the human organism, from conception to death. Two fundamental processes of change can be distinguished in ontogenesis: development and aging. The study of both the synchronic and diachronic relationship between development and aging is one of the most important tasks of an ontogenetic psychology. This should be done in view of the potential interactions between the biological, psychological and social levels of organization in the course of human ontogenesis. (Schroots, 1982, p. 73)

Truly an ambitious program that foundered initially on the problematic distinction between the basic concepts of *information* (for development) and *entropy* (for aging), but essentially this definition is my research agenda far into the future.

The management of the NIPG/TNO, however, was not really charmed by my attempts at basic theory formation and ordered me, therefore, to do some applied research in the care of the elderly. With the feelings of homesickness at USC still fresh in my mind, I then decided to study the supposedly (in)dependence and loneliness of older people with the help of a special assessment method, for I had understood perfectly well that the study of the life course (ontogeny) and the emotional life of people, unlike cognition, required special techniques. From this period dates the first experimental version of the Life-line Interview Method (LIM), which is a direct elaboration of my work at USC (Schroots, 1984).

Order

I gradually adapted and started the much-dreaded career. Gerontology is typically a field in which you can move up in spite of expertise and of academic weight. Of the four researchers who were occupied with the elderly, I was chosen to coordinate the research. For the first time in my life I came into direct contact with the soul-destroying order of bureaucracy, which is not at all interested in innovative, creative research, which should, of course, be its primary interest. Out of intellectual boredom, I started writing essays about life and time—that is, *The Art of Becoming* and *The Nature of Time,* all 14 of which have been published in the *Dutch Psychologist* and that in principle contain my credo as researcher (Schroots, 1985/1986). From this period stems my ''discovery'' of Prigogine as the creator of a new paradigm in science, which would be also of important relevance to geropsychology (see my essay *Will* in the June 1985 issue of the *Dutch Psychologist*). However, the peace and order of my bureaucratic research grave—the ''Schrootshoop'' (scrapheap) as I said in jest—was not of long duration, for once more a letter from Jim Birren created the much-needed excitement in my orderly life.

Order out of Chaos

At that time Jim Birren was director of both the Andrus Gerontology Center and the Andrew Norman Institute (ANI) for Advanced Study in Gerontology and Geriatrics. Every year a limited number of promising investigators from different disciplines in gerontology were invited to spend their sabbatical at the ANI in freedom, peace, and quiet. This was a rather unique institute, consequently, with unique opportunities for discussion and reflection, the more so because the theme of the academic year 1985–1986 turned out to be *Theories of Aging.* The letter from Jim Birren was an invitation plus a generous grant for the coming academic year. Such an honorable invitation happens only once in a lifetime, and naively I took the letter right away to the NIPG/TNO management, who I believed would think it to be an honor. The management, however, was not amused and forbade me to accept the invitation with the spurious argument that I was indispensable for the coordination of some junior researchers who, by the way, had not asked for my coordinatorship. (The last couple of years, and out of necessity, I had therefore restricted my leadership style to laissez-faire, which in the long run is very frustrating for both parties). However, thanks to external pressure the management had to back down and as a final compromise I was permitted to go for a minisabbatical of six months at the ANI. Much later I realized that I had to pay a price for it.

My study at the ANI was an unforgettable experience and a beautiful illustration of Prigogine's revolutionary theorem about order out of chaos through self-organization. To start with the chaos, I had resolved to write a third series of essays on growth and senescence, in which changes of form would be discussed as a continuation of my previous essays on life and time. These essays, then, would be my required contribution to the ANI book, *Emergent Theories of Aging,* that Jim Birren had planned for that year. It was tradition at the ANI that draft versions of various contributions were discussed at length during weekly lunch meetings. In view of the outstanding academic qualities of fellows and guests like Vern Bengtson, Caleb Finch, and Warner Schaie, the multidisciplinary ANI meetings ensured scholarly discussions. Anxiously, therefore, I presented my newest ideas about growth and senescence on the basis of metaphors of life and time. I probably should not have done this, for it soon became clear that the group of 12 fellows didn't really appreciate my ''natural philosophy'' approach of the ''natural science'' subject of growth and senescence, with the exception of Gary Kenyon, the philosopher of our group, and James Henry, the Jungian animal physiologist, who noted that my essays reminded him most of the French seventeenth-century philosopher Montaigne. Aside from the compliment, the judgement of the fellows was anything but positive. *Exit* Schroots. I felt hurt, misunderstood, and ashamed, especially in relation to Jim Birren, who had so much confidence in me and my abilities.

I still had two months left to sort things out. In a last and desperate effort I decided to write a so-called scientific paper on growth and senescence. I then worked like a maniac day and night on the chapter ''On Growing, Formative Change and Aging'' (Schroots, 1988), which still has the typical features of an essay, because when I began the chapter, I didn't know how it would end. Essentially, my contribution is about Prigogine's revolutionary interpretation of the second law of thermodynamics, which states that there is an increase of entropy, disorder, or chaos with age in living systems, resulting in the system's death. Prigogine, however, postulates that internal or external fluctuations of dynamic systems can pass a critical point—the transformation, bifurcation, or branching point—and create order out of disorder through a process of self-organization—that is, a process by which a structure or pattern of change emerges with the passage of time. From this metatheoretical perspective, I inferred that the aging of living systems can be conceived as a nonlinear series of transformations (literally ''changes of form'') into higher and/or lower order structures or processes, showing a progressive trend toward more disorder than order over the life span and resulting in the system's death.

The inspiration for ''On Growing, Formative Change and Aging,'' perhaps the most creative paper that I have written so far, stems directly from my study of metaphors. In particular, the metaphor of life as a branching tree proved to be very fruitful for the further development of ontogenetic psychology and gerodynamics, which formed the breeding ground of my branching theory and the Life-line Interview Method (LIM, Schroots, 1995a, 1995b, 1996). During the time I was writing my chapter I felt very lonely. Great was my shock when I found that Gene Yates had written an excellent chapter about nearly the same subject (only from a biophysical perspective) in Birren's and Bengtson's *Emergent Theories of Aging,* published by Springer in 1988. Looking back I should have had more faith in my own theory.

E Cinere Resurgo

When I returned to The Netherlands I felt for the first time in years at ease in gerontology. At last I gained insight into the gerontological hodgepodge of facts and details that lacked any theoretical idea. Self-confident, I started implementing the research program Preventive Health Care for the Elderly, which focused on the Early Assessment of the Dementia Syndrome. The project was subsidized by the Prevention Foundation *(Preventiefonds)* and implemented in close collaboration with the Department of Psychiatry of the Free University, Amsterdam. When I began the project, I promptly had a déjà vu—I had done similar research on children under the title of ''Minimal Brain Dysfunction.'' If I replaced the term ''MBD'' in my old reports with ''Dementia Syndrome,'' nobody would notice the trick, I thought. My playful imagination at that time showed, and still shows, something about the complete lack of communication between child psychologists and geropsychologists, who strictly speaking have common roots in the same discipline of developmental science. It also shows that geropsychology still trails child psychology by about 10 to 15 years.

My growing self-confidence was nourished by three invitations, respectively, for the honorary chair in geropsychology at the University of Utrecht, for the part-time position of senior lecturer of gerontology at the University of Wageningen, Department of Epidemiology and Public Health (as successor to Robert van Zonneveld, the nestor of socio-medical gerontology in The Netherlands), and for the vice chair of the program committee of the Netherlands Society of Gerontology (NVG, *Nederlandse Vereniging voor Gerontologie*) in preparation of its 40th Jubilee Congress. After much deliberation I decided to accept the Wageningen invitation, not only because of its pleasant work climate but also because I had the naive belief that at this university with experts in the field of forestry I could further develop my Branching theory. Much later I understood that my choice of Wageningen University was in fact the postponed solution of my adolescent career choice problem.

As usual the NIPG/TNO management was not very happy with my decision, which was ultimately based on my choice of science instead of academic prestige. Once again the management tried to thwart my scientific ambitions, and once again it had to back down. Also the program development of the NVG Jubilee Congress didn't go smoothly, because of the political struggle between medical and social gerontologists, and in spite of the fact that the congress was organized professionally by Clemens Walta, at that time director of the Post Graduate Institute of Education in the Social Sciences, with whom I had previously worked productively. In the final analysis, the 40th Jubilee Congress was a success, thanks to the contributions of international speakers like Jim Birren, Bob Butler, Tom Cole, and Alvar Svanborg, and thanks also to the many participants of thematic and multidisciplinary paper and poster sessions. The most important papers have been published in two books: *Health and Aging,* edited by Schroots, Birren, and Svanborg (Springer/Swets & Zeitlinger, 1988), and *Gezond Zijn Is Ouder Worden* (Healthy Aging), edited by Schroots, Bouma, Braam, Groeneveld, Ringoir, and Tempelman. Calmly and glowing with self-confidence, I left in November of 1987 for the Annual Scientific Meeting of the Gerontological Society of America.

When I came home at the beginning of December, I found two identical letters from the NIPG/TNO management in my mailbox, one an express letter and the other a registered letter, both of which summoned me to contact the management as soon as possible. The next morning, at 9:00 a.m. sharp and my head full of jet lag, I was told that I was not formally but *de facto* suspended for an indefinite period of time ''because of the unbearable work situation of my coworkers/junior-researchers.'' Also, I was forbidden to speak with my coworkers, so that from that moment all contacts had been broken off. For the time being I would draw my salary regularly.

I was completely dazed; I didn't understand it at all, and I went home in shock. My paid ''holidays''—interspersed with work, illness, and misery—continued for two and a half years. I felt more and more isolated. Also I got to know extensively the organizational violence of the TNO personnel department attached to the NIPG, a research institute that studies prevention but doesn't practice it. I hope never again to go through such a miserable period, all the more so because practically the same thing happened to my beloved less than three months after it happened to me. To this day I can only guess at the motives underlying the management's decision to provoke a labor conflict like that. Some colleagues consider it a bureaucratic stupidity, followed by new stupidities over and over again; others say that I was the first victim of two reorganizations that would lead to the final shutdown of the NIPG in the 1990s. I don't know, but the combination of these two explanations seems most probable to me. The awful thing, however, is that my reputation in The Netherlands was seriously damaged. My appointment as honorary chair in human gerontology at the University of Amsterdam (Faculty of Medicine and Psychology) didn't go through for this reason.

In spite of the fact that I became totally destroyed, I persevered in my attempts to penetrate to the core of gerontology. Because of my essays on life and time (Schroots 1985/1986) I had a special interest in the relationship between physical, biological, psychological, and social age and time on the one hand and the aging of living systems on the other. Full of hubris, I had resolved, therefore, to study this relationship further. Starting from Prigogine's dynamic systems theory, my search for knowledge led to a supplement of various types of ''classical'' calendar time with ''intrinsic time,'' which—in combination with calendar time—is a measure of *intrinsic aging.* The modern quest for *markers of aging* has its theoretical origins in this new concept of time. In these difficult days, Jim Birren, who was a big support, and I collaborated on the article "The Nature of Time: Implications for Research on Aging" (Schroots & Birren, 1988), the most abstract paper of my career. In this period I also made another discovery: If you cannot do empirical research, then it's worth the effort to explore theoretical issues. In gerontology there are plenty of subject matters.

After the NIPG/TNO management made futile attempts for two years to keep me under control, my eyes were opened and I finally dared to face the possibility of a definitive farewell. The opening of my eyes is not only a metaphor, because in the summer of 1989 I was saved from blindness by extremely painful surgery on the retina of my left eye. Collaborating with Clemens Walta, who happened to be interested in my plans for the future, I quietly developed the concept of what later would be called the European Research Institute on Health and Aging (ERGO, *Europees Researchinstituut voor Gezondheid en Ouder worden*). When I took some distance from the NIPG/TNO and my life was again going in the right direction, one of the most beautiful gifts in life was happening to me: a daughter had been born to us, Anna Johanna Maria Schroots. This gift of God, as my love and I are calling her, made a very good balance for the bitter pill that my self-selected farewell to the NIPG/TNO meant to me, in spite of the final verdict of the cantonal judge that TNO was predominantly to blame for the state of affairs. On May 15, 1990, I was out of work but in possession of a golden handshake, two and a half years of unemployment benefits, and a very traumatic experience. From that time stems my motto *E Cinere Resurgo,* out of ashes I emerge.

ERGO

Emerging out of ashes wasn't easy. I soon realized that the structural placing of ERGO in a larger research organization was absolutely necessary to get subsidies. To establish ERGO at the University of Amsterdam, and because my honorary chair didn't go through, I offered to teach a free course of human gerontology at the Department of Psychology. I am a born teacher and I love to pass on knowledge. Since October of 1990 I give, therefore, as adjunct professor of human gerontology, graduate courses for students of psychology, medicine, and sociology; I am also supervising the training and theses of interested students. In exchange for teaching I was entitled to the use of some basic facilities, which would speed up the further development of ERGO.

One of my first achievements was the organization by ERGO (in collaboration with Jim Birren and Clemens Walta) of an international conference (invitational colloquium and public symposium) on cross-national, multidisciplinary, and longitudinal research on healthy aging (May 1991). The international forum of leading researchers (Jim Birren, Dorothy Field, Jim Fozard, Eino Heikkinen, Han Kemper, Ursula Lehr, John McKinlay, Peter Molenaar, Pat Rabbitt, Georg Rudinger, Warner Schaie, E. Steinhagen-Thiessen, Hans Thomae, Gene Yates, and many others) was, in the final analysis, responsible for the scientific success of the ERGO conference (Schroots, 1993). Most unfortunately, I could not participate in my own conference because I was hospitalized again, but this time for surgery on the retina of my right eye. Bad luck, the more so because millions of public money for longitudinal research on healthy aging was not given to ERGO, and that only because ERGO, according to the former ministry of Welfare, Health, and Cultural Affairs (WVC) was unsatisfactorily embedded in the University of Amsterdam (UvA).

Yet not everything was trouble and affliction. Life had another big surprise in store for my beloved and me through the birth of our younger daughter, Eva Julia Schroots. We were beside ourselves with joy; I always wanted to have girls, because boys—as I remembered from my MBD research—are much too vulnerable and more certainly so if they are born of older parents. I also believe that I can get along much better with girls than with boys, especially when I think back to all my quarreling and fighting with my brothers. At that time I also gave in to my scientific interest in the ''soft'' sides of psychology. Thanks to Jim Birren's advocacy of a more autobiographical approach in geropsychology, an informal group was formed of academics who were primarily interested in the experience of aging. The Schwarzwald group, named after the place of our first meeting in Germany in 1991, consisted of Jim and Betty Birren (United States), Gary Kenyon (Canada), Willi Mader (Germany), Jean-Eric Ruth (Finland, deceased in 1997), Torbjorn Svensson (Sweden), and myself. Our group has met several times since then and produced the book *Aging and Biography: Explorations in Adult Development*. My contribution consisted of the theoretical exploration of the *fractal* structure of lives—that is, the self-concept or underlying identity of the self throughout life, which integrates an individual's experiences across time, and is conceived in terms of self-organization (gerodynamics), self-similarity (branching theory), and self-structuring (Life-line Interview Method; Schroots, 1996).

After the successful conference (and lost battle for public funding), ERGO focused especially hard on the European fleshpots, supported in this respect by the ever good-humored member of the board, Karel Slootman, who as director of business development of an international survey company knew his way in the Brussels bureaucracy of European Commission (EC) and Directorates General. In preparation for European research on healthy aging, a steering committee was founded, on the initiative of ERGO, consisting of Drs. Rocío Fernández-Ballesteros (Autonoma University of Madrid), Georg Rudinger (University of Bonn), and myself (chair). Helped by a small grant from the EC we organized a couple of workshops in Brussels and Bonn, with a view to search for European partners and to develop a common grant proposal. That's how I ended up, little by little, at the beginning of the 1990s, in the world of European gerontology (if there is such a thing), with the whole lot of national sentiments, language barriers, and organizational problems.

Even though The Netherlands is a welfare state, ample Dutch unemployment benefits come to an end too. At the end of 1992 I was facing minimum welfare, not a pleasant prospect for a researcher with a partner and two little children. The University of Amsterdam didn't offer me a job, and national funding of European research didn't show any prospects, in spite of my two successful workshops. It looked as if I would have to find a job for a living and I had to stop trying to do gerontological research through ERGO. I indulged in all kinds of fantasies about how to live my life in the future; I was thinking of starting my own rented deck chair business so that in the winter at least I would have time to study my favorite, geropsychology. However, the European network of researchers and ERGO's steering committee created a troubled conscience in me. To leave my colleagues in decent order, I decided to make a final attempt to qualify for a so-called Concerted Action within the framework of the very competitive BIOMED program of the European Commission. In a last desperate effort—the odds were less than 10%—I submitted the grant proposal for EuGeron: EU Concerted Action on Gerontology, in which seven member states of the European Union participated. After I had sent my proposal at the end of February 1993 by express delivery to the EC in Brussels, I felt immensely relieved. At last, I could think again about my future and not feel guilty. I had done the best I could, nobody could blame me for anything, a sequel was not likely at all, and the world was before me. Schluss, finished, that's the end, I believed, until the next day when Dolf Kohnstamm (chair of developmental psychology at the University of Leiden) called me and asked whether I would be interested in replacing an associate professor of life-span psychology for a few months while she was ill.

Yes, I was interested, and suddenly the world looked much less gloomy. For the last time, while we still could afford it, my love and I decided to go on an extensive vacation with our daughters Anna and Eva.

When I came home, an official letter of the European Commission was in my mailbox, and the message was that ERGO would receive 270,000.00 ECU (Euros) for the implementation of the EuGeron project. I started laughing and crying at the same time. Now that I had finally found some peace, I had to go back to the European arena. I considered for a moment, just for a moment, to return the money.

The rest of the ERGO story runs parallel to the developments of EuGeron and the follow-up project EXCELSA (Cross-European Longitudinal Study of Aging) that started in 1998 (for an overview, see *Aging in Europe,* edited by Schroots, Fernandez-Ballesteros & Rudinger, IOS Press, 1999). In spite of EuGeron's success, ERGO still is unsatisfactorily embedded in the existing university order. I have my doubts whether this will ever happen.

Sum

The Latin verb *sum* means "I am," and in English it also means "summary." Both meanings denote the essence, the core of a person. From the very beginning I have constructed my autobiography around the meaning of my name: I was born in the ruins of Rotterdam, I explored the local garbage dumps, and from rusty nails and waste wood I constructed a workbench. The association between my name and the concept of aging as deterioration, disintegration, disorder, chaos, and entropy is not difficult to see. In retrospect it took a long time before I threw myself with all my heart into gerontology, and that is not the fault of Jim Birren, my lifelong friend and mentor.

My career has not gone smoothly; many times I was in sackcloth and ashes, but I have learned from my own branching theory that order can arise out of disorder and that aging has also positive aspects, which is called "maturing": *E Cinere Resurgo,* out of ashes I emerge. From childhood I chose the life of a free spirit in science, two attitudes that are not easy to reconcile. Only much later in my career have I realized that free spirits in science have to pay a price, in my case a financially insecure life. Also this aspect of my life has its origins in the ontogenetic and dynamic principles of branching theory, on which I have worked for a long time and which only recently is beginning to bear fruit (Schroots & Yates, 1999). Thank God that Marla, my love, has always supported me in the realization of my scientific ideal.

Ergo means "therefore" in Latin, and, therefore, ERGO doesn't escape either from the laws of gerodynamics: internal and external fluctuations disturb the dynamic equilibrium, but ERGO has not passed a critical point yet. The crucial question is this: Is ERGO dying a slow death after the branching point and is it deteriorating into a lower order system, or is it transformed into a higher order structure, embedded in the existing university order? I don't hazard a prophecy; it is not necessary either, because *E Cinere Resurgo, Ergo, Sum Johannes J. F. Schroots.*

References

Schroots, J. J. F. (1972). Prediktie, inferentie en decisie: Een evaluatie van de neuropsychologische test [Prediction, inference and decision: An evaluation of the neuropsychological test]. *Ned. T. Psychol., 27,* 309–340.

Schroots, J. J. F. (1979). *Leidse Diagnostische Test (LDT). Deel 5: Cognitieve ontwikkeling, leervermogen en schoolprestaties* [Leiden Diagnostic Test (LDT). Vol. 5: Cognitive development, learning potential and school achievement]. Lisse: Swets & Zeitlinger, 1979.

Schroots, J. J. F. (1982). Ontogenetische psychologie: Een eerste kennismaking [First introduction to ontogenetic psychology]. *De Psycholoog, 17,* 68–81.

Schroots, J. J. F. (1984). The affective consequences of technological change for older persons. In P. K. Robinson, J. Livingston, & J. E. Birren (Eds.), *Aging and technological advances* (pp. 237–247). New York: Plenum Press.

Schroots, J. J. F. (1985/1986). *Essays on "The art of becoming" and "The nature of time."* Presented at the 1985–1986 seminar on "Theories of aging," Andrew Norman Institute for Advanced Study in Gerontology and Geriatrics. Los Angeles: University of Southern California, Andrus Gerontology Center [Published in Dutch: *De Psycholoog, 20/21,* 1985/1986].

Schroots, J. J. F. (1988). On growing, formative change and aging. In J. E. Birren & V. L. Bengtson (Eds.), *Emergent theories of aging* (pp. 299–329). New York: Springer.

Schroots, J. J. F. (1991). Metaphors of aging and complexity. In G. M. Kenyon, J. E. Birren, & J. J. F. Schroots (Eds.), *Metaphors of aging in science and the humanities* (pp. 219–243). New York: Springer.

Schroots, J. J. F. (Ed.). (1993). *Aging, health and competence: The next generation of longitudinal research.* Amsterdam: Elsevier Science Publishers.

Schroots, J. J. F. (1995a). Psychological models of aging. *Canadian Journal on Aging, 14,* 44–66.

Schroots, J. J. F. (1995b). Gerodynamics: Toward a branching theory of aging. *Canadian Journal on Aging, 14,* 74–81.

Schroots, J. J. F. (1996). The fractal structure of lives: Continuity and discontinuity in autobiography. In J. E. Birren, G. M. Kenyon, J.-E. Ruth, J. J. F. Schroots, & T. Svensson (Eds.), *Aging and biography: Explorations in adult development* (pp. 117–130). New York: Springer.

Schroots, J. J. F., & Birren, J. E. (1988). The nature of time: Implications for research on aging. *Comprehensive Gerontology C, 2,* 1–29.

Schroots, J. J. F., & Yates, F. E. (1999). On the dynamics of development and aging. In V. L. Bengtson & K. W. Schaie (Eds.), *Handbook of theories of aging* (pp. 417–433). New York: Springer.

Chapter 21
ONE STEP AHEAD:
An Autobiography

Joel Shanan

To look back, at the fin de siècle of "our" 20th century, into my life to recall events over a period of more than 70 years appears rather threatening. I cannot present a sequence of personal events and endeavors to contribute to progress in clinical and research geropsychology without stressing that whatever I did and did not achieve is only to be understood by the peculiar course of the life of a twentieth-century central European Jew who had managed to survive the Holocaust. Particularly, my career development makes sense only if one takes into account that it occurred in the just emerging but quickly growing Israeli society composed of preponderantly young people. I consider it a privilege to have been among the first in that society to participate in creative efforts to promote mental health and the welfare of people in their second half of life. To the extent that I succeeded, it was possible through the not always easy integration of my clinical work with teaching and research in life-span development.

Wanderjahre: Years of Wandering

Getting started on my computer, I note that this is May 7, 1997. May 7 is a date that may not mean much to most people under the age of 60. For those who *can* remember, it is the day of Nazi Germany's official surrender: May 7, 1945, which ended six years of war in Europe. On May 7, 1945, I had been attending, on my first leave from a Swiss refugee camp at Caux sur Montreux, a piano recital in Montreux on the beautiful shores of Lac Leman, Lake Geneva. Right in the middle, the concert was interrupted with an announcement that Germany had surrendered and that Hitler was dead. Today it is hard to describe the complexity of feelings of someone who only a few months before had been lucky enough to get to Switzerland from the now so notorious concentration camp of Bergen Belsen. Paradoxically, my own immediate reaction to that dramatic announcement was that *now* that Hitler and Nazism were dead, *I* had made it! So *now* I could die quietly. In fact, the closeness to death for years had made me feel tired and old.

When the last of the German concentration camps had been liberated by the allied armies, the incredible atrocities of the Holocaust perpetrated by the Germans and their quite willing helpers from other nations had been brought to the consciousness of the world, mainly by the BBC broadcasts. In Europe many listened but few could believe. Even today,

50 years later, many find it hard to believe that the Holocaust *really* took place and that it bereaved the Jewish population, between 1933 and 1945, of six million brothers and sisters, parents and children—more than a third of its total prewar number. These victims, among them my mother and almost all the rest of my wider family, were deprived of the opportunity to grow up and old. Living through this Holocaust—unmatched in history not only in its extent relative to the size of the target population but also in its step-by-step, diabolically planned cruelties—has undoubtedly played its part in shaping the course of my life.

Those were years of total uncertainty—not only of what had become of my mother, sister, and the rest of the family, but also of what could happen to me tomorrow. Only after the war was I able to find out that my sister had, after years in camp, arrived in Palestine. Until this day I have never found out what became of my mother and all the others. My father had died in Vienna shortly after I had left Austria, following the "Anschluss," the annexation of Austria by Nazi Germany.

Vienna, Austria, is the city where I grew up in a well-protected environment, although I was born in Budapest. From there my parents moved to Vienna after the 1919 pogroms. At age 18 I graduated from high school. I had learned a lot about biology, higher math, Latin, history, and German and French literature. Yet I knew little about the real world and people. The values that had been transmitted to us from grade school on, particularly in high school, were rather universalistic, intellectually elitistic, but definitely social at the same time. When I finished high school it was clear that as a high school graduate (probably less than 5% of an age cohort at that time) the purpose of my life was not to become important or rich but to help people in need and to advance science. We did not receive any education or guidance for what today is known as career development.

The occupation of Austria by Nazi Germany seemed to put an end to such ideals. When Hitler entered Austria in March 1938, I was 18½ years old, a medical student who had just passed his first exams in anatomy, physics, and chemistry. Of course I was not allowed to continue my studies but was lucky to be able to leave Vienna shortly after the Anschluss. Because of anti-Semitic legislation in Slovakia too, where I had emigrated, it became impossible to continue my studies. I worked as long as possible as an office clerk, later did physical work on a farm, then on a railway station, and finally ended up ended up in a forced labor camp.

When deportations started in Slovakia in the spring of 1942, I escaped illegally to Hungary. Caught there, I spent the next six months in prison. When released I was returned by the Hungarian police to the Slovak border, but I turned around at night and after an adventurous night walk of about 25 miles arrived in Budapest. There I stayed "underground" until the Germans, who in March 1944 had occupied Hungary, reached me there too. A few months later I found myself transported in cattle cars to Bergen Belsen concentration camp.

During these "wander years," to put it euphemistically, I met all sorts of people whom as a medical student or doctor I would possibly have seen only as patients. One thing that they had in common, apparently characteristic of human beings, was that they were able to suffer physically and mentally, sometimes beyond any imagination. Yet to give in passively to what seemed to be inevitable circumstances was close to writing one's own death sentence. Only by coping psychologically could one enhance one's chances to survive even in the most dehumanizing situations—such as in the KZ—and to maintain one's image as a human being.

And so it happened that it was in the concentration and death camp of Bergen Belsen that I received my first lessons in psychology, especially life-span psychology. In my "block" there happened to be a Hungarian psychiatrist, Leopold Szondi, who offered a "seminar" to interested younger inmates. Although I felt quite old at 25, I participated. When we arrived from Bergen Belsen in Switzerland, Szondi published his thoughts under the title *Schicksalsanalyse* (Fate analysis) (Szondi, 1944). He proposed to understand human development as "fate" from *before* conception until death. He analyzed first the personality of the parents, what presumably genetically determined complementarity of motives had attracted them to each other. He then looked into the dynamics of their interaction as "determinants' of subsequent 'Fate'" (i.e., personality development of the offspring). Before the war he had gathered cross-sectional, psychological test data of hundreds of people ranging from childhood to old age. He tried to show that personality, sexual attraction, interpersonal and professional development, and even the vulnerability to certain illnesses were shaping the course of life, guided by an inner logic. For somebody whose career and personal development had been derailed for seven years, it was comforting to hear that development does not stop at an early age and that it continues over throughout the life span guided mostly by those inner motivating forces rather than by external circumstances only.

Lehrjahre: Years of Apprenticeship

When I arrived a few months later, in the early postwar period, the British still ruled Palestine and the economic and political situation there was bad. I did not know Hebrew and only very little auto-didactically acquired English. I found a job as a cook in a home for maladjusted refugee children. There I learned a lot from naive observation about the development of such children. I also was able to enroll at the Hebrew University (total student body in 1945 was about 500). Of course, there was no school of medicine. So I took up psychology and special education—two fields that seemed to me most fit, after medicine, to give my life a meaning and to justify my survival. They could provide skills necessary to relieve and possibly to prevent human suffering. During my readings, I hit on the writings of C. G. Jung. I discovered that some of Szondis ideas about human development were very close to Jung's. The latter too conceived development as stretching over the life span and emphasized the personally and socially positive aspects of maturity at midlife. Next I discovered Erikson and was very impressed by his brilliant effort to integrate Freudian psychology with essentially psycho-sociological thinking. He was the third author from whom I learned that development was multiply determined and did not stop with physical maturity. My attention was also drawn to the fact that development was embedded in narrower and broader social contexts and that the interaction of intrapsychic forces with their surroundings determined the course of development at each stage.

It took only a little over two years to find myself again torn away from studies and in war, one that resulted in the realization of the United Nations (UN) resolution to create the state of Israel. This time I participated as a quickly trained infantry man in Jerusalem, which was encircled and besieged by armies and armed units from all neighboring Arab countries. They shelled the holy city heavily and came close to destroying it and the Jewish state *in statu nascendi,* as it appeared to be a helpless newborn, so to speak.

During that war I met and married Naomi, my spouse now for 50 years. She was the firstborn girl in one of the oldest collective settlements, kibbutzim, and a veteran driver of the British ATS in Africa during World War II. She too had joined the fighting forces in Jerusalem. Later she graduated from the Jerusalem Teachers College and started teaching immigrant children. Ultimately she became an artist. I was released from the army in 1949 and was able to return to my studies. In 1951 I graduated from the Hebrew University and took my first job as a civilian selection officer in the newly established psychological unit of the brand new Israeli Defense Army. On that job I became closely acquainted with a problem in psychological assessment that even today has not been satisfactorily resolved: the problem of assessing people from a culture different from the Western one. Today we know the problem still exists for the aged and chronically impaired who may also be considered as subcultural groups. For them too, more satisfactory solutions are required.

My first encounter with that problem was shocking and left a lasting impact on my later clinical work and research. This was the time when the Yemenite Jews were brought to Israel by operation ''Magic Carpet.'' Most of them could read the Bible in Hebrew but spoke only Arabic. They knew little about Western culture and modern life or technology. They were true desert people. When they came to the army there was total discommunication and one did not know what to do with them. Because at the time there were no better trained psychologists around, I was assigned the job of devising a battery of tests that would enable us to learn something about the mental abilities of these new immigrants. Because they did not know Hebrew it had to be a nonverbal battery. So we selected some parts of the Wechsler Bellevue Intelligence Test, which then was the dernier cri in nonverbal testing, as well as some easier items from the Ravens Matrix. In addition, we built some nonverbal reasoning tests of our own. None of these differentiated between the hundreds of recruits we tested. In fact, they all looked retarded. Nevertheless they were enrolled in the army and were put in a three-month experimental training camp. There, in addition to military training, they got special Hebrew lessons and an opportunity to get experience in the new culture. To each unit, a psychologist was attached as an observer who also worked with the training personnel. Three months later, then hard to believe but true, most of these ''retarded'' new immigrant recruits had learned Hebrew; they started to understand the purpose and workings of the army and also, to some extent, the style of interpersonal relations that was so different from those they were used to. They also improved on the psychological tests but still did poorly in comparison to their real-life performance. Twenty years later, when doing rehabilitation research on aging poststroke patients, I was very much reminded of this army experience.

In 1952, after my MA thesis on treatment classes had been published in the first Hebrew journal of educational psychology *Megamot* (Trends), I was offered a scholarship to study in the United States. I chose to study at the University of Chicago, which offered academically high level innovative programs, especially in clinical and personality psychology. The leading faculty figures included M. I. Stein and William Henry, pioneers in cross-cultural research on the TAT as well as of its use in the study of adult development and creativity; Don Fiske and Don Campbell, who were the first to look into the intricate relationships between intra- and interindividual variability at any point in time and over time; J. G. Miller, who applied and modified Bertalanffy's General Systems theory; and last but not least, David Shakow, who may be truly considered one of the most important founders of clinical psychology in the United States. He was an early trailblazer of schizophrenia research and the first to design controlled clinical research on the process of classical psychoanalysis. He was also the first to draw attention in a 1938 article to what in the 1960s was to become known as ''cohort effects.''

The person who was to become my personal advisor, later a lifelong friend and mentor in geropsychology, was Bernice Neugarten from the then recently established Committee on Human Development. The faculty of the committee were devoted to the then not very popular idea of viewing the human as a psychologically active individual moving through life, embedded from conception to death in an ever-changing special social cultural environment. It was this approach and Bernice's persistent but modest and yet charismatic personality that led the leaders of that group and their students to get involved in the study of adult development from early through middle and later adulthood. From a developmental point of view they agreed with both of the then popular trends, behaviorism and psychoanalysis, on the importance of early development for the understanding of adolescent and adult behavior. Yet they stressed that an understanding of the later stages of development (i.e, middle and late adulthood and old age) was also necessary to fully understand the place of earlier stages in the course of individual life-span development.

My four years at the University of Chicago, from 1952 to 1956, were a counterclimax to my experience of European culture and its horrible corollaries during World War II. The Hutchins atmosphere at the University of Chicago, in class and on the campus, promoted not only freedom of thought and creative thinking but a type of camaraderie and free exchange of thought between teachers and students that was completely new for me. It reminded me of descriptions of the atmosphere of European universities in the early Renaissance. The emphasis on intellectual excellence and on devotion to creative advancement of science in contrast to an emphasis on rationalism and preservation of earlier achievements reinforced some of the central values I had absorbed during my Viennese high school years. Last but not least, the day-by-day encounter with American democracy and American technology had a significant impact on my personal and professional development. I was greatly impressed by the relatively fast change that had occurred—at least at the academic level—from an effort to enhance know-how to a curriculum by providing tools that encouraged the student to learn ''how to know.'' Not less deeply was I impressed by the way in which U.S. democracy had managed to defend itself against McCarthy and his antidemocratic and anti-Semitic ideas, which were just at the peak of influence during those years. Those were also exciting years in terms of the development of our little family, which turned from a diad into a triad when our son, Amir, was born.

During my internship at the Illinois Neuro-Psychiatric Institute under the guidance of David Shakow, I became convinced that a thorough acquaintance with adult personality and cognitive and family development was as necessary for a clinical psychologist as information about early childhood and adolescent development or personality dynamics. To understand, assess, and bring about constructive change of behavior at any point of human development, one has not only to know the developmental antecedents, but one also has to have some information on what can be expected in the following stages. My experience during my internship thus complemented what I had learned in class and contributed significantly to my becoming a clinical and developmental psychologist who during the next three decades was committed to integrate the helping aspects of his profession with a need for constant search and research to improve knowledge of when and how to help.

In 1956 I received, at the age of 37, my PhD in psychology and thus became, if not the first, one of the very first Israelis who had received a postwar education in psychology in the United States. I knew that during that period the psychology department of the Hebrew University had been closed but did not know that a Department of Psychiatry had just been established by two American scholars at the Hadassa Hebrew University Hospital. It was quite a surprise for me to receive, even before I had completed my PhD, an invitation to serve there as chief psychologist and to organize psychological services in the new department and in the university hospital as well as to teach psychology on the faculty of medicine, established only a few years previously. I proudly accepted this offer, which held the promise of combining clinical with academic work and creating something new in Israel. Not without hesitation I had turned down some quite attractive offers from U.S. universities. In the fall of 1956, after having completed my PhD, we left with a mixture of joy and sadness our student housing in the GI barracks at the Midway in Chicago. We left behind many wonderful friends, faculty, and students. When the leaves started falling we sailed on the *Ile de France* to Europe. With little Amir in his stroller we crossed France and Italy by train and arrived by ship in Haifa, Israel.

The Middle Years—Clinical Work, Teaching, and the Beginnings of Research From Early to Middle Adulthood

When I arrived in Israel there were only few psychologists and even fewer psychiatrists around. Practically all psychologists, not more than a hundred (1:15,000 persons), focused on educational problems of children or on guidance and occupational choice. One would expect just that in a new country in which the number of immigrants nearly equaled the number of Jews who had been in the country before 1948. There were also a few clinicians, most of whom had earned their degrees in pre–World War II Europe. Psychology courses were taught at the Hebrew University within the framework of the School of Education. An independent department of psychology did not exist. However, there existed a Psychological Association, founded a few years earlier. It encouraged the newly established government agencies to promote the advancement of children and youth. In a country of immigrants who had just escaped the Holocaust or other anti-Semitic measures in some Arab countries and the Soviet Union, the emphasis was on the future. In retrospect I can confess that I felt slightly uncomfortable when people asked me about my main interests. I probably sounded quite defensive when trying to explain why I thought that one had also to know something about adult and family development to help and advance the parents of those children about whose intellectual development and psychosocial well-being everybody was so concerned.

I had no idea that in that very year, 1956, the Israel Gerontological Society had been founded by some physicians and social workers, who had been active mostly in the care and treatment of elderly immigrants. At that time, people over 65 years old consisted of not more than 4 to 5% of the total population. Life expectancy was yet an unknown term, but people over age 50 were for all practical purposes considered old! Attention was paid mostly to economic, social, and medical problems. Who had the time to think about the *psychology* of adults, aging or the aged! It took about a decade until I was able to start with the help of my graduate students a series of partly cross-cultural studies on self-perception of parental responsibility and coping style. I doubt whether the findings, though published, were ever used by the responsible educational authorities, which focused nearly exclusively on the integration of children. Until today I believe many failures of integration programs, in the United States too, were because of this attitude toward parents and adults in general as the desert generation, thought lost anyway for the promised land.

In the hospital the problem was a different one: Psychiatry in a general hospital was something completely new. The idea by itself was considered somewhat deviant because ''crazy'' people belonged in a psychiatric hospital or a ''house of crazy people'' (*Irrenhaus,* etc.), as it was called in most European languages. What had psychiatrists or psychologists to do in a respectable university hospital for normal sick people? Moreover, the difference between a psychologist and a psychiatrist was not clear to most physicians and other personnel. Compared to the psychiatrist, the psychologist was in an even worse position because he or she was not even a ''medical'' but only a ''paramedical'' person.

I soon realized these odds but decided to put into action what I had learned in Chicago. The founders of the psychiatry department were James Mann and Milton Rosenbaum, two distinguished clinicians and research psychiatrists from the United States who brought psychosomatics to the University Hospital, introducing psychological aspects to medicine in Israel. I was invited to participate in case and assessment conferences, mainly at the prestigious Department of Internal Medicine but later also at other departments. Increasingly, doctors were ready to acknowledge that psychological assessment techniques, observation and tests coupled with a therapeutic approach based on an understanding of adult psychosocial development could be helpful in a medical context too. To the extent that I became accepted as a clinician, the readiness to accept some of my suggestions to control for age and sociocultural background in psychophysiological research became acceptable too.

Hesitant attitudes started to change in the late 1950s. I was lucky to receive a three-year research grant from the National Institute of Mental Health (NIMH) for a multidisciplinary study of transient amenorrhea. It promised to assess the differential effects of personality factors, especially coping style and self-perception, as well as hormonal (stress and sex), social-cultural, dietary, and climatic factors in the occurrence of temporary loss of menstruation in young women who had come from abroad to Israel for a year. In the course of this study, it became possible to predict (from psychological variables and hormonal analyses assessed 10 days after arrival in Israel and then six months later) the occurrence and cessation of amenorrhea. Twenty years later, this study was still quoted in the European literature as of grande valeur on account of its methodology and findings.

In the course of this study, I learned a lot about the advantages and drawbacks of longitudinal multidisciplinary research. More important, however, for my own future development I had been able to establish and to refine my thinking on coping style as a manifestation of ego functioning. I also developed a sentence completion technique, a semiprojective measure of coping style and its components, as well as reliable rating systems for interview material and projective tests such as Murray's TAT. During the following decades these techniques were to complement questionnaires as tools in studies of psycho-pathology and normal development of middle-aged and older adults in Israel as well as abroad. With the latter, however, I could get started only in the early 60s—again in the context of psychosomatic and rehabilitation research.

Through my clinical work and budding research activities, the new approach to development as ranging over the life span, rather than from birth to five years or to adolescence, became known in Israel. In retrospect it is interesting to note that it was the helping professions that took day-by-day responsibility of the patient and the client in need, nursing and social work, which were the first to sympathize with this approach. Thus I was asked to teach and to establish a curriculum in psychology and human development by the School of Nursing and the Paul Baerwald School of Social Work, then newly established as part of the Hebrew University. The medical school adopted this pattern only somewhat later. The Department of Psychology has kept its distance from the idea of ''development beyond adolescence'' until this very day. There exist now, however, gerontology programs in other Israeli universities, notably Tel Aviv and Bar Ilan University.

In 1967 I discontinued teaching in the schools of nursing and social work. I felt that the time had come to assign more time to research as well as to the growing teaching obligations in the new Department of Psychology, where graduate, including clinical, programs had been started in the early 1960s. From then until my retirement, my teaching obligations—clinical and research—were divided between psychiatry and psychology, between medical school and the faculty of social sciences. Over the years the emphasis of my seminar teaching shifted from clinical and personality in the 1960s to adult development and aging in the 1970s and 1980s. Asked to continue my research seminars on aging after my retirement, I am now, at 79, the oldest teacher at the Hebrew University. Many of my seminar students did and are still doing masters and doctoral theses in the area of adult development and aging. However, in retrospect I feel that the major social impact of my and my students' teaching revealed itself in the knowledge and attitudes about life-span development and aging that we taught at the schools of medicine, nursing, and social work. Last but not least, the practicum courses and clinical internships for psychology, medical, nursing, and social work students at the Department of Psychiatry in Hadassa University Hospital promoted these attitudes on a clinical level. Quite a few of my graduate students are now holding important positions in Israel, the United States, and Europe. Some of my work is now continued there.

Passing on to the 1960s, I would like to mention that Pressey and Kuhlen's pioneering textbook, *Psychological Development Through the Lifespan,* had appeared just when I started teaching in 1957. I was very impressed and immediately used it in my courses at the School of Social Work. Two years later, in 1959, James Birren's first and monumental *Handbook of Aging and the Individual* appeared (Birren, 1959). It equaled in organization and in depth of thought such classics as Stevens's *Handbook of Experimental Psychology* and Carmichael's *Handbook of Child Psychology.* Birren's handbook delineated for me both the limits and the problematics of geropsychology as a science as well as a field of application. If one looks back at geropsychological research today, one finds that most of its themes and techniques are rooted in the points raised by Birren's own chapter and other contributions to that handbook. Significant for the development of my own thinking and work became, in addition to Jim Birren's introductory chapter, those contributed by Klaus Riegel and Ralph Gerard, whose personality- and system-oriented approach to neurophysiology had already impressed me as his student during my internship at the Illinois Neuropsychiatric Institute. Last but not least to be mentioned is Kuhlen's concluding chapter, which stressed the importance of the search for patterns rather than averages within a dynamic framework of personality development.

Cumming and Henry's *Growing Old* (Cumming & Henry, 1961) and Bernice Neugarten's *Personality in Middle and Later Life* (Neugarten, 1964) were published in the early 1960s. Of course, I was familiar with both their theoretical content and their findings. Both Henry and Neugarten had been my teachers, and most of the other contributors had been my friends as graduate students. Most of the central ideas, such as ''disengagement'' and techniques, such as the controlled use of projective techniques like the TAT, reported in this collection of papers had been discussed in research seminars so that all of the doctoral students had the feeling of having contributed a little bit to that pioneering effort. Until today I believe that the concept of disengagement as defined by Henry is valuable in the understanding of the processes of aging. It does not contradict at all the idea of a need for activity. It has not been understood by many of Henry's students and even less by students of his students—that it strictly referred to intrapsychic processes and stressed that actual disengagement from social reality was to occur only in the very latest stages of aging. There was, of course, another reason for the resistance to the idea of disengagement stemming from the conflicting findings in this field. Paradoxically for an idiographically oriented clinician like Henry, he had overlooked the possibility that disengagement may not be a universal phenomenon but more characteristic of some sectors such as the well educated and less so for the poorly educated class or any other subcultural groups whose development and fate in life was dictated from birth on by effects of limited availability of resources. This, in fact, we could show later in our own longitudinal studies of aging (Shanan, 1985). Thomae's longitudinal findings in Germany (Thomae, 1995) as well some of Schaie's and Costa's longitudinal findings lend themselves to a similar interpretation.

During the mid-1960s I got my first chance to do a geropsychogical research proper. Medical research partners who got interested in the psychodynamics of postcoronary infarct patients, middle-aged men, agreed to include in the study quasi-experimental controls, persons with stomach ulcers, and patients of the same age, sex, and origin who had spent a similar period of time in the hospital but who were not suspect of psychophysiological symptoms. On the basis of these data, I was able to describe for the first time in Israel certain aspects of coping style, personality, and cognitive functioning of Israeli men in their 40s and 50s. This publication, as well as some preliminary publications on a study of poststroke patients and their families in which I had been responsible for the psychosocial part, came to the attention of senior officials of the Institute for Social Security of the State of Israel, which had become interested in the psychological aspects of transition to retirement. Maybe this was a sign that the generation that had founded the state and laid the foundations of its major institutions felt the onset of an aging process. Whatever the reasons, a substantial grant by that institute, followed by another one from the Labour Federation, enabled me to organize a study of more than 100 Israelis aged 46 to 65 and approximately five years later to replicate it on a population cohort of similar size and of identical chronological age, born five years after the first group. Because each of the two samples was composed in terms of a balanced block design, it was possible to obtain information on age trends for all possible combinations of sex, educational level, and cultural origin. It turned out that level of education was the most important determinant of attitudes toward retirement, more so than cultural origin, which was important only in the less educated group. The findings, reported in 1968 in two volumes in Hebrew, were used quite extensively in ''preparation for retirement'' projects and in the media. Some of them still serve today as a major quasi-normative information for people aged 46 to 65 on such frequently used instruments as the Wechsler Bellvue Adult Intelligence Test, Shanan's Sentence Completion Test, and objectively scorable measures of TAT stories as well as of a scorable, semistructured life interview.

Getting Older—Longitudinal Research From Middle to Later Adulthood

A significant turn in my career development and my capacity to contribute to the development of geropsychology beyond the narrow borders of Israel occurred in 1969. In that year I happened to present at the Eighth International Congress of Gerontology in Washington, DC, what seemed to me just another paper on my still cross-sectional findings on aging. It came to the attention of Hans Thomae and Ursula Lehr, who had just started a major study of aging in Bonn. We met and quickly found out that we had not only many common interests but also some common denominators in our basic thinking and assumptions. We tended to look for patterns of personality development rather than only for average changes of personality traits or parameters of cognitive functioning. Another common ground we found was in the stress on the individual as an actively coping person rather than as responding only or mostly to external stimulation. Thomae referred to *Alternsstile und Altersschicksale* (styles and fates of aging), whereas my own work (Shanan, 1985, 1988, 1991, 1995) emphasized types of aging trajectories characterized by different coping styles, within given cultural contexts. Ruth and Coleman (1996) have, in their recent chapter in the fourth edition of the *Handbook of Aging,* come to a similar conclusion. As a member of the founding executive of the then newly established Society for the Study of (human) Behavioral Development, I also had the privilege of becoming more closely acquainted with a number of outstanding European and American scholars as well as to become actively involved in the journal of that organization. Deplorably that organization and the journal shifted back after a decade, when most of its founding members were out of office, returning to the traditional emphasis on child and adolescent development. As an ex-European it was fascinating to find out that during these years and the 1970s gerontological research in the United States was significantly advanced by a group of ex-Europeans such as K. Riegel, P. Baltes, G. Labouvie-Vief, and, last but not least, K. W. Schaie, who has significantly advanced methodological thinking in the area of longitudinal research and has complemented it by a longitudinal project on cognitive development unparalleled in the history of psychology in scope and length of follow-up.

After a heart attack in the early 1970s, I had to slow down for a while and worked mostly on the analysis of my earlier data on aging. I complemented my earlier data on younger adulthood with a six-year longitudinal study on student development in medical school, where I had established a selection and follow-up unit in the late 1960s. Some of the more interesting findings were that the course of development for women and men was differently paced at all stages during the six years of medical studies. Another not less important finding was that suicide attempts and suicide had been completely eliminated and psychiatric cases nearly entirely eliminated since the selection system, which mainly focused on personality and coping style, had been introduced.

With completion of these studies and a one-year follow-up on 1000 immigrant students, it had become possible to compare coping style in Israeli men and women as to three stages of adult development during the 20s—that is, during early career development: the period of parenthood, middle adulthood, and the later years. Only in the second half of the 1970s was I able to turn my studies of aging into a longitudinal one. This was made possible by reexamining the persons I had studied in 1967 and 1972. The newly founded Brookdale Institute for Aging and Human Development in Jerusalem, of which I was part from its beginnings in 1974 until 1980, became the home of the Jerusalem Study of Middle Age and Aging that was then known as the JESMA.

In 1979 I had to undergo some major cancer surgery just shortly after our only son had left to study in the United States. It was the hard way to complement what I had learned about the empty-nest period and about coping with potentially fatal illness. From then on until the late 1980s, the JESMA was continued at the Human Development Institute of the Department of Psychology at Hebrew University, supported by the Volkswagen Foundation. A continued interchange of ideas—with Hans Thomae and his group in Bonn, with Joep Munnichs from Nijmegen and Eva Beverfeldt from the Norwegian Institute of Gerontology, as well as with a number of gerontologists from the United States—added greatly to my capacity to digest the findings of the JESMA. The complex techniques of investigation and the major findings of the JESMA have been published in a ''Contributions to Human Development'' series monograph, *Personality Types and Culture in Later Adulthood* (Shanan, 1985). Among its unique features is the concurrent use of different techniques of data gathering and of analysis. Some multivariate designs as proposed by Schaie (1977) were used on discrete variables along with a Q-analysis, which made it possible to look at the aging individual as a whole, to delineate different configurations of personality that we were not hesitant to view as types (Shanan, 1985) and to identify related courses of development. A paper was presented at the 1988 Sandoz Lectures (Shanan, 1988) and a series of later papers, including one on aging of the Holocaust survivors in our JESMA sample, complemented findings reported in the monograph.

Retirement and After—''Vanity, All Is Vanity''?

The papers from the 1990s (Shanan 1991, 1995) were all written after my official retirement from the hospital and from the university and can be viewed as representative of my present positions. They were written after I had undergone another life-threatening and—even more so—body-image-threatening event—major bypass heart surgery at age 72. I have to add I was amazed how quickly it was possible to recover from that blow. As I have tried to show, my present positions are deeply rooted in my educational experiences, mostly at the University of Chicago, but probably also reflect some of my own personal experiences in peace and war, in health and illness, as well as my intellectual, my scientific, and, not less important, my personal interaction with a number of colleagues from different countries. Events like cancer surgery in 1979, open-heart surgery in 1991, and my spouse's prolonged health problems certainly slowed down my efforts to make up for the seven years I had lost during World War II. They did not deter me from the path I had chosen, however.

My present positions reflect my basic human, scientific, and especially geropsychological values. They are possibly more skeptical and more complex than those with which I started my career. To begin with, it is certainly important to obtain normative or at least quasi-normative average information on separate parameters of cognitive and personality functioning. But it appears at least as important, theoretically and practically, to identify specific trajectories of development as related to both personality configurations and patterns of environmental, socioeconomic, and cultural conditions. The latter are indispensible in most cases of clinical and social intervention and in the planning of preventive measures. A clear distinction should be made between average trends and type-specific and culture-specific development, especially in cases of long-term physical or mental impairment such as blindness (Behar & Shanan, 1997) or late developmental effects of adult trauma, an area in which too little research has been carried out.

Second, a distinction should be made between stability—if such a thing exists at all in human behavior—and continuity versus discontinuity. With regard to this parameter an ipsative approach rather than a normative one is not only important but imperative. As we learned from our own studies, from the clinic, and from other major aging projects, people may considerably differ in continuity and discontinuity of different traits, as well as in their overall personality manifestations at different stages of their development, and still maintain their identity. A lot is still to be learned about the nature of change and who is likely to change, when and in which way, and under what circumstances. To put it reversely: We still have a long way to go in identifying the common parameters of processes of aging across cultural and temporal variation.

Here a word of caution is in place with regard to cohort and cultural differences in general. These differences are important mostly in the comparison of average values and average trends. Yet they conceal the fact that cohort effects are most obvious under conditions of change and stress and tend to disappear under conditions of relative cultural stability, in particular when different birth cohorts have been exposed to identical or similar access to socioeconomic or genetic resources. Access to educational experiences turned out to be in all our studies *the* most important marker variable in determining the individual style of coping, and consequently, via a more or less active personality, the pace, timing, and character of the course of development. This maybe is one of the major lessons to be learned from our studies in Israel (i.e., in a quickly changing environment). I would also consider it a contribution that we were able to demonstrate that the concurrent use of complex and single-variable approaches, as well the concurrent use of different measurement instruments for one trait and the concurrent use of different techniques of statistical analysis, can point to the relative advantage and disadvantage of each and thus lead possibly to more specific, sophisticated, and valid conclusions.

Looking back over 50 years it is obvious that tremendous changes have taken place. Life expectancy has increased everywhere, in the Western world particularly. The number of people over 65 has increased by tens of percents. The need for social and, one may add, psychological services has increased concomitantly. Gerontological associations, national and international, have grown and improved in quality and in terms of their educational and political impact. The number of journals has increased, and even in a little country like Israel there now exist two official journals on gerontology. It is my feeling that psychologists have contributed significantly during that period in research and teaching. However, they have not quite kept up with social workers and medical and paramedical professionals in the field of service delivery. This is certainly true for Israel. Psychology graduates prefer to work with younger people or to engage in ivory tower research. I was careful to avoid this path during all my scientific and professional career.

A respectable amount of information has been gathered during this period on personality development during the second half of life. From my ego-analytical and system-theoretical point of view, great progress has been made in the theoretical approach to problems of aging and personality. However, without wanting to be cynical it appears to me that some theoretical and empirical approaches, which during my student and early career years were considered deviant, are nowadays regarded as progressive. This reflects undoubtedly the change in zeitgeist in psychology. Koch and Shakow noticed this change 35 years ago. Psychology started then to move from a rigidly self-conscious search for the ''truly'' scientific (i.e., experimental method rooted in one pure theory) to a readiness to face a variety of substantive issues and to a more liberal use of techniques of investigation. On the negative side it appears that research and teaching in geropsychology has fallen back, for a variety of reasons, into the basic mistake of the child development movement: isolation from other phases of development. From a purely scientific point of view there is absolutely no need for such isolatory trends.

A personal life review presents, as Goethe long ago noticed, a concoction of ''fiction and truth.'' The reviewer cannot be quite sure where the distinction between the two is to be drawn. This is probably true of all historical and biographical writing. It is hard to determine what we have repressed, what we have omitted, and what—to serve our present aims—has been transformed in memory and how. Consequently, it is also hard to know at ''true time'' what is new or if new, how new, what is likely to hold up, and what is likely to be discarded by posterity forever. Milan Kundera considers the problem a serious one, particularly at a time when all of us are compelled to compete with computer speed to succeed. This, as he hints, tends to increase exhibition on one hand and speedy forgetting on the other hand. Yet in personality development and the development of science I personally feel that a certain amount of forgetting is necessary to make place for the new, for development to take place. So may I be forgiven for having forgotten to mention some editorial and other offices I have held, some professional wars I fought, or some persons and events that might have contributed to what I was able to contribute. I leave it up to the reader to decide whether I did or did not contribute to the advancement of geropsychology from what she or he has read in the story I have told here. Only the reader can decide what, from her or his vantage point, was a major contribution.

Should it turn out that I have made a contribution at all beyond trying to help people in trouble, I personally do not see it in any specific piece of work but mainly in my efforts to question the accepted, to generate a better understanding of the course of life and, ultimately, of human nature. If I have been at least partly successful in transmitting some of the knowledge and experience I gained, some of my skepsis and my faith in geropsychology, then my teaching activities, risk-taking acts of publication, and the emotions and efforts invested in sheer personal contacts have not been in vain.

References

Behar, E., & Shanan, J. (1997). Long lasting blindness, availability of resources and early aging. *Perceptual and Motor Skills, 84,* 675–688.

Birren, J. E. (Ed.). (1959). *Handbook of aging and the individual.* Chicago: University of Chicago Press.

Cumming, E., & Henry, W. E. (1961). *Growing old.* New York: Basic Books.

Neugarten, B. L. (1964). *Personality in middle and later life.* New York: Atherton.

Ruth, J. E., & Coleman, P. (1996). Personality and aging: Coping and management of self in later life. In J. E. Birren & K. W. Schaie (Eds.), *Handbook of the psychology of aging* (4th ed., pp. 308–322). New York: Academic Press.

Schaie, K. W. (1977). Quasi-experimental research designs in the psychology of aging. In J. E. Birren & K. W. Schaie (Eds.), *Handbook of the psychology of aging* (pp. 39–58). New York: Van Nostrand Reinhold.

Shanan, J. (1985). *Personality types and culture in later adulthood.* Basel: Karger.

Shanan, J. (1988). Coping style, personality and aging. In M. Bergener, M. Ermini, & H. B. Staehelin (Eds.), *The 1988 Sandoz lectures in gerontology, crossroads in aging* (pp. 221–232). London: Academic Press.

Shanan, J. (1991). Who and how: Some unanswered questions in adult development. *Journal of Gerontology, Psychological Sciences, 46*(6), 309–316.

Shanan, J. (1995). Verarbeitung von belastungen (Coping with stress). In A. Kruse & R. Schmitz-Scherzer, *Psychologie der Lebensalter (Psychology of the Life Span)* (pp. 61–69). Darmstadt: Steinkopff.

Thomae, H. (1995). Die Bonner gerontologische laengsschnittstudie (The Bonn Longitudinal Study of Aging-BOLSA). *Zeitschrift fuer Gerontologie, 26*(3), 142–151.

Chapter 22
CONSISTENT CURIOSITY ABOUT HUMAN LIVES

Hans Thomae

Writing an autobiography, contrary to telling it in a narrative interview, is influenced more or less explicitly by some reconstruction of the past from present points of view. When focusing on the past, as much as this is possible, I might state that my early as well as my later views of my life were determined by an interaction of consistency and change. Consistent experiences in childhood and adolescence were related to my mother's continuous efforts to give her sons chances for higher education although the economic situation of the family and the lack of any public or private support of less wealthy families interfered with these efforts. Consistency in experience during this stage of life was also provided by my father's concerns about growing debts and increasing economic pressure.

Background

Because of my mother's efforts, I visited the Alte Gymnasium at Würzburg (in Bavaria). The experience of change was offered by the influence of some Nazi groups in this school around 1930 and the different reactions of teachers and peers to their activities. More important, however, were internal changes that resulted in a deep identification with Christian beliefs and values followed by increasing doubts in the validity of these views. Physical events also contributed to this experience of change in the context of consistency. At the time of Hitler's rise to power (January 1933) I suffered from acute signs of heart insufficiency, which made it necessary for me to stay at home for 10 weeks.

Training

When I left high school (Altes Gymnasium) in 1935, my family moved to Berlin where I entered the university with the aim of graduating with a degree in psychology and philosophy. The doctorate in one of these offered my only possibility to obtain a degree in these fields. The diploma for psychology was introduced during World War II when I had already finished my studies.

From the limited knowledge available at that time for an average adolescent about changes at far distant universities, I was completely unaware of the deep changes in the department of psychology of the University of Berlin, which took place after 1933. Wolfgang Köhler, Kurt Lewin, and all the other famous members of the Berlin School of gestalt psychology had left. The introductory course was given by P. B. Rieffert, who had contributed to the application of psychology in the German army during World War I. In experimental psychology I was trained by Dr. Firgau, a former coworker of Narziss Ach at Göttingen. Only four students took the course, of which I was the only German one. The others came from India, Greece, and another country and had applied for a scholarship to hear Wolfgang Köhler, Kurt Lewin, or Kurt Koffka. For German students psychology was not a favorite subject in these early years of the Nazi regime.

Aside from my activities at the university I had to look for odd jobs in order to contribute to the costs of my study and living. This double role made it difficult to take regard of the terrible political developments of the years preceding World War II. The somewhat steady state defined by the efforts to meet the challenges of these two roles was stopped a few weeks before my 21st birthday. After a 3000-meter run at the campus, I had the first incidence of heavy intestinal hemorrhages. Although many specialists tried to find the cause of these sometimes life-threatening events, and although half of my stomach and the duodenum was removed at D-Day 1944, these physical problems continued to come back again and again until my early 70s—with increasing intermissions, however.

These physical problems added new challenges to my life; on the other hand, they may have saved my life as I never was rated as suitable for military service. On the advice of one of my doctors I left the sometimes stressing atmosphere of the German capital and enrolled at Bonn University in the summer of 1938. There Erich Rothacker was director of the seminar of philosophy as well as of the Institute of Psychology. During my first term Rothacker's book *Levels of Personality* was published, which included a chapter titled ''Aging and Maturation.'' The last term was defined as a level of development including mastery and wisdom. I myself did not pay much attention to this aspect of Rothacker's work and wrote my doctoral dissertation on problems of consciousness on the basis of experiments on subconscious perception.

Beginning of the Career

At the beginning of the war Bonn University was closed. I accepted Philipp Lersch's invitation to come to Leipzig and work as a junior assistant at the famous Wundt Institute. The chair of Wundt had been vacant for years because of several interventions of the Nazi Party in favor of an old member of it. The faculty resisted, however. As Lersch had worked as a psychologist within the German army before Hitler's rise to power, the faculty members favoring him were successful finally. Lersch was a representative of the *geisteswissenschaftliche* psychology, or humanistic psychology. However, one of his publications was based on experiments on facial expression. He tried to bridge the gap between his approach and the traditional Wundtian one and supported any effort to promote experimental research. This was why he asked me to revise the files on the huge apparatus existing in the institute, as these had been lost during the years of an absence of a director. Both the files and most of the apparatus were burned during an allied air raid in 1943.

In 1941 two neurologists working at the Hospital of the German Air Force came to Lersch and told him that they wanted to repeat the productive collaboration between neurology and psychology that had existed during World War I. During that time the neurologist Kurt Goldstein and the psychologist Ademar Gelb from the University of Frankfurt studied the adjustment of brain-injured soldiers to their deficit and documented in very valuable publications (Gelb & Goldstein, 1920) the great capacity of the human brain to compensate losses of function in one region by processes that Goldstein later used in New York as an argument for his theory of personality development. As I was very much fascinated by the publications of Goldstein and Gelb in the *Zeitschrift für Psychologie,* I asked Lersch to suggest my name as the psychologist in the new neurological team. Everybody agreed aside from the administrators of the Air Force Hospital. Due to my medical history, they were not ready to engage me—neither as a soldier nor as a civilian employee.

Because of Lersch's kindness, I could take a longer leave together with my wife, Ingeborg (born Klamroth), and my daughter, Barbara, from the frustration and a new incidence of the old physical problem. During this time I finished the outline of a book titled *General Principles of Motivation and Decision,* which I had prepared before by interviews and experiments on motive states such as hunger or stress in a waiting situation. This book was accepted by the faculty for philosophy and science of the University of Leipzig as "Habilitation Thesis"—a prerequisite for the entrance into an academic career as existing in Germany then and now.

Chances and Hopes After the War

When the Leipzig Institute was destroyed I was conscripted for service in a camp in which delinquent boys were to be resocialized. There I could make the first observations on the ways people try to cope with different situations. After the war I could continue these observations in a Bavarian institution for homeless boys. Many of them had lost or left their parents at the end of the war or after it. Some of them did not accept the chance to stay and learn an occupation. They left the home and continued to circulate between the four military zones of Germany, which were not yet separated by an Iron Curtain. U.S. military police brought many of them when they had crossed the border between the Soviet and U.S. zones. But instead of staying they preferred to look for some GIs who gave them cigarettes and chocolate, which they could sell at the black market. In order to survive by adjusting to the present conditions, they developed very unique techniques. The observation of these and other ways of responding to the situation is the basis of my own conceptualization of coping, which tries to avoid the translation of behavior into traits as this behavior loses its plasticity by this translation. In 1953 I published findings from these observations in *Psychologische Forschung,* the former *Journal of the Gestalt Psychology.* The topic of coping remained a consistent concern for me.

In 1949 Erich Rothacker asked me to come back to Bonn as lecturer and senior assistant. It was a unique opportunity to organize an institute beginning with the ruins left from an air raid in 1944. When I came, two rooms filled with books were already available. Within the next year we moved to a separate section of the main building, which had 14 rooms. A donation of the U.S. military government enabled us to buy many American textbooks, handbooks, and monographs in experimental, developmental, personality, and social psychology.

From the experience in working with delinquency I was suggested by one of the new German government agencies to the allied military government of West Germany for an interdisciplinary group, which was supposed to study the training of social workers in France, the United Kingdom, and the United States. This study group was in line with the general policy of reeducation adopted in West Germany by the United States six years after the war.

During our stay in the United Kingdom, I was able to learn very much about new developments in sociology and psychology and could visit the laboratory of H. J. Eysenck at the Maudsley Hospital. After our group had moved to Liverpool I had a very heavy recurrence of hermorrhage. Due to the efficiency of the British Health Service I was brought to a hospital where I was treated for two weeks. As I had to lie down quietly according to the strict medical regulations I had a good chance to study doctor–patient relationships. From these and former experiences I felt somewhat on safe grounds later when I worked with medical specialists.

After this unhappy end of my visit to the United Kingdom, I wanted to discontinue my participation in the group studying the training of social workers in three western countries. Therefore I did not visit France in this context. The United States partners of the project encouraged me, however, to participate in the group's visit to America. In June 1951 I followed the other group members to New York and Washington, DC. There the representative of the sponsoring government agency told me that I was free to make my choices among the places to be visited. As only four weeks were available, I selected the University of Chicago and the State University of Iowa at Iowa City. There I hoped to meet former coworkers of Kurt Lewin in the Child Welfare Research Station. The four years after Lewin's death obviously were enough to remove any memory of this scientist and make this state university to a headquarter of neo-behaviorism.

At the University of Chicago I met Bruno Bettelheim and L. L. Thurstone. These certainly were representatives of very different approaches to psychology, but perhaps I believed at this time that an integration of such opposite trends would be possible. At least I tried to integrate psychometric and psychographic approaches in the planning of the psychological section of an interdisciplinary study of the development of children born at the end of World War II. This longitudinal study was initiated by Wilhelm Hagen, an official in the Public Health Administration of the federal government of West Germany at Bonn. Hagen had started a study of this kind in the 1920s and 1930s in the Ruhr area. As he was fired by the Nazis due to his leftist past he made a second and very successful trial when he became responsible for social medicine in the new government. Together with pediatricians, child psychiatrists, psychologists, and social workers we followed 3000 children born around 1945 from their 6th to their 16th year.

The money needed for this project was attained by Hagen from Marshall Plan funds as he could convince the committee in charge that it would not make much sense to spend millions of dollars from the German economy without knowing if the health of the German youth had not sustained permanent damage from the deprivations during and after the war. Our findings disconfirmed hypotheses of this kind and pointed to a high degree of plasticity in the physical and mental development in childhood and adolescence. This was especially true for a subgroup of our sample, which had been exposed to high stresses as the parents of these children had to leave their homes in those eastern parts of the former ''Reich,'' which were turned over to Russia or Poland after the war (Coerper, Hagen, & Thomae, 1954). This longitudinal study pointed also to the interaction of consistency and change of behavior in childhood and adolescence. Dependent on the stability of the social environment— especially that of the family—the cognitive and personality development of our subjects showed a more or less steady pace from infancy to adolescence. Additionally there was much evidence for a high degree of interindividual variability, which initiated doubts on the conceptualization of development in terms of universal stages.

For my scientific development it was also important that a grant from the World Health Organization (WHO) enabled me to visit some of the centers of longitudinal research on children in the United States, such as at Berkeley, California; Denver, Colorado; Yellow-springs, Ohio; New Haven, Connecticut; and Boston, Massachusetts. In the fall of 1952, the chance to study the files of the Child Guidance Study and the Adolescence Growth Study at Berkeley influenced my work not only for the psychological section of the longitudinal study on postwar children, but 12 years later also for the planning of the Bonn Longitudinal Study of Aging.

Toward a Life-Span Approach to Development

Before my second visit to the States, I published a book called *Personality: A Dynamic Interpretation* (1951). Following the theories of G. W. Allport and Gardner Murphy, I stressed the need to conceptualize personality both in terms of processes and structure. Aside from basic processes such as activation, orientation, and chronification, I hypothesized some secondary processes especially for young and middle adulthood. In my argumentation I used the methods as applied in Charlotte Bühler's classical book on the human life cycle as a psychological problem in which she used historical biographies as well as case histories as documents. In the same way I conceptualized personality changes like deepening or flattening of emotions, or differences in the extension or redaction of the psychological life space. On the basis of Lytton Strachey's biography of Florence Nightingale, I pointed to a process of getting increasingly matter-of-fact minded as a stage toward professional maturity. This way, my interest in development was extended from childhood and adolescence into adulthood.

In December 1953 I moved from Bonn to the University of Erlangen in Bavaria where I had been appointed as professor of psychology and head of the Department of Psychology. Again I had to start with the beginning in organizing an institute. This did not prevent me from applying for a grant from the newly refounded *Deutsche Forschungsgemeinschaft* (German Research Association) in order to collect autobiographies of white-collar employees in the 30- to 50-year-old age group. The information was obtained by the use of semistructured interviews. One of the most active coworkers in this project was Ursula Lehr, with whom I published some of our first findings in *Vita Humana*. They could have been used to raise the issue of the mid-life crisis. From the interview data we received from a subsample of the longitudinal study on postwar children and from adolescents born at the beginning of the war as well as from young adults who had been drafted at the age of 16 years at the end of the war, I was very cautious, however, to assign a climax of stresses and conflicts to a specific age group.

I founded the journal *Vita Humana* (from 1964 known as *Human Development*) in 1958 due the interest of Dr. Heinz Karger, a famous medical publisher who had emigrated from Berlin to Basel (Switzerland) after Hitler's rise to power. The idea of the journal was to encourage scientists from medicine, psychology, sociology, and related fields to exchange information on the human life cycle. H. E. Jones from Berkeley supported my efforts by contributing very valuable reports on the progress of Berkeley's longitudinal studies on young adulthood (Jones, 1958). J. E. Anderson from the Minnesota Institute of Child Welfare opened the first issue with a paper titled ''A Developmental Model of Aging'' (Anderson, 1958). Other members of the editorial board were J. E. Birren, Charlotte Bühler, R. J. Havighurst, L. W. Sontag, and A. T. Welford.

Some of these colleagues I met at the Fourth International Congress of Gerontology (1957) in Merano, Italy. Since that time I had a good relationship with Nathan Shock. Few German colleagues belonged to the first members of the editorial board of *Vita Humana,* as the life-span approach was not popular at that time in this country. One member of this board was Curt Bondy, who after his exile in the United States had been appointed as director of the former institute of William Stern at the University of Hamburg. Bondy initiated and directed the German standardization of the Wechsler Intelligence Scales. Furthermore he initiated and guided the first larger study on the attitudes of older people from Northern Germany. Some of the findings of these studies were published by Klaus Riegel (1958) in *Vita Humana.* This colleague also contributed to the first issues of this journal with a German review of the findings of psychogerontology, mainly from the United States.

A second German colleague belonging to the editorial board of *Vita Humana* was H. v. Bracken, who had published several articles on mental and personality development in middle and late adulthood. The small number of Germans on this board shows the almost complete lack of interest in development beyond adolescence. Also, before the war there had been few studies on this stage of life, one of which was done by Fritz Giese at Stuttgart in 1930. The topic was the beginning of the awareness of aging. On average it was dated to include the age span 35–39 years.

During the Erlangen years I became involved in another larger publication project. I edited the *Handbuch der Psychologie,* Volume 3 (Developmental Psychology), which was the first of the 12 volumes of this handbook. In the initial chapter on the concept of development, I reviewed as many existing definitions as I could. As a result of an analysis of these definitions, I suggested a rather broad one: "Development is a series of changes observed in the context of the human life cycle" (Thomae, 1959). Although this conceptualization looks very vague at first, it is very precise in distinguishing developmental changes from those studied—for example, the psychology of information processing. Only if observed changes are analyzed in the context of the human life cycle do they become developmental phenomena. Changes are studied in many areas of psychology. Their developmental aspects become evident as soon as they are analyzed in relation to certain points or sequences of the human life cycle.

The parsimonious character of the definition allows for the inclusion of maturational processes as well as for adaption to environmental changes during the whole life cycle. The term *behavior* in the definition includes both overt and covert behavior. Development from this point of view is not an abstract process in time, it is a series of events observed in the longitudinal study of individuals or retrospective reports such as autobiographies. Today, there are some tendencies to supplement broad definitions such as ours with a more or less long list of criteria (e.g., by identifying life-span development by constructs such as optimization or selection; Baltes, 1997). Definitions such as these may be used to conceptualize specific forms of development. This phenomenon must be studied, however, in its broadest meaning, including cases with no optimization or no selection. Scientists, especially psychologists, should not aim at construing ethical, biological, or social norms from which individual sequences of changes of behavior during the life span are evaluated. I emphasized this parsimonious and value-free conceptualization of development again and again, most extensively in 1979 in a discussion of Wohlwill's effort to reduce the meaning of development to maturational processes in childhood (Thomae, 1979).

Teaching at Erlangen was a time of consistency of scientific activity and one of gradual progress. In 1955, change in many aspects of my life and that of my family returned. Two days after the birth of my son Friedrich, I was informed from a colleague from the medical school at Erlangen that the baby was suffering from Down's syndrome. Another colleague from the same school tried to comfort me by "one of the most confirmed opinions of pediatrics," according to which the life expectancy of children with a Down's syndrome is limited to 15 years. Due to the efforts of my wife and my mother-in-law (who lived in our home for more than 40 years), Friedrich not only survived so far, but he also developed in a way quite different from the monstrous images of mentally retarded children and adults found in classic German textbooks of psychopathology. He learned to write and to read and is quite popular in our small Bonn suburb. As most of his peers, he is quite cute in operating any kind of appliances for getting entertainment or information on national affairs.

The Bonn Longitudinal Study of Aging (BoLSA)

In 1959 I came back again to Bonn University as professor of psychology and head of the department. The faculty in psychology was very small at that time. In my class I had to cover subjects like psychology of learning, motivation, personality, developmental psychology, and social psychology. Educational psychology and industrial and clinical psychology were represented by professors from other institutes or by lecturers. As the number of students rose from 90 to 500 within four years, it was reduced by administrative regulations. The faculty was increased slowly by Professor A. Däumling for clinical psychology, R. Bergler for social psychology, and Ursula Lehr for developmental psychology.

The most important research project between 1964 and 1980 was the planning and carrying out of the Bonn Longitudinal Study of Aging (BoLSA). For its design I applied the model of the Berkeley Child Guidance Study to the analysis of development in late life. To provide the best possible climate the tests, interviews and medical check-ups were distributed over five days. A lengthy semistructured interview was taken at the first, the second, and the fifth day, the testing took place at the fourth, the medical checkup at the third day.

In agreement with the scientific attitude of H. E. Jones, but also with that of pioneers of longitudinal research on aging such as E. W. Busse, no special hypothesis was formulated before the start of the study. As in the Bethesda Study on Normal Aging (Birren, Butler, Greenhouse, Sokoloff, & Yarrow, 1963), a number of questions were raised when the methods were selected. Implicitly a cognitive theory of behavior was decisive in putting the greatest emphasis on interviews and their systematic analysis by rating scales. This way we tried to assess at each of the seven measurement points (1965–1980) how the participants perceived their present situation, their past, and their future. After three measurement points, this implicit cognitive theory was formulated explicitly in three postulates: the first one states that behavior is the outcome of the situation as perceived rather than that of the objective situation; the second postulate points to the interaction of cognitive and motivational systems in the perception of present, past, and future; the third one stresses that homeostatic principles are effective in guiding this motivation-cognition interaction in the process of adjustment to daily hassles (R. S. Lazarus) as well as to major stresses in old age (Thomae, 1970, 1992).

Another theoretical topic guided the assessment of the social network of our subjects. This was defined by the conflict between the disengagement theory and the activity theory of aging. As we were involved in a cross-national study in which these alternate theories were going to be tested (Havighurst, Munnichs, Neugarten, & Thomae, 1969), we applied the interview schedule and the rating scales from this project for the measurement of degree and kind of social participation of the BoLSA participants. Furthermore a competence theoretical orientation became integrated into our approach after the first measurement point. Summarizing these remarks on the scientific basis of BoLSA, I might say that our theoretical orientation emerged from the first encounters with our subjects and became explicitly formulated in the final interpretation of the study.

The initial sample consisted of 220 women and men, born between 1890 and 1895 and between 1900 and 1905, respectively. The number dropped, mainly due to the death of 50 participants in 1980. The social background was mainly that of lower middle class. They had received an average of 9.5 years of education.

The money for the study came from the Volkswagen Foundation. This was established in the early 1960s when the Volkswagen Company, formerly owned by the German state, was changed into a private stock corporation. My application was approved for the first three years, as it was at that time one of very few applications for the funding of specific research projects. In the first years the new foundation received mainly requests for the payment of expensive scientific apparatuses and library buildings. In any case, there was no special program for the funding of research on aging available in Germany at the beginning of BoLSA. The Volkswagen Foundation developed such a program at the beginning of the 1970s but closed it again 10 years later in favor of other interest groups.

BoLSA's findings were published in four to five books and about 250 papers. Regarding consistency and change in cognitive functioning, we confirmed the close relationship between level of functioning and educational background. Especially in tests measuring crystallized intelligence, those with 12 or more years of education remained at a rather high level whereas those with fewer years of education received declining scores after 12 to 15 years. The correlations between education and fluid intelligence were also significant. At the beginning of the study, women scored significantly lower in cognitive tests. They gained, however, much from the repeated measurement design although at some of the measurement points we exchanged the WAIS scales with the Raven scales.

Health as assessed in the medical checkup correlated significantly with cognitive functioning, whereas this was not true for health as perceived by the participants themselves. This health measure was related to degree of satisfaction and to ways of coping with everyday problems. In terms of the conflict between activity theory and disengagement theory, the longitudinal analysis of our data disconfirmed generalizing statements about the relationship between the degree of social activity and life satisfaction. A different approach was recommended by Lehr and Minnemann (1987) in their analysis of the social network data from the first measurement points. They showed the effect of social status, personality, and social role on the relationships between life satisfaction on the one hand and activity versus disengagement on the other hand.

The 1980s: A Decade of Growth in Gerontology

An important aspect in the development of geropsychology in Germany is related to the founding of the (West) German Society of Gerontology in 1966. Previous plans for the establishment of an exclusively medical organization could be interfered. Due to the cooperation of the first president of the Gerontological Society, the Professor for Internal Medicine René Schubert, the sociologist K. Specht, and myself, a real interdisciplinary structure of this society and of its meetings could be achieved. In 1977 I was elected president of this society and became deeply involved in the organization of the Twelfth International Congress of Gerontology (Hamburg, 1981). During my term as president, the council of the Germany Gerontological Society wrote to all deans of medical schools in (West) German universities and recommended the founding of chairs for geriatrics with reference to the demographic development and to existing models in the United Kingdom, Italy, and the Scandinavian countries. This appeal was less successful, however, than appeals to the behavioral and social science departments. In the early 1980s, several former members of the BoLSA staff became professors of gerontology or developmental psychology with an emphasis on the adult stage of life. Aside from these developments, existing chairs for differential or developmental psychology changed their main interest to research and teaching on psycho-gerontological problems.

An important step for the progress of gerontology in Germany was the appointment of Paul B. Baltes as director of the Max Planck Institute for Education and Human Development at Berlin and that of M. M. Baltes as professor of gerontopsychology at the Free University of Berlin.

In 1986 Ursula Lehr became the director of a newly founded institute of gerontology at the University of Heidelberg and was active in asking for resources for research on aging at this university and others. This activity increased when she was appointed federal minister (secretary) for health, family, youth, and women in 1988. Many projects were started or planned during her term. Due to the reduction of financial resources after the German reunion in 1989, few of these projects survived to the end of the 1990s. One of them is the Berlin Study on Aging in which P. B. Baltes, M. M. Baltes, A. M. Mayer, and many other scientists from medicine, psychology, and sociology are cooperating in studying the development of old-old Berlin citizens (age at the beginning of the study: 70 to 105 years). Another project planned at the end of the 1980s was the Interdisciplinary Study on Development in Adulthood (ILSE), which is going on in three universities in West Germany (Heidelberg, Bonn, Erlangen) and two in East Germany (Leipzig and Rostock). Two cohorts (1930 and 1950) are included with the aim of tracing cohort and other conditions of health and well-being in old age. This means that the design is a longitudinal one and hopefully will be implemented until the year 2013, 20 years after the beginning of ILSE. As I was involved in both the planning of this study and its guidance during the difficult early years, the conflict between desire for activity and disengagement is becoming a problem for me.

The largest project started during Ursula Lehr's term as secretary of health, family, youth, and women was concerned with the establishment of a German Center for Research on Aging at Heidelberg. Although the interdisciplinary scientific committee for the preparation of this center completed its work two years after its appointment in 1989, it took seven years until it was founded by an agreement between the federal government of Germany and the state of Baden-Württemberg, to which the University of Heidelberg belongs. As the representatives of molecular biology and of different medical disciplines had supported the plans for a national institute on aging, we gave these fields a high priority within the committee for the preparation for this center. Due to the great financial problems that the federal and the state governments in Germany were facing since the middle of the 1990s, the expected expenses for these biological and medical-clinical departments were evaluated as too high. Therefore, the preliminary structure of the center includes three departments, two of which are devoted to the psychological and social aspects of aging. The first department, according to my recommendation, is devoted to research on life-span development, which is responsible for the continuation of the ILSE project. A second department is concerned with social and ecological problems, the third one with the epidemiology of aging with an emphasis on somatic diseases. In 1995 Ursula Lehr was appointed founding director of the center. In 1998 Peter Martin came back from Iowa State University to Germany. Before he had spent several years doing research on the Georgian Centenarian Study, where he had graduated from Bonn University. He was appointed director of the department for research on development.

The Bonn School of Gerontology

After Ursula Lehr was appointed as founding director of the German center of research on aging, Andreas Kruse, a former coworker of Lehr's at Bonn as well as at Heidelberg, came back from the University of Greifswald as director of the Institute of Gerontology at Heidelberg. Kruse is one of the brightest young men in behavioral and social gerontology, and he is closely associated with our work at Bonn. Aside from an analysis of BoLSA data on coping with health problems, for which he received the first E. W. Busse Award for young scientists in 1987, he published very valuable studies on the coping abilities of patients suffering from stroke. At a ceremony on the occasion of R. Schmitz-Scherzer's retirement in

January 1998, Kruse mentioned that five generations of gerontologists so far came from the Bonn Institute of Psychology. I myself was assigned the position of the great-great-grandfather, Ursula Lehr that of the second-generation leader. He could have mentioned for this generation also Franz Weinert, who had specialized in problems of learning during his time at Bonn and initiated a series of research projects on aging and memory as director of the Max Planck Institute for Psychological Research at Munich. The third generation consists mainly of former coworkers of BoLSA, such as R. Schmitz-Scherzer, Ingrid and G. Tismer, N. Erlemeier, M. Renner, and others. Aside from the BoLSA team, Georg Rudinger belongs to the third generation. He took continuous efforts in analyzing BoLSA data on cognitive tests in their social and biographical contexts and working on a cross-sectional study. The sample of this study consisted of more than 700 women and men from 18 to 81 years of age. Calendar age explained the variance of the test scores to the same degree as education. Altogether 77% of the variance was not explained by age. After I had retired and Ursula Lehr had moved to Heidelberg, Rudinger was the only professor at Bonn who continued research on aging. He was very active also in the methodological preparation of ILSE and the analysis of its data. Internationally he is well known from his role in EXCELSA, Cross-European Longitudinal Study of Aging.

Another former coworker of mine, H. J. Fisseni, belongs to this third generation too. He started with research on the perceived life space of residents of homes for the aged and contributed to the analysis of BoLSA data in terms of a cognitive theory of aging. He also wrote a very well-known textbook on personality psychology.

Finally I should mention E. Olbrich, who was trained at Bonn, worked with Ursula Lehr at the University of Cologne (1972–1976), and returned with her to Bonn before he became professor of the University of Gießen and some years later of Erlangen. He used his experience from Bonn for his research at the University of Erlangen.

The fourth generation of former Bonn gerontologists is represented by Insa Fooken, who specialized in gender differences on aging. Kruse assigned himself to the fifth generation. Aside from him there are quite a few young gerontologists who work in the Bonn tradition. One of them is W. F. Schneider, who interviewed and tested the old survivors of BoLSA almost 20 years after the beginning of the study and focused on the future time perspective of these octo- and nonagenarians. Another member of this youngest generation is Brigitte Stappen, who contributed to research on mourning by a short-term longitudinal study.

Most of my and Ursula Lehr's former students experienced the fascination of research on late life already in their early years. Therefore, many of them will be more successful at solving some of the problems that I might have approached if time would have permitted. Most of them will be able to do so as professors of developmental psychology or gerontology at universities and schools for social work.

Concluding Remarks

The interaction between consistency and change that determined my biography from the beginning was going on through my academic life. Consistent was my interest in how life proceeds from birth to death. Change was permanent regarding the focus of this interest, which moved from childhood into old age by my 40s. So far, the study of aging accounts for two thirds of my scientific work.

Compared to more recent standards, my family life was consistent. When my wife died in 1983 we had lived together for 46 years. Change came from different encounters and from challenges, such as raising a mentally retarded son.

Consistency and change were present also in my relationships with friends and colleagues. Jim Birren brought me the new American Psychological Association book on aging published in 1956 when I was sitting at the Grand Place at Brussels during the Fifteenth International Congress of Psychology in 1957. I was lucky enough to meet him and Betty on many occasions on both sides of the ocean. I also had a long-lasting relationship with Bob Havighurst and Bernice Neugarten. I learned much from them. The same is true for more than 30 years of friendship with Joel Shanan from Jerusalem, who often came to Bonn when I did not see him at Jerusalem. Death ended my close relations with H. E. Jones. I wonder what we might have accomplished if he had not left this planet so early.

Some time ago, two excellent young gerontologists from Berlin questioned whether life satisfaction in old age as stated in many studies around the world should not be evaluated as a symptom of ''protective illusions.'' As aging is associated increasingly with negative events, one should expect a decline of psychological well-being. From my own perspective, the death of my wife and the social and economic problems to be expected for my son after my death might have decreased my life satisfaction. On the other hand, the freedom—so far—from the lifelong hemorrhages and some attained knowledge about how to get control of them brought some compensation. This is even more true for the deepened continuation of a long partnership with Ursula Lehr, whom I married in 1998. Continuous contacts with colleagues from at home and abroad add to this positive balance in my feelings. Old age makes it even easier to come along with colleagues who earlier had been competitors in the fight for resources in funding research projects.

Maybe this positive balance between brighter and darker outlooks in my life belongs to those protective illusions. My present research activities deal with the role of illusions of this kind during the whole life span. So far, I have found that humans classify illusions as irrational ways of dealing with life. On the other hand, there are cues to the insight that humans cannot live without illusions at any stage of life.

At the age of 40 I hypothesized that the most gratifying way of looking to the future consists of a cognitive extension of the present time into the next months or years. The integration of the present and the next part of future is the best way of meeting forthcoming events. From this point of view, why should we not be grateful for whatever contributes to our life satisfaction in old age? Satisfaction with the present makes it easier to take the next step.

References

Anderson, J. E. (1958). A developmental model for aging. *Vita Humana 1*, 5–18.

Baltes, P. B. (1997). On the incomplete architecture in human ontogeny: Selection, optimization, and compenzation, as foundation of developmental theory. *American Psychologist, 52*, 366–380.

Birren, J. B., Butler, R., Greenhouse, S. W., Sokoloff, L., & Yarrow, M. (Eds.). (1963). *Human aging: A biological and behavioral study.* Bethesda, MD: U.S. Department of Health, Education, and Welfare.

Cloerper, C., Hagen, W., & Thomae, H. (Eds.). (1954). *Deutsche Nachkriegskinder. Methoden und erste Ergebnisse der deutschen Längsschnittuntersuchungen über die körperliche und seelische Entwicklung im Schulkindalter* (German Postwar children: Methods and first results of the German longitudinal studies on the physical and psychological development in school age). Stuttgart: Thieme.

Gelb, A., & Goldstein, K. (1920). *Psychologische Analysen hirnpathologischer Fälle.* (Psychological analyses of brain-pathological cases). Leipzig: J. A. Barth.

Havighurst, R. J., Munnichs, J. M. A., Neugarten, B. L., & Thomae, H. (Eds.). (1969). *Adjustment to retirement: A crossnational study.* Assen (NL): Van Gorcum.

Jones, H. E. (1958). Consistency and change in early maturity. *Vita Humana, 1,* 43–52.

Lehr, U., & Minnemann, E. (1987). Veränderung von Quantität und Qualität sozialer Kontakte vom 7. zum 9. Lebensjahrzehnt. In U. Lehr & H. Thomae (Eds.), *Formen seelischen alterns* (pp. 80–91). Stuttgart: Enke.

Riegel, K. (1958). Ergebnisse und Probleme der psychologischen Alternsforschung. *Vita Humana, 1,* 52–64, 111–127, 204–243.

Thomae, H. (1959). Entwicklungsbegriff und Entwicklungstheorie. In H. Thomae (Ed.), *Handbuch der psychologie* (2d ed., pp. 1–18). Göttingen: Verlag für Psychologie.

Thomae, H. (1970). Theory of aging and cognitive theory of personality. *Human Development, 13,* 1–16.

Thomae, H. (1979). The concept of development and life-span developmental psychology. In P. B. Baltes (Ed.), *Life-span development and behavior* (Vol. 2, pp. 281–312). New York: Academic Press.

Thomae, H. (1992). Contributions of longitudinal research to a cognitive theory of adjustment to aging. *European Journal of Personality Psychology, 6,* 157–175.

Thomae, H. (1998). The nomothetic-idiographic issue: Roots and steps toward an integrative approach. *World Psychology, 2* (in print).

Chapter 23
TRANSMISSION AND TRANSMUTATION

Lillian E. Troll

Looking back, it seems inevitable that I would become a life-span developmental psychologist, perhaps especially one with an interest in life-span family development. Two influences started me off—my mother and the University of Chicago—and later events just tweaked the trajectory thereafter.

When my mother was 14, at the beginning of this century, she came to America from Latvia by herself because she could not get an education there and an education was what she wanted most in life. It took her several years to help bring over the rest of her family—her mother and siblings—and then she finally got to college. First she enrolled at Michigan Agricultural College (now Michigan State University), where she met and married my father, who was a student there. Then, when he graduated, she transferred to the University of Chicago—he had promised to finance her schooling if she married him. Unfortunately, my birth a year later postponed her educational aspirations for another dozen years, partly because of the prevailing belief that mothers should not be college students and partly because my father got a position in Canada.

We moved back to Chicago from Canada when I was 12 and my mother nearing 40. Nevertheless she was persuasive enough to convince the University of Chicago to accept her back as a regular student. Because this was during the Depression and my father could not find a job in Chicago—he left his good one in Canada because my mother didn't like living there—she turned from her original dreams for a literary education to the more practical profession of social work. She went to work for the Jewish Children's Bureau when she graduated and remained there until she retired at 80. Thus during my high school years I was surrounded by her textbooks and heard vivid stories about her cases. My interest in human behavior and human problems had begun.

I was an undergraduate at the University of Chicago between 1933 and 1937 and a graduate student from 1938 until I went to Washington in 1941, six months before the United States entered World War II. Two major components of the atmosphere on campus during those years were a fervor to improve the world and a passion for tackling theoretical issues. I remember peace marches and lengthy political discussions, and I also remember being inspired by renowned teachers—whenever they were back on campus from Washington, where they were part of Franklin Roosevelt's New Deal team.

Although I changed my major several times, first English and then anthropology, I finally settled on a joint psychology and premedical program in my junior year. I had decided that the best way to improve the world was to produce better citizens, which in turn meant understanding the processes of human development. In that era of what now seems naive and optimistic psychology, it appeared possible to improve the quality of humans and thus society through scientifically based child rearing. This led me to the study of child development under the erudite Helen Koch.

I should add that I was also elitist. When I was not admitted to the University of Chicago Medical School, in large part because of restrictive quotas, I decided not to settle for any lesser medical school but to accept Dr. Koch's offer of a fellowship in child psychology. Fellowships were rare and highly prized at that time. Also, because I was elitist, I skipped a master's degree to head straight for a PhD. This decision had practical consequences 20 years later because my salary had been set at the bachelor's level and did not cover my needs.

The Committee on Human Development was just being formed when I was in graduate school, and like most new programs of that time at the University of Chicago it offered almost unlimited opportunities for combining different fields of study. In addition to courses in neurology and biology, I studied psychology, sociology, education, and anthropology. It seemed to me important to know about all these fields to find out how to change human beings.

My proposed dissertation on the development of an improved test of music ability by the use of factor analysis may not seem to fit these intentions of studying the theory of human development. One explanation for this choice had nothing to do with my trajectory but because I was going to marry a musician. The other explanation is that factor analysis had enormous prestige on campus at that time because L. L. Thurstone, its creator, was an eminent faculty member. It seemed like the way to find out about everything. I passed prelims in early 1940 and my dissertation proposal was accepted soon thereafter.

Test Construction

But the war intervened. While I was busy reviewing the literature on music ability and developing appropriate tests for my battery, I was asked by my previous statistics professor, Marion Richardson, to take an upcoming civil service exam for a job in Washington. This would be in the office of personnel research that he was starting in the War Department. During the Depression one did not turn down any possibility of a job. Besides, I was young and certain I could easily finish a dissertation while working—I had worked at one job or another all through high school and college, mostly piano teaching and various kinds of office work. When the telegram arrived asking me to report on July 1, 1941, my fiancé and I got married and drove off to Washington.

By the time war was declared that December, our personnel research section had prepared a starting battery of basic classification tests for the recruits pouring into the several armed services. In fact, a core group of test constructors had been working on these tests many months before I arrived. One of my ancillary assignments was running the section library, and I was astonished to find that while I and my fellow students had been marching for peace, our government had been printing field manuals and technical manuals to train us for war. I find it strange now that I had not been horrified then at participating in a war effort. Nor did I sense as much incongruity as I might now between my pacifist, universalist beliefs and my job in the War Department. When the construct of "tolerance of ambiguity" appeared on the psychological scene many years later, it made perfect sense to me.

During the months and years of the war we were busy constructing one new test after another: general classification tests, officer candidate tests, mechanical aptitude tests, clerical aptitude tests, driver tests. I personally made up the Women's Army Corps (WAC) test and started to develop a test for spies before the creation of the OSS (precursor to the Central Intelligence Agency) transferred this project to them. In the beginning, our group served all the branches of the armed services, but soon both the navy and the air force formed their own units, recruiting personnel from our original cadre of about 30 psychologists. (By the end of the war there were at least three times as many.) Most of the men were eventually given officer's commissions but we few women—about six of us in the beginning and not many more later—remained in a civilian status. In the early 1940s, only a few of us muttered about sex discrimination, even though as civilians we did not share in the privileges that the men did. For one thing, we could not try out the tests in military installations and thus did not get to travel.

Although assigning enlistees to appropriate slots for human destruction was a far cry from developing better children and improving the world, it was intellectually stimulating and involved the application of much of what we had learned in psychology. We became a proud tight-knit group. We liked to think we were very smart and vied with each other on how well we scored on each new test we designed. We worked long hours (and for a while we worked seven days a week) and saw few people outside our own group, which included our spouses at weekly parties. I was not the only one who married when I got the job.

My primary assignment was in the editorial section helping put finishing touches on all the tests before they were sent out for trial, but I also participated in test construction and eventually produced a two-volume statistical manual that summarized the results of our efforts. In the last year of the war, we wrote the history of army testing—the various tests were parceled out to us in apparently random fashion. My assignment was the Signal Corps Radio Operator's test, whose first version had been created during World War I.

My dissertation on music ability, on the other hand, did not get finished. The long hours of work had something to do with this, but also I had reached the point where I needed to transcribe the battery onto a record, and I did not know how to go about this. Away from campus, I had no contact with recording studios.

By early 1945 we knew our work was about over and started thinking about our futures. Most of us were at the same professional stage of PhDMT (minus thesis), and the men returned to campus to finish PhDs and then moved on to distinguished faculty and research positions. Not the women, though. Ruth Churchill, my immediate superior from the time I arrived in Washington in 1941, and I both became pregnant. We joined the host of American women who had been employed during the war years but now felt drawn to domesticity. Ruth and I went on maternity leave shortly before her son and my daughter were born in November and December 1945, respectively. Although Ruth "finished up" her degree a few years later and went on to start a pioneer student testing and classification program at Antioch College, where she eventually rose to a high administrative post, I did not return to serious career activities for almost a decade. Eventually, though, all of us did return to work.

The Newton Experience

From 1945 to 1955, as a suburban housewife following my husband's career moves from city to city, I tried to apply my earlier academic studies in child development to rearing my own children, but otherwise I was in a different world. I felt sure that my studies had taught me how to be a good mother, but it proved harder than I thought and was different from what I expected. Meanwhile friends reported that the American Psychological Association (APA) office wanted to know what had happened to me because I had not kept up my membership. In fact, my children did not know I was a psychologist until they were almost grown. During those years, the closest I came to a psychological career was founding a nursery school in the New Jersey suburb where we lived in the early 1950s. I tried to model this school on the wonderful University of Chicago nursery school where I had trained and worked as a graduate student, but I found this to be absurd in a suburban setting with lots of space to play and lots of children to play with. Our nursery school—my partner was a neighbor who had been a journalist but also was now primarily a mother and housewife—was not a success that first year, financially or otherwise, but it did do better a few years later, perhaps because the burgeoning fertility of the 1950s made suburban mothers more interested in help with their children. By that time, however, I and my family had moved to the Boston area.

When my youngest child started kindergarten in Newton, Massachusetts, in 1955, I was fortuitously offered a short-term job to substitute for an incapacitated school psychologist in the Newton public schools—I had worked as a school psychologist in the Chicago public schools the year before I started graduate school. By that time I was very ready to go back, at least part time. In the new zeitgeist, married women were not supposed to have careers and I only expected to work for a few weeks until the staff member I was replacing recovered her health. In fact, I would not have accepted the job if it were full time or permanent. But the person I replaced never returned, and three years later I was still there and given tenure. By the time I left in 1963, my experiences in that job had profoundly changed my thinking about human development and my career perspective.

For one thing, in graduate school 15 years earlier we had looked at development as the child developing and the mother supervising, and we believed that all we had to do was see that mothers followed the right rules—or at least find the right rules for them to follow. Besides, although we might not have agreed with Arnold Gesell that development was largely an unfolding of predetermined patterns, we did seem to believe that the point of child rearing was mainly to avoid wrong moves. We also seemed to be more concerned with the reliability and validity of the tests we used to determine where the children were than with how they got to be that way.

Primarily, my experiences in Newton enlarged my frame from mother–child dyads to whole families and communities. As I worked with the hundreds of children that were referred to me each year, diagnosing their problems and treating many of them and their parents, I was struck with how often the behaviors for which the children were referred were similar to the behaviors I observed in their parents and siblings and even their grandparents and aunts and cousins. I was also impressed with the complexity of family interactions and relationships.

Later, when I turned to the literature, I discovered that I was not the only one at that time starting to wonder about our earlier individual and nuclear family suppositions. Jules Henry, for example, was moving in with families of schizophrenic children to look beyond a disease model; psychologists at the Mental Research Institute in Palo Alto, California, were observing the interactions of whole nuclear families and finding that schizophrenic children were representatives of their family dynamics—that the children were merely the ''identified patients.'' A few psychiatrists were talking about family causations of mental illness as opposed to ''inborn'' defects. (We are seeing another reversal of this trend now.)

The literature assumed that the family similarities and dynamics applied only in the case of the mentally ill, but when I thought about my experiences with ''normal'' people in Newton, I was sure that very similar processes characterized all children and all families. I could see it in my own family. This interest in family similarities, finally, enlarged my focus from child development to adult development and finally life-span development. Coincidentally, I was finding that I could learn more from clinical, qualitative kinds of approaches than from the standardized tests that had formed the bulwark of my training.

My change in perspective would probably not have happened if it were not for the policy of Edward Landy, the head of our Newton school psychology program. He insisted that we not only work with children and teachers as was—and probably still is—standard practice for school psychologists, but also that we at least communicate with the parents. This policy affected me differently from the way it did the other psychologists on the staff, because my colleagues were all young adults, most not yet married, who tended to identify with the children against the parents. But I was now at the age and life stage of the parents, and it was they with whom I found myself identifying. At my first interviews with parents, for example, I expected to find them ogres who were the causes of their children's problems. When we started talking, however, I knew immediately that they—and I—were at the same place, as much victims as causes. This was an astonishing discovery. With this new perspective, I did not have to battle villains but we could work together toward solving problems.

Clinical Psychology

I was noticing the same change in perspective in my concurrent training as a clinical psychologist. My clients were not only the children but whole nuclear families and, in fact, extended families as well. I tried to explain this to the psychiatrist who was training me but I think he, like my colleagues, was too young to see the point. This was my second round of training as a clinical psychologist. In the year between my bachelor's degree and starting graduate school, I had the good fortune to be an intern at the Michael Reese Hospital Psychological Clinic, working primarily with Samuel Beck, who had recently become famous for his work on the Rorschach test. In general, my clinical experience had more theoretical than practical consequences. Although I worked as a clinician in Newton and also later in Detroit, I generally felt that I had too many questions about what I was doing to be comfortable. It is true that I seemed to be helping my clients, but how? What was I doing that was right? Such questions drove me to research rather than practice whenever I had a choice. In part, my questioning derived from the early sparks of inquiry engendered at the University of Chicago, but also in part it came from the lack of explanatory power provided by prevailing theories for my own and others' dilemmas in child rearing and marital relations and more generally in social policies.

Back to the University of Chicago

If my second major career influence was the University of Chicago campus in the 1930s and my third the school psychology department of the Newton Public Schools in the 1950s, the fourth was my return to the university in the 1960s. Because I had left graduate school for the war effort more than 20 years earlier, I was way beyond the statute of limitations and thus fortunate to be accepted back as a doctoral student at almost the same level at which I had left. (The parallel to my mother's experience has not escaped me.)

When I had moved to Boston in the 1950s, Helen Koch had done her best to promote the completion of my doctorate by arranging for me to work jointly with her at the University of Chicago and John Whiting at Harvard. This arrangement did provide a modicum of direction and access to good libraries, but my job combined with responsibilities for a husband and three children and a big suburban house kept me from moving expeditiously on the new dissertation I now wanted to do involving personality and family transmission.

Sadly, my musical aptitude battery has never been recorded. It has been in a folder in my top file drawer for more than half a century. After the war I lost enthusiasm for assessing musical aptitude, which did not have high priority in the postwar era of technical and commercial priorities. Even my husband had turned from music to electronic engineering. Sometime in the 1970s a Japanese psychologist visiting Wayne State University where I then taught told me my battery would be of interest to people in his country where detection of musical ability was important. He asked me to send him my tests but somehow I never got around to doing so.

It was the breakup of our marriage in 1963 and my consequent need for a higher income to support our children that finally pushed me to renewed scholarly effort. I had also been advised to leave Boston for financial and legal reasons connected to the divorce and decided to move to Palo Alto to be near my sister and parents. Because I planned to work at Stanford in an arrangement like that I had with John Whiting, it was desirable to get family help with my early teenage children, who were caught up in the avant garde of the hippie movement in Boston—and who then plunged into the middle of the even more encompassing movement in California.

At this point gerontological issues entered the picture. I was told that I could not get a degree at Stanford because I was too old—over 45. I could go to Berkeley, but that would mean starting graduate school all over again, and my interviewer at Berkeley advised me to return to Chicago. When I wrote Bernice Neugarten, then the chair of the Committee on Human Development, I was welcomed back. The committee agreed that I could do a master's thesis in Palo Alto, where I wanted to stay until my middle child finished high school, and that this would be a pilot study for a new dissertation on personality similarities between children and their parents. The only other stipulations were that I take an updated statistics course and write three reviews of the literature (covering 25 years) on infancy, adolescence, and aging. I found this assignment stimulating and it proved to be a good preparation for all the literature reviews I was to do in the future. Foremost among these was a decade review of research on the family of later life, which I eventually expanded into a volume together with Robert and Sheila Atchley (Troll, Miller, & Atchley, 1979).

When my daughter Jeannie graduated high school in June and went off to college in Vermont, therefore, I left my oldest child in a theater company in Palo Alto and the youngest in a hippie-oriented high school in the foothills and drove back over the Rockies to Chicago in my derelict car, surprised when I made it against my mechanics' advice.

I should mention that during those two years in California I had my first experience as a gerontologist, courtesy of Bernice Neugarten. I had planned to continue working as a school psychologist in California and, in fact, was offered a job as one in Menlo Park near where we lived but was told I could not get a California school psychology license without further preparation—that my Massachusetts license could not be transferred. Only many years later did I find that I could have gotten a California license by applying to a special office in Sacramento. But then I would not have gotten my feet wet as a gerontologist. Serendipity!

For a few months I administered psychological tests to San Francisco Veterans Administration Hospital patients in a study under the direction of Jack Blumenkrantz, a psychologist who had a research project to diagnose carotid artery blockages that could impair cognitive functioning. Later I worked with a psychiatrist, Donald Freedman, in a California Department of Mental Hygiene study of the route to mental hospitals for people over 55. We interviewed representatives of nine counties about their current practices with disturbed older patients. This state study was affiliated with the Langley Porter Institute and Marjorie Lowenthal's project on commitment policies for older people exhibiting behavioral abnormalities. I learned enough about the difference between acute and chronic brain syndromes to make me skeptical about the Alzheimer's disease bandwagon when it sprang up a few years later. I learned that many apparent dementias are the result of such acute conditions as cardiac infarctions, diabetes, electrolyte imbalances, and alcoholism and can be reversed by prompt medical treatment. Unfortunately, prevailing beliefs about the inevitability of dementia with aging and laws based on these beliefs led to immediate and unreversible institutionalization, precluding that necessary medical treatment. At the end of our study we published a policy guidebook for treating older disturbed patients that was intended to be used in general hospitals, it is hoped to prevent some of the abuses we had found.

When I arrived back at the University of Chicago in July of 1965, I found myself in the middle of the student revolution. Students for a Democratic Society, the vanguard of the student movement in the 1960s, had been started by Richard Flacks, and it was his research project on youth and social change (with coinvestigator Bernice Neugarten) that I directed while finishing my degree. In fact, I obtained the data for my new dissertation on personality similarities between college students and their parents from these largely open-ended individual interviews with the two generations of Chicagoans; half of the students were activists and half controls, half men and half women. My stepwise multivariate analysis of codings of a dozen values and personality characteristics showed that a significant proportion of the variance of the student's scores was removed when the scores of both parents were entered into the analysis first.

Thus the hypotheses about family similarities that I had formed while working with elementary school children and their young adult parents in Newton seemed to fit the college-age youth and their middle-aged parents in Chicago. There were husband-wife similarities and parent-child similarities. In later postdoctoral three-generation studies, I even found grandparent-grandchild similarities and was able to demonstrate family transmission by way of path analyses. My first focus was family transmission, because that is what struck me most in my Newton observations. A focus on family relationships, attachment, and emotions evolved later.

The Detroit Years

After I completed my dissertation in 1967, published as Troll, Neugarten, and Kraines (1969), I moved to Detroit in 1967 to expand the life-span program of teaching and research on the family at the Merrill-Palmer Institute. Three years later, however, financial problems at Merrill-Palmer led to my moving a few blocks away to the psychology department at Wayne State University. Carolyn Shantz, whose area was infancy and early childhood, and I both joined an already vigorous developmental area in that department. Others of our colleagues at Merrill-Palmer joined the education and sociology departments at Wayne State, and we continued to work together for another five years.

I believe that our developmental psychology program was one of the few in the country that truly focused on the life span. I myself taught overview courses in life-span development (from conception to death) as well as courses in infancy, in early childhood, in adolescence, in adulthood, in aging, and in death and dying. Much of my research during those years used an open-ended questionnaire I developed to study three-generation, same-sex lineages (grandmother, daughter, granddaughter and grandfather, son, grandson). I used a set of 12 stem questions ranging from "tell me what you are like" to "describe a man (or woman) and tell what he (or she) is like." I wanted measures that simulated the clinical sessions in which I had first observed family similarities. Use of three-point ratings cumulated over 12 questions enabled me to measure such issues as cognitive and affective similarities (e.g., Troll, Lycacki, & Smith, 1975) and gender shifts in motivation and power over the generations. I also became interested in the attachment of adults to other family members (Troll & Smith, 1976), which I am studying to this day.

When I was asked by Bernice Neugarten and the Brooks-Cole Publishing Company to write a volume for their new life-span developmental series, I decided to do one on adult development, there being no text yet that distinguished adulthood from old age. This was a stimulating task; the book evolved from my class notes and experiences (Troll, 1975, 1985). Surprisingly, the second edition of this book is still in print even though it should long ago have been updated. Instead of going on to publish a full-scale text on adult development, I decided to write one that encompassed aging as well (Troll, 1982). This book unfortunately is no longer in print; I feel it is my magnum opus.

We never know how much of our own thinking derives from others, but I cannot stress sufficiently how indebted I am to Bernice Neugarten, a true pioneer in adult development and aging. I am one of her many students who climbed on her shoulders. Although we had been graduate students together in the late 1930s and I might not have been as impressed with her as her younger students, it did not work out that way. She was impressive. It was her adult development and aging course that established the groundwork for most later texts and research. She continued to open new vistas in the years that followed, perpetually asking new questions and posing new hypotheses and theories.

Even though I am chronologically a generation older than most of Bernice's students who form the "Chicago mafia," I have enjoyed my association with that lively group over the years and number its members among my closest colleagues and friends: Margaret Huyck, David Gutmann, Sheldon Tobin, Vern Bengtson, Barbara Turner, Gunhild Hagestad, David Chiriboga, Eva and Boaz Kahana are some but not all of these. At annual meetings of the APA and the Gerontological Society of America (GSA) for many years I would discover that my latest brainstorms and theoretical enthusiasms were shared by Margaret Huyck. Vern Bengtson started his three-generation study at the University of Southern California a couple of years after I finished my two-generation dissertation and about the time I started exploring three generations on my own. We have often been colleagues and collaborators ever since. My current work on modified extended families derives from his database, which he has generously made available to me. For many years, my interactions with Gunhild Hagestad enriched my thinking on generations. My thoughts on adult development were influenced by the seminal thinking of David Gutmann just as those on personhood in late life were influenced by Sheldon Tobin.

The Women's Movement and Gender Differences

Although gender differences were intrinsic to any developmental processes I studied, they did not become a central interest in my own thinking and research until the women's movement in the early 1970s. While I was only mildly involved in direct political activities like the organization of the National Organization of Women (NOW) chapter in Detroit, the repercussions of such involvement were major. Just as I had read intensively when I became interested in family transmission, I now read all that I could find about gender inequalities, starting with Betty Friedan's *The Feminine Mystique* (1964). These early spirited feminist writings provided an important shift in my perspective on human relationships and also helped me personally to soften some of my felt inadequacy from the divorce. I was the first among my friends and acquaintances whose marriage had "failed" and was convinced that there was something wrong with me.

My activities in the area of women's studies have been of two kinds. One has had to do with organizing psychological symposia and books to stimulate thinking about gender differences in aging and the aging of women. With my Merrill-Palmer colleague Joan Israel, we inaugurated the first conference on aging women at the University of Michigan—Wayne State University Gerontological Society. This resulted in a 1976 volume published by the Institute of Gerontology, *No Longer Young: The Older Woman in America* (Troll, Lycacki, & Smith, 1975). Following this conference, I edited a book on the aging of women with Joan

Israel and her husband, Kenneth, a psychiatrist, (Troll, Israel, & Israel, 1977) for which I recruited think pieces from a number of friends—there was as yet no available empirical literature from which to draw. (Our publisher, Prentice-Hall, objected to our proposed title *The Aging Woman* because nobody would want to buy it.)

In the following years, I organized numerous symposia at the meetings of the Gerontological Society and the American Psychological Association, among others. A 1984 empirical paper on generational changes in motivation and power cited earlier was included in a volume of the American Association for the Advancement of Science edited by Stamm and Ryff. Most recently, I coedited *Women Growing Older* with Barbara Turner (Turner & Troll, 1994).

I mentioned that the women's movement affected me in two ways. At this point, it is difficult to separate my twin interests of life-span family development and aging women as they have intermingled—that is, in trying to stimulate others to think about gender differences in aging, I have directed some of my own research to issues of aging women. One of my goals has been revising the thinking about older women—and of course men—as passive recipients of family actions to seeing the total family dynamics. In other words, my views of families as interacting wholes that I initially saw from the children's perspective I now also saw from the perspective of the oldest generations.

I myself had been an early example of the "returning woman" to education and careers, which I encountered during the 1970s. When I started teaching at Wayne State University, my classes were burgeoning with returning veterans on the GI bill and returning women whose children were now grown and whose ambitions had been postponed during the postwar era of domesticity and child rearing. I was 51 when I finished my PhD and went to Merrill-Palmer. My earlier decision to return to work at the Newton schools had been looked on with surprise and sometimes dismay among my friends. The wife of a Harvard mathematics professor took me out to lunch to ask me why I was doing this. I found myself telling her that I thought that otherwise my education would have been a waste, but I don't know why I said this and I'm still not sure I believe it. She and eventually all the others in that group did the same thing within the next few years—finishing degrees they had abandoned for marriage and family and starting new careers. Some of them rose rapidly in academic and other pursuits, and the phenomenon became a subject of study in itself.

When I was 60, I was offered a position as full professor with tenure at Rutgers University to chair one of the four psychology departments in its multicollege system. In fact, the department I chaired, in which I was the only woman faculty member, was in University College, which was primarily for adult students who were often employed during the day. I moved to New Jersey in 1975. As I had found at Wayne State, the many returning students, both men and women, were a delight to teach because of their enthusiasm and dedication. Some of my graduate students both at Wayne State and Rutgers also tended to be somewhat older than the traditional students just out of college; many were married women and a few had children. It was no surprise, therefore, that they would be drawn to studying family relations and adult development. I found their dissertations exciting in that they expanded my own interests. Only a few have chosen careers in academia, but Victoria Bedford, my last doctoral student at Rutgers, whose work is about sibling relationships, almost makes me feel I have started something.

Retirement Years: The Oldest-Old and Extended Families

My mother lived with me the last nine years of her life—she died at 93. This living situation turned out to be a difficult experience for both of us. She had been happiest when she was working and continually regretted that she had not accepted an offer to remain in her agency part time after she turned 80. When she died, therefore, I expected to feel a sense of relief, but instead I was taken aback to find myself severely depressed. As I had done earlier when confronted with unexpected situations, I turned to the literature and found almost nothing about the effect of the death of parents when one is in later life—I was almost 70 when she died, so I decided to study this phenomenon after my upcoming compulsory retirement at age 70. (My father had died at 78 and my sister, early, at 57.)

The preretirement years were difficult not only because of my mother's death but also because I had to make a decision about where to live and work. I could have stayed around Rutgers but serendipitously was asked to fill in at San Jose State University in California for David Chiriboga, who was about to move to Texas. I made a quick decision. Moving back to California would enable me to taper off my academic affiliation instead of cutting it off abruptly. It also would enable me to accept Colleen Johnson's invitation to work with her in San Francisco. Last but not least, two of my children and all my grandchildren were then in the Bay Area. To cap it all, my daughter met somebody who wanted to sublease her house in Palo Alto for a year, and I was able to sell my house in New Jersey in two weeks. It was an overdetermined situation. I moved before the end of the month and taught my first class at San Jose as soon as I got there from the airport.

I only stayed at San Jose a year because it was more interesting at the University of California, San Francisco (UCSF), working with Colleen on her longitudinal study of the oldest-old—people over 85. While I have interviewed a few respondents, most of my input has consisted of analyzing personality and family issues (e.g., Troll & Skaff, 1997; Johnson & Troll, 1992, 1994). I have been an adjunct professor at UCSF for more than 10 years now and will probably continue at an increasingly reduced pace so long as I remain competent. Using the rich data provided by open-ended interviews to answer questions that intrigue me seems a wonderful way to spend my retirement years.

One of my reasons for being pleased to be affiliated with UCSF was that I planned to start investigating the effect of the death of a parent in 1986, the year I moved back to California. Instead of using a sample recruited from obituaries—my first plan—I was invited by Vern Bengtson to study the families in his University of Southern California longitudinal three-generation study, which included extensive data on grandparents, their children, and their adult grandchildren. There were 10 families in which the oldest generation had died after the beginning of the study. So far, however, I presented only one paper on my original theme of death of parents. When I started reading the 150 protocols of family members and interviewing several survivors in each of the 10 families, I was struck more by the drama of the family relationships than the more limited information about grief and mourning. I shifted my focus from death of parents to extended-family integration. I am in the process of writing a book on which families stay together over time and which do not, and why.

I have sometimes compared my retirement situation to that of the gentlemen scholars of the eighteenth century. My annuity, though not large as I worked in academia only a comparatively few years, is sufficient to enable me to "play" with ideas and research. I have been enjoying this postretirement work so much that I am sorry my mother did not take the opportunity to remain active and creative after 80. Some of my friends and colleagues look for totally different pursuits in their retirement years but others, like me, can't think of anything better than being able to play in a way they never could while they were bound to the pressures and restrictions of academic or professional systems.

Developmental and Historical Processes

In looking back over my career, I see that I have been influenced both by history and by my own development. When I started college in the Depression, I chose a school that happened to be two blocks from where my family lived. That the University of Chicago was such a stimulating place at that time was an unanticipated bonus. I did not choose to go there because of its atmosphere, but I did flourish in that atmosphere. World War II turned me aside from developmental studies, but I was fortunate to find creative work as a psychologist surrounded by intelligent and creative colleagues. The postwar domestic era moved me into noncareer but vital experiences of a suburban wife and mother so that I was ready to rethink the dogma of my earlier developmental theories when confronted by the new experiences of the Newton schools psychology program. Finally my close encounters with the student and women's movements had profound effects on my academic interests.

Developmentally, I was a PhD-MT and a new bride when I went to Washington and fit right in with the rest of the staff, most of whom were also newly married. I was still of child-bearing age after the war when everybody seemed to be turning to domestic life and enjoying the luxuries of all the new appliances and products that appeared. I was older than the others in the Newton office and open to hearing the voices of the parents and other family members instead of just the teachers and the children. It enabled me to appreciate what I was seeing in larger family dynamics. I became a grandmother when I started my academic career and enjoyed teaching and working on issues of later family life. Finally, I have been able to experience my own aging, and I think this has contributed to my understanding of gerontological processes in ways younger gerontologists do not have available. And talking about family similarities, my oldest granddaughter has just graduated from medical school and is about to start a residency in psychiatry. My son's specialty is family medicine.

References

Friedan, B. (1964). *The feminine mystique.* New York: Dell.

Institute of Gerontology, The University of Michigan, Wayne State University. (1976). *No longer young: The older woman in America.* Occasional papers in gerontology, No. 11.

Johnson, C. L., & Troll, L. E. (1992, 1994). Family functioning in late late life. *Journal of Gerontology: Psychological Sciences, 47*(3), 566–572.

Troll, L. E. (1975, 1985). *Development in early and middle adulthood.* Monterey, CA: Brooks/Cole.

Troll, L. E. (1982). *Continuations: Development after 20.* Monterey, CA: Brooks/Cole.

Troll, L. E., Israel, J., & Israel, K. (1977). *Looking ahead: A woman's guide to the problems and joys of growing older.* Englewood Cliffs, NJ: Prentice-Hall.

Troll, L., Lycacki, H., & Smith, J. (1975). Development of the cognitively complex woman over generations. In Institute of Gerontology, *No longer young: The older woman in America* (pp. 81–88). Detroit: The University of Michigan—Wayne State University.

Troll, L. E., Miller, S., & Atchley, R. (1979). *Families of later life.* Belmont, CA: Wadsworth.

Troll, L. E., Neugarten, B., & Kraines, R. (1969). Similarities in values and other personality characteristics in college students and their parents. *Merrill-Palmer Quarterly, 15,* 323–336.

Troll, L. E., & Skaff, M. (1997). Perceived continuity of self in very old age. *Psychology and Aging, 12*(1), 162–169.

Troll, L. E., & Smith, J. (1976). Attachment through the life span. *Human Development, 4*(1), 67–74.

Turner, B. F., & Troll, L. E. (1994). *Women growing older.* Newport Beach, CA: Sage.

·

Chapter 24
EPILOGUE:
The Global Emergence of Geropsychology

Linda Fagan Dubin

As the autobiographies and historical perspectives in previous chapters have eloquently described, the birth of geropsychology experienced a long gestation and difficult and prolonged labor. The field is still in its infancy. Demographic trends from ancient times to the threshold of the twenty-first century (as illustrated in the figures presented in this chapter) indicate that few people lived past 50 years of age at the beginning of the twentieth century. Thus, it is not surprising that there was minimal interest in issues regarding elderly people in any region of the world, except for the religious and philosophical issues regarding death. It is quite remarkable that the contributors to this volume, who were young in the prewar period, were foresighted enough to perceive the importance of understanding the latter portion of the continuum of the life span. Even at a time when child development was a major focus of psychology, these geropsychologists recognized that aging represents an important aspect of the developmental spectrum.

After World War II (especially after 1950), the proportion of the population living past 65, and even past 85 years of age, increased dramatically. A corresponding rise in study of geropsychology has been observed. Figures 24-1 through 24-4 show global demographic changes projected into the twenty-first century in the United States and other regions of the world. Changes in life expectancy from ancient to current times are illustrated in Figure 24-5. Figure 24-6 shows the effect of these changes on median age through the approximate period of U.S. history.

In the second half of the twentieth century, scholars and lay people became more interested in the physical, psychological, and social changes and challenges associated with living to be old. Although elderly individuals experience the burden of ill health disproportionately, the associated economic and social costs fall on younger members of every culture. Faced with projections of significant increases in the world's elderly population, societies have begun to take notice and to respond to the need for more information and understanding of relevant issues.

Autobiographies of experts around the world represent a good place to begin an analysis of issues related to geropsychology. The individuals represented in this volume have devoted their careers to understanding various aspects of elderly individuals. Their immersion in focal issues of geropsychology surely provided insight and foresight, which ultimately yielded a special perspective with respect to their own aging.

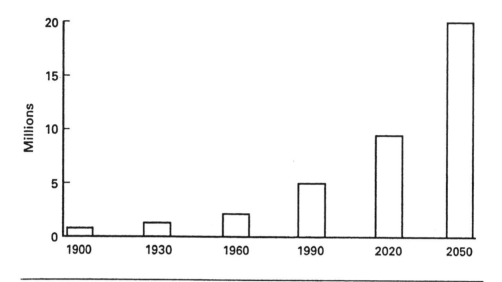

Figure 24-1. U.S. Population Age 85 and Older, 1900–2050.
Source: U.S. Bureau of the Census, *Decennial census,* 1900–1980; projections, 1990–2050,
Current Population Report, P-25, October 1982.

This chapter augments the autobiographical material with biographical information solicited from their colleagues, ''offspring,'' and disciples toward our goal of understanding the historical origins of geropsychology. In this endeavor we search for information and nuance, which yields not only a global review but also enriches our ability to address the practical issues involved in dealing with the significant demographic changes that affect us. By incorporating the psychological needs of elderly persons, a balanced and practical understanding of the full developmental spectrum, including end-of-life issues, will emerge.

Serendipity and circumstance play an enormous role in influencing human thought and endeavor. The previous chapters have indicated that the intellectual climate of a period, chance meeting of associates, wars, and changing demographics determined or altered the course of psychogerontology. A variety of themes, stops and starts, and practical considerations emerge as a reflection of events and sociocultural differences around the world.

The World Health Organization (WHO) defined health as ''a state of physical, mental, and social well-being, and not merely the absence of disease or injury,'' recognizing the global importance of psychological determinants of health and well-being in all people of all ages. Public health is concerned with assuring the conditions in which people can be healthy. Models that identify the multiple determinants of health cite several areas in which psychosocial and environmental variables interact to determine health status. The United Nations Assembly on Aging developed the goal to ''add life to years rather than adding years to life,'' proposing a focus on quality-of-life issues among elderly persons.

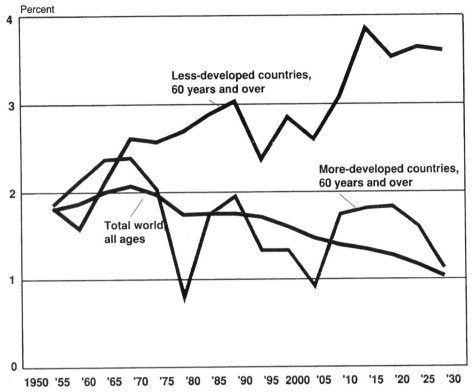

Average Annual Percent Growth

Figure 24-2. Elderly Population Growing Fastest in Developing Countries. From U.S. Department of Commerce, Bureau of the Census, 1996.

This chapter reviews the historical emergence of geropsychology in the context of the culture and climate of various countries. Readers can formulate hypotheses that focus on the following questions:

- Why was there little interest in geropsychology before 1950?
- What major themes influenced areas of study?
- What practical issues influenced research?
- How did the social and spiritual climate affect ideas?
- How and when did geropsychology become institutionalized/professionalized?
- What lessons can be learned and what are the future implications?

Interdisciplinary interaction, cross-fertilization, and timing, as revealed in this volume, characterize the development and evolution of psychogerontology. At a time when elderly populations are aging around the world, the analysis of problems and needs related to aging can be applied to the development of programs and policies that can improve the well-being not only of the aged but of society at large.

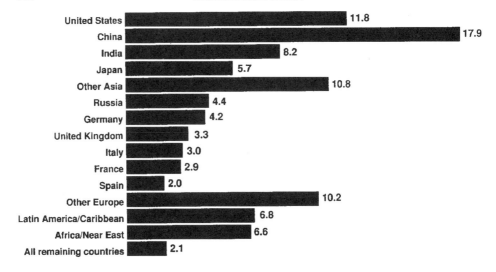

Figure 24-3. The Oldest-Old: Percent Distribution of World Population 75 Years and Over. From U.S. Department of Commerce, Bureau of the Census, 1996.

Procedures and Problems

This chapter presents qualitative data collected from contributors in many countries. International experts in psychogerontology were asked to nominate correspondents for a historical survey of the field. The nominees were sent questionnaires developed to identify important individuals, publications, and events in the respondents' countries. The survey also sought to reveal the cultural climate in which the historical origins of psychogerontology were fostered or impeded. The questionnaire included the items listed next.

History of Geropsychology: Correspondents' Questionnaire

1. In your opinion, who were the first psychologists in your country interested in geropsychology?
2. What position did he or she occupy?
3. What are the dates of the person's life?
4. What aspects was he or she concerned with?
5. What notable publications resulted?
6. What research did he or she do?
7. Did he or she have any colleagues or students who continued the line of interest?
8. For what was he or she particularly noted?
9. What was the academic climate within which geropsychology developed?
10. Was there a set of ideas that helped or hindered the development of geropsychology?
11. Have any applications developed?
12. Is there a publication you regard as initiating the field?

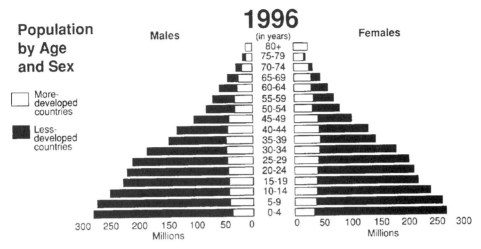

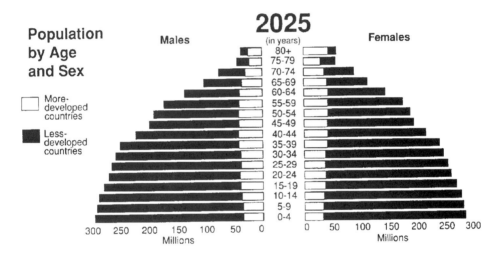

Figure 24-4. The Changing Global Age Structure. From U.S. Department of Commerce, Bureau of the Census, 1996.

13. Are there any societies, associations, or organizations with sections devoted to geropsychology in your country?
14. Have there been any conferences on the psychology of aging in your country that you regard as of historical significance?

Approximately 20 questionnaires were reviewed.[1] Because systematic sampling was not feasible, it is not known whether responses reflect the opinions of other colleagues in the various countries. Table 24-1 summarizes the results of the international survey. The first question often produced several nominees, but economy of space in the table required

---

[1] Some questionnaires were incomplete; additional information was gleaned from informal sources.

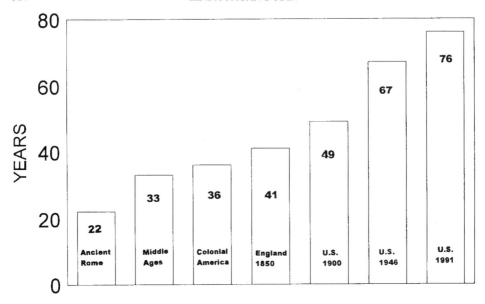

Figure 24-5. Human life expectancy at birth from ancient to modern times. Adapted from U.S. National Center for Health Statistics, Washington, DC.

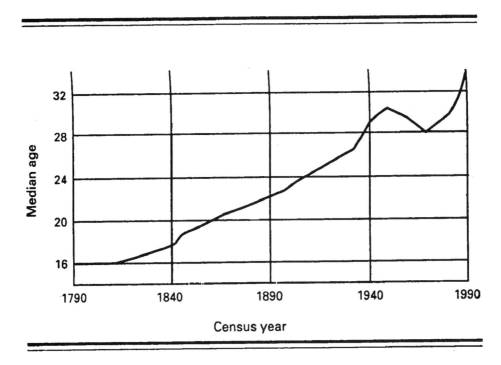

Figure 24-6. Median age of U.S. population, 1790–1990. From *Statistical Bulletin,* Metropolitan Life Insurance Co. Used with permission.

selection, which was done by consensus of the present editors (Birren and Schroots). The omission of psychogerontologists is not intended to devalue the significance of their work. Tabulation was difficult: Responses were often incomplete and in variable format. Nevertheless, several distinctive patterns emerged. Chronological trend analysis in the context of world events, as well as regional patterns and recurrent themes, were reviewed and categorized (as shown later in Table 24-2).

Results

As described elsewhere in this volume, contributions to the field were sparse before 1950. Populations had low proportions of old people and focus on child development predominated. Infant mortality, infectious disease, and social conditions demanded more immediate attention. Trends in human longevity are also related to technological changes during the period. The present survey revealed the effects of war, depression, and other economic factors in the first half of the twentieth century.

Trend Analysis

The impact of the world wars on research in Europe was reflected in differential patterns of activity globally during those periods, as shown in Table 24-1. Before the turn of the twentieth century, Francis Galton's 1884 health exhibit in London included subjects up to 80 years of age. In 1899 Paul Ranschburg, a physician and professor of neurology and psychiatry at Budapest Medical School, developed an experimental psychology laboratory and the Institute of Psychology at the Hungarian Academy of Sciences where he studied cognitive functions and memory pathology in elderly persons. (However, his work does not seem to have been translated until after 1950.) No other significant European work was reported before the contributions of Charlotte Bühler in the 1930s. The Nazi regime and World War II curtailed her research, which related to the so-called dynamic phases of life, not just in youth, but into maturity; she ultimately fled to the United States with her husband and colleague, Karl Bühler.

Meanwhile, in the United States, the first reported dissertation in the field of psychogerontology was submitted by Helen Hubbert (1915, Johns Hopkins University), especially noteworthy in light of the paucity of women in the professions. G. S. Hall, retired president of Clark University, wrote the book *Senescence: The Last Half of Life* in 1922. In 1927, Miles, professor of psychology at Stanford University, received foundation grant support for work on the relationship of skills to aging. Funding allowed Terman (longitudinal studies of gifted children) and others to develop a strong research program in geropsychology at Stanford. Longitudinal studies and research protégés were spawned, and many young investigators found financial support during the Depression.

In 1937 Cowdry (a histocytologist) organized the first Conference on Aging at Woods Hole, Massachusetts, and in 1941 the United States Public Health Service funded a research program on aging and sponsored a conference: Mental Health in Later Maturity. Even in the United States, however, World War II took its toll and no further significant activity was apparent until 1946 when the American Psychological Association (APA) developed a division on adult development of aging.

In Asia the earliest work reported was that of Kakusho Tachibana of Osaka University in Japan, who conducted research that culminated in his 1927 publication *A Training Process of Old Persons—On Speed of Motor Action.* He interviewed longevous persons (commended by the emperor) and patients at *Yokufu-en,* a nursing home established after the 1923 earthquake. However, World War II disrupted his work after military authorities

Table 24-1—*Key Contributions to the Global Emergence of Geropsychology*

Country	Person/Personal	Affiliations
Australia	Elsie Harwood [b. 1911; DPhil., 1957]	U. of Queensland [Psychology]; Reader, Honorary Research Consultant; coauthor: Naylor.
	George Naylor [Ph.D., (M. Sc: Geology, 1952); died 1980]	U. of Queensland [Psychology]: Reader, Honorary Research Consultant, Visiting professor: U. of Wyoming, 1955; coauthor: Harwood.
Austria	Charlotte Bühler	U. of Vienna [Psychology] [1930s]; colleagues: Karl Bühler, Hans Thomae.
Canada	David Schonfield [1920–1995]	U. of Calgary [Occupational psychology].
	Blossom Wigdor	U. of Toronto, McGill University (1952–1979) [Psychology]; first editor-in-chief of the "Canadian J. on Aging" (1982).
China	Shulian Xu [b. July 9, 1921]	Research Fellow, Institute of Psychology, Chinese Academy of Sciences; colleagues: Z. Wu, C. Sun.
Germany	William Stern [publications 1923, 1931]	Stern (1931); Giese (1928).
	Hans Thomae [b. July 31, 1915]	U. of Bonn: Psychology (Director, 1960–1983); colleagues: Ursula Lehr, Schmitz-Scherzert, Kruse; U. of Iowa: Martin.
Greece	Lambos Houssiadas [b. April 18, 1925]	U. of Thessaloniki: Professor of Psychology; colleagues: Natsopoulos, Efremidou.
Hungary	Paul Ranschburg [1870–1945]	Budapest Medical School, 1918; M.D., Neurology, Psychiatry; colleague: Szondi.
India	P. V. Ramamurti [b. September 13, 1936]	Sri Venkateswara U. Tirupati [Psych.] prof., Dir. Center for Research on Aging; colleagues: Jamuna, Reddy.

Interests and Research Aspects	Seminal Publications
Longitudinal studies of aging [Operation Retirement, UQOR], initiated in 1965; intellectual, emotional, and social changes in aging and retirement, e.g., speed of perception, learning.	Longitudinal Study in Gerontology [1963–1995]: "Recall and recognition in elderly and young subjects," 1969 [with G. Naylor]; "Old dogs, new tricks," 1975 [with G. Naylor]; "Being a patient in a nursing home," 1980.
Operation Retirement [UQOR], initiated in 1965; intellectual, emotional, and social changes in aging (speed of perception), learning.	Naylor–Harwood Adult Intelligence Scale—NHAIS, 1972; 1963–1995: Longitudinal Study in Gerontology, 1966–1986; "Old dogs, new tricks" in *Psychology Today*, 1975.
Developmental psychology, dynamic phases of life, not just in youth, but into maturity.	"Der menschliche Lebenslauf als psychologisches Problem" (The course of human life as a psychological problem), 1933.
Memory changes with age; limitations of perceptual span; conflicting conclusions and theories; applications; stereotyping.	"Field training of older people" [1956].
Mental health, elder abuse, advocate; health and medical issues.	"Age differences in retention of learning" [Wigdor & Wimer, 1958].
Aging of cognitive function (memory, thinking, intelligence and attention); mental health of the elderly (subjective well-being, marriage satisfaction); personality and self-concept.	Xu et al. (1985). Changes in some of 20–90 year-old adults' memory activities: "Acta Psychologica Sinica" 2, 154–161; Xu et al. (1987): "Psychology of Aging," Academic Press.
Relationship between heredity and environmental factors ("heredity predisposes, environment fulfills"); active coping.	"Die menshliche Personlichkeit" (The Human Personality) [editor], 1923.
Systematic studies on development in middle and late adulthood [longitudinal studies]; personality development in a life-span perspective; stress and coping; cognitive theory of adjustment to aging; processes on decision making; biographical research.	1958: Longitudinal research on middle-aged employees [with U. Lehr, Vita Humana]; 1970: Theory of aging and cognitive theory of personality, Human Development 13: 1–16; "Psychologie des Alterns" (Psychology of Aging), 1972, translated into other languages 1996; Findings from the Bonn Longitudinal Study of Aging (1950–1970).
Cognitive development [old age]; cognitive egocentricity in older individuals; effects of retirement in the family life of older people. Work with graduate students and associates included studies with aphasic, Parkinson's, and Alzheimer's patients.	"Advanced Age and Performance" (1974).
Experimental psychology laboratory— Institute of Psychology of the Hungarian Academy of Sciences [1899]; cognitive functions in the elderly; experimental methods for psychological study of "backward children"/developmental deficits; pathology of memory.	Trans: Neurological/psychiatric diseases of old people [1967]; trans: An introduction to social gerontology [1978].
Perception of personal futurity, psychological aspects of care giving and disability among the elderly, health behavior of centenarians, mental health, determinants of successful aging, effects of spirituality/religion (e.g., Karma), characteristics of longevous persons.	Perspectives of geropsychology in India: a review [1995]; previous reviews 1984, 1987, 1993.

Continued on next page

LINDA FAGAN DUBIN

Table 24-1—*continued*

Country	Person/Personal	Affiliations
Italy	Marcello Cesa-Bianchi [b. 1926]	Milan U., Medical School, Institute of Psychology; M.D.: Prof. of Psychology/Neuropsychiatry; colleagues: Pravettoni, G. Cesa-Bianchi, Vecchia.
Japan	Kakusho Tachibana [1900–1978]	Osaka U., So-Ai Women's College and Yokkufu-en [visiting researcher]: Prof. of Psychology; colleagues: Matataro Matsumoto [Tokyo U.], Dr. Fufiro Amako [head physician of Yokufu-en].
Netherlands	Joep M. A. Munnichs [b. 1927]	Prof. and Chair in Psychogerontology, Catholic University, Nijmegen (KUN).
Norway	Eva Beverfelt	Norsk gerontologisk institutt [NGI]: Director/ Associates at the Norwegian Institute of gerontology; colleague: Sol Seim [Oslo].
Spain	Rocio Fernando-Ballesteros [b. March 21, 1939]	U. of Madrid; Prof. of psychology, Director of Programs on Gerontology; colleagues: Gonzalez; R y Caler, M.D.
Sweden	Jan Helander [b. 1930]	Psychology Prof.: Goteborg University; colleagues: Berg, Melin.
United Kingdom	A. T. Welford (1914–1995)	Director of the Nuffield Research Unit into Problems on Aging, Cambridge, England [1950–1960?].
	K. F. H. Murrell	Nuffield Research Unit in Industrial Gerontology (1952–1959?); Professor, U. of Wales Institute of Science and Technology, engineer.
United States	G. S. Hall [1844–1922]	Professor of Psychology, President of Clark U.
	W. R. Miles [b. 1885]	Professor of Psychology, Stanford U.
	Sydney Pressey [b. 1888]	Yale University: Prof. psychology; colleague: Raymond Kuhlen.

Interests and Research Aspects	Seminal Publications
Perception and applied psychology; developmental psychology; eventually geropsychology [1950]. Research into cognitive, affective, and emotional aspects in the context of life-span developmental psychology (experimental and psycho-social methods).	Founded journal "Richerce di Psicologia." Editor "Psicologia della Senescenza" ["Psychology of Senescence" (1978)]. "Psicologia dell'Invecchiamento" (Psychology of Aging).
Motor performance; interviewed longevity persons commended by the Emperor and nursing home patients of Yokufu-en; 1930s: color preferences, word associations, esthetics, religions, retrospection; history of stereotyping of aging in Japan; established nursing homes and educational institutions that train care-givers and home-helpers of the elderly.	A training process of old persons—on speed of motor action. "Japanese J. of Psychology" 2 (1927): 635–653.
Subjective experiences of aging, perspective in later life; holistic, interdisciplinary social approaches in gerontology.	"Old age and finitude" [1966, thesis].
Quality of life; social awareness of elderly; special needs. By fostering international contacts enhanced the status/role of social gerontology. Use of WAIS applied [White Papers of Ministries and Central Government].	
Environment, behavior and aging, stereotypes/ageism, learning potential/ reserve capacity, successful aging, quality of life.	"Aging Assessment in Psicoadiagnostico" [1983]; Assessment of Resident Setting [1986]; "Training effects on intelligence of older persons" [1995].
Intelligence and aging in a life-span perspective.	On Age and Mental Test Behaviour. "Actz Psychologicz Gothoburgensis" VII (1967) [first doctoral dissertation on geropsychology].
Human skills; experimental studies of human performance changes with age.	"Skill and Age" (1951).
Ergonomics; found variations according to age.	Major Problems of Industrial Gerontology. "J. Gerontology" 14: 216–221 (1959).
Broad issues of aging; promoter of new ideas in an era of little interest in aging.	"Senescence: The last half of life" [1922].
Miles, a member of the National Academy of Sciences, had a foundation grant for research on aging [1927]. He was interested in the relationship of skills to aging.	"Measures of certain abilities throughout the life span" [PNAS: 17(1931)].
Pressey, interested in aging and development, was founding president of the Division on Adult Development and Aging of the American Psychological Association.	"Life: a Psychological Survey" (Pressey et al., 1939).

Entries are excerpted from materials submitted by the nominators, whose contributions are gratefully acknowledged. Complete information was not always available.

requisitioned the building. In China and India aging research was initiated later in the century.

It is interesting to note that several women are represented among the pioneers of psychogerontology (e.g., in Australia, Austria, Canada, China, Norway, and the United States). Although no representative or random sampling was performed, there seemed to be a greater proportion of female psychogerontologists (almost one third) than in other professional and academic fields of the period. One might speculate that the traditional role of women as caregivers of both children and elderly people influenced the gender distribution.

Themes

Although research in geropsychology was sparse between 1900 and 1950, the responses of this international survey suggested a broad range of topics and disciplines as areas from which geropsychology emerged:

- Cognitive issues: memory, perception, intelligence
- Developmental continuum/life-span approaches
- Experimental psychology
- Medical and pathology concerns (e.g., dementia, psychotherapy)
- Mental health: depression, stress, coping
- Occupational issues, especially in Canada and the United Kingdom
- Performance and skills
- Personality
- Social and social service
- Spirituality and the elderly population, especially in Asia.

Table 24-2 summarizes the geographic distribution of topics and the investigators providing the foundations for the emergence of the field of psychogerontology/geropsychology.

The climate of spirituality found in Asian cultures was consistently noted by the Japanese, Chinese, and Indian contributors, who mentioned the ambiance of Buddhism, Confucianism, and Karma. Ramamurti, professor of psychology at Sri Venkateswara University Tirupati (India), has been especially interested in the perception of personal futurity and the effects of religion and spirituality on elderly persons. Issues of charity and filial responsibility no doubt played a role in the appreciation of well-being and social support needs of elderly populations.

Intelligence and memory changes with aging were recurrent themes, especially evident in the work of Eva Beverfelt, Norwegian director of the *Norsk gerontologisk institutt* (NGI), and Jan Helander, professor of psychology at Goteborg University in Sweden. In fact, this area of interest was widespread (e.g., Harwood and Naylor in Australia, Houssiadas in Greece, Terman at Stanford University in the United States, and Xu in China).

Early work in psychogerontology often derived from medical issues facing the mental health of elderly persons and was conducted by physicians (e.g., Ranschburg in Hungary, Cesa-Bianchi in Italy, and Fernando-Ballesteros in Spain) or in a climate of clinical psychology (e.g., Munnichs in the Netherlands). In other cases, the goal of understanding the psychology of elderly persons related to social goals, particularly in Sweden and Norway, as well as in Spain. Many investigators expressed concern with stereotypes of the aged. India continues to address the issue of social supports in its welfare policy, as have many countries in recent years. Increasing numbers of countries have developed public old age/disability/survivors programs. Retirement issues were a specific focus of Harwood and Naylor in

Table 24-2—*Origins of Psychogerontology*

Theme	Psychogerontologist	Country
Clinical	Cesa-Bianchi	Italy
(mental health, pathology)	Houssiadas	Greece
	Ranschburg	Hungary
	Wigdor	Canada
Cognition	Harwood, Naylor	Australia
(intelligence, memory,	Thomae	Germany
perception, performance)	Houssiadas	Greece
	Schonfeld	Canada
	Helander	Sweden
	Tachibana	Japan
	Xu	China
Experimental	Ranschburg	Hungary
	Welford	England
Life span	Bühler	Austria
(heredity/environment)	Stern, Thomae	Germany
	Cesa-Bianchi	Italy
	Fernando-	
	Ballesteros	Spain
	Helander	Sweden
	Hall, Miles, Pressey	United States
Occupation retirement	Murrell, Welford	England
	Hossiadas	Greece
Personality	Thomae	Germany
	Xu	China
Social	Stern, Thomae	Germany
(care giving, coping, support)	Munnichs	Netherlands
	Beverfelt	Norway
	Helander	Sweden
	Ramamurti	India
	Tachibana	Japan
Spiritual	Ramamurti	India
	Tachibana	Japan

Australia (Operation Retirement) and Houssiadas in Greece. Figure 24-7 illustrates the growth of old age assistance programs globally.

The influence of postwar productivity efforts in the 1950s was apparent in England and Wales. A. T. Welford, director of the Nuffield research unit in Cambridge, conducted experimental studies on human performance changes with age. K. F. H. Murrell, an engineer and professor of the University of Wales Institute of Science and Technology, found variations in relation to age in his ergonomics studies.

Post-1950 Activity

In the second half of the twentieth century there was increased interest in gerontological issues. The first conference to organize the international association of geropsychologists convened in Belgium in 1949, resulting in the Congress of the International Association of Gerontology, which held subsequent conferences following that in St. Louis (1951). The American Psychological Association (APA) held a conference on the psychological aspects

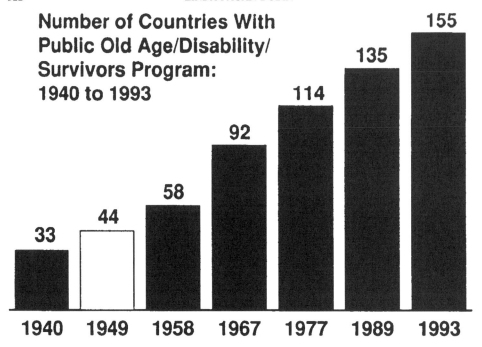

Number of Countries With Public Old Age/Disability/Survivors Program: 1940 to 1993

Figure 24-7. The Spread of Public Old Age Security. From U.S. Department of Commerce, Bureau of the Census, 1996.

of aging in 1955. During the 1970s there was a plethora of conferences on a variety of relevant issues:

- International Association of Gerontology (IAG) conferences: Kiev (1972), Jerusalem (1975), Tokyo (1978)
- European symposia: Dubrovnik (1976), Ystad (1977), Krakow (1979), Avignon (1979)

After 1980, the number of publications, organizations, conferences, and psychogerontologists seemed to grow exponentially and is expected to increase into the twenty-first century, consistent with the observed and projected growth of aging and old populations.

Implications and Applications

Psychology is one of the multiple determinants of health and successful aging in every culture. The elderly population is growing, in numbers and proportion of the world's population. Needs of this vulnerable group are having an impact, not only on individuals but on societies around the globe. Economic issues of burgeoning costs of end-of-life medical care, long-term care, and threats to Social Security (e.g., in the United States) have taken center stage. However, knowledge regarding the psychosocial and mental health issues related to the elderly are essential to the development of meaningful policy. Understanding the dynamics of mental and physical well-being and psychoneuroimmunological interrelationships provides us with an opportunity to address problems more efficiently and effectively. Insight toward improving geriatric psychology in program planning for the aged might involve education, social support, exercise, and other psychogerontological applications.

Beneficial health effects of physical and mental activity, stress reduction, and social support have been reported. The slow-down-and-take-it-easy recommendation for retirement has been superseded by the use-it-or-lose-it concept, documented to be relevant across the life span. Education and environmental enrichment have been shown to have positive effects, not only on cognitive function but also on brain anatomy. Physical education programs could improve not only musculoskeletal strength and ability but also psychological well-being. Relaxation and stress-reduction studies might draw from the many cultures that have given us tai chi, yoga, meditation, and biofeedback—leading to a better understanding of the psychological health of elderly people and to a positive golden-age experience.

Today, countries around the world are compelled to address issues in geriatric health care and psychosocial services. Costs to society—especially for caregivers—are high. In this era of global communication and transportation, information satellites and diversity within national cultures, countries can learn from one another. Youth of most cultures cannot fully comprehend the needs of older persons, but increasing numbers of the young and middle-aged are becoming old. Perhaps autobiographies of those who have studied the older population will yield insight and understanding that foster an optimal state of mind for the aged and, ultimately, for our aging societies. Countries may be guided by the authors' lessons in the formulation of humane, comprehensive strategies and policies for promoting the holistic health of elderly people.

Summary

This chapter has provided a global, historical review and analysis of contributions from experts in the field. The information collected has been placed in the context of demographic changes, world events, and economic factors.

The survey was derived from a nominated international pool of geropsychologists who were asked to address their knowledge of key people, events, and cultural climate in their countries. This perspective was solicited to supplement the autobiographical material of the other chapters. Information was tabulated, summarized, and analyzed for emerging trends and themes. Hypotheses related to demographic changes, gender role, cultural ambiance, and economical issues are proposed. Significant historical events and conferences are noted.

The goal of this historical report was to begin to interpret and understand the origins of interest and intellectual thought giving rise to the field of geropsychology. Implications of the findings provide the basis for recommendations and applications in public health policy.

This appendix contains brief sketches of early leaders in psychology, both deceased and alive, who furthered the development of geropsychology through their own research, the encouragement of students, or the development of relevant theory. It is regretted that more of them could not have been included in the volume because of the lack of space. Perhaps a future volume may represent their efforts adequately. In most instances the sketches have been prepared by a person in the same country. We appreciate very much their efforts in preparing the biosketches. For a few, when no one could be located to do this, an outsider prepared the sketch by consulting library sources.

Austria
Charlotte Bühler
1893–1974

Charlotte Bühler was born in Berlin in 1893 and worked on research in Munich, where in 1916 she married Karl Bühler (1879–1963), who was an equally famous scientist. They settled in Austria, and she started working at the Educational Institute of Vienna in 1923. In 1924–1925 she obtained a scholarship in the United States and made contacts, which finally led the Rockefeller-Foundation, from 1926 on, to finance researchers like her in Vienna. Among them were Else Frenkel, Felix Lazarsfeld, and Rene Spitz. In 1938 Bühler immigrated to Norway and then moved to the United States in 1940, where she decided to settle. She was associated with several American universities, such as the University of Southern California School of Medicine. Together with Abraham Maslow, Carl Rogers, and others, she established the foundation for the Association for Humanistic Psychology in 1962.

Bühler accomplished a worthwhile contribution to developmental psychology, specifically to life-span developmental psychology, as we know it today. She prepared the way for opening the subject by concentrating on dynamic processes in childhood and youth and by exploring the time of maturity, particularly referring to her research results about the life cycle. Bühler's studies showed that ''individual becoming'' cannot be exclusively seen as registering something new, but that every biography has also phases of movement and stagnation. The dynamic of human life is carried out in a dialectical process of moving and being still, turning to the new and episodically holding onto the familiar, taking on a duty and consequently reaching fullfillment. To these aspects Charlotte Bühler formulated biographical characteristics (aiming for a goal in human activities, the pressure of needs, the dualism of human intentions, etc.) that were recognized later by several researchers. She recognized that self-realization, orderliness of biographical decisions, actions, and experiences were very important facts in human development, and she wrote this as far back as 1959. Furthermore, she emphasized the importance of reflecting possibilities, barriers, and the finality of one's own actions in old age, as well as individual finiteness.

Bühler was famous internationally for her specialized work with toddlers, small children, and youth, as well as offering constructive methods of applying modern psychology, and for her research on the dynamics of the life cycle in general. Among several publications special importance was reached by her books *Der Menschliche Lebenslauf als Psychologisches Problem* (The Course of Human Life as a Psychological Problem), *Kindheit und Jugend* (Childhood and Youth), *Das Seelenleben des Jugendlichen* (The Mental State of Young People), and *Psychologie im Leben unserer Zeit* (Psychology for Contemporary Living).

References

Bühler, C. (1928). *Kindheit und jugend* (Childhood and youth) (1st ed.). Jena: Gustav Fischer.

Bühler, C. (1933). *Der Menschliche lebenslauf als psychologisches problem* (The course of human life as a psychological problem). Leipzig.

Bühler, C. (1962). *Psychologie im leben unserer zeit* (Psychology for contemporary living). München, Zürich (English version, 1968. New York: Hawthorn Books).

Bühler, C. (1967). *Das Seelenleben des jugendlichen* (The mental state of young people) (6th ed.). Stuttgart.

Bühler, C., & Massarik, F. (Eds.). (1968). *The course of human life.* New York.

Bühler, K. (1929). *Die krise der psychologie* (The crisis in psychology). Jena: Gustav Fischer.

—Christiane Bahr

Canada
A. E. David Schonfield
1920–1995

David Schonfield's long and productive career, notable for its diversity and broad range of contributions to aging research, training, and professional service, established him as one of the founders of Canadian gerontology and the country's pioneering geropsychologist. His concern was more with people and process than starting institutions or formal programs. He advanced Canadian geropsychology as a creative researcher, able administrator, outstanding teacher, and active organizer of Canadian gerontology.

Following wartime service (1942–1945) with the British Ministry of Information and work during the postwar period (1945–1948) with the Control Commission for Germany, Schonfield received the MA degree from Cambridge University in psychology and moral sciences in 1950, and in 1951 he received a postgraduate diploma in abnormal psychology from the University of London. His work from 1949 to 1950 as a research assistant at Cambridge's Nuffield Unit on Aging led to his first gerontological publication, *Training of Older People in Industry.* He spent the next several years in professional service roles in the United Kingdom, as an assistant lecturer at the Maudsley Hospital (1951), as an educational psychologist in Bolton (1951–1955), and as a clinical psychologist at Cambridge United Hospitals and Fulbourn. This diverse professional experience, and the influence Sir Frederick Bartlett's work on skill development at Cambridge, initiated a career characterized by broad research interests, an emphasis on personal experience as a critical guide for psychogerontological research, and an abiding recognition of the importance of translating lab findings into real-world solutions for older persons. Emigrating to Canada in 1957, Schonfield was appointed to the faculty for educational psychology at the University of Calgary. In 1960, psychology was created as a separate department with Schonfield as its founding head, a department to which he remained a vital contributor until his death in 1995.

Schonfield's scholarly activities were centered on an internationally recognized core research program on the effects of aging on memory, and they included his classic 1966 demonstration with Robertson that age-related memory loss is attributable in large measure to a decline in the ability to retrieve memories from storage. Driven by a curiosity that seldom distinguished between professional and personal life, nor between paid service and retirement, Schonfield's experience-derived hypotheses about aging led him beyond his core cognitive interests to study and to write on personality, social gerontology, attitudes toward aging and older people, skill training, retirement, recreation, the issues faced by aging women, and teaching the psychology of aging. This same diversity of research interests also provided him with a broad common ground for working with others to advance professional gerontology in Canada. He was one of the founders of the Canadian Association on Gerontology and was its first vice president, the first associate editor for psychology of the *Canadian Journal on Aging,* a member of the editorial board of several leading gerontology journals, and a prominent advocate for aging research in the Canadian Psychological Association. His many contributions to aging research were recognized by fellowship in both the Canadian Psychological Association and the Gerontological Society of America, as well as numerous national awards.

Of Schonfield's many contributions to geropsychology, perhaps the most extensive was made through the thousands of students whom he taught about aging and the many graduate students he supervised. A truly gifted teacher and mentor who used a lively sense of humor as a pedagogical tool, Schonfield was one of the first to offer a university course on the psychology of aging. Beyond their knowledge of aging research, he cared passionately that his students think critically, write clearly, behave ethically, and recognize that in research getting the question right is as important as getting the answer right. Through his many students who went on to academic careers in Canada and the United States, David Schonfield's achievements as an inspirational teacher in conjunction with those in research and professional service constitute an enduring legacy to academic geropsychology in North America.

References

Schonfield, A. E. D. (1974). Translations in gerontology—From lab to life: Utilizing information. *American Psychologist, 29,* 796–801.

Schonfield, A. E. D. (1982). Who is stereotyping whom and why? *The Gerontologist, 22,* 267–272.

Schonfield, A. E. D., & Robertson, E. A. (1966). Memory storage and aging. *Canadian Journal of Psychology, 20,* 228–236.

—Donald Kline and Larry Wenger

China
Heqin Chen
1892–1982

Heqin Chen was an educational and child psychologist. He was born in Zhejiang Province, China. He graduated from Tsing Hua University in 1914 and Johns Hopkins University of the United States in 1917. His master's degree was awarded by Columbia University in 1919.

Heqin Chen was interested in the psychology and education of children. He was the founder of infancy education. He also conducted a few studies on the psychology of aging. He built a kindergarten as an experimental base for the study of the characters of physio-psychological development in children. He emphasized the principle of combining theory with practice and established a complete system of infancy education and normal child education. He suggested conducting a style of "active education" and reformed the tendency of leaving practice in traditional education.

He published many books for children and designed toys and educational equipment. He valued foster teachers and researchers. He established an infancy normal school. From the 1920s through the 1950s, he organized several academic societies, such as the Society of Study for Infancy Education, the Society of Child Education of China, and the Society of Infancy Education of China. He was the editor in chief of child education publications. He published many books and articles, including *The Method of Intelligence Test, Principle of Test* (1921), and "Learning Abilities of the Elderly" (1923), which is a worthy study on cognitive function of the elderly in China during the 1920s. He also published *The Study on Child Mentality* and *Family Education* in 1925.

Heqin Chen was the chief director of the Educational Society of China in 1927 and the president of Nanjing Normal College from 1949 to 1959. He was the honorary chair of the Educational Society of China in 1979 and the honorary chief director of the Society of the Study for Infancy Education.

Heqin Chen's educational practice and ideas had a great influence on educational and intellectual circles of China from the 1920s through the 1940s.

References

Chen, H. Q. (1922). The method of learning comprehension. *Mentality, 1*(2), 1–12.

Chen, H. Q. (1923). Learning abilities of the elderly. *Mentality, 2*(1), 1–11.

Chen, H. Q. (1923). The suggestion of child. *Mentality, 2*(3), 1–10.

—Zhenyun Wu

Germany
Erich Rothacker
1888–1965

Erich Rothacker was born in Pforzheim. His father was the owner of a commercial firm in Naples, so Erich Rothacker spent his childhood in Germany and Italy. He studied at the faculties of medicine and philosophy in Strasbourg, Berlin, Munich, Kiel, and Tübingen. During his university studies he visited lectures in anatomy, physiology, psychiatry, biology, philosophy, history of art, and psychology. He wrote his philosophical dissertation in 1909 and habilitated in 1919 at Heidelberg. There he got a lectureship for the history of philosophy in 1922 and became an extraordinary professor in 1924. From 1929 to 1945 he was director of the Psychological Institute in Bonn. Principal bibliographical references for the philosophical and psychological work of Erich Rothacker are *Die Schichten der Persönlichkeit* (1938), *Probleme der Kulturanthropologie* (1942), "Psychologie und Anthropologie" (1957), *Philosophische Anthropologie* (1964), and *Zur Genealogie des menschlichen Bewußtseins* (1966).

The work of Erich Rothacker was important for life-span developmental psychology and gerontology because of its explication of the following theoretical perspectives: (a) the conceptual distinction between different dimensions of personality and development, (b) the definition of psychological development as a continuously lasting process across the whole life span, and (c) the hypothesis of a possible crossing over between the curves of physiological growth and psychological maturity in old age, conceptualizing psychological changes across the life span as the result of former developmental processes in earlier periods of individual biography (maturity). These theoretical perspectives are delineated in the book *Die Schichten der Persönlichkeit.*

A. Rothacker distinguishes between two dimensions of personality and development: a physiological dimension and a psychological dimension. Development is defined in the sense of positive change, in particular growth and differentiation of functions, abilities, and skills, respectively increasing maturity of personality (the term "maturity" is explicitly not intended to refer to realizing genetic information or to endogenously determined development). Processes of development on these two dimensions differ in various aspects. Therefore, processes of physiological and psychological development must be analyzed separately.

B. The development of *physiological functions* is restricted to the first half of life. Physiological development (in the sense of growth and differentiation) is completed during the third decade. Early adulthood is analyzed from the perspective of physical capacity; middle adulthood and especially late adulthood are analyzed from the perspective of physiological losses and impairments.

In contrast to this perspective, the development of *psychological functions and abilities* (as possibilities or potentials) is understood as a process *going on across the whole life span.* Even in late adulthood people are seen as generally open for new experiences that may give new impulse for further development.

C. Generally, new experiences can be made across the whole life span. Coping consciously with developmental tasks and reflecting opportunities and possibilities, which are given in different life situations, are seen as indicators of a "mature" personality. Processes of change on the physiological and psychological dimensions follow different rules: Whereas changes in physiological processes in old age are characterized by losses and impairment, changes in psychological processes might offer possibilities for coping effectively with new experiences and might include increasing maturity. It is exactly this crossing over between the curves of physiological growth and psychological maturity that requires a definition of development, which reflects the multidimensionality of developmental processes.

References

Rothacker, E. (1938). *Die Schichten der Persönlichkeit (Layers of personality)*. Leipzig: Barth.

Rothacker, E. (1942). *Probleme der Kulturanthropologie (Problems of cultural anthropology)*. Bonn: Bouvier.

Rothacker, E. (1957). Psychologie und Anthropologie *(Psychology and anthropology)*. *Jahrbuch für Psychologie und Psychotherapie, 5,* 275–283.

Rothacker, E. (1964). *Philosophische Anthropologie (Philosophical anthropology)*. Bonn: Bouvier.

Rothacker, E. (1966). *Zur Genealogie des menschlichen Bewußtseins (Geneology of human consciousness)*. Bonn: Bouvier.

—Andreas Kruse

Greece
Lambros Houssiadas
b. 1925

Lambros Houssiadas received his BA degree in classics from the Aristotle University of Thessaloniki (1951) and his PhD in psychology from the University of Leeds in the United Kingdom. His doctoral research was concerned with the perception of causality. In 1961 he was elected associate professor by the psychology department at the University of Adelaide, Australia, where he taught the course in developmental psychology for four years (1961–1965). In the same year, he received an honorary (Ad Eundum Gradum) PhD from the University of Adelaide. It was during his teaching of this course that he developed a strong interest in the aging process as he realized that identification of "development" with childhood and adolescence left out all the important changes that take place in maturity and old age. He thus extended the content of the developmental course to include the entire life span.

In 1965 Houssiadas was elected professor of psychology at the University of Thessaloniki. He was the first psychologist in Greece to occupy a chair of psychology; before that, psychology was taught by philosophers. Being the only academic psychologist in Greece at that time, he considered it his responsibility to promote both teaching and research in psychology. Shortly after his appointment to the chair, Houssiadas cooperated with A. T. Welford in organizing an international conference in psychology at the Aristotle University of Thessaloniki on decision making and age (August 1967). It was the first conference in psychology to be held in Greece, and it can be considered a significant event for the development of Greek psychology. The papers of the conference were subsequently edited by A. T. Welford and J. E. Birren in 1969 and published in the fourth volume of the Interdisciplinary Topics in Gerontology Series with the title *Decision Making and Age*.

For a number of years, the psychology of aging was taught only at the joint Department of Philosophy, Education, and Psychology of the Aristotle University of Thessaloniki as an optional undergraduate course. Thanks to Houssiadas's continuous efforts and influence, psychology of aging has been included in the graduate program of developmental and cognitive psychology of the School of Psychology of the Aristotle University of Thessaloniki since 1993. Although he did not publish any major work on aging in his early years, he is recognized as the founder of contemporary psychology and psychology of aging in Greece.

Houssiadas is still active in geropsychological research, participating in European research programs such as EXCELSA (Cross European Longitudinal Study of Aging) and contributing with papers regarding aging in Greece (Houssiadas, 1999, in press a, b). He is also an active member of the Geriatric and Gerontological Society of Northern Greece, together with other members of the School of Psychology of the Aristotle University. Their participation in the activities of this society is a significant development toward making geropsychology an integral part of the gerontological sciences in Greece.

References

Houssiadas, L. (1999). Aging in Greece. In J. J. F. Schroots, R. Fernandez-Ballesteros, & G. Rudinger (Eds.), *Aging in Europe*. Biomedical Health Research Series. Amsterdam: IOS Press.

Houssiadas, L. (in press a). Prochorimeni ilikia: Mithi kai pragmatikotites [Advanced age: Myths and realities]. Thessaloniki: Geriatric and Gerontological Society of Northern Greece.

Houssiadas, L. (in press b). Psichologiki proetimasia yia tin prossarmogi stin "trite ilikia" [Psychological preparedness to the "third age"]. In G. N. Christodoulou (Ed.), *Triti ilikia: Psichokinonika ke viologika provlemata* [Third Age: Psychosocial and biological problems]. Athens: University of Athens Press.

Welford, A. T., & Birren, J. E. (Eds.). (1969). *Decision making and age*. New York: Karger.

—Anastasia Efklides

Hungary
Paul Ranschburg
1870–1945

Paul Ranschburg had outstanding merits in the organization of institutional bases of psychology in Hungary. In 1889, he established the first laboratory for psychological research at the psychiatric clinic of the Medical School of Budapest, where he was working as a psychiatrist and a university reader. Looking over the complex experimental methods of this laboratory with special emphasis on psychophysiology and psychopathology, it is worthy to mention Ranschburg's critical reservations concerning the radical behaviorism as well as the upward striving psychoanalysis.

In 1928 Ranschburg founded the Hungarian Association of Psychology and became its first president. He also initiated the *Hungarian Review of Psychology*. His pioneering work and his personal influence reinforced the traditional interest and participation of the medical profession in psychology.

Ranschburg's scientific preoccupation concerned mainly the investigation of cognitive functions and performances and the quantitative analysis of their normal and pathological aspects. He elaborated ingenious mental tests and put into practice a great variety of laboratory instruments, among them his most innovative device—the Ranschburg mnemometer—which was constructed as early as 1900. He applied the equipment in his greatly appreciated study in developmental psychology: *Data to the Psychology of Old Age*. Soon he reported on his experiments in the field of normal and faulty memory processes and in 1901 he revealed, as one source of forgetting, the mechanism of reciprocal inhibition of homogenous stimuli, the "Ranschburg effect."

In 1902 the laboratory was attached to the Institute for special education of backward children and Ranschburg extended his research to the learning processes of disabled children and to specific developmental deficits like dyscalculia, dyslexia, and dysgraphia. From this center evolved the Training College for teachers of disabled children and in the 1950s certain laboratories of the Academic Institute of Psychology.

In 1918 Ranschburg was appointed to a professorship. Generations of enthusiastic scholars were rallying around him; one of his most famous disciples was Leopold Szondi.

Ranschburg's work was appreciated in many European countries and in 1927 the Psychological Abstracts from the United States asked for his contribution.

References

Ranschburg, P. (1899). *Data to the psychophysiology of old age* I.–II. Orvosi Hetilap.

Ranschburg, P. (1900). Über qualitative und quantitative Veränderungen geistiger Vorgänge in hohen Greisenalter in Allg. Zeitschr. für Psychiatrie [On qualitative and quantitative mental changes in senectitude].

Ranschburg, P. (1911). *Das kranke Gedächtnis* [Pathology of memory]. Leipzig: J. A. Barth.

Ranschburg, P. (1923). *Az emberi elme* [The human mind]. I.–II.

—E. Moussong-Kovacs

India
P. V. Ramamurti
b. 1936

Born in 1936 in the city of Madras in South India, Panruti Vallam Ramamurti graduated with honors in psychology from the Madras Christian College in 1956 and took a diploma in anthropology from the Madras University in 1956. He discontinued research to serve on the faculty of his alma mater. Finally in 1959 he joined Sri Venkateswara University at Tirupati along with two other colleagues, to organize a postgraduate department of psychology.

Ramamurti renewed his research effort in aging part time at Sri Venkateswara University and published the first papers in geropsychology in India—''Bilateral Transfer in a Mirror Drawing Task in the Old and the Young'' (1963), ''A Study of Figure Reversals in the Old and the Young'' (1964), and ''Behavioural Rigidity and Frequency of Figure Reversals in the Old'' (1964). He was awarded what came to be known as the first doctoral degree in aging in India for his dissertation on ''Factors Related to Adjustment (Coping) of Urban Aged Men,'' submitted to his university in 1968. He was also one of the first to receive funding from the Indian Council of Social Science Research for a major research project on role availability, utilization, and satisfaction in the rural aged. Eager to provide postgraduate instruction in geropsychology, in 1977 he was responsible for starting, for the first time in India, a specialization paper at the master's level on the psychology of aging.

Marking the occasion of the international year of the elderly in 1982, Ramamurti, along with friends in the fields of biology and medicine, became a founding member of the Association of Gerontology, India, and later became its second president. Backed by the strength of the association and by his role as president, he successfully urged several funding agencies (such as the University Grants Commission and the Indian Council of Social Science Research) to treat research in aging as a priority. In 1983 he spent a semester as a Fulbright fellow under the tutelage of Professor James E. Birren at the Andrew Norman Institute of Advanced Study, Andrus Gerontology Center, University of California, Los Angeles, to develop a simple method of indexing individual aging changes as a ratio of an elder's present performance to his best (past) performance.

Eager to promote psycho-social research on the aged in India, soon after his return from United States, Ramamurti successfully prevailed on the authorities of his university to start, for the first time in India, a Centre for Research on Aging in the Department of Psychology during 1983–1984 to promote teaching, research, and extension in psycho-social aging. It became a model for the others to follow. The organization of an interdisciplinary study group on aging provided a forum for promoting scholars from sister disciplines of anthropology, sociology, homescience, and population studies taking to aging research. His lucid and entertaining presentations, keynote lectures, and inaugural addresses at interuniversity colloquia, conferences, seminars and symposia, as well as on radio, on television, and in print inspired scholars and the public alike and drew their attention to gerontology. The following years brought an upsurge of research, mostly due to his inspired effort in bringing scholars from diverse fields into the fold of aging research in India.

As a chief promoter of research and training in aging in India, Ramamurti attracted the University Grants Commission in 1990, which identified his department for special assistance to strengthen research and teaching in life-span development with an emphasis on aging. He successively reviewed Indian literature in psycho-social aging in 1984, 1992, and 1995. His hundred-odd research articles, covering the length and breadth of geropsychology, and a score of funded research projects have significantly contributed to the origin, growth, and development of Indian geropsychology. A recipient of many honors and awards for his work, Ramamurti brought scientific knowledge within easy reach of the general population through his brief handouts, the best known of them being the popular ''Ten Commandments of Happy Aging'' that has been translated into many Indian languages.

References

Ramamurti, P. V., & Jamuna, D. (1993). Developments and research on aging in India. In Erdman B. Palmore (Ed.), *Developments and research on aging—An international handbook* (pp. 145–158). West Port: Greenwood Press.

Ramamurti, P. V., & Jamuna, D. (1995). Perspectives of geropsychology in India: A review. *Indian Psychological Abstracts and Reviews, 2*(2), 207–267.

—D. Jamuna

Italy
Marcello Cesa-Bianchi
b. 1926

For the past 40 years Cesa-Bianchi has had a great influence on Italian psychology, its subject matter for research and study, and its organization, especially in medical education. He earned his MD in 1949, completed his postgraduate studies in psychology in 1952, and focused on neuropsychiatry in 1956. He became professor of psychology in 1956 and full professor in 1965. In 1953 he developed the Institute of Psychology of the Municipality of Milan, and in 1956 he founded the Institute of Psychology of the Medical School, Milan University. In 1982 he founded the postgraduate school of clinical psychology. More than of 50 of his students have become full or associate professors of psychology in Italian universities.

In 1970 Cesa-Bianchi was appointed editor of a relevant series of psychological books (Franco Angeli, Milano) that has published about 200 volumes. In 1977 he also founded the journal *Ricerche di Psicologia*. He has authored or edited 38 books and about 1100 articles concerning experimental and psycho-social studies, some of which are in the context of international and cross-cultural projects.

His research interests were initially in the fields of perception and applied psychology, but soon he acquired a strong interest in developmental psychology, dealing initially with infancy and adolescence but soon focusing on the psychology of aging. In 1950 he was the first Italian psychologist to start a research program in geropsychology. The main contributions of Cesa-Bianchi and his students in this area dealt with the following topics:

1. *Psychology of aging*. They explored life-span developmental psychology, dealing mainly with cognitive, affective, motivational processes. They helped to reveal that aging does not necessarily mean loss and illness, and that, through constancy and vicarious processes and brain plasticity, human behavior may maintain a high efficiency until a very old age.
2. *Psychology of old people*. Studying extended samples of the Italian population, they showed a great variability in the psychological processing of old people and determined that this variability is linked to a variety of genetic, developmental, medical, and social factors. Moreover, they confirmed the role and importance of exercise, creativity, and interpersonal and intergenerational relationships in determining a good quality of life and in establishing an old-age culture (Cesa-Bianchi & Vecchi, 1998).

References

Cesa-Bianchi, M. (Ed.). (1978). *Psicologia della Senescenza* [Psychology of senescence]. Milano: Franco Angeli.

Cesa-Bianchi, M. (1987). *Psicologia dell'Invecchiamento* [Psychology of aging]. Roma: Nuova Italia Scientifica.

Cesa-Bianchi, M., Pravettoni, G., & Cesa-Bianchi, G. (1997). "I: invecchiamento. Il contributo di quarant'anni di ricerche" [Psychological aging: The contribution of forty years of research]. *Giornale di Gerontologia, 45,* 313–321.

Cesa-Bianchi, M., & Vecchi, T. (Ed.). (1998). *Elementi di Psicogerontologia* [Elements of psychogerontology]. Milano: Franco Angeli.

—Marco Poli

Japan
Kakusho Tachibana
1900–1978

Tachibana was an early pioneer in the psychology of aging and gerontology in Japan. He wrote the first article on geropsychology in an academic journal in that country, and in 1927 he focused his experiments on the learning process of motor action using older participants.

M. Matsumoto, a professor at Tokyo University, advised him to devote himself to studying the psychology of aging, but the conditions of the psychological experiment and research on aged persons were very difficult for any researcher in 1920s. Tachibana found opportunities to interview many older people, especially at a nursing home, Yokufuen, that was established after the great Tokyo earthquake of 1923. F. Amako, the chief physician of Yokufuen, started publishing a series of science reports, *Bulletin of Yokufuen,* in 1930. Tachibana contributed many articles on his psychological studies, until the requisition of Yokufuen buildings during the World War II by the military authorities.

His great book, *Gerontology—Problems and Investigations* (1971) led the field, comprehensively covering basic psychological studies, sociological research, phenomenological consideration on many dying poems, and educational practice for senior citizens to find their roles in society. Out of his studies and consideration, Tachibana claimed that old age involved features such as egocentricity, *unentfaltete Vielheit,* segregation, and subjectivity. Later, he suggested that the attitudes and behavior of old people were characterized by loneliness, resignation, and tranquility, which were also important elements of the religious-aesthetic concept, *Sabi,* in the early modern culture of Japan. (The origin of the word *Sabi* was *Sabighisa* (loneliness). However, it has been used to express the aesthetic worth of elegant and quiet simplicity in aging people.) His other impressive book, *Pursuit of Aging* (1975), emphasized the wealth and beauty of aging and aimed to enlighten people about how to integrate their own lives in a mature and satisfying way.

He rendered great service by establishing the Japan Gerontological Society in 1959 and the Japan Socio-Gerontological Society in 1959. Beginning in the 1950s, he also advised younger researchers on the psychology of aging and gerontology as a professor at Osaka University. He also contributed much toward holding the 11th International Congress of Gerontology in Tokyo in 1978. He passed away on the last day of the same month as the conference. The experimental study at Yokufuen was continued by a group led by K. Nagashima, a professor at Nippon University. Tachibana's viewpoint on *Sabi* has influenced this author to analyze the contents of *guided autobiography* in the cultural context of Japan.

Tachibana's autobiography essentially represents the early history of geropsychology in Japan. Many consider him to be the greatest psychologist on aging and the most devoted educator for the older population in Japan during the twentieth century.

References

Tachibana, K. (1927). On learning process of the aged. *Japanese Journal of Psychology, 2,* 635–653.

Tachibana, K. (1971). *Gerontology—Problems and investigations.* Tokyo: Seishin–shobo.

Tachibana, K. (1975). *Pursuit of aging.* Tokyo: Seishin–shobo.

—Koichi Yamamoto

The Netherlands
Joep M. A. Munnichs
b. 1927

Munnichs is the nestor of psychogerontology in The Netherlands. He studied psychology at the Catholic University, Nijmegen (KUN) (1947–1955), received his doctorate (cum laude) at the KUN in 1964 (his thesis was titled "Old Age and Finitude"), and held the only chair in psychogerontology in The Netherlands, initially (1972) in the Department of Developmental Psychology and from 1976 to 1990 as head of the Interdepartmental Group of Social Gerontology, KUN. Munnichs is the initiator and editor in chief (1970–1990) of the (Netherlands) *Journal of Gerontology and Geriatrics (TvG&G)*. His efforts led to the founding of the division of social gerontology of the Netherlands Psychological Association (NIP) and he became its first chair in 1972. Because of his merits of many years in the field of geropsychology and social gerontology, he was presented with an honorary membership to the NIP when he was given emeritus status in 1990.

During his study of psychology, Munnichs developed a long-standing interest in the psychology of aging, particularly in the subjective experience of aging. Inspired by the observations of the Swiss physician Vischer in *Seelische Wandlungen beim alternden Menschen* (Psychological changes in aging individuals, 1961), he becamed interested in the phenomenon of time perspective in later life. This theme forms the basis of his thesis on the finitude of human existence as experienced in the second half of life. An important aspect of the thesis is that both qualitative and quantiative data have been used for analysis.

In his publications Munnichs emphasizes the experiential and social aspects of aging as opposed to the so-called deficit model, which focuses on cognitive decline. He believes that a holistic, interdisciplinary approach in gerontology is necessary to do justice to the aged by treating them as fully human beings. As emeritus professor, Joep Munnichs is engaged on the study of (autobiography) and thanatology.

References

Munnichs, J. M. A. (1966). *Old age and finitude.* Basel: Karger.

Munnichs, J. M. A., Mussen, P., Olbrich, E., & Coleman, P. G. (Eds.). (1985). *Lifespan and change in a gerontological perspective.* New York: Academic Press.

Munnichs, J. M. A., & Uildriks, G. (Ed.) (1989). *Psychogerontologie: Een inleidend leerboek* [Psychogerontology: An introductory textbook]. Deventer (NL): Van Loghum Slaterus.

—Johannes J. F. Schroots

Russia
Ivan Petrovich Pavlov
1849–1936

Pavlov was professor of physiology and director of the department of physiology of the Institute of Experimental Medicine, 1890–1925, and professor in the Military Medical Academy 1890–1925, in St. Petersburg, Russia. In 1904 he was awarded the Nobel Prize in physiology for his research on the brain and higher nervous system.

He was the son of a village priest in the district of Ryasan in Russia, and after dropping out of the theological seminary in 1870 he studied science at the University of St. Petersburg. In 1875 he studied medicine at the Military Medicine Academy in St. Petersburg, completing his medical studies in 1879 and his dissertation for the doctor of medicine degree in 1883.

While identified as a physiologist, Pavlov, had a profound effect on the development of psychology in the 20th century. He is best known for his research on conditioned reflexes, and his research on conditioning provided a pathway for experimental psychologists to establish a new perspective about the organization of behavior. Thus behaviorism was born with the physiologist Pavlov as the grandfather. Pavlov viewed the brain system as the integrating organ of the body, placing it in an important position with regard to regulating physiological functions as well as behavior. In this regard he was a pioneer at a time when most western physiologists were viewing the brain as passive in important bodily functions.

Pavlov's view of the dominant regulatory function of the brain is well expressed in his own words.

> The activity of the nervous system is directed, on the one hand, towards unification, integrating the work of all the parts of the organism, and, on the other, towards connecting the organism with the surrounding milieu, towards an equilibrium between the system of the organism and the external conditions (Pavlov, 1930, p. 207)

His integrative approach to the nervous system is further seen in a statement attributed to him, ''We are now coming to think of the mind, the soul, and matter as all one, and with this view there will be no necessity for a choice between them'' (Gantt, 1928, p. 25).

Pavlov's (1941) research on conditioned reflexes was so influential in American psychology that he was invited to contribute a chapter in a volume published by Clark University Press on *Psychologies of 1930,* edited by Carl Murchison. His chapter was titled, ''A Brief Outline of the Higher Nervous Activity.''

Late in his career (1928–1936), Pavlov turned to applying the principles he derived from the study of conditioned reflexes to psychiatric problems. He even interpreted the phenomenon of hypnosis in terms of ''irradiated inhibition.'' Coming into contact with disabilities of old age, he sought to interpret some observed behavior as due to a decrease in excitatory processes. He believed that the old established reflexes would have priority because there is exclusion of other collateral and simultaneous stimuli. He said,

> I look at some object which I need, take it and do not see anything touching or near it—this is why I unnecessarily strike other objects. This is erroneously called senile distraction, on the contrary it is concentration, involuntary, passive, defective. Thus the old man, dressing and at the same time thinking about something or talking to someone, goes out without his cap, takes the wrong article, leave his clothes unbuttoned, etc., etc. (Pavlov, 1932, as quoted in Gantt, 1941, p. 109).

He also noted that, ''A marked loss of memory for things of the present—a usual phenomenon in normal old age—is due to the reduced mobility of the excitatory process especially or its inertness owing to age, etc.'' (Pavlov, 1935, as quoted in Gantt, 1941, p. 179). Thus Pavlov, as a physiologist, contributed to the science of psychology of aging by offering explanations of phenomena that he linked with aging by invoking the relative strength of excitatory and inhibitory processes.

References

Gantt, W. H. (1928). Ivan P. Pavlov: A biographical sketch. In I. V. Pavlov, *Lectures on conditioned reflexes* (Vol. 1, pp. 11–31). New York: International Publishers.

Pavlov, I. P. (1928). *Lectures on conditioned reflexes* (W. H. Gantt, Trans. & Ed., Vol. 1). New York: International Publishers.

Pavlov, I. P. (1930). A brief outline of the higher nervous activity. In C. Murchison (Ed.), *Psychologies of 1930* (pp. 207–220). Worcester, MA: Clark University Press.

Pavlov, I. P. (1941). *Lectures on conditioned reflexes: Conditioned reflexes and psychiatry.* (W. H. Gantt, Trans. & Ed., Vol. 2). New York: International Publishers.

—James E. Birren

Sweden
Jan Helander
b. 1930

As the first Swedish psychologist professionally interested in aging, Jan Helander has had a great influence on the early development of gerontological psychology and gerontology in Sweden (Helander, 1967). He got his PhD in psychology from the University of Gothenburg in 1967. At that time in Sweden there was no education in aging available at any university and his background was therefore in cognitive psychology, psychobiology, genetics, and statistics.

In the late 1960s, Jan Helander was appointed associate professor in psychology at the University of Gothenburg. There he taught gerontology to a large number of undergraduate and graduate students; of them some became researchers but most chose to become clinical psychologists. In 1976 he became the founding director of the Gerontology Centre in Lund, and a couple of years later he left the centre to become an independent lecturer in gerontology. With the move to Lund and the Gerontology Centre, he left the academic field and turned to more general lecturing and writing on aging and old age care. He was a frequent traveler all over Sweden lecturing for old age care personnel, decision makers, retiree organizations, and so forth. He also appeared as a guest on many radio and television programs. He wrote several popular books on aging. For a long period he was a member of the board of governors for the Swedish Red Cross. During six years, from 1976 to 1981, Jan Helander was chair of the European Social and Behavioural Sciences Section of the International Association of Gerontology.

Jan Helander dedicated his dissertation ''On Age and Mental Test Behaviour'' to ''the memory of Maria, sister in the gate.'' In one of his lectures he told that Maria was the most important factor behind his interest in aging.

> I met her when I was six years old. She was in her sixties and we were very close friends. She really understood me and we played together a lot. She worked with the Church of Sweden trying to provide food and clothing to starving middle-aged men during the deep depression in the 1930s. I met these men and had some friends among them but I was too young to understand what I saw. Long afterwards I realised that Maria was an extraordinary person, not only in my own life.

The main theme in Jan Helander's writing and lecturing is that one should view aging in a life-span perspective and that old age is a normal part of life. According to him it is especially important to see that old, old-old, and very old people still have resources that are important to them, to younger generations, and the society as whole (Helander, 1991).

References

Helander, J. (1967). On age and mental test behaviour. Göteborg: Acta psychologica gothoburgensis.

Helander, J. (1991). Att leva medan tiden går [To live while time passes]. Stockholm: Natur & Kultur.

—Stig Berg

Switzerland
Carl Gustav Jung
1875–1961

Carl G. Jung studied medicine at the University of Basel and started his education and career as a psychiatrist at the Burghölzli Psychiatric Hospital in Zürich under the direction of Bleuler. At the turn of the century he discovered the work of Freud and went to visit him in Vienna in 1907. In 1909 Jung and Freud were special guests of Granville Stanley Hall at the 20th anniversary of the foundation of the Clark University. Although Jung did not accept Freud's doctrine without reservation, he played an eminent role in the Psychoanalytic Association of which he was the first president. The elaboration of his own ideas led to the break with Freud and the psychoanalytic movement in 1913. From the end of 1913 to 1919, Jung lived rather isolated from the scientific and professional community. He undertook his own self-analysis in an often painful and threatening exploration of feelings and images that erupted from the unconscious.

The devotion to his private practice and the support and love of his wife, lovers, and friends kept him upright in the darkest period of his life. He emerged from this creative illness with new psychotherapeutic tools and a number of ideas and insights that he elaborated in the years thereafter. At the end of his life, Jung defined his dreams and visions at the time of his self-analysis as "the prima materia for a lifetime's work." He wrote, "It has taken me virtually forty-five years to distill within the vessel of my scientific work the things I experienced and wrote down at that time" (1961, p. 199).

Jung became the founder of analytical psychology (Jung, 1966, 1972). In the early 1930s, he presented an outline of a life-span developmental theory that highly reflected his personal experiences. He divided the human life cycle into two halfs and four eras (childhood, young adulthood, middle adulthood, and old age) separated by transitional stages (adolescence, the noon of life, and the late life transition). Each era has its own basic theme, developmental tasks and goals. The goal of the first half of life is the involvement in the external world, becoming somebody in the society. The basic dynamics and themes of development in childhood, adolescence, and early adulthood are described by metaphors as "growth, expansion and nature." Some creative people who one-sidedly cultivate their potentialities in search of a successful involvement in the outside world may face a so-called crisis of the noon of life around the age of 40. At the height of their lives, these individuals become aware of the finitude of life and the demands of their internal world. This is the beginning of the individuation process, the accomplishment of which is the developmental goal of the second half of life, namely coming to selfhood, in which one achieves a definite sense of one's incomparable uniqueness. The dynamics and imperatives of the afternoon of life are "dying, contraction and culture." The individuation process is a spiritual and culture creating quest, which includes the discovery of uneducated and repressed personal qualities in oneself (the Shadow and the personal unconscious) becoming aware of the possibility that one's achievements in roles and functions in the society (the Persona) may mask an inner void, coming to terms with the archetypal, contrasexual figure of the Anima (in men) or Animus (in women), and finally the realization of the Self in the continuing dialogue with the archetypes of the Wise Old Man (in men) or the Great Mother (in women). Jung never gave a clearly structured description of the individuation process and its final state.

The rootedness of Jung's scientific writings in his personal life experiences and his stress on the not easily accessible impersonal universal structures of the psyche prevented his view on the development in the midlife transition and middle adulthood from becoming very influential in the main stream adult developmental psychology. Traces of Jungian influence can be found in Levinson's theory of the seasons of life, Gould's theory of the evolution of adult consciousness, and in Tornstam's gerotranscendence theory.

References

Jung, C. G. (1972). *The structure and dynamics of the psyche.* (Collected Works, Vol. 8). London: Routledge & Kegan Paul.

Jung, C. G. (1961). *Memories, dreams and reflections.* New York: Pantheon Books.

Jung, C. G. (1966). *Two essays in analytical psychology.* (Collected Works, Vol. 7). London: Routledge & Kegan Paul.

—Alfons Marcoen

United Kingdom
Alan Traviss Welford
1914–1995

A. T. Welford was an experimental psychologist based for the first 30 years of his professional life in Cambridge. His contribution to geropsychology began when he returned from a year in Princeton in 1946 and became director of the Nuffield Unit for Research into Problems of Ageing. His mission was to transfer to this new field the research methodology related to skilled performance developed at Cambridge under the impetus of war. It had been predicted, correctly, that the rebuilding of the country would stretch the efforts of the available workforce for many years. It was hoped that knowledge might be developed that would help to make older workers more effective. The objective was practical but the procedures were theoretically oriented. The evidence came from performance comparisons, mainly in the laboratory, between small groups of people of different ages through the working life span. The concept of information handling was used and the emphasis was on translation processes between receptors and effectors. The picture that emerged was that deterioration with age is continuous for information processing and for short-term memory, but this need not affect performance at work if demand is below capacity. A useful generalization is that noise in the information channel increases with age and this has implications for optimal job design and for training for older workers. The Nuffield Unit had a life of about 10 years, and the final report was published in 1958 (Welford, 1958).

In 1965 he edited, with J. E. Birren, a survey of all gerontology up to that time (Welford & Birren, 1965). Welford then did extensive work on his more general experimental psychology interests, notably choice reaction times and the psychological refractory period; his magnum opus on human skill was published in 1968.

He spent a sabbatical year at the University of Adelaide in 1964 as a commonwealth visiting professor and occupied a specially created chair there for more than a decade from 1968. Here he continued his interest in aging and wrote extensively about wider aspects such as motivation, effort, human relations, retirement and so on, always in the context of skilled performance.

In addition to his work on geropsychology and experimental psychology, he made a lasting contribution to ergonomics. He was the founding editor of the journal *Ergonomics,* the first chair of the UK Ergonomics Research Society, and, later, president of the Ergonomics Society of Australia and New Zealand. A more detailed description of his academic achievements and a complete list of his publications can be found in Singleton (1997).

References

Singleton, W. T. (1997). A. T. Welford—A commemmorative review. *Ergonomics, 40*(2), 125–140.

Welford, A. T. (1958). *Ageing and human skill.* Oxford: University Press.

Welford, A. T. (1968). *Fundamentals of skill.* London: Methuen.

Welford, A. T., & Birren, J. E. (Eds.). (1965). *Behavior, Aging and the Nervous System.* Springfield, IL: Thomas.

—W. T. Singleton

United States
Granville Stanley Hall
1844–1924

G. Stanley Hall had a great influence on American psychology, its subject matter for research and study, and its professional organization. His PhD, awarded in 1878, was the first doctorate awarded for psychological research in the United States. He opened the laboratory of psychology at Johns Hopkins University in 1883 and initiated the *American Journal of Psychology* in 1887. His efforts led to the founding of the American Psychological Association, and he became its first president in 1892. From his position as president of Clark University (1888–1920), he was able to influence the directions taken by the emerging science.

Hall's interest in developmental psychology was expressed in the publication of his two-volume work, *Adolescence,* which was published in 1904. After he retired as president of Clark University in 1920, he turned his attention to writing his book on aging that was published in 1922, *Senescence: The Second Half of Life.* In the introduction to the book on senescence he revealed that he had a long-standing interest in the subject of aging: "In fact ever since I published my *Adolescence* in 1904 I have hoped to live to complement it by a study of senescence." His book was a thorough review of the available literature ranging from philosophy through biology and medicine to psychology. In relation to aging, Hall was mainly preoccupied by the subject of death and included in the book the results of a survey he had done about attitudes toward death.

He clearly regarded life as divided into stages:

> 1) childhood, 2) adolescence from puberty to full nubility, 3) middle life or the prime, when we are at the apex of our aggregate of powers, ranging from twenty-five or thirty to forty or forty-five and comprising thus the fifteen or twenty years not commonly called our best, 4) senescence which begins in the early forties or before in woman, and 5) senectitude, the post-climacteric or old age proper (Hall, 1922, p. vii)

References

Hall, G. S. (1904). *Adolescence: Its psychology and its relations to physiology, anthropology, sociology, sex, crime, religion, and education* (Vols. 1–2). New York: Appleton.

Hall, G. S. (1922). *Senescence: The last half of life.* New York: Appleton.

—James E. Birren

Index

Numbers in italics refer to listings in reference section.

ABOUT THE EDITORS

James E. Birren, PhD, is associate director of the UCLA Center on Aging; adjunct professor of Medicine/Gerontology; and adjunct professor, Department of Psychiatry and Biobehavioral Sciences, University of California, Los Angeles. He is professor emeritus of Psychology and Gerontology of the University of Southern California, where he served as the founding executive director and dean of the Ethel Percy Andrus Gerontology Center. He received his MA and PhD in psychology from Northwestern University and was a fellow at the Center for Advanced Study in the Behavioral Sciences at Stanford University. His awards include the Brookdale Foundation Award for Gerontological Research and the Distinguished Scientific Contribution Award of the American Psychological Association. He has published extensively about the psychology of aging and has more than 250 publications in academic journals and books. He has served as editor of the internationally recognized *Handbook of the Psychology of Aging* and the *Encyclopedia of Gerontology.*

Johannes J. F. Schroots, PhD, is director of ERGO, European Research Institute on Health and Aging; adjunct professor of Human Gerontology, University of Amsterdam; and senior researcher of Geropsychology, Free University Amsterdam. He is the European council member and project leader for The Netherlands of EXCELSA, Cross-European Longitudinal Study of Aging; former project leader of EuGeron, European Community Concerted Action on Gerontology: Aging, Health and Competence; and former coordinator of the TNO department of Preventive Health Care for the Elderly. His research and teaching concentrates on multidisciplinary issues of health and aging. He received his MA in experimental, industrial, and organizational psychology and his PhD in social science from Free University Amsterdam. He was a fellow at the Andrew Norman Institute for Advanced Study in Gerontology and an International Fogerty fellow at the Ethel Percy Andrus Gerontology Center, University of Southern California. He is coeditor of books on aging and has published scientific articles on the psychology of aging. He is a fellow of the Gerontological Society of America.